The McGraw-Hill Handbook of Interest, Yields, and Returns

Lawrence R. Rosen

McGraw-Hill, Inc.

New York   San Francisco   Washington, D.C.   Auckland   Bogotá
Caracas   Lisbon   London   Madrid   Mexico City   Milan
Montreal   New Delhi   San Juan   Singapore
Sydney   Tokyo   Toronto

Library of Congress Cataloging-in-Publication Data

Rosen, Lawrence R.
    The McGraw-Hill handbook of interest, yields, and returns /
Lawrence R. Rosen
        p.   cm.
    Includes bibliographical references and index.
    ISBN 0-07-053766-6 (acid-free paper)
    1. Interest—Handbooks, manuals, etc.   2. Investments—Handbooks,
manuals, etc.   I. Title.
HG1621.R67   1994
332.6—dc20   94-17595
                                                              CIP

1 2 3 4 5 6 7 8 9 0   DOC/DOC   9 0 9 8 7 6 5 4

ISBN 0-07-053766-6

*The sponsoring editor for this book was Betsy N. Brown, the editing
supervisor was David E. Fogarty, and the production supervisor was
Suzanne W. Babeuf. It was set in Baskerville by Inkwell Publishing
Services.*

Printed and bound by R. R. Donnelley & Sons Company.

To
Dr. Melvin Bloom, Professor of Mathematics, Miami
University (my mathematics professor)

Edward M. Cowett, L.L.B., President, I.O.S., Ltd.
(my dear friend and mentor)

And to the memory of two dedicated and
outstanding professors, who sharpened my
intellectual curiosity:

Dr. Eugene S. Klise, Professor of Money and
Banking, Miami University

Dr. George C. Grosscup, Jr., Professor of Economics
and Statistics, Miami University

Contents

Preface

You can do only three things with your money: spend it, lend it, or invest it. No matter which course you choose, this book will help you do it better.

Making an investment without understanding *yield to maturity* and *current yield*, or managing a business without comprehending *internal rate of return* and *discounted cash flow techniques*, would be as foolish as attempting to navigate the high seas without a compass.

This book contains all the necessary information traditionally associated with the time value of money, including present and future values of single investments, the various forms of series of payments or investment (annuities), as well as discounting, compound, and simple interest. However, that is only the beginning: This material constitutes less than 20 percent of the book, which goes far beyond the customary approach. For example, here's the kind of information you will find in this book.

Suppose that you are now 46 and planning to retire when you reach 65. You figure that, starting *now*, you must save $500 per month (at 12 percent interest) to have the funds you will need. What will happen to the amount you must save each month if you procrastinate for, let's say, 5 years? That is, instead of saving $500 per month starting at age 46, how much more would you have to save each month if you want to start until 51. Take a guess. Five percent more? Ten percent more?

The answer is 100 percent more! That's right, if you wait 5 years you will then have to save $1000 per month, not $500.

That's the kind of practical information you will find in this book. And to find the answers, you needn't (unless you so desire) spend hours manipulating complicated formulas. Of course, all the formulas and methods of solving them are included in case you ever want to use them, but simple graphs throughout allow you to find complicated solutions in seconds instead of hours. For the example, see Fig. P.1. For the example we are considering, enter the graph at age 46 on the left vertical axis (under the "age" column) and draw a line horizontally across the page to the "5-year delay" curve. Then, from the point of intersection with that curve, continue the line down (vertically) to the bottom horizontal line. That point on the bottom line, just over 100 percent, is the percentage by which you must increase your annual savings to make up for the 5-year delay. See the dashed line on the graph. That's all there is to it—you don't have to do any math at all! In Chap. 27 the method of calculation is described and another graph shows the results for an 8 percent earnings rate.

This book is especially suitable for people who want to make intelligent investment and borrowing decisions—whether as individuals or for businesses or organizations. A few of the many types of investment questions that this book will help you answer include:

- Why does the annual percentage rate (APR) quoted by lenders in most instances understate the true cost of borrowing?

- How much difference does it make if an investment compounds more frequently than annually—for example, quarterly or continuously?

- Which is better, a bank money market account or one offered by a mutual fund?

- How can I obtain tax-sheltered investment distributions?

- What is the *true return* that can be used to compare all forms of investment, including stocks, bonds, and real estate? How do the internal rate of return (IRR) and associated measures actually work?

- *To retire in comfort*, how much must I invest and when, and what rate of earnings must I achieve?

- Should I pay off (*refinance*) my present home mortgage and take a new one at 8 percent with 3 points?

- Is a *reverse mortgage* (whereby a senior homeowner receives a monthly income for life) a good deal? What is it really costing me or my estate?

- My retirement savings are about $150,000; how much can I withdraw each year so that the withdrawals will last for my expected life span?

- If I withdraw more money each year from my savings or investments than those investments earn, when will I run out of capital?

- Why does a 6 percent *add-on* or *discount* loan really cost much, much more? How much more?

- What are the pros and cons of *accelerating the repayment* of my home mortgage or other loan?

Age   Years until funds needed

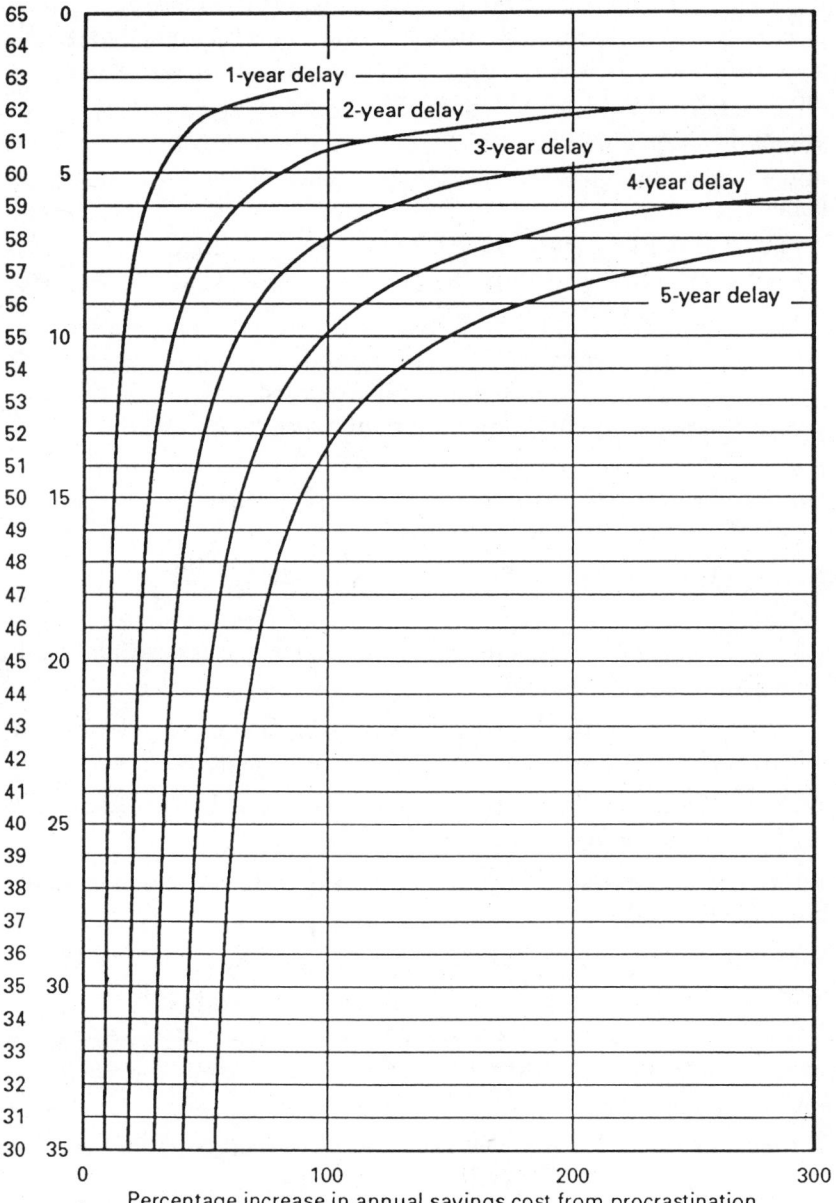

Percentage increase in annual savings cost from procrastination

Figure P.1. How delays in starting a savings program affect the cost. (Money earns 12 percent.)

- If I buy an investment *real estate* property, with 75 percent of the purchase price supplied by a mortgage loan, how much are my annual payments of principal and interest? Should I amortize the loan in 20 years or pay interest-only? How long will my *tax shelter* last?

- Should I buy *bonds*? If yes, which are more desirable, discounts, bonds at par, premiums, governments, corporates, or municipal (tax-exempt) issues?

- Which should I buy, a *noncallable* 30-year bond yielding 10 percent to maturity, or a 30-year callable bond of the same issuer, yielding 10.4 percent, which is noncallable for 5 years?

- What is an acceptable method for valuing and analyzing the interest-rate risk of such financial instruments as callable bonds, put bonds, zero-coupon bonds, single-premium deferred annuities, and certificates of deposit?

- How can I control the risk level of an entire portfolio of bonds using the *modified duration* measure?

- How can I use *convexity* to find bonds which will *increase* in price more than they will *decrease*, for a given change in rates?

- Why will *callable* bonds decrease in price more than they will increase, for a given change in interest rates?

- How can using an *option pricing model* provide better control of portfolio risk and uncover profitable investment opportunities?

- What are the *tax implications* of bond purchases, and how do taxes affect my investment decisions?

- Which is riskier, a *discount* bond bought to earn 12 percent or a *premium* bond bought at the same yield?

- Which is riskier, a 30-year bond bought to yield 13 percent or a 15-year bond bought with the same return?

- I can buy bonds yielding 12 percent or utility common stocks with good records of dividend increases that yield 7 percent. Which is the better buy?

- GNMAs and other mortgage-backed securities seem to offer higher yields than Treasuries; what's the catch?

- How can I bring my bond investments under tight control?

- How are yield to maturity, zero-coupon spot rate, and forward rate linked?

- My business is considering expanding; how can *capital budgeting* and *weighted-average cost of capital* help me make the right decision?

- What are the implications of price-earnings changes on my stock investments?

- How do *reinvestment assumptions* matter in making intelligent decisions?

- Why do so many sources erroneously state that for an investor to actually achieve IRR or YTM, one *must* reinvest at the rate of IRR?

This book is meant to help you form an accurate picture of the financial implications of everyday money decisions. It provides *quick* answers to everyday questions about interest that will be useful to savers, businesspeople, borrowers, investment brokers, accountants, lawyers, lenders, car buyers, financial planners, and homeowners.

Graphs (as well as formulas with examples of applications) serve those who consider themselves "nonmathematical" and others who, though perfectly capable of performing complex mathematical calculations, will welcome this *speedy* reference source. Its unique graphs make it possible to solve complicated money problems in seconds, or problems may be solved by use of the basic formulas and tables that are included.

Readers whose last exposure to equation solving was in the dimly remembered past of schooldays may be pleasantly surprised by the clarity and elegance of the simple explanations. But no attention need be paid to the "mathematics of interest." *Anyone who can read simple graphs will find this a handy sourcebook.*

The author has yet to meet anyone who became wealthy or maximized his or her assets by putting money in the bank at a fixed rate of interest. To create wealth and maximize one's assets, one will normally need to invest. There are all kinds of potential investments that one can make. And there are all kinds of brokers hoping to sell you one. To name several potential investments, there are:

Common stocks	Preferred Stocks
Corporate bonds	Municipal bonds
Real estate	Zero-coupon bonds
Money market accounts	Certificates of deposit
Mortgage-backed bonds	Oil and gas drilling funds

How does one decide where to put his or her money? Brokers always have an optimistic view of whatever it is that they are selling. They are hardly likely to be a good source of unbiased knowledge and wisdom. The answer is that one should decide for oneself by analyzing the available options and making one's own decisions.

This book gives you the tools you need to make important decisions concerning your financial well-being. For example, among the following available investments—stock, bond, and real estate—which would be the best investment for you—assuming that in each case you hold the investment for 15 years?

A *common stock* in a conservative utility company sells at $100 per share and currently pays a dividend of $10 per year. You are considering buying 10 shares. Your analysis (which should include analysts' forecasts) suggests that the dividend rate and earnings per share are likely to increase at a rate of 5 percent per year. It is assumed that the market value of the stock over the long term will also increase at the same rate as the annual dividend increase, that is, 5 percent per year. The pretax cash return is the $10 dividend divided by the $100 share price, that is, 10 percent.

Alternatively, would it be better to buy a *corporate bond* for $800 that matures in 15 years at $1000 and pays $120 per year in interest? The initial pretax cash return is the annual interest of $120 divided by the $800 price, that is, 15 percent.

Or you could invest in an *office building.* The purchase can be made with 75 percent borrowed funds (e.g., $3000) and 25 percent cash investment (i.e., $1000). The loan terms on the borrowed funds are: 12 percent interest per year; 25-year amortization. Assume that you eventually sell the property at a 12 percent capitalization rate; that is, the sale price is 8.3 times (i.e., 100 +12) the then income. Both annual rents and expenses are expected to increase at an annual inflation rate of 6 percent. The current annual cash distribution (e.g., $17.50 per year) is 1.75 percent of the cash investment (e.g., $1000).

The following table summarizes the known facts about the three investment alternatives.

	Common stock	Corporate bond	Office building
Cash investment	$1000	$800	$1000
Distributable cash (dividend, interest, net rent after loan payment)	100	120	17.50
Rate of increase per year of:			
Dividend and earnings per share	5%		
Interest (bond)		0%	
Rents and expenses			6%
Loan terms for office building:			
Total purchase price			$4000
Loan amount			$3000
Interest rate on loan			12%
Years of loan amortization			25
Initial pretax cash return on cash invested	10%	15%	1¾%

At this point, which investment looks best to you? There are certainly a wide range of conditions and initial cash returns from which to choose: from 1.75 to as high as 15 percent.

The broker for the *common stock* will probably talk to you in terms of price-earnings ratios, dividend payout, and current yield. The *real estate* broker may speak in terms of cash-on-cash return, equity buildup, and tax savings. Confusing? Yes. Does it need to be? No!

Fortunately, there is a common denominator to which all forms of investment may be reduced—a single number that acts as a measure of comparison among investment possibilities A, B, C, etc. That measure is the *internal rate of return* (IRR). This book tells you all about it. It is expressed as a percentage. *It is like the interest rate earned on a bank account.*

Refer back to the three potential investments just described, the common stock, the corporate bond, and the office building. Which one do you think is the best investment assuming that the risks are more or less the same? Let's see what the *internal rate of return* tells us about choosing among the three alternatives:

Common stock IRR	15.0%
Corporate bond IRR	15.5%
Real estate IRR	19.7%

The IRRs described above are all before taxes. But what about Uncle Sam's share of the profits? The government's cut does matter, and the after-tax result of the investment is what counts to you. If you are in a 28 percent tax bracket, the after-tax IRRs for these investments are

Common stock IRR	11.4%
Corporate bond IRR	11.3%
Real estate IRR	21.3%

Now with this knowledge, and assuming that you had a little more confidence in what IRR really means, isn't it much easier to make the most rational and intelligent choice? And isn't it surprising that the real estate investment with the lowest initial cash return, 1.75 percent, surfaces as the after-tax leader by an overwhelming margin.

The actual calculation of IRR is complex, but within the capability of most people. However, some of the calculations are impossible to perform by solving ordinary equations and require the use of trial-and-error methods, moderately priced calculators, or computer software.

The beauty of this book is that even the most complex IRR calculations have been reduced to simple graphs that anybody can use to find answers in seconds. This book will make you a better informed investor. I guarantee it!

About 45,000,000 computer calculations were performed to prepare the graphs in this book. By having the book, you will be investing like a computer whiz—without having to learn how to use a computer. And if you have a computer, this book will help you make better use of it.

The time value of money: The single most important concept that one can master to facilitate a successful career in business, banking, securities, investment real estate, among others, is *the time value of money.* Knowledge of this essential subject is equally important to any individual in managing his or her own financial holdings and to anyone who either borrows or lends money or who operates as a manager or leader of a business organization. Swimming the competitive waters of business without mastery of the concept of the time value of money is like trying to navigate the proverbial creek without a paddle. The most important and valuable business academic course ever taken by the author was called "Mathematics of Finance," and its subject was the time value of money. Its usefulness and value have endured throughout the author's financial and business career, which has included serving as president of an international investment securities firm, managing a multimillion-dollar portfolio of bonds and stocks, acquiring and managing an eight-figure real estate and securities investment portfolio, consulting as an expert witness in financial matters, and founding a computer financial software firm.

The concept of the time value of money is simple enough—in fact, it is known to almost everyone and is characterized by the saying, "A bird in the hand is worth two in the bush." From a monetary standpoint, it means simply that a dollar in hand today is more valuable than one which is due in the future. The obvious reason is that with a dollar in hand today, one can invest it and produce earnings—and that makes it more valuable than a dollar due in the future.

Economists refer to *opportunity cost* as the difference in value between money due at two different periods of time. It is the lost benefit from having to wait to receive the money until a future date. It is the interest forfeited by not having the money to invest at an earlier date.

Though the concept of time value is simple, the calculations involved in applying the concept to real situations can be complicated. Whenever possible, in finding solutions to time-value-of-money problems, several methods of approach are provided.

The first such method requires almost no mathematical ability on the part of the reader: it requires only the ability to use a graph to find the solution to the problem. Scores of graphs are provided for finding solutions to such time-value situations as:

1. **Present and future values of single sums**
   Future value of a single sum
   Rate of interest needed to accumulate a specific future sum
   Present value of a future sum
   Rate needed to discount a future sum to a specific present value
   How long it takes money to double
   At what interest rate money will double

2. **Present and future values of a series of cash flows**
   Future value of a level-payment series
   Level payment needed to accumulate a specific future sum
   Present value of a level-payment series
   Rate needed to have a certain present value of a level-payment series

3. **Unique financial planning solutions**
   How long invested money will last after withdrawals at various rates
   Conversion of nominal interest rates to effective annual yields
   How much one needs to invest at various rates to achieve a financial
   goal, assuming that the annual investment is increased each year

4. **Loans from both borrower and lender viewpoints**
   The monthly payment required to pay off a loan
   How big a loan various level payments will support

5. **Yields to maturity on fixed-income and bond investments**
   What yield to maturity or yield to call will be earned by a bond with
   various maturities and purchase prices
   What price must be paid to buy a bond based on various maturities,
   coupon payments, and call or redemption provisions

6. **Internal rate of return to analyze investments**
   What internal rate of return is provided by an investment in stocks
   What internal rate of return is provided by an investment in real estate
   How internal rate of return or yield to maturity for bonds is calculated

Alternative methods (to the graphs) are included, such as pertinent formulas or equations for finding answers to time-value-of-money situations. The formulas can be solved by using the time-value factors in Appendix 1, logarithms as discussed in Appendix 2, electronic calculators which have the ability to find powers and roots, or personal computers.

Acknowledgments

The author's thanks and appreciation are extended to the following persons for their contribution of time, material, or both to the research for this book: James G. Weber, Vice President, Systems and Programming, J. J. B. Hilliard,

W. L. Lyons, Inc.; Tim Zink, Senior Attorney, Federal Reserve Bank of St. Louis; Steve Hueghlin, Founder and Vice President, Gabriele, Hueghlin & Cashman; Peter Murray, Director of Professional Qualifications, MSRB, Municipal Securities Rulemaking Board; Sheila Stoke, Controller, Bank of Louisville; Bill Fenwick, J. J. B. Hilliard, W. L. Lyons, Inc.; Orson Oliver, President, Bank of Louisville; Anthony F. Herbst, University of Texas, Professor of Finance and C. R. and D. S. Carter Chairholder; Jay Brandt, Associate Professor of Finance, Department of Economics and Finance, University of Louisville School of Business; Hon. Romano L. Mazzoli, U.S. House of Representatives; Jennifer McLaughlin, staff assistant, Office of Congressman Mazzoli; Steve Gagel, Fellow, Society of Actuaries, F.S.A., Mercer-Meidinger-Hansen; Kathie Pellegrini, F.S.A., Mercer-Meidinger-Hansen; Kathryn McGrath, U.S. Securities and Exchange Commission; Jay Frandsen, Professor of Mathematics, Jefferson County, Kentucky; Steve Gwin, Fellow, Society of Actuaries, Capital Holding Corp.; Joya Maria Kaler, Regional Sales Representative, Commerce Clearing House; Cal Johnson, Quantitative Analyst, Equity Derivatives, Salomon Brothers; Edward Musikantow, Managing Director, Morgan Stanley & Co.; Marian White, Product Publicity Coordinator, Hewlett Packard; Phyllis Hunefeld, Executive Assistant, Federal Reserve Bank of St. Louis (Louisville Branch); Erroll Frank, Superintendent of Schools, Hamilton County, Ohio; A. J. Warner, Partner and First Vice President, J. C. Bradford & Company; Shawn D. Rosen, Associate, Hewitt Associates; Glenda Neely, Librarian, University of Louisville; Betsy Brown, Senior Editor, McGraw-Hill; Rae Shepherd-Shlechter, Interlibrary Librarian, Louisville Public Library.

These people all took time from their busy schedules to provide either advice, research material, or both—for which I am grateful and indebted.

LAWRENCE R. ROSEN
Louisville, Kentucky

1

Simple and Compound Interest and Effective Rates

A million dollars is a lot of money, inflation notwithstanding. There are those whose lifetime ambition is to become a millionaire. Others would simply like to make an additional million. And some are just curious about what it would take to become a millionaire or to make $1 million. For all these, Fig. 1.1 shows how to use compound interest to make $1 million. To see how to use this graph, suppose that Arnie Andersen has 20 high-earning years in which to make his million. He thinks he can earn 12 percent on his investments. He plans to reinvest all the income from his investments to earn more interest, dividends, and rents. How much must he invest each month to achieve his $1 million goal?

Refer to Fig. 1.1. The vertical axis represents the *monthly investment* amount. The horizontal axis represents the *number of years* it will take to accumulate $1 million at various rates of interest and monthly investment amounts. The curves each represent the nominal *annual interest rate* that the monthly investments will earn. Arnie Andersen would enter the graph on the horizontal axis at the point labeled *A*, proceed vertically to the 12 percent curve (point *B*), and then continue horizontally toward the left axis, reaching it at point *C*. Point *C* is the monthly investment amount, $1011.

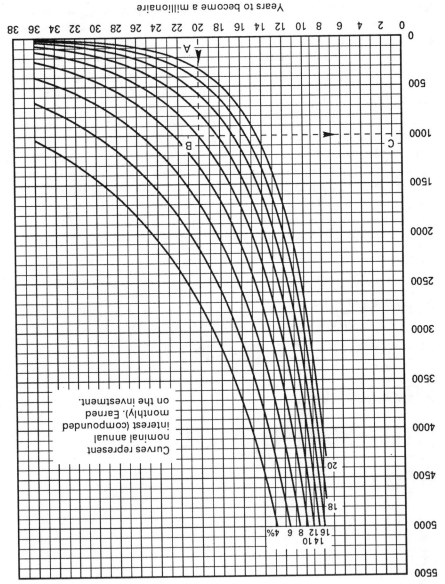

Monthly investment $

Years to become a millionaire

Figure 1.1. How to use compound interest to make $1 million. Example: To obtain $1 million in 20 years, at 12 percent annual interest (compounded monthly) after tax, it takes a monthly investment of about $1011 (see dashed line on graph).

That's all there is to it: If Arnie invests $1011 per month for 20 years at 12 percent interest, his account will be worth a cool $1 million.

To make a million, an almost unlimited number of other combinations are possible of monthly investment amounts, rates of interest, and time periods. Examples include investing $841 per month at 10 percent for 24 years, or $78 per month at 14 percent for 36 years, etc.

Keep in mind, of course, that there may be income taxes to be paid on the interest earnings. To offset the tax liability, use the interest-rate curve that represents the after-tax rate to be earned. For example, if you expect to earn 10 percent before taxes and your combined state and federal tax bracket is 40 percent, you should use the 6 percent curve (60 percent of 10 percent is 6 percent, where 60 percent is the portion of the interest income that is retained after taxes of 40 percent are paid).

Such is the power of interest compounding: Just $1011 per month can grow into $1 million in 20 years at 12 percent interest. *Compound interest* is one type of interest; the other type is *simple interest*.

Simple and Compound Interest

Simple interest is earned only on the original principal. Simple interest may be contrasted with compound interest, where interest is earned on both interest and principal. We just saw that $1011 per month can grow to $1 million at compound interest. At simple interest, all the interest earned is spent, nothing is reinvested, and the account balance after 20 years is a relatively meager $242,640 (1011 × 20 years × 12 months) rather than $1 million. In addition to the account balance, at simple interest, the interest received and spent over the 20 years would have been about $315,766. The account balance and the interest spent combined are about $442,000 less than the $1 million that would be accumulated if interest were reinvested. So, the pleasure of spending has a great opportunity cost!

Generally it is easy to grasp concepts involving interest by relating them to bank accounts with which we are all familiar. If you have a savings account, and each time interest is credited to the account you withdraw the interest and spend it, then you are receiving simple interest. Nothing is being reinvested—and nothing is compounding. If, on the other hand, you allow the interest credited to the account to remain in the account, and that interest itself begins to earn interest, then you are both reinvesting your interest and it is compounding. In the financial community, the terms *compounding* and *reinvesting* are used synonymously.

We shall now take a look at the formulas for simple interest and compound interest, and then at graphs that can be used to find the value of accounts in which interest is compounding.

Simple Annual Interest

If you invest $1000 today at 4 percent simple annual interest, after 1 year the account will be worth $1040; after 2 years, it will be worth $1080, and so on. The formula is

$$I = PiT$$

where I = interest earned
P = principal (e. g., $1000)
i = rate of annual interest (e.g., 4 percent, or 0.04)
T = time in years (e.g., 1 year)

Thus, for the example given, after 1 year the interest earned (I) will be $1000 × 0.04 × 1, or $40. That is,

$$I = (\$1000) (0.04) (1) = \$40$$

The value of the account, S, is the original principal ($1000) plus the interest earned ($40). Thus,

$$S = P + I$$

since $I = PiT$, then

$$S = P + PiT \quad \text{or} \quad S = P (1 + iT)$$

After 2 years, the value of the account, at 4 percent simple annual interest, is

$$S = P (1 + iT)$$
$$= \$1000 [1 + (0.04) (2)]$$
$$= \$1000 [1.08]$$
$$= \$1080$$

This calculation purposely fails to take into consideration, however, any interest earned in the second year on the $40 interest from the first year. Interest paid only on the original principal is called *simple interest*. Another way of looking at the question of simple versus compound interest is in terms of *reinvestment*. When an investor takes receipt of the periodic interest or income and spends it (as with a bank account where interest checks are mailed to the investor, or a stock which sends dividends to the stockholder), it is a *simple interest* situation. On the other hand, when the investor *reinvests* by letting the interest remain in the account, to earn interest on the interest, that is a *compound interest* situation. Thus compound interest includes interest earned on both accumulated interest and the original principal.

Table 1.1. Compound Interest

Year	Principal at start year	Annual interest earned during year at 4% (P/T)	Value at end of year (P+I)
1	$1000.00	$40.00	$1040.00
2	1040.00	41.60	1081.60
3	1081.60	43.26	1124.86
4	1124.86	44.99	1169.86
5	1169.86	46.79	1216.65
6	1216.65	48.67	1265.32
7	1265.32	50.61	1315.93
8	1315.93	52.64	1368.57
9	1368.57	54.74	1423.31
10	1423.31	56.93	1480.24

Compound Interest

For the same example as we have been discussing ($P = \$1000$, $i = 0.04$), over a 10-year period of time, the annual interest and accumulated value of the account if invested at compound interest are shown in Table 1.1.

To determine the value of an account, S, after a period of years n (e.g., 10), with an original investment, P (e.g., $1,000), at an annual compound interest rate of i (e.g., 0.04), the formula is

$$S = P(1+i)^n$$
$$= \$1000 (1.04)^{10}$$
$$= \$1000 (1.480244) = \$1480.24$$

The value of $(1 + i)^n$ at various rates of i and for various values of n is shown in Appendix 1, Table 6, column 1. The table shows, for instance, how $1.00 will grow at a rate of 4 percent compounded annually. The value at the end of 10 periods will be $1.48.

If tables are not available, the value of $(1 + i)^n$ can be determined by using logarithms, which are explained in Appendix 2. For example, the method for determining the value, x, of $(1.04)^{10}$, that is, 1.04 multiplied by itself 9 times, is

$$\text{Log } x = 10 \text{ Log } 1.04$$
$$\text{Log } x = 10 (0.017033)$$
$$\text{Log } x = 0.170330$$
$$x = 1.48023$$

How to use logarithms to solve problems is explained at the beginning of Appendix 2. Logarithms are particularly useful when working with powers or roots of numbers. If the battery goes dead on your calculator, you don't need to stop thinking. Just turn to Appendix 2 (or get new batteries).

The Power of Compounding

Figure 1.2 shows how long it will take a single investment to double in value at various compound earnings rates. The dashed line shows that a single invest-ment today of $1000, with earnings compounded at 8 percent per year, will double after 9 years. This result can be checked or obtained by the formula

$$S = P (1 + i)^n$$

$$= \$1000(1.08)^9$$

$$= \$1000(1.999004) = \$1999$$

An excellent rule of thumb for mentally calculating the approximate length of time it takes money to double is the *rule of 72*:

$$T = \frac{72}{i}$$

where T = approximate time

i = compound annual growth or interest rate

Example: Doubling Money. How long will it take for $5000 to grow to $10,000 at 10 percent compound annual interest?

$$T = \frac{72}{i} = \frac{72}{10} = 7.2 \text{ years}$$

The corollary to the question above is: At what rate of interest i must $5000 be invested in order to double in 10 years? In this case, the quick mental method is to divide 72 by the number of years n:

$$i = \frac{72}{n} = \frac{72}{10} = 7.2 \%$$

Thus, the rule of 72 may be used to find either the interest rate required or the time period needed in order for money to double.

The answers obtained by the rule of 72 are approximate. The closer the rate of interest is to 8 percent, the more accurate is the estimate given by use of the rule. As the rate of interest increases above 8 percent, the accuracy of the rule diminishes progressively. A more precise result for rates of 20 percent or higher is obtained by substituting 78 for 72 in the rule.

Percent per year

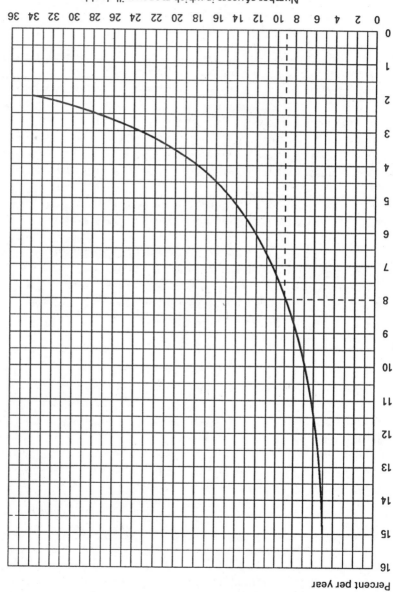

Number of years in which money will double

Figure 1.2. How long it will take a single investment to double in value at various annual compound earnings rates.

Example: Using the Rule of 78. At 20 percent interest compounded annually, how long will it take an investment to double? By the rule of 72, the answer is 3.6 years. The actual answer is 3.8 years. The rule of 78 suggests 3.9 years, which is closer to the correct answer than that provided by the rule of 72. So, use the rule of 78 for interest rates above 20 percent per year.

The rule of 72 or 78 can also be used to determine the discount rate which is necessary to obtain a present value of about one-half of a given future value. Present values are discussed in Chap. 2.

Table 1.2 shows the value of a lump-sum investment of $1 after selected numbers of years at rates of annual compound earnings from 1 to 15 percent. From the table, $1 invested today, with earnings at 8 percent reinvested annually, would grow to $4.66 in 20 years. One hundred dollars would increase to $466, $1000 to $4660, and $10,000 to $46,600. The compound interest formula, again, is:

$$S = P (1 + i)^n$$

where n = number of years (think of n as the *number*)

S = value after n years (think of S as the *sum* or future value)

P = original investment (*principal*) or *present value*)

i = compound annual growth rate (*interest*)

Figures 1.3 and 1.4 show the values of a single investment of $1, $1000, after periods from zero to 30 years under annual compound interest rates from 1 to 14 percent.

Notice that there are four variables in the compound interest formula: S, P, i, and n. If any three of the variables are known, the fourth can be calculated. The unknown variable can be found by formula, by the use of the graphs, from the tables in Appendix I (see Tables 1–20 at the back of the book), or by using an electronic calculator or computer.

Example: Finding an Unknown Future Value. How much will $1 be worth after 16 years if it earns 3 percent compound annual interest? As the dashed line in Fig. 1.3 shows, the value would be $1.60. From the formula,

$$S = P (1 + i)^n$$
$$= 1 (1.03)^{16}$$
$$= 1 (1.604706) = \$1.60$$

The value of $(1.03)^{16}$ can also be found in Appendix 1, Table 5 (3 percent rate) in the column headed "Amount of 1" in the row for 16 periods. Or it may be found by using logarithms (see Appendix 2), or by using an electronic calculator or a computer.

Table 1.2. Growth of $1 at Compound Annual Interest

	Annual interest compound rate														
Yrs	1%	2%	3%	4%	5%	6%	7%	8%	9%	10%	11%	12%	13%	14%	15%
1	1.01	1.02	1.03	1.04	1.05	1.06	1.07	1.08	1.09	1.10	1.11	1.12	1.13	1.14	1.15
2	1.02	1.04	1.06	1.08	1.10	1.12	1.14	1.17	1.19	1.21	1.23	1.25	1.25	1.30	1.32
3	1.03	1.06	1.09	1.12	1.16	1.19	1.23	1.26	1.30	1.33	1.37	1.40	1.44	1.48	1.52
4	1.04	1.08	1.13	1.17	1.22	1.26	1.31	1.36	1.41	1.46	1.52	1.57	1.63	1.69	1.75
5	1.05	1.10	1.16	1.22	1.28	1.34	1.40	1.47	1.54	1.61	1.69	1.76	1.84	1.93	2.01
6	1.06	1.13	1.19	1.27	1.34	1.42	1.50	1.59	1.68	1.77	1.87	1.97	2.08	2.19	2.31
7	1.07	1.15	1.23	1.32	1.41	1.50	1.61	1.71	1.83	1.95	2.08	2.21	2.35	2.50	2.66
8	1.08	1.17	1.27	1.37	1.48	1.59	1.72	1.85	1.99	2.14	2.30	2.48	2.66	2.85	3.06
9	1.09	1.20	1.30	1.42	1.55	1.69	1.84	2.00	2.17	2.36	2.56	2.77	3.00	3.25	3.52
10	1.10	1.22	1.34	1.48	1.63	1.79	1.97	2.16	2.37	2.59	2.84	3.11	3.39	3.71	4.05
11	1.12	1.24	1.38	1.54	1.71	1.90	2.10	2.33	2.58	2.85	3.15	3.48	3.84	4.23	4.65
12	1.13	1.27	1.43	1.60	1.80	2.01	2.25	2.52	2.81	3.14	3.50	3.90	4.33	4.82	5.35
13	1.14	1.29	1.47	1.67	1.89	2.13	2.41	2.72	3.07	3.45	3.88	4.36	4.90	5.49	6.15
14	1.15	1.32	1.51	1.73	1.98	2.26	2.58	2.94	3.34	3.80	4.31	4.89	5.53	6.26	7.08
15	1.16	1.35	1.56	1.80	2.08	2.40	2.76	3.17	3.64	4.18	4.78	5.47	6.25	7.14	8.14
16	1.17	1.37	1.60	1.87	2.18	2.54	2.95	3.43	3.97	4.59	5.31	6.13	7.07	8.14	9.36
17	1.18	1.40	1.65	1.95	2.29	2.69	3.16	3.70	4.33	5.05	5.90	6.87	7.99	9.28	10.76
18	1.20	1.43	1.70	2.03	2.41	2.85	3.38	4.00	4.72	5.56	6.54	7.69	9.02	10.58	12.38
19	1.21	1.46	1.75	2.11	2.53	3.03	3.62	4.32	5.14	6.12	7.26	8.61	10.20	12.06	14.23
20	1.22	1.49	1.81	2.19	2.65	3.21	3.87	4.66	5.60	6.73	8.06	9.65	11.52	13.74	16.37
21	1.23	1.52	1.86	2.28	2.79	3.40	4.14	5.03	6.11	7.40	8.95	10.80	13.02	15.67	18.82
22	1.24	1.55	1.92	2.37	2.93	3.60	4.43	5.44	6.66	8.14	9.93	12.10	14.71	17.86	21.64
23	1.26	1.58	1.97	2.46	3.07	3.82	4.74	5.87	7.26	8.95	11.03	13.55	16.63	20.36	24.89
24	1.27	1.61	2.03	2.56	3.23	4.05	5.07	6.34	7.91	9.85	12.24	15.18	18.79	23.21	28.63
25	1.28	1.64	2.09	2.67	3.39	4.29	5.43	6.85	8.62	10.83	13.59	17.00	21.23	26.46	32.92
26	1.30	1.67	2.16	2.77	3.56	4.55	5.81	7.40	9.40	11.92	15.08	19.04	23.99	30.17	37.86
27	1.31	1.71	2.22	2.88	3.73	4.82	6.21	7.99	10.25	13.11	16.74	21.32	27.11	34.39	43.54
28	1.32	1.74	2.29	3.00	3.92	5.11	6.65	8.63	11.17	14.42	18.58	23.88	30.63	39.20	50.07
29	1.33	1.78	2.36	3.12	4.12	5.42	7.11	9.32	12.17	15.86	20.62	26.75	34.62	44.69	57.58
30	1.35	1.81	2.43	3.24	4.32	5.74	7.61	10.06	13.27	17.45	22.89	29.96	39.12	50.95	66.21
31	1.36	1.85	2.50	3.37	4.54	6.09	8.15	10.87	14.46	19.19	25.41	33.56	44.20	58.08	76.14
32	1.37	1.88	2.58	3.51	4.76	6.45	8.72	11.74	15.76	21.11	28.21	37.58	49.95	66.21	87.57
33	1.39	1.92	2.65	3.65	5.00	6.84	9.33	12.68	17.18	23.23	31.31	42.09	56.44	75.48	100.70
34	1.40	1.96	2.73	3.79	5.25	7.25	9.98	13.69	18.73	25.55	34.75	47.14	63.78	86.05	115.80
35	1.42	2.00	2.81	3.95	5.52	7.69	10.68	14.79	20.41	28.10	38.57	52.80	72.07	98.10	133.18
36	1.43	2.04	2.90	4.10	5.79	8.15	11.42	15.97	22.25	30.91	42.82	59.14	81.44	111.83	153.15
37	1.45	2.08	2.99	4.27	6.08	8.64	12.22	17.25	24.25	34.00	47.53	66.23	92.02	127.49	176.12
38	1.46	2.12	3.07	4.44	6.39	9.15	13.08	18.63	26.44	37.40	52.76	74.18	103.99	145.34	202.54
39	1.47	2.16	3.17	4.62	6.70	9.70	13.99	20.12	28.82	41.14	58.56	83.08	117.51	165.69	232.92
40	1.49	2.21	3.26	4.80	7.04	10.29	14.97	21.72	31.41	45.26	65.00	93.05	132.78	188.88	267.86

Similarly, a $1000 investment at 3 percent would be worth $1600 after 16 years, and an original investment of $10,000 would be worth about $16,000 after the same length of time.

Number of years

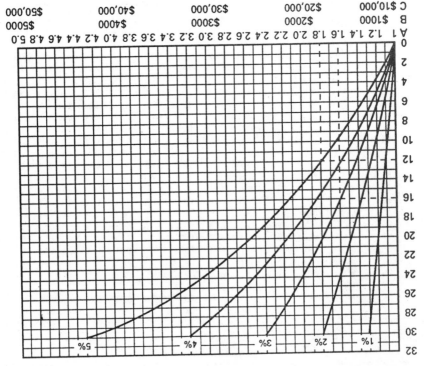

Figure 1.3. Single investments at 1 to 5 percent compound annual interest rates.

Value of a single investment of (A) $1, (B) $1000, or (C) $10,000 at various compound growth rates

Example: Finding an Unknown Number of Years. Tommy Thurston has $10,000 today and estimates that he can earn 5 percent per year compounded. How many years will it take for his nest egg to reach $18,000 if no withdrawals are made?

To find the solution using Fig. 1.3, restate the problem as follows: At 5 percent annual compound interest, how long will it take an investment of $1 ($10,000) to increase to $1.80 ($18,000), or to multiply by a factor of 1.8 ($18,000 divided by 10,000)? As the dashed line in Fig. 1.3 shows, it will take about 12 years.

Using the formula, the solution is found

$$\frac{S}{P} = (1 + i)^n$$

$$\frac{\$18,000}{\$10,000} = (1 + 0.05)^n$$

$$1.8 = 1.05^n$$

Thus the problem is to find n where the rate is 5 percent and 1.05^n is 1.8. See Appendix 1, Table 7. Scan the first column "Amount of 1—How $1 left at compound interest will grow" until you find 1.8 or as close as possible to it. The result for 12 years is 1.795, and for 13 years it is 1.886. So n is slightly greater than 12 years. Another way to solve for an unknown exponent is to use logarithms. Using logarithms (see Appendix 2),

$$n = \frac{\text{Log } S/P}{\text{Log } (1 + i)} = \frac{\text{Log } 18,000/10,000}{\text{Log } 1.05} = \frac{\text{Log } 1.8}{\text{Log } 1.05} = \frac{0.25527}{0.02119} = 12.05 \text{ years}$$

Example: Finding an Unknown Present Value. José Santiago's goal is to have $50,000 at the end of 18 years. Assuming that he can earn 8 percent compounded annually, how much must he invest today?

Refer to Fig. 1.4. Starting on the left vertical side of the figure at 18 years, proceed—as the dashed line indicates—across to the 8 percent curve, then down (vertically) to the base. The figure shows that $1 will grow to $4 after 18 years at the 8 percent compounded annually. The problem, then, is as follows, what is the sum x that must be invested today to reach $50,000 after 18 years at 8 percent compounded:

$$\frac{\$1}{\$4} = \frac{x}{\$50,000}$$

$$\$4x = \$50,000$$

$$x = \$12,500$$

Hence $12,500 invested today, at 8 percent compounded annually, will be worth $50,000 after 18 years.
The solution by formula is

$$S = P(1 + i)^n$$

$$P = \frac{S}{(1 + i)^n} = \frac{\$50,000}{(1.08)^{18}} = \frac{\$50,000}{3.996019} = 12,512.45$$

The value $(1.08)^{18}$ is found by any of the following means:

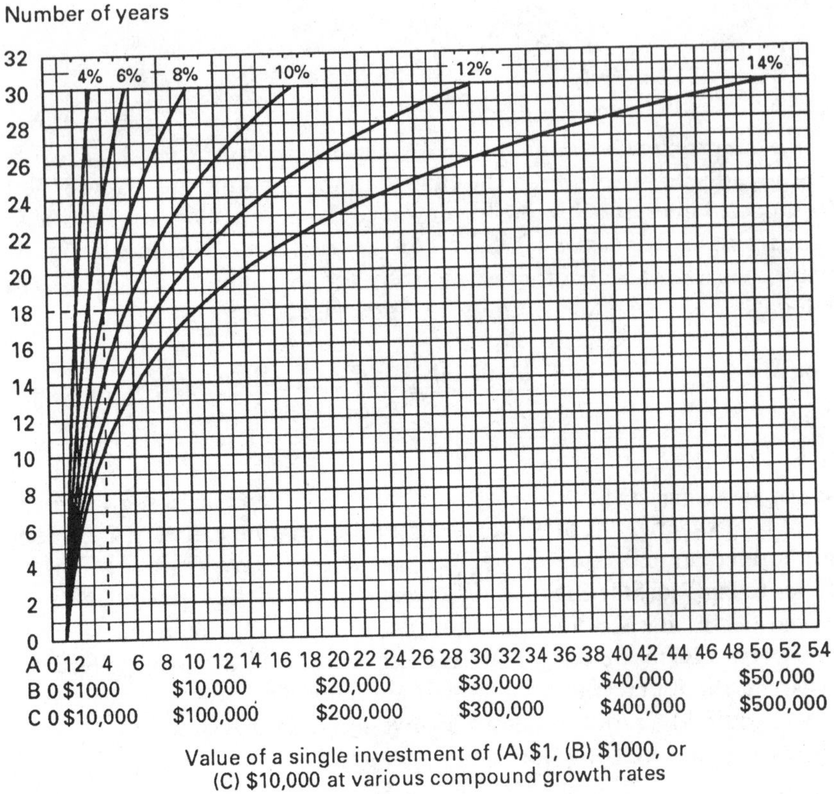
Number of years
32
30
28
26
24
22
20
18
16
14
12
10
8
6
4
2
0
4% 6% 8% 10% 12% 14%
A 0 1 2 4 6 8 10 12 14 16 18 20 22 24 26 28 30 32 34 36 38 40 42 44 46 48 50 52 54
B 0 $1000 $10,000 $20,000 $30,000 $40,000 $50,000
C 0 $10,000 $100,000 $200,000 $300,000 $400,000 $500,000
Value of a single investment of (A) $1, (B) $1000, or
(C) $10,000 at various compound growth rates

Figure 1.4. Single investments at 4 to 14 percent compound annual interest rates.

1. From Appendix 1, Table 10, 8 percent rate, under the column headed "Amount of 1" adjacent to 18 periods (of time)
2. Using an electronic calculator, computer; or
3. Using logarithms (see Appendix 2). Using logs, the solution is

$$\begin{aligned} \text{Log}\,(1.08)^{18} &= 18\ \text{Log}\,(1.08) \\ &= 18\,(0.003342) \\ &= 0.060156 \\ \text{antilog}\ 0.060156 &= 3.9944 \end{aligned}$$

Example: Finding an Unknown Rate of Interest. Joan Fontaine wants to retire in 8 years. To do so, however, she needs a nest egg of $300,000 to tide her over her retirement years in the style in which she wishes to live. She has $105,167.71 now, so, she needs to multipty her capital by 2.85 or almost 3 times ($300,000 divided by 105,167.71). At what rate, after taxes, must Joan invest to achieve her goal?

Number of years

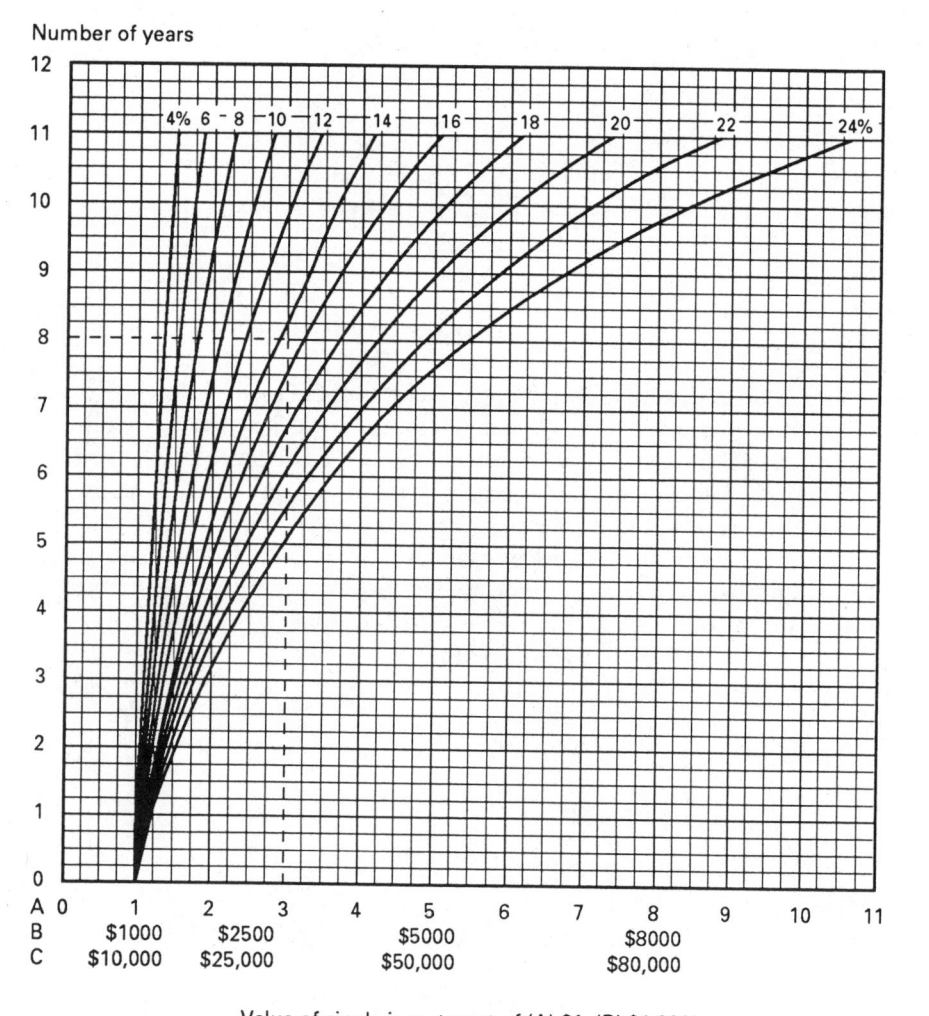

Value of single investment of (A) $1; (B) $1,000;
or (C) $10,000 at various compound growth rates

Figure 1.5. Single investments at 4 to 22 percent compound annual interest rates.

Figure 1.5 shows the future values of a single investment at rates from 4 percent to 22 percent compounded annually. Entering the graph along the left vertical axis at the 8-year point, mentally draw a horizontal line across the graph. Then, on the bottom horizontal axis, find the point where the value is 2.85 (or almost 3) and mentally draw a vertical line from that point up to where it intersects the previously drawn horizontal line representing 8 years.

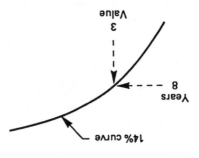

The value of the curve at or closest to that point of intersection is the rate of interest Joan must earn—about 14 percent. Notice that the point of intersection lies right on the 14 percent curve. (If the point of intersection lay midway between the 13 percent and 14 percent curves, then the appropriate rate would be about 13.5 percent, etc.)

Using the graph, the solution is easy. However, solving the problem using the formula is a bit more complicated. For those readers who are interested, it uses the familiar equation,

$$S = P (1 + i)^n$$

We know that

$$S = \$300,000$$

$$P = \$105,167.71$$

$$n = 8 \text{ years}$$

Hence

$$\$300,000 = \$105,167.71(1 + i)^8$$

$$(1 + i)^8 = \frac{\$300,000}{\$105,167.71}$$

$$(1 + i)^8 = 2.85259$$

There are several ways of finding the rate, i. The tables in Appendix 1 may be scanned, looking at the line adjacent to 8 periods and the value in the first column, "Amount of $1." Scan through the tables seeking a value in the first column, alongside 8 periods. Table 16, rate 14 percent, comes very close, with a value of 2.85286. Thus, using the tables of factors, 14 percent is the value sought.

Another way of finding i is to make use of logarithms, as described in Appendix 2:

$$\text{Log } 2.85259 = 8 \text{ Log } (1 + i)$$

$$\text{Log } (1 + i) = \frac{\text{Log } 2.85259}{8}$$

Log 2.85259 = 0.45524 (by interpolation between 0.45515 and 0.45530)

Thus,

$$\text{Log } (1 + i) = \frac{0.45524}{8}$$

$$\text{Log } (1 + i) = 0.056905$$

The number whose Log is 0.056905 is 1.140. Thus

$$1 + i = 1.140$$

and

$$i = 0.14 \quad \text{or} \quad 14\%$$

By any method, Joan Fontaine needs an investment that will yield 14 percent after taxes in order to achieve her objective. Using the graphs is, of course, the fastest and easiest method, so that's the way to go if precision is not required and an approximation will do.

And if you want real convenience, a computer software program called THE FINANCIAL AND INTEREST CALCULATOR, available from the author, provides almost instantaneous solutions to most time-value-of-money problems. The software may be ordered (using the order form in this book) directly from the publisher, Larry Rosen Co., 7008 Springdale Road, Louisville, KY 40241.

Effective Annual Rates and Frequency of Compounding

The basic compound interest formula, $S = P(1 + i)^n$, assumes that the interest is compounded annually. However, other compounding periods are frequently encountered. For example, policies at savings institutions vary—some may compound interest daily, monthly, or even continuously. Bond calculations are usually based on semiannual compounding. To handle other-than-annual periods of compounding, the basic compound interest formula is modified to the following:

$$S = P\left(1 + \frac{i}{m}\right)^{mn}$$

where S = the value of principal and interest, after $n \times m$ periods of compounding—the sum or future value

P = the original principal or investment

n = the number of years

m = the number of compounding periods during one basis year (i.e., 2 for semiannual, 4 for quarterly, etc.); the basis year may be 360, 365, or 366 days.

i = the compound annual growth rate (the *nominal* annual rate)

Example: Finding Future Value with Interest Compounded Semiannually. How much would a $1000 investment be worth at a 3 percent annual (or nominal) rate if compounded semiannually for 16 years?

$$S = P\left(1 + \frac{i}{m}\right)^{nm}$$

$$= \$1000\left(1 + \frac{0.03}{2}\right)^{(16)(2)}$$

$$= \$1000\,(1.015)^{32}$$

$$= \$1000\,(1.610324) = \$1610.32$$

This result of semiannual compounding, $1610.32, compares to $1604.71 at annual compound interest. The future value at a monthly or daily rate of compounding would be even greater, as follows:

Monthly compounding:

$$S = P\left(1 + \frac{i}{m}\right)^{nm}$$

$$= \$1000\left(1 + \frac{0.03}{12}\right)^{(16)(12)}$$

$$= \$1000\,(1.0025)^{192}$$

$$= \$1000\,(1.6151)$$

$$= \$1615.11$$

Daily compounding:

$$S = P\left(1 + \frac{i}{m}\right)^{nm}$$

$$= 1000\,(1 + 0.03365)^{(16)(365)}$$

$$= 1000 \ (1.0000822)^{5840}$$

$$= 1000 \ (1.61604)$$

$$= \$1616.04$$

Daily compounding is sometimes used by financial institutions on the basis of a 360-day year, rather than 365 days. A 360-day year calculation involves less frequent compounding, thus providing the depositor with less interest and costing the financial institution less money. Obviously, other things being equal, it is better to put one's money on deposit with a bank that compounds daily on the basis of a 365-day year.

Continuous Compounding*

Financial institutions may choose to pay interest on the basis of compounding interest *continuously*—365 days per year, 24 hours per day, 60 minutes per hour, etc. The formula for such continuous compounding is:

$$S = Pe^{rt}$$

where S = the sum at the future date or maturity of both principal and interest—the future value

P = the principal—the original investment or present value

e = the base for natural logarithms, about 2.7182818 (e represents an infinite series†)

r = nominal rate of annual interest

t = number of years (time)

Example: Finding Future Value with Continuous Compounding Interest.
Shana McCarthy invests $1000 at 8 percent compounded continuously. How much will her account be worth at the end of 2 years?

$$S = P \ (e)^{rt}$$

$$= \$1000 \ (2.7182818)^{(0.08)(2)}$$

$$= \$1000 \ (1.17351)$$

$$= \$1173.51$$

---

*To convert continuous and periodic rates see section on conversions starting on p. 31.

†$e = \lim_{x \to 0} (1 + x)^{(1/x)} = 1 + 1 + \frac{1}{2!} + \frac{1}{3!} + \frac{1}{4!} + \frac{1}{5!} + \ldots = 2.7182818 \ldots$ (This definition is given for the sake of completeness; it can be ignored in that it is not necessary to understand it in order to solve problems involving continuous compounding of interest.)

Effective Annual Yield

For a given nominal rate of interest—say, 8 percent—the more frequently the interest is compounded, the more interest will be earned and the greater will be the effective yield. The *effective yield* is determined from

$$Y = \left(1 + \frac{r}{m}\right)^m - 1$$

where Y = effective annual yield
   r = conventional or nominal yield (rate)
   m = number of periods of compounding per year in the basis year (360, 365, or 366 days)

When the time period is 1 year, the effective annual rate is simply the interest earned divided by the original principal. For example, if $8160 in interest is earned on an original principal of $100,000, the effective rate is 8.16 percent. To put it another way, if the nominal rate is 8.16 percent and compounding is annually, then the effective rate is also 8.16 percent.

Consider the results of investing $100,000 for 1 year at a nominal rate of 8 percent annual interest, with compounding occurring annually, semiannually, quarterly, monthly, daily on a 360-day basis, daily on a 365-day basis, and continuously, as shown in Table 1.3. Obviously, if alternative investments have the same nominal (e.g., 8 percent) rate of interest, the one that compounds more frequently will produce the greater yield and will have the higher effective annual rate.

However, if the nominal rates are not the same (e.g., 8 percent and 7 percent), surprising results may occur: Better yields might result in some instances from a lower nominal rate and more frequent compounding than from a higher nominal rate with less frequent compounding.

Table 1.3. Nominal versus Effective Rates

Compounding frequency	Compounds per year m	Result of investing $100,000 at 8% compounded	Increase from previous %	Multiplier	Effective annual yield
Annual	1	$108,000.00		$(1.08)^1$	8.00%
Semiannual	2	$108,160.00	$160.00	$(1.04)^2$	8.16%
Quarterly	4	$108,243.22	83.22	$(1.02)^4$	8.24%
Monthly	12	$108,299.95	56.73	$(1.00667)^{12}$	8.30%
Daily, 360-day year	360	$108,327.74	27.79	$(1.000222)^{360}$	8.33%
Daily, 365-day year	365	$108,327.76	0.01	$(1.000219)^{365}$	8.33%
Continuously	Infinite	$108,328.71	0.95	$e^{0.08}$	8.33%

$+ \ e^{0.08} = (1.083287)$

Example: Finding the Effective Annual Yield. Ted Travis has $100,000 to invest. Bank A offers him a nominal rate of 10 percent with monthly compounding. A competitor, Bank B, offers 10.2 percent with annual compounding. Which deposit should Travis select? What is the effective annual rate offered by each bank? How much would his account contain at each bank at the end of 1 year?

At Bank A, the value of the account after 1 year is

$$S = P\left(1 + \frac{i}{m}\right)^{mn}$$

$$= \$100,000\left(1 + \frac{0.10}{12}\right)^{(1)(12)}$$

$$= \$100,000 \,(1.104171)$$

$$= \$110,471$$

and the effective annual yield is

$$Y = \left(1 + \frac{r}{m}\right)^m - 1$$

$$= \left(1 + \frac{0.10}{12}\right)^{12} - 1$$

$$= 0.1047 \text{ or } 10.47\%$$

At Bank B, the value of the account after 1 year is

$$S = P\left(1 + \frac{i}{m}\right)^{mn}$$

$$= \$100,000\left(1 + \frac{0.102}{1}\right)^{(1)(1)}$$

$$= \$100,000 \,(1.102)$$

$$= \$110,200$$

and the effective annual yield is

$$Y = \left(1 + \frac{r}{m}\right)^m - 1$$

$$= \left(1 + \frac{0.102}{1}\right)^{(1)(1)} - 1$$

$$= 0.102 \text{ or } 10.20\%$$

Thus Travis would earn an extra $271 ($110,471 less $110,200) by depositing his funds with Bank A, even though it quotes only a 10 percent nominal rate compared to the 10.2 percent of Bank B.

Effective Rates versus Nominal Rates

Figure 1.6 shows that the greatest effect of compounding more frequently than annually is in the change from annual to semiannual. Each increase in the number of times interest compounds per year results in an increase in the effective rate, but the magnitude of the increase diminishes with more frequent compounding.

Example: Finding the Effective Annual Rate.   A bank offers a 10.0 percent nominal rate of interest. What would the effective rate be if interest were compounded daily (365-day year) rather than annually? Enter Fig. 1.6 on the bottom axis at the 10.0 percent nominal rate; proceed vertically to the intersection with the curve for daily compounding; then proceed horizontally to the left axis. At the left axis the value is 10.52 percent, which is the effective annual rate.

The solution by formula is

$$Y = \left(1 + \frac{r}{m}\right)^m - 1$$

$$= \left(1 + \frac{0.1}{365}\right)^{365} - 1$$

$$= (1 + 0.000274)^{365} - 1$$

$$= 1.10516 - 1$$

$$= 0.010516 \quad \text{or} \quad 10.516\%$$

, How significant is this seemingly meager difference between nominal rates and effective rates? Possibly quite astounding. Consider the effect of investing $100,000 for 15 years: at 10 percent nominal rate (10 percent compounded annually); and at 10 percent nominal rate compounded daily (365-day year), which as we have seen is a 10.516 percent effective annual yield.

Result of investing at 10.0% $417,725
Result of investing at 10.516%   448,102
Increase from higher effective rate $ 30,377

Compared to the initial investment of $100,000, the future value is increased by some 30 percent, or $30,377, by investing at a rate that is

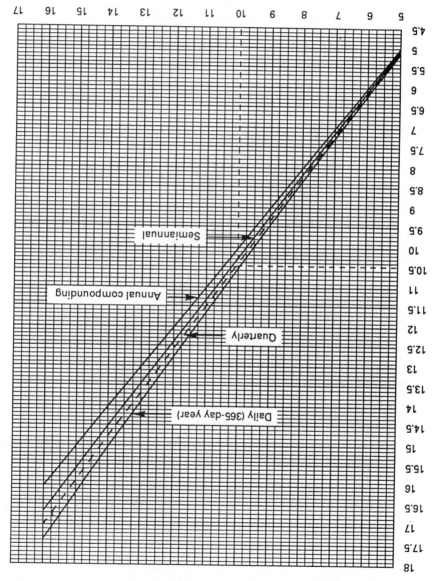

Effective annual rate

Figure 1.6. Effective rates versus nominal rates: Curves represent frequency of compounding.

Nominal rate

compounded more frequently, resulting in a higher effective rate by just over $1/_2$ of 1 percent. *The bottom line is a $30,000 gift just by selecting daily rather than annual compounding.*

Effects of Changes in Compounding Frequency

We have examined the effects of changes in compounding frequency on the future value of a single investment. Changes in compounding frequency have comparable effects on other time-value-of-money situations which are described in subsequent chapters. The effects of more frequent compounding are:

A reduction in the present value of a future single sum

A reduction in the present value of a series of payments (annuity)

An increase in the periodic loan payment to pay off a loan

An increase in the amount of interest paid on an installment loan

An increase in the number of years to pay off a loan

Using Tables with Various Periods of Compounding

Tables 1–20 in Appendix 1 provide factors for $(1 + i)^n$ or "how $1 left at compound interest will grow."

Example: Effects of Changes in Compounding Frequency. How much will $100,000 be worth at 8 percent nominal interest, if interest compounds annually, semiannually, and quarterly? Again, the future value formula for periodic compounding is required: $S = P(1 + i/m)^{nm}$. For annual compounding, using the formula gives

$$S = \$100,000 \left(1 + \frac{0.08}{1}\right)^{(1)(1)}$$

$$= \$100,000 \,(1.08)$$

$$= \$108,000$$

Using Appendix 1, Table 10 (The 8 percent table for 1 period of time), the factor for 1.08^1 is 1.08:

$$\$100,000 \,(1.08) = \$108,000$$

For semiannual compounding, using the formula gives

$$S = \$100,000 \left(1 + \frac{0.08}{2}\right)^{(1)(2)}$$

$$= \$100,000 (1.04)^2$$

$$= \$108,160$$

Using Appendix 1, Table 6 (note that the 4 percent table is used for 2 periods of time), the factor for 1.04^2 is 1.081600:

$$S = \$100,000 (1.081600)$$

$$= \$108,160$$

For quarterly compounding, using the formula gives

$$S = \$100,000 \left(1 + \frac{0.08}{4}\right)^{(1)(4)}$$

$$= \$100,000 (1.0824322)$$

$$= \$108,243.22$$

Using Appendix 1, Table 4 (the 2 percent table with 4 time periods), the factor for 1.02^4 is 1.082432:

$$S = \$100,000 (1.082432)$$

$$= \$108,243.20$$

Thus, to use the tables of factors (Tables A1-1 to A1-20 in Appendix 1) as a shortcut, two adjustments are required. First, the nominal annual rate must be divided by the number of times per year that interest is compounded. This gives the interest rate heading of the table to be used. Second, the number of years involved must be multiplied by the number of times per year that interest is compounded. This provides the time "periods" to be used in the tables.

Using Tables of Factors When the Desired Period Is Not Listed

In some cases, the number of periods of time desired may exceed the number of periods listed in the tables. Suppose, for example, that the factor for 200 periods is needed but the tables only go up to 150 periods. In that case, factors for two periods may be multiplied together to give the desired factor. That is, one may multiply the factors for 100 and 100, or 120 and 80, or 110 and 90, etc., in order to obtain the factor for 200. (This procedure works because of the law of exponents, $a^2 \times a^3 = a^5$; and $a^{200} = (a)^{120}(a)^{80}$. To multiply exponents with the same base (e.g., a), add the exponents (e.g., $120 + 80$). For example, in the 8 percent table, the factor for 30 periods (10.062656) is equal to the product of the factors for 10 years (2.158924) times the factor for 20 years (4.660957).

Money Market Accounts

Banks, savings & loans, etc., express the rates they pay to depositors in a wide variety of ways. Richard Morse, a Kansas State University professor, analyzed 28 advertisements by financial institutions and found 11 different ways of expressing the annual rate, 10 ways of expressing yield, and 7 methods of compounding interest.

To maximize your earnings (without increasing your risk), be sure to determine the *effective annual rate.* As we have already discussed, to find the effective rate, you must know the frequency of compounding, as well as the nominal rate.

How does the institution determine the amount of money at any given moment (the "balance") to which the interest rate applies? Some institutions do not credit deposits immediately, but delay for one or more days before giving the depositor credit for good funds. Obviously, an institution that follows such practices, other things being equal, is a less desirable place to make deposits than one that gives immediate credit.

Another factor to consider is the minimum balance required in the account, which if violated results in penalties or charges. The minimum balance may also determine the level of the interest rate with which you will be credited by firms that offer tiered rates.

Still another point involves the method the bank uses to calculate the balance. The most favorable choice from the depositor's point of view is the *average daily balance method.* Here, the bank takes the ending balance for each day in the cycle and then divides by the number of days in the cycle. Let's say that the average daily balance for a 30-day cycle is $1000. That amount is then taken as the amount on deposit for the number of days in the cycle and the interest rate to be credited is applied to it. Other things being equal, avoid banks that pay interest based on the *minimum or lowest balance on deposit each day.* Another, trickier way of saying the same thing is: "Interest paid on the highest balance on deposit for the entire period." Of course, what isn't readily apparent is that this really means, "Interest is paid on the *minimum balance.*"

Money market funds, such as those sponsored by various families of mutual funds (Fidelity, Scudder, Federated, etc.) are definite competitors for checking account funds. These funds quote (according to rules established by the Securities and Exchange Commission or SEC) both a *yield* and an *effective yield*. The yield typically is the rate earned (from net income) for a 7-day time period (ending date announced), multiplied by 52 (actually, 365 divided by 7) to obtain an annualized amount. Thus, if the 7-day figure is 0.0015, that is, $^{15}/1000$ of 1 percent, the "yield" when multiplied by 52 is 7.8 percent. However, this does not give effect to the frequency of interest compounding, which in the case of most funds is daily although the results are only posted monthly. The "effective yield" which reflects the results of daily compounding would be 8.135 percent. This is based on daily compounding of the daily rate of 0.000214. It is this 8.135 effective yield that should be compared to other offerings such as bank money market checking accounts. (SEC rules prescribe that the weekly, 7-day yield be converted to the annual effective yield using a 365-day year (SEC Release 33-6753).

In the author's experience, banks post their money market checking rates based on what other banks are paying, and banks, in general, are not at all competitive with mutual fund-sponsored money market accounts. Most mutual fund accounts offer free check writing with a minimum check of $100 or so, and assess no charges for writing too many checks, or for letting one's balance fall below the required minimum. On the other hand, bank offerings may be insured by the Federal Deposit Insurance Corporation (FDIC) up to certain deposit limits, and the mutual fund accounts are generally not insured by anyone.

The mutual fund yields quoted, regardless of whether they are called "yield" or "effective yield," are *after* the applicable fund expenses. These expenses include a management fee, usually somewhere in the vicinity of $^1/_2$ of 1 percent of assets, and various expenses such as accounting, legal, shareholder reports, mailing costs, etc. There may also be a sales commission or "load" that is applied directly to the investment and reduces the amount of shares purchased or redemption proceeds received. In addition, some funds charge what is known as a 12-B(1) fee, which is named for the section of the enabling securities act that permits this practice. 12-B(1) fees are sales-and-promotion-type expenses that the fund itself pays for, rather than the sponsoring organization which receives the management fees. However, as the yield figures are after all such expenses, it is the effective yield which should be compared to the bank's effective yield or other alternatives. After all, the bank's *effective yield is what the depositor receives.* It doesn't matter to the depositor how much the bank spends on advertising or how much it pays its president. *On the other hand, with the mutual fund money market account, the level of fees is likely to matter in the long run,* especially as it will affect the performance of one such fund relative to another over an extended time period. Therefore, in the author's judgment, one should stay away from money market funds with sales loads, funds with 12-B(1) fees, and funds with high ratios of expenses to assets (those that exceed roughly $\frac{3}{4}$ of 1 percent per year, including the management fee).

Sources of information about fees, earnings, etc., of money market funds include *Weisenberger's Investment Companies*, available in most libraries. *Morningstar Mutual Funds*, as well as *Donoghue Reports* (available for a fee from The Donoghue Organization, Inc., P.O. Box 540, Holliston, MA 01746).

A bank checking account that pays, say, 5.25 percent interest is likely to figure the monthly credit as follows:

$$I = P \left(\frac{r}{D}\right)_n$$

where I = interest credited for the month

P = average daily balance for the cycle of n days

r = rate per year quoted

D = days in a year (360 results in more interest to the depositor than 365)

n = number of days in the cycle (for the year should total 365, or 366 in a leap year)

Some banks don't even bother to inform depositors of the rate of interest being paid, though the Truth in Savings Act has improved disclosures. Samples of monthly statements issued by two banks, are shown as Figs. 1.7 and 1.8.

When the interest rate is not stated, it can be determined as follows:

```
IN CASE OF ERRORS OR QUESTIONS ABOUT YOUR ELECTRONIC
FUNDS TRANFERS, DIRECT INQUIRIES TO: 502-XXX-XXXX, AND WE
WILL GET AN ANSWER QUICKLY. YOUR BUSINESS IS BIG BUSINESS
TO US.
*****************CHECKING ACCOUNT SUMMARY*****************
PREVIOUS BALANCE      3,038.27    AVERAGE BALANCE
+  CREDITS    0             .00
-  DEBITS     0             .00
+  SERVICE CHARGES          .00
+  INTEREST PAID          11.61    YTD INTEREST PAID
ENDING BALANCE        3,049.88                      369.27
***************CHECKING ACCOUNT TRANSACTIONS***************
DEPOSITS AND OTHER CREDITS
DATE . . . AMOUNT . TRANSACTION DESCRIPTION
11/25               11.61   INTEREST PAID
****************CUSTOMER BALANCE SUMMARY****************
DATE . . . BALANCE      DATE . . . BALANCE
10/25      3,038.27     11/24      3,049.88
```

Figure 1.7. Some bank statements do not show an interest rate.

```
******************** ACCOUNT SUMMARY ********************

BALANCE LAST STATEMENT 1,301.16    AVERAGE BALANCE   1,301.16
  0 DEPOSITS & CREDITS      0.00   AVG COLL BALANCE 1,301.16
  0 CHECKS & OTHER CHARGES 0.00
    INTEREST PAID           5.61   YTD INTEREST PAID    98.16
    SERVICE CHARGE          0.00
BALANCE AS OF 11/30      1,306.77  CURRENT INTEREST RATE 5.25%

*************** DEPOSITS AND OTHER INCREASES *************

    DATE        AMOUNT    DESCRIPTION          TRACE NUMBER

    11/30        5.61     INTEREST PAID          0000000


**************** DAILY BALANCE SUMMARY ****************


    DATE        BALANCE            DATE        BALANCE

    10/31       1,301.16           11/30       1,306.77
```

Figure 1.8. A bank statement that does not show the effective rate at which interest is paid.

$$r = \left(\frac{I}{n}\right)\left(\frac{1}{P}\right)(D)$$

where r = rate per year quoted
I = interest credited for the month
n = number of days in the cycle
P = average daily balance for the cycle of n days
D = number of days in a year

Thus, if the interest for the month is $11.61 and the average balance for the month is $3038.35, as shown on the statement in Fig. 1.7, the rate is

$$r = \left(\frac{I}{n}\right)\left(\frac{1}{P}\right)(D)$$

$$= \left(\frac{\$11.61}{30}\right)\left(\frac{1}{\$3038.35}\right)(360) = 0.0458508 \text{ or } 4.585\%$$

However, the interest in this case is credited to the account each month. So the monthly rate is the nominal annual rate of 4.585 percent divided by 12, that is, 0.00382083 per month. The *effective rate* is then

$$(1.00382083)^{12} - 1 = 0.046826 \text{ or } 4.683\%$$

In contrast, another bank for the same month indicates on its monthly statement (see Fig. 1.8) that it pays a "current interest rate" of 5.25 percent. The interest paid was $5.61 for the month, and the average balance was $1301.16. The stated "current interest rate" can be determined as follows:

$$r = \left(\frac{I}{n}\right)\left(\frac{1}{P}\right)(D)$$

$$= \left(\frac{5.61}{30}\right)\left(\frac{1}{\$1301.16}\right)(365) = 0.05246 \text{ or } 5.25\% \text{(rounded)}$$

Here, again, interest is paid and compounded monthly, so the effective annual rate is:

$$\left(1 + \frac{0.05246}{12}\right)^{12} - 1 = 0.05374 \text{ or } 5.37\% \text{ (rounded)}$$

Neither bank's offering compared favorably to the interest rates being paid, at the time about 7.5 percent, by the money market mutual funds of the mutual fund organizations. Of course, if one needs to be able to write checks for less than $100, one has little choice but to keep a bank account. And just try to borrow money from a mutual fund group!

In the examples just cited, interestingly enough, the bank which pays the undisclosed effective annual rate of 4.683 percent requires a $1000 *minimum balance,* while the bank which pays the higher 5.37 percent requires $2000 minimum collected balance. So the slightly higher rate is mitigated by the fact that an additional $1000 has to be tied up at, let's say, 2.5 percent per year less interest rate than is available elsewhere. This means lost revenue on, let's say, an extra $1000 average balance, of about $2.0833 per month, or , $25 per year. This lost opportunity cost of investing for a higher rate on the larger minimum balance of $1000 significantly reduces the attractiveness of the bank that pays 5.37 percent. Assume, for example, that the average monthly balance is $2500. Then the monthly interest is

$$I = P\left(\frac{r}{D}\right)^{(n)} = (\$2500)\left(\frac{0.0525}{365}\right)(30) = \$10.78$$

The lost interest for the month due to having an extra $1000 tied up at the lower interest rate is $2.08. Thus the net interest earned, $10.78 less the opportunity lost of $2.08, is $8.70.

If we refigure the rate earned based on $8.70 in interest and an average $2500 balance, we find:

$$r = \left(\frac{I}{n}\right)\left(\frac{1}{P}\right)(D) = \left(\frac{8.70}{30}\right)\left(\frac{1}{2500}\right)(365) = 4.23\%$$

This 4.23 nominal percentage rate is an effective annual rate of 4.31 percent. So, we find an illusion: The bank stating that it pays 5.25 percent (with a $2000 minimum collected balance) is really not as attractive as the bank that does not say what it is paying but that actually has an effective annual yield of 4.683 percent with a minimum $1000 balance.

The Truth in Savings Act

The purpose of the *Truth in Savings Act* of 1991 (12 U.S.C. 4301 et seq., Pub. L. 102-242) is to require the clear and uniform disclosure of: (1) the rates of interest which are payable on deposit accounts by depository institutions; and (2) the fees that are assessable against deposit accounts, so that consumers can make a meaningful comparison between the competing claims of depository institutions with regard to depository accounts. Generally, each advertisement (announcement, or solicitation initiated by an depository institution or deposit broker relating to any demand or interest-bearing account offered by an insured depository institution which includes any reference to a specific rate of interest deposited) shall state: (1) the annual percentage yield; (2) the period during which such annual percentage yield is in effect; (3) all minimum account balance and time requirements which must be met in order to earn the advertised yield; (4) the minimum amount of the initial deposit which is required to open the account in order to obtain the yield advertised, if such minimum amount is greater than the minimum balance necessary to earn the advertised yield; (5) a statement that regular fees or other conditions could reduce the yield; (6) a statement that an interest penalty is required for early withdrawal. In addition, each institution must maintain (and provide customers upon demand) a schedule of fees, charges, interest rates, and terms and conditions that includes the following additional information: (1) any annual rate of simple interest; (2) the frequency with which interest is compounded and credited; (3) a clear description of the method used to determine the balance on which interest is paid; (4) a statement, if applicable, that any interest which has accrued but has not been credited to an account at the time of a withdrawal from the account will not be paid by the depository institution or credited to the account by reason of such withdrawal.

Misleading descriptions of free or no-cost accounts are prohibited, and misleading or inaccurate advertisements, etc., are prohibited.

Each depository institution must include on or with each periodic statement provided to each account holder the following information: (1) the annual percentage yield earned; (2) the amount of interest earned; (3) the amount of any fees or charges imposed; (4) the number of days in the reporting period.

Compliance with the act is under the control of the Federal Reserve Banks, the Federal Deposit Insurance Corporation, the Office of Thrift Supervision, and the National Credit Union Administration Board. Civil liabilities are imposed for violating the act, and legal actions may be brought in any U.S. district court, or in any other court of competent jurisdiction, within 1 year after the date of the occurrence of the violation involved.

Disclosure of annual percentage yield (APY) as required by the act utilizes the compound interest formula discussed earlier, and is calculated in two different ways, the first for account and advertising purposes, the second for periodic statements to customers.

In general, the annual percentage yield for account disclosures and for advertising is an annualized rate that reflects the relationship between the amount of interest that would be earned by the consumer for the term of the account and the amount of principal used to calculate that interest. The calculation of annual percentage yield is based on the actual number of days in the term of the account. For accounts without a stated maturity date (such as a typical savings or transaction account), the calculation must be based on an assumed term of 365 days. In determining the total interest figure to be used in the formula, assume that all principal and interest remain on deposit for the entire term and that no other transactions (deposits or withdrawals) occur during the term. For time accounts that are offered in multiples of months, base the number of days on either the actual number of days during the applicable period, or the number of days that would occur for any actual sequence of that many calendar months. With the latter rule, use the same number of days to calculate the dollar amount of interest earned on the account that is used in the annual percentage yield formula (where "interest" is divided by "principal"). This assumption is not used if an institution requires, as a condition of the account, that consumers withdraw interest during the term. In such a case, the interest (and annual percentage yield calculation) must reflect that requirement.

The "annual percentage yield earned" for periodic statements reflects the relationship between the *amount of interest actually earned* on the consumer's account during the statement period and the *average daily balance* in the account for the statement period. The calculation is performed using the compound interest formula, where "balance" is the average daily balance in the account for the period; "interest earned" is the actual amount of interest earned on the account for the period; and "days in period" is the actual number of days for the period.

For *stepped-rate accounts* (different rates apply in succeeding periods, where the rates are known at the time the account is opened), each interest rate is assumed to be in effect for the length of time provided for in the deposit contract.

For *variable-rate accounts* without an introductory premium or discounted rate, the calculation is based only on the initial interest rate in effect when the account is opened (or advertised). Variable-rate accounts with an introductory premium (or discount) rate must be calculated like a stepped-rate account.

For *tiered-rate accounts* (different rates apply to specified balance levels), an annual percentage yield (or a range of annual percentage yields, if appropriate) must be disclosed for each balance tier.

Implementation of the act in mid-1993 has helped correct many of the disclosure abuses by U.S. domestic institutions described earlier in this chapter.

Conversions between Continuous and Periodic Rates

A continuous rate may be converted to an equivalent effective periodic compound rate, or vice versa by using the following formula.

$$Pe^{[i_1 n]} = P\left(1 + \frac{i_2}{m}\right)^{mn}$$

or

$$e^{i_1} = \left(1 + \frac{i_2}{m}\right)^{m}$$

and

$$i_1 = m \ln\left(1 + \frac{i_2}{m}\right)$$

and

$$i_2 = m\left(e^{i_1/m} - 1\right)$$

where P = present value
e = 2.71828
i_1 = continuously compounded interest rate
m = number of times per year that interest is compounded
i_2 = equivalent rate with compounding m times per year
n = years of compounding
ln = natural logarithm

Example: Finding the Continuous Rate. Bank Bountiful advertises that its super-savings account pays 8 percent interest compounded quarterly. What is the equivalent continuously compounded rate of interest?

$$i_1 = m \ln\left(1 + \frac{i_2}{m}\right)$$

$$i_1 = 4 \ln\left(1 + \frac{0.08}{4}\right)$$

$$= 4 \ln(1.02)$$

$$= 4\,(0.0198)$$

$$= 0.07921 \quad \text{or} \quad 7.921\%$$

Example: Finding the Periodic Rate. Sensitive Savings & Loan calculates that it can afford to pay interest on savings accounts at 7.921 percent, compounded continuously. But it reasons that it would be better to advertise a higher rate with quarterly compounding. What is the equivalent rate?

$$i_2 = m\,(e^{i_1/m} - 1) = 4\,(e^{\,0.07921/4} - 1) = 4\,(1.02 - 1) = 0.08 \quad \text{or} \quad 8\%$$

Appendix: Semilog Graphs

The growth rate of an investment at a constant compounding rate appears to be a sharply increasing (convex) curve as shown in Fig. 1.9, which depicts the growth of $1000 over a 10-year period at 10 percent interest, compounded annually. The actual values at the end of each year are:

Initial investment: $1000

Annual constant growth rate: 10.0%

Year	End-of-year value
1	$1100.000
2	1210.000
3	1331.000
4	1464.100
5	1610.510
6	1771.561
7	1948.717
8	2143.589
9	2357.948
10	2593.742

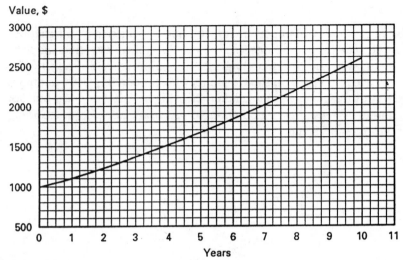

Figure 1.9. Compound growth: nonlog presentation.

However, if the same data is plotting on semilogarithmic (log-linear) paper, the result is a straight line, as shown in Fig. 1.10.

The significance of this is that growth at a constant rate of compound interest can be plotted on semilog paper, if only the values of two points are known, since the result will be a straight line connecting (and extending before and beyond) those two points.

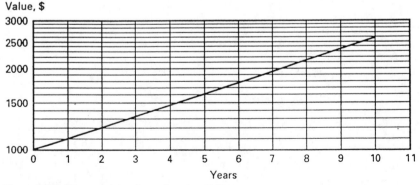

Figure 1.10. Compound growth: semilog presentation.

Summary

A substantial amount of important information is contained in this chapter: how to calculate compound interest; the vast differences over time made by small changes in the compounding rate; the importance of knowing the true effective rate based on the frequency of compounding; how to obtain the most advantageous money market checking account; and last but not least, how to be a walking computer and do accurate mental compounding using the rules of 72 and 78.

2

Present Value of Future Income

Single-Payment Promissory Note

Frank Ford owns a promissory note that he received from the sale of his car. The maker of the promissory note promises to pay $1000 two years from today without interest. Frank needs cash today, however, and he takes the promissory note to his bank, and he asks the bank to purchase the note for cash today.

The banker, Charles Bennington, explains that he cannot pay $1000 for the note; its *present value* is less than that. Bennington says that the bank will buy the note at its present (or *discounted*) value, however. Bank practice, Bennington explains, requires him to receive a return when the note is finally collected equivalent to what the money would have earned if it had been invested at 10 percent compounded annually. As money market conditions change, the amount the bank has to earn changes, as the rate of return includes not only the appropriate risk-free rate, but also compensation for the risk that the note will not be paid, and an allowance for the bank's overhead or cost of doing business.

The problem, then, is to determine the present value of a note with a maturity value of $1000 due 2 years hence and with a discounted interest rate of 10 percent.

Present Value

If the note is *discounted at simple annual* (as opposed to compound) *interest*, the present value is determined as:

$$P = S (1 + iT)^{-1}$$

where P = principal or original investment
     S = sum of future value
     i = simple annual interest rate
     T = term in years

For this example,

$$P = S (1 + iT)^{-1}$$

$$= \$1000 \ [1 + (0.10)(2)]^{-1}$$

$$= \$1000 \ (0.8333)$$

$$= \$833.33$$

However, Mr. Bennington is not interested in discounting the note at simple interest, and insists that it must be discounted at compound interest. The formulas for discounting at compound annual interest are:

$$S = P\left(1 + \frac{i}{m}\right)^{nm} \quad \text{and} \quad P = S\left(1 + \frac{i}{m}\right)^{-nm}$$

where S = value of principal and interest, after n multiplied by m periods of compounding: the sum or future value ($1000)
     P = original principal or investment
     n = number of years (2)
     m = number of compounding periods in 1 year (e.g., semiannual = 2; quarterly = 4, etc.) (1 in the example)
     i = compound annual growth rate (10% or 0.10)

Thus

$$P = S\left(1 + \frac{i}{m}\right)^{-nm}$$

$$= \$1000 \left(1 + \frac{0.10}{1}\right)^{-2} = \$1000 \ (1.1)^{-2} = \$1000 \ (0.826446287)$$

$$= \$826.44$$

Therefore, $826.44 is the amount the bank will pay Frank to acquire the note. The values for $(1 + i)^n$ used in the formula are given in Appendix 1.

Example: Finding the Present Value of a Sum Due in the Future. Figure 2.1 may be used to find the present value of a single future payment. Assume that $1000 is due 9 years from today. What is the present value discounted at 12 percent interest, compounded annually?

As the dashed line shows, the present value is $360.

Value today dollars

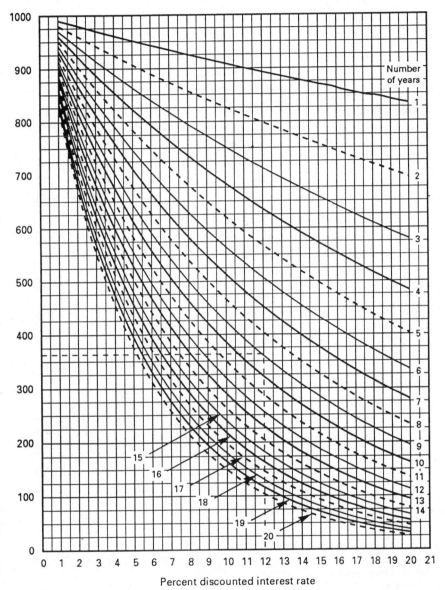

Figure 2.1. How much $1000 due in the future is worth today. Example: $1000 due and payable 20 years from today, discounted at 20 percent compound interest per year, is worth only $26 now.

The problem may be represented by a *time line* as follows:*

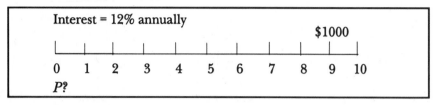

The solution by formula is:

$$P = S\left(1 + \frac{i}{m}\right)^{-(n)(m)}$$

$$= \$1000\left(1 + \frac{0.12}{1}\right)^{-(9)(1)}$$

$$= \$1000\,(0.360610)$$

$$= \$360.61$$

where P = present value
S = maturity value
n = time from the present until maturity
i = discounted interest rate
m = number of times interest is compounded per year

* Throughout this book (and throughout your investing lifetime), it will be useful to visualize situations involving money and interest by constructing a simple time line. A time line that depicts the value of $1000 ten years hence at 8 percent annual interest is:

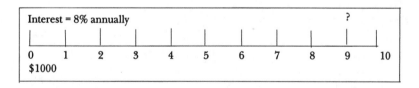

The cash outflows of money ($1000) as well as present values are shown below the line, and cash inflows as well as future values are shown above the line. The value to be determined is shown by a "?".

It is important to distinguish between the receipt or expenditure of money at the beginning or at the end of a time period. In the time line example above, $1000 is expended or invested at the beginning of the first time period (year, in this example)—point zero. The desired future value is at the end of the tenth year. The use of a time line helps one to keep in mind the exact timing of cash flows, whether such flows be at the beginning or at the end of time periods.

Time lines are employed frequently in this book, and the reader is encouraged to draw his or her own time lines to better visualize the nature of specific money and interest situations.

The value of $(1.12)^{-9}$ in the formula may be found in four ways:

1. Using Table 14 in Appendix 1, 12 percent rate, fourth column; adjacent to the 9th period in that column, the value is 0.360610.

2. Using logarithms as described in Appendix 2, the value of $(1 + 0.12)^{-9}$ is

$$\frac{1}{1.12^9}$$

Thus, $9 (\log 1.12) = 9 (0.04922) = 0.44298$

The number whose log is 0.44298 = 2.7735; and 1/2.7735 = 0.360555.

3. Using an electronic calculator, the value is 0.36061. Typically, enter 1.12; then enter –9 and press the key marked y^x.

4. Using a computer, the value is 0.36061. (Typically, the notation is 1.12^–9<Enter>).

How Present Value Is Affected by Changes in *i* and *n*

The present value is *increased* whenever *i* (the rate of interest or discount) is *decreased*. Refer to Fig. 2.1. On the 20-year curve, when the interest rate is reduced from 20 percent to 10 percent, the present value is increased from about $25 to about $150. Also, the present value *increases* whenever the number of years of discounting is *decreased*. For example, at a 20 percent interest rate, when the number of years decreases from 20 to 1, the present value increases from about $25 to about $830.

On the other hand, the present value *decreases* when *i* *increases* and when *n* increases. In other words, the change in present value is inversely proportional to changes in *i* or *n*.

Remember, whenever all of the values except one in the formula (*S*, *P*, *n*, *i*, *m*) are known, the missing value can be found. If either the discount rate (*i*) or the number of years (*n*) is unknown, then both the present value and the future value must be known. The procedure for finding the missing item is exactly as described in Chap. 1.

Example: Finding Present Value with Semiannual Compounding.   Bill Buyer buys a car from Sam Seller, and as part of the purchase price Bill gives a promissory note that reads in part: "I promise to pay to the order of Sam Seller the sum of $10,000 plus interest at maturity 3 years from this date at the rate of 4 percent, compounded annually." On the day of the sale Sam Seller takes the note to his bank, which agrees to buy the note from him at a value determined by discounting at 12 percent, compounded semiannually. How much does Sam receive?

This is really two problems. The first is to determine how much Bill will pay at the maturity of the note in 3 years. The second is what is the present value of that amount.

Refer to Fig. 1.4. Enter the graph on the vertical axis at the 3-year point, proceed horizontally to the 4 percent curve, then down to the bottom axis, where the point of intersection is about 1.12. The $10,000 present value is multiplied by about 1.12 to obtain a future value of about $11,200. Now, turn to Fig. 2.2. Start on the bottom axis at the 12 percent rate, proceed vertically to the curve for 3 years, then horizontally to the left axis. The reading at the left axis is about $710 per $1000. Since we want to know the present value of $11,200, the answer is 11.2 times 710, that is, $7952. (As the graph is based on annual compounding, $7952 can be expected to be a bit higher than the result by formula using semiannual compounding.)

Using the formula, the amount Bill will pay in 3 years is:

$$S = P(1 + i)^n$$

$$= \$10,000 (1 + 0.04)^3$$

$$= \$10,000 (1.124864)$$

$$= \$11,248.64$$

[The value of $(1 + 0.04)^3$ can be found in Table 6 of Appendix 1; by using Appendix 2 to find the value of $(3)(\log 1.04)$; by using an electronic calculator, or by using a computer.]

The problem is represented by the following time line:

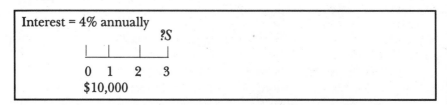

Then the question is, what is the present value of $11,248.64 due in 3 years discounted at 12 percent, with semiannual compounding? This can be visualized using the following time line:

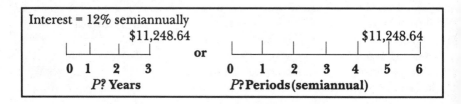

Value today

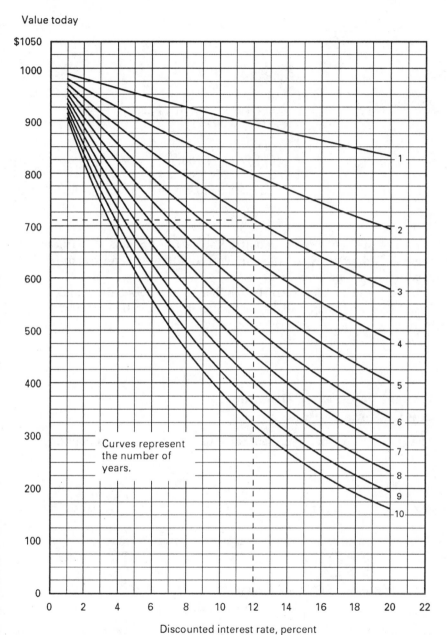

Discounted interest rate, percent

Figure 2.2. How much $1000 in the future is worth today (expanded).

The solution using the formula is:

$$P = S\left(1 + \frac{i}{m}\right)^{-(n)(m)}$$

$$= \$11,248.64\left(1 + \frac{0.12}{2}\right)^{-(3)(2)}$$

$$= \$11,248.64 \, (1.06)^{-6}$$

$$= \$11,248.64 \, (0.704961)$$

$$= \$7929.85$$

The value of $(1.06)^{-6}$ can be found in Table 8 of Appendix 1; by finding the value of [1 divided by the value of 6(log 1.06)] in Appendix 2; or by using a calculator or computer.

Thus, it can be seen even though Sam is to receive compound interest from Bill as well as the $10,000 face amount, Sam can realize only $7929.85 by selling the note. The magnitude of this reduction is due to the below-market interest rate that Sam agreed to accept!

Present Value when Discounting at a Continuous Rate

The formula for finding present value under continuous discounting is:

$$P = S(e)^{-rt}$$

where S = sum at the future date or maturity of both principal and interest: the future value

P = principal: original investment or present value

e = base for natural logarithms, about 2.7182818 (e represents an infinite series)

r = nominal rate of annual interest

t = number of years (time)

Example: Finding Present Value When Discounting at a Continuous Rate. Ho Ming holds a note promising to pay him $1,000,000 30 years hence. A bank is willing to buy the note from him discounted at a 12 percent continuous rate. How much will Ho Ming receive if he sells the note?

$$P = S(e)^{-rt}$$

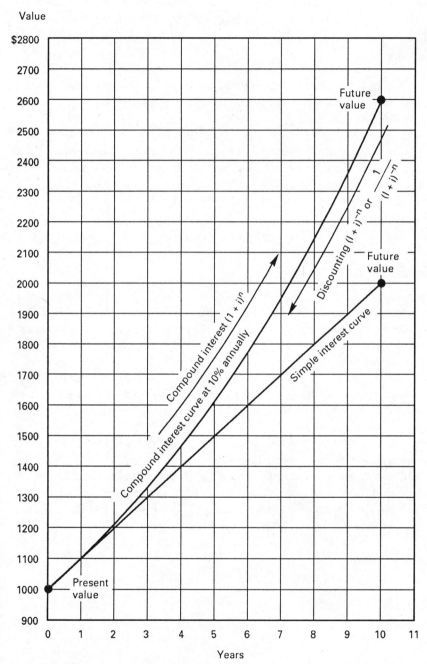

Figure 2.3. Relationship between present and future values.

$$= \$1,000,000 \; (e)^{-(0.12)(30)}$$

$$= \$1,000,000 \; (0.02732)$$
$$= \$27,323.72$$

When is \$1,000,000 worth only \$27,000? The answer, obviously, is when the money is due 30 years from now and money is worth 12 percent compounded continuously.

This principle has commercial applications in promotions, advertising, and giveaway schemes, where large sums are promised, but in reality, those large sums are future face values of money. Frequently, zero-coupon bonds are the instrument which is offered, and the face value of the bonds is the prominently advertised amount. Chapter 19 offers further insight about zero-coupon bonds.

Conclusion

Present values and future values work together; in fact, one is simply the reciprocal or inverse of the other. That is, to find the future value, S, one must multiply P by $(1+i)^n$. And to find the present value, one must multiply S by $1/(1+i)^n$. Another way to view the situation is shown in Fig. 2.3. Starting at the lower left corner of the figure, \$1000 is the present value at point 0. From that point there are two ways to proceed upward with the passing of time, by the compound interest curve or by the simple interest curve. Either way, the application of time and interest creates an ever-increasing future value.

Comparison of the value at any point in time shows the dynamic growth of compound interest versus simple interest.

On the other hand, starting from the upper right-hand corner of the figure and following the curve down to the left shows the effect of discounting. With the application of time and the discount rate, the present value becomes ever smaller.

3

Present Value
of a Series
# of Future Payments

Installment Promissory Note

A car dealer sells a car on the installment plan. The buyer agrees to pay $100 a month for 36 months, without interest. However, the seller needs his money today to buy more cars and pay bills. He takes the promissory note to the bank and seeks to sell the note for cash.

The banker explains, as he did to the owner of the single-payment promissory note in Chap. 2, that the $3600 of future payments is worth less than that today. The bank is willing to purchase the promissory note for cash by paying an amount that will earn the bank 12 percent, compounded monthly, on the price it pays. The banker wishes to find the discounted present value of a series of payments or an annuity. An *annuity* is a sequence of equal payments made at equal intervals of time. A *simple,* or *ordinary, annuity* requires that the conversion intervals (number of times interest is compounded per year) correspond to the payments—semiannual compounding and semiannual payments, monthly compounding and monthly payments, etc. The *present value* is the total value of all the payments at the beginning of the term, i.e., one payment interval before the first payment. To find the amount, the banker calculates the present value of this simple annuity.

Present Value of a Simple Annuity

The present value of a simple annuity, A, is

$$A = R\left[\frac{1 - (1 + i/m)^{-(n)(m)}}{i/m}\right]$$

where (with values for our example in parentheses):

A = present value of a series of equal payments (annuity)
i = annual or nominal interest rate (12%, or 0.12)
m = number of times interest is compounded per year (12)
R = amount of each regular future periodic payment ($100)
n = number of years (3)

Thus, for our example,

$$A = R\left[\frac{1 - (1 + i/m)^{-(n)(m)}}{i/m}\right]$$

$$A = \$100\left[\frac{1 - (1 + 0.12/12)^{-(3)(12)}}{0.12/12}\right]$$

$$= \$100\,(30.1075) = \$3010.75$$

The bank will pay the seller $3010.75 today for the promissory note.
The value of

$$\frac{1 - (1 + i/m)^{-(n)(m)}}{i/m}$$

may be found in Appendix 1, under the column "Present worth of 1 per period: what $1 payable periodically is worth today." For this purpose, the values of i and n already reflect adjustment by m.

Alternatively, Fig. 3.1 may be used.

Example: Finding the Present Value of a Simple Annuity. An installment contract provided initially for 180 payments of $100 each without interest at the rate of one payment per month. Twenty-nine payments have already been made, and the owner of the contract now wishes to obtain the present value from a bank. If the bank agrees to buy the contract at 8 percent discounted annually, how much will the seller receive?

Enter Fig. 3.1 at 151 months (which is 180 less 29) and proceed vertically as the dashed line shows; at the 8 percent curve, move horizontally to determine the value today, $95. However, $95 is the value of 151 payments

Value today (dollars)

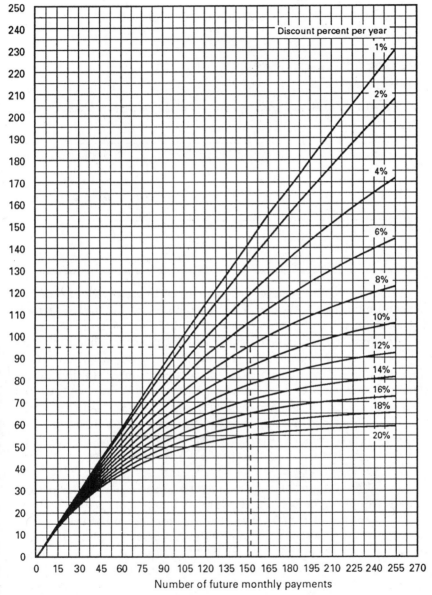

Figure 3.1. How much future payments of $1.00 per month are worth today.

of $1.00 per month. The value for payments of $100 per month is, therefore, $95 times $100, or about $9500. (The computer solution, using the author's FINANCIAL AND INTEREST CALCULATOR, is $9500.03.)

Time Line for an Ordinary Annuity

The nature of an ordinary annuity can easily be grasped by constructing a time line:

Interest = 12%, compounded monthly (i.e., 1% per period)
$R = \$100$

```
         R    R    R    R    R    R    R    R    R    R
  |___|____|____|____|____|____|____|____|____|____|___|
  0    1    2    3    4    5    6    7    8    9    10
  P?
```

This time line represent an ordinary annuity of 10 payments of R, the first payment commencing at the end of the first time period and the last payment being made at the end of the tenth time period. The present value to be determined is at one interval before the first payment. The time line respresents the present value of an annuity of 10 payments at the end of each month of $100 each, with interest discounted at 1 percent per month. Note that for the ordinary annuity formula to be applicable, the value of m must apply to both the compounding frequency and the frequency of payments. In this example, interest is compounded monthly, and payments are made monthly.

Example: Finding the Present Value of a Simple Annuity. What is the present value of the 10 monthly payments of $100 described above with interest discounted at 1 percent per month?

Figure 3.1 does not present a clear picture for such a short time period. Enter the figure on the horizontal axis at 10 months, proceed vertically to the 12 percent (annual rate) curve, then horizontally to the vertical axis, where the point of intersection appears to be about $9. Since $9 would represent the present value of an annuity of $1 per period, the present value of $100 per period would be 100 times $9, or about $900.

The solution by formula is:

$$A = R\left[\frac{1 - (1 + i/m)^{-(n)(m)}}{i/m}\right]$$

$$= \$100 \left[\frac{1 - (1 + 0.12/12)^{-(10/12)(12)}}{0.12/12} \right]$$

$$= \$100 \left[\frac{1 - (1.01)^{-10}}{0.01} \right]$$

$$= \$100 \left[\frac{1 - 0.905287}{0.01} \right]$$

$$= \$100 \ (9.471304)$$

$$= \$947.13$$

The 9.471304 value of

$$\frac{1 - (1 + i/m)^{-(n)(m)}}{i/m}$$

may be found in column 5 of Table 2 of Appendix 1, 1 percent rate, on the line for 10 periods. Or it may be found by using logs, following the procedure described in Appendix 2, or by using a calculator or computer.

The formula for simple annuities is derived from discounting the individual payment amounts and the algebraic formula for the value of a series. So it is not surprising that $947.13 is also the value obtained by taking the sum of the discounted value of each $100 payment for the appropriate time period at 1 percent per month. This is shown in Table 3.1.

Table 3.1. Discounted Present Value
of Simple Annuity Cash Flows

Payment amount, $100; interest rate
per month, 0.01

Time periods to discount	Discount factor	Present value
10	0.90529	$ 90.53
9	0.91434	91.43
8	0.92348	92.35
7	0.93272	93.27
6	0.94205	94.20
5	0.95147	95.15
4	0.96098	96.10
3	0.97059	97.06
2	0.98030	98.03
1	0.99010	99.01
Total		$947.13

Annuity Due

The payments of an *annuity due* start at the *beginning* of each payment interval. (So far, our discussion of a simple annuity has involved payments at the *end* of each payment interval.) The present value on the day of the first payment, *A*, can be found most easily by adding to the first payment (which is cash) the present value of the remaining payments (which are one less than the total number of payments). The future value, *V*, of an annuity due is determined at one interval after the last payment. The following time line depicts an annuity due:

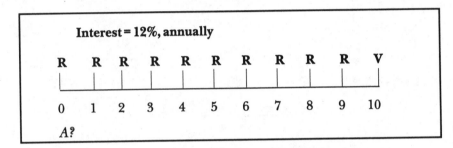

The formula for the present value of an annuity due is:

$$A = R\left\{1 + \left[\frac{1 - (1 + i/m)^{-[(n)(m)-1]}}{i/m}\right]\right\}$$

where   *A* = present value of a series of equal payments (annuity)
           i = annual or nominal interest rate
          m = number of times interest is compounded per year
          R = amount of each regular future periodic payment
          n = number of years
   (*n*)(*m*) − 1 = number of payments less one

The factor is for one time period less than the number of payments (because the first payment at the beginning of the first time interval is handled separately). For an annuity due, the adjustment to the formula for an ordinary or simple annuity is to add the first payment (which is cash) to the present value of the remaining payments.

    Example: Finding the Present Value of an Annuity Due. Irene Sokolov buys a vacant lot for speculation and agrees to pay the seller $5000 without interest, with payments to be made at the beginning of each 3 months for 9 years. Money is worth 6 percent per year. What is the present value of this annuity due?

A time line for this situation is:

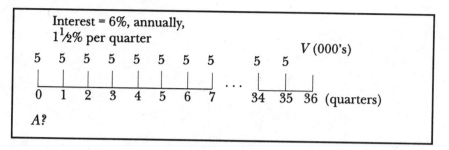

By formula, the present value of this annuity due is:

$$A = R\left\{1 + \left[\frac{1 - (1 + i/m)^{-[(n)(m)-1]}}{i/m}\right]\right\}$$

$$= \$5000 \left\{1 + \left[\frac{1 - (1 + 0.06/4)^{-[(9)(4)-1]}}{0.06/4}\right]\right\}$$

$$= \$5000 \left\{1 + \left[\frac{1 - (1.015)^{-35}}{0.015}\right]\right\}$$

$$= \$5000 \left\{1 + \left[\frac{1 - 0.59387}{0.015}\right]\right\}$$

$$= \$5000 \,(1 + 27.07559) = \$140,377.97$$

Thus, the present value of the land under the stated conditions is $140,377.97. The value of the bracketed term,

$$\left[\frac{1 - (1 + 0.06/4)^{-[(9)(4)-1]}}{0.06/4}\right]$$

can be found in Table 3 of Appendix 1, $1\frac{1}{2}$ percent rates in the fifth column, on the line for 35 periods. The table shows 27.075594. The value can also be determined by calculator or computer.

The present value could have been determined by applying the compound discount factor $(1 + i)^{-n}$ to each of the 35 individual cash flows, which when added to the first payment at the beginning of the initial time interval would have equaled the same $140,377.97. Consider how much simpler than that procedure is the use of the annuity method.

4

How Monthly
Investments and
Annuities Grow

The Value of
Monthly Investments
at Various Rates

The value of $100 monthly investments after 24, 48, . . . , 240 monthly investments at various rates of compound earnings growth is shown in Table. 4.1. It may be seen that investments in a savings account of $100 per month at a nominal annual rate of 12 percent (compounded at 1 percent per month) would be worth $98,926 after 240 months.

Any amount per month (e.g., $50) may be multiplied by the *multiplication factor* in the second part of Table 4.1 (at 8 percent nominal annual growth for 180 months, the factor is 346.038) to obtain the total investment account value after completion of the specified number of monthly payments (e.g., 180). In this example—$50 per month for 180 months at 8 percent nominal compound earnings per year—the value is $50 × 346.038, or $17,301.90.

Future Value of a Simple Annuity

As explained in Chap. 3, an annuity is a sequence of *equal* payments made at *equal* intervals of time. A simple annuity requires that the conversion intervals (number of times interest is compounded per year) correspond with the payments—semiannual compounding and semiannual payments,

Table 4.1. Future Value of a Monthly Annuity

Nominal annual interest	24	48	72	Months 96	120	180	240
	Value of an Account after $100 Investments Each Month						
4%	$2494	$5196	$8,122	$11,292	$14,725	$24,609	$36,677
6%	2543	5410	8,641	12,283	16,388	29,082	46,204
8%	2593	5635	9,203	13,387	18,295	34,604	58,902
10%	2645	5872	9,811	14,618	20,484	41,447	75,937
12%	2697	6122	10,471	15,993	23,004	49,958	98,926
14%	2751	6386	11,187	17,529	25,907	60,579	130,117
16%	2807	6664	11,964	19,248	29,257	73,873	172,644
18%	2863	6957	12,808	21,172	33,129	90,562	230,885
20%	2921	7265	13,725	23,329	37,610	111,570	310,965
	Value of an Account after Monthly Investments of $1.00 (Multiplication Factor)						
4%	$24.943	$51.960	$81.223	$112.919	$147.250	$246.090	$366.775
6%	25.432	54.098	86.409	122.829	163.879	290.819	462.041
8%	25.933	56.350	92.025	133.869	182.946	346.038	589.020
10%	26.447	58.722	98.111	146.181	204.845	414.470	759.369
12%	26.973	61.223	104.710	159.927	230.039	499.580	989.255
14%	27.513	63.858	111.868	175.290	259.069	605.786	1301.166
16%	28.066	66.636	119.639	192.476	292.571	738.730	1726.442
18%	28.634	69.565	128.077	211.720	331.288	905.625	2308.854
20%	29.215	72.655	137.257	233.289	376.095	1115.700	3109.652

monthly compounding and monthly payments, etc. The future value is the total value of all the payments at the end of the term; i.e., the value on the day of the last payment.

$$S = R \left[\frac{(1 + i/m)^{(n)(m)} - 1}{i/m} \right]$$

where S = future value of a series of equal payments (annuity) after n payments

i = annual or nominal compound interest rate

m = number of times interest is compounded per year and number of investments per year

R = amount of each regular future periodic payment

n = number of years

nm = total number of investments or payments in n years

The *multiplication factor* (see Appendix 1, amount of $1 per period) is the bracketed value in the formula:

$$\frac{(1 + i/m)^{(n)(m)} - 1}{i/m}$$

Example: Finding the Future Value of an Annuity. Pat McPherson invests $100 per month for 180 months; the investment earns 6 percent annual interest (compounded monthly). How much is the account worth at the time of the last investment?

Refer to Fig. 4.1. As the dashed line shows, 180 investments on successive months of $100 each, growing at 6 percent compounded annual interest, produces an account value of about $29,082.

Example: Finding the Periodic Investment in an Annuity. The graphs may also be used in reverse. That is, if one wishes to have $20,000 some years from now, for how many months would one have to invest $100 per month if one can earn only 4 percent per annum on one's investment?

Refer again to Fig. 4.1. As shown by the dotted lines on the figure, proceed vertically from $200 (or $20,000) on the base of the graph to the 4 percent curve, then horizontally to the left side of the graph to determine the answer: 154 months.

The value of monthly investments of amounts other than $100 may also be determined from Fig. 4.1. For example, the value of $200 per month is twice the amount shown in the figure, the value of $50 per month is 50 percent of the amount in the figure, and so on.

Example: How Long Does It Take to Accumulate a Specified Future Sum?
Wanda Blake wants to have $30,000 in the future. She has innumerable possibilities for achieving the goal, including investing $100 per month at 8 percent, $100 at 6 percent, $100 at 4 percent, $50 at 10 percent, or $50 at 8 percent. For how many months must investments be made?

Using Fig. 4.1, the answers can quickly be found:
At 8 percent, 165 monthly investments of $100 are required.
At 10 percent, 151 monthly investments of $100 are required.
At 6 percent, 184 monthly investments of $100 are required.
At 4 percent, 208 monthly investments of $100 are required.
At 10 percent, 216 monthly investments of $50 are required.
At 8 percent, 242 monthly investments of $50 are required.

Figures 4.2 through 4.7 show the annual investments needed to accumulate capital of various amounts at 5, 8, and 10 percent.

Remember that, for a simple or ordinary annuity, the number of investments per year and the frequency of compounding *must* be in harmony, as illustrated in Table 4.2.

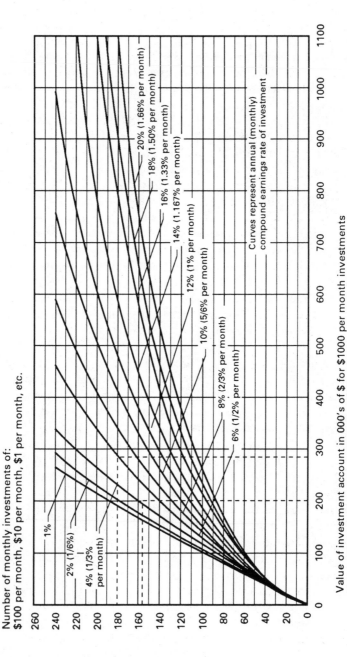

Figure 4.1. How monthly investments grow.

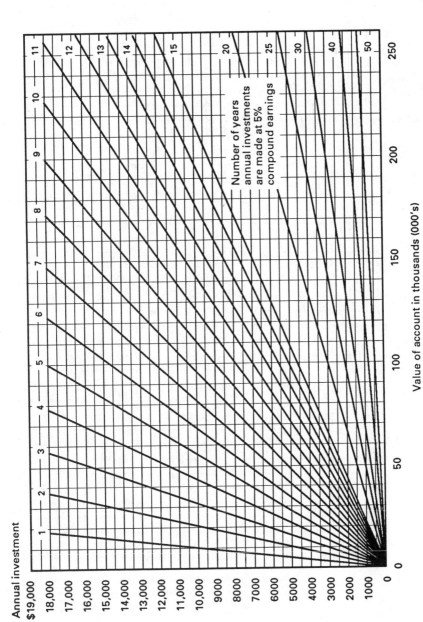

Figure 4.2. Annual investments to accumulate capital (to $260,000) at 5 percent.

57

Annual investment

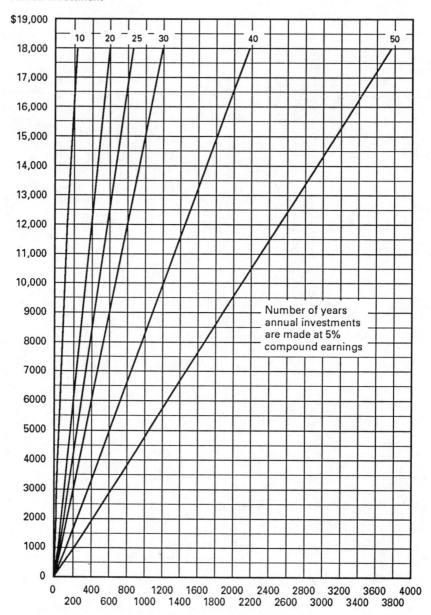

Capital sum accumulated (000's of dollars)

Figure 4.3. Annual investments to accumulate capital (to $4,000,000) at 5 percent.

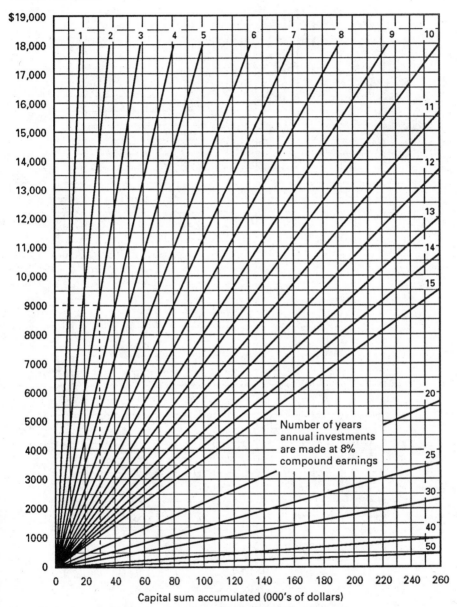

Figure 4.4. Annual investments to accumulate capital (to $260,000) at 8 percent.

Annual investment

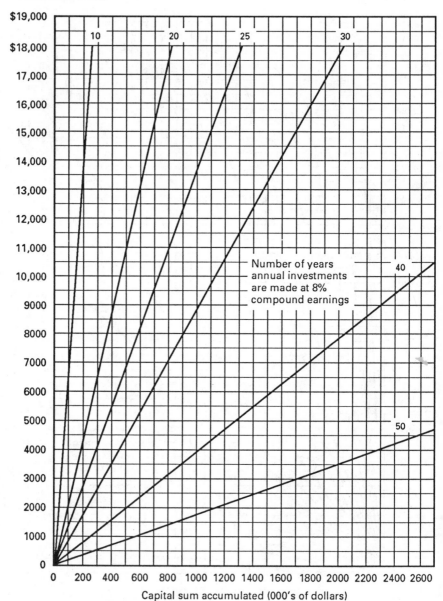

Figure 4.5. Annual investments to accumulate capital (to $2,600,000) at 8 percent.

Annual investment

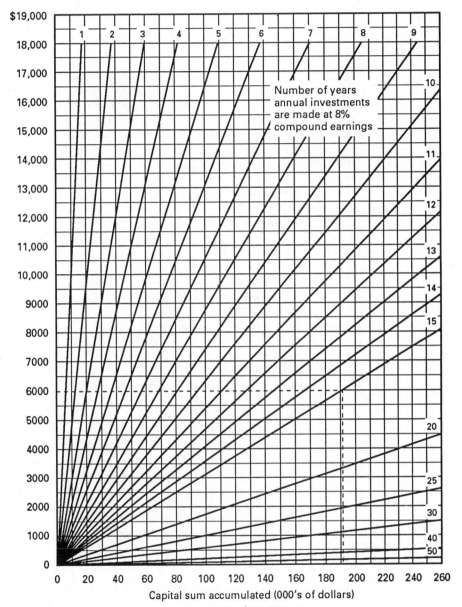

Figure 4.6. Annual investments to accumulate capital (to $260,000) at 8 percent.

Annual investment

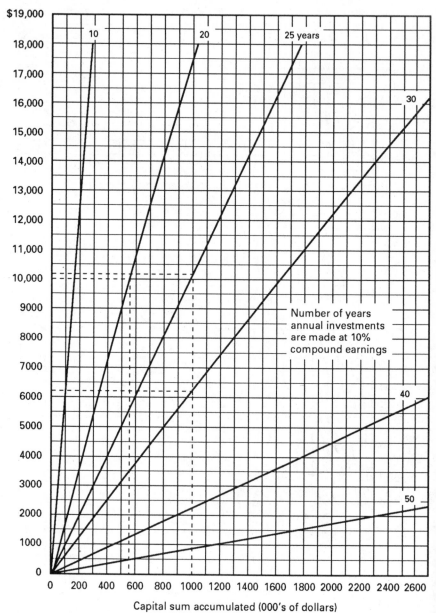

Figure 4.7. Annual investments to accumulate capital (to $2,600,000) at 10 percent.

Example: Finding the Periodic Rate.   What is the periodic rate of interest when the annual nominal rate is 18 percent, and interest is compounded monthly (12 times per year)?

From Table. 4.2, as shown in the last column on the line for 18 percent, the nominal annual rate is 1.5 percent.

Example: Finding the Future Value of an Annuity.   Starting at age 45, Roger Smith puts away $10,000 per year for 20 years at 10 percent compound interest. How much is his account worth when he retires at age 65?

Figure 4.7 provides an immediate solution. On the left vertical axis, enter at the $10,000-per-year point; proceed horizontally to the 20-year curve, then vertically down to the bottom horizontal axis, where the point of intersection is about $570,000. Thus, Roger's account is worth $570,000 when he retires.

Table 4.2. Simple Annuities: Harmony between Rate and Compounding Frequency

Nominal annual interest rate, %	Number of times interest is compounded per year and number of investments per year				
	1	2	4	6	12
	Rate of interest per time period, %				
1	1	0.50	0.250	0.167	0.083
2	2	1.00	0.500	0.333	0.167
3	3	1.50	0.750	0.500	0.250
4	4	2.00	1.000	0.667	0.333
5	5	2.50	1.250	0.833	0.417
6	6	3.00	1.500	1.000	0.500
7	7	3.50	1.750	1.167	0.583
8	8	4.00	2.000	1.333	0.667
9	9	4.50	2.250	1.500	0.750
10	10	5.00	2.500	1.667	0.833
11	11	5.50	2.750	1.833	0.917
12	12	6.00	3.000	2.000	1.000
13	13	6.50	3.250	2.167	1.083
14	14	7.00	3.500	2.333	1.167
15	15	7.50	3.750	2.500	1.250
16	16	8.00	4.000	2.667	1.333
17	17	8.50	4.250	2.833	1.417
18	18	9.00	4.500	3.000	1.500
19	19	9.50	4.750	3.167	1.583
20	20	10.00	5.000	3.333	1.667
21	21	10.50	5.250	3.500	1.750
22	22	11.00	5.500	3.667	1.833
23	23	11.50	5.750	3.833	1.917

A time line reveals the following:

```
 Interest = 8%, annually
                                                        S?
   10m    10    10    10    10    10      10    10    10    10
 |_____|_____|_____|_____|_____|_____     |_____|_____|_____|
                                       . . .
    1     2     3     4     5     6       17    18    19    20
 P
```

We can also find the answer by using the formula for the future value of an annuity:

$$S = R\left[\frac{(1 + i/m)^{(n)(m)} - 1}{i/m}\right]$$

$$= \$10,000\left[\frac{(1 + 0.1/1)^{(20)(1)} - 1}{0.1/1}\right]$$

$$= \$10,000\left(\frac{6.72750 - 1}{0.1}\right)$$

$$= \$10,000 \, (57.2750)$$

$$= \$572,750$$

Table 12 of Appendix 1 contains the 57.274999 value of the factor

$$\left[\frac{(1 + 0.1/1)^{(20)(1)} - 1}{0.1/1}\right]$$

The factor can also be found by using the logarithms (see Appendix 2), or by using an electronic calculator or a computer.

Interpolating to Find Future Values

Sometimes, values in tables must be interpolated to find a needed factor, as the following example demonstrates.

Example: Finding the Future Value of an Annuity. Sally Sanchez can afford to save $500 per month from her salary. If she invests it to earn a nominal 10 percent, compounded monthly, how much will her savings be worth in 15 years?

First, refer to Fig. 4.6. Enter the graph on the left axis at $6000 per year (Sally's $500 monthly investment times 12 times per year); proceed horizontally to the curve representing 15 years, then drop vertically to the bottom axis, where the point of intersection is just past $190,000.

The value determined from this figure (or from Fig. 4.1) is based on annual compounding. Since Sally is actually investing at 0.8333 percent monthly (10 percent nominal annual rate), solution by formula can be expected to produce a larger value due to the benefit of the more frequent compounding. By formula, the calculations are:

$$S = R \left[\frac{(1 + i/m)^{(n)(m)} - 1}{i/m} \right]$$

$$= \$500 \left[\frac{(1 + 0.1/12)^{(15)(12)} - 1}{0.1/12} \right]$$

$$= \$500 \left(\frac{(1.00833)^{(180)} - 1}{0.00833} \right)$$

$$= \$500 \left(\frac{4.45392 - 1}{0.00833} \right)$$

$$= \$500 \left(\frac{3.451392}{0.00833} \right)$$

$$= \$207,235$$

$207,235 is the future value that Sally will accumulate.

The value of the factor for

$$\frac{(1.00833)^{(180)} - 1}{0.00833}$$

can also be found in Tables 1 and 2 in Appendix 1 by interpolating between the values for ½ percent and 1 percent per period (using 180 periods), as shown in Table 4.3. The missing value for 0.833 lies about (0.00333/0.005) of the way between the factor values for 0.500 and 1.000. That is,

$$\frac{\text{Difference between factors for 0.500 and 0.833}}{\text{Difference between factors for 0.500 and 1.000}} = \frac{0.00333}{0.005} = 0.666$$

Table 4.3. Interpolating in Tables for the Missing Factor

	Rate, %		Table factor	
Difference of	⌐ 1.000		499.580197 ⌐	Difference of
0.005	[0.833 ⌐	Difference of	?	208.7614
	⌐ 0.500 ⌐	0.00333	290.818712 ⌐	

The missing value lies about two-thirds or 0.666 of the way between the factors. Now,

$$0.666 \times 208.7614 = 139.0351 \text{ adjustment}$$

The adjustment is added to the factor for 0.500 to obtain the factor for the missing 0.833 percent.

Factor for 0.500	290.818712
Plus adjustment	139.035149
Factor for 0.833 by interpolation	429.853861

(Note that this adjustment is for future value tables; for present value tables, the adjustment is subtracted.)

The factor value using a computer or electronic calculator is 414.47031, which is significantly different from the value determined by interpolation. This variance is due to the lack of closeness between the two available tables (0.5 percent and 1.0 percent). However, voluminous tables of factors (for example, Financial Publishing Company's *Financial Compound Interest and Annuity Tables*) are available which would have given a precise factor for 0.8333 percent. Sally's $500 per month multiplied by the interpolated factor is $214,926.93, about $7692 in error from the more accurate calculation. If the tables in Appendix 1 do not show a value close enough to the desired amount, and if an electronic calculator or computer that can calculate powers is not available, a more accurate factor can be determined using logarithms. In this case, we find the factor as follows:

Log 1.00833 = 0.00359	(by interpolation in the log table)	
Times	180	
Antilog 0.64602 = 4.42600		
Less	1.00000	
Numerator of factor	3.42600 + 0.00833 = 411.28451	

This factor of 411.28451 is much closer to the precise value (414.47) than that obtained by interpolation from Appendix 1 (429.85).

Time Period for a Simple Annuity

The equation for finding the number of time periods for a simple annuity is a bit complicated, but it can be solved with a little effort:

$$nm = \log\left[\frac{S(i/m)}{R} + 1\right]\Big/\log\left(1 + \frac{i}{m}\right)$$

where n = number of years
$\quad R$ = amount of each regular future periodic payment
$\quad S$ = future value of a series of equal payments (annuity)
$\quad i$ = annual or nominal interest rate
$\quad m$ = number of times interest is compounded per year
$\quad nm$ = number of investments of R

Example: Finding the Number of Time Periods in an Annuity. Stacey and Jeff are newlyweds and decide to begin saving in order to accumulate funds for the down payment on a house. They decide that they need to accumulate a down payment of $30,000. They can afford to save $750 per month, and they can earn 8.0 percent annually, compounded monthly. How long will it take them to accumulate the down payment?

In Fig. 4.4, we can mentally draw a horizontal line starting from $9000 on the left axis; then draw a vertical line starting from $30,000 on the bottom horizontal axis. The curve where the two lines intersect is the curve for the appropriate number of years: the 3-year curve, indicating about 36 months.

The solution by formula is

$$= \log\left[\frac{\$30,000\,(0.08/12)}{750} + 1\right]\Big/\log\left(1 + \frac{0.80}{12}\right)$$

$$= \log\,(0.266667 + 1)/\log\,(1.006667)$$

$$= \frac{0.023639}{0.00664}$$

$$= 35.58 \text{ months}$$

Table 10 in Appendix 1 can also be used to find an approximate solution. Regular investments of $750 per month equal $9000 per year. The $30,000 future sum divided by the $9000 annual investment means a multiplier of 3.33 times. In the table, scan the second column, "Amount of 1 per period," for the values closest to 3.3333.

The value for 4 periods is 4.5061.

The value for x periods is 3.3333.

The value for 3 periods is 3.2464.

Thus the number of years seems to lie between 3 and 4, and to be much closer to 3 than to 4. Interpolation narrows the value to 3.069 years, or about 36.8 months. The variance from 35.58 months determined earlier is due to interpolation.

Periodic Payment in a Sinking Fund

Often an investor wants to know how much he or she must save or invest in order to accumulate a specific future sum. Or one may wish to make regular investments in order to build up a specific sum to repay a debt, such as a mortgage. This kind of account is a simple annuity known as a *sinking fund*. The formula for finding the regular investment or periodic payment needed is:

$$R = S \left[\frac{i/m}{(1 + i/m)^{(nm)} - 1} \right]$$

where R = regular periodic payment required
S = sum due in the future
i = nominal annual interest
m = number of payments each year
n = number of annual payments

Example: Finding the Regular Investment or Periodic Payment in a Sinking Fund. Don Mackey owes $10,000, to be repaid in a single lump-sum payment about 10 years from now. How much should Don set aside each year over the next 10 years in order to build up a sinking fund of $10,000 ten years hence, if his annual deposits earn 6 percent compound?

Using the formula,

$$R = S \left[\frac{i/m}{(1 + i/m)^{(nm)} - 1)} \right]$$

where S = $10,000
i = 6% or 0.06
m = 1
n = 10

Thus,

$$R = \$10,000 \left[\frac{0.06/1}{(1 + 0.06/1)^{(10)(1)} - 1} \right]$$

$$= \$10,000 \, (0.075867982)$$

$$= \$758.68 \text{ per year}$$

If Don invests $758.68 at 6 percent compounded annually each year, at the end of 10 years his investment account will contain principal, interest, and interest-on-interest of $10,000, the desired amount.

The value of the factor,

$$\left[\frac{i/m}{(1 + i/m)^{(nm)} - 1} \right]$$

may be found in Table 8 of Appendix 1 under the column titled "Sinking fund: periodic deposit that will grow to $1 at a future date."

Figure 4.1 also provides a solution. Enter the graph on the left axis at 120 months; proceed horizontally to the curve for 6 percent per year interest, then down to the bottom axis, where the future value is found to be about $16,384 (for the $100-per-month investment). A simple proportion is all that is needed to find the monthly investment that will grow to $10,000 (instead of $16,384) in 10 years at 6 percent annual interest. Here's that proportion:

$$\frac{\$10,000}{\$16,384} = \frac{X}{\$100}$$

$$(\$100)(\$10,000) = (\$16,384)(X)$$

$$X = \frac{\$1,000,000}{\$16,384} = \$61.035$$

Thus, $61.035 is the monthly amount of investment required. And, per year, the requirement is $732.42. (This value from Fig. 4.1 compares to the formula calculation of $758.68. The difference is due to two reason: First, the graph is based on monthly compounding and the formula [and problem] used annual compounding; second, reading the graph is not an exact science.)

Example: Finding the Regular Investment Needed to Accumulate $1,000,000?
How much would you have to invest each year to accumulate $1,000,000 in 30 years, if your investment compounds annually at 10 percent? Refer to Fig. 4.7. Enter the graph on the bottom axis at $1,000,000; proceed vertically to the curve for 30 years; then proceed horizontally to the left axis, where the annual investment required is about $6100.

By formula, the solution is:

$$R = S \left[\frac{(i/m)}{(1 + i/m)^{(nm)} - 1)} \right]$$

$$= \$1,000,000 \left[\frac{(0.1/1)}{(1 + 0.1/1)^{(30)(1)} - 1} \right]$$

$$= \$1,000,000 \left[\frac{(0.1)}{(1.1)^{(30)(1)} - 1} \right]$$

$$= \$1,000,000 \left[\frac{(0.1)}{17.45 - 1} \right]$$

$$= \$1,000,000 \, (0.006079) = \$6079.25 \text{ per year}$$

The factor,
$$\left[\frac{(i/m)}{(1 + i/m)^{(n)(m)} - 1} \right]$$

is found in Appendix 1, Table 12, 10 percent rate, under the column, "Sinking fund–periodic deposit that will grow to $1 at future date," adjacent to 30 periods, as 0.006079. This factor, multiplied by $1,000,000, is the $6079 regular annual investment. The factor could also be found using logs, or with a calculator or computer.

Example: How Long Does It Take to Accumulate $1,000,000 with Equal Annual Investments?   Edward Michals wants to retire with $1,000,000. He is confident that he can earn 10 percent annually on his investments. He thinks he can save about $10,100 per year. How log will it take him to reach his goal of $1,000,000?

Enter Fig. 4.7 and draw a horizontal line starting at the left axis at $10,100. Then draw a vertical line up from $1,000,000 on the bottom axis. The curve closest to the point where the two lines intersect is the curve for the number of years we seek. In this case it is 25 years.

Alternately, a solution may be found in the Appendix 1 tables. First, divide S, the future value, by R, the regular payment. Let X represent the multiplication factor used in the tables.

$$X = \frac{S}{R} = \frac{\$1,000,000}{\$10,100} = 99.01$$

Here, 99.01 represents the multiplication factor; that is, $1 must grow into $99.01 to satisfy the set of given facts.

Using Table 12, 10 percent rate, and the column, "Amount of 1 per period," scan down the column until the value closest to 99.01 is found. We see that 25 years (periods) has a value of 98.347 and 26 years has a value of 109.18. So, about 25 years would be required.

Finally, solution by formula is a bit tricky. The formula is:

$$n = \log\left[\frac{S(i/m)}{R} + 1\right] \bigg/ \log\left(1 + \frac{i}{m}\right)$$

where n = number of years
R = amount of each regular future periodic payment
S = future value of a series of equal payments (annuity)
i = annual or nominal interest rate
m = number of times interest is compounded per year
nm = number of investments

Here, S = \$1,000,000
i = 10% or 0.10
m = 1
R = \$10,100

So,

$$n = \log\left[\frac{\$1,000,000\,(0.1)}{\$10,100} + 1\right] \bigg/ \log\,(1.1)$$

$$= \log\left[\frac{\$100,000}{\$10,100} + 1\right] \bigg/ \log\,(1.1)$$

$$= \frac{\log\,(9.90 + 1)}{\log\,(1.1)}$$

$$= \frac{\log\,(10.9)}{\log\,(1.1)}$$

$$= \frac{1.03743}{0.04139}$$

$$= 25.06 \text{ years}$$

Annuity Due—Future Value

An *annuity due* is an annuity where the first investment or payment is made at the beginning of the first time period and future payments are made at the beginning of each subsequent time period. The future value of an annuity due (at a point in time *one interval after the last payment*) can be found by multiplying R by $(1 + i/m)^m$.

$$V = \left[1 + \left(\frac{i}{m} \right) \right] (R) \left[\frac{\left\{ 1 + (i/m) \right\}^{nm} - 1}{(i/m)} \right]$$

where V = future value of a series of equal payments (annuity)

i = annual or nominal interest rate

m = number of times interest is compounded per year, and the number of payments per year

R = amount of each regular future periodic payment

n = number of years

The following time line depicts an annuity due:

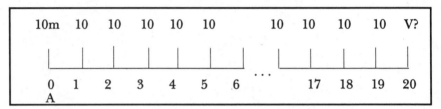

Example: Future Value of an Annuity Due. Mr. Worth sells some land and is to receive $5000 at the *beginning* of each 3 months for 9 years. If he invests the receipts at 6 percent, compounded quarterly, how much will he have at the end of 9 years?

A time line will help visualize the problem:

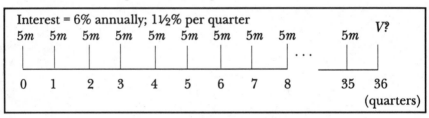

The solution by formula for finding the future value is:

$$V = \left[1 + \left(\frac{i}{m} \right) \right] (R) \left[\frac{(1 + i/m)^{(n)(m)} - 1}{i/m} \right]$$

$$= \left[1 + \left(\frac{0.06}{4} \right) \right] (\$5000) \left[\frac{(1 + (0.06/4)^{(9)(4)} - 1}{0.06/4} \right]$$

$$= (1.015)\ (\$5000) \left[\frac{(1.015)^{36} - 1}{0.06/4} \right]$$

$$= (\$5075) \left[\frac{1.709140 - 1}{0.015} \right]$$

$$= (\$5075) \left[\frac{0.709140}{0.015} \right]$$

$$= (\$5075)\,(47.275969)$$

$$= \$239,925.54$$

The value of

$$\left[\frac{(1 + i/m)^{(n)(m)} - 1}{i/m} \right]$$

may be found in Table 3 of Appendix 1, 1½ percent rate, in column 2, "Amount of $1 per period," on the line for 36 periods as 47.275969. Or it may be found using a calculator or computer.

The $239,925.54 future value could have been found by applying the compound interest formula $(1 + i)^n$ to each of the 36 cash flow figures to determine their value at the end of 36 periods, and then taking the sum of all of them. The annuity formula is a much easier and more elegant method of arriving at the same result.

Conclusion

In the chapter we have calculated the future value of both ordinary annuities and annuities due. We have found that with any three of four variables given (future sum, time, interest rate, and regular payment), the missing item can be calculated. And we have found solutions by various methods, including graphs, tables of factors, log table, and by formula.

Now that we know that the $10,100 per year will produce $1,000,000 in 25 years at 10 percent annual compounding, it is time to figure out from where the $10,100 will come, as well as determine the investment medium where 10 percent earnings can be safely secured.

5
Deferred Annuities

In preceding chapters we have worked with both simple or ordinary annuities as well as annuities due. The initial investment or regular payment (sometimes referred to as *rent* or *rents*) begins at either the end (simple annuity) or beginning (annuity due) of the first time interval.

Regular payments in a *deferred annuity* do not begin until two or more time intervals have elapsed. The term of a deferred annuity begins at some future time. For example, an annuity of quarterly payments which have been deferred for 6 years has the beginning of its term 6 years hence; the first payment is at $6\frac{1}{4}$ years. The sequence of payments depicted in the following time line shows an annuity, A, whose term has been deferred for eight periods. The present value is indicated by X, and the future value by S. The annuity begins at the end of the eighth period, and continues for 16 regular payments.

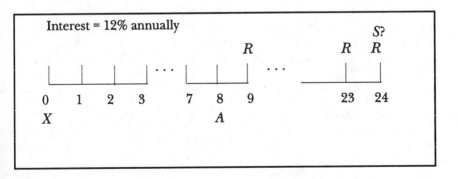

Future Value of a Deferred Annuity

The future value of a deferred annuity is the same as the future value of an ordinary or simple annuity. The period of deferral has no effect on the computation of the future value of a deferred annuity. Thus, the future value of a deferred annuity may be determined by any of the methods described in Chap. 4.

Example: Future Value of a Deferred Annuity.   A school district is worried about replacing its computer systems. The district expects to receive more revenue from taxes starting 2 years from now. At that time, it plans to invest $100,000 per year for 10 years in a fund, which it expects to earn 8 percent, compounded annually. What will be the value of the fund after the 10 years of payments? In other words, what is the future value of a 10-year annuity of $100,000 per year deferred 2 years, at 8 percent, with semiannual interest?

The time line is:

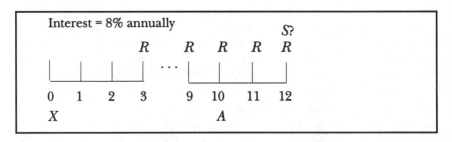

The future value may be found by using Fig. 4.5. Enter the graph at $10,000 on the left vertical axis; proceed horizontally to the 10-year curve, then down to the intersection of the bottom horizontal axis, where the value is just under $150,000. Since $150,000 is the value for $10,000 annual investments (as compared to the actual case of $100,000), it must be multiplied by 10 to determine the $1,500,000 future value of $100,000 per year. The future value may also be determined by formula, tables, calculator, or computer. The more precise value from the formula, described in Chap. 4, is $1,448,656.25.

Present Value of a Deferred Annuity

Determining the value today of a deferred annuity is a two-part process. First, the present value of the regular payments is determined at one interval before the first payment. This is shown on the time line as *A*. Then the value of A is discounted to today, where it is represented on the time line as X. The present value of the ordinary annuity at A is found by any of the methods described in Chap. 3. Then X, the present value of A, is calculated at point 0 by the method outline in Chap. 2.

Example: Finding the Present Value of a Deferred Annuity. Grandfather George wants to provide an annuity that will provide his grandson, Shawn, with a monthly income of $2000 for 48 months to take care of 4 years of college. Shawn will not need the first annual installment until 48 months from today. If the investment earns a nominal annual rate of 12 percent, compounded monthly, how much does Grandfather need to invest today?

The following time line depicts the situation. First, one must find the value at A; then discount the amount so obtained to point 0. The value at A can be found using Fig. 3.1. Draw a vertical line up from 48 months on the bottom horizontal axis of the figure to the intersection with the 1 percent (per month) curve; then proceed horizontally to the left vertical axis to the point of intersection, about $38. Thus $38 of present value represents $1 of monthly annuity income, and $2000 of monthly income would require about $76,000 as the value of A (by calculator, $75,948).

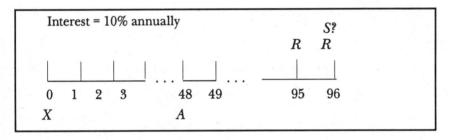

The value of X at point 0 is the value of $76,000 discounted for 48 monthly periods (4 years) at 1 percent per month (12 percent per year, compounded monthly). This can be found using Fig. 2.1. Enter the figure on the bottom horizontal axis at 12 percent annual interest; proceed vertically to the 4-year curve (for 4 years); then move horizontally to the left axis, where the point of intersection is at $620, which represents $620 in present value per $1000 of future value. Applying that 0.62 ratio to $76,000 indicates $47,120 (which is 0.62 times $76,000) as the amount needed.

By formula, computer, or calculator, the computed values are $75,947.92 as the value of A and $47,107.49 as the value of X. The formulas are the same as those used in previous chapters and need not be repeated here.

In this example, Shawn will receive $2000 per month for 4 years, a total of $96,000. To provide this benefit, under the terms stated, only about $47,000 is needed today.

Deferred annuities can be purchased commercially from financial institutions such as insurance companies, or they may be self-created and funded. Annuities are not guaranteed by any federal agency.

Of great importance with respect to deferred annuities is the need to obtain the maximum possible rate of interest or return on the investment that is consistent with the risk one can afford to bear. There is considerable competition among financial institutions in the terms which they offer. So it is *wise to investigate carefully*. The terms offered by the vendors can then be compared to what an investor can do for himself by investing directly in carefully chosen bonds, certificates of deposit, or other investments. Only then will the investor know that a wise course of action has been chosen.

6

How Long Will
My Capital Last?

Life Expectancy
of an Investment
with Equal
Annual
Withdrawals

A basic problem that faces investors—especially investors in a mutual fund periodic or automatic withdrawal plan—is the depletion or exhaustion of the investor's capital that occurs if the rate of withdrawal exceeds the rate of earnings on the capital. In such a case, the investor will eventually have no capital remaining.

Table 6.1 shows how long an original capital of $100,000 will Last, before being reduced to zero, if:

1. Annual withdrawals or redemptions from the original capital are made at 6 percent ($6000), 8 percent ($8000), and 10 percent ($10,000); and

2. The original capital remaining after the withdrawals grows at compound annual interest rates of 4, 6, 8, 10, and 12 percent, compounded annually.

Example: How Long Will My Capital Last?   Raoul Diego places $100,000 in a retirement account and earns 8 percent on his capital, but he withdraws $10,000 per year, that is, 10 percent of the original capital. How Long will his capital last?

Table 6.1. How Long Will My Capital Last?

Annual withdrawal		Compound rate of growth of capital				
		4%	6%	8%	10%	12%
Rate %	Amount	Number of Years until Capital Depleted				
6	$ 6000	28	Never	Never*	Never*	Never*
8	8000	17	23	Never	Never*	Never*
10	10,000	13	15	20	Never*	Never*

* The original capital will increase.

Refer to Table 6.1. Under the 8 percent column, and on the line for 10 percent withdrawals, is the answer, 20 years.

Example: 8 Percent Earned; 10 Percent Withdrawn.   Mrs. Eldridge has today $100,000 of original capital. It is invested to earn an 8 percent compound annual rate of interest. If Mrs. Eldridge withdraws 10 percent of the original capital, i.e., $10,000 per year, year after year, after how many years from today will the original capital be reduced to zero?

We can solve this problem using Figs. 6.1 and 6.2. Enger Fig. 6.1 on the left vertical axis at the 10 percent point for annual withdrawals; then proceed horizontally to 8 percent curve (annual earnings); then drop vertically to the bottom axis. At the bottom axis the point of intersection is about 21 years, which is how long the capital will last.

If the original capital were $1,000,000, and the annual withdrawals were $100,000, the capital would be dissipated in the same 21 years.

The solution can also be found by using the following formula for *capital withdrawals*:

$$x = \frac{i/m}{1 - (1 + i/m)^{-nm}}$$

where x = percentage of original capital withdrawn annually
   i = nominal annual compound earnings rate of remaining capital
   m = number of times interest is compounded annually and number of withdrawals per year
   n = number of years before capital is exhausted
   nm = number of withdrawals and number of time periods

In this example,

$$x = \frac{\text{amount of each periodic withdrawal}}{\text{original capital}} = \frac{\$10,000}{\$10,000} = 0.1$$

Therefore,

Percent of original capital withdrawn annually

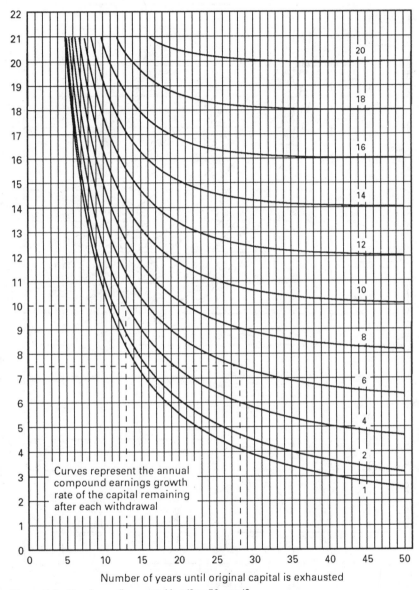

Number of years until original capital is exhausted

Figure 6.1. How long will my capital last (2 to 50 years)?

Percent of original capital withdrawn annually

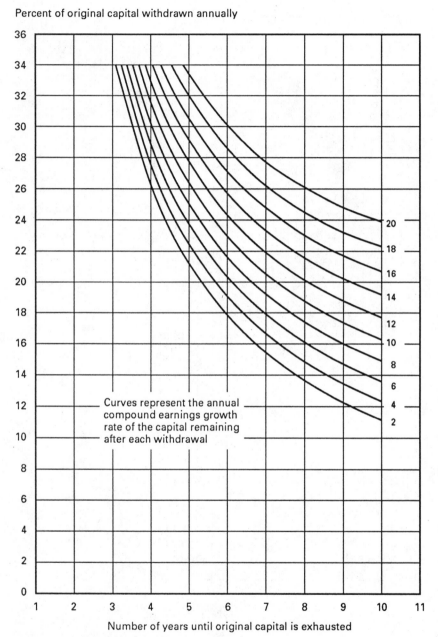

Figure 6.2. How long will my capital last (1 to 10 years)?

$$x = \frac{i/m}{1 - (1 + i/m)^{-nm}}$$

$$0.1 = \frac{0.08/1}{1 - (1 + 0.08/1)^{-(n)(1)}}$$

$$= \frac{0.08}{1 - (1 + 0.08/1)^{-(n)(1)}}$$

$$0.1 \left[1 - (1.08)^{-n} \right] = 0.08$$

$$\left[1 - (1.08)^{-n} \right] = 0.8$$

$$-1.08^{-n} = -0.2$$

$$+1.08^{-n} = +0.2$$

$$\frac{1}{1.08^n} = 0.2$$

$$1 = (+0.2)(1.08)^n$$

$$1.08^n = \frac{1}{0.2}$$

$$(n)(\log 1.08) = \log 5$$

$$n = \frac{\log 5}{\log 1.08}$$

$$= 20.91 \text{ years}$$

The value of the factor

$$x = \frac{i/m}{1 - (1 + i/m)^{-nm}}$$

may also be found in the tables in Appendix 1 in the last column, "Partial Payment: annuity worth $1 today–periodic payment necessary to pay off a loan of $1." Using Table 10, 8 percent rate, scan down the column until the values nearest to 0.1 are found. (The value of the factor is, in this instance, known and is 0.1.) The value for 20 periods in 0.1018, and for 21 periods it is 0.0998. Thus, the number of annual periods is almost 21.

Still another way to solve this problem is to use Table 6.2. In the 8 percent (earning rate) column, proceed down the column until the value closest to the withdrawal rate of 10 percent is found (9.98 percent). Then, in that row, proceed horizontally to the first column, where the number of years that the capital will last is displayed: 21 years.

Example: 6 Percent Earned; 7.5 Percent Withdrawn. Imogene Spend-thrift invests her $1,000,000 portfolio to earn 6 percent and withdraws 7.5 percent ($75,000) of the original capital each year. When will she run out of money?

Refer to Fig. 6.1. The dashed line shows that if 7.5 percent of original capital (e.g., $1,000,000) is withdrawn annually ($75,000), and the original capital remaining grows at an annual compound rate of 6 percent, Ms. Spendthrift's original capital will be exhausted in about 28 years.

The number of years may also be found in Appendix Table 8, 6 percent rate. The table to use is the one corresponding to i, the compound interest rate. Scan the last column for the nearest values of x, the withdrawal rate—in this case, 0.075. The closest periods are 27 and 28 years.

Example: How Much Capital Is Needed? Frank Ford can invest his money to earn 10 percent and wishes to have an income (including exhaustion of capital) of $100,000 per year for at least 13 years. How much original capital is required?

On Fig 6.1, move vertically (see dashed line on figure) up from 13 years to the 10 percent curve and then across horizontally to the left margin. The point where the horizontal line intersects the left axis of the graph is 14 percent. Mr. Ford may withdraw 14 percent of his original capital per year.

The remaining question is: "How much original capital is needed?" We know that 14 percent of x, the original capital, is $100,000 per year. Therefore, $714,285.71 is required. (If $0.14x = \$100,000$, then $x = \$100,000 \div 0.14 = \$714,285.71$.)

Life Expectancy and Death Rates

How much capital to withdraw or the percentage of total capital to withdraw should be considered in terms of one's life expectancy. Table 6.3 provides some insight into the question of the number of years for which one should plan. This table is based on massive groups of people who are essentially healthy.

Table 6.2. What Percent of My Capital Can Be Withdrawn Annually?*

Years that capital will last	4%	6%	8%	10%	12%	14%	16%	18%	20%
1	104.0	106.0	108.0	110.0	112.0	114.0	116.0	118.0	120.0
2	53.02	54.54	56.08	57.62	59.17	60.73	62.3	63.9	65.5
3	36.03	37.41	38.80	40.21	41.63	43.07	44.5	46.0	47.5
4	27.55	28.86	30.19	31.55	32.92	34.32	35.7	37.2	38.6
5	22.46	23.74	25.05	26.38	27.74	29.13	30.5	32.0	33.4
6	19.08	20.34	21.63	22.96	24.32	25.72	27.1	28.6	30.1
7	16.66	17.91	19.21	20.54	21.91	23.32	24.8	26.2	27.7
8	14.85	16.10	17.40	18.74	20.13	21.56	23.0	24.5	26.1
9	13.45	14.70	16.01	17.36	18.77	20.22	21.7	23.2	24.8
10	12.33	13.59	14.90	16.27	17.70	19.17	20.7	22.3	23.9
11	11.41	12.68	14.01	15.40	16.84	18.34	19.9	21.5	23.1
12	10.66	11.93	13.27	14.68	16.14	17.67	19.2	20.9	22.5
13	10.01	11.30	12.65	14.08	15.57	17.12	18.7	20.4	22.1
14	9.47	10.76	12.13	13.57	15.09	16.66	18.3	20.0	21.7
15	8.99	10.30	11.68	13.15	14.68	16.28	17.9	19.6	21.4
16	8.58	9.90	11.30	12.78	14.34	15.96	17.6	19.4	21.1
17	8.22	9.54	10.96	12.47	14.05	15.69	17.4	19.1	20.9
18	7.90	9.24	10.67	12.19	13.79	15.46	17.2	19.0	20.8
19	7.61	8.96	10.41	11.95	13.58	15.27	17.0	18.8	20.6
20	7.36	8.72	10.19	11.75	13.39	15.10	16.9	18.7	20.5
21	7.13	8.50	9.98	11.56	13.22	14.95	16.7	18.6	20.4
22	6.92	8.30	9.80	11.40	13.08	14.83	16.6	18.5	20.4
23	6.73	8.13	9.64	11.26	12.96	14.72	16.5	18.4	20.3
24	6.56	7.97	9.50	11.13	12.85	14.63	16.5	18.3	20.3
25	6.40	7.82	9.37	11.02	12.75	14.55	16.4	18.3	20.2
26	6.26	7.69	9.25	10.92	12.67	14.48	16.3	18.2	20.2
27	6.12	7.57	9.14	10.83	12.59	14.42	16.3	18.2	20.1
28	6.00	7.46	9.05	10.75	12.52	14.37	16.3	18.2	20.1
29	5.89	7.36	8.96	10.67	12.47	14.32	16.2	18.1	20.1
30	5.78	7.26	8.88	10.61	12.41	14.28	16.2	18.1	20.1
31	5.69	7.18	8.81	10.55	12.37	14.25	16.2	18.1	20.1
32	5.59	7.10	8.75	10.50	12.33	14.21	16.1	18.1	20.1
33	5.51	7.03	8.69	10.45	12.29	14.19	16.1	18.1	20.0
34	5.43	6.96	8.63	10.41	12.26	14.16	16.1	18.1	20.0
35	5.36	6.90	8.58	10.37	12.23	14.14	16.1	18.1	20.0
36	5.29	6.84	8.53	10.33	12.21	14.13	16.1	18.0	20.0
37	5.22	6.79	8.49	10.30	12.18	14.11	16.1	18.0	20.0
38	5.16	6.74	8.45	10.27	12.16	14.10	16.1	18.0	20.0
39	5.11	6.69	8.42	10.25	12.15	14.09	16.0	18.0	20.0
40	5.05	6.65	8.39	10.23	12.13	14.07	16.0	18.0	20.0
41	5.00	6.61	8.36	10.20	12.12	14.07	16.0	18.0	20.0
42	4.95	6.57	8.33	10.19	12.10	14.06	16.0	18.0	20.0
43	4.91	6.53	8.30	10.17	12.09	14.05	16.0	18.0	20.0
44	4.87	6.50	8.28	10.15	12.08	14.04	16.0	18.0	20.0
45	4.83	6.47	8.26	10.14	12.07	14.04	16.0	18.0	20.0
46	4.79	6.44	8.24	10.13	12.07	14.03	16.0	18.0	20.0

Table 6.2. What Percent of My Capital Can Be Withdrawn Annually?* *(Continued)*

Years that capital will last	4%	6%	8%	10%	12%	14%	16%	18%	20%
				Earning rate of original and remaining capital					
47	4.75	6.41	8.22	10.11	12.06	14.03	16.0	18.0	20.0
48	4.72	6.39	8.20	10.10	12.05	14.03	16.0	18.0	20.0
49	4.69	6.37	8.19	10.09	12.05	14.02	16.0	18.0	20.0
50	4.66	6.34	8.17	10.09	12.04	14.02	16.0	18.0	20.0
51	4.63	6.32	8.16	10.08	12.04	14.02	16.0	18.0	20.0
52	4.60	6.30	8.15	10.97	12.03	14.02	16.0	18.0	20.0
53	4.57	6.29	8.14	10.06	12.03	14.01	16.0	18.0	20.0
54	4.55	6.27	8.13	10.06	12.03	14.01	16.0	18.0	20.0

*Values in table are percent of capital withdrawn annually.

Life expectancy, happily, has increased considerably in recent years. The 1958 C.S.O. Basic Table, for example, showed at age 65, a life expectancy for males of 13.95 years, as compared to an expectancy from the 1983 tables for males of 16.19 years. For females, the 1958 expectancy of 13.95 years increased, in the 1983 results, to 20.78 years.

What about Inflation?

With inflation seemingly a built-in fact of life, it is prudent to make retirement plans with some appropriate allowance for its ravaging effect. Specifically, to cope with inflation, increase the annual withdrawal that one makes from one's capital by the anticipated rate of inflation. Thus, one's retirement income (from withdrawal from capital) will increase each year at the rate of inflation, keeping the purchasing power of the withdrawals intact.

At a 5 percent rate of inflation, the analysis may be performed by using Fig. 6.3. For example, a retiree with a $1,000,000 nest egg plans to withdraw 10 percent ($100,000) the first year of his retirement. Assuming that inflation is 5 percent per year, and that this capital earns 10 percent each year, over an expected life span of 15 years, how much can he withdraw each year? Enter Fig. 6.3 at the bottom horizontal axis at 15 years, proceed vertically to the 10 percent (earnings rate on capital) curve, then go horizontally to the left to the intersection with the left vertical axis. That point, 10 percent, shows that he may withdraw 10 percent of his capital the first year and increase the withdrawals each year by the 5 percent rate of inflation. The capital will last for and be reduced to zero in 15 years.

Table 6.3. Group Annuity Mortality Table, and Life Expectancy, 1983

Age	Deaths per 1000	Life expectancy	Age	Deaths per 1000	Life expectancy	Age	Deaths per 1000	Life expectancy
				Males				
1	0.34	75.95	38	1.04	39.88	75	44.60	9.65
2	0.34	74.98	39	1.13	38.92	76	49.39	9.10
3	0.34	74.00	40	1.24	37.96	77	54.76	8.58
4	0.34	73.03	41	1.37	37.01	78	60.68	8.07
5	0.34	72.05	42	1.53	36.06	79	67.13	7.60
6	0.32	71.08	43	1.72	35.12	80	74.07	7.14
7	0.30	70.10	44	1.93	34.18	81	81.48	6.71
8	0.29	69.12	45	2.18	33.24	82	89.32	6.31
9	0.29	68.14	46	2.47	32.32	83	97.53	5.93
10	0.29	67.16	47	2.79	31.40	84	106.05	5.57
11	0.30	66.18	48	3.14	30.48	85	114.84	5.23
12	0.30	65.20	49	3.51	29.58	86	124.17	4.91
13	0.31	64.22	50	3.91	28.68	87	133.87	4.60
14	0.32	63.24	51	4.32	27.80	88	144.07	4.32
15	0.33	62.26	52	4.76	26.92	89	154.86	4.04
16	0.33	61.28	53	5.20	26.05	90	166.31	3.78
17	0.34	60.30	54	5.66	25.18	91	178.21	3.54
18	0.35	59.32	55	6.13	24.32	92	190.46	3.30
19	0.37	58.34	56	6.62	23.47	93	203.01	3.08
20	0.38	57.36	57	7.14	22.63	94	217.90	2.86
21	0.39	56.38	58	7.72	21.79	95	234.09	2.66
22	0.41	55.41	59	8.38	20.96	96	248.44	2.48
23	0.42	54.43	60	9.16	20.14	97	263.95	2.30
24	0.44	53.45	61	10.06	19.33	98	280.80	2.12
25	0.46	52.48	62	11.13	18.52	99	299.15	1.95
26	0.49	51.50	63	12.39	17.73	100	319.19	1.78
27	0.51	50.53	64	13.87	16.95	101	341.09	1.61
28	0.54	49.55	65	15.59	16.19	102	365.05	1.44
29	0.57	48.58	66	17.58	15.45	103	393.10	1.28
30	0.61	47.61	67	19.80	14.73	104	427.26	1.10
31	0.64	46.63	68	22.23	14.02	105	469.53	.92
32	0.69	45.66	69	24.82	13.34	106	521.94	.74
33	0.73	44.70	70	27.53	12.68	107	586.52	.55
34	0.79	43.73	71	30.35	12.04	108	665.27	.33
35	0.86	42.76	72	33.37	11.42	109	1000.00	.00
36	0.91	41.80	73	36.68	10.81			
37	0.97	40.84	74	40.39	10.22			

Table 6.3. Group Annuity Mortality Table, and Life Expectancy, 1983 (*Continued*)

Age	Deaths per 1000	Life expectancy	Age	Deaths per 1000	Life expectancy	Age	Deaths per 1000	Life expectancy
				Females				
1	0.17	82.45	38	0.57	45.96	75	23.99	12.87
2	0.17	81.46	39	0.62	44.99	76	27.18	12.19
3	0.17	80.48	40	0.67	44.02	77	30.67	11.53
4	0.17	79.49	41	0.72	43.05	78	34.46	10.89
5	0.17	78.50	42	0.78	42.08	79	38.55	10.28
6	0.14	77.52	43	0.84	41.11	80	42.95	9.70
7	0.12	76.53	44	0.92	40.15	81	47.66	9.13
8	0.10	75.54	45	1.01	39.18	82	52.69	8.59
9	0.10	74.54	46	1.12	38.22	83	58.07	8.07
10	0.10	73.55	47	1.24	37.27	84	63.81	7.56
11	0.10	72.56	48	1.37	36.31	85	69.92	7.08
12	0.11	71.57	49	1.51	35.36	86	76.57	6.61
13	0.12	70.57	50	1.65	34.41	87	84.46	6.16
14	0.13	69.58	51	1.79	33.47	88	91.94	5.73
15	0.14	68.59	52	1.95	32.53	89	101.35	5.31
16	0.15	67.60	53	2.12	31.60	90	111.75	4.90
17	0.16	66.61	54	2.32	30.66	91	123.08	4.52
18	0.17	65.62	55	2.54	29.73	92	135.63	4.16
19	0.18	64.63	56	2.80	28.81	93	149.58	3.81
20	0.19	63.65	57	3.10	27.89	94	165.10	3.48
21	0.20	62.66	58	3.44	26.98	95	182.42	3.17
22	0.21	61.67	59	3.82	26.07	96	201.76	2.87
23	0.23	60.68	60	4.24	25.17	97	222.04	2.60
24	0.24	59.70	61	4.70	24.28	98	243.90	2.34
25	0.25	58.71	62	5.21	23.39	99	268.19	2.09
26	0.27	57.73	63	5.77	22.51	100	295.19	1.86
27	0.28	56.74	64	6.39	21.65	101	325.23	1.64
28	0.39	55.76	65	7.06	20.78	102	358.90	1.43
29	0.32	54.77	66	7.82	19.93	103	395.84	1.24
30	0.34	53.79	67	8.68	19.09	104	438.36	1.05
31	0.36	52.81	68	9.70	18.26	105	487.82	.86
32	0.39	51.83	69	10.92	17.44	106	545.89	.68
33	0.41	50.85	70	12.39	16.63	107	614.31	.50
34	0.44	49.87	71	14.13	15.84	108	694.88	.31
35	0.48	48.89	72	16.16	15.06	109	1000.00	.00
36	0.50	47.92	73	18.48	14.31			
37	0.54	46.94	74	21.09	13.58			

SOURCE: 1983 Group Annuity Mortality Table for Males and Females of the Group Annuity Mortality Committee of the Society of Actuaries. Provided by Kathie Pellegrini, FSA, of Mercer-Meidinger-Hansen, NC.

Percent of original capital withdrawn in the first year,
increased annually at the rate of inflation

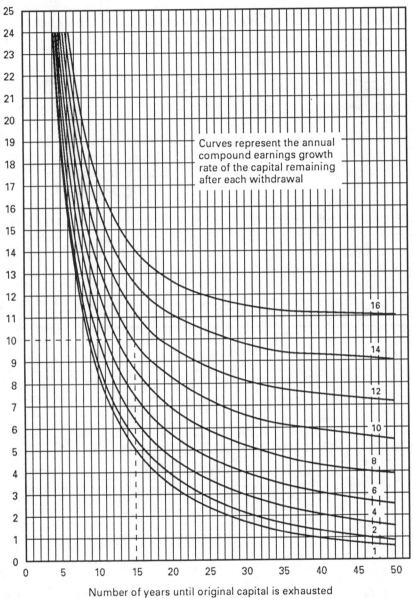

Number of years until original capital is exhausted

Figure 6.3. How long will my capital last with 5 percent inflation? Example: With $1,000,000 in
capital, 10 percent ($100,000) can be withdrawn the first year, $105,000 the second year, increaasing
each year by 5 percent (the inflation rate), provided the remaining capital after withdrawals grows at 10
percent.

The full details of the previous example are shown n Table 6.4. The following summarizes the financial effects for the retiree with capital of $1,000,000. It highlights the astounding differences between accumulation, withdrawals that ignore inflation, and withdrawals that reflect inflation. The results at the end of 15 years, with 5 percent inflation and 10 percent earnings on capital, are:

With no withdrawals	$4,177,248
With withdrawals at a flat 10% of original capital	1,000,000
With withdrawals increasing each year by the rate of inflation	(19,392)

Although the inflation-protecting withdrawals deplete the capital over 15 years, remember that this result was intended. That depletion is the price that has to be paid for receiving $657,856 more in withdrawals than the $1,500,000 that would have been received at the noninflationary flat withdrawal rate of $100,000 per year.

Certainly, with no prospect of inflation ceasing to be a factor in our lives, every financial plan should make allowances for its effects. Figure 6.3 and Table 6.5 (for 5 percent inflation), and Fig. 6.4 and Table 6.6 (for 10 percent inflation) will facilitate proper planning.

Table 6.4. Capital Withdrawals with Inflation

1,000,000 capital available at start of withdrawals
5.00% inflation
10.00% earnings
10.00% rate of withdrawal

	Without inflation			With inflation			
Years	Capital with no withdrawals	Withdrawals without inflation	Capital remaining after withdrawals	Capital at beginning	Earnings	With withdrawals	Capital at end
0	$1,000,000						
1	1,100,000	$100,000	$1,000,000	$1,000,000	$100,000	$100,000	$1,000,000
2	1,210,000	100,000	1,000,000	1,000,000	100,000	105,000	995,000
3	1,331,000	100,000	1,000,000	995,000	99,500	110,250	984,250
4	1,464,100	100,000	1,000,000	984,250	98,425	115,763	966,912
5	1,610,510	100,000	1,000,000	966,912	96,691	121,551	942,053
6	1,771,561	100,000	1,000,000	942,053	94,205	127,628	908,630
7	1,948,717	100,000	1,000,000	908,630	90,863	134,010	865,484
8	2,143,589	100,000	1,000,000	865,484	86,548	140,710	811,322
9	2,357,948	100,000	1,000,000	811,322	81,132	147,746	744,709
10	2,593,742	100,000	1,000,000	744,709	74,471	155,133	664,047
11	2,853,117	100,000	1,000,000	664,047	66,405	162,889	567,562
12	3,138,428	100,000	1,000,000	567,562	56,756	171,034	453,284
13	3,452,271	100,000	1,000,000	453,284	45,328	179,586	319,027
14	3,797,498	100,000	1,000,000	319,027	31,093	188,565	162,365
15	4,177,248	100,000	1,000,000	162,365	16,236	197,993	(19,392)
16	4,594,973	100,000	1,000,000	(19,392)	(1,939)	207,893	(229,224)

Table 6.5. What Percent of Capital Can I Withdraw Annually with Inflation at 5.0% per Year?

Years that capital will last	Earnings rate of original and remaining capital																			
	1%	2%	3%	4%	5%	6%	7%	8%	9%	10%	11%	12%	13%	14%	15%	16%	17%	18%	19%	20%
1	101.0	102.0	103.0	104.0	105.0	106.0	107.0	108.0	109.0	110.0	111.0	112.0	113.0	114.0	115.0	116.0	117.0	118.0	119.0	120.0
2	49.5	50.3	51.0	51.8	52.5	53.3	54.0	54.8	55.5	56.3	57.0	57.8	58.6	59.3	60.1	60.9	61.7	62.4	63.2	64.0
3	32.4	33.0	33.7	34.3	35.0	35.7	36.3	37.0	37.7	38.4	39.1	39.8	40.5	41.2	41.9	42.6	43.3	44.0	44.7	45.4
4	23.8	24.4	25.0	25.6	26.3	26.9	27.5	28.2	28.8	29.4	30.1	30.8	31.4	32.1	32.8	33.5	34.2	34.8	35.5	36.2
5	18.7	19.2	19.8	20.4	21.0	21.6	22.2	22.8	23.5	24.1	24.7	25.4	26.0	26.7	27.4	28.0	28.7	29.4	30.1	30.8
6	15.2	15.8	16.4	16.9	17.5	18.1	18.7	19.3	19.9	20.5	21.2	21.8	22.5	23.1	23.8	24.4	25.1	25.8	26.5	27.2
7	12.8	13.3	13.9	14.4	15.0	15.6	16.2	16.8	17.4	18.0	18.6	19.3	19.9	20.6	21.2	21.9	22.6	23.3	24.0	24.7
8	11.0	11.5	12.0	12.6	13.1	13.7	14.3	14.9	15.5	16.1	16.7	17.4	18.0	18.7	19.3	20.0	20.7	21.4	22.1	22.9
9	9.6	10.1	10.6	11.1	11.7	12.2	12.8	13.4	14.0	14.6	15.2	15.9	16.5	17.2	17.9	18.6	19.3	20.0	20.7	21.4
10	8.4	8.9	9.4	10.0	10.5	11.1	11.6	12.2	12.8	13.4	14.1	14.7	15.4	16.1	16.7	17.4	18.2	18.9	19.6	20.4
11	7.5	8.0	8.5	9.0	9.5	10.1	10.7	11.3	11.9	12.5	13.1	13.8	14.4	15.1	15.8	16.5	17.2	18.0	18.7	19.5
12	6.7	7.2	7.7	8.2	8.8	9.3	9.9	10.5	11.1	11.7	12.3	13.0	13.7	14.3	15.1	15.8	16.5	17.3	18.0	18.8
13	6.1	6.6	7.0	7.5	8.1	8.6	9.2	9.8	10.4	11.0	11.7	12.3	13.0	13.7	14.4	15.1	15.9	16.7	17.4	18.2
14	5.5	6.0	6.5	7.0	7.5	8.0	8.6	9.2	9.8	10.4	11.1	11.8	12.5	13.2	13.9	14.6	15.4	16.2	16.9	17.7
15	5.1	5.5	6.0	6.5	7.0	7.5	8.1	8.7	9.3	10.0	10.6	11.3	12.0	12.7	13.4	14.2	14.9	15.7	16.5	17.3
16	4.6	5.1	5.6	6.0	6.6	7.1	7.7	8.3	8.9	9.5	10.2	10.9	11.6	12.3	13.0	13.8	14.6	15.4	16.2	17.0
17	4.3	4.7	5.2	5.7	6.2	6.7	7.3	7.9	8.5	9.1	9.8	10.5	11.2	12.0	12.7	13.5	14.3	15.1	15.9	16.7
18	4.0	4.4	4.8	5.3	5.8	6.4	6.9	7.5	8.2	8.8	9.5	10.2	10.9	11.7	12.4	13.2	14.0	14.8	15.6	16.5
19	3.7	4.1	4.5	5.0	5.5	6.1	6.6	7.2	7.9	8.5	9.2	9.9	10.6	11.4	12.2	13.0	13.8	14.6	15.4	16.3
20	3.4	3.8	4.3	4.7	5.3	5.8	6.4	7.0	7.6	8.3	8.9	9.7	10.4	11.2	11.9	12.7	13.6	14.4	15.2	16.1
21	3.2	3.6	4.0	4.5	5.0	5.5	6.1	6.7	7.4	8.0	8.7	9.4	10.2	10.9	11.7	12.5	13.4	14.2	15.1	16.0
22	3.0	3.4	3.8	4.3	4.8	5.3	5.9	6.5	7.1	7.8	8.5	9.2	10.0	10.8	11.6	12.4	13.2	14.1	15.0	15.8
23	2.8	3.2	3.6	4.1	4.6	5.1	5.7	6.3	6.9	7.6	8.3	9.1	9.8	10.6	11.4	12.2	13.1	14.0	14.8	15.7
24	2.6	3.0	3.4	3.9	4.4	4.9	5.5	6.1	6.8	7.4	8.1	8.9	9.7	10.5	11.3	12.1	13.0	13.8	14.7	15.6

Table 6.5. What Percent of Capital Can I Withdraw Annually with Inflation at 5.0% per Year? (Continued)

Years that capital will last	Earnings rate of original and remaining capital																			
	1%	2%	3%	4%	5%	6%	7%	8%	9%	10%	11%	12%	13%	14%	15%	16%	17%	18%	19%	20%
25	2.4	2.8	3.2	3.7	4.2	4.7	5.3	5.9	6.6	7.3	8.0	8.7	9.5	10.3	11.1	12.0	12.9	13.7	14.6	15.6
26	2.3	2.7	3.1	3.5	4.0	4.6	5.2	5.8	6.4	7.1	7.9	8.6	9.4	10.2	11.0	11.9	12.8	13.7	14.6	15.5
27	2.2	2.5	2.9	3.4	3.9	4.4	5.0	5.6	6.3	7.0	7.7	8.5	9.3	10.1	10.9	11.8	12.7	13.6	14.5	15.4
28	2.0	2.4	2.8	3.3	3.8	4.3	4.9	5.5	6.2	6.9	7.6	8.4	9.2	10.0	10.8	11.7	12.6	13.5	14.4	15.4
29	1.9	2.3	2.7	3.1	3.6	4.2	4.7	5.4	6.0	6.8	7.5	8.3	9.1	9.9	10.8	11.6	12.5	13.5	14.4	15.3
30	1.8	2.2	2.6	3.0	3.5	4.0	4.6	5.3	5.9	6.6	7.4	8.2	9.0	9.8	10.7	11.6	12.5	13.4	14.3	15.3
31	1.7	2.1	2.5	2.9	3.4	3.9	4.5	5.2	5.8	6.5	7.3	8.1	8.9	9.8	10.6	11.5	12.4	13.4	14.3	15.2
32	1.6	2.0	2.4	2.8	3.3	3.8	4.4	5.1	5.7	6.5	7.2	8.0	8.8	9.7	10.6	11.5	12.4	13.3	14.3	15.2
33	1.5	1.9	2.3	2.7	3.2	3.7	4.3	5.0	5.6	6.4	7.1	7.9	8.8	9.6	10.5	11.4	12.3	13.3	14.2	15.2
34	1.5	1.8	2.2	2.6	3.1	3.6	4.2	4.9	5.6	6.3	7.1	7.9	8.7	9.6	10.5	11.4	12.3	13.3	14.2	15.2
35	1.4	1.7	2.1	2.5	3.0	3.5	4.1	4.8	5.5	6.2	7.0	7.8	8.7	9.5	10.4	11.3	12.3	13.2	14.2	15.1
36	1.3	1.6	2.0	2.4	2.9	3.5	4.1	4.7	5.4	6.2	6.9	7.8	8.6	9.5	10.4	11.3	12.2	13.2	14.2	15.1
37	1.2	1.6	1.9	2.4	2.8	3.4	4.0	4.6	5.3	6.1	6.9	7.7	8.6	9.5	10.4	11.3	12.2	13.2	14.1	15.1
38	1.2	1.5	1.9	2.3	2.8	3.3	3.9	4.6	5.3	6.0	6.8	7.7	8.5	9.4	10.3	11.3	12.2	13.2	14.1	15.1
39	1.1	1.4	1.8	2.2	2.7	3.2	3.8	4.5	5.2	6.0	6.8	7.6	8.5	9.4	10.3	11.2	12.2	13.1	14.1	15.1
40	1.1	1.4	1.7	2.1	2.6	3.2	3.8	4.4	5.2	5.9	6.7	7.6	8.4	9.3	10.3	11.2	12.2	13.1	14.1	15.1
41	1.0	1.3	1.7	2.1	2.6	3.1	3.7	4.4	5.1	5.9	6.7	7.5	8.4	9.3	10.2	11.2	12.1	13.1	14.1	15.1
42	1.0	1.3	1.6	2.0	2.5	3.0	3.7	4.3	5.1	5.8	6.6	7.5	8.4	9.3	10.2	11.2	12.1	13.1	14.1	15.1
43	0.9	1.2	1.6	2.0	2.4	3.0	3.6	4.3	5.0	5.8	6.6	7.5	8.4	9.3	10.2	11.2	12.1	13.1	14.1	15.0
44	0.9	1.2	1.5	1.9	2.4	2.9	3.5	4.2	5.0	5.7	6.6	7.4	8.3	9.2	10.2	11.1	12.1	13.1	14.1	15.0
45	0.8	1.1	1.5	1.9	2.3	2.9	3.5	4.2	4.9	5.7	6.5	7.4	8.3	9.2	10.2	11.1	12.1	13.1	14.1	15.0
46	0.8	1.1	1.4	1.8	2.3	2.8	3.4	4.1	4.9	5.7	6.5	7.4	8.3	9.2	10.2	11.1	12.1	13.1	14.0	15.0
47	0.8	1.0	1.4	1.8	2.2	2.8	3.4	4.1	4.8	5.6	6.5	7.4	8.3	9.2	10.1	11.1	12.1	13.1	14.0	15.0
48	0.7	1.0	1.3	1.7	2.2	2.7	3.4	4.0	4.8	5.6	6.4	7.3	8.2	9.2	10.1	11.1	12.1	13.0	14.0	15.0
49	0.7	1.0	1.3	1.7	2.1	2.7	3.3	4.0	4.8	5.6	6.4	7.3	8.2	9.2	10.1	11.1	12.1	13.0	14.0	15.0
50	0.7	0.9	1.2	1.6	2.1	2.6	3.3	4.0	4.7	5.5	6.4	7.3	8.2	9.1	10.1	11.1	12.1	13.0	14.0	15.0

Percent of original capital withdrawn in the first year,
increased annually at the rate of inflation

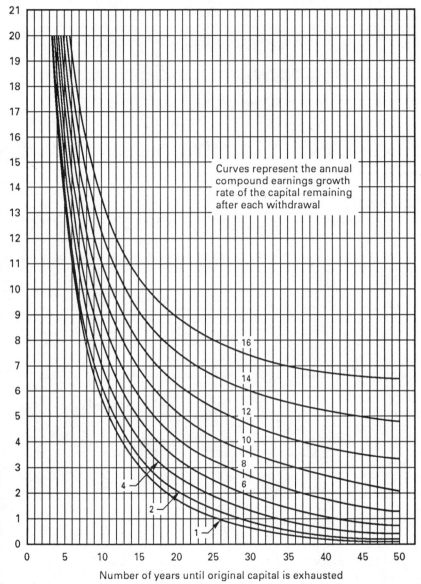

Curves represent the annual
compound earnings growth
rate of the capital remaining
after each withdrawal

Number of years until original capital is exhausted

Figure 6.4. How long will my capital last with 10 percent inflation?

Table 6.6. What Percent of Capital Can I Withdraw Annually with Inflation at 10.0% per Year?

Years that capital will last	Earnings rate of original and remaining capital																			
	1%	2%	3%	4%	5%	6%	7%	8%	9%	10%	11%	12%	13%	14%	15%	16%	17%	18%	19%	20%
1	101.0	102.0	103.0	104.0	105.0	106.0	107.0	108.0	109.0	110.0	111.0	112.0	113.0	114.0	115.0	116.0	117.0	118.0	119.0	120.0
2	48.3	49.1	49.8	50.5	51.3	52.0	52.8	53.5	54.3	55.0	55.8	56.5	57.3	58.0	58.8	59.5	60.3	61.1	61.8	62.4
3	30.8	31.5	32.1	32.7	33.4	34.0	34.7	35.3	36.0	36.7	37.3	38.0	38.7	39.4	40.0	40.7	41.4	42.1	42.8	43.5
4	22.1	22.7	23.3	23.9	24.4	25.0	25.7	26.3	26.9	27.5	28.1	28.8	29.4	30.0	30.7	31.3	32.0	32.7	33.3	34.0
5	16.9	17.4	18.0	18.5	19.1	19.7	20.2	20.8	21.4	22.0	22.6	23.2	23.8	24.5	25.1	25.7	26.4	27.0	27.7	28.3
6	13.5	14.0	14.5	15.0	15.5	16.1	16.6	17.2	17.8	18.3	18.9	19.5	20.1	20.7	21.4	22.0	22.6	23.3	23.9	24.6
7	11.0	11.5	12.0	12.5	13.0	13.5	14.0	14.6	15.1	15.7	16.3	16.9	17.5	18.1	18.7	19.3	20.0	20.6	21.3	21.9
8	9.2	9.6	10.1	10.6	11.1	11.6	12.1	12.6	13.2	13.8	14.3	14.9	15.5	16.1	16.7	17.3	18.0	18.6	19.3	19.9
9	7.8	8.2	8.7	9.1	9.6	10.1	10.6	11.1	11.7	12.2	12.8	13.4	13.9	14.6	15.2	15.8	16.4	17.1	17.7	18.4
10	6.7	7.1	7.5	8.0	8.4	8.9	9.4	9.9	10.5	11.0	11.6	12.1	12.7	13.3	13.9	14.6	15.2	15.9	16.5	17.2
11	5.8	6.2	6.6	7.0	7.5	8.0	8.4	8.9	9.5	10.0	10.6	11.1	11.7	12.3	12.9	13.6	14.2	14.9	15.5	16.2
12	5.0	5.4	5.8	6.2	6.7	7.1	7.6	8.1	8.6	9.2	9.7	10.3	10.9	11.5	12.1	12.7	13.4	14.1	14.7	15.4
13	4.4	4.8	5.2	5.6	6.0	6.5	6.9	7.4	7.9	8.5	9.0	9.6	10.2	10.8	11.4	12.0	12.7	13.4	14.1	14.8
14	3.9	4.3	4.6	5.0	5.4	5.9	6.3	6.8	7.3	7.9	8.4	9.0	9.6	10.2	10.8	11.4	12.1	12.8	13.5	14.2
15	3.5	3.8	4.2	4.5	5.0	5.4	5.8	6.3	6.8	7.3	7.9	8.4	9.0	9.6	10.3	10.9	11.6	12.3	13.0	13.7
16	3.1	3.4	3.8	4.1	4.5	4.9	5.4	5.9	6.4	6.9	7.4	8.0	8.6	9.2	9.8	10.5	11.2	11.9	12.6	13.3
17	2.8	3.1	3.4	3.8	4.1	4.6	5.0	5.5	6.0	6.5	7.0	7.6	8.2	8.8	9.4	10.1	10.8	11.5	12.2	13.0
18	2.5	2.8	3.1	3.4	3.8	4.2	4.7	5.1	5.6	6.1	6.7	7.2	7.8	8.4	9.1	9.7	10.4	11.2	11.9	12.6
19	2.2	2.5	2.8	3.2	3.5	3.9	4.3	4.8	5.3	5.8	6.3	6.9	7.5	8.1	8.8	9.4	10.1	10.9	11.6	12.4
20	2.0	2.3	2.6	2.9	3.3	3.6	4.1	4.5	5.0	5.5	6.0	6.6	7.2	7.8	8.5	9.2	9.9	10.6	11.4	12.1
21	1.8	2.1	2.4	2.7	3.0	3.4	3.8	4.3	4.7	5.2	5.8	6.3	6.9	7.6	8.2	8.9	9.6	10.4	11.1	11.9
22	1.6	1.9	2.2	2.5	2.8	3.2	3.6	4.0	4.5	5.0	5.5	6.1	6.7	7.3	8.0	8.7	9.4	10.2	10.9	11.7
23	1.5	1.7	2.0	2.3	2.6	3.0	3.4	3.8	4.3	4.8	5.3	5.9	6.5	7.1	7.8	8.5	9.2	10.0	10.8	11.6

26	11.2	10.3	9.5	8.8	8.0	7.3	6.6	6.0	5.3	4.8	4.2	3.7	3.3	2.9	2.5	2.1	1.8	1.5	1.3	1.1
27	11.1	10.2	9.4	8.6	7.9	7.2	6.5	5.8	5.2	4.6	4.1	3.6	3.1	2.7	2.3	2.0	1.7	1.4	1.2	1.0
28	11.0	10.1	9.3	8.5	7.8	7.0	6.3	5.7	5.0	4.5	3.9	3.4	3.0	2.6	2.2	1.9	1.6	1.3	1.1	0.9
29	10.9	10.0	9.2	8.4	7.6	6.9	6.2	5.5	4.9	4.3	3.8	3.3	2.8	2.4	2.1	1.8	1.5	1.2	1.0	0.8
30	10.8	9.9	9.1	8.3	7.5	6.8	6.1	5.4	4.8	4.2	3.7	3.2	2.7	2.3	2.0	1.6	1.4	1.1	0.9	0.8
31	10.7	9.9	9.0	8.2	7.4	6.7	6.0	5.3	4.7	4.1	3.5	3.1	2.6	2.2	1.9	1.5	1.3	1.0	0.9	0.7
32	10.7	9.8	8.9	8.1	7.3	6.6	5.9	5.2	4.6	4.0	3.4	2.9	2.5	2.1	1.8	1.5	1.2	1.0	0.8	0.6
33	10.6	9.7	8.8	8.1	7.3	6.5	5.8	5.1	4.5	3.9	3.3	2.8	2.4	2.0	1.7	1.4	1.1	0.9	0.7	0.6
34	10.5	9.7	8.8	8.0	7.2	6.4	5.7	5.0	4.4	3.8	3.2	2.7	2.3	1.9	1.6	1.3	1.0	0.8	0.7	0.5
35	10.5	9.6	8.7	7.9	7.1	6.3	5.6	4.9	4.3	3.7	3.1	2.7	2.2	1.8	1.5	1.2	1.0	0.8	0.6	0.5
36	10.5	9.6	8.7	7.9	7.0	6.3	5.5	4.8	4.2	3.6	3.1	2.6	2.1	1.8	1.4	1.2	0.9	0.7	0.6	0.4
37	10.4	9.5	8.6	7.8	7.0	6.2	5.5	4.8	4.1	3.5	3.0	2.5	2.1	1.7	1.4	1.1	0.9	0.7	0.5	0.4
38	10.4	9.5	8.6	7.7	6.9	6.1	5.4	4.7	4.0	3.4	2.9	2.4	2.0	1.6	1.3	1.0	0.8	0.6	0.5	0.4
39	10.3	9.4	8.6	7.7	6.9	6.1	5.3	4.6	4.0	3.4	2.8	2.3	1.9	1.5	1.2	1.0	0.8	0.6	0.4	0.3
40	10.3	9.4	8.5	7.6	6.8	6.0	5.3	4.6	3.9	3.3	2.8	2.3	1.8	1.5	1.2	0.9	0.7	0.5	0.4	0.3
41	10.3	9.4	8.5	7.6	6.8	6.0	5.2	4.5	3.8	3.2	2.7	2.2	1.8	1.4	1.1	0.9	0.7	0.5	0.4	0.3
42	10.3	9.3	8.4	7.6	6.7	5.9	5.1	4.4	3.8	3.2	2.6	2.1	1.7	1.4	1.1	0.8	0.6	0.5	0.4	0.3
43	10.2	9.3	8.4	7.5	6.7	5.9	5.1	4.4	3.7	3.1	2.6	2.1	1.7	1.3	1.0	0.8	0.6	0.4	0.3	0.2
44	10.2	9.3	8.4	7.5	6.6	5.8	5.0	4.3	3.7	3.0	2.5	2.0	1.6	1.3	1.0	0.7	0.6	0.4	0.3	0.2
45	10.2	9.3	8.4	7.5	6.6	5.8	5.0	4.3	3.6	3.0	2.4	2.0	1.6	1.2	0.9	0.7	0.5	0.4	0.3	0.2
46	10.2	9.2	8.3	7.4	6.6	5.7	5.0	4.2	3.5	2.9	2.4	1.9	1.5	1.2	0.9	0.7	0.5	0.4	0.3	0.2
47	10.2	9.2	8.3	7.4	6.5	5.7	4.9	4.2	3.5	2.9	2.3	1.9	1.5	1.1	0.9	0.6	0.5	0.3	0.2	0.2
48	10.2	9.2	8.3	7.4	6.5	5.7	4.9	4.1	3.5	2.8	2.3	1.8	1.4	1.1	0.8	0.6	0.4	0.3	0.2	0.2
49	10.1	9.2	8.3	7.4	6.5	5.6	4.8	4.1	3.4	2.8	2.2	1.8	1.4	1.0	0.8	0.6	0.4	0.3	0.2	0.1
50	10.1	9.2	8.2	7.3	6.5	5.6	4.8	4.1	3.4	2.7	2.2	1.7	1.3	1.0	0.7	0.5	0.4	0.3	0.2	0.1

7

Mortgage Loans, Depreciation, Tax Shelters, and Mortgage-Backed Securities

Mortgage Loans

Loans secured by mortgages or liens are a factor in most peoples' lives. The repayment of most loans secured by a first mortgage on real estate or liens on automobiles is by level or equal payments over the life of the mortgage. Each payment represents both an interest and a principal payment. At the time of the final payment, the outstanding loan balance is extinguished. Such loans are called *self-amortizing*. Other loans whose payment schedules do not repay the debt by equal payments are said to be *balloons*.

Figure 7.1 shows how the *interest* portion of each payment on a $200,000 loan predominates in the early years of payments and how in later years the proportion of each payment that is applied to reduction of principal increases. The relationship between principal and interest depicted in the graph is typical of all level-payment loans.

Two types of questions frequently arise in connection with mortgage loans:

Loan balance at beginning of year

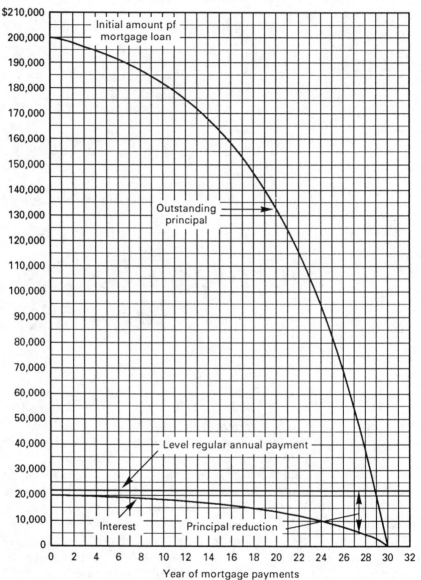

Figure 7.1. Comparison of loan balance, principal, and interest.

1. Frieda Fuerst can afford to pay x dollars per month toward a loan. If interest is y percent, how much can she borrow today, assuming that she can repay the loan over z years?

2. Sam Sutton wants to buy a house with a loan of x dollars; the interst rate is y percent, and the repayment period is z years. How much are his annual (or monthly) repayments?

Both of these problems may be solved by using Fig. 7.2 or Table 7.1.

Example: Finding the Periodic Payment to Repay a Loan.   Holly Hernandez wishes to buy a house that will carry a mortgage loan of $100,000 at 6 percent interest over 20 years. How much are her annual loan payments?

Enter Fig. 7.2 on the base line at 20 years; move vertically to the 6 percent loan interest curve, then horizontally to 8.7 percent. This 8.7 percent times the amount of the loan, $100,000, is the annual payment, about $8700. The exact amount is $8718.46 for annual repayments, and at ½ percent per month interest for 240 months, the monthly payment is $716.43.

The equation or formula for finding the periodic payment to pay off a mortgage loan is the same as that for finding the regular payment in an ordinary annuity, and involves the same process as described in Chap. 6:

$$R = A\left[\frac{i/m}{1 - (1 + i/m)^{-nm}}\right]$$

where R = regular investment or the periodic payment
A = amount borrowed (present value of the annuity)
i = nominal annual compound earnings rate of remaining capital
m = number of times interest is compounded annually and number of payments per year
n = number of years to pay off loan
nm = number of loan payments

In this example,

$$R = A\left[\frac{i/m}{1 - (1 + i/m)^{-nm}}\right] = \$100,000\left[\frac{0.06/1}{1 - (1 + 0.06/1)^{-(20)(1)}}\right]$$

$$= \$100,000\left[\frac{0.06}{1 - (1.06)^{-20}}\right] = \$100,000\left[\frac{0.06}{0.68820}\right]$$

$$= \$100,000\,(0.08718) = \$8718.46$$

Annual payment as percent of initial loan

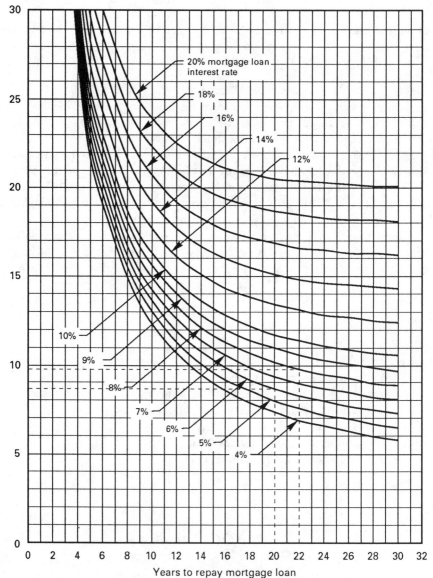

Years to repay mortgage loan

Figure 7.2. Mortgage loan repayments or constant annual repayments.

Table 7.1. Constant Annual Loan Repayments

Annual Principal and Interest Payment as Percentage of Original Loan (Annual Constant)

Annual interest rate %	Years to repay loan														
	2	4	6	8	10	12	14	16	18	20	22	24	26	28	30
20	65.5	38.6	30.1	26.1	23.9	22.5	21.7	21.1	20.8	20.5	20.4	20.3	20.2	20.1	20.1
18	63.9	37.2	28.6	24.5	22.3	20.9	20.0	19.4	19.0	18.7	18.5	18.3	18.2	18.2	18.1
16	62.3	35.7	27.1	23.0	20.7	19.2	18.3	17.6	17.2	16.9	16.6	16.5	16.3	16.3	16.2
14	60.7	34.3	25.7	21.6	19.2	17.7	16.7	16.0	15.5	15.1	14.8	14.6	14.5	14.4	14.3
12	59.2	32.9	24.3	20.1	17.7	16.1	15.1	14.3	13.8	13.4	13.1	12.8	12.7	12.5	12.4
11	58.4	32.2	23.6	19.4	17.0	15.4	14.3	13.6	13.0	12.6	12.2	12.0	11.8	11.6	11.5
10	57.6	31.5	23.0	18.7	16.3	14.7	13.6	12.8	12.2	11.7	11.4	11.1	10.9	10.7	10.6
9	56.8	30.9	22.3	18.1	15.6	14.0	12.8	12.0	11.4	11.0	10.6	10.3	10.1	9.9	9.7
8	56.1	30.2	21.6	17.4	14.9	13.3	12.1	11.3	10.7	10.2	9.8	9.5	9.3	9.0	8.9
7	55.3	29.5	21.0	16.7	14.2	12.6	11.4	10.6	9.9	9.4	9.0	8.7	8.5	8.2	8.1
6	54.5	28.9	20.3	16.1	13.6	11.9	10.8	9.9	9.2	8.7	8.3	8.0	7.7	7.5	7.3
5	53.8	28.2	19.7	15.5	13.0	11.3	10.1	9.2	8.6	8.0	7.6	7.2	7.0	6.7	6.5
4	53.0	27.5	19.1	14.9	12.3	10.7	9.5	8.6	7.9	7.4	6.9	6.6	6.3	6.0	5.8
3	52.3	26.9	18.5	14.2	11.7	10.0	8.9	8.0	7.3	6.7	6.3	5.9	5.6	5.3	5.1
2	51.5	26.3	17.9	13.7	11.1	9.5	8.3	7.4	6.7	6.1	5.7	5.3	5.0	4.7	4.5

The value of the factor

$$\frac{i/m}{1 - (1 + i/m)^{-nm}}$$

is found as 0.087184 in Appendix 1, Table 8, 6 percent rate, in the column, "Partial payment—annuity worth $1 today, periodic payment necessary to pay off a loan of $1," the sixth column, for 20 periods.

Example: Finding an Affordable Amount to Borrow. Betsy Bridges can afford to pay $250 per month ($3000 per year) to repay a mortgage loan. If interest costs are 8 percent and she can obtain a 22-year repayment period, what size loan may she secure?

Enter Fig. 7.2 along the base at 22 years; move vertically to the 8 percent curve, then horizontally to the left axis. The point of intersection, 9.8 percent, is the annual repayment as a percentage of the original loan. To find the loan amount, x:

$$0.098x = \$3000$$

$$x = \frac{3000}{0.098} = \$30,612$$

Ms. Bridges can borrow about $30,612 and pay off the loan over 22 years at 8 percent interest by making annual payments of $3000. The precise amount with annual repayments is $30,602.23, and with $250 monthly repayments, the loan size increases to $31,010.52.

To solve this problem by formula, the method is the same as finding the present value of an ordinary annuity. The formula is:

$$A = R \left[\frac{1 - (1 + i/m)^{-(n)(m)}}{i/m} \right]$$

where A = present value of a series of equal payments (annuity): loan amount

R = amount of each regular future periodic payment

i = annual or nominal interest rate

m = number of payments per year

n = number of years

Here,

$$A = R \left[\frac{1 - (1 + i/m)^{-(n)(m)}}{i/m} \right] = \$3000 \left[\frac{1 - (1 + 0.08/1)^{-(22)(1)}}{0.08/1} \right]$$

$$= \$3000 \left[\frac{1 - (1.08)^{-22}}{0.08} \right]$$

$$= \$3000 \, (10.20074)$$

$$= \$30,602.23$$

Appendix 1, Table 10, 8 percent rate, in the fifth column for 22 periods, "Present worth of $1 per period," contains the factor, 10.200743.

Depreciation Allowances

The maximum allowable depreciation rates which may be applied to real property under the Tax Reform Act of 1986 vary depending on what year the asset was placed in service, what type of asset it is, and whether the taxpayer has made an election to take normal or another rate of depreciation.

For buildings bought or constructed after 1986, if such buildings are residential rental property where at least 80 percent of the gross rentals come from dwelling units, then 27.5-year straight-line depreciation is prescribed by MACRS, the Modified Accelerated Cost Recovery System of the Internal Revenue Code.

For other nonqualifying residential and for nonresidential (e.g., commercial and industrial) property, 31.5-year straight-line depreciation is mandated.*

Various declining-balance methods of depreciation apply to nonreal or personal property.

Various other rates and methods of depreciation apply to property placed in service prior to 1987. These include 200 percent and 150 percent declining-balance methods and useful lives as short as 15 years. These rates continue to apply to assets of eligible owners. New purchasers are required to use the substantially less attractive 27.5- and 39-year lives.

Depreciation is a bookkeeping entry and is not a cash expenditure (at the time of the entry), even though it is a tax deduction. On the other hand, mortgage loan principal repayments are a cash expenditure, but are not tax deductible.

To the extent that depreciation exceeds mortgage loan principal repayments, a *tax-sheltered cash flow* is created—that is, the owner receives cash in excess of his or her taxable income. Conversely, if loan principal repayments exceed depreciation, a negative situation results in that the owner's taxable income is greater than his or her cash receipts.

Figure 7.3 shows—as a percentage of the original loan—the reduction in outstanding principal that occurs as the result of each annual loan repayment.

Example: How Much Is Loan Principal Reduced?   A mortgage loan is for 30 years at 8 percent. How much is the original loan principal reduced as a result of the sixth annual level payment?

Figure 7.3 shows the answer: about 1.3 percent. The graph also shows—as a percentage of the original depreciable amount—each year's allowable depreciation.

The reduction in loan principal that takes place in any given year or time period is the difference between the outstanding loan principal at the beginning of the time period and that at the end of the time period. The outstanding principal at any particular time represents the one lump sum which would pay off the debt at that moment. In other words, the outstanding principal equals *the present value of all remaining payments*. In this example, the reduction in principal from the sixth payment is equal to the difference between the outstanding loan principal at the end of 5 years (A_1) and that at the end of 6 years (A_2). A time line will help us visualize the situation:

---

*For nonresidential real property placed in service after May 12, 1993, 39 years replaced 31.5-year depreciation.

Percent

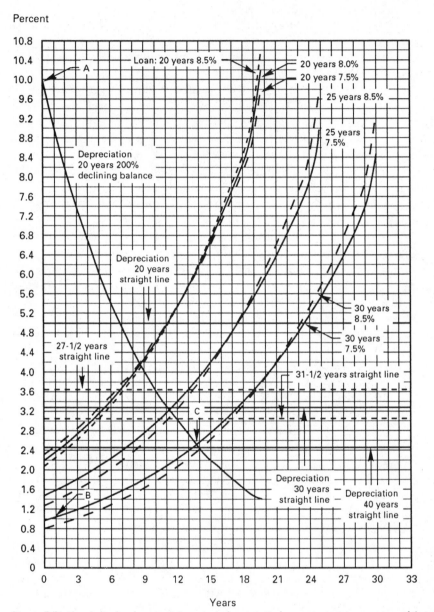

Figure 7.3. Tax shelter breakeven point: mortgage loan principal repayments as a percentage of the original loan (depreciation expressed as a percentage of the original value of the depreciable asset).

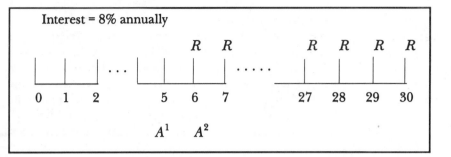

The debt reduction (x) from the sixth payment is A_1 less A_2.

The formula for *the amount of principal included in a single payment* is:

$$x = R\left(\frac{1 - (1 + i/m)^{-(n_1)(m)}}{i/m}\right) - R\left(\frac{1 - (1 + i/m)^{-(n_2)(m)}}{i/m}\right)$$

where x = amount of principal repayment

    R = level annual loan payment

    i = nominal annual interest rate

    m = compounding frequency (and number of payments per year)

    n_1 = number of years of the original mortgage less the number of the payment

where one wishes to find x (in the example, the number of payments from 6 to 30, i.e., 25); and $n_2 = n_1$ plus 1 year (in the example, the number of payments from 7 through 30, i.e., 24).

$$x = R\left\{\frac{1 - [1 + (0.08/1)]^{-25}}{0.08}\right\} - R\left\{\frac{1 - [1 + (0.08/1)]^{-24}}{0.08}\right\}$$

$$= R\,(10.674776) - R\,(10.528758)$$

$$= R\,(0.146018)$$

If the original loan were \$100,000 then the annual debt payment, R, would be \$8882.74. The principal reduction from the sixth payment would be:

$$\$8882.74 \times 0.146018 = \$1297.04$$

And \$1297.04 as a percentage of the original \$100,000 loan is 1.297 percent, or about 1.3 percent.

The values of the factors are found in Appendix 1, Table 10, 8 percent, in the fifth column, "Present worth of \$1 per period," on the lines for 25 and 24 periods as 10.674776 and 10.528758. The difference between the two factors multiplied by the periodic regular payment equals the principal reduction from the payment. Using the tables in this instance is quick and easy and certainly takes much less time than solving the formula.

Example: Constructing a Loan Amortization Schedule. A loan is made for $100,000 for 1 year with a nominal interest rate of 12 percent to be paid monthly. Repayments are at the end of each month. Construct a loan amortization schedule. A *loan amortization schedule* shows each payment, and allocates each payment to interest and to principal reduction. Then the outstanding balance is adjusted by the amount of principal reduction.

First the monthly repayment amount is calculated to be $8884.88. The steps in preparing the schedule are:

1. Determine the regular payment.
2. Multiply the periodic interest rate times the current outstanding balance. This gives the interest expense applicable to the current payment.
3. Deduct the interest expense from the regular payment. The difference is the amount of loan principal reduction that occurs from this payment.
4. Deduct the loan principal payment from the previous outstanding balance to obtain the current outstanding balance.
5. Keep repeating the above steps until the schedule is complete. The details are displayed in Table 7.2.

For a longer time period—say, 36 months—at 10.5 percent per year interest, and a $90,000 initial loan, the monthly payment is $2925.22. An

Table 7.2. Loan Amortization Schedule

Loan amount, $100,000.00
Monthly interest rate, 1.00%
Months to repay, 12
Loan monthly payment, $8884.88

	Beginning balance	Interest	Principal	Ending balance
1	$100,000.00	$1,000.00	$7,884.88	$92,115.12
2	92,115.12	921.15	7,963.73	84,151.39
3	84,151.39	841.51	8,043.26	76,108.03
4	76,108.03	761.08	8,123.80	67,984.23
5	67,984.23	679.84	8,205.04	59,779.19
6	59,779.19	597.79	8,287.09	51,492.11
7	51,492.11	514.92	8,369.96	43,122.15
8	43,122.15	431.22	8,453.66	34,668.49
9	34,668.49	346.68	8,538.19	26,130.30
10	26,130.30	261.30	8,623.58	17,506.72
11	17,506.72	175.07	8,709.81	8,796.91
12	8,796.91	87.97	8,796.91	(.00)

amortization schedule for the first 3 years with a mid-year first payment is shown in Table 7.3

Example: Finding Annual Depreciation.   If property is depreciated over 20 years using the 200 percent declining-balance method, what percent depreciation deduction may be made for the third year? As Fig. 7.3 shows, about 8.1 percent.

The original amount depreciable and the original loan amount may be nearly equal or quite different. If such original amounts are quite different, the graph percentages for each apply to unlike original sums. If such original amounts are nearly equal, however, then the graph percentages may be directly compared to each other.

It is often the case that the original amounts (depreciation and mortgage loan) are approximately equal, as is shown in the following hypothetical case.

Property purchase price	$ 1,000,000
Value of land (not depreciable)	300,000
Value of building (depreciable amount)	$ 700,000
First mortgage loan at 70% of purchase	$ 700,000

Figure 7.3 gives an overall view of the relationship between various rates of depreciation and various mortgage loan terms. Figures 7.4 through 7.13 are more detailed and should be used for particular cases:

Fig. 7.4, 7.5% loan and 20, 27.5, and 31.5-year depreciation

Fig. 7.5, 7.5% loan and 27.5, 30, and 31.5-year depreciation

Fig. 7.6, 7.5% loan and 27.5, 31.5, and 40-year depreciation

Fig. 7.7, 8.0% loan and 20, 27.5, and 31.5-year depreciation

Fig. 7.8, 8.0% loan and 27.5, 30, and 31.5-year depreciation

Fig. 7.9, 8.0% loan and 27.5, 31.5, and 40-year depreciation

Fig. 7.10, 8.5% loan and 20, 27.5, and 31.5-year depreciation

Fig. 7.11, 8.5% loan and 27.5, 30, and 31.5-year depreciation

Fig. 7.12, 8.5% loan and 27.5, 31.5, and 40-year depreciation

Fig. 7.13, 11% loan and 27.5, and 31.5-year depreciation

The number of years over which real property may be depreciated, and the method of depreciation that may be applied, have been the source of continual change by the Congress. It is likely that depreciation rules will continue to be altered frequently in the future as well.

Table 7.3. Loan Amortization Schedule, 36 Months

Loan amount, $90,000.00
Interest rate, 10.5%
Months to repay, 36

		Payment	Interest	Principal	New balance
Year 1	July 1	$ 2,925.22	$ 787.50	$ 2,137.72	$87,862.28
	Aug. 1	2,925.22	768.79	2,156.43	85,705.85
	Sept. 1	2,925.22	749.93	2,175.29	83,530.56
	Oct. 1	2,925.22	730.89	2,194.33	81,336.23
	Nov. 1	2,925.22	711.69	2,213.53	79,122.70
	Dec. 1	2,925.22	692.32	2,232.90	76,889.80
	Year	$17,551.32	$4,441.13	$13,110.19	$76,889.80
Year 2	Jan. 1	2,925.22	672.79	2,252.43	74,637.37
	Feb. 1	2,925.22	653.08	2,272.14	72,365.23
	Mar. 1	2,925.22	633.20	2,292.02	70,073.21
	Apr. 1	2,925.22	613.14	2,312.08	67,761.13
	May 1	2,925.22	592.91	2,332.31	65,428.82
	June 1	2,925.22	572.50	2,352.72	63,076.10
	July 1	2,925.22	551.92	2,373.30	60,702.80
	Aug. 1	2,925.22	531.15	2,394.07	58,308.73
	Sept. 1	2,925.22	510.20	2,415.02	55,893.71
	Oct. 1	2,925.22	489.07	2,436.15	53,457.56
	Nov. 1	2,925.22	467.75	2,457.47	51,000.09
	Dec. 1	2,925.22	446.25	2,478.97	48,521.12
	Year	$35,102.64	$6,733.95	$28,368.69	$48,521.12
Year 3	Jan. 1	2,925.22	424.56	2,500.66	46,020.46
	Feb. 1	2,925.22	402.68	2,522.54	43,497.92
	Mar. 1	2,925.22	380.61	2,544.61	40,953.31
	Apr. 1	2,925.22	358.34	2,566.88	38,386.43
	May 1	2,925.22	335.88	2,589.34	35,797.09
	June 1	2,925.22	313.22	2,612.00	33,185.09
	July 1	2,925.22	290.37	2,634.85	30,550.24
	Aug. 1	2,925.22	267.31	2,657.91	27,892.33
	Sept. 1	2,925.22	244.06	2,681.16	25,211.17
	Oct. 1	2,925.22	220.60	2,704.62	22,506.55
	Nov. 1	2,925.22	196.93	2,728.29	19,778.26
	Dec. 1	2,925.22	173.06	2,752.16	17,026.10
	Year	$35,102.64	$3,607.62	$31,495.02	$17,026.10
Year 4	Jan. 1	2,925.22	148.98	2,776.24	14,249.86
	Feb. 1	2,925.22	124.69	2,800.53	11,449.33
	Mar. 1	2,925.22	100.18	2,825.04	8,624.29
	Apr. 1	2,925.22	75.46	2,849.76	5,774.53
	May 1	2,925.22	50.53	2,874.69	2,899.84
	June 1	2,925.21	25.37	2,899.84	0.00
	Year	$17,551.31	$ 525.21	$17,026.10	$ 0.00

SOURCE: FINANCIAL AND INTEREST CALCULATOR (computer software), Larry Rosen Co., 1989.

Percent

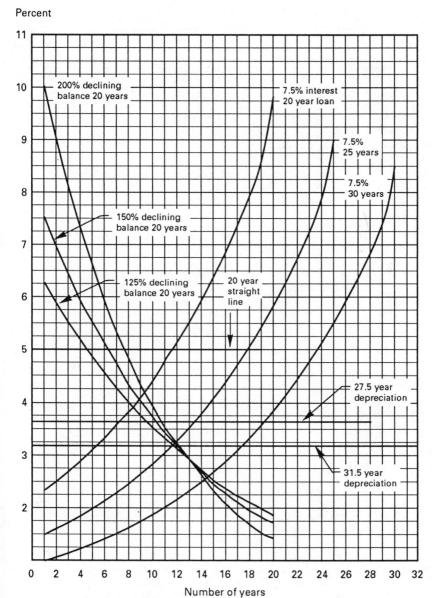

Number of years

Figure 7.4. Mortgage loan principal repayments and depreciation expressed as a percentage of the original value of the loan and depreciable asset: 7.5 percent loan, 20-, 27.5-, and 31.5-year depreciation.

Percent

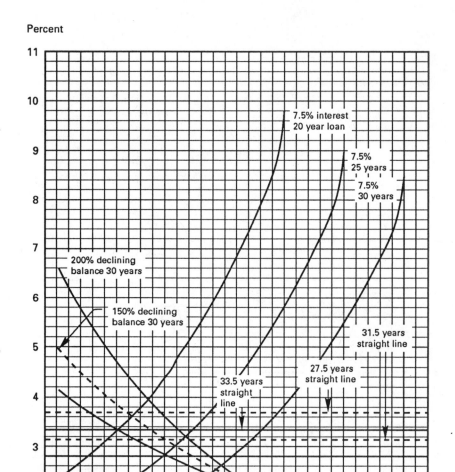

Number of years

Figure 7.5. Mortgage loan principal repayments and depreciation expressed as a percentage of the original value of the loan and depreciable asset: 7.5 percent loan, 27.5-, 30-, and 31.5-year depreciation.

Percent

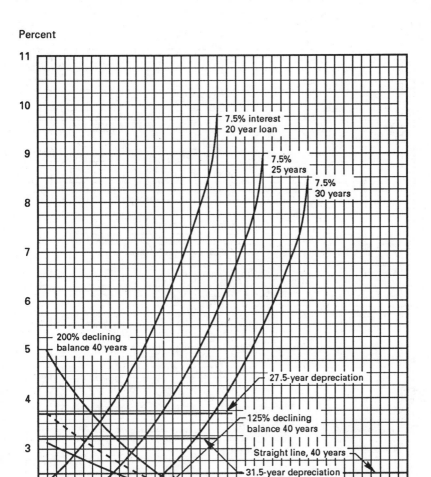

Number of years

Figure 7.6. Mortgage loan principal repayments and depreciation expressed as a percentage of the original value of the loan and depreciable asset: 7.5 percent loan, 27.5-, 31.5-, and 40-year depreciation.

Percent

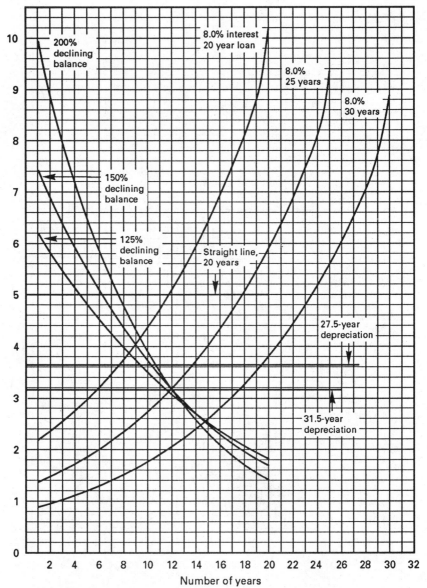

Figure 7.7. Mortgage loan principal repayments and depreciation expressed as a percentage of the original value of the loan and depreciable asset: 8 percent loan, 20-, 27.5-, and 31.5-year depreciation.

Percent

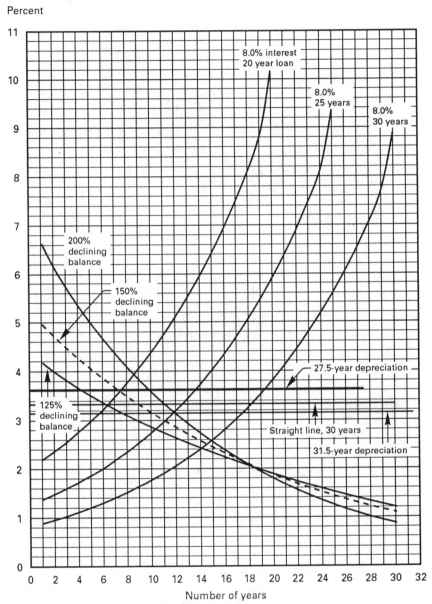

Figure 7.8. Mortgage loan principal repayments and depreciation expressed as a percentage of the original value of the loan and depreciable asset: 8 percent loan, 27.5-, 30-, and 31.5-year depreciation.

Percent

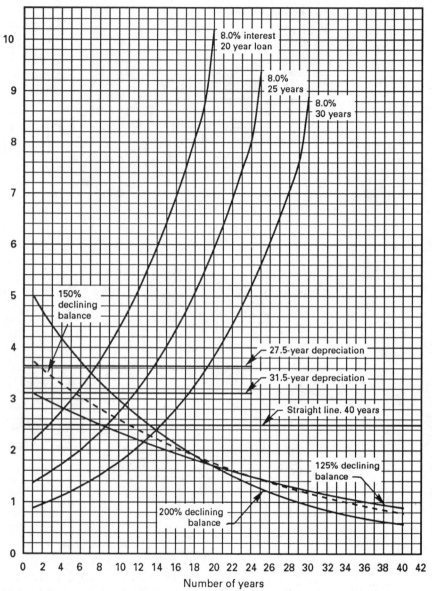

Figure 7.9. Mortgage loan principal repayments and depreciation expressed as a percentage of the original value of the loan and depreciable asset: 8 percent loan, 27.5-, 31.5-, and 40-year depreciation.

Percent

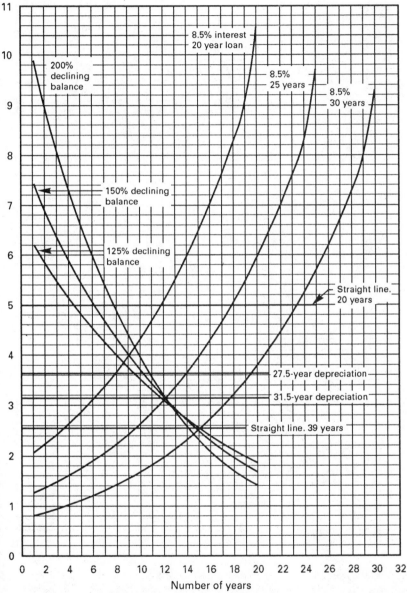

Figure 7.10. Mortgage loan principal repayments and depreciation expressed as a percentage of the original value of the loan and depreciable asset: 8.5 percent loan, 20-, 27.5-, 31.5-, and 39-year depreciation.

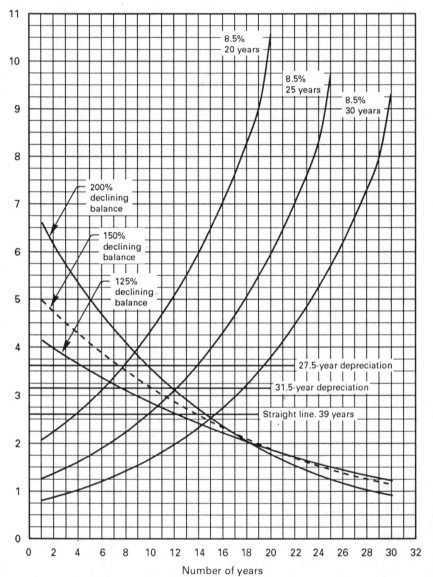

Percent

Figure 7.11. Mortgage loan principal repayments and depreciation expressed as a percentage of the original value of the loan and depreciable asset: 8.5 percent loan, 27.5-, 30-, 31.5-, and 39-year depreciation.

Percent

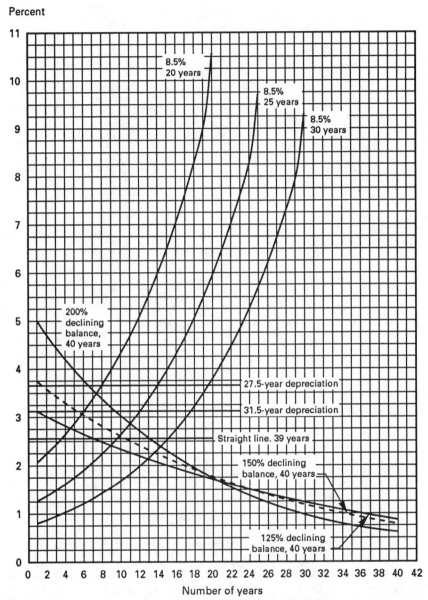

Figure 7.12. Mortgage loan principal repayments and depreciation expressed as a percentage of the original value of the loan and depreciable asset: 8.5 percent loan, 27.5-, 31.5-, 39-, and 40-year depreciation.

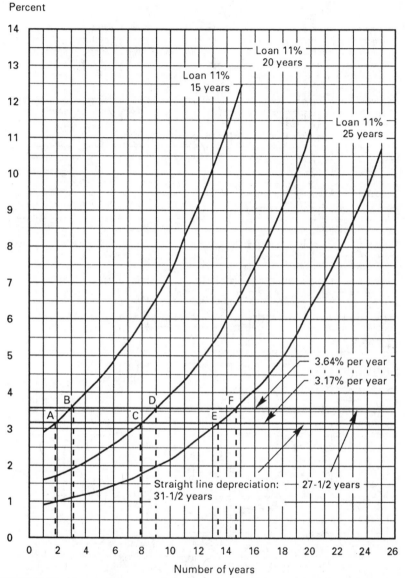

Percent

Figure 7.13. Mortgage loan principal repayments and depreciation expressed as a percentage of the original value of the loan and depreciable asset: 11 percent loan, 27.5-, and 31.5-year depreciation.

Tax Shelters

Refer to Fig. 7.3. Assume the following:

1. 200 percent, 20-year, declining-balance depreciation is used.
2. The mortgage loan is for 30 years at 7.5 percent.
3. The original amount depreciable is equal to the original loan.

In the first year, if this method of depreciation is allowed, what tax shelter exists?

The depreciation expressed as a percentage of the original depreciable amount (e.g., $700,000) is 10 percent, or $70,000 (point A on the figure). The portion of the loan payment that reduces the principal of the original loan (e.g., $700,000) is 0.96 percent, or $6720 (point B on the graph). Hence, the tax-sheltered cash receipts—the excess of depreciation over loan principal repayment—is 9.04 percent (10.0 less 0.96 percent), or $63,280.

For the same example, after how many years would tax-sheltered cash receipts no longer be created?

When the depreciation line on the figure crosses the loan line, the two are equal and no tax-sheltered cash receipts are created. This occurs at point C, which is approximately the fourteenth year. At this point, the owner might wish to consider refinancing the property—the new loan would commence with low annual principal payments and restore the tax shelter. Alternatively, the owner might wish to enter a tax-free exchange for a larger, more expensive property.*

Example: Finding the Principal Portion of a Loan Payment.   Michael Metaxos has a 20-year mortgage loan, originally $100,000. Interest is at 8 percent, and payments are made annually. How much of the eighth annual payment (of $10,185.22) reduces the outstanding loan (x)?

The formula for *the amount of principal in a single payment* is:

$$x = R\left(\frac{1 - (1 + i/m)^{-(n_2)(m)}}{i/m}\right) - R\left(\frac{1 - (1 + i/m)^{-(n_1)(m)}}{i/m}\right)$$

where x = amount of principal repayment
   R = level annual loan payment ($10,185.22)
   i = nominal annual interest rate (0.08)
   m = compounding frequency (and number of payments per year) (1)
   n_1 = number of payments of the original mortgage less the number of the payment where one wishes to find x (13)
   n_2 = n_1 plus 1 payment (12)

*Refer to Internal Revenue code S1031 for details of tax-free or like kind exchanges.

The effect of the formula is that the first term represents the loan balance just prior to the current payment, and the last term represents the loan balance just after the current payment. For this example,

$$x = R\left(\frac{1 - (1 + 0.08/1)^{-(13)(1)}}{0.08/1}\right) - R\left(\frac{1 - (1 + 0.08/1)^{-(12)(1)}}{0.08/1}\right)$$

$$= \$10,185.22\ (7.9037759416) - \$10,185.22\ (7.5360780169)$$

$$= \$10,185.22\ (7.9037759416 - 7.5360780169)$$

$$= \$10,185.22\ (0.3676979247)$$

$$= \$3745.12$$

The effect of the formula, in this example, is to subtract the loan balance remaining after eight payments from the balance after seven payments.

Straight-Line Depreciation

The *straight-line depreciation* formula for determining the annual percentage of depreciation relative to the original depreciable amount is:

$$x = \frac{1}{n}$$

where x = annual depreciation percentage of original depreciable amount
n = number of years of useful life.

Example: Finding Annual Straight-Line Depreciation. What is the annual percentage depreciation if 31.5 years is the useful life?

$$x = \frac{1}{n} = \frac{1}{31.5} = 3.17\%$$

Declining-Balance Depreciation

The formula for determining the annual depreciation amount using *declining-balance depreciation* is:

$$X_n = ry\,(1 - r)^{N-1}$$

where X_n = declining-balance depreciation in the Nth year

r = rate of declining-balance depreciation (relative to straight-line) times the straight-line rate of depreciation

y = original amount to be depreciated

n = year in which the depreciation amount is to be found

Example: Finding Declining-Balance Depreciation. John Olson has an asset which qualifies for 200 percent declining-balance depreciation over a 20-year life, and an original cost of $100,000. What depreciation can Mr. Owner claim in the fifth year?

$$x_n = ry\,(1-r)^{\,N-1}$$

$$= (2)\,(0.05)\,(\$100,000)\,[1-(2)\,(0.05)]^{5-1}$$

$$= 0.1\,(\$100,000)\,(0.9)^4$$

$$= \$6561.00 \qquad \text{or } 6.56\% \text{ of the original depreciable amount.}$$

Tax Shelter Longevity

Refer to Fig. 7.13, 11 percent loan, 27.5- and 31.5-year depreciation. The point at which principal repayment equals annual depreciation is indicated by the letters A through F on the graph for each combination of loan (15-, 20-, and 25-year maturities with level amortization) and depreciation. It is at those points that the tax shelter of the investment evaporates.

It is apparent from inspecting the figure that *the longer the term of the loan, the longer the tax shelter endures.* For example, with a 15-year loan and 31.5-year depreciation, the tax shelter lasts less than 2 years; but with a 25-year loan, the tax shelter endures for a little over 13 years.

This does not mean that the longer-term loan should be blindly chosen as the best. The overall investment results from a financed asset are complex and will be delved into in depth later in this book. Internal rate of return analysis, discussed later, will show the optimum loan to seek.

Evaluating Mortgage-Backed Securities

Mortgage loans are generally originated by savings & loans, mortgage bankers, and commercial and mutual savings banks, but these originators may not desire to hold the mortgage loans in their portfolios, because, among other reasons, the duration of the debt (an asset of the lender) may far exceed the duration of the lender's liabilities (e.g., deposits). The shifting of loans from originator to investors also facilitates geographic diversity in the demand for loans; for example, there may be a high demand for loans to support new construction in the Sun Belt, and a high demand for portfolio investment in New England. So the originator sells the loan, and may or may not continue to service it after the sale. Typically, similar type loans (with somewhat homogenous characteristics) are then pooled and sold to institutional and individual investors by securities brokers. The origination of loans can be quite profitable for the originator, as it benefits by up-front points paid by the borrower, and continuing mortgage servicing fees, usually expressed as a percentage of the outstanding mortgage loan balance. And these fees are earned despite only a temporary commitment of funds to the loan by the originator, as the originator's funds are replenished when the loan is sold in the secondary market. The multifaceted involvement of government in the mortgage market facilitates this unloading of mortgage loans by originators in order to foster the socially desirable objective of providing housing for the nation. This involvement includes loan insurance or guarantees, as well as the use of government agencies or affiliates to acquire the loans and issue certificates of such agencies to the public, as, for example, GNMA certificates, and the like.

A wide variety of mortgage pass-through instruments are available for investment. Generally, these are pools of mortgages, administered by a financial institution, where the payments made by the mortgagor (borrower) of principal and interest are passed through to investors. Investors acquire a piece of the pool by purchasing a participation certificate (PC), either at original issuance or in the secondary market. Payments of interest and principal by the mortgagor may or may not be insured by an external source, such as the Federal Housing Administration (FHA), or guaranteed by the Veteran's Administration (VA) or Farmers Home Administration (FmHA).

Intermediaries play a major role in the secondary market, by reselling mortgages frequently by pooling groups of loans and selling participation to the public in the form of mortgage-backed securities (MBSs). Three federal agencies play major roles as intermediaries. Mortgage-backed securities may be *guaranteed* by an external source such as the Government National Mortgage Association (GNMA, or Ginnie Mae). Purchases in enormous volume of secondary-market mortgage loans are made by the Federal Home Loan Mortgage Corporation (FHLMC, or Freddie Mac) and The Federal National Mortgage Association (FNMA, or Fannie Mae). FNMA and FHLMC then issue a variety of securities to replenish their funds and continue the process.

The volume of mortgage borrowing in the United States dwarfs other forms of borrowing, including both corporate and tax-exempt bonds, as shown in Fig. 7.14.

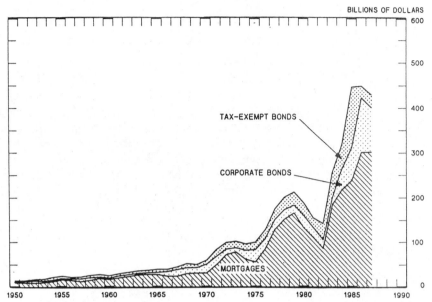

Figure 7.14. Long-term annual borrowing, private domestic nonfinancial sectors. (SOURCE: Board of Governors of the Federal Reserve, 1988 Historical Chartbook.)

Mortgages from an Investor's Viewpoint

The secondary markets for *pass-throughs* of participation certificates (PCs), mortgage-backed securities (MBSs), and pay-throughs (PTs) developed to attempt to alleviate four concerns of institutional investors with respect to investing directly in individual mortgage loans (direct investment):

1. Transaction costs for direct investing are higher because interest and principal is paid monthly rather than semiannually.
2. The cash flows from direct investment are highly uncertain because the borrower can make additional principal payments at any time, or pay off the entire loan in advance.
3. Direct investment is less marketable than a conventional security.
4. Direct investment may entail the additional cost of pursuing delinquent borrowers and foreclosing.

Pass-throughs may be generally classified as either *agency* issues (which predominate) or *conventional* or *private* issues.

Agency Issues

The principal agencies are GNMA, Freddie Mac, and Fannie Mae.

GNMA.   Timely payment of principal and interest is guaranteed by the full faith and credit of the United States. Ginnie Mae is a wholly owned instrumentality of the United States within the Department of Housing and Urban Development. GNMA certificates include *only* mortgages which are FHA insured and VA guaranteed. GNMA offerings include a wide variety, including: ARMs (adjustable-rate mortgages), Midgets (15-year securities), GPMs (graduated-payment mortgages, which after 5 years become the equivalent of a fixed-rate fully amortizing loan), Mobile Homes (which have a higher servicing fee than other GNMAs), Buy-downs, and FHA projects (based on 40-year multifamily-project loans). GNMA offerings may either be GNMA Is (single-family loans) or GNMA IIs (both single- and multifamily). Other technical distinctions also exist between the I and II categories.

Freddie Mac.   Freddie Mac's are mostly conventional mortgage pools. Generally, Freddie Mac guarantees only the timely payment of interest; principal payment is guaranteed only to the extent that it will be paid within 1 year of the due date. A Freddie Mac guarantee is not a U.S. government guarantee. Freddie Mac was chartered on July 24, 1970, as the result of Title III of the Emergency Home Finance Act of 1970, as amended, 12 U.S.C., sections 1451–1459 (the Freddie Mac Act). The Financial Institutions Reform, Recovery, and Enforcement Act of 1989 modified its capital structure and the composition of its board of directors. A description of five major categories of Freddie Mac securities follows:

1. PCs. These generally consist of first-lien, conventional residential mortgages. They represent undivided interests in pools of such loans and pay interest and pass-through principal monthly.

2. Gold PCs. These enhanced securities pass through a first payment to investors 45 days after issuance, compared to 75 days for PCs. They also offer a guarantee of timely payment of both interest and scheduled principal, and the pass-through of actual rather than predicted prepayments.

3. Giant Mortgage Participation Certificates (Giant PCs). These represent ownership of a pool which consists of two or more PCs, and/or other Giant PCs. Giant PCs may be principal only or interest only.

4. Collateralized Mortgage Obligations (CMOs). These are general debt obligations of Freddie Mac secured by specified mortgages.

5. Mortgage Cash Flow Obligations (MCFs). These are general debt obligations of Freddie Mac based on specific mortgages.

Fannie Mae. Fannie Mae guarantees timely payment of both principal and interest. A Fannie Mae guaranty is not a U.S. obligation. Fannie Mae is one of the largest corporations in the United States, based on assets. It is the nation's largest supplier of funds for home mortgages. It was incorporated in 1938 under Title II of the National Housing Act, which was revised as the Federal National Mortgage Association Charter Act in 1954. Fannie Mae issues a variety of short-term notes and debentures, as well as mortgage-backed securities (MBSs) and stripped mortgage-backed securities:

1. Mortgage-backed securities. Most MBSs are issued through lender swap transactions, where securities are traded for pools of mortgages placed in trust. MBSs represent an undivided interest in both principal and interest receipts.

2. Stripped mortgage-backed securities (SMBSs). There are separate classes for principal and interest, or other variations of divided rights to the cash flows from the underlying mortgages.

Conventional or Private Issues

The other major category of mortgage-related securities (besides agencies) are those which are conventionally or privately issued. These are issued by investment banking firms, banks, and others. Major issuers include: Citicorp, Salomon Brothers, Sears Mortgage Securities, Norwest Mortgage Securities, Bank of America, Travelers Insurance, and others.

These securities are not guaranteed by the U.S. government or by the agencies, but may have credit enhancement features, which reduce but do not eliminate credit risk, including:

1. Insurance from a mortgage insurance company

2. Letters of credit or guarantees from commercial banks

3. Subordinated interests

These securities, unlike those of the agencies, generally are evaluated by such credit reporters as Standard and Poor's and Moody's.

Evaluating Yields on Mortgage-Related Securities

The problem with evaluating yields with respect to mortgage-related securities (MRSs) is the uncertainty of future cash flows. To find the internal rate of return (IRR) or yield to maturity (YTM), one must know the cash flows (after reduction by servicing fees). The uncertainty for MRSs is due to principal prepayments. Mortgage borrowers have the right to prepay principal, all or in part, at any time. Borrowers may simply make extra payments from time to time, or they may sell the property underlying the loan and prepay the loan in its entirety. Other complications exist as well, for example, when a borrower defaults or fire or other casualty destroys the property and an insurer pays off the loan. If a defaulted loan is guaranteed, the terms of the guarantee may force the guarantor to immediately prepay the loan. Imagine the chagrin of investors who purchased such bonds at premiums. The level of interest rates strongly influences the rate of discretionary prepayments, because when rates drop significantly below the stated loan interest rates, intelligent borrowers refinance their loans at the lower rates, which results in full prepayment.

Thus investors in MRSs have a risk analogous to that of investors in callable bonds, a *call risk*. The borrower's right to prepay is tantamount to owning a call option to repay the remaining mortgage debt at any time, and the owner of an MRS is effectively short that call option. However, because MRS loans may be prepaid for reasons other than changes in interest rates, an uncertainty exists that is not present in evaluating callable bonds. Additionally, some borrowers may not prepay and refinance even though interest-rate levels are such that such a decision is irrational. So, some of the variations from the callable bond situation result in early prepayment (e.g., fire), and others are the reverse (e.g., failure to prepay when it would be economically advantageous).

Twelve-Year Prepayment Quotes

A conventional method by which many participants in the securities industry have quoted yields on MRSs is on the basis of an assumed *12-year prepaid life*. This 12-year assumption was based on historical experience of actual prepayments. This convention is described in contradictory ways within the securities industry. Some participants say it means that, after 12 years, one-half the MRS portfolio will have paid off their loans. That is, it is the number of years that elapsed (in the past) until one-half the original principal balance was left in the pool. The more generalized opinion is that all the mortgages in a pool will prepay in full at the end of 12 years. In the later case, the assumption is that regularly scheduled principal payments occur for 12 years, at which point the entire remaining principal balance is prepaid. The only good thing the author can find to say about either method is that it is easy to compute the YTM or IRR with those assumptions. So, if a broker tries to sell you an MRS based on a 12-year average life assumption, balk! The assumption is simply worthless. This approach ignores both the coupon rate on the mortgage and the number of years that have elapsed since the mortgage pool's origination. This approach has been replaced by another method, the FHA prepayment experience.

FHA Prepayment Experience

The FHA method is based on the prepayment experience for 30-year FHA-insured mortgages and is derived from a probability survival table (for loans) of the FHA. This approach, though dubious, is still widely used. FHA experience forecasts the prepayment rate of a mortgage pool relative to the historical prepayment and default experience of mortgages originated in a given year. When this method is used, a mortgage pool's prepayment rate is expressed as a percentage of FHA experience. A rate of 150 percent means that the mortgages in a specific pool are paying off principal at a rate 1.5 times faster than 100 percent FHA experience generally. A rate of 50 percent means that the pool's loans are paying off at one-half the rate of FHA experience. A sample of the FHA experience table for a year selected at random is given in Table 7.4.

The FHA experience table is based on the age of the mortgage and ignores the coupon rate on the loans. It is based on assumable FHA and VA loans, which is appropriate for GNMAs but not for issuances of Freddie Mac and Fannie Mae. *Most important, however, is the fact that applying factors of FHA experience for an individual pool to FHA experience is based on historical data.* The author is aware of no evidence that this record of historical results can be used successfully for predicting the future.

An offering by a broker may take the form shown in Table 7.5. Only with a *par* Ginnie Mae is there so little difference among the projected yields at various FHA repayment rates. But with *discount* Ginnie Maes, as prepayments speed up, yield increases. Conversely, with *premium* Ginnie Maes, as prepayments speed up, yield decreases. These essential facts are easy to remember. *With a discount bond, the sooner the amount of the discount is recovered, the higher is the yield to the purchaser. With a premium bond, the longer one enjoys the higher coupon yield, that is, the longer it takes for the bond to be paid off, the better is the yield.*

With MRSs, always determine the minimum YTM that can be experienced. With a discount bond, this will be at a zero percent FHA rate (no prepayments). With a premium bond, this will be with immediate prepayment. Par bonds will be indifferent to the prepayment rate. Unless there is some reason that immediate prepayment is a possibility (such as a pool with only one bond, or a pool where the coupon rates are far in excess of current market rates), a more realistic measure would be the YTM based on a 300 or 350 percent FHA rate.

Table 7.4. FHA Experience Table

Years after origination	Surviving percentage of loans	Cumulative percentage of original loans repaid	100% FHA experience (during year repaid), %
0	100.0	0.0	0.0
1	98.8	1.2	1.2
2	95.2	4.8	3.6
3	90.1	9.9	5.1
4	85.0	15.0	5.1
5	79.8	20.2	5.2
6	76.7	23.3	3.1
7	69.8	30.2	6.9
8	65.2	34.8	4.6
9	61.1	38.9	4.1
10	57.5	42.5	3.6
11	54.0	46.0	3.5
12	50.7	49.3	3.3
13	47.7	52.3	3.0
14	44.9	55.1	2.8
15	42.2	57.8	2.7
16	39.5	60.5	2.7
17	36.8	63.2	2.7
18	34.2	65.8	2.6
19	31.5	68.5	2.7
20	28.9	71.1	2.6
21	26.4	73.6	2.5
22	24.0	76.0	2.4
23	21.7	78.3	2.3
24	19.7	80.3	2.0
25	17.4	82.6	2.3
26	15.5	84.5	1.9
27	13.7	86.3	1.8
28	12.1	87.9	1.6
29	10.0	90.0	2.1
30	8.0	92.0	2.0
31	0.0	100.0	8.0

An adage in the brokerage market is that the life of an MRS is as follows:

For discounts, 15 years or so

For premiums, 9 years or so

For very speedy premiums, 5 years or so

For slow discounts, 18 years or so

One broker suggests subtracting the age of the Ginnie Mae (settlement date less dated date) from the preceding figures to obtain the approximate remaining expected life.

Table 7.5. GNMA Offering Sheet (Secondary Market)

Quantity (par value when originally issued)	$100,000	
Balance remaining ($20,000 of principal has been repaid)	$80,000	
Current factor (A + B)	80.00%	
Pool number (each pool has its own identification)	#16007	
Interest rate (this is ½% less than the average mortgage rate of the pool, to provide for the servicing fee)	11.00%	
Current offering price (set by the seller or dealer) ($1000 per bond)	100	
Accured interest (from last payment to settlement date) [(B) (E/12) (14/30)]; where 14 days have elapsed since last payment.	$342.22	
Total amount due if offering is accepted [(C) (A) + G]	$80,342.22	
Past FHA experience (prepayment rate; 0% means no prepayments; 50% means half the average rate, etc.)		
i. Over past 2 years	50.00%	
ii. Over past 1 year	75.00%	
iii. Over past 6 months	100.00%	
iv. Since original issuance of this pool	70.00%	
The foregoing shows that in recent times the prepayment rate for this pool has accelerated.		
Range of projected YTMs:	BEY is	YTM is
i. At future FHA experience of 300%, bond equivalent YTM	11.115%	10.866%
ii. At future experience of 100%, bond equivalent YTM is	11.167%	10.916%
iii. At future experience of 0%, bond equivalent YTM is	11.191%	10.939%
Bond equivalent yield is higher due to monthly (versus semiannual) payment of interest and principal.		
Servicing mortgage co.: Joyful Savings and Loan (the location of the mortgage company may have little relationship to the location of the properties securing the mortgage loans in the pool).		
Geographic location. Sun Valley, Sun Belt (Demographic figures are available showing the rate of housing turnover for specific areas.)		
Dated date (date of formation of this pool)	10/1/1990	
Due date	10/15/2020	
Time elapsed (from dated date to settlement date, years)	4.917	
Settlement date	9/15/1995	

Enough said about FHA experience. It is important to recognize its deficiencies.

Constant Prepayment Factors

Another measure of prepayment is the *conditional* or *constant prepayment rate* (CPR). This assumes that the principal is prepaid at some constant rate. Usually, CPR refers to an annualized rate, while the terms *single monthly mortality* (SMM) and *constant monthly prepayment* (CMP) are used for monthly rates of prepayment. It assumes that a constant fraction of the *remaining* principal is prepaid each time interval. It is based on the historic prepayment experience and the economic environment. Its advantage is that it is simple to use. Its disadvantage is that it is highly subjective. For example, if a mortgage pool prepays at a SMM of 1 percent, then 1 percent of the outstanding balance, after subtracting scheduled principal payments, will be prepaid in each month. The CPR will be a bit less than 12 times the SMM (due to the effect of monthly compounding). For example, a 1 percent per month SMM corresponds to an 11.36 percent CPR. The conversion formula for a *single monthly mortality* (SMM) is:

$$SMM = 1 - (1 - CPR)^{1/12}$$

where SMM = single monthly mortality rate
CPR = constant repayment rate

A disadvantage of this method is that it fails to consider the effect of age on prepayments, including the relatively low prepayment levels that exemplify newer loans.

Public Securities Association

The Public Securities Administration (PSA) represents dealers in U.S. securities, including mortgage-related securities. The use of the PSA standard prepayment model as a benchmark has generally replaced the approaches discussed above. The PSA model combines the FHA survivorship schedules with the CPR method. The PSA benchmark (referred to as 100 percent PSA) assumes a series of CPRs that commence at $^2/_{10}$ of 1 percent for the first month (about 2.4 percent per year) and that increase by $^2/_{10}$ of 1 percent each month thereafter, until 30 months after the mortgage loan's origination, from which point the rate then attained, 6 percent CPR, is used thereafter. The effect of this is that the rate of assumed prepayment using the PSA method will be about the same as FHA Experience (100 percent) during the first 8 or 9 years; then it will be more than the FHA Experience until about 22 or 23 years; and from then until the 30-year maturity, PSA will be less than FHA. A projected 200 percent PSA means that the CPR in any month will be twice the standard CPR (at 100 percent PSA). For example, the CPR would be $^4/_{10}$ of 1 percent in month 1, at 200 percent PSA. The 100 percent PSA model for *constant repayment rate* (CPR) can be expressed as follows:

$$\text{If } t < 30, \text{ then CPR} = \frac{0.06t}{30}$$

$$\text{If } t > 30, \text{ then CPR} = 0.06$$

where t is the number of months elapsed since mortgage loan origination.

Faster or slower prepayment speeds make reference to some percentage of the PSA. For example, 200 percent PSA means two times the CPR of the PSA prepayment rate. The CPR converts to an SMM by using the formula presented previously.

Example. Find CPR and SMM Assuming 200 Percent PSA for the Twentieth Month.

$$CPR = \frac{0.06t}{30} = \frac{0.06\,(20)}{30} = 0.04$$

$$200\%\ PSA = 2.0\,(0.04) = 0.08$$

$$SMM = 1 - (1 - 0.08)^{1/12} = 0.006924$$

The PSA standard prepayment model is a benchmark, not a model for forecasting prepayments. It has assisted in standardizing quotations for MRSs and is easily understood. Its most significant limitation is that it fails to recognize the characteristics of the underlying mortgages in a particular pool, such as for example, whether such loans are at premiums, discounts, or par, whether they are GNMAs or conventional loans, etc.

Econometric Prepayment Models

Various Wall Street firms and some investment advisory firms have developed models that project prepayment rates as a function of selected economic variables. The PSA, through Knight-Ridder, makes available prepayment rates determined by the models of such firms as Salomon Brothers, Bear Stearns, Citicorp, Dean Witter, First Boston, Goldman Sachs, Kidder Peabody, Merrill, Morgan Stanley, Paine Webber, Prudential Bache, and Shearson. The output of these models is converted to rates expressed as a percentage of PSA. There is considerable variance among the projected rates of the various firms.

Among the non-interest-rate factors that cause prepayment rates to rise are: plant closures, company mergers and takeovers, poor economic conditions, divorces, tornadoes, floods, and fires. And on the interest rate scene, prepayments will increase (assuming rational borrowers) when rates fall below the interest rate paid by the borrower, adjusted for refinancing costs.

An econometric prepayment model generally projects SMMs for each remaining month of the mortgage security, and attempts to reflect such variables as changing patterns of housing turnover, variations in prepayment according to the time the loan has been in effect (aging), etc. These

SMMs are usually converted to an equivalent averaged CPR or percentage of PSA (since, for sales purposes, it is expected that such a rate will be quoted).

Industry sources find econometric models to be preferable to using other means of predicting prepayments because past prepayment levels are frequently an unreliable indicator of future prepayment levels.

Cash Flows of a Loan with Regular Prepayments

Before the true return (IRR or YTM) can be found for an investment in a mortgage-backed security, the projected cash flow schedule for the investment must be derived. Earlier in this chapter we developed loan amortization schedules. That is all that is entailed here, except that two new twists are added to the old cocktail as the result of prepayments. Use the SMM (single monthly mortality) to multiply by the mortgage balance (less scheduled principal payment) at the beginning of each time period to find the prepayment amount. Each month the required principal and interest amount is reduced commensurate with the prepayments which have occurred. The new required payment each month is based on the time remaining from the present to the original maturity and the then outstanding balance.

Example: Find the Cash Flows to a Mortgage Investor. Find the cash flows to an investor for the first 10 months, where the initial loan is $100,000, with 10 percent annual interest, a 6 percent CPR, and assuming that prepayments are at 150 percent of PSA. See Table 7.6. Cash flows will be substantially affected by changes in the multiple of the PSA rate at which prepayments are assumed. The higher the PSA rate, the more of the early payments are represented by principal and the less is the portion represented by interest. The relationships may be seen in Fig. 7.15, which shows for the 30-year life of a GNMA the breakdown each year among principal (including prepayments), interest, and servicing fee. Inspection of the figure shows that at a zero PSA rate (no prepayments), the annual cash flows are level, although the breakdown among the components changes. As time passes, more of each payment reduces principal and less is interest. As prepayments increase, the level of cash flows in the early years is greater, and a higher portion of such cash flows reduces the loan principal. The mirror image of principal repayment is the status of the outstanding loan balance, which diminishes most rapidly at the highest PSA level and remans highest at the zero PSA rate.

Once the cash flow of an MBS has been estimated, the IRR or YTM is determined in the conventional manner. This yield is sometimes referred to in the case of MBSs as a *cash flow yield*, to distinguish it from *bond*

Table 7.6 Cash Flow to Investor with 150% PSA Repayments

→   0.50000% annual servicing fee percentage
→ $100,000.00 loan amount   →   10.000% annual interest
      0.83333% interest rate per month
→   360 months to repay   →   6.000% CPR
      0.50% monthly prepayment as percentage of current balance
      $877.57157 loan monthly payment amount (without prepayments, initially)
SMM = $1 - (1 - CPR) \exp{^1\!/_{12}} = 0.0051430$
PSA = →   150.00% (multiple of 100% PSA assumed)

Mo. (n)	100% PSA CPR	SMM	Monthly payment factor	Beginning balance	Interest	Scheduled principal	Principal prepayment	Mortgage Service fee	investor cash flow	Ending balance
ab	c	d	e	f	g	h	i	j	k	l
1	0.0020	0.0022503	1.00000	$100,000	$833	$44.24	$ 25.02	$41.67	$861	$99,931
2	0.0040	0.0025014	0.99975	99,931	833	44.60	50.08	41.64	886	99,836
3	0.0060	0.0007531	0.99925	99,836	832	44.94	75.15	41.60	910	99,716
4	0.0080	0.0010055	0.99850	99,716	831	45.29	100.22	41.55	935	99,570
5	0.0100	0.0012587	0.99749	99,570	830	45.62	125.27	41.49	959	99,400
356	0.0600	0.0078284	0.06896	295	2	58.06	1.86	0.12	62	235
357	0.0600	0.0078284	0.06842	235	2	58.08	1.39	0.10	61	176
358	0.0600	0.0078284	0.06789	176	1	58.11	0.92	0.07	60	117
359	0.0600	0.0078284	0.06735	117	1	58.14	0.46	0.05	60	58
360	0.0600	0.0078284	0.06683	58	0	58.16	0.00	0.02	59	0

Note a. For simplicity, only the first and last few months are shown.

Note b. The mortgage payment factor is based on the previous month's SMM.

Note c. The computation is: (0.06)(A)/30, or if month > 30, 0.06.

Note d. $1 - [1 - (c * PSA\ multiple)]^{(^1\!/_{12})}$.

Note e. $(1- D_{n-1})(E_{n-1})$.

Note f. L_{n-1}.

Note g. (f) (interest rate per month).

Note h. (monthly payment) (E - G).

Note i. (F - H)(D).

Note j. (Annual servicing fee/12)(F).

Note k. H + I + G - J.

Note l. F - H - I.

equivalent yield (BEY). To convert from IRR to BEY, a standard procedure is followed, which adjusts the monthly payment yield to an equivalent semiannual yield, which is then multiplied by 2 (by convention) to obtain the BEY. Thus the formula for *bond equivalent yield for an MBS* is:

$$BEY = 2\,[(1 + i)^6 - 1]$$

where BEY = bond equivalent yield
       i = monthly interest rate that equates the MBSs cash flows to the initial or current price

Annual cash flows
per $1,000 face

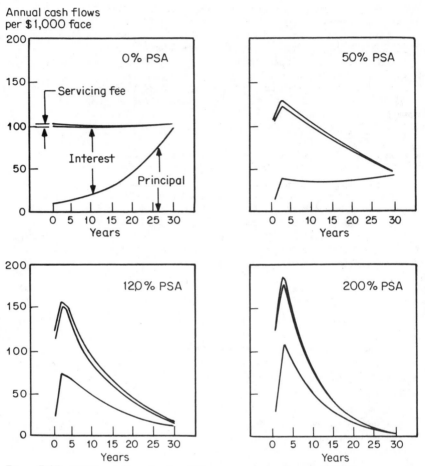

Figure 7.15. GNMA cash flows at various PSA prepayment rates (9 percent GNMA).

Example: Finding the Bond Equivalent Yield. Find the BEY for an MBS priced at $875, where the monthly IRR is 75/100 of 1 percent.

$$BEY = 2\,[(1 + i)^6 - 1]$$

$$= 2\,[(1 + 0.0075)^6 - 1] = 9.1704\%$$

In placing bids for MBSs, the investor has to determine the price he or she is willing to pay. Generally, the starting point is the desired BEY. In order to calculate the price, the BEY must be first converted to a monthly IRR by solving the above BEY formula for i, that is, by using the following monthly MBS interest rate formula to find i.

$$i = [1 + (0.5) (BEY)]^{1/6} - 1$$

where i = monthly interest rate (monthly IRR)

BEY =

bond equivalent yield of the MBS

Example. An investor wants to acquire an MBS to obtain a BEY of 9 percent. At what rate must the investor discount the prospective cash flows of the MBS?

$$i = [1 + (0.5) (BEY)]^{1/6} - 1$$

$$= [1 + (0.5) (0.09)]^{1/6} - 1 = 0.007363$$

Thus, the cash flows must be discounted at a monthly rate of 0.7363 percent.

Time Spread or Elapsed Time

Fundamental to the concepts of "x-year prepayment quotations" and similar measures to attempt to quantify the projected yields of MBSs is the technique coined *time spread* by its proponent in 1936, Kenneth E. Boulding ("Time and Investments," *Economica*, Vol. 3, pp. 196–220, 1936), and which is also referred to in actuarial literature as *elapsed time*.

The relevance of elapsed time is:

1. When it is used with IRR, elapsed time is a measure of how long, on average, the initial investment remains invested.

2. Elapsed time provides the date or point in time at which a *single* amount (equal to the sum of the undiscounted cash flows) would be equivalent at the IRR to the actual series of cash flows; for example, if there are cash flows for a period of 30 years, with an IRR of i, and the elapsed time, ET, is determined to be 12 years, it means that a lump sum (equal to the sum, undiscounted, of the cash flows) invested at 12 years is nearly equivalent to the entire series of cash flows discounted or accumulated at the IRR. In the case of a GNMA or MBS, this means (if the projected cash flows including estimated prepayments are accurate) that the proposed investment in the GNMA is equivalent to investing the same sum in an alternate bond with ET years until maturity and a single payoff amount at that time (as with a zero-coupon bond).

Assuming that initially a negative cash flow occurs (the investment), followed by a series of positive cash flows (the positive cash flows), the approximate formula (the precise formula follows soon) for finding elapsed time is:

$$\mathrm{ET}_a = \frac{\displaystyle\sum_{k=1}^{t} n_k\, r_k}{\displaystyle\sum r_k}$$

where ET = elapsed time

ET_a = approximation of elapsed time

k = counter, from 1 to t

t = total number of cash flows

n_k = number of periods to cash flow 1, cash flow 2, ..., cash flow n

r_k = amount of cash flow 1, cash flow 2, ... , cash flow n

Consider the set of cash flows shown in Table 7.7 and find the approximate elapsed time. Applying the approximation formula for ET,

$$\mathrm{ET}_a = \frac{\displaystyle\sum_{k=1}^{t} n_k\, r_k}{\displaystyle\sum r_k}$$

$$= \frac{9000}{2000} = 4.5 \text{ years (or periods)}$$

The approximation method overstates the amount of ET; for a more accurate measure, a second term is deducted from the approximate amount, as follows:

$$\mathrm{ET} = \mathrm{ET}_a - \left[\frac{i}{2}\left(\frac{\displaystyle\sum_{k=1}^{t}[n_k^2 r_k]}{\displaystyle\sum_{k=1} r_k} - \mathrm{ET}_a{}^2\right)\right] = 4.5 - \left[\frac{0.169082}{2}\left(\frac{42,000}{2,000} - 4.5^2\right)\right]$$

Table 7.7. Approximate Elapsed Time Determination

Initial investment = $1000
IRR = 16.9082%

Year n	Cash flow r	$(n)\,(r)$
1	0	0
2	100	200
3	200	600
4	300	1200
5	1400	7000
Sum	2000	9000

$$= 4.5 - (0.169082)(0.375) = 4.436 \text{ years (or periods)}$$

The determination of the value of the product of years squared and the individual cash flows is shown in Table 7.8.

When the cash flows are discounted to a point 4.436 years from the commencement date, their sum is $1,999.68, which, of course, is nearly $2,000, the sum of the undiscounted cash flows.

These principles may be applied to the FHA experience table (Table 7.4). The resulting factors for finding elapsed time or time spread are shown in Table 7.9. ET for the FHA experience table, based on a nominal annual rate of 9 percent, is as follows.

$$ET_a = \frac{2,854,664}{232,089} = 12.2999 \text{ years}$$

and

$$ET = 12.2999 - \left[\frac{0.0913}{2} \left(\frac{52,106,881}{232,089} - 12.2999^2 \right) \right] = 8.95 \text{ years}$$

This means that $232,089 due in about 8.95 years is equivalent to the entire range of principal and interest cash flows for the 30-year FHA projection, where the IRR is 9.13 percent. (Actually, as shown in Table 7.9, 9.6 years (versus 8.95) produces an exact result.)

In practice, with GNMAs several nuances exist which need to be reckoned with for complete accuracy. The first is a delay factor reulting from the fact that a time period (often quoted at about 45 delays) elapses from the time a principal and interest payment is made by the mortgagor until the payment is passed through to an investor in a mortgage-backed security. The second is a result of the ½ of 1 percent servicing fee that is retained by the loan servicing agent. The underlying mortgage will bear a coupon rate—say, 10½ percent—that is ½ percent higher than the coupon rate of the mortgage-backed security. This means that the actual principal amortization of the underlying mortgage will occur based on

Table 7.8. Elapsed Time Determination

Initial investmet = $1000
IRR = 16.9082%

Year n	Cash flow r	$(n)(r)$	Year squared n^2	$n^2 \times r$
1	0	0	1	0
2	100	200	4	400
3	200	600	9	1,800
4	300	1,200	16	4,800
5	1,400	7,000	25	35,000
Sum	2,000	9,000		42,000

Table 7.9. Elapsed Time or Time Spread Based on FHA Experience (Table 7.4)

$100,000 original loan
0.75% monthly interest, 9% per year
9.3807% equivalent annual interest

Years after origination a	Surviving percentage of loans c	Cumulative percentage of original loans repaid e	FHA experience (during year repaid), % g	During year principal repaid h	Col. a times col. h i	Loan balance at beginning of year j	Interest during year k	Cash flow col. h + col. k l	Col. a times col. l m	Col. a squared times col. h n	Col. a squared times col. l o	At IRR of 9.12981% value of all CFs disct'd to ET 9.6369 years p	At IRR 9.12981% value of all CFs disct'd. to time 0
0	100.0	0.0	0.0	0	0	100,000	0	0	0	0	0	0	0
1	98.8	1.2	1.2	1,200	1,200	98,800	9,324	10,524	10,524	1,200	10,524	22,383	9,644
2	95.2	4.8	3.6	3,600	7,200	95,200	9,099	12,699	25,399	14,400	50,797	24,748	10,663
3	90.1	9.9	5.1	5,100	15,300	90,100	8,691	13,791	41,374	45,900	124,121	24,628	10,611
4	85.0	15.0	5.1	5,100	20,400	85,000	8,213	13,313	53,251	81,600	213,005	21,785	9,386
5	79.8	20.2	5.2	5,200	26,000	79,800	7,730	12,930	64,648	130,000	323,242	19,388	8,354
6	76.7	23.3	3.1	3,100	18,600	76,700	7,340	10,440	62,642	111,600	375,854	14,345	6,181
7	69.8	30.2	6.9	6,900	48,300	69,800	6,871	13,771	96,399	338,100	674,796	17,339	7,471
8	65.2	34.8	4.6	4,600	36,800	65,200	6,332	10,932	87,456	294,400	699,646	12,613	5,434

13	47.7	52.3	3.0	3,000	39,000	47,700	4,615	7,615	98,999	507,000	1,286,986	5,676	2,446
14	44.9	55.1	2.8	2,800	39,200	44,900	4,343	7,143	100,006	548,800	1,400,079	4,879	2,102
15	42.2	57.8	2.7	2,700	40,500	42,200	4,085	6,785	101,779	607,500	1,526,690	4,247	1,830
16	39.5	60.5	2.7	2,700	43,200	39,500	3,832	6,532	104,512	691,200	1,672,195	3,746	1,614
17	36.8	63.2	2.7	2,700	45,900	36,800	3,579	6,279	106,738	780,300	1,814,554	3,300	1,422
18	34.2	65.8	2.6	2,600	46,800	34,200	3,330	5,930	106,743	842,400	1,921,367	2,856	1,231
19	31.5	68.5	2.7	2,700	51,300	31,500	3,082	5,782	109,850	974,700	2,087,142	2,551	1,099
20	28.9	71.1	2.6	2,600	52,000	28,900	2,833	5,433	108,659	1,040,000	2,173,187	2,197	947
21	26.4	73.6	2.5	2,500	52,500	26,400	2,594	5,094	106,969	1,102,500	2,246,348	1,887	813
22	24.0	76.0	2.4	2,400	52,800	24,000	2,364	4,764	104,807	1,161,600	2,305,744	1,618	697
23	21.7	78.3	2.3	2,300	52,900	21,700	2,143	4,443	102,200	1,216,700	2,350,605	1,383	596
24	19.7	80.3	2.0	2,000	48,000	19,700	1,942	3,942	94,603	1,152,000	2,270,478	1,124	484
25	17.4	82.6	2.3	2,300	57,500	17,400	1,740	4,040	101,003	1,437,500	2,525,074	1,056	455
26	15.5	84.5	1.9	1,900	49,400	15,500	1,543	3,443	89,521	1,284,400	2,327,551	824	355
27	13.7	86.3	1.8	1,800	48,600	13,700	1,370	3,170	85,579	1,312,200	2,310,624	695	300
28	12.1	87.9	1.6	1,600	44,800	12,100	1,210	2,810	78,683	1,254,400	2,203,125	565	243
29	10.0	90.0	2.1	2,100	60,900	10,000	1,037	3,137	90,960	1,766,100	2,637,852	578	249
30	8.0	92.0	2.0	2,000	60,000	8,000	844	2,844	85,328	1,800,000	2,559,836	480	207
31	0.0	100.0	8.0	8,000	248,000	0	375	8,375	259,632	7,688,000	8,048,594	1,295	558
Sum			100.00	100,000	1,458,100		132,089	232,089	2,854,664	29,775,300	52,106,881	232,090	100,000

a $10\frac{1}{2}$ percent coupon. Additionally, if the yield calculation performed is based on monthly payments, which it should be, the resulting yield is conventionally adjusted from monthly to a bond equivalent basis, that is, a semiannual rate.

Finally, the computation of the average life (within the investment community) is frequently (if not invariably) based only on the undiscounted principal payments, not on principal and interest. On the other hand, Macaulay duration (discussed in detail in subsequent chapters), which is not typically used in figuring price-yield quotations on MBSs, does include all cash flows, and is based on the discounted present values of such cash flows. If average life were defined to include all cash flows, then its computation would be the same as that of elapsed time or time spread.

In calculating quoted yields on MBSs, the industry practice generally seems to be to treat the security as having a synthetic maturity date equal to the present date plus the average life. The yield to maturity is calculated using the coupon rate and price to that synthetic date, and the yield is converted from monthly to that of a bond equivalent semiannual basis.

Collateralized Mortgage Obligations

Collateralized Mortgage Obligations (CMOs) were introduced to attempt to eliminate some of the principal prepayment uncertainty that investors perceive in addressing the mortgage pass-through offerings of GNMA and others. CMO offerings vary, but in general, they represent a classification into *tranches* of varying rights and priorities to either interest or principal. Among the features that may be present in a tranche (backed by mortgages) are: shorter final maturity, enhanced call protection, and semiannual (rather than monthly) interest payments. CMOs may be collateralized either by whole loan mortgages or by pass-through securities. Evaluaton of a CMO generally entails investigating three items. First, the underlying portfolio that collateralizes the issue must be scrutinized for both credit and cash flow characteristics. Second, the method must be ascertained by which each tranche passes through interest and principal. Finally, special features require checking, including guarantees of the sponsor of the CMO. Two classifications within CMOs are IOs (bonds which pay interest only) and POs (which pay principal only).*

---

*One individual company of the author's acquaintance had to write off as a loss tens of millions of dollars in one quarter due to its CMO investment in IOs. Rates fell, and the loans were prematurely paid off, leaving no more interst to be paid.

Other Measures of Return and Evaluation for MBSs

An MBS is really two securities, one which provides the net receipts of principal and interest payments, and another, a short call option which gives the borrower the right to prepay. Evaluating such an instrument is analogous to the principles discussed later regarding callable bonds. As the result of the uncertainty of cash flows, and the compensation for giving the borrower an implicit call option to prepay, the BEYs of an MBS are generally higher than those of Treasuries, even for GNMAs, which are backed by the full faith and credit of the United States.* Whether the yields are sufficiently high depends on the rate of prepayment. To quantify what a reasonable price or yield should be, an option pricing model should be used as described in Chap. 18. The value of the short option is then deducted from the value of the MBS (assuming no prepayments) to obtain the value of the actual MBS.

MBSs can also be evaluated by various measures of the expected life of the security, including average life and Macaulay duration. As with bonds, price and yield behavior can be quantified using measures of duration, convexity, and volatility. These are discussed later.

The investment characteristics and price-yield behavior of MBSs are more complex than for straight bonds, as we have seen. Their cash flows are uncertain and must be predicted by methodical procedures in order to obtain estimations of likely yield. Because of the complexity surrounding MBSs, opportunities exist for astute investors to obtain relatively better returns as compared to other bonds. By the same token, however, investors must be prepared to analyze prospective MBS investments carefully in order not to be unpleasantly surprised by unfavorable results from adverse prepayment activity.

---

*The lower level of liquidity of MBSs as compared to Treasuries also contributes to the difference in yields between the two investments.

8

Mortgage Points, Reverse Mortgages, Home Equity Conversions, and Annuities

Mortgage Points

Mortgage Lenders often attempt to charge borrowers an up-front, one-time fee that may range up to 3 percent, 4 percent, or even more of the full amount of the loan. These fees are referred to as *points*. The number of points that may be charged reflects the greed of the lender, on the one hand, and what the traffic will bear, on the other. Points may also be levied as a result of laws or regulations.

State usury laws (or FHA, VA, GNMA, or Freddie Mac regulations) sometimes set a maximum interest rate that is below prevailing national mortgage rates. In such a case the granting of loans would practically cease without a special solution, because a significant portion of mortgage loans are sold by the originator to other financial institutions in the national market. Such loans would have to be discounted to bring the yield to the secondary market purchaser to competitive national levels.

To compensate for an artificially low rate of interest on real estate mortgages, where the borrower is paying the maximum allowable interest rate, which is below national prevailing rates, the following chain of events may take place.

The *buyer* (borrower) may pay an additional fee (expressed as a percentage of the loan) to the lender under the guise of a "service fee" or some other type of fee (as opposed to interest).

Alternatively, the *seller* of the property may pay "points" expressed as a percentage of the loan (1 percent equals 1 point) to the lender. The seller compensates by increasing the price at which he or she sells the property to the buyer.

Example: Loan without points.　Peter Pacher borrows $100,000, to be repaid in 20 annual level payments, including principal and interest at a nominal annual rate of 8 percent. Annual payments are $10,185.22. What is the true rate of interest (annual percentage rate), APR?

In this case, where the full loan amount is disbursed and no points are charged, the APR is the same as the nominal annual stated rate, or 8 percent.

Example: Loan with points.　George Granger obtains the same loan as Peter Pacher in the previous example, except that George pays 2 percent of the loan as "points" to the lender, that is, $2000 (0.02 × $100,000). In this case,

Net cash to the borrower	$98,000
Annual payment	10,185.22

The *APR of a loan with points* is determined from

$$A = R \left[\frac{1 - (1 + i/m)^{-(n)(m)}}{i/m} \right]$$

where　A = amount of the loan less the dollar value of points charged (if PV is the amount of the loan without points, and P is the dollar value of the points charged, then $A = PV - P$, and $P = PV - A$)

i = annual or nominal interest rate (APR)

m = number of times interest is compounded per year

R = amount of each regular future periodic payment

n = number of years

For this example,

$$\left[\frac{1 - (1 + i/m)^{-(n)(m)}}{i/m} \right] [\$10,185.22] = \$98,000$$

$$\left[\frac{1 - (1 + i/m)^{-(n)(m)}}{i/m} \right] = 9.621804$$

By interpolation from Appendix 1, Tables 10 and 11,

8 percent	9.818147
x percent	9.621804
9 percent	9.128545

$$\frac{0.493259}{0.689602} = \frac{x}{1.0}$$

$$= 0.71528$$

The annual percentage rate is $9.0 - 0.71528$, that is, 8.28472 percent. Thus the effect of the buyer paying 2 points at the inception of this particular loan is to increase the APR from 8.0 percent to 8.28472 percent. (By computer, using the software, FINANCIAL AND INTEREST CALCULATOR, the solution is 8.273 percent.)

Effect of Points

When points are charged by a lender, the effect to the borrower is to increase the cost, and the effect to the lender is to increase the yield. For example, if a loan is stated as a 9.5 percent loan, and points are charged, the lender will earn a rate higher than 9.5 percent. By the same token, the borrower will pay more than 9.5 percent. The loan payments are computed on the basis of the full mortgage loan amount. The fact is that the lender loans the borrower a lesser sum than the full loan amount (less by the dollar amount of fees resulting from the points charged). This results in an increase in the lender's yield produced by the mortgage payments relative to the reduced size of the loan.

The annual percentage rate or *effective yield* is determined by equating the actual amount of the loan ($100,000 less $2000 in the example) to the periodic repayments ($10,185.22 annually in the example) discounted at a rate equal to the APR (8.273 percent in the example). If the loan calls for equal periodic repayments, the actual amount of the loan is equated to the present value of an annuity with a discount rate equal to the APR. The formula as stated earlier in this chapter is solved for i.

How Many Points to Charge to Increase Yield to Desired Level

Lenders may wish to determine how many points to charge to increase their yield on a loan to a desired level. The earlier example was for a 20-year, $100,000 loan, at 8 percent interest, with annual payments of $10,185.22. The lender wants to charge points to bring its yield to 9 percent instead of the stated 8 percent. How many points must the lender charge? The formula is the same as for finding the present value of an annuity,

$$A = R \left[\frac{1 - (1 + i/m)^{-(n)(m)}}{i/m} \right]$$

However, i is now given as 0.09 (9 percent). Therefore,

$$A = \$10,185.22 \left[\frac{1 - (1.09)^{-(20)}}{0.09} \right] = \$92,976.25$$

The amount to charge, \$7023.75, is determined from the formula

$$P = Z - A$$

where P = points (dollar value)
Z = present value of original loan without points
A = original loan amount after reduction by dollar value of points

Thus,

$$P = \$100,000 - \$92,976.25 = \$7023.75$$

The points to be charged to increase the lender's yield (and the borrower's cost) to 9 percent are

$$\frac{P}{Z} (100) = \frac{\$7023.75}{\$100,000} (100) = 7.024 \text{ points}$$

Rules of Thumb

Conventional wisdom in the lending business is that 1 point is equivalent to about $1/8$ of 1 percent increase in APR. Thus a charge of 4 points increases the effective cost of a loan by $1/2$ of 1 percent ($4 \times 1/8$). Like so many adages, this rule of thumb is sometimes true and many times false. Applying the adage to the example just given, 7 points would indicate an increase in the APR of 7 times $1/8$, or 0.88 percent. The actual increase in the APR is 1 percent. Therefore, in this case, relying on the rule of thumb would be misleading. The danger of using rules of thumb is that the user may not know the underlying assumptions, and, if current assumptions are not similar, the rule of thumb may be highly inaccurate. (In all probability, the rule of thumb was based on long-term loans of 25 or 30 years without prepayment, at interest-rate levels in the 7 to 10 percent range, with a modest number of points charged, e.g., less than 3. To the extent that deviations occur from those critical assumptions, the rule of thumb becomes less and less accurate.) *Therefore it is recommended that this old rule of thumb not be relied upon.* Instead, both borrowers and lenders should compute the APR of a loan involving points using the methods described. And be certain to use realistic assumptions about *early prepayment,* as the APR that lenders quote (based on Regulation Z of the Federal Reserve Board) is based on *the loan being held to maturity. With a given number of points, the shorter the time period the loan is held, the higher becomes the APR.* This important effect is logical: If one pays $5000 in points and the loan is held for 30 years, the average cost of the points per year is only $166.70. But if the loan is prepaid in 5 years, then the cost of the points is $1000 per year. Similarly, the APR of the loan increases with shorter repayment periods.

How Mortgage Points Increase the APR

Figure 8.1 provides a convenient way to determine the effect of points on the annual percentage rate.

Example: Finding the increase in APR due to points. If a 10-year loan at 10 percent interest is made without points being charged, the annual percentage rate is, in fact, 10 percent. What happens to the APR if 4 points are charged? Enter Fig. 8.1 on the left vertical axis at 4 points; proceed horizontally to the 10-year curve; then drop vertically to the bottom axis, where the point of intersection gives the new APR, just under 11.0 percent. The actual answer is 10.96 percent by computer calculation, using the author's software, FINANCIAL AND INTEREST CALCULATOR. One of the many programs included in the software, called "Mortgage Points," solves just this type of problem. Figure 8.2 is a printout which illustrates how easy it is to use the software to find the true cost of a loan that carries points.

Reverse Mortgages and Home Equity Conversion

The cover of the slick, four-color brochure proclaims, "PRESERVE YOUR FINANCIAL INDEPENDENCE WITH TAX-FREE INCOME FOR LIFE."

That's quite a statement! Who wouldn't want to preserve their financial independence? And who doesn't want tax-free income for life? This program (offered by an insurance company) appears to be the best thing that's happened since apple pie and motherhood. But is it really?

The program is called a *reverse mortgage* or *home equity conversion* plan. Most people are familiar with conventional mortgage loans. The borrower typically makes a level monthly payment, which in the early years is mostly

Number of loan points charged

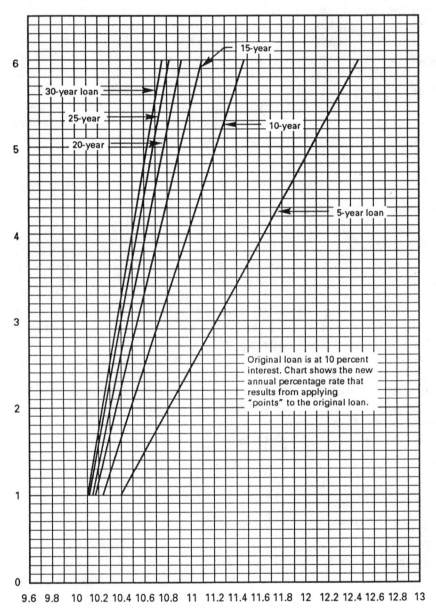

Figure 8.1. How mortgage points increase the annual percentage rate.

```
                    Larry Rosen's
                 Mortgage points effect
                      Calculator
                   Copyright 1986


How much is the fact amount of the loan? [ 100,000 ]

How many points are to be charged? [ 4 ]

Over how many years is the loan to be repaid? [ 10 ]

Do you wish the program to calculate your annual loan
repayment (Y or N?) Y

Net loan after points is: 96,000

Annual loan repayment is: 16,274.54

IRR = 10.9614%

Print above data? (Y / N)?
```

Figure 8.2. Printout illustrating the effect of mortgage points. Underlined figures are calculated by the software. Amounts in brackets are supplied by the user. (SOURCE: *Financial and Interest Calculator, Larry Rosen Co. 1984–1989.*)

interest. The outstanding loan balance gradually declines, mostly in the last few years of the loan, and eventually the loan payments extinguish or "pay off" the loan.

With a reverse mortgage, the process works in the opposite fashion. Generally, the homeowner has already gone through the conventional loan process and has either paid off or nearly paid off the loan. The homeowner now owns his or her home free and clear (or nearly so) of any loans. Now the homeowner would like to get some additional benefit from the paid-up home besides living in it. The reverse mortgage is made to order for this situation. A lender steps in, remortgages the house with a first lien, and promises some or all of the following benefits to the homeowner-borrower:

- Homeowner receives monthly payments free of federal or state income tax.
- A line of credit for additional money.
- The right to continue to own and live in the dwelling for life.
- Monthly payments which continue for the rest of the borrower's life or borrowers' lives (both husband and wife may be the borrowers).
- No obligation for the loan principal or interest to be repaid as long as the borrower (or borrower's spouse) lives in the house (or in some cases for a longer period).

- When the loan is repaid, the borrower still gets the benefit of the then equity in the home and gets full benefit of the appreciation in value, if any, that has occurred.

- A guaranty from the lender that the amount of the loan that has to be repaid will never be more than the home's value.

- Proceeds may be used for any purpose including: pay off old loan, buy a car, send grandchild to college, hire in-home health care help, pay off bills, make reparis to home, purchase long-term care insurance, or take a trip.

Can any program really be this good? What's the catch? There may not be a catch, but beware! The real question is not whether all the features offered are desirable, but rather, *what the program is going to cost* relative to the benefits. Obviously, it would not be a good deal to receive $100 per year for life starting at age 66 if $200,000 is to be deducted from the value of the borrower's house at death, thus reducing the value of the borrower's estate by substantially more than the benefits received.

The Insurance Element

The program is both a loan and an insurance policy. The insurance element eliminates several risks, including one major risk: that the loan balance will exceed the value of the house. This risk is partially dependent on the rate at which the value of the house increases (or decreases), which is obviously outside the control of the lender. The risk also depends on the rate of interest charged by the lender on the loan advances, which is controlled by market factors which establish interest rate levels. *The risk is controlled by regulating the size of the monthly payments* that will be made, relative to the value of the house at inception of the loan, which limits the buildup of the loan balance. The size of the monthly payments may be thought of as being dependent on: (1) a portion or percentage of the value of the house at the inception of the loan (call it "initial loan-to-value ratio"); and (2) the mortality or life expectancy of the borrowers. For the lender, the lower the loan-to-value ratio, and the shorter the life expectancy of the borrowers, the lower is the risk that the loan will ever exceed the value of the house. For the borrower, who will never have to repay more than the value of the house, the higher the payments, and the longer he or she lives in the house, the better is the financial arrangement.

The Risk of How Long the Loan Will Last.   The life expectancy of a husband and wife at age 66 is given in joint-and-survivorship annuity tables. These tables show the average number of years lived by those who reach a given age. For a person age 66, average life expectancy is about 22 years (per

Group Annuity 90 Tables). Note that actuarial experience for *annuitants* (as compared to the general populace) is that annuitants live longer. Therefore, life expectancy tables for annuitants must be used; not the tables used for calculation of normal life insurance premiums. [Note, however, that in the program insured by Housing and Urban Development (HUD), this is not the case; 1979–1981 female mortality tables are the basis of the actuarial calculations. The HUD reasoning: "the initial cost of a home equity conversion mortgage (reverse mortgage) is much lower than the cost of a life annuity, so that it is likely that the reverse mortgage program will appeal to a broader segment of the elderly homeowner population than those who expect to be long-lived." The HUD-sponsored program is discussed later in this chapter.] Technically, premiums are calculated on the basis of the actual number of people living each year per the actuarial tables rather than on the average life expectancy. Contrary to the popular belief that life expectancy is widely used in actuarial calculations, its use is to compare alternative tables of mortality.

Perhaps having money adds to life expectancy, because people who have the benefit of a regular annuity income tend to live longer. There is no doubt that the life expectancy of annuitants is greater than that of nonannuitants. It is likely that people who can afford to buy an annuity may be wealthier than average, and thus can afford better medical care, and therefore live longer. And, of course, people in ill health are less likely to buy an annuity, the benefits of which cease at death.

IRS tables are used to determine the taxable portion of each conventional annuity payment. Note that a reverse mortgage is *not* a conventional annuity. It is merely a loan from the lender to the borrower and is not subject to being partially taxed as are conventional annuity payments. The higher the life expectancy in the IRS tables, the higher is the tax that has to be paid each year by conventional annuitants. Thus the IRS tables may tend to err on the high side of life expectancy. The IRS tables compute taxation on the presumption that payments of a joint-and-survivorship annuity starting at age 66 will be made for about 24 years (actually 24.1 years), that is, to age 90. You don't have to be an actuary to know that among most couples who are 66, one partner is not likely to survive to age 90. Even though one may not live to be 90, one has to pay tax on the conventional annuity *as if* one will live that long.

Effective July 1986, the IRS adopted unisex actuarial tables—a major change since women live longer than men, and the sexes have always been treated differently in determining mortality and life expectancies. A free IRS publication, *Pension and Annuity Income* (Publication 575), explains the taxation requirements for conventional annuities. Write P.O. Box 9903, Bloomington, IL 61799 to obtain a copy.

With a reverse mortgage, the length of the loan is equal to a maximum of the joint life expectancy of the borrower or borrowers (e.g., a husband and wife), or may be for the term of just one life. Since the loan must be repaid when the borrowers leave the house permanently, as defined by the lender, the actual loan duration may be less than life expectancy. If one borrower dies and the other goes into a nursing home, the loan will have to be repaid, even though both parties have not died.*

The Risk of the Loan Balance Exceeding the Home Value.   The reverse mortgage lender tells the borrowers how much their monthly or annual tax-free payments will be. The lender makes this determination so that it is unlikely that the loan balance will exceed the house value over the expected duration of the loan. The lower the loan payments, the lower the buildup of the loan balance and the longer the time period until the loan balance will equal the value of the house. A graphic display of a typical loan compared to house values is shown in Fig. 8.3.

The lender sets the monthly payments (or loan-to-value ratio) so that the expected loan balance will not exceed the expected house value during the expected life of the loan. However, higher-than-expected interest charges to the borrower (if the loan has an adjustable rate) could make the loan balance equal the house value in a shorter time period. This could happen, for example, if market rates exceed the lender's estimates. Some borrowers will live longer than the average expectancy. And when, as a result of higher rates or longer life, the loan balance exceeds the house value, the lender then incurs the additional cost of forgiving the part of the loan balance that exceeds the proceeds from the sale of the house. For example, assume that the monthly payment is $267, the borrowers are aged 66, their life expectancy is 15 years, and the last living borrower actually lives for 20 years, or 5 years more than the life expectancy estimated at the time the loan originated. At the end of 15 years the loan balance equals the house value. The additional payments for the last five years, the interest on those payments, and the interest on the prior loan balance will still be charged to the loan account. However, these charges will only wind up being paid to the insurance company or lender to the extent of the increase in value of the house from the equality point where the loan balance equals the house value. Note that the excess of the loan account over the value of the house (after sales costs) is a debt which never gets paid to the lender. It is forgiven or never existed. The lender must either insure against this risk with an external insurer, or self-insure against this risk.

---

*Some lenders compete for business by softening the restrictions. For example, the loan may not have to be repaid until some months after both parties vacate the house.

Dollars

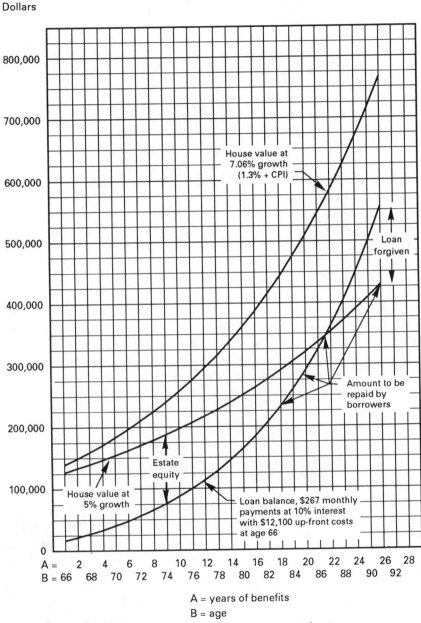

A = years of benefits
B = age

Figure 8.3. Reverse mortgage: amount repayable—insurance company plan.

The Borrower's Analysis

From the borrower's point of view, the reverse mortgage loan should be considered in terms of the *internal rate of return* (IRR): the interest rate that equates his costs to his benefits. In making this determination, the borrower may assume several different scenarios regarding how long the payments will be made by the lender. For example, what is the IRR for the joint life expectancy of the borrowers? What is the IRR for 5 years in excess of that, and for 10 years in excess, and for 5 years less than the life expectancy? If life expectancy is 15 years, what is the IRR that equates costs and benefits for 10, 15, 20, and 25 years? Naturally, the longer the time period, the longer the borrower will receive benefits.

Many banks, insurance companies, and mortgage lenders offer reverse mortgage loans. There are many different types of programs. *It is critical to evaluate the different possibilities in order to determine which program offers the best deal and, in fact, to determine whether to take any loan at all.*

The basis for making the comparison is to find the internal rate of return, the interest rate that equates the cash received (benefits expected to be received) to the cash expended (cost of the loan.) In this case the "costs" of the loan are the amount of the loan, or other amount, that has to be repaid, for example, upon moving or at death. This amount, which may be less than the loan balance but never more, is paid by the borrower or the borrower's estate, directly or as a deduction from the proceeds of the sale of the house. For analysis, consider the loan cost to be the future loan balance that has to be repaid.* The "benefits" of the loan are the monthly payments made to the borrower for as many years as such payments occur. The interest rate which equates the present value of the benefits to the present value of the costs is the IRR. From the lender's viewpoint, the IRR is the rate of profit on the funds expended. From the borrower's standpoint, the IRR is the cost to receive the benefits offered.

The basis for determining the amount of loan that will have to be repaid when the borrowers leave the house or die is shown in Fig. 8.3. The loan balance is based on the actual proposal of the insurance company at the beginning of this section, namely, $267 monthly payments, starting at age 66, with up-front costs of $12,100 and interest charged at 10 percent (2 percent over the assumed 10-year Treasury bond rate of 8 percent). With an initial value of the house of $130,000 and appreciation of the house at 5 percent, it is not until 22 years have elapsed, or age 88 of the borrower, that the loan balance exceeds the house value. It is only at that point that the insurance feature comes into play as the insurer forfeits charges to the loan account which exceed the value of the house.

---

*For analysis, the loan account balance that has to be repaid in the future is the lesser of the loan account balance or the net value of the house after selling costs.

•le 8.1. Reverse Mortgage: Amount of Loan Forgiven

2,100 = initial loan
$267 = monthly loan advances to borrowers
0.00% = interest rate charged on loan account
0,000 = initial value of house
5.00% = annual percentage increase in value of house
5.76% = CPI growth rate
　12 = times interest is compounded per year

r Amount of $1	Amount of $1 per period	Loan account balance			House value		Amount of loan forgiven
		From up-front charges	From monthly advances	Loan total	At 93% of 5.00% growth	At 7.06% growth	
		$ 12,100					
$ 1.105	$12.566	13,367	$ 3,355	$ 16,722	$126,945	$139,178	0
1.220	26.447	14,767	7,061	21,828	133,292	149,004	0
1.348	41.782	16,313	11,156	27,469	139,957	159,524	0
1.489	58.722	18,021	15,679	33,700	146,955	170,786	0
1.645	77.437	19,908	20,676	40,584	154,302	182,844	0
1.818	98.111	21,993	26,196	48,189	162,018	195,752	0
2.008	120.950	24,296	32,294	56,590	170,118	209,572	0
2.218	146.181	26,840	39,030	65,870	178,624	224,368	0
2.450	174.054	29,650	46,472	76,123	187,556	240,209	0
2.707	204.845	32,755	54,694	87,449	196,933	257,167	0
2.991	238.860	36,185	63,776	99,961	206,780	275,323	0
3.304	276.438	39,974	73,809	113,783	217,119	294,761	0
3.650	317.950	44,160	84,893	129,053	227,975	315,571	0
4.032	363.809	48,784	97,137	145,921	239,374	337,851	0
4.454	414.470	53,892	110,664	164,556	251,342	361,703	0
4.920	470.436	59,536	125,607	185,142	263,910	387,239	0
5.436	532.263	65,770	142,114	207,884	277,105	414,578	0
6.005	600.563	72,657	160,350	233,007	290,960	443,847	0
6.633	676.016	80,265	180,496	260,761	305,508	475,183	0
7.328	759.369	88,670	202,751	291,421	320,784	508,731	0
8.095	851.450	97,955	227,337	325,292	336,823	544,647	0
8.943	953.174	108,212	254,497	362,709	353,664	583,099	9,045
9.880	1,065.549	119,543	284,502	404,044	371,347	624,266	32,697
10.914	1,189.692	132,061	317,648	449,708	389,915	668,339	59,794
12.057	1,326.833	145,889	354,265	500,154	409,410	715,524	90,743
13.319	1,478.336	161,166	394,716	555,881	429,881	766,040	126,000

Table 8.1 shows that the first year in which part of the loan balance has to be forgiven is 22 years hence, where the loan balance exceeds the value of the house (at 5 percent growth) by $9045. This occurs when the borrower is 88 years old.

Table 8.2. Reverse Mortgage: True Cost

15.715% = internal rate of return or interest rate
10.00% = 10-year treasury rate *plus* 2% charged by lender on balance in loan account
$130,000 = value of house at loan inception
$3,000 = fixed fee charged by lender at loan inception to loan account for appraisals
7.00% = additional fee charged by lender as percentage of house value at inception of loan
$267 = monthly benefit to borrower which is paid by lender
$3,204 = annual benefits to borrower
15 = years that benefits are paid (life expectancy or otherwise)
12 = number of times interest is compounded per year (e.g., 12 = monthly)
5.00% = annual percentage rate at which the value of the house is assumed to increase
5.76% = CPI growth rate, 1979–1987

Years that benefits are paid, n	Loan account balance at end of life expectancy	House value at CPI + 1.3% growth rate	93% of actual value of house assuming growth at rate specified above	Lesser of values	Present value factor for n years, at rate of 15.72%	Present value of "lesser of values" to be repaid by borrower	Factor for present value of benefits at annual rate of 15.72%	Present value of benefits of $3,024 per year	Benefits less cost
			Amount estate must repay is lesser of:						
15.0	$164,556	$361,703	$251,342	$164,556	0.11198	$18,428	5.752	$18,428	0
10	87,449	257,167	196,933	87,449	0.23233	20,317	5.028	16,109	$(4,207)
11	99,961	275,323	206,780	99,961	0.20078	20,070	5.221	16,728	(3,342)
12	113,783	294,761	217,119	113,783	0.17351	19,742	5.386	17,257	(3,485)
13	129,053	315,571	227,975	129,053	0.14995	19,351	5.527	17,710	(1,641)
14	145,921	337,851	239,374	145,921	0.12958	18,909	5.648	18,097	(812)
15	164,556	361,703	251,342	164,556	0.11198	18,428	5.752	18,428	0
16	185,142	387,239	263,910	185,142	0.09678	17,917	5.840	18,711	794

Year									
20	291,421	508,731	320,784	291,421	0.05398	15,730	6.063	19,430	3,700
21	325,292	544,647	336,823	325,292	0.04665	15,174	6.124	19,620	4,446
22	362,709	583,099	353,664	353,664	0.04031	14,257	6.158	19,731	5,474
23	404,044	624,266	371,347	371,347	0.03484	12,937	6.188	19,826	6,890
24	449,708	668,339	389,915	389,915	0.03011	11,739	6.213	19,907	8,169
25	500,154	715,524	409,410	409,410	0.02602	10,652	6.235	19,977	9,325

No. of years of benefits   15
Present value of benefits to be received from lender $18,428
Present value of cost of lesser of loan, house, etc. $18,428
Net present value of benefits less costs   0

How could the insurance company's plan be improved? If the monthly benefits are increased, the loan balance will increase and the insurance feature will become more meaningful. If the up-front costs are reduced, the loan balance will be reduced and the benefits could be increased. And if the rate of interest charged increases, the loan balance will increase at a faster pace. In other words, the increase in the loan balance depends on up-front costs, the monthly payment, the interest rate, and the time the loan is in effect.

The details of a proposal made to the author by the Home Income Security Plan, a servicemark of Capital Holding, are shown in Table 8.2. The author represented that he and his wife were each 66 years of age and that the current market value of their house was $130,000. The insurance proposal offered a tax-free loan of $267 per month. Payments are to continue as long as one of the borrowers lives in the house. The other features of the plan are those cited at the beginning of this chapter. The up-front costs charged to the borrower's loan account are $3000 for closing costs, appraisals, etc., and, in addition, a whopping 7 percent of the value of the house as a fee for "risk." Thus the up-front costs charged to the borrowers are $12,000—$3000 plus 7 percent of $130,000. All costs, including the up-front costs, each $267 monthly payment or loan, as well as interest are charged to the borrower's loan account. The interest rate charged is the 10-year Treasury bond rate plus 2 percent. Thus, if the Treasury rate is 8 percent, the loan interest rate is 10 percent.

The true cost of the insurance company program, including interest charges, risk fee, and other costs, equates to a 15.715 percent annual percentage rate or internal rate of return—provided interest charges continue at the equivalent of 10 percent and monthly payments continue for 15 years. After 15 years, the borrowers would be 81 years old. Refer to Table 8.2. On the line for 15 years of benefits, note that $18,428 is both the present value of: (1) costs, that is, "lesser of values to be repaid by borrower" and (2) benefits, that is, "benefits of $3204 per year." The IRR of 15.715 percent is the rate which causes the present value of costs and benefits to equal each other. The meaning of this is that the insurance company-sponsored reverse mortgage program is going to cost the borrowers 15.715 percent, under the stated assumptions, including interest charges at 10 percent on the loan account, and a benefit period of 15 years.

The true cost of this reverse mortgage for various time periods is shown in Table 8.3. If the borrowers only live to receive benefits for 10 years, then the IRR or true cost of the program will be 20.449 percent per year. At 15 years, the IRR is 15.715 percent, etc. The longer the benefits are actually received, the less costly and thus the more advantageous the program becomes. Of course, the value of the lower cost is exceeded by the benefits

Table 8.3. IRR for Various Benefit Periods: Insurance Company Reverse Mortgage

IRR represents the cost to the borrowers of the program

Lesser of values, S	Annual benefits, R	S/R	From Appendix 1: approx. IRR	Years of benefits	True IRR by trial and error (%)
$ 87,449	$3,204	27.294	18+	10	20.449
164,556	3,204	51.360	16–	15	15.715
291,421	3,204	90.955	14–	20	13.893
409,410	3,204	127.781	12–	25	11.664

The present value of $267 per month at the IRR rate shown, compounded monthly, equals the present value of the "lesser of values" discounted to the present at the IRR rate with annual compounding. For simplicity, the monthly payments are treated as being made at the end of each month. In fact they are made at the beginning of each month. Whether payments are treated as being made at the beginning or end of the month has a minimal effect on the results.

of enjoying a long life. (Capital Holding stopped offering reverse mortgages in April 1993.)*

Finding the IRR for a Reverse Mortgage

Actually calculating the internal rate of return requires a trial-and-error approach. However, a very close approximation of the IRR can be obtained from the tables in Appendix 1 using the following approach.

There are two sides to the equation of present value, one for costs, and the other for benefits. The cost is the present value of the "lesser of values" that the borrowers must repay. This "lesser of values" is multiplied by the discount factor for a single sum. The formula for the present value of a single sum is

$$P = S \left(1 + \frac{i}{m}\right)^{-(n)(m)}$$

where P = present value
S = maturity value (the "lesser of values" in this case)
n = time from the present until maturity

*A company representative blamed SEC accounting rules for the withdrawal of Capital Holding (now called Providian) from the reverse mortgage market. Specifically, the problem relates to the inability to amortize business procurement costs over the life of the loan. Another insurance company, Providential in San Francisco, describes a different SEC accounting problem related to the inability to accrue interest as income in a normal lender manner.

i = discounted interest rate

The benefit is the present value of the monthly payments of $267. That monthly benefit is multiplied by the factor for "present worth of $1 per period." The formula for the present value of a simple annuity is

$$A = R \left[\frac{1 - (1 + i/m)^{-(n)(m)}}{i/m} \right]$$

where A = present value of a series of equal payments
   i = annual or nominal interest rate
   m = number of times interest is compounded per year
   R = amount of each regular future periodic payment
   n = number of years

The essence of the solution is that

$$P = A$$

in the above two formulas. Therefore,

$$S(1 + \frac{i}{m})^{-(n)(m)} = R \left[\frac{1 - (1 + i/m)^{-(n)(m)}}{i/m} \right]$$

$$\frac{S}{R} = \left[\frac{1 - (1 + i/m)^{-(n)(m)}}{(i/m)(1 + i/m)^{-(n)(m)}} \right]$$

This can be reduced to

$$\frac{S}{R} = \left[\frac{(1 + i/m)^{(n)(m)} - 1}{(i/m)} \right]$$

which is the formula for the future value of a simple annuity. Thus, if the value of S/R is found, then Appendix 1 tables can be used to find a close approximation to the IRR. For example, if S/R is 18.419 for a 10-year program, scan the second column of the tables (amount of $1 per period) on the 10-year line looking for that value. Table 15, Rate of 13 percent, shows 18.419749. Thus the IRR would be 13 percent. This method is followed in Table 8.3 to obtain the IRRs for various benefit periods.

The short-cut method described above of approximating the IRR saves a substantial amount of time in finding the true IRR. Notice that as the benefit period lengthens, the IRR falls—and thus the true cost of the program to the borrower falls as well. *The moral is that if you don't expect to live at least an average life span, then a reverse mortgage is probably not for you.*

How the pure cost of an annuity is determined is shown in Table 8.4. The pure cost is a function of the number of people who die each year, elapsed time, and the value of money. An insurance company adds commissions and other overhead and profit to the pure cost. The calculation of the present value (P) of all benefits to be paid in year 2 is

$$P = (P_b)\,(f)\,(B)$$

where N_L = number living

N_{Lb} = number living at the beginning of the time period (e.g., year 1)

N_d = number dying during the year

$P_b = 1 - (N_d/N_L)$ = probability of a benefit payment during the year

f = discount factor, present value of a single sum

B = benefits payment during the year

Thus, for year 2,

$$P = 1 - \left(\frac{\$178{,}059}{\$8{,}165{,}359}\right)(1 + 0.0875)^{-1}\,(\$3204)$$

$$= (0.9781934)\,(0.91954)\,(\$3204)$$

$$= \$2827$$

Thus, the present value needed today, $2827, takes care of the payment of benefits in year 2. This is, in other words, the proportion of the populace that are living, multiplied by the benefit to be paid in year 2, discounted to the present at the value of money. The present value of claims is computed in similar fashion for each subsequent year until everyone has died and there are no more benefits to be paid. The sum total of all the present values is the grand total of money needed to fund the payment of all the future benefits. This is $23,881. This $23,881 would be a pure no-load annuity which when invested at 8.75 percent interest would produce exactly enough money to pay out the expected benefits. In this case $23,881 represents the net single premium required to provide benefits of $3204 per year to an individual male, starting at age 66. The rate per $1000 of annual benefit is $23,881 divided by $3204, that is, $7.45 per $1000 of annual benefit.

With a joint-and-survivorship annuity, the probability of either party being alive in a given year is greater than the probability for either individual alone. If, in a given year, the male has a probability of death of 2 percent and the female, 1.5 percent, then the probability of one of the parties being alive is [1 − (0.02) (0.015)], that is, 0.9997, or 99.97 percent. Individually, the male has a chance of living of 98 percent and the female, 98.5 percent. As a result of this actuarial phenomenon, the cost of providing joint-and-survivorship benefits is much greater than that of providing an

Table 8.4. Pure Cost of an Individual Annuity (Excludes Cost of Overhead and Profit)

8.75% = interest rate
$3,204 = annual payments

Year	Age Male	Age Female	Number living*	Number dying*	Probability of pmt (male)	Discount factor at 8.75% (male)	Present value of pmt (male)
	5	10	10,000,000	3,700			
1	65	70	8,165,359	164,875			
2	66	71	8,000,484	178,059	0.980	0.920	$2,887
3	67	72	7,822,425	191,579	0.958	0.846	2,595
4	68	73	7,630,846	205,354	0.935	0.778	2,328
5	69	74	7,425,492	219,282	0.928	0.715	2,126
6	70	75	7,206,210	233,243	0.883	0.657	1,859
7	71	76	6,972,967	247,094	0.854	0.605	1,654
8	72	77	6,725,873	260,668	0.824	0.556	1,467
9	73	78	6,465,205	273,776	0.792	0.511	1,297
10	74	79	6,191,429	286,205	0.758	0.470	1,142
11	75	80	5,905,224	297,724	0.723	0.432	1,002
12	76	81	5,607,500	308,082	0.687	0.397	875
13	77	82	5,299,418	317,016	0.649	0.365	760
14	78	83	4,982,402	324,260	0.610	0.336	657
15	79	84	4,658,142	329,550	0.570	0.309	565
16	80	85	4,328,592	332,639	0.530	0.284	483
17	81	86	3,995,953	333,306	0.489	0.261	410
18	82	87	3,662,647	331,363	0.449	0.240	345
19	83	88	3,331,284	326,669	0.408	0.221	289
20	84	89	3,004,615	319,141	0.368	0.203	240
21	85	90	2,685,474	308,768	0.329	0.187	197
22	86	91	2,376,706	295,615	0.291	0.172	160
23	87	92	2,081,091	279,836	0.255	0.158	129
24	88	93	1,801,255	261,676	0.221	0.145	103
25	89	94	1,539,579	241,469	0.189	0.134	81
26	90	95	1,298,110	219,643	0.159	0.123	63
27	91	96	1,078,467	196,701	0.132	0.113	48
28	92	97	881.766	173,206	0.108	0.104	36
29	93	98	708,560	149,756	0.087	0.095	27
30	94	99	558,802	126,952	0.068	0.088	19
31	95	100	431,850	105,349	0.053	0.081	14
32	96	101	326,502	85,432	0.040	0.074	10
33	97	102	241,070	67,582	0.030	0.068	6
34	98	103	173,488	52,049	0.021	0.063	4
35	99	104	121,439	38,945	0.015	0.058	3
36	100	105	82,494	28,246	0.010	0.053	2
37	101	106	54,248	19,804	0.007	0.049	1
38	102	107	34,439	13,395	0.004	0.045	1
39	103	108	21,044	8,709	0.003	0.041	0
40	104	109	12,335	5,425	0.002	0.038	0
41	105	110	6,910	3,226	0.001	0.035	0

Table 8.4. Pure Cost of an Individual Annuity (Excludes Cost of Overhead and Profit) (Continued)

42	106	111	3,684	1,824	0.000	0.032	0
43	107	112	1,860	975	0.000	0.030	0
44	108	113	885	498	0.000	0.027	0
45	109	114	394	231	0.000	0.025	0
46	110	115	162	101	0.000	0.023	0
47	111	116	61	41	0.000	0.021	0
48	112	117	20	15	0.000	0.019	0
49	113	118	5	4	0.000	0.018	0
50	114	119	1	1	0.000	0.016	0

Net single premium required to provide benefits $23,881

Cost per $1,000 of benefits $7.45

SOURCE: 1955 American Annuity Table.

individual annuity. And the actual cost to buy an annuity will include markups for the sponsor's overhead, including commissions and profit.

Alternatives to the Reverse Mortgage

The sales features of the insurance company reverse mortgage, such as "tax-free income for life" and "preserve your financial independence," are undeniably attractive. The question, however, is what is the best means of achieving such desirable goals. Alternatives to reverse mortgages cited by some include:

Trading down. Proponents suggest that older homeowners trade down to a smaller house and invest for income the difference between the after-tax proceeds of the large home and the smaller. If they're older than 55, they may qualify for a $125,000 capital-gains exemption. (But the costs of trading down are great; brokerage commissions to both sell the old home and buy the new, as well as related title searches and policies, moving expenses, etc.)

Sell to children. The homeowners sell their house to their children in return for a lifetime annuity—and continue living there. This arrangement eliminates the lender. Although the house can be pledged to support the loan which the child invests to make the payments to the parent, not many children are so wealthy that they can pay a parent a lifetime annuity. Expenses of this method would include all the usual costs of obtaining a mortgage loan, including title search, policy, etc. Potential tax liabilities on the sale to the children would also have to be explored.

Home equity line of credit. Yet another alternative is a home equity line of credit. If homeowners can get a home equity line of credit, they might be better off than with a reverse mortgage. Such homeowners would need a high annual income to qualify. Before granting home equity lines of credit, lenders normally require an ability to repay at least the interest on the loan as such interest accrues. Another problem is that such loans normally have a finite maturity of 7 years or so. Minimum family income requirements (often $40,000 to $50,000) may have to be met as well. Such loans have few fees; some have none. A typical homeowner of 75 with an income of $8000 probably wouldn't qualify—and might not be able to make the monthly payments required of such a loan. Such a homeowner could lose his or her house if the loan is called when the borrower(s) leave the house. The borrower must plan to remain in the house for many years, otherwise because of the high front-end costs, a reverse mortgage is an unwise selection.

Annuity. Another alternative to entering into a reverse mortgage loan agreement is to borrow the money to buy a joint-and-survivorship annuity in an amount which will provide the same after-tax cash benefits. Such an annuity is payable for the lives of the two insureds (and will not cease when departure from a house occurs). It can be for the same dollar value per year as the reverse mortgage would provide. A portion of each joint-and-survivorship annuity payment is subject to taxation, but the balance is not taxed and is treated as a "return of capital." IRS tables show, for each age and payment, how much is nontaxable.

Finding the Taxable Portion of an Annuity Benefit

The formula for determining the taxable portion of each annuity benefit received is

$$T = 1 - \frac{C}{(R)\,(n)}$$

where T = taxable portion of each annuity benefit received
   C = cost to acquire the annuity, i.e., net single premium (say, $35,941 or $11.22 per $1000)
   R = annual benefit to be received (say, $3204 per year)
   n = number of years of benefits per IRS tables (at age 66 for both parties, the value of n is 24.1, indicating 24.1 years of benefits)

Where both parties are 66,

$$T = 1 - \frac{\$35,941}{(\$3204)(24.1)}$$

$$= 1 - \frac{\$35,941}{\$77,216.40}$$

$$= 1 - 0.46546$$

$$= 0.53454 \quad \text{or} \quad 53.454\%$$

Thus, of each annual annuity benefit received of $3204, 53.454 percent or $1712.67 would be taxable as interest income and the balance would be treated as a nontaxable return of capital. Over the entire 24.1 years of predicted benefits, the situation is

Total payments, $3204 times 24.1 years	$77,216.40
Taxable portion, 53.454% of total	41,275.25
Nontaxed return of capital	$35,941.15

As indicated above, the entire original cost, $35,941.15, of the net single premium is recovered by nontaxed benefits over the IRS's assumed life span. However, if the annuitant dies before receiving 24.1 years of benefits, all of the cost of the annuity will not have been recovered for tax purposes.

The best method of comparing a reverse mortgage to a conventional annuity is to assume that the net single premium to buy the annuity is borrowed, and that interest is simply added to the borrowed balance. The annual benefits (while the borrower lives) of the reverse mortgage and the annuity are set equal to each other. Then determine the IRR. The program with the lowest IRR is the least expensive and is the best—other things being equal. Another measure of the relative merits of each is to compare the respective outstanding loan balances at the time when the benefits cease at death. Since the value of the house will be the same under either method, an accurate measure is that of the accumulated loan balance. The program with the smallest accumulated loan balance is the best.

The loan balance for various time periods can be found in Table 8.2 in the column "Loan balance at the end of life expectancy." For a 23-year life expectancy (age 89), the accumulated loan balance with the reverse mortgage is $404,044.

With an annuity benefit of $267 per month purchased for a net single premium of $35,941, and if interest costs are 10 percent per year, after 23 years the loan balance would be $355,082. (Prudential Insurance Company quoted the author $35,131.58 for the same benefit, and Travellers quoted $38,101.13.)

Table 8.5. Comparison of Reverse Mortgage to Annuity

10.00% =	10-year Treasury rate *plus* 2 percent charged by lender on balance in loan account
$130,000 =	value of house at loan inception
$3,000 =	fixed fee charged by lender at loan inception to loan account for appraisals, closing fee, etc.
7.00% =	additional fee charged as percentage of house value at inception of loan
$267.00 =	monthly benefit to borrower which is paid by lender
$3,204 =	annual benefits to borrower
12 =	number of times interest is compounded per year (e.g., 12 = monthly)
35,941 =	net single premium joint and survivorship for $267 per month before tax
40,243 =	net single premium joint and survivorship for $298.96 before tax which provides after-tax benefits of $267 per month in a 20% tax bracket

Years that benefits are paid	Loan account balance at end from monthly benefits	Loan account balance at end from up-front costs	Total reverse mtg. loan account balance	Bank loan to buy annuity— loan balance	Loan balance reverse mtg. less bank loan to buy annuity
1	$ 3,355	$ 13,367	$ 16,722	$ 44,457	$(27,735)
2	7,061	14,767	21,828	49,112	(27,284)
3	11,156	16,313	27,469	54,255	(26,786)
4	15,679	18,021	33,700	59,936	(26,236)
5	20,676	19,908	40,584	66,212	(25,628)
6	26,196	21,993	48,189	73,146	(24,957)
7	32,294	24,296	56,590	80,805	(24,215)
8	39,030	26,840	65,870	89,266	(23,396)
9	46,472	29,650	76,123	98,614	(22,491)
10	54,694	32,755	87,449	108,940	(21,491)
11	63,776	36,185	99,961	120,347	(20,386)
12	73,809	39,974	113,783	132,949	(19,166)
13	84,893	44,160	129,053	146,871	(17,818)
14	97,137	48,784	145,921	162,250	(16,329)
15	110,664	53,892	164,556	179,240	(14,684)
16	125,607	59,536	185,142	198,009	(12,866)
17	142,114	65,770	207,884	218,743	(10,859)
18	160,350	72,657	233,007	241,648	(8,641)
19	180,496	80,265	260,761	266,951	(6,190)
20	202,751	88,670	291,421	294,905	(3,484)
21	227,337	97,955	325,292	325,785	(493)
22	254,497	108,212	362,709	359,899	2,810
23	284,502	119,543	404,044	397,585	6,459
24	317,648	132,061	449,708	439,218	10,491
25	354,265	145,889	500,154	485,209	14,944
26	394,716	161,166	555,881	536,017	19,864
27	439,403	178,042	617,444	592,145	25,299
28	488,769	196,685	685,454	654,151	31,303
29	543,304	217,280	760,585	722,649	37,936
30	603,550	240,033	843,583	798,319	45,263
31	670,105	265,167	935,272	881,914	53,358

However, it is best to compare the respective loan balances annually, because variations will occur and the plan that seems best after one time period may be worse after another. Table 8.5 does just that.

The true cost or IRR of the conventional annuity is calculated in a manner similar to that of the reverse mortgage.

Finding the IRR for a Conventional Annuity

To find the true cost or IRR of a conventional annuity requires a trial-and-error process, but a very close approximation can be obtained from the tables in Appendix 1 using the following approach.

There are two sides to the equation of present value, one for costs, the other for benefits. The *cost* is the present value of the "loan balance" that the borrowers' estate must repay at death to the bank from which the funds were borrowed. That "loan balance" is multiplied by the discount factor for a single sum. The formula for the present value of a single sum is

$$P = S (1 + i/m)^{-(n)(m)}$$

where P = present value
S = maturity value (the "lesser of values" in this case)
n = time from the present until maturity
i = discounted interest rate

The *benefit* is the present value of the monthly payments of $267. That monthly benefit is multiplied by the factor for "present worth of $1 per period." The formula for the present value of a simple annuity is

$$A = R \left[\frac{1 - (1 + i/m)^{-(n)(m)}}{i/m} \right]$$

where A = present value of a series of equal payments
i = annual or nominal interest rate
m = number of times interest is compounded per year
R = amount of each regular future periodic payment
n = number of years

The essence of the solution is that

$$P = A$$

in the above two formulas. Therefore,

$$S \left(1 + \frac{i}{m}\right)^{-(n)(m)} = R \left[\frac{1 - (1 + i/m)^{-(n)(m)}}{i/m}\right]$$

$$\frac{S}{R} = \left[\frac{1 - (1 + i/m)^{-(n)(m)}}{(i/m)(1 + i/m)^{-(n)(m)}}\right]$$

This can be reduced to

$$\frac{S}{R} = \left[\frac{(1 + i/m)^{(n)(m)} - 1}{(i/m)}\right]$$

which is the formula for the future value of a simple annuity.

Thus, if the value of S/R is found, then Appendix 1 tables can be used to find a close approximation to the IRR. For example, if S/R is 18.419 for a 10-year program, scan the second column of the tables (amount of $1 per period) on the 10-year line looking for that value. Table 15, rate of 13 percent, shows 18.419749. Thus the IRR would be 13 percent. This method is followed in Table 8.6 to obtain the IRRs for various benefit periods.

The true IRRs for the conventional annuity purchase using bank funding for the acquisition are shown in Table 8.7. Notice that the cost of the annuity in Table 8.7 is $40,243. The cost has been increased, and the benefits as well, in order to provide an *after-tax annuity* monthly benefit which equals the *tax-free loan benefit* of the reverse mortgage. This procedure will be explained in the next section.

Finally, the comparison in Table 8.8 of the IRRs of a conventional annuity and a reverse mortgage shows that in three of the four benefit periods evaluated, the conventional annuity produces superior after-tax results.

Table 8.6. IRR for Various Benefit Periods: Conventional Annuity

(IRR represents the cost to the borrowers of the program)
$35,941 = net single premium for joint-and-survivorship annuity which provides
monthly benefits of $267 for life
$10.00% = interest rate charged by lender of premium

True IRR (%)	Years	Loan balance, S	Annual benefits, R	S/R	From Appendix 1, approx. IRR	Present value of annuity	Present value of loan	PV annual less PV loan
22.3063	10	$ 93,222	$3,204	29.095	18+	$12,446	$12,446	0
14.8136	15	150,134	3,204	46.858	15−	18,905	18,905	0
12.3987	20	241,793	3,204	75.466	12+	23,346	23,346	0
11.3961	25	389,410	3,204	121.539	11+	26,222	26,222	0

Table 8.7. IRR for Various Benefit Periods for a Conventional Annuity to Yield After-Tax Benefits Comparable to a Reverse Mortgage

(IRR represents the cost to the borrowers of the program)
$40,243 = net single premium for joint-and-survivorship annuity which provides monthly benefits of $267 for life
$10.00% = interest rate charged by lender of premium

True IRR (%)	Years	Loan balance, S	Annual benefits, R	S/R	From Appendix 1, approx. IRR	Present value of annuity	Present value of loan	PV annual less PV loan
24.5867	10	$104,380	$3,204	32.578	18+	$11,585	$11,585	0
16.1881	15	168,105	3,204	52.467	17−	17,707	17,707	0
13.3669	20	270,735	3,204	84.499	13.5	22,020	22,020	0
12.1328	25	436,021	3,204	136.086	12+	24,900	24,900	0

Determining the After-Tax Benefit of a Purchased Annuity

Since the insurance company reverse mortgage program provides benefits in the form of a nontaxable loan, the purchase of a conventional annuity should be of the proper amount to yield the same *after-tax* benefits. However, as discussed previously, part of each annuity benefit received is taxable. The following method calculates the gross benefit needed to produce the desired after-tax annuity.

Let y = Pretax amount of monthly benefit needed to provide $267 per month after taxes, where

53.454% = percentage of each benefit that is taxable per IRS tables

20.00% = tax bracket of borrower (annuitant)

Then

$$y - (0.53454y)(0.2) = \$267$$

Table 8.8. IRR Comparison of Annuity versus Reverse Mortgage

True IRR, conventional annuity (%)	True IRR, reverse mortgage (%)	Conventional less reverse mortgage (%)	Years of benefits
24.587	20.449	4.14	10
16.188	15.715	0.47	15
13.367	13.893	−0.53	20
12.133	11.664	0.47	25

$$0.8931y = \$267$$

$$y = \$298.96$$

Thus, $298.96 of gross monthly benefit will yield $267 after tax. And the net single premium to buy an after-tax benefit of $267 is

$$\frac{\$298.96}{\$267.00} \times \$35,941 = \$40,243$$

The loan balance built up in the reverse mortgage account for the first 21 years (to age 87) is less than with the acquisition of a conventional annuity by borrowing the money. So for most homeowners, who have a normal life expectancy of 22 years or so from age 66, the annuity may be more attractive. It is not until the twenty-second year (age 88) that the benefits of the bank loan exceed those of the reverse mortgage. The longer the borrower lives and receives benefits, the more beneficial the bank loan plan becomes.* After 24 years of benefits, the bank/annuity plan is $10,491 ahead of the reverse mortgage; and after 30 years, the difference is $45,263. The loan balance details may be inspected in Table 8.5. These loan balance amounts for the conventional annuity are with the annuity size increased in order to provide after-tax monthly benefits equal to those of the reverse mortgage. However, it must also be remembered that the owners of a conventional joint-and-survivorship annuity will leave no estate. There are no residual benefits to pass to one's heirs. So, if leaving benefits to one's heirs is an important consideration, this points to the bank-HUD plan as the plan of choice rather than a loan plus purchase of an annuity. (One may also consider the purchase of an annuity with a period of years (say, 10 or 15) and certain (obligatory) payments (either to the annuitants or their estate) and compare that to the bank-HUD plan. Naturally, the monthly benefits for a given premium cost are less with a years-certain annuity than for an annuity which stops at death.

HUD Reverse Mortgage Program

The U.S. Department of Housing and Urban Development (HUD) began a program in 1989 to insure mortgages on the homes of persons age 62 or older, which enables the homeowners to convert the equity in their primary residences into cash. The program is called "Home Equity Conversion Mortgage (HECM) Insurance." It is popularly referred to as a "reverse

---

*The loan balance from the reverse mortgage is limited, however, to a maximum of the value of the house.

mortgage." This program was established as the result of a Congressional act which added new Section 255 to the National Housing Act. Borrowers under the HECM plan must own their home free and clear of loans, or nearly so, and must attend an informative counseling session.

The program rules were adopted after thorough investigation including comments from such organizations as the American Association of Retired Persons (AARP), the National Council on the Aging (NCOA), the Mortgage Bankers Association (MBA), the American Bankers Association (ABA), the Federal National Mortgage Association (FNMA), the Federal Home Loan Mortgage Corp. (FHLMC), the State of Connecticut, the Rhode Island Housing and Mortgage Finance Corp., The Virginia Housing Development Authority, the Georgia Residential Finance Authority, the Ohio Department of Aging, Capital Holding Corp., Riggs National Bank, Suncoast Schools Federal Credit Union, Eden Council for Hope and Opportunity of Walnut Creek, California, and Catholic Social Service of Tucson. The program began with a trial involving 2500 loans. As of this writing, some 6000 loans have been made, and the Federal Housing Administration is authorized to guarantee 25,000 loans.

Characteristics of the HUD Program

Under the HUD program the loans are made by commercial lenders (banks, S&Ls, mortgage bankers, and finance companies) who transfer certain of the risks to HUD. Table 8.9 lists lenders who offer reverse mortgages or provide counseling. Many aspects of the program have been standardized and are compulsory for a lender to obtain a certificate of insurance from HUD. However, lenders are free to make some decisions, including the interest rate charged as well as payment options offered to borrowers.

The program allows homeowners to convert the equity in a home into cash that does not have to be repaid until the borrower moves or dies.

There are three basic forms of payment plans that HUD will insure, including "tenure," "term," and "line of credit." Regardless of the payment option selected, the insureds may continue to live in the house until they move, sell the house, or die.

They may sell their property at any time, retaining any proceeds that exceed the amount necessary to pay off the mortgage.

Insureds cannot be forced to sell their home to pay off the mortgage.

HUD insures the lender against the risk that the mortgage balance may grow to exceed the value of the property.

The *tenure* option provides monthly payments to an insured as long as the homeowner occupies the home as a principal residence.

Table 8.9. Lenders Offering Reverse Mortgages and Counselors

At press time the following lenders actually offered or have offered reverse mortgages. However, every lender which is approved to offer HUD-FHA loan programs can provide a reverse mortgage thorough HUD-FHA if the lender wishes to do so and takes the necessary steps to qualify with HUD. All of the lenders which have no footnotes after their names offer the standard HUD-FHA Home Equity Conversion Mortgage (HECM).

	Location	Phone number
Alabama		
Homestead Mortgage	Columbus, GA	(404) 324-2274
United Savings Bank	Anniston	(205) 237-6668
Unity Mortgage	Birmingham	(205) 969-0426
Arizona		
Directors Mortgage	Riverside, CA	(800) 442-4966
First Mortgage Corporation	Tempe	(800) 456-0569
Sun American Mortgage	Mesa	(602) 832-4343
Reverse Mortgage Program[c]	Tucson	(602) 623-0344
	Phoenix	(602) 997-6105
California		
ARCS Mortgage, Inc.	Bakersfield	(805) 395-0785
	Calabasas	(818) 880-2890
	Canoga Park	(818) 884-6988
	Cerritos	(213) 924-7707
	Covina	(818) 331-0991
	Fresno	(209) 432-2727
	Lancaster	(805) 945-3641
	Merced	(209) 384-8650
	Modesto	(209) 575-4801
	Paso Robles	(805) 238-5004
	Petaluma	(707) 765-1318
	Pleasanton	(415) 847-2082
	Prunedale	(408) 755-7940
	Redding	(916) 223-2065
	Roseville	(916) 781-2727
	San Diego	(619) 279-1701
	San Luis Obispo	(805) 543-2727
	Santa Barbara	(805) 965-6699
	Santa Maria	(805) 928-5727
	Santa Rosa	(707) 546-4456
	Sonora	(209) 532-2727
	Stockton	(209) 474-6161
	Temecula	(714) 695-2727
	Ukiah	(707) 462-3757
	Vallejo	(707) 462-3757
	Van Nuys	(818) 787-7720
	Victorville	(619) 951-2333
Bank of Lodi	Lodi	(209) 367-2075
Beachfront Funding	San Clemente	(714) 492-5000
CFE Mortgage	Pasadena	(818) 577-0233
Directors Mortgage	Riverside	(800) 442-4966

NOTE: Footnotes appear at the end of the table.

Table 8.9. Lenders Offering Reverse Mortgages and Counselors (*Continued*)

	Location	Phone number
California (Continued)		
Farwest Mortgage Bankers	Placentia	(714) 579-1117
	Redondo Beach	(310) 316-8503
First California Mortgage	Petaluma	(707) 792-2700
Interstate Mortgage	Upland	(714) 982-4424
Mical Mortgage	San Diego	(619) 452-8200
Northpoint Mortgage	Fresno	(209) 225-2255
Providential Home Income[b1]	San Francisco	(800) 441-4428
Unity Mortgage	Atlanta, GA	(800) 235-3767
Western Residential Lending	Sacramento	(916) 381-2000
Freedom Home Equity Prtnrs[b]	Irvine	(800) 637-3336
Transamerica HomeFirst[b]	San Francisco	(800) 538-5569
ECHO Housing[c]	Oakland	(510) 271-7931
HIP[c]	San Mateo	(415) 348-6660
Independent Living[c]	San Francisco	(415) 863-0581
Project Match[c]	Santa Clara	(408) 287-7121
Colorado		
Directors Mortgage	Riverside, CA	(800) 442-4966
Unity Mortgage	Boulder	(303) 938-6832
	Boulder	(800) 358-8012
	Colorado Springs	(719) 380-8045
	Englewood	(303) 798-7275
Wendover Funding	Englewood	(303) 843-0480
Connecticut		
Amerifirst Mortgage	Hempstead, NY	(800) 473-6167
Constitution Mtg. Bankers	Meriden	(203) 237-0077
	Niantic, CT	(203) 739-0549
Farmers & Mech. Bank[f]	Middletown	(203) 346-9677
Peoples Bank[f]	Hartford	(203) 527-7144
		(800) 338-7366
Delaware		
Boulevard Mortgage	Philadelphia, PA	(215) 331-6900
Home Mortgage Center	Abingdon, MD	(410) 515-9393
International Mortgage	Baltimore, MD	(410) 581-7806
District of Columbia		
International Mortgage	Baltimore, MD	(410) 581-7806
Unity Mortgage	Rockville, MD	(800) 368-3245
Florida		
Brasota Mortgage	Bradenton	(813) 746-6119
Builders Financial, Ltd.	Plantation	(305) 476-8181
Congress Funding Corp.	Pinellas Park	(813) 725-0700
Creative Financing	Pt. St. Lucie	(407) 335-3446
Homeowners & Investors Svcs.	Lake Worth	(407) 533-6070
IDL Mortgage Corporation	Fort Myers	(813) 482-8686
	Bradenton	(813) 746-9900
Navy Orlando Fed. Cred. Un.	Orlando	(407) 644-1100
Pinnacle Financial	Orlando	(407) 578-2000
		(800) 421-5626

Table 8.9. Lenders Offering Reverse Mortgages and Counselors (*Continued*)

	Location	Phone number
Florida (Continued)		
Pointe Savings Bank	Boca Raton	(407) 480-9443
Unity Mortgage	Atlanta, GA	(800) 235-3767
Georgia		
Homestead Mortgage	Columbus	(404) 324-2274
Tucker Federal	Tucker	(404) 938-1222
Unity Mortgage	Atlanta	(800) 235-3767
Hawaii		
ARCS Mortgage	Kailua	(808) 263-6602
First Hawaiian Mtg.	Honolulu	(808) 536-8899
	Kaiwa-Kona	(808) 329-7777
	Kahului	(808) 871-7195
	Kamuela	(808) 885-7700
	Aiea	(808) 483-5511
	Merced	(209) 725-8590
	Roseville	(916) 786-6400
U.S. Financial Mtg. Corp.	Tahoe City, CA	(916) 581-5626
Liberty Bank	Honolulu	(808) 527-9337
Idaho		
Directors Mortgage	Riverside, CA	(800) 442-4966
Investors West Mortgage	Boise	(208) 345-8153
		(800) 281-3338
Illinois		
Dependable Mortgage Co.	Calumet City	(708) 862-5969
Directors Mortgage	Riverside, CA	(800) 442-4966
First Suburban Mortgage	Inverness	(708) 934-1111
NBD Mortgage	Troy, MI	(313) 828-4694
Senior Income Rev. Mtg.	Chicago	(800) 774-6266
WestAmerica Mortgage Co.	Oakbrook Terrace	(708) 916-9299
Indiana		
Unity Mortgage	Indianapolis	(319) 240-0025
Iowa		
Allied Mortgage	Des Moines	(515) 224-7100
Commercial Federal	Omaha	(401) 554-9200
Unity Mortgage	Atlanta, GA	(800) 235-3767
Kansas		
James B. Nutter & Co.	Kansas City	(816) 531-2345
Kentucky		
Tri-County Mortgage	Corbin	(606) 523-1076
Maine		
Maine State Housing Auth.	Augusta	(207) 623-2981
Unity Mortgage	Atlanta, GA	(800) 235-3767
Maryland		
Carroll County Bank	Westminster	(301) 848-8100

Table 8.9. Lenders Offering Reverse Mortgages and Counselors (*Continued*)

	Location	Phone number
Maryland (*Continued*)		
HEC of Annapolis	Annapolis	(410) 269-4322
		(800) 310-4322
Home Mortgage Center	Kensington	(410) 515-9393
International Mortgage	Baltimore	(410) 581-7806
	Cumberland	(301) 777-1400
Unity Mortgage	Rockville	(800) 368-3254
Massachusetts		
H.O.M.E.[c]	Boston	(617) 924-6875
Michigan		
Bay Creek Mortgage	Traverse City	(616) 941-7171
Unity Mortgage	Southfield	(313) 262-1492
Reverse Mortgage	Southfield	(800) 433-8485
Minnesota		
Directors Mortgage	Riverside, CA	(800) 442-4966
Heigl Mortgage	Bloomington	(612) 831-6644
Richfield Bank and Trust	Richfield	(612) 861-8339
Missouri		
James B. Nutter & Company	Kansas City	(816) 531-2345
Unity Mortgage	Atlanta, GA	(800) 235-3767
Montana		
Intermountain Mortgage	Billings	(406) 652-3000
Board of Housing[x]	Helena	(406) 444-3040
Nebraska		
Commercial Federal	Omaha	(402) 554-9200
Nevada		
Directors Mortgage	Riverside, CA	(800) 442-4966
WestAmerica Mortgage	Las Vegas, NV	(702) 796-7990
New Hampshire		
Cheshire Co. Savings Bank	Keene	(603) 352-2502
Chittenden Bank	Burlington, VT	(802) 660-2123
Unity Mortgage	Bedford	(800) 832-5251
N.H. Housing Fin. Agency[x]	Manchester	(603) 472-8623
New Jersey		
Amerifirst Mortgage	Hempstead, NY	(800) 473-6467
ARCS Mortgage	Hoboken	(201) 795-0100
Boulevard Mortgage	Philadelphia, PA	(215) 331-6900
Hart Mortgage	Wanague	(201) 492-2328
	Marlton	(800) 666-4133
Interchange State	Saddlebrook	(201) 845-5600
Pioneer Mortgage	Haddon Heights	(609) 546-1700
		(800) 222-0057
Boiling Springs S&L[f]	Rutherford	(201) 939-5000

Table 8.9. Lenders Offering Reverse Mortgages and Counselors (*Continued*)

	Location	Phone number
New Mexico		
Sunwest Bank	Albuquerque	(505) 765-2211
New York		
Amerifirst Mortgage	Hempstead	(800) 473-6467
ARCS/Bank of New York	Newburgh	(914) 566-0100
Home Mortage Corporation	Levittown	(516) 796-6100
	Flushing/Queens	(718) 997-7000
	Westchester	(914) 948-4111
Onondaga Savings Bank	Syracuse	(315) 424-4011
Rockwell Equities	Jericho	(516) 334-7900
Counseling for HEC^c	Hempstead	(516) 485-5600
Westchester Res. Hsg.^{c}	White Plains	(914) 428-0953
North Carolina		
Centura Bank	Rocky Mount	(800) 426-7073
Financial First Fed. Sv. Bk.	Burlington	(919) 227-8861
First Federal Savings	Charlotte	(704) 335-4400
Tidewater First Fin. Group	Virginia Beach, VA	(804) 456-0155
Wendover Funding	Greensboro	(800) 476-7200
North Dakota		
Directors Mortgage	Riverside, CA	(800) 442-4966
Ohio		
Unity Mortgage	Columbus, OH	(800) 528-9189
	Hudson, OH	(800) 826-6983
Oklahoma		
Unity Mortgage	Oklahoma City	(800) 336-3135
Oregon		
ARCS Mortgage	Grants Pass	(503) 471-2727
	Medford	(503) 770-2727
	Roseburg	(800) 640-4773
Directors Mortgage	Riverside, CA	(800) 442-4966
Unity Mortgage	Atlanta, GA	(800) 235-3767
Pennsylvania		
Boulevard Mortgage	Philadelphia	(215) 331-6900
Hart Mortgage Corporation	Ft. Washington	(800) 666-4133
Home Mortgage	Abingdon, MD	(410) 515-9393
Integra Mortgage	Pittsburgh	(412) 553-7757
International Mortgage	Cumberland	(301) 777-1400
Pioneer Mortgage	Haddon, NJ	(609) 546-1700
		(800) 222-0057
Unity Mortgage	Atlanta, GA	(800) 235-3757
Rhode Island		
Rhode Island Housing	Providence	(401) 751-5566
South Carolina		
American Federal Bank	Greenville	(803) 255-7434
		(800) 726-6837

Table 8.9. Lenders Offering Reverse Mortgages and Counselors (*Continued*)

	Location	Phone number
South Carolina (Continued)		
First Citizens Mtg. Corp.	Columbia	(803) 733-2747
First Federal	Spartanburg	(803) 582-2391
Utah		
AIM Mortgage, Inc.	Salt Lake City	(801) 487-2586
Directors Mortgage	Riverside, CA	(800) 442-4966
Vermont		
Chittenden Bank	Burlington	(802) 660-2123
Unity Mortgage	Bedford	(800) 832-5251
Virginia		
Ameribanc Savings	Annandale	(703) 658-5500
Beach Fed Mortgage	Virginia Beach	(804) 499-8300
Crestar Mortgage Corp.	Virginia Beach	(804) 498-8702
First Bancorp Mortgage	Newport News	(804) 599-3273
First Savings Mortgage	Vienna	(703) 883-9010
Home Mortgage Center	Falls Church	(703) 671-1414
International Mortgage	Baltimore, MD	(410) 581-7806
Mortgage Capital Investors	Springfield	(703) 941-0711
Tidewater First Fin. Group	Virginia Beach	(800) 282-4326
Unity Mortgage	Rockville, MD	(800) 368-3254
Washington		
ARCS Mortgage	Bellevue	(206) 462-7055
	Lynnwood	(206) 744-2727
Directors Mortgage	Riverside, CA	(800) 422-4966
Investors Mortgage	Boise, ID	(208) 345-8153
West Virginia		
International Mortgage	Cumberland	(301) 777-1400
Tidewater First Fin. Group	Virginia Beach	(800) 282-4326
Wyoming		
Unity Mortgage	Boulder, CO	(800) 358-8012

[c]Provides independent counseling for prospective borrowers as required by the HUD-FHA program.

[j]Offers fixed-term privately sponsored program, not HUD-FHA. Repayment is required at the end of the fixed term.

[p]Offers private program, not HUD-FHA.

[p1]Offers both private program and HUD-FHA.

[x]State sponsored lender to borrowers with incomes below established limits.

The *term* option provides monthly payments for a fixed period selected by the insured.

The *line-of-credit* option (which may be combined with tenure or term options) permits the insured to draw money at times and in amounts of the insured's own choosing, up to a maximum amount.

Lump-sum draws may be made, and the payment plan may be altered.

Since the payments—regardless of the option selected—*are a loan, they are not taxable* for income tax purposes. Nor are the interest charges to the loan account deductible for a cash-basis taxpayer until such charges are paid.* If the interest is simply added to your mortgage balance, the interest is not tax deductible until you actually pay off the loan.

Finding the Monthly Reverse Mortgage Payment

Finding the monthly annuity or reverse mortgage payment for a tenure (lifetime) option plan is not unduly complicated. The formula is

$$P_1 = f(V)$$

where P_1 = principal limit (preliminary)—the maximum gross present value of loan allowable under the HUD insurance arrangement

V = allowable house value—the lesser of the appraised value or the maximum allowed by statute for the area where the house is located ($151,725 maximum at the time of writing). (These values will increase periodically.)

f = factor supplied by HUD, which reflects the following assumptions:
(1) Expected appreciation rate of the house = 4%/year
(2) Variance of the appreciation rate = 1%
(3) Terminations due to death, move-outs, and refinancings = 1.3 times the mortality rate
(4) Discount (interest) rate = mortgage interest rate less $1/2$%
(5) Mortality data from the 1979–1981 female mortality tables, based on Census data published by the U.S. Department of Health and Human Services. These values and assumptions are subject to further refinement as the result of analysis of the data from the trial program. As the result, the factors (f) are expected to change periodically.

---

*Home equity debt may affect the deductibility of interest payments. Check current regulations limiting deductibility of interest on home equity debt. See IRS Publication 936, Home Mortgage Interest Deductions.

Values of f for representative situations are shown in Table 8.10. More comprehensive tables exist for a wide variety of interest rates.

$$P_2 = P_1 - C$$

where P_2 = net principal limit (maximum lump-sum loan) at inception

C = authorized costs, including:

Mortgage insurance initial premium of 2% of allowable house value appraisal

Title examination

Title insurance

Recording fees

Mortgagee's (lender's) title insurance

Repair administrative fee, if any

Initial payments to or on behalf of the borrower, including any funds set aside from the principal limit for monthly servicing fees of the lender (such set-aside is the present value of the fixed monthly fee to the borrower's 100th birthday, discounted at rate i as defined below).

Funds in a line of credit

First-year property charges

Finally, the last step is

$$R = P_2 \left[\frac{i}{1 - (1 + i)^{-n}} \right] [\, (1 + i)^{-1}\,]$$

where R = regular monthly payment

r = expected annual interest rate agreed to between borrower and lender

i = $(r + 0.5\%/12)$ where 0.5% is the annual rate applied to the outstanding loan balance for monthly insurance premium (MIP)

n = number of months from inception until youngest borrower would reach age 100.

Also,

$$i = \frac{(r + 0.5)}{12}$$

Appendix 1 contains factors for the following part of the formula under "Annuity worth $1 today."

$$\frac{i}{1 - (1 + i)^{-n}}$$

Table 8.10. Factors for HUD Insured Loan to Determine Borrower's Principal Limit

Factor and Shared Appreciation Loan Premium Points

Age	Interest rate (%)									
	8.000	9.000	10.000	10.500	11.000	12.000	12.125	12.250	12.375	12.500
62	.371-36	.302-46	.247-50+	.224-50+	.204-50+	.170-50+	.166-50+	.163-50+	.159-50+	.156-50+
63	.382-35	.313-44	.258-50+	.234-50+	.214-50+	.179-50+	.175-50+	.171-50+	.167-50+	.164-50+
64	.393-33	.324-42	.268-50+	.245-50+	.224-50+	.188-50+	.184-50+	.180-50+	.176-50+	.173-50+
65	.405-31	.336-40	.280-50	.256-50+	.234-50+	.197-50+	.193-50+	.189-50+	.186-50+	.182-50+
66	.417-30	.348-39	.291-48	.267-50+	.245-50+	.208-50+	.203-50+	.199-50+	.195-50+	.192-50+
67	.429-28	.360-37	.303-46	.279-50+	.257-50+	.218-50+	.214-50+	.210-50+	.206-50+	.202-50+
68	.442-27	.373-35	.316-44	.291-49	.268-50+	.230-50+	.225-50+	.221-50+	.217-50+	.213-50+
69	.454-25	.386-33	.329-42	.304-47	.281-50+	.241-50+	.237-50+	.233-50+	.228-50+	.224-50+
70	.467-23	.400-31	.342-40	.317-45	.294-50	.254-50+	.249-50+	.245-50+	.240-50+	.236-50+
71	.481-22	.413-30	.356-38	.331-43	.307-48	.267-50+	.262-50+	.257-50+	.253-50+	.249-50+
72	.494-20	.428-28	.370-36	.345-41	.321-45	.280-50+	.275-50+	.271-50+	.266-50+	.262-50+
73	.508-19	.442-26	.385-34	.360-39	.336-43	.294-50+	.289-50+	.285-50+	.280-50+	.276-50+
74	.522-18	.457-24	.400-32	.375-37	.351-41	.309-50+	.304-50+	.299-50+	.295-50+	.290-50+
75	.537-16	.472-23	.416-30	.390-35	.367-39	.324-49	.319-50	.314-50+	.310-50+	.305-50+
76	.551-15	.488-21	.432-29	.407-33	.383-37	.340-46	.335-47	.330-49	.325-50	.321-50+
77	.566-14	.504-20	.448-27	.423-31	.399-35	.356-44	.351-45	.346-46	.342-47	.337-49

78	.581-12	.520-18	.465-25	.440-29	.417-33	.373-41	.368-42	.363-43	.359-45	.354-46
79	.596-11	.536-16	.482-23	.458-27	.434-30	.391-39	.386-40	.381-41	.376-42	.371-43
80	.611-10	.553-15	.500-21	.475-25	.452-28	.409-36	.404-37	.399-39	.394-40	.389-41
81	.626-09	.569-13	.517-19	.493-23	.470-26	.427-34	.422-35	.417-36	.412-37	.408-38
82	.641-08	.586-12	.535-17	.511-20	.488-24	.446-31	.441-32	.436-33	.431-34	.426-35
83	.656-06	.603-10	.553-15	.529-18	.507-21	.465-28	.460-29	.455-30	.450-31	.445-32
84	.671-05	.619-09	.571-13	.548-16	.526-19	.484-25	.479-26	.474-27	.470-28	.465-29
85	.686-95–	.636-07	.589-11	.566-13	.545-16	.504-22	.499-23	.494-24	.489-25	.485-26
86	.700-05–	.652-06	.607-09	.585-11	.564-13	.524-19	.519-20	.514-20	.509-21	.505-22
87	.715-05–	.668-05–	.624-07	.603-08	.583-10	.543-15	.539-16	.534-16	.529-17	.525-18
88	.729-05–	.685-05–	.642-05–	.622-06	.602-07	.564-11	.559-12	.554-12	.550-13	.545-13
89	.743-05–	.701-05–	.660-05–	.640-05–	.621-05–	.584-07	.580-08	.575-08	.571-08	.566-09
90	.757-05–	.717-05–	.678-05–	.659-05–	.641-05–	.605-05–	.601-05–	.596-05	.592-05	.588-05
91	.772-05–	.734-05–	.697-05–	.679-05–	.661-05–	.627-05–	.622-05–	.618-95–	.614-05–	.610-05–
92	.786-05–	.750-05–	.716-05–	.699-05–	.682-05–	.649-05–	.645-05–	.641-05–	.637-05–	.633-05–
93	.800-05–	.767-05–	.735-05–	.719-05–	.703-05–	.672-05–	.668-05–	.665-05–	.661-05–	.657-05–
94	.816-05–	.785-05–	.755-05–	.741-05–	.726-05–	.697-05–	.694-05–	.690-05–	.687-05–	.683-05–
95	.832-05–	.805-05–	.778-05–	.764-05–	.751-05–	.725-05–	.722-05–	.719-05–	.715-05–	.712-05–
96	.832-05–	.805-05–	.778-05–	.764-05–	.751-05–	.725-05–	.722-05–	.719-05–	.715-05–	.712-05–
97	.832-05–	.805-05–	.778-05–	.764-05–	.751-05–	.725-05–	.722-05–	.719-05–	.715-05–	.712-05–
98	.832-05–	.805-05–	.778-05–	.764-05–	.751-05–	.725-05–	.722-05–	.719-05–	.715-05–	.712-05–
99	.832-05–	.805-05–	.778-05–	.764-05–	.751-05–	.725-05–	.722-05+	.719-05–	.715-05–	.712-05–

The following part of the formula (also found in Appendix 1) is necessary in order to adjust for the fact that the payments to the borrower are made at the *beginning* of each month:

$$(1 + i)^{-1}$$

Example: Finding the monthly payment for a reverse mortgage with tenure option. What is the maximum monthly payment amount for a couple aged 75 and 80, provided their house is worth $100,000, in a $101,250-maximum-value area? The cost of HUD's up-front insurance fee is 2 percent of the $100,000 value; and appraisal, title examination, and insurance and other costs excluding the HUD fee are $1500. The interest rate on the loan agreed to between the borrowers and the lender is 10 percent per year excluding the one-half of 1 percent annual HUD insurance premium. The age of the youngest borrower must be used to determine the factor f. Table 8.10 provides f as 0.416. Thus,

$$P_1 = f(V)$$

$$= 0.416 \, (\$100,000) = \$41,600$$

and

$$P_2 = P_1 - C$$

$$= \$41,600 - \$3500 = \$38,100$$

Then,

$$R = P_2 \left[\frac{i}{1 - (1 + i)^{-n}} \right] (1 + i)^{-1}$$

$$= \$38,100 \left[\frac{0.015/12}{1 - (1 + 0.105/12)^{-300}} \right] \left(1 + \frac{0.105}{12} \right)^{-1}$$

$$= \$38,100 \left[\frac{0.00875}{1 - (1 + 0.00875)^{-300}} \right] (1 + 0.00875)^{-1}$$

$$= \$38,100 \left[\frac{0.00875}{1 - 0.07327} \right] (0.99133)$$

$$= \$38,100 \, (0.00944) \, (0.99133) = \$356.61$$

Thus, $356.61 is the monthly payment amount that these homeowners can receive tax-free until they sell the house, move, or die.

Example: Finding the monthly payment with term option. Use the same assumptions as in the previous example, except that the loan is for a term option of 10 years.

Starting with the value $38,100 from the previous example, that is, $P_2 =$ $38,100 as the present value, find the monthly payment where the rate is 10.5 percent per year, compounded monthly, with payments at the *beginning* of each month for 120 months.

$$R = (A) \left[\frac{i/m}{1 - (1 + i/m)^{-nm}} \right] \left(1 + \frac{0.105}{12} \right)^{-1}$$

where R = amount of each regular future periodic payment
  i = annual or nominal interest rate
  m = number of times interest is compounded per year
  n = number of years
  A = present value of the series of equal payments

$$R = (\$38,100) \left[\frac{0.015/12}{1 - (1 + 0.105/12)^{-(10)(12)}} \right] \left(1 + \frac{0.105}{12} \right)^{-1}$$

$$= (\$38,100) \left[\frac{0.00875}{1 - (1 + 0.00875)^{-(10)(12)}} \right] (1 + 0.00875)^{-1}$$

$$= \$38,100 \left[\frac{0.00875}{1 - 0.35154} \right] (0.991326)$$

$$= \$38,100 \ (0.013493) \ (0.991326) = \$509.64$$

Thus $509.64 is the monthly payment amount for a 10-year term with payments made at the beginning of each month. For an alternative method of calculation, the values of the principal parts of the formula may be found in Appendix 1. By the same method, the monthly payment for a 90-month term would be $608.11, and for a 180-month term they would be $417.50.

Line of Credit

A line of credit can be combined with monthly payments by setting aside a portion of the principal limit for a line of credit. The net principal limit is then used to calculate monthly payments in the usual manner. The amount set aside for the line of credit becomes the initial principal limit for the line of credit. The amount increases each month by the compounding rate (i). The borrower can receive payments from the line of credit as long as the portion of the outstanding balance attributable to the line of credit (including accrued interest and MIP) does not exceed the principal limit for the line of credit. The combined principal limit for the monthly payments plus the principal limit for the line of credit equals the principal limit for a tenure or term payment plan without a line of credit.

Shared Appreciation Mortgages

In exchange for sharing a stated portion of a property's net appreciated value (if any), at the time that a mortgage is due and payable or prepaid, the borrower may receive a *lower* interest rate than for a comparable mortgage without shared appreciation and, consequently, may receive higher payments. HUD rules severely limit the extent to which lenders can share in appreciation.

Example: Bank-HUD plan. Consider a similar set of circumstances to the case explored at the beginning of this chapter with the insurance company plan. We have a husband and wife, each age 66. Their house is valued at $130,000. The bank and borrower agree to an interest rate of 10.5 percent per year; together with a continuing HUD insurance fee of 0.5 percent of the loan balance, the rate at which the loan balance will increase is 11 percent per year, compounded monthly. The initial insurance (HUD) fee is 2 percent of the maximum claim amount. The fee in this case is 2 percent of the maximum claim amount of $91, 650, that, $1833.00. Additional costs for appraisal, title insurance, etc., are $1667. Total up-front costs are $3500. The loan factor (Table 8.10) is .0267. Thus the initial principal limit (maximum amount that can be borrowed in a lump sum or present value of future monthly payments to age 100) is $24,470 (i.e., 0.267 × $91,650). The total monthly payments are $195.19, from which a service fee of $20 per month is deducted, providing a monthly benefit to the borrowers of $175.19. [This compared to the insurance-sponsored (Home Income Security Plan of Capital Holding Co.) monthly benefit for a house value of $91,650 for a couple aged 66 of $184.00.] The calculations for determining the above are by the same method as described previously in this chapter.

What about the significance of the continuing charge for MIP (monthly insurance premium), which is charged at the annual rate of one-half of 1 percent of the loan balance. Refer to Table 8.11. The MIP charge is only

able 8.11. Bank-HUD Plan: Reverse Mortgage

ge of youngest borrower:	66	Initial property value: $130,000
terest rate:	10.500%	Expected appreciation: 4%
aximum claim amount:	$91,650	Initial line of credit: $0
itial principal limit:	$24,470	Monthly payment: $175.19
eginning mortgage balance:	$3,500	Monthly servicing fee: $20.00
		Total payment and fee $195.19

		Annual totals			End-of-year projections			
ear	Age	SVC fee*	Payment†	MIP‡	Interest	Loan bal.	Line of credit	Prin. limit§	Property value¶
1	66	$240	$2,102	$ 25	$ 524	$ 6,392	0	$ 27,301	$135,200
2	67	240	2,102	40	844	9,618	0	30,460	140,608
3	68	240	2,102	57	1,200	13,218	0	33,985	146,232
4	69	240	2,102	76	1,598	17,234	0	37,918	152,081
5	70	240	2,102	97	2,041	21,715	0	42,306	158,164
6	71	240	2,102	121	2,536	26,714	0	47,202	164,491
7	72	240	2,102	147	3,089	32,292	0	52,664	171,071
8	73	240	2,102	176	3,705	38,515	0	58,758	177,913
9	74	240	2,102	209	4,392	45,459	0	65,558	185,030
10	75	240	2,102	246	5,159	53,206	0	73,144	192,431
11	76	240	2,102	286	6,015	61,850	0	81,608	200,129
12	77	240	2,102	332	6,970	71,494	0	91,052	208,134
13	78	240	2,102	383	8,035	82,253	0	101,588	216,459
14	79	240	2,102	439	9,223	94,258	0	113,344	225,117
15	80	240	2,102	502	10,549	107,652	0	126,460	234,122
16	81	240	2,102	573	12,029	122,596	0	141,094	243,487
17	82	240	2,102	651	13,680	139,270	0	157,421	253,227
18	82	240	2,102	739	15,521	157,873	0	175,638	263,356
19	84	240	2,102	837	17,576	178,628	0	195,963	273,890
20	85	240	2,102	946	19,869	201,785	0	218,639	284,846
21	86	240	2,102	1,068	22,427	227,622	0	243,940	296,239
22	87	240	2,102	1,204	25,281	256,449	0	272,169	308,089
23	88	240	2,102	1,355	28,465	288,612	0	303,664	320,413
24	89	240	2,102	1,525	32,018	324,496	0	338,803	333,229
25	90	240	2,102	1,713	35,981	364,533	0	378,009	346,558
26	91	240	2,102	1,924	40,404	409,203	0	421,752	360,421
27	92	240	2,102	2,159	45,338	459,042	0	470,557	374,837
28	93	240	2,102	2,421	50,843	514,649	0	525,009	389,831
29	94	240	2,102	2,714	56,985	576,690	0	585,763	405,424
30	95	240	2,102	3,040	63,838	645,911	0	653,547	421,641
31	96	240	2,102	3,404	71,484	723,141	0	729,174	438,507
32	97	240	2,102	3,810	80,015	809,309	0	813,554	456,047
33	98	240	2,102	4,263	89,533	905,448	0	907,697	474,289
34	99	240	2,102	4,769	100,153	1,012,712	0	1,012,712	493,261

*$20 per month, regardless of size of loan or monthly payments.

†Payments are at the beginning of each month.

‡One-half of 1% of loan balance is the continuing mortgage insurance premium.

§Principal limit increases at 11%, compounded monthly (10.5% loan rate plus 0.5% M.I.P.).

¶Increases at 4%, compounded annually.

Dollars

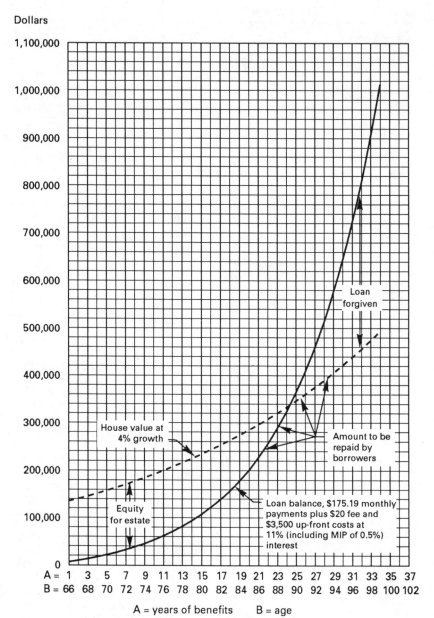

Figure 8.4. Reverse mortgage: amount repayable—bank-HUD plan.

about $25 in the first year, but by the twenty-first year it is over $1000. The net present value of the MIP (at 10.5 percent) is $1999 for the first 22 years (which is about the life expectancy of the couple). This $1999 divided by the maximum claim amount of $91,650 is 2.18 percent. Thus, one may consider the HUD insurance cost (including the 2 percent up-front fee) to be an adjusted up-front cost of about 4.18 percent of the maximum claim amount. (This contrasts to the insurance plan's up-front costs for this house value of $3000 plus 7 percent of $91,650, that is, $9415.50. This works out to about 10.27 percent for the insurance plan.)

At what point is it likely that the loan account balance will exceed the value of the house? Refer to both Table 8.11 and the pictorial representation of the data in Fig. 8.4. The point at which the loan balance curve crosses the curve for the value of the house is in the twenty-fourth or twenty-fifth year. If the borrowers die or leave the house before that, there will be some equity for their estate (i.e., the house proceeds will exceed the loan amount repaid). If the borrowers die after that, the excess of the loan amount over the proceeds of the house is not repaid by the borrowers; it is paid for by HUD. *It is apparent that the actuarial construction of the plan is such that the insurer will not have any claims most of the time, as the value of the house exceeds the loan amount for a normal life expectancy.*

IRR or APR of Bank-HUD Plan

Finally, we come to the critical question: What is the internal rate of return (or annual percentage rate) for the bank-HUD plan? (For the insurance plan considered earlier, we determined that the IRR is 15.715 percent for 15 years of payments, so we will use 15 years of payments in this case as well—at which point the borrowers, if alive, will be 81.)

A time line aids in visualizing the situation:

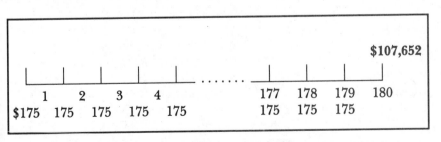

The question is: What is the interest rate which equates equal monthly payments of $175.19 at the beginning of each month for 180 months to the future loan account balance of $107,652? That annual IRR or APR rate is 14.027 percent. *Thus, the Bank-HUD program offers considerably less cost in these instances to the borrowers than the insurance plan.*

The IRR or APR calculation is as follows:

$$S = R \left[\frac{(1 + i/m)^{(n)(m)} - 1}{(i/m)} \right] \left(1 + \frac{i}{m} \right)$$

where S = future value of a series of equal payments (annuity)
i = annual or nominal interest rate
m = number of times interest is compounded per year
R = amount of each regular future periodic payment
n = number of years

Thus,

$$\$107,652 = \$175.19 \left[\frac{(1 + i/12)^{(15)(12)} - 1}{(i/12)} \right] (1 + i)$$

$$\$614.49 = \left[\frac{(1 + i/12)^{(15)(12)} - 1}{(i/12)} \right] (1 + i)$$

Appendix 1 allows an approximation of i if one uses an annual payment assumption (rather than a monthly one). Calculator solutions are rapid, even with old models. (Find the interest rate for an annuity due when future value and monthly payments are known.) Trial-and-error solution produces a value of i of 0.01169, which when multiplied by 12 to obtain an annual rate, is 14.027 percent.

Conclusion

The reverse mortgage fulfills a vital need: the desire of senior citizens to have more disposable income for as long as they live in their home, without running the risk of having the income cease if they continue to live too long. There are no simple alternatives to a reverse mortgage plan for achieving the same objectives. There is a choice, however, between insurance company plans such as TransAmerica's and bank-HUD plans. One of the key elements in deciding among the alternative offerings (and borrowers should definitely shop around) is the APR or IRR of the respective plans. The higher the APR or IRR, the more the plan is going to cost the borrowers and, other things being equal, the plan with the lowest IRR or APR is the best. The fact that the bank-HUD plan at the moment of this writing offers a substantially lower IRR or APR than the insurance company plan does not mean that the situation may not reverse itself next week, next month, or next year. Profit-motivated insurance companies may be expected to react quickly to competitive forces and price their products in a manner to compete effectively—if consumers use their intelligence to shun the more expensive offerings.

Present regulations are such that the HUD-insured loans, at least in the case of high-value homes (say, over $150,000 in value), will produce lower monthly benefits because HUD currently sets an upper limit on the value of the house* that HUD will recognize that is less than the values insurance companies or other lenders will acknowledge. Insurance company plans do not set such a limit and accordingly are in a position to offer much higher monthly payment amounts for high-value homes. Nevertheless, the APR or IRR for each dollar of benefit may or may not be much higher.

It is an obligation of both bank lenders and insurance company sponsors of these reverse mortgage plans to provide a disclosure statement showing the APR or IRR of the plan. Practice seems to be that the disclosure statement is given at the closing transaction when the loan documents are signed, etc. *It is suggested that prospective reverse mortgage mortgagors (borrowers) ask for an advance copy of the APR disclosure statement before making up their minds* as to which plan to take.

For homeowners who have spent a good part of their lives making payments to build up equity in a house, a reverse mortgage program allows them to reap the benefits of their thriftiness by receiving monthly payments in their retirement years. It is a program that is destined to become a major part of the U.S. financial scene, and in the years ahead it is predicted that the words "reverse mortgage" will become as well known as "IRA" or "Keogh" or "pension plan."

Additional Sources of Information†

Additional information may be obtained from the following sources:

AARP Home Equity Information Center
Consumer Affairs Section
American Association of Retired Persons
601 E Street NW
Washington, DC 20049

*The upper limit varies geographically.

†The first step is to determine a local lender which participates in the HUD-FHA revenue mortgage program. As lenders seem to come and go from the reverse mortgage lending area, call your nearest Housing and Urban Development (HUD) office to find out the names of participating nearby lenders. (Look in the Blue Pages under federal government for Housing and Urban Development.)

(202) 434-3525
(800) 424-3410

Advising Older Homeowners on Home Equity Conversion: A Guide for Attorneys

Home Equity Conversion for the Elderly: An Analysis for Lenders

The Unique Asset: A Home Equity Conversion Guide for Financial Advisors

Home-Made Money

American Bar Association
Commission on Legal Problems of the Elderly
1800 M Street, NW
Washington, DC 20036
(202) 331-2297

Attorney's Guide to Home Equity Conversion

National Center for Home Equity Conversion
7373 147th Street, W, Ste. 115
Apple Valley, MN 55124
(612) 953-4474

A Financial Guide to the Individual Reverse Mortgage Account

Sale Leaseback Guide and Model Documents

Deferred Payment Loans for Home Repairs and Improvements: A Program Development and Operations Handbook

Insurance Companies offering plans:

American Homestead Mortgage Corp.
305 Fellowship Rd.,
Mt. Laurel, NJ 08054
(609) 866-0800

Capital Holding Corp. (terminated loan program)
680 Fourth Ave.
Louisville, KY 40201
(502) 560-2000

Freedom Home Equity Partners
2500 Michelson Dr., Ste. 410
Irvine, CA

Life Capital Corp.
San Francisco

State Housing Authorities, including:

Connecticut Department on Aging
175 Main Street
Hartford, CT 06106
(800) 443-9946

Federation for Community Planning
614 Superior Ave., N.W., Ste. 300
Cleveland, OH 44113

Ohio Department of Aging
50 W. Broad St., 9th Floor
Columbus, OH 43215
(614) 466-9651

Providential Home Income Plan
Providential Corp.
3 Embarcadero Center
San Francisco, CA 94111
(300) 441-4428

TransAmerica HomeFirst (CA, PA, NJ, NY)
San Francisco, CA
(800) 538-5569

Western Reserve Area Agency on Aging
1030 Euclid Ave., Ste. 318
Cleveland, OH 44115
(216) 621-8010

New Jersey Division on Aging
(800) 792-8820

Rhode Island Department of Elderly Affairs
79 Washington Street
Providence, RI 02903
(401) 277-6552

Virginia Housing Development Authority
13 S. 13th St.
Richmond, VA 23219

Maryland DHCD-CDA
45 Calvert St.
Annapolis, MD 21401

Western Reserve Area Agency on Aging
1030 Euclid Avenue, Ste. 318
Cleveland, OH 44115
(216) 621-8010

Canada:

Canada Home Income Plan
Vancouver, B.C.
Toronto, Ontario

Home Earnings Reverse Mortgage
(Offices throughout Canada)

9

Loan Repayments and the True Cost of a Loan

The Truth in Lending and Fair Credit Billing acts require lenders, in most instances, to disclose the annual percentage rate (APR) that a borrower is charged. The APR is equivalent to the nominal annual interest rate that a borrower experiences by repaying the loan in the agreed manner. In calculating the APR, the compounding frequency is based on the shortest time interval between the borrower's loan repayments. For example, if a borrower repays monthly, the compounding frequency is 12 times per year. The APR is the periodic rate (e.g., 0.01) multiplied by the number of times interest is compounded per year (e.g., 12). Regulation Z issued by the Board of Governors of the Federal Reserve System contains details of government regulation for promoting the informed use of consumer credit by requiring disclosures about its terms and cost.

Why are there so many types of loans, add-ons, discount, loans with points, etc.? The variety of loans is at least partially a relic of the "good old days" (for lenders)—before the Truth in Lending Act. Lenders are in the business of selling a product. Instead of VCRs or camcorders, the product that lenders sell is dreams. And to fulfill some dreams, the product required is money. Furthermore, it is easier to sell money when a lender can say: "We can offer you our 8 percent discount loan for 60 months" than it is to say "Our installment loan will cost you an APR of 22.28 percent." Add-on loans and their cousins, "discount loans," have the common feature that borrowers pay back more than they borrow. And since the loan is paid back in installments (usually monthly), the entire loan balance is outstanding only for the first time period (month). After that, the loan principal is gradually reduced with each installment payment. Hence the true cost of the loan (APR) is much higher (even double or triple) the stated rate attached to the term "add-on" or "discount" (as in an 8 percent discount loan for 60 months). On the other hand, lenders are not free to loan at whatever the traffic will bear; they are limited in the rates they can charge by state law (sometimes referred to as usury laws) and by what must be disclosed according to the Federal Reserve's Regulation Z. And that partially explains why lenders are active lobbyists.

Real Estate Loan: Finding the Annual Repayment

The formula for finding the annual repayment for a regular mortgage loan is

$$R = S \left[\frac{i/m}{(1 + i/m)^{nm} - 1} \right]$$

when the future value is known, or

$$R = A \left[\frac{i/m}{1 - (1 + i/m)^{-nm}} \right]$$

when the present value is known,

where R = amount of each regular future periodic payment
S = future value of series of equal payments (annuity)
i = annual or nominal interest rate
m = number of times interest is compounded per year
n = number of years
A = present value of the series of equal payments

Example: Finding the installment payment for a real estate mortgage loan. Susan Shaw borrows a sum, A, and agrees to repay it in n annual installments of R each. This is typical of the real estate mortgage loans described in Chap. 7 (see Fig. 7.2). The amount of the mortgage loan A is \$200,000. Annual interest i is 6 percent, with repayment by 20 annual installments, n. We want to find the annual repayment, R.

The value of the factor

$$\left[\frac{i/m}{1 - (1 + i/m)^{-nm}} \right]$$

is given in Table 8 of Appendix 1, "partial payment, annuity worth $1 today." This factor is frequently referred to in real estate circles as the *annual constant*. The solution, then, is

$$R = \$200,000 \left[\frac{0.06/1}{1 - (1 + 0.06/1)^{-20}} \right] = \$200,000 \, [0.087184] = \$17,436.91$$

Real Estate Loan: Finding the Amount That Can Be Borrowed

When the amount to be calculated is the sum which can be borrowed, A, with the loan to be repaid by regular fixed repayments of a specified amount, R, over a period of n regular payments including a rate of compound interest of i, then the formula is

$$A = R \left[\frac{1 - (1 + i/m)^{-nm}}{i/m} \right]$$

where A = present value of a series of equal payments (annuity)
  i = annual or nominal interest rate
  m = number of times interest is compounded per year
  R = amount of each regular future periodic payment
  n = number of years

  Example: Finding the amount that can be borrowed. Determine the amount that can be borrowed today, providing annual repayments of principal and interest of $3000 are to be made for 22 years at 8 percent nominal annual compound interest on the unpaid balance.

$$A = R \left[\frac{1 - (1 + i/m)^{-nm}}{i/m} \right]$$

$$= \$3000 \left[\frac{1 - (1.08)^{-22}}{0.08} \right]$$

$$= \$3000 \, (10.200743) = \$30,602.23$$

The amount the borrower can obtain today is $30,602.23. (See Chap. 8 for a discussion of mortgage points, which, if applicable, affect the calculation.)

Add-on (or Discount) Loan

With an add-on or discount loan, the lender begins with the amount that the borrower will receive (P) in cash, e.g., $10,000. To this is added interest (I) on the $10,000 at the add-on or discount rate, e.g., 10 percent (i) for some period of time (t), say, 90 days. To determine the face amount of the loan (or the promissory note), first interest is calculated and then that interest is added to the cash the borrower receives.

Example: Finding the size of an add-on loan. A borrower receives $10,000, at 10 percent, for 90 days. What is the amount of the add-on loan?

First the interest (I_1) is found, as follows:

$$I_1 = Pit$$

$$= \$10,000 \, (0.1) \frac{90}{365}$$

$$= \$246.58$$

Then the interest on the interest (I_2) is added:

$$I_2 = \$246.58 \, (0.1) \left(\frac{90}{365} \right) = \$6.08$$

The borrower will be asked to sign a note for $10,252.58, the sum of the cash, interest, and interest on interest, as follows:

Cash received by borrower	$10,000.00
Interest on $10,000	246.58
Interest on interest	6.08
Total face amount of loan	$10,252.66

Thus the borrower receives $10,000 and pays back $10,252.66 after 90 days.

Example: Find the APR for the above-described add-on loan. The APR is found by solving for i, using the now-familiar formula,

$$S = P \, (1 + i)^n$$

$$(1 + i)^n = \frac{S}{P} = \frac{\$10,252.66}{\$10,000.00} = 1.0253$$

$$(1 + i)^{90/365} = 1.0253$$

$$\log (1 + i) = \frac{\log 1.2053}{(90/365)} = \frac{0.01083}{0.24658} = 0.04392$$

$$(1 + i) = 1.10649$$

$$i = 0.10649 \quad or \quad 10.649\%$$

Thus, the true annual interest rate is 10.649 percent for this so-called 10 percent discount or add-on loan.

In actual banking practice, this type of loan would probably be repaid over a longer period of time and by monthly installments. It is similar to the "discount installment loan" described later in this chapter. Banking practice varies as to whether 360 days or 365 days is used as the length of a year.

A generalized formula for finding the APR of an add-on type loan, as just described, using natural logarithms (ln), is

$$i = e^{[\ln(S/P)]/n} - 1$$

where i = annual percentage rate
   S = face amount of the note
   P = cash received by borrower
   n = time in years of the loan

Discount Note

With a discount note, the interest, as determined, is deducted from the face amount of the note to determine the cash received by the borrower.

Example. Benjamin Barber signs a note for a 10 percent discount loan of $10,000 to be repaid after 2 years. The bank computes 2 years' interest at 10 percent per year, for a total of 20 percent, then multiplies this times the note face amount of $10,000 to obtain $2000 in interest. This $2000 is deducted from the $10,000 note face, S, and the borrower receives the difference of $8000 in cash, P. What is the annual percentage or true annual compound interest rate, i?

$$i = e^{[\ln(S/P)]/n} - 1$$

$$i = e^{[\ln(\$10,000/\$8,000)]/2} - 1 = e^{0.11157} - 1 = 1.11803 - 1 = 0.11803$$

The true annual interest rate of this 10 percent discount loan is thus 11.8 percent.

In banking practice, this type of loan would probably be for a shorter time period, e.g., 90 days. Alternatively, the loan might be calculated as follows: The borrower desires $8000 cash for 90 days. The bank charges a rate of 10 percent discount (i.e., 2.5 percent for 90 days). Then 100 percent less 2.5 percent equals 97.5 percent, and $8000 divided by 0.975 is $8205.13. The note which the borrower signs and the amount he repays at the expiration of 90 days is $8205.13. This, then, is equivalent to a 10.813 percent APR.

Open Note, Interest Paid at Maturity

An open note, with interest paid at maturity, is a straight, nongimmicked, loan (in computer terminology, WYSIWYG—or, what you see is what you get).

Example: Finding the APR of an open note. Benjamin Barber obtains $10,000 in cash and agrees to repay, 1 year later, $10,000 plus interest at 10 percent, $1000. What is the APR?

In this example, the stated interest rate of 10 percent is the true annual percentage rate.

$$S = P(1 + i)^n$$

$$\$11{,}000 = \$10{,}000\,(1 + i)^1$$

$$(1 + i)^1 = 1.1$$

$$i = 0.1 \quad or \quad 10\%$$

Add-on Installment Loan

A borrower needs $10,000 cash, which she obtains by agreeing to repay principal and interest computed by the lender as follows:

Amount of cash loan	$10,000 (A)
Interest.	6%, add-on
Number of years over which note is repaid in equal periodic installments	5 years
Number of periodic repayments	5
Repayments (compounding frequency) per year . . .	1
Interest (6%) times years (5)	30%
Note signed by borrower	$13,000 ($10,000 + $3,000)
Annual repayment ($13,000/5)	$2,600 (R)

The true cost of this 6 percent add-on installment repayment loan can be computed approximately, but quickly, as follows:

$$A = R \left[\frac{1 - (1 + i/m)^{-nm}}{i/m} \right]$$

where A = present value of a series of equal payments (annuity)
i = annual or nominal interest rate
m = number of times interest is compounded per year

R = amount of each regular future periodic payment

n = number of years

Here

$$\left[\frac{1 - (1 + i/m)^{-5}}{i/m}\right] = \frac{A}{R} = \frac{\$10,000}{\$2600} = 3.84615$$

Checking the Appendix 1 tables under the column "What $1 payable periodically is worth today," on the line for five periods, we find that the factor 3.8461 lies between 9 and 10 percent. The value of the factor for 9 percent is 3.889151, and for 10 percent it is 3.790786. Then, by interpolation, the interest rate is approximately 9.44 percent (by computer, 9.4349 percent). This result may be checked by applying the formula:

$$A = R \left[\frac{1 - (1 + i/m)^{-nm}}{i/m}\right]$$

$$= \$2600 \left(\frac{1 - 1.0944^{-5}}{0.0944}\right) = \$10,000.63$$

The *true rate* of 9.44 percent is *significantly higher* than is *implied* simply by the phrase "6 percent add-on."

The relationship between the APR and the quoted add-on installment repayment rate is not fixed. It varies according to the level of the rate, the number of repayments, and the time involved. One can obtain an idea of this varying relationship from the following table:

Number of repayments	Add-on rate (%)	APR (12 × monthly rate (%)
1	10.000	10.000
2	7.620	10.000
3	6.870	10.000
4	6.550	10.000
5	6.370	10.000
36	3.000	5.625
36	4.000	7.500
36	5.000	9.000
36	6.000	11.125
36	7.000	12.750
36	8.000	14.250

Any add-on rate, discount rate, etc., must be converted to a true APR in order to see the true cost (or profitability, for a lender) of a loan or investment. Add-on rates are used by banks, finance companies, and other firms in conjunction with installment repayment loans.

Example: finding the number of payments in an installment loan. Sally Tang wishes to buy a boat for $1000 and to borrow the entire sum. The APR that she will pay will depend on various factors, including the current money market, her personal financial condition, etc. Assume that the applicable APR is 15 percent. Sally can afford to pay monthly installments of $62.50 to retire the debt. How many monthly payments will she be required to make?

Refer to Fig. 9.1. The point at which the line extended vertically from 6.25 percent meets the line extended horizontally from 15 percent APR provides the solution. See the dashed lines on Fig. 9.1. Eighteen monthly payments are required. (The computer solution, using the FINANCIAL AND INTEREST CALCULATOR software published by the author, is 17.96 percent.)

Example: Finding the monthly payment. Franklin Pierce is willing to provide a loan of $1000 and requires 36 equal monthly repayments. He charges 10 percent APR. How much will the monthly payments be to repay the loan? Enter Fig. 9.1 at 10 percent APR, move horizontally to the curve for 36 monthly repayments, then vertically down to the bottom axis. About 3.25 percent of the original loan, that is, $32.50 per month, will be required.

This problem may also be solved by formula, as follows:

$$R = A \left[\frac{i/m}{1 - (1 + i/m)^{-nm}} \right]$$

where R = amount of each regular future periodic payment
$\quad i$ = periodic interest rate
$\quad m$ = number of times interest is compounded per year
$\quad n$ = number of years
$\quad A$ = present value of the series of equal payments

Here

$$R = \$1000 \left[\frac{0.00833}{1 - (1.00833)^{-36}} \right] = \$1000 \left(\frac{0.00833}{0.258172} \right)$$

$$= \$32.27 \text{ per month for 36 months}$$

The computer solution using the FINANCIAL AND INTEREST CALCULATOR is also $32.27.

Annual percentage rate

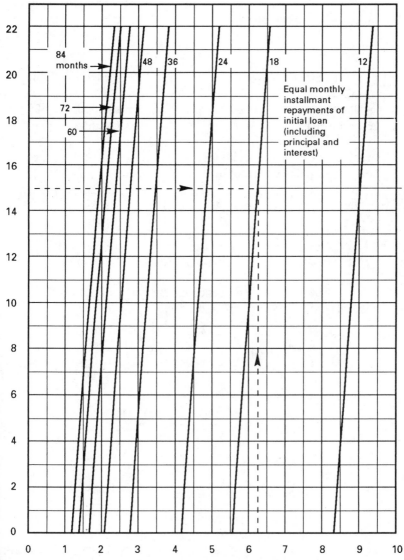

Monthly repayment as percent of initial loan
(to pay off loan in full with interest charged at the indicated annual percentage rate)

Figure 9.1. Installment loan repayments: 12 to 84 monthly repayments.

The factor for $\frac{5}{6}$ percent per month is not shown in Tables 1–14. However, 10 percent per year is shown. An approximate answer using Table 12 of Appendix 1 can be obtained based on 10 percent per year and three annual installment repayments, as follows:

$$R = \$1000 \ (0.4021) = \$402.10 \text{ per year}$$

The approximate monthly payment is then $402.10 divided by 12 to give $33.51 per month.

Example: Finding the APR of an add-on loan. Sue Smith obtains $1000 at 6 percent add-on, repayable in 36 equal monthly installments (n). Find the APR.

The amount of the note Ms. Smith must sign, and the monthly repayment amount, must first be found, as follows:

Cash to borrower	$1000 ($A$)
6 percent × 3 years	18%, add-on
Add-on interest (0.18 × $1000)	$180
Note is for ($1000 + $180)	$1,180
Monthly repayments ($1180/36 months)	$32.78 ($R$)

The APR, using Fig. 9.2, is 11.1 percent (see the dashed lines on Fig. 9.2).

Using formulas, the APR is found as follows:

$$A = R \left[\frac{1 - (1 + i/m)^{-nm}}{i/m} \right]$$

$$\$1000 = 32.78 \left[\frac{1 - (1 + i/m)^{-36}}{i/m} \right]$$

$$30.5064 = \left[\frac{1 - (1 + i/m)^{-36}}{i/m} \right]$$

Using Appendix 1, Table 2 (36 months), the factor (bracketed expression in the formula) for 1 percent per month is 30.1075. And Table 1 for $\frac{1}{2}$ percent shows 32.8710 as the factor. Our periodic rate lies between $\frac{1}{2}$ percent and 1 percent per month. Interpolation provides the approximate solution:

0.50%	32.8710	30.5064	32.8710
x	30.5064	−30.1075	−30.1075
1.00%	30.1075	0.3989	2.7635

Annual percentage rate

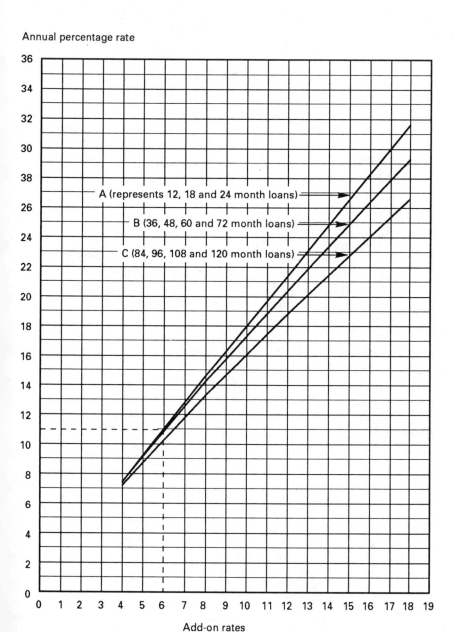

Add-on rates

Figure 9.2. Add-on loan rates converted to APR and vice versa.

$$\frac{0.3989}{2.7635} = \frac{x}{0.5}$$

$$x = 0.072173 \quad \text{or} \quad 7.217\%$$

$$x = 1.0 - 0.0721 = 0.9279\% \text{ per month}$$

$$0.9279\% \times 12 = 11.1348\% \text{ per year}$$

This is the APR for the loan. Solution by computer or formula is 11.082 percent, which is more accurate than interpolating to determine the result.

Prepaying an Installment Loan

Continuing the previous example ($1000 cash received, 36 monthly repayments of $32.78 each, APR about 11.1 percent), if the borrower wishes to repay the loan in full after having made, let us say, 12 of the 36 payments, how much will she be required to pay, and what, then, will be the APR she actually experiences?

When loans are prepaid, lenders use a "sum-of-the-digits" system (generally referred to as the *Rule of 78*) to determine how much the lender will retain of the interest calculated initially.

For the borrower, deductibility for income tax purposes of interest expense, calculated under the rule of 78, is subject to the instructions of Revenue Procedures 84-30, 84-27, and 84-28. Form 3115 also must be filed with the borrower's tax return.

The interest (i) initially calculated was $180. The sum of the digits of the 36 monthly installments is:

$$36 + 35 + 34 \ldots +1 = 666$$

The *sum of the digits* formula is

$$X = \left(\frac{N+1}{2}\right)(N)$$

where N = number of periodic payments
       X = sum of the digits for the originally scheduled term of the loan

In this example,

$$X = \left(\frac{36+1}{2}\right)(36) = 666$$

Twelve installment payments have been made. To find the portion of the $180 interest that is *unearned* by the lender (and is to be credited to the borrower) as the result of the prepayment of the loan, deduct 12 (payments made, or months elapsed) from the 36-month original term, that is, 24. The formula for the *rule of 78* or *sum-of-the-digits method of determining unearned interest* is

$$X_u = \left(\frac{U+1}{2}\right)(U)$$

where X = sum of the digits (666)

N = number of payments

U = months for which interest is unearned (24)

I = interest originally charged by the lender for the full term

The sum of the digits (X_u) for U, that is, $24 + 23 + \ldots + 1$ is:

$$X_u = \left(\frac{U+1}{2}\right)(U) = \left(\frac{24+1}{2}\right)(24) = 300$$

The formula for the unearned interest, I_u, (to be paid by the lender to the borrower) is

$$I_u = \frac{X_u}{X}(I) = \frac{300}{666}(\$180) = \$81.08$$

The payoff amount, which the lender requires of the borrower, is found as follows:

Original note	$1180.00
Less: payments made (12 × $32.78).....................	− 393.36
Balance	$ 786.64
Less: unearned interest (I_u)	− 81.08
Net to Pay Off Loan	$ 705.56

The APR if the loan is thus prepaid is

$$A = R\left[\frac{1 - (1 + i/m)^{-nm}}{i/m}\right] + x\left[1 + \left(\frac{i}{m}\right)\right]^{-nm}$$

where A = cash received ($1000)

i = periodic interest rate

m = number of payments and times interest is compounded per year (12)

R = amount of each regular future periodic payment ($32.78)

n = number of years (1)

$m \times i$ = what we seek to find, the APR

x = the payment amount to extinguish the debt ($705.56)

$$\$1000 = 32.78 \left[\frac{1 - (1 + i/m)^{-12}}{i/m} \right] + 705.56 \left[1 + \left(\frac{i}{m}\right) \right]^{-12}$$

$$30.5064 = \left[\frac{1 - (1 + i/m)^{-12}}{i/m} \right] + 21.5241 \left[1 + \left(\frac{i}{m}\right) \right]^{-12}$$

$$i = 0.0095$$

$12i$ = about 11.4%, the APR

The solution is found by trial and error by substituting values for i in the right-hand side of the equation until the value substituted causes the right side of the equation to equal 30.5064.

Thus, the APR effectively charged the borrower (11.4 percent) at prepayment is slightly higher than that of the APR (11.1 percent) which would have been applicable had the loan been carried to maturity.

In the preceding example, a 36-month loan was prepaid after 12 months, with the borrower's refund of prepaid interest calculated by the sum-of-the-digits method. But what if the borrower prepaid even earlier, after only 6 months, or later, after 24 months? *When the borrower's refund is determined by the sum-of-the-digits or rule of 78 method, the earlier the borrower repays the loan, the higher is the effective annual percentage rate (APR) to the lender.* In the preceding example (36-month add-on loan), the facts are as follows:

Month in which prepayment occurs	APR (or IRR)
6	11.555%
12	11.400%
24	11.181%
36	11.135%

No particular position has been taken by the Federal Reserve for or against the rule of 78, and any special disclosure of the higher costs to borrowers that can result from prepayment, according to Tim Zink, Senior Economist at the Federal Reserve Bank of St. Louis. A cursory check of loan documents used by various banks shows that the rule of 78 is in current use, and *borrowers are not advised of the higher APR that will result from prepayment.*

The popularity (among lenders, certainly, not borrowers) of add-on and discount loans has diminished in the United States due to the requirements of Regulation Z of the U.S. Federal Reserve Board (enacted July 1, 1969) to disclose the APR. APR and IRR (discussed throughout much of the remainder of the book) are virtually synonymous. *Think of APR as IRR calculated using a compounding frequency equal to whatever the shortest time interval is that occurs between various payments* at irregular time intervals.

It benefits a U.S. lender very little, as a sales gimmick, to magnanimously offer a borrower a 6 percent add-on loan, when the law requires the lender to disclose that the APR is really approximately double that. The rule of 78 applies to refunding prepaid interest charges (evolving from such loans as add-ons and discounts), and the higher costs to borrowers resulting from the use of the rule of 78 by lenders *ought* to be required disclosure.

The rule of 78 obtains its name from applying the sum-of-the-digits method to a 1-year loan, the sum of the digits in such event (12 + 11 + ... + 1) being 78.

Example: Finding the APR of a discount note. Stacey Sumner needs $1000, which a bank agrees to lend her at 6 percent, discount, repayable in 36 equal monthly installments. The bank requires her to sign a note for $1219.51, calculated as follows:

Cash to be borrowed	$1000 (A)
The discount, 6% × 3 years	18%
100% − 18% discount	82%
$1000/0.82, the amount of the note	$1219.51
Monthly repayments ($1219.51/36 months)	$33.87
The stated discount rate	6%

The APR can be determined in several ways. Using Fig. 9.3, enter the figure on the horizontal axis at the 6 percent discount rate. Proceed vertically to the 36-month curve, then horizontally to the left to the vertical axis, where the APR is found to be about 12 percent.

The APR can also be found by formula:

$$A = R \left[\frac{1 - (1 + i/m)^{-nm}}{i/m} \right]$$

$$\$1000 = 33.78 \left[\frac{1 - (1 + i/m)^{-36}}{i/m} \right]$$

$$\left[\frac{1 - (1 + i/m)^{-36}}{i/m} \right] = 29.5246$$

Annual percentage rate

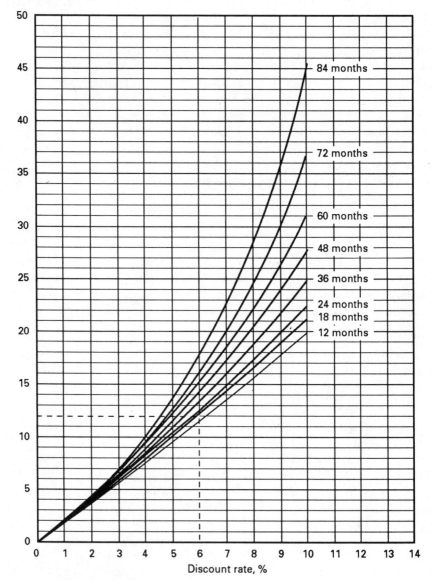

Figure 9.3. Discount rates converted to APR and vice versa.

Checking the Appendix 1 tables, one finds for the factor in brackets, for 36 periods,

$$1\% = 30.1075$$

$$1\tfrac{1}{2}\% = 27.6607$$

$$\text{Actual factor} = 29.5246$$

Thus the monthly APR is between 1 and $1\tfrac{1}{2}$ percent. Interpolation produces:

30.1075	1.0%
29.5246	y
27.6607	1.5%

$$\frac{1.8369}{2.4468} = \frac{x}{0.5}$$

$$x = 0.38089$$

The monthly rate, y is 1.5 percent – 0.38089, that is, 1.1192 percent. A monthly rate of 1.1192 percent times 12 months is the APR of 13.43 percent. (The computer solution, using THE FINANCIAL AND INTEREST CALCULATOR, is 13.3649 percent.)

Biweekly Repayment of Mortgage Loans

"Join our biweekly mortgage-saver system and save $94,000 in payments for every $100,000 of loan." So reads the come-on. This is what it is all about.

Normally, mortgage loans are repaid on a monthly basis, that is, 12 payments per year. If the monthly loan payment is $500, then total annual payments of principal and interest are $6000.

However, if payments are made biweekly, the $250 is paid every 2 weeks. Total annual payments are 26 × $250, or $6500.

Two forces are at work in the biweekly system: First, payments are increased by 8.333 percent per year (e.g., $6500 versus $6000); second, payments are made about half a month sooner. The effect of these two forces is a substantially faster payoff of the loan. For example, a $100,000 loan at 10 percent annual interest requires monthly payments of principal and interest of $877.57 to pay off in 30 years. If the payments are halved but made every other week, the payment becomes $438.79, the periodic rate is 0.1 ÷ 26 times per year, or 0.00385, and the loan pays off in only 21 years.

Promoters of this biweekly payment system will point out that it "saves you" 9 years of payments, that is, 108 payments of $877.57, a purported "savings" of $94,778 in payments of principal and interest. and these same promoters have some method of charging you for a service that allows you to reap these "savings."

However, there really aren't any savings at all. No matter how you look at it, whether you have a customary loan or a biweekly one, you are still paying the same 10 percent annual rate of interest on the unpaid balance of your loan. *With the biweekly system you spend 8.333 percent more and you pay a little sooner.* The extra $877.57 in annual payments under the biweekly payment approach accounts for the bulk of the reduction in the time it takes to pay off the loan. If the extra $877.57 annual payment ($877.57 ÷ 52 = $16.8764 per week) were simply put into a savings account earning 10 percent per year (periodic weekly rate of 0.1 ÷ 52 = 0.00192) for 30 years [(52)(30) = 1560 weeks], then the value of the savings account after 30 years will be $166,982.17.

There is another way to look at this matter. The future "savings" of $877.57 per month is from the 253rd month to the 360th month. The following time line presents the information:

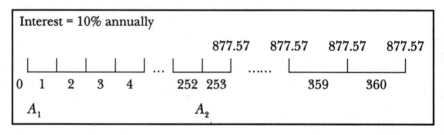

The present value, today, of the future savings is determined as follows. The value of A_2 is the present value of an annuity of 108 payments of $877.57, each discounted at 10 percent, compounded monthly. This is $62,333.23. And the value today (at A_1) is the value of the $62,333.23 discounted for 252 monthly periods at 10 percent, compounded monthly. This is $7700. *Thus $7700 is the present value, today, of the future savings.*

Now, what does it *cost* to obtain those savings? The cost is $16.8764 per week for 19 years and 1 month, that is, 992 weeks. The following time line shows present value:

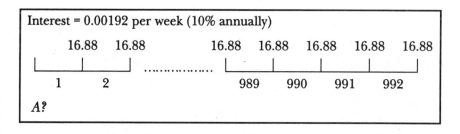

The cost in terms of present value of the weekly payments of $16.88 is $7470.81. Also, there is the additional cost of having to pay $877.57 one-half month early each and every month for 21 years. Interest cost for one month is $877.57 × 0.1/12 = $7.313. So interest on $877.57 for ½ month is $3.65654. The extra cost from paying ½ month earlier each month is the present value of an annuity of $3.65654 for 252 months at 10 percent nominal, compounded monthly, or $384. Further, the two cost elements, $7471 + $384 = $7855, approximate the $7700 present value of the benefit of 9 years less in future payments. (The slight differences between cost and benefits are due to rounding of numbers that were used in the calculations.) In other words, the *benefit and the cost are about equal.* The old saying, "You pay for what you get," holds true in the case of biweekly mortgages.

Adjustable-Rate and Graduated-Payment Mortgages

Long-term mortgage lenders have suffered great financial reverses in periods of high short-term interest rates because of their fixed-rate loan portfolios. When the fixed-rate loans happen to be at lower rates than current short-term rates, the lenders face a profit squeeze as their cost of funds exceeds their income from the low-interest fixed-rate assets. Adjustable-rate and graduated-payment loans are means of helping the lenders match their cost of funds to their income.

The interest rate on an adjustable-rate mortgage (ARM) is adjusted periodically, usually based on an index such as short-term Treasury bill rates. The provisions of an ARM vary considerably from lender to lender. The rates may be adjusted annually over a 5-year period and thereafter remain unchanged, or they may remain fixed for one or more years and then be adjusted either annually or at some other interval. Frequently, the change in interest rate is capped and is limited to no more than two percentage points per year and 6 percent over the life of the loan. Some ARMs may be convertible to a fixed-rate loan at certain times and for specified fees.

Why do people accept ARMs when in a period of rising rates the cost of the loan will frequently increase? One reason is that lenders push them. Another is that ARMs often carry a lower (than fixed-rate) initial interest rate. The low initial rate is sometimes called a "teaser." In the retail business it would be called a "loss leader."

The interest rate on a *graduated-payment mortgage* (GPM) can be either fixed or adjustable. Payments on GPMs in the early years are less than for conventional loans, then gradually increase and level off after about 5 years. GPMs may offer some benefit to borrowers who reasonably expect to have a continuously increasing income. But if the expected increase in income does not occur, there could be problems.

To Refinance or Not to Refinance, That Is the Question

Barnard Baruch, the great financier and advisor to Presidents, when asked for his views of the market, is reported to have said: "It will fluctuate my good man, it will fluctuate." As markets fluctuate, so do interest rates. And as interest rates decline from time to time, borrowers are well advised to consider whether it is profitable to refinance their loans. The same principles are involved in refinancing mortgage or other loans as are operative in the municipal, government, and corporate bond markets. Based on the interplay between lower rates and the cost of effecting the transaction, there is a point at which it becomes profitable for the borrower to pay off the old loan with the proceeds of a new one.

The Texas Instruments (TI) *Application Guide for the Financial Investment Analyst* (a business calculator) poses the following example.

"Four years ago, a buyer financed a home with a 30-year, *12* percent, fixed-rate mortgage for the amount of $140,000. The monthly payments are $1440.06, and the loan carries a penalty of 1 percent of the loan balance if paid off before it matures.

"Now mortgage rates have dropped, and the buyer can refinance the balance of $137,547.44 over 25 years at $9\frac{7}{8}$ percent. The monthly payments will be $1237.79, and the new loan carries a 1.5 percent penalty if paid off before it matures.

"Refinancing charges include $3000 in origination and other fees, 2 points of the new loan amount, and the 1 percent penalty for paying off the existing loan.

"Is the refinancing option favorable if *the buyer plans to sell the home in 5 years* and the buyer's other investments earn an average of 8 percent interest compounded monthly?"

Table 9.1 summarizes the above information.

Refinancing Strategy

The strategy is to find the present value of the future costs of both loans. If the present value of the cost of the proposed loan is less than that of the existing loan, it is profitable to refinance. The discount rate used in determining present value is the presumed rate that could be earned by the borrower with the savings that result from the refinancing. In other words, the discount rate is the rate at which the borrower could presumably invest the savings as they occur. Determination of the present value requires calculating the outstanding principal balance on the loans on dates other than the maturity date of the loan. For this example, the calculation is shown in Table 9.2. On the basis just described, the present value of the savings that will result from refinancing the loan is $4379.72 at a discount rate of 8 percent per year. In other words, the refinancing benefit is 8 percent on the improved cash flows and $4379.72 in addition. But how much more is that?

Another way of evaluating the refinancing proposal is to compare the IRRs of the two loans. The IRRs for the two loans and the cash flows that are relevant in calculating the IRR are shown in Table 9.1. The actual calculation is left to the reader. The IRR in the case of a loan is akin to the APR (annual percentage rate). Obviously, the lower the IRR or APR, the better it is for the borrower. In this case, the IRR for the existing loan is 12.14 percent; for the refinancing proposal the IRR is 11.50 percent. The loan with the lower IRR, the proposed loan, is the better choice. Thus the IRR or APR tells us the same thing as the TI approach: Refinance! Table 9.3 shows yet another approach, analyzing the incremental cash flows. There it is shown that the IRR of the incremental cash flows is over 27 percent on the new money employed in refinancing (using the TI approach where new money is employed to pay for the refinancing costs).

The benefits of refinancing and a summary of the present value approach to analyzing another situation *where the monthly payments are kept constant and the new loan is $160,024* are shown in Table 9.4 and Fig. 9.4, Part A. The column "Incremental difference" shows the change in cash flows that result from refinancing. The net present value of $2029 resulting from refinancing (after 8 percent discounting) shows that refinancing is desirable. The present value of $2029 clearly applies to the incremental cash flows. Thus, it is seen that the end result of finding the present value of the cash flows of each loan (old and proposed) is the same as finding the present value of the incremental cash flows. This means that one could set aside the necessary funds, $12,872, to fund (at 8 percent growth, compounded monthly) the future additional costs of the refinancing ($19,177 sixty months hence) and still have left over, currently, the present value savings from refinancing of $2029.

Table 9.1. Whether to Refinance a Mortgage Loan: Texas Instruments Example

	Original loan	Proposed loan	Incrementa new cash
Given information:			
Present balance of loan	$137,547.44		
Monthly payment of principal and interest	$1,440.06	$1,237.79	
Stated interest rate on loan	12.000%	9.875%	
Years remaining until maturity of loan	26	25	
Original loan amount at inception of loan	$140,000.00	$137,547.44	
Number of years from now that loan will be paid off when house is sold	5	5	
Calculated information (See Table 9.2):			
Outstanding principal 5 years hence	$132,272.78	$129,374.68	
Payoff fees of 1% and 1½ on loans	1,322.73	1,940.62	
Principal in 5 years with payoff fee	$133,595.51	$131,315.30	
Costs to refinance:			
Origination fee		3,000.00	
Points (2%) of new loan amount		2,750.95	
Payoff fee on existing loan (1%)		1,375.47	
Total out-of-pocket costs		$7,126.42	
Summary of cash flows:	$137,547.44	$137,547.44	
Loan fees paid at inception		(7,126.42)	
Total initial cash flow	$137,547.44	$130,421.02	$(7,126.4
Monthly cash flows for 59 months	(1,440.06)	(1,237.79)	202.2
Cash flow in sixtieth month:			
Monthly payment	(1,440.06)	(1,237.79)	
Loan payoff	(133,595.51)	(131,315.30)	
Total in sixtieth month	$(135,035.57)	$(132,553.09)	$2,482.4
TI's NPV calculation based on these cash flows:			
Cash flow 0	0.00	$(7,126.42)	
Cash flows 1–50	$(1,440.06)	(1,237.79)	
Cash flow 60	(135,035.57)	(132,553.09)	
Discount rate used	8.00%	8.00%	
Net present value	$(160,692.20)	$(156,312.48)	
Savings by refinancing		4,379.72	
Reconciliation of TI method:			
Present value of $1,440.06 – $1,237.79 savings per month at 8% annual rate for 60 months ($202.27 savings per month)		$9,975.64	
Less: Out-of-pocket transaction costs		(7,126.42)	
Plus: Present value of savings on payoff in 5 years ($133,595.51 - 131,315.30) at 8%		1,530.50	
Total savings (at present value)		$4,379.72	
Other solutions:			
IRR (using total initial cash flow)	12.14%	11.50%	

*The respective present values are $89,670.70 and $88,140.20, a difference of $1,530.50.

Table 9.2. Finding Outstanding Principal on a Loan

The outstanding principal on a loan is determined by finding the present value of the remaining payments at the date on which the outstanding principal is sought. In the case of the refinancing situation presented in Table 9.1, the calculation is as follows:

	Original loan	Proposed new loan
Monthly payment amount	$1,440.06	$1,237.79
Number of months remaining at that point, 5 years hence	252	240
Discount rate	12.00%	9.875%
Present value factor*	91.8527	104.5200
Outstanding principal (monthly payment amount × present value factor)	$132,273	$129,374

*The present value factor is

$$\frac{1 - (1 + i/m)^{-nm}}{i/m}$$

The present value factor for an annuity may also be found in Appendix 1 under the column "Present worth of 1 per period."

The Texas Instruments Calculator Approach

In the author's opinion, the TI approach is somewhat unrealistic in assuming that the borrower will pay the out-of-pocket costs of the new loan in cash. In reality, customary practice and experience indicate that these costs will be included in the face amount of the new and larger loan. It is also likely that the borrower will seek to obtain some immediate cash flow benefit from the refinancing by increasing the size of the new loan beyond that necessary merely to pay the costs associated with refinancing.

The TI method, employed in Part B of Fig 9.4, is shown for comparison. The TI method, as we have seen, requires the borrower to part with cash to fund certain transaction costs and, circumstances permitting, results in a *lower* monthly payment than is required by the old loan. Here the loan balance of the existing loan is kept constant. Part B also shows that it is

Table 9.3. IRR of Refinancing Savings

Another means of approaching the question of refinancing is to look at the incremental changes that result from the refinancing—that is, the additional cash spent or the additional cash saved.

In the case of the TI example, the incremental changes are shown in Table 9.1 in the last column, under the heading "Incremental new cash."

The end result of the refinancing (using the TI example) is an IRR of 27.62% on the incremental new funds employed.

Table 9.4. Reconciliation of Net Present Value

	Existing loan retained	Refinance new	Incremental difference	When?
Outstanding loan principal at end, including payoff fee	$133,596	$152,773	($19,177)	60 months
Monthly payments	1,440	1,440	0	
Cash received at loan closing	0	14,900	14,900	Now

New loan principal	$160,024	
Less:		
Origination fees	(3,000)	
Points	(3,200)	
Payoff an old loan	(1,375)	
Total fees	$(7,576)	
New loan less fees	152,448	
Old loan principal	137,547	
Plus: Payoff fee	0.00	see above
Total old loan	$137,547	
Net new money	14,900	

Net present value at 8% discount	$(19,142)	$(4,431)	$15,089	
IRR	n/a	9.970%	5.057%	
Discount factor for 60 months at 8% per year			0.67121	
Outstanding loan to be repaid 60 months hence of $19,177 discounted at 8% per year				$(12,872)
Cash in pocket from refinancing at closing				14,900
Net present value				$ 2,029

favorable to refinance. The borrower expends $7126 to pay points, origination fees, and the payoff fee on the old loan. The loan amount remains the same at $137,547.44, but the monthly principal-and-interest payment declines to $1237.79. At a discount rate of 8 percent for determining present value, the transaction provides a gain of $4380 in current dollars.

After-Tax Results of Refinancing

The after-tax results of refinancing, like the after-tax results of almost all financial decisions, are the important consideration. After-tax refinancing results are automatically calculated in a few seconds using the author's computer spreadsheet program, MORTGAGE LOANS—IS IT TIME TO REFINANCE?, a printout from which is shown as Fig. 9.5. It computes the benefits or cost taking taxes into consideration. The example shown is for a borrower in a 30 percent tax bracket. After-tax analysis produces a vast

Two approaches to refinancing are used: part A, where the monthly loan payment is kept constant, the new loan principal exceeds that of the old, and the borrower puts cash in his or her pocket as the result of the refinancing (after deducting all associated costs); and Part B, where the loan principal amount is kept constant, the monthly payments are reduced with the new loan, and the borrower expends cash (at the time of refinancing) to pay the applicable fees.

The software determines which loan (existing or proposed) has the lowest discounted present value of after-tax costs. The loan with the lower costs is the desired loan. If it is the proposed loan, then refinancing is in order and will be profitable to the borrower.

← indicates that numeric entry by the user is required, and PV indicates the present value. All numbers not marked with an arrow are computed by the software.

Data Entry Section

0.0%	←	tax bracket of borrower for ordinary income
8.000%	←	annual interest rate for determining PV of both loans
		[This is the after-tax rate at which savings from refinancing can be invested by the borrower (the PV rate)]
5	←	number of years loans are likely to be kept (before sale of house, etc.)

Existing Loan

360	←	number of months of original loan
$1,440.06	←	monthly payment (pretax)
312	←	months remaining on existing loan
$137,547.44	←	present loan balance
1.00%	←	payoff penalty as percent of present loan balance
12.00%	←	interest rate per year on original loan

Possible New Loan

25	←	years for amortizing new loan
9.875%	←	interest rate per year on possible new loan
$1,237.79		monthly payment with no increase in loan size

(Continued)

Figure 9.4. To refinance or not ... pretax. (*SOURCE: Larry Rosen Co., copyright © 1990.*)

Costs to Obtain the New Loan

$3,000.00	← origination fees ($) including appraisal
2.00%	← points (as percent of new loan amount)
1.50%	← payoff penalty on new loan

Part A: Retain the same monthly payment amount for the new loan and increase the loan size

$132,273	Loan balance of existing loan at payoff 60 months hence when 252.0 payments remain
133,596	Loan balance of existing loan at payoff 60 months hence with payoff fees
71,022	PV of monthly payments of existing loan with payoff 60 months hence at discount rate of 8.000%
89,671	PV of loan balance less fees with payoff 60 months hence at discount rate of 8.000%
$160,693	Total PV of existing loan with repayment in 60 months
$160,023.74	New loan amount, which can be borrowed for 300.0 months with monthly payments of $1440.06 and interest of 9.875% per year
150,515	Loan balance of proposed loan at payoff 60 months hence when 240.0 payments remain
152,773	Loan balance of proposed loan with payoff fees of 1.500%
71,022	PV of monthly payments of proposed loan with payoff 60 months hence at 8.000% per year
102,543	PV of new loan less fees with payoff 60 months hence at 8.000% per year
$173,564	Total PV of proposed loan before current transaction costs and benefits of new cash
$160,693	Total PV of existing loan (cost to keep existing loan)
$173,564	Total PV of proposed loan (cost if refinanced)
$(12,872)	Preliminary PV of cost of existing loan less PV of cost of new loan (favorable to refinance if plus) (before considering new cash received and cash expended at closing.)
$137,547.79	Present balance of existing loan at 12.000% for 312.0 months

Figure 9.4. (Continued)

<u>160,023.74</u>	New loan amount, which can be borrowed for 300 months with monthly payments of $1440.06 and interest of 9.875% per year
22,475.95	Difference; if negative, can't profitably refinance
$ 6,200.47	Total cost of loan origination fee and points on new loan amount
$153,823.27	New loan less costs (but before paying off the existing loan and payoff fees)
<u>138,922.91</u>	Old loan plus payoff penalty of $1,375 on existing loan
$ 14,900.35	After Paying off old loan including payoff fee on old loan. This is the present value of the new loan less costs and repayment of the old loan. This is how much money the borrower can put in his or her pocket from refinancing and still have the same monthly principal and interest payment of 1,440.06 per month.
<u>(12,871.60)</u>	Preliminary PV of new loan
$ <u>2,028.75</u>	Total present value of refinancing (favorable if plus)

Part B: Loan principal remains unchanged with the new loan, and the borrower must expend cash to pay fees (This is the method used by Texas Instruments)

Existing loan:

$132,273	Loan balance of existing loan at payoff 60 months hence when 252.0 payments remain
133,596	Loan balance of existing loan at payoff 60 months hence with payoff fees
71,022	PV of monthly payments of existing loan with payoff 60 months hence
<u>89,671</u>	PV of loan balance less fees with payoff 60 months hence
$160,693	Total PV of existing loan

Proposed New Loan:

$129,374	Loan balance of proposed loan at payoff 60 months hence when 240.0 payments remain
131,315	Loan balance of proposed loan with payoff fees of 1.500%

(Continued)

Figure 9.4. *(Continued)*

61,046	PV of monthly payments of existing loan with payoff 60 months hence at 8.000% per year
88,140	PV of new loan including fees with payoff 60 months hence at 8.000% per year
7,126	PV of current costs (origination, points, etc.) (paid in cash by the borrower)
$156,313	Total PV of proposed loan

Summary of Part B:

$160,693	Total PV of existing loan (cost to keep existing loan)
$156,313	Total PV of proposed loan (cost if refinanced)
$ 4,380	Existing PV less proposed PV: favorable if plus; unfavorable if minus (This is the present value of refinancing.)

Figure 9.4. *(Continued)*

change in the results. (The software can be obtained directly from the publisher, Larry Rosen Co., 7008 Springdale Road, Louisville, KY 40241.) The spreadsheet program calculates in seconds a very complex problem that would otherwise take a minimum of hours to compute.

The refinancing is analyzed based on keeping the *same monthly payment* for the new loan as for the old one. Circumstances permitting, this allows new cash to be gained by the borrower. This approach is shown in Part A of Fig. 9.4. The loan amount for the new loan exceeds that of the old loan. The borrower walks away from the refinancing closing with $14,902 in cash.

In terms of the example, the refinancing is favorable in that the borrower pays off the old loan, all costs of refinancing, and puts $14,902 in his or her pocket. Further, the monthly payment on the new loan remains unchanged at $1440.06, and the new, larger loan ($160,023.74) is paid off in 25 years (compared to 26 years for the old loan). Note, however, that the new loan payoff including penalty at the end of 60 months is $152,773 versus only $133,596 for the existing loan. At a discount rate for determining present value of 8 percent, the transaction provides a gain of $2028.75 in current dollars on a zero-tax basis as shown in Fig. 9.4. However, on an *after-tax basis*, as shown in Fig. 9.5, the gain jumps to $2270.83 (after discounting the cash flows at 8 percent).

The foregoing explanation applies to all loans, including level-payment loans (LPLs), graduated-payment mortgages (GPMs), price-level-adjusted mortgages (PLAMs), and shared-appreciation mortgage loans (SAMs).

An LPL has a fixed monthly payment that remains the same throughout the life of the loan. The loan may or may not be self-amortizing. In a

Introduction:
The approach to refinancing is as follows: the monthly loan payment is kept constant, – the new loan principal exceeds that of the old loan; and the borrower puts cash in his/her pocket as the result of the refinancing.

Method: Determine which loan (existing or proposed) has the lowest present value of after-tax costs. The loan with the lowest discount present value of after-tax costs is the desired loan. If it is the proposed loan, the refinancing is in order and will be profitable. Effect is given to the tax savings resulting from deductibles as follows:

Currently deductible: prepayment penalty	non-deductible: origination fee appraisal fee	Deductible ratably over loan life interest and 'points' paid prepaid interest

Enter data only in the section which follows:
PV indicates the "present value."

← indicates numeric entry by user is required

Data Entry Section:

30.0%	←	tax bracket of borrower for ordinary income
8.000%	←	annual interest rate for determining PV of both loans. This is the rate at which the savings from refinancing can be invested by the borrower.
5	←	number of years loans are to be kept before sale of the property, new financing, etc.
1	←	Starting month (1 to 12) in first year

Existing Loan Data Entry:

360	←	number of months of original loan
1,440.06	←	monthly payments (pre-tax)
312	←	months remaining on existing loan at starting month
26.0		no entry (whole years remaining rounded up)
$137,547.44	←	present loan balance (at starting month)
1.00%	←	pay-off penalty as % of the loan balance at pay-off time.
12.000%	←	interest rate per year on original loan
1.000%		no entry (rate per month)
1.010		no entry (1 plus rate per month)

(Continued)

Figure 9.5. To refinance or not ... after tax. (SOURCE: *Mortgage Loans–Is It Time to Refinance, Larry Rosen Co., copyright © 1990.*)

4	no entry (years elapsed since loan origination)
60	no entry (cut-off month for existing loan)
70.000%	no entry (retention % of income after tax)
132,273	no entry (cut-off months; ending balance)
708	no entry (cut-off month)

Proposed New Loan

1,440.06	no entry (unless monthly payment on new loan is to be different from that of existing loan)
25 ←	years for amortizing new loan 300 total months
9.875% ←	interest rate per year on possible new loan
1,237.79	no entry: monthly pmt if no increase in loan size per mo
160,024	no entry: NEW LOAN AMOUNT
60	no entry: (cut-off month for proposed loan)
$3,000.00 ←	origination fees ($) including appraisal, etc.
2.00% ←	points as % of new loan amount
1.50% ←	pay-off penalty on new loan
150,515	no entry: balance at cut-off date

[this concludes the data entry section: no user entries beyond this]

Retains the same monthly payment amount for the new loan and increases the loan size.

				Existing Loan				
Year no.	No. mos.	Loan balance at beg. of the year	Loan balance at end of the year	Reduction in loan principal for the year	Interest for the year	After tax pmts for year	Discount factor till beginning	PV of after tax pmts
1	12	137,547	136,729	(819)	16,462	12,342	11.4958	11,824
2	12	136,729	135,806	(923)	16,358	12,373	10.6148	10,945
3	12	135,806	134,766	(1,040)	16,241	12,409	9.8013	10,135
4	12	134,766	133,594	(1,172)	16,109	12,448	9.0501	9,388
5	12	133,594	132,273	(1,321)	15,960	12,493	8.3565	8,700
6	0	0	0	0	0	0	0.0000	0
40	0	0	0	0	0	0	0.0000	0
totals				(5,274)	81,130	62,065		50,991

total payments	86,404		after tax payments	62,065
principal	(5,274)		interest after tax	(56,791)
interest	(81,130)		principal	(5,274)
Reconciliation	(0)			(0)

Figure 9.5. (Continued)

		Proposed Loan						
Year no.	No. mos.	Loan balance at beg. of the year	Loan balance at end of the year	Reduction in loan principal for the year	Interest for the year	After tax pmts for year	Discount factor till beginning	PV of after tax pmts
1	12	160,024	158,477	(1,547)	15,734	12,561	11.4958	12,033
2	12	158,477	156,770	(1,707)	15,574	12,609	10.6148	11,153
3	12	156,770	154,886	(1,883)	15,397	12,662	9.8013	10,342
4	12	154,886	152,808	(2,078)	15,203	12,720	9.0501	9,593
5	12	152,808	150,515	(2,293)	14,988	12,784	8.3565	8,903
6	0	0	0	0	(150,015)	0	150,015	0.0000	0
40	0	0	0	0	0	0	0.0000	0
totals						76,895	213,850	52,023

Present Value Analysis of Refinancing		
	Existing loan	Proposed loan
PV of monthly payments (After Tax)	50,991	52,023
Loan balance at pay-off	132,273	150,515
Penalty for pay-off	1,323	2,258
Pay-off amt 60 mos. hence	133,596	152,773
Amts due 60 mos. hence		
PV of loan principal	88,783	101,027
PV of prepayment penalty (A.T.)	621	1,061
PV of loan principal pmt (after tax)	89,405	102,088
Preliminary PV of loans	140,396	154,111
Difference in PV of loans (above)		(13,716)
Proceeds of refinancing		160,024
Repay old loan		(137,547)
Current costs (not incl. in PV above)		

	Gross	PV Tax Savings	
Prepay penalty on existing loan	(1,375)	413	(963)
Points charged on new loan	(3,200)	673	(2,527)
Origination fees on new loan	(3,000)	0	(3,000)

TOTAL PRESENT BENEFIT (+) COST (-) OF
REFINANCING   2,270.83

(at present value discount rate of 8.000% per year)

Cash Flow Summary from Refinancing:	
Current:	
Proceeds of new loan	$160,024
Less: old loan balance	(137,547)
Less: pay-off penalty on old	(1,375)
Less: origination fees	(3,000)
Less: 'points'	(3,200)
Current new cash from refinancing	14,902

(Continued)

Figure 9.5. (Continued)

Future:	
Old loan monthly payment of principal and interest	1,440
Less: new loan monthly payment	(1,440)
Difference in monthly payments	0
Pay-off of Loans:	
Pay-off balance of old loan, including penalty	133,596
Pay-off balance of new loan, including penalty	152,773
Difference in pay-off amounts	(19,177)

Figure 9.5. (Continued)

self-amortizing loan the entire loan principal is repaid by the fixed monthly payments. A loan which is not self-amortizing is often called a "balloon loan" because a balance remains at maturity which has not been paid off by the regular monthly payments. The largest balloon loan would be an "interest-only loan" where fixed payment consist of only interest on the outstanding balance, without any amortization of principal.

With a GPM the early payments are reduced below those on a fixed-payment loan and later payments are raised above the level of standard loan payments. A GPM normally bears the same rate of interest as an LPL. for a significant number of years, commencing at loan inception, the annual payments are less than the interest charges and the deficiency is charged to the loan principal, which rises each year (instead of falling as in an LPL). Thus, "negative amortization" occurs for a period of years. Eventually, however, the situation reverses and the loan balance is amortized over the remainder of the loan term.

A PLAM carries a nominal interest rate that is usually quite low—say, 3 percent—and periodically the remaining outstanding balance of the loan is adjusted (upward) by the amount of inflation that has occurred since the last adjustment, and the payments are then adjusted to amortize the loan over its remaining life. The PLAM is also characterized by negative amortization for a significant number of years.

A SAM also provides a low nominal rate of interest; in return, the lender receives a share of the appreciation of the mortgage property. The size of the share is negotiable. The lower the nominal rate of interest charged, the higher is the likely share of appreciation taken by the lender. The probable outside limit on the share of the appreciation demanded by the lender is, at loan inception, the ratio of the loan to the value of the property.

Income tax effects become quite complicated for GPMs, PLAMs, and SAMs. For cash-basis (as opposed to accrual-basis) taxpayers, the IRS does not allow a deduction for interest until it is actually paid. For GPMs and PLAMs, only the interest actually paid during a year is deductible during that year. The excess interest (the amount of negative amortization) is not currrently deductible. For SAMs the contingent interest (interest resulting from the sharing aspect of the loan) is deductible only when the property is eventually sold, and then not if one refinances with a new conventional loan that covers the original SAM and contingent interest. Readers are cautioned to consult a professional tax advisor for the latest ramifications of the deductibility of interest payments.

The Federal Reserve APR Understates True Rate

The Truth-in-Lending Act (Title I of the Federal Consumer Protection Act of 1968) and Regulation Z (issued in 1969 by the Board of Governors of the Federal Reserve System) require disclosure by lenders to borrowers of interest rates charged on loans.

The annual percentage rate (APR), following the dictates of Regulation Z, causes the APR to *understate* the actual effective interest rate charged to the borrower. One Federal Reserve official states that this is not a problem because (to quote the act): "The informed use of credit results from an awareness of the cost thereof by consumers. It is the purpose of this title to assure a meaningful disclosure of credit terms so that the consumer will be able to *compare more readily* the various credit terms available to him and avoid the uninformed use of credit, and to protect the consumer against inaccurate and unfair credit billing and credit card practices." This official indicates that the error is unimportant because the same methodology is used in judging all loans and therefore applies to all lenders. This author disagrees and feels that *the Federal Reserve should revise Regulation Z* and require the disclosure of the *effective* annual rate as well as or in lieu of the *nominal* annual rate.

The basis of the understatement is the Regulation Z method of determining APR by multiplying the periodic interest rate by the number of compounding periods per year—e.g., multiplying by 12 when monthly payments are required or by 2 when payments are made semiannually. In other words, the APR, as defined, is the *nominal* annual rate rather than the *effective* annual rate.

Following the Regulation Z method (called the "actuarial method" by the Federal Reserve) will result in understating the true effective rate of interest charged in all cases where the loan payment frequency is less than annual.

A full discussion of this subject is contained in Anthony Herbst's article, "Truth in Lending, Regulation Z: Comments on Closed-End Contract Interest Rate Disclosure Requirements," in the *Journal of Bank Research*, vol. 3, no. 2, pp. 95–101, Summer 1972. This article also criticizes the Regulation Z policy of allowing (in undefined exceptional circumstances) an approximation method of determining the APR called the "constant-ratio" formula. Herbst compares the results of the constant-ratio formula to two other approximation methods, "the residuary method" and the "direct-ratio" method. He concludes that "if Title I and Regulation Z continue to require that the nominal rather than effective annual rate be disclosed, then use of the direct ratio approximation rather than the constant ratio formula should be allowed generally."

Example: Finding the APR by approved and unapproved methods. Suppose that $100,000 is borrowed and is repaid by 24 monthly payments of $4682 each. What is the APR (the IRR), the effective annual rate, and the rate by the constant-ratio, residuary, and direct-ratio methods?

APR or IRR. The periodic monthly rate which solves the APR or IRR equation is 0.00954697. Multiplied by 12 periods per year, this is a nominal annual rate of 11.4564 percent.

Effective annual rate. The effective annual rate is

$$(1 + 0.00954697)^{12} - 1 = 1.120775 - 1 = 12.0775\%$$

Note that the effective annual rate is 62.1 one-hundredths of 1 percent greater than the APR or IRR. Dr. Herbst reports in the article mentioned above that for any effective monthly interest rate of greater than 0.609 percent, the nominal rate understates the effective rate by more than 0.25 percent. (It is to be noted that the Truth in Lending Act states: "The disclosure of an APR is accurate ... if the rate disclosed is within a tolerance not greater than one-eighth of one percent more or less than the actual rate or rounded to the nearest one-fourth of one percent.")

Residuary method. The formula is

$$r_e = \frac{2\,(m)\,(I)}{P\,(t+1) - I\,(t-1)}$$

where r_e = estimated effective annual rate
       m = number of payment periods per year
       t = total number of payments
       P = amount financed
       I = monetary interest charge, $[(r)(t) - P]$
       r = periodic payment of principal and interest

thus,

$$r_e = \frac{2\,(m)\,(I)}{P\,(t+1) - I\,(t-1)} = \frac{(2)\,(12)\,(\$12{,}368)}{\$100{,}000\,(25) - (\$12{,}368)\,(23)} = 13.4\%$$

Constant-ratio method. The formula is

$$r_e = \frac{2\,(m)\,(I)}{P\,(t+1)} = \frac{\$296,832}{\$2,500,000} = 11.873\%$$

Direct-ratio method. The formula is

$$r_e = \frac{6\,(m)\,(I)}{3P\,(t+1) + I\,(t-1)} = \frac{\$890,496}{\$7,784,464} = 11.439\%$$

Of the three approximation methods, the constant-ratio method comes closest to the 12.0775 percent effective annual rate. But the direct-ratio approximation is closer to the nominal annual rate. In summary:

Effective annual rate:	12.0775%
Nominal Annual rate:	11.4564%
Difference:	0.6211%

	Percent	Difference between effective annual and approximation (%)	Difference between nominal annual and approximation (%)
Residuary method	13.4000	(1.3225)	(1.9436)
Constant ratio	11.8730	0.2045	(0.4166)
Direct ratio	11.4390	0.6385	0.0174

The immediate and principal limitation of the residuary, constant, and direct approximation methods is that they are useful only for approximating self-amortizing, level-payment loans.

In Chap. 25, two other measures of the cost of borrowing or the return on investment are described, the *geometric mean* and the *average discounted rate of return.*

10

Variable and General Annuities and Perpetuities

Ordinary annuities involve a series of level or equal payments (sometimes called *rents*) for some stated number of periods of time. Another type of series is that where the payments are of an increasing or decreasing nature.

Decreasing Annuities

First let us consider a decreasing annuity. In a *decreasing annuity*, each successive payment is lower by a fixed amount than the preceding payment. An example is:

Annual periods	Amount of payment
1	$110,000
2	80,000
3	50,000
4	20,000

Each annual payment is $30,000 less than the previous year's payment. Another way to look at this series of payments is as a group of four annuities:

one of $20,000 for four periods; one of $30,000 for three periods, one of $30,000 for two periods, and finally a single payment of $30,000. A time line will crystallize the situation:

```
┌─────────────────────────────────────────────────────────────┐
│              Interest = 10% annually                          │
│              (000s omitted)                                   │
│                 30                                            │
│                 30          30                                │
│                 30          30          30                    │
│                 20          20          20          20        │
│          └─────────┬───────────┬───────────┬───────────┘      │
│                    1           2           3           4       │
│                                                               │
│           A?                                                  │
└─────────────────────────────────────────────────────────────┘
```

In the above example, what is the value today of the decreasing annuity if money is worth 10 percent annually? The present value of these payments is readily seen as the present value of the four distinct annuities, and a quick solution to the problem is found by using the factors in Table 12 of Appendix 1, in the fifth column, "Present worth of $1 per period." Each separate annuity uses the following formula:

$$A = R \left[\frac{1 - (1 + i/m)^{-(n)(m)}}{i/m} \right]$$

where A = present value of a series of equal payments (annuity)
i = annual or nominal interest rate
m = number of times interest is compounded per year
R = amount of each regular future periodic payment
n = number of years

for the example above,

A = $20,000 (3.169865) + $30,000 (2.486851) + $30,000 (1.735537)
    + $30,000 (0.909090)

    = $63,397.3 + $74,605.53 + $52,066.11 + $27,272.70

    = $217,341.64

Discounted cash flow provides another method of finding the same answer. In this case the sum of each year's cash flows is discounted to the present and the sum of the four flows is the total present value. The value of the factor for the present worth of $1 is found in Table 12 of Appendix 1 in the fourth column, "Present worth of $1."

The formula for finding the present value by the discounted cash flow approach is

$$A = \frac{R_1}{(1+i)^1} + \frac{R_2}{(1+i)^2} + \cdots + \frac{R_n}{(1+i)^n}$$

where A = present value
$\quad R$ = irregular payment
$\quad i$ = periodic interest rate
$\quad n$ = number of periods

The solution is presented in Table 10.1. The sum of the present values of the four cash flows discounted to the present is $217,342.

Increasing Annuities

The present or future value of an *increasing annuity* can be determined by a similar method of breaking up and analyzing the payments.

Example 1: Finding the future value of an increasing annuity. George St. Clair decides to invest for his daughter's education 5 years before she is due to start college. He puts away $5000 at the end of the first year, and increases the annual investment by $3000 each subsequent year. How much will be accumulated when the fifth payment is made, if the investment earns 10 percent, compounded annually?

A time line again comes to the rescue:

Table 10.1. Discounted Cash Flow

Annual periods	Amount of payment	Present worth of $1	Value today
1	$110,000	$0.90909	$100,000
2	80,000	0.82645	66,116
3	50,000	0.75131	37,566
4	20,000	0.68301	13,660
			$217,342

The total future values, S, is the sum of the future value of annuities of $5000 for 5 years, $3000 for 4 years, $3000 for 3 years, $3000 for 2 years, and $3000 in cash. Again, Table 12, Appendix 1, contains factors which contribute to the speedy resolution of the problem, this time, in the second column, "Amount of $1 per period." As shown in Table 10.2, the account, into which $55,000 has been invested, will be worth $63,678 at the end of 5 years.

The solution may also be found by aggregating the future value of each year's payments, using the familiar compound interest formula:

$$S = R_1 (1 + i)^1 + R_2 (1 + i)^2 \cdots + R_n (1 + i)^n$$

where S = future value
R = irregular payment
i = periodic interest rate
n = number of periods

The future value is $63,678, as calculated in Table 10.3.

As we have just seen, the present or future value of an increasing or decreasing annuity may be determined by either of two methods: (1) the sum of the values of several annuities; or (2) discounted or compounded cash flows. A third, short-cut method is explained in the next section.

Table 10.2. Future Value of Increasing Annuity: Series of Annuities

Annual periods	Amount of payment	Amount of $1 per period	Future value in 5 years
5	$50,000	$6.10510	$30,526
4	3,000	4.64100	13,923
3	3,000	3.31000	9,930
2	3,000	2.10000	6,300
1	3,000	1.00000	3,000
			$63,678

Table 10.3. Future Value of Increasing Annuity: Accumulating Cash Flows

Annual periods	Amount of payment	Amount of $1 per period	Future value
4	$ 5,000	$1.46410	$ 7,320
3	8,000	1.33100	10,648
2	11,000	1.21000	13,310
1	14,000	1.10000	15,400
0	17,000	1.000000	17,000
			$63,678

Annuities That Increase at a Fixed Rate

In this era of inflationary expectations, it is often desirable to consider a series of payments that increase at a fixed or set percentage rate. An example will make the subject clear. If Steve MacLeod saves $1000 in the first year, and each year thereafter he saves 5 percent more than in the preceding year, how much will his money be worth after n years? In this case, his investment in the second year is $1050, in the third year it is $1102.50, etc. The future value of the account is the future value of an annuity that is increasing at a fixed rate of 5 percent. Besides the rate of increase of the amount of the investment, the rate of interest earned on the investment also is relevant.

Future Value of an Annuity That Increases at a Fixed Rate

An annuity is a sequence of equal payments made at equal intervals of time. This increasing annuity requires that the conversion intervals (number of times interest is compounded per year) correspond with the payments—e.g., annual compounding and annual payments, monthly compounding and monthly payments, etc. The future value is the total value of all the payments, including compounded interest, at the end of the term—that is, the value on the day of the last payment. The formula for the future value of an increasing annuity is

$$S = R \left(\frac{(1+i)^{n-1}\left\{1 - [(1+r)/(1+i)]^n\right\}}{1 - [(1+r)/(1+i)]} \right)$$

where S = future value of a series of increasing payments (annuity)
  r = rate per year at which the amount of payment is increased
  R = amount of the first year's payment
  n = number of years
  k = number of payments less one payment
  i = annual or nominal interest rate earned on invested assets

Another way of expressing the formula (which is more suitable for computer programming) is

$$S = (R) \left[\sum_{n=0}^{k} (1 + r)^n (1 + i)^{k-n} \right]$$

Example: Finding the future value of an increasing annuity. Sue and Sam want to take a trip around the world in 5 years. They prepare a budget and figure they can save $1000 at the end of the first year; and each year thereafter they will save 6 percent more than in the preceding year. If their investment account makes 10 percent after taxes, how much will they have in their account after 5 years?

Table 10.4 shows the details of the calculation, and the answer: $6807.

Present Value of an Increasing Annuity

Closely related to the future value of an increasing annuity is its present value, the formula for which is

$$P = R \left(\frac{1/(1 + i) \left\{ 1 - [(1 + r)/(1 + i)]^n \right\}}{1 - [(1 + r)/(1 + i)]} \right)$$

To obtain a better idea of the dynamic compounding power of *both* an increasing periodic investment *and* compound interest, refer to Table 10.5. In each case, the first-year investment is $1000, and the annual investment increases from year to year by 6 percent. At various interest rates (6, 8, 10, and 12 percent), the table shows the accumulated value at the end of various periods of time (5, 10, 15, and 20 years). Over 20 years, at 12 percent interest, the $38,993 invested would grow to $107,319. This is 195 percent more paid in ($38,993) than if $1000 per year had been invested ($20,000) without

Table 10.4. Annuity That Increases at a Fixed Rate

$1000 = investment during the first year
6.00% = investment increase from year to year
10.00% = interest rate earned

Year	Annual investment	Balance at beg. of year	Interest for the year	Balance at end of year
1	$1000	0	0	$1000
2	1060	$1000	$100	2160
3	1124	2160	216	3500
4	1191	3500	350	5041
5	1262	5041	504	6807

Table 10.5. Annuity Increasing 6 Percent per Year at Various Interest Rates

6% = annual rate of increase of the amount invested
$1,000 = first-year investment

Interest rate (%)	Total value of the accumulated sum			
	5 years	10 years	15 years	20 years
6	$6,312	$16,895	$33,914	$ 60,512
8	6,555	18,404	38,781	72,691
10	6,807	20,072	44,517	88,009
12	7,068	21,917	51,283	107,319
Amount invested	5,975	13,972	24,673	38,993

At 0% per year increase in the amount invested:

	5 years	10 years	15 years	20 years
At 6% interest	$5,637	$13,181	$23,276	$ 36,786
Amount invested	5,000	10,000	15,000	20,000
Ratio of *amount invested* at 6% growth versus 0 growth	119.5%	139.7%	164.5%	195.0%
Ratio of *value of a/c* with 6% growth in amt. invested versus no growth—all at 6% interest	112.0%	128.2%	145.7%	164.5%

increase each year. It is 164.5 percent more (when the money earns 6 percent) with the increasing investment ($60,512) than if the investment remained static at $1000 per year ($36,786). Thus the dynamics of dual compounding are evident.

The FINANCIAL AND INTEREST CALCULATOR computer software includes a program called "Increasing Annuity Calculator," which solves such problems in seconds. For example, what is the value of the account if the first-year investment is $1200, and it increases at 8 percent each year for 20 years? The money earns 7 percent. The solution using the computer software is shown in Table 10.6.

Using the formula, the calculation is

$$S = R \left(\frac{(1+i)^{n-1}\{1 - [(1+r)/(1+i)]^n\}}{1 - [(1+r)/(1+i)]} \right)$$

$$= \$1200 \left(\frac{(1.07)^{19}\{1 - [(1.08)/(1.07)]^{20}\}}{1 - [(1.08)/(1.07)]} \right)$$

Table 10.6. Finding the future Value of an Increasing Annuity

Larry Rosen's
INCREASING ANNUITY CALCULATOR
Copyright © 1990
(Note: User entries are underlined)

What is the annual investment or payment (e.g., 1200)? <u>1200</u>

What is the total number of years (e.g., 20)? <u>20</u>

What is the periodic increase in the regular savings or payment amount (in decimal form, e.g., 0.08 for 8 percent)? <u>0.08</u>

What is the interest rate earned (decimal form, e.g., 0.07)? <u>0.07</u>

CALCULATING, PLEASE WAIT ...

The accumulated sum is 94952.72

Print the details (Y/N)?, <u>Y</u>

Turn on printer

$$= \$1200 \left\{ \frac{(3.61653)\,[1 - (1.00935)^{20}]}{1 - 1.00935} \right\}$$

$$= \$1200 \left[\frac{(3.61653)\,(1 - 1.20448)}{1 - 1.00935} \right]$$

$$= \$1200 \, \frac{(3.61653)\,(-0.20448)}{-0.00935}$$

$$= \$1200 \, \frac{-0.73951}{-0.00935} = \$1200 \,(79.127) = \$94{,}952.72$$

Needless to say, the computer solution offers certain advantages to doing the calculation by formula.

Supercompounding

King Ivan, the ancient king of Babaland, nearing the end of his lengthy life, summoned his two sons to his bedside. Desiring to determine which of his sons he should appoint as his principal heir, the king posed to his sons the following problem.

"In the first situation, we would invest 1,000,000 shekels the first year, and each year thereafter, for 10 years, we would make an additional investment, 4 percent greater than that of the previous year. And the assets thus acquired would themselves grow by 6 percent each and every year.

"Alternatively, we would again invest 1,000,000 shekels the first year, and each year for the next 10 years we would increase the investment by 6 percent over that of the previous year, and the assets would grow at only 4 percent each year.

"If you, my son, were to become king, which of the two alternatives would you select in order to provide the most money for our kingdom's treasury?" What would you have chosen if you were given the choice?

Actually, to determine the correct choice, you do not need a computer, or even a calculator; in fact, neither paper nor pencil is required. The choices are equivalent. The accumulated value of an investment at rate x with an annual increase in the amount invested of y percent over the previous year's investment will always equal the same amount as an investment at rate y with an annual increase in the amount invested of x percent.

Accumulating funds by increasing the periodic investment by a stated percentage, and having the entire accumulated fund grow at compound interest, is a powerful method of accumulating capital. Figure 10.1 illustrates the dynamics of such investing.

Example: Supercompounding. Wanda Beresohn invests $1000 the first year, and increases the investment in each subsequent year by 10 percent. Wanda wants to accumulate $1 million by the end of 30 years. What rate must she earn on the invested assets?

Refer to Fig. 10.1. Enter the graph on the vertical axis at the $1,000 (000) point, and draw a horizontal line across the graph. Then, find the 30-year point on the horizontal axis, and draw a vertical line up the page. The closest curve to the point where the two lines intersect is the required rate the assets must earn, that is, 15.16 percent.

Perpetuities

A *perpetuity* is an annuity that continues forever. Since the payments never end, it is impossible to determine the future value of a perpetuity. The present value is determinable using the following formula:

$$A = \frac{R}{I}$$

where A = present value
R = regular payment
i = periodic interest rate

The derivation of this formula is based on the formula for the present value of an ordinary annuity,

Value (000's)

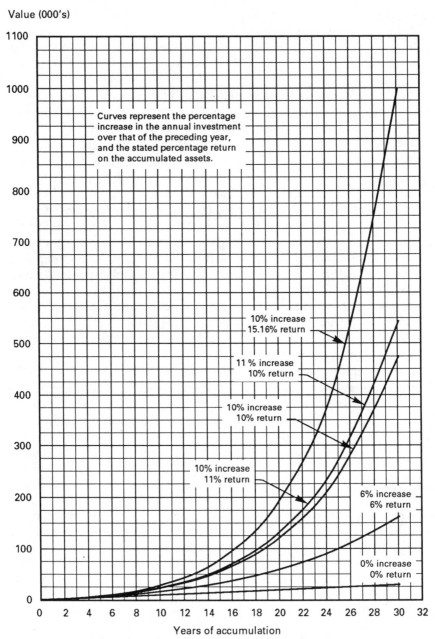

Years of accumulation

Figure 10.1. Supercompounding ($1000 is the first year's investment).

$$A = R \left[\frac{1 - (1 + i/m)^{-(n)(m)}}{i/m} \right]$$

$$= \frac{R}{i} - \frac{R}{i}(1 + i)^{-n}$$

As n approaches infinity, $(1+i)^{-n}$ approaches 0.

Example: Perpetuity present value. Peter Finch wishes to establish an endowment to provide a \$20,000-per-year scholarship honoring himself. The first award and payment is to be made 1 year from now. If the invested funds earn 8 percent, compounded annually, how much is needed?

$$A = \frac{R}{I} = \frac{\$20,000}{0.08}$$

$$= \$250,000$$

Thus, \$250,000 invested at 8 percent will provided a \$20,000-per-year endowment in perpetuity.

In Europe, there are publicly traded bonds called *perpetuals* or *perpetual annuities*. They are usually redeemable at par after a specified future date, but only at the borrower's option. In England a similar instrument is called a *consol*.

In the fixed-income markets, perpetuals represent an extreme in terms of longevity, maturity, or duration. As such, other factors being equal, their prices would be more volatile than any fixed-maturity debt instruments. That is, for a given percentage change in market interest rates, the percentage price change of a perpetual would be greater than for any fixed-maturity bond.

General Annuities

Earlier discussions have been about ordinary or simple annuities where the number of payments per year corresponded to the number of times interest is compounded per year—for example, payments are monthly and interest is compounded monthly, or payments are semiannual and interest is compounded twice per year. The formulas with which we have been working for ordinary annuities require equality between the number of payments per year and the number of times interest is compounded. In real life, however, situations occur where such equality does not exist. For a *general annuity*, the payment interval and conversion interval are not equal.

Fortunately, the present value or future value of a general annuity can be found by converting it to an equivalent simple annuity.

Effective Yield or Rate

The effective rate is an interest rate, which when compounded *annually*, produces the identical amount of interest as the nominal, stated, or conventional rate, when the nominal rate is compounded m times per year. The following formula calculates the annual *effective rate*:

$$Y = \left(1 + \frac{r}{m}\right)^m - 1$$

where Y = effective annual yield
r = nominal or conventional yield (rate)
m = number of periods of compounding per year

This equation expressing the relationship between effective annual yield and nominal yield can be rearranged to

$$r = m\,[(1 + Y^{1/m} - 1]$$

Example: Finding an Equivalent rate. Money is worth a nominal rate of 4 percent, compounded twice per year. What is the *equation* for the equivalent rate compounded quarterly?

If X = the equivalent rate per *quarter*, then

$$(1 + X)^4 = (1.02)^2$$

Example: Finding an Equivalent rate. What is the equation for the equivalent rate compounded annually?

If X = the equivalent rate per year, then

$$(1 + X) = (1.02)^2$$

Example: Finding an equivalent rate. What is the equation for the equivalent rate compounded monthly?

If X = the equivalent rate per month, then

$$(1 + X)^{12} = (1.02)^2$$

Example: Finding the nominal rate, given the effective rate, and vice versa. If the effective rate is 10 percent, what is the equivalent nominal, conventional or stated rate, compounded quarterly?

$$r = m\,[(1 + Y)^{1/m} - 1]$$

$$= 4\,[(1 + 0.1^{1/4} - 1]$$

$$= 0.09645 \quad \text{or} \quad 9.645\%$$

Thus, a nominal annual rate of 9.645 percent, compounded quarterly, is equivalent to 10 percent. This equality is shown by the *effective yield formula*, as follows:

$$Y = \left(1 + \frac{r}{m}\right)^m - 1$$

where Y = effective annual yield
r = nominal or conventional yield (rate)
m = number of periods of compounding per year

Here

$$Y = \left(1 + \frac{r}{m}\right)^m - 1$$

$$= \left(1 + \frac{0.0965}{4}\right)^4 - 1 = 0.10 \quad \text{or} \quad 10\%$$

With a general annuity, the basic procedure is to use the simple annuity formula corresponding to the payment interval, and substitute the equivalent rate, based on compounding frequency, for (i/m). Several examples will clarify the situation.

Example. Stan Smith deposits $100 at the end of each 6 months for 8 years into an account which earns a stated 4 percent per year, compounded quarterly. How much will be in the account at the end of 8 years?

The formula for the *future value of a simple anuity* is

$$S = R\left[\frac{(1 + i/m)^{(n)(m)} - 1}{i/m}\right]$$

where S = future value of a series of equal payments (annuity)
i = annual or nominal interest rate
m = number of times interest is compounded per year
R = amount of each regular future periodic payment
n = number of years

If this were a simple annuity, i/m would be 0.04/4. But this is not a simple annuity, because interest is compounded quarterly and the payments are made semiannually. This conflict is resolved by finding the *equivalent rate* (which corresponds to the payment interval). Let x = the rate per 6 months which is equivalent to 4 percent compounded quarterly. Then

$$(1 + x)^2 = \left(1 + \frac{0.04}{4}\right)^4$$

$$= (1.01)^4$$

$$(1 + x) = (1.01)^2$$

$$= 1.02010$$

$$x = 0.0201$$

The value of x represents the equivalent rate per 6 months (the payment interval is semiannual) and can be substituted into the simple annuity formula for (i/m). The formula is

$$S = R \left[\frac{(1 + i/m)^{(n)(m)} - 1}{i/m}\right]$$

$$= \$100 \left[\frac{(1.0201)^{(8)(2)} - 1}{0.0201}\right]$$

$$= \frac{\$100 \left[(1.0201)^{(16)} - 1\right]}{0.0201}$$

$$= \$100 \,(18.65377) = \$1865.38$$

It is possible to manipulate the formula in such a manner that the use of factors in the tables in Appendix 1 may be employed. In the preceding example, the manipulated formula would be

$$S = 100 \left[\frac{(1.01)^{32} - 1}{0.01}\right] \left[\frac{0.01}{(1.01)^2 - 1}\right]$$

The value of the expression

$$\left[\frac{(1.01)^{32} - 1}{0.01}\right]$$

is found in Appendix 1, Table 2, "Amount of $1 per period," for 32 periods, as 37.494067. And the value of the expression

$$\left[\frac{0.01}{(1.01)^2 - 1}\right]$$

is found in the column "Sinking fund" for 2 periods as 0.497512. Then $S = 100(37.494067)\,(0.497512) = \$1865.37$.

Example: Finding the present value of a general annuity. Sean Egan enters into a contract to buy property with payments of $4000 at the end of each quarter for 10 years. What is the equivalent cash price of the property if the value of money is 6 percent, compounded monthly?

The formula for the present value of a simple or ordinary annuity is

$$A = R \left[\frac{1 - (1 + i/m)^{-nm}}{i/m} \right]$$

where A = present value of a series of equal payments (annuity)
i = periodic interest rate
m = number of times interest is compounded per year
R = amount of each regular future periodic payment
n = number of years

If this were a simple annuity, (i/m) would be 0.06/12. But this is not a simple annuity, because interest is compounded monthly and the payments are made quarterly. This conflict is resolved by finding the equivalent rate (which corresponds to the quarterly payment interval). Let x be the rate per quarter which is equivalent to 6 percent, compounded monthly. Then

$$(1 + x)^4 = \left(1 + \frac{0.06}{12} \right)^{12}$$

$$= (1.005)^{12}$$

$$(1 + x) = (1.005)^3$$

$$= 1.015075$$

$$x = 0.015075$$

The value of x represents the equivalent rate per quarter and can be substituted into the simple annuity formula for (i/m).

The solution is

$$A = R \left[\frac{1 - (1 + i/m)^{-nm}}{i/m} \right]$$

$$= \$4000 \left[\frac{1 - (1.015075)^{-(10)(4)}}{0.015075} \right]$$

$$= \$4000 \left(\frac{1 - 0.549635}{0.015075} \right)$$

$$= \$4000 \,(29.874929) = \$119{,}499.72$$

Thus $119,499.72 is the current or present value of the property.

It is possible to manipulate the formula in such a manner that the use of factors in the tables in Appendix 1 may be employed. In the previous example, the manipulated formula is

$$A = \$4,000 \left[\frac{1 - (1.005)^{-120}}{0.005}\right] \left[\frac{0.005}{(1.005)^3 - 1}\right]$$

The value of the expression

$$\left[\frac{1 - (1.005)^{-120}}{0.005}\right]$$

is found in Appendix 1, Table 1, "Present worth of $1 per period," for 120 periods, as 90.073453. The value of the expression

$$\left[\frac{0.005}{(1.005)^3 - 1}\right]$$

is found in the column "Sinking fund" for 3 periods as 0.36672. Then

$$A = \$4000 \,(90.073453)\,(0.336672) = \$119,499.37$$

Example: Finding the present value of a general annuity. How much must be invested at 6 percent, compounded *semiannually*, to allow *quarterly* payments to be made of $1500 for 7 years?

The formula for the present value of a simple or ordinary annuity is

$$A = R \left[\frac{1 - (1 + i/m)^{-nm}}{i/m}\right]$$

where A = present value of a series of equal payments (annuity)
   i = periodic interest rate
   m = number of times interest is compounded per year
   R = amount of each regular future periodic payment
   n = number of years

If this were a simple annuity, (i/m) would be $(0.06/2)$. But this is not a simple annuity, because interest is compounded semiannually and the payments are made quarterly. This conflict is resolved by finding the equivalent rate (which corresponds to the payment interval). Let x be the rate per quarter which is equivalent to 6 percent, compounded semiannually. Then

$$(1 + x)^4 = \left(1 + \frac{0.06}{2}\right)^2$$

$$= (1.03)^2$$

$$(1 + x) = (1.03)^{0.5}$$

$$x = 1.014889 - 1 = 0.014889$$

The value of x represents the equivalent rate per quarter and can be substituted into the simple annuity formula for present value. The solution is

$$A = R \left[\frac{1 - (1 + i/m)^{-nm}}{i/m} \right]$$

$$= \$1500 \left[\frac{1 - (1.04889)^{-(7)(4)}}{0.014889} \right]$$

$$= \$1500 \, (22.760335) = \$34,140.50$$

Thus $34,140.50 is the present value that will provide the requisite $1500 per quarter for 7 years.

Example: Finding the payment of a general annuity. What equal payments can be provided at the end of each *quarter* for 8 years by an investment account which contains $35,000 and earns a nominal 4 percent, compounded *semiannually?*

The formula for finding the regular payment for an ordinary annuity is

$$R = A \left[\frac{i/m}{1 - (1 + i/m)^{-nm}} \right]$$

where A = present value of a series of equal payments (annuity)
i = periodic interest rate
m = number of times interest is compounded per year
R = amount of each regular future periodic payment
n = number of years

If this were a simple annuity, (i/m) would be $(0.04/2)$. But this is not a simple annuity, because interest is compounded semiannually and the payments are made quarterly. This conflict is resolved by finding the equivalent rate (which corresponds to the payment interval). Let x be the rate per quarter which is equivalent to 4 percent, compounded semiannually. Then

$$(1 + x)^4 = \left(1 + \frac{0.04}{2} \right)^2$$

$$= (1.02)^2$$

$$(1 + x) = (1.02)^{0.5}$$

$$x = 1.00995 - 1 = 0.00955$$

The value of x represents the equivalent rate per quarter and can be substituted into the simple annuity formula for present value. The solution is

$$R = \$35,000 \left[\frac{i/m}{1 - (1 + i/m)^{-32}} \right]$$

$$= \$35,000 \left[\frac{0.00955/m}{1 - (1.00955)^{-32}} \right]$$

$$= \$35,000 \left[\frac{0.00955}{0.26255} \right] = \$1274.55$$

Thus $1274.55 is the regular payment which can be made at the end of each quarter for 8 years from a $35,000 fund that earns interest at 4 percent compounded quarterly.

Conclusion

Life is not so uncomplicated as to allow a simple formula such as that for ordinary annuities to be the inevitable solution to problems. Payments may be irregular in amount (increasing or decreasing annuities), or the interval at which interest is compounded may differ from the frequency at which payments are made (general annuity). In this chapter, we have discovered the means of coping with these complexities.

11

Interest, Dividends, T-Bills, and Equivalent Yields

Investors or savers who desire to keep money invested at attractive and competitive rates should keep abreast of ever-changing "money market" conditions.

Money market conditions are reported daily in financial newspapers. The manner in which prices are reported is shown in Fig. 11.1.

The Money Market

Investors must be aware of the way the money market functions, as changes in interest-rate levels cause changes in the market prices of debt securities and also affect the market prices (discounted present values) of stocks.

Short-term U.S. government issues (T-bills, for example) and prime short-term commercial paper comprise the bulk of the money market, which is characterized by the short-term nature of its activity as compared to the capital markets (long-term bonds). Money market instruments are close substitutes for cash and for each other, and are a principal medium of temporary investment by banks, businesses, insurance companies, and others. Other money market media include negotiable time certificates of deposit (CDs), federal funds, banker's acceptances, repos, and call loans.

Money market instruments in the global markets of today also include non-U.S.-currency-denominated paper, including (but not limited to) British sterling, Australian dollars, New Zealand kiwis, Japanese yen, German

Money Rates

Prime Rate 9.00	Commercial Paper (range):	Eurodollar Rates:
Base interest rate charged by major U.S. commercial banks on loans to corporations.	Dealers:	(Secondary Market)
	30-180 days 6.375-6.20	Overnight 6.125-6.25
Discount Rate 6.00	Corporate Issuers:	1 month 6.375-6.50
Rate charged by Federal Reserve System on loans to depository institutions.	30-270 days 6.24-6.09	3 months 6.375-6.50
	Discount rate for unsecured notes of top-credit corporations sold directly or through dealers.	6 months..............................6.4375-6.5625
Federal Funds Rate:		1 Year..............................6.9375-7.0625
High 6.25 Low 6.125 Close 6.25		Rates paid on dollar deposits outside the U.S.
Rates on overnight loans among financial institutions.	Certificates of Deposit:	
	($100,000 minimum)	London Interbank Offered Rates:
Bankers Acceptances:	30 days 6.15	3 months 6.50
30 days..............................6.33	90 days 6.18	6 months 6.625
60 days..............................6.25	180 days 6.20	The average of rates paid on dollar deposits.
90 days..............................6.20	Rates paid on new certificates of major commercial banks, usually in blocks of $1 million or more.	
120 days..............................6.22		Treasury Bill Auction Results:
150 days..............................6.22		3 months (as of Mar. 18)..............5.83
180 days..............................6.21	Broker Call Loans 8.00-8.50	6 months (as of Mar. 18)..............5.82
Discount rate on business credits backed and sold by banks to finance trade.	Rate charged on short-term loans to brokerage dealers backed by securities.	Average discount rate for Treasury bills in minimum units of $10,000.
		Source: Telerate Systems Inc.

Figure 11.1. Money rates. (*Reprinted with permission from Investor's Business Daily.*)

marks, and European Currency Units (ECUs).* Investing in a CD, bill, bond, note, or other paper denominated in a currency other than one's native currency is actually a double investment—one investment in the relevant currency, the other in the instrument itself.

Certificates of Deposit (CDs) are negotiable or nonnegotiable certificates given by a commercial bank in exchange for a time deposit. Regulation Q of the Federal Reserve Board formerly prescribed the maximum rate of interest that may be paid by member banks on certain time and savings deposits made in the United States. Now such restrictions have been lifted, but Regulation Q still prescribes that no interest may be paid by member banks on demand deposits as defined by Regulation D. The Office of the Comptroller of the Currency regulates nonmember national banks, and the states regulate state-chartered banks.

*The value of an ECU, which was introduced in 1979, is established by European Monetary System ("EMS") on the basis of specified amounts of the currencies of member countries of the European Community. At the time of writing the 12 countries included: Germany, Great Britain, France, Italy, Holland, Belgium, Luxembourg, Denmark, Ireland, Greece, Spain, and Portugal. The portion of an ECU that a single currency represents is adjusted from time to time and reflects the size of the underlying economy of that currency. Thus the deutsche mark has the greatest impact on the value of the ECU. To find the ECU's value in U.S. dollars, each component currency (e.g., $0.6\frac{1}{2}$ deutsche marks, 1.332 French francs, etc.) is valued, in this case, in U.S. dollars, at current foreign exchange rates and the sum is the value of an ECU expressed in dollars. From time to time the "currency basket" is realigned to reflect underlying economic changes in the domestic currencies of the constituents.

Federal funds mean the deposit balances of member banks and other depository institutions at the Federal Reserve Bank. The Monetary Control Act of 1980 governs deposits at the Fed by depository institutions. Since some banks may have more on deposit than is required, and other banks may be deficient in deposits with the Fed, trading in federal funds takes place. Transactions take place through federal funds houses. The daily volume of transactions is in multi-billions of dollars. Federal funds are also used extensively for other purposes, including large transactions in government issues. With federal funds, settlement of transactions between a buyer and seller may be done on a same-day basis. The rate of interest charged on loans of federal funds is called the *Fed funds rate*, and it is the benchmark rate for money market instruments.

A *banker's acceptance* begins as a draft drawn by, let us say, an exporter against his customer, ordering him to pay a specified sum either at sight or after a specified period of time for goods that have been purchased. When the customer takes possession of the goods, he simultaneously endorses the draft with the word "accepted" and his signature. With this endorsement, the draft becomes an acceptance. The exporter may find it difficult to sell or discount the acceptance if the customer is not well known. Therefore, arrangements are often made for drafts to be drawn against the customer's bank. When such a draft is accepted by the customer's bank, it is known as a banker's acceptance. These acceptances are then traded through banker's acceptance houses.

Commercial paper consists of short-term promissory notes of business firms, which are sold by commercial paper houses to their customers.

Call loans are bank loans to brokers or dealers against listed or government securities as collateral. The proceeds of these loans are used by brokers to finance customers' margin (loan) accounts and by dealers to carry securities they are distributing or which they hold in inventory.

Repurchase agreements ("repos") typically originate between market makers in government paper and investors, as a means of financing the inventory of the market makers. Such financing is cheaper for the market maker in governments than borrowing from banks at the dealer loan rate. Repos are also offered by banks and brokerage houses to customers, usually as an overnight investment.

From an investor's viewpoint, loans in the repo market are well secured by top-quality paper and offer yields higher than overnight CDs. Banks which offer repos generally price them off the Fed funds rate—that is, at a lesser yield than the Fed funds rate. The lesser yield is the bank or issuer's "spread."

Reverse repos ("reverses") are just the opposite of repos. Here, the market maker lends its money to a bank and receives securities and interest on the transaction. Banks which are members of the Federal Reserve System are not subject to reserve requirements for issuance of repos. This makes lending via repos attractive to the issuing bank, and allows the bank to offer a higher yield on a repo than on a deposit.

Eurodollars are U.S. dollars on deposit outside the United States. For example, a U.S. person's U.S. dollar account at Union Bank of Switzerland is a Eurodollar account.

Current Yield: Stocks

Stock market closing prices include other interesting data besides the pertinent high, low, and closing prices themselves. In the transactions listed in Fig. 11.2, the 1.68 after the company name abbreviation "DetEd" indicates that the annual dividend per share of this common stock is at the rate of $1.68 per year. The current yield from dividends is 1.68 divided by the market price of 24.875, or 6.8 percent. The formula

$$CY = \frac{DIV}{P}$$

where CY= current yield (annual)
     DIV = indicated annual dividend (normally current quarterly rate × 4)
     P = current price per share

For the example above,

$$CY = \frac{\text{annual dividend (i.e., \$1.68)}}{\text{current price (\$24.875)}} = 6.75\%$$

The "yield" column in the price quotation in Fig. 11.2 indicates that the current yield is 6.8 percent. Many newspapers, however, do not provide the calculated current yield, which, of course, changes daily with the price of the stock.

The highest price at which Deere (common stock), as shown in Fig. 11.2, has traded during the year is $64.25, and the lowest price was $44. A P/E (price-earnings) ratio of 12 indicates that the market price is 12 times the company's annual earnings per share. During the day, 1,452,100 shares traded. The highest price at which the shares traded during this particular week was 55.125. The closing price at the end of the day's trading was 55.125. The stock closed $1.625 higher than at the close of the previous day's trading.

52-Weeks High	Low	Name and Dividend	Sales 100s	Yield Pct.	P/E Ratio	Week's High	Week's Low	Last	Net Chg.
25⅛	14⅛	DCNY .40e	662	2.7	...	15¼	d14⅛	15	− ⅜
30⅜	24⅛	DPL 2.24	2924	7.4	10	u30⅜	29¾	30¼	+ ⅜
23⅞	16⅝	DQE 1.28	2537	5.7	11	22½	22⅛	22⅜	.....
18¾	12¼	Dallas .66	552	4.7	59	14⅜	14	14⅛	− ⅛
42⅞	33⅛	DanaCp 1.60	2421	4.7	9	34¼	33⅛	34¼	+ ¾
18⅜	12⅜	Danher	864	...	9	15½	14⅝	15½	+ ¾
15½	7⅞	Daniel .18	634	1.5	23	13⅜	11½	12	− 1
19½	13¼	DataGn	2447	...	...	13¾	d13¼	13⅝	.....
6¼	3¼	Datapt	3983	...	...	4⅞	3¼	3¾	− 1⅛
25	15¾	Datpt pf4.94	219	30.4	...	18	16	16¼	− 1½
8⅛	3⅜	DtaDsg .12j	2589	...	...	5⅛	4⅝	5	+ ¼
17¼	12	DavWtr .28	220	1.9	23	14½	13⅞	14⅜	+ ¼
65½	38⅝	DaytHd 1.12	10083	1.7	17	u65½	62½	65	+ ⅛
84½	73¼	DPL pf 7.48	111	8.9	...	u84½	82½	84	+ 1¼
86½	74⅛	DPL pf 7.70	z20	9.2	...	83½	83½	83½	.....
83	72	DPL pf 7.37	z6100	8.9	...	u83	81½	83	+ 1½
37⅞	28⅛	DeanFd .66	1346	2.0	14	33⅜	32⅝	33⅛	.....
9½	8½	DWGI .88	x5087	10.1	...	8⅞	8⅝	8¾	− ⅛
64¼	44	Deere 1.40	14521	2.5	12	55⅛	52¾	55⅛	+ 1⅝
18¾	15½	DelVal 1.86	322	10.1	10	18½	18	18½	+ ¼
20	16⅞	DelmPL 1.50	749	7.7	12	19½	19⅛	19½	+ ¼
85¾	46½	DeltaAr 1.20a	8584	1.8	7	66½	63½	66	+ ¾
18	8¾	DeltaW .30	517	2.6	8	11¾	11¼	11⅝	− ⅛
6¼	4	Deltona	405	...	...	5⅛	4⅝	5⅛	+ ½
35⅜	23½	Deluxe 1.04	3836	3.0	20	34½	33¼	34⅜	+ ⅞
32⅞	23⅞	DensMf 1.32	x1598	5.3	10	25¾	24⅝	24⅞	− ½
52½	32¼	DeSoto .40	8073	.8	...	48⅜	38¾	47⅜	+ 8½
25	15¾	DetEd 1.68	17905	6.8	...	u25	23⅞	24⅞	+ ¾
136	89¾	DetE pf5.50	...	...	...	...	...	...	...
95¼	84	DetE pf 9.32	z2910	9.9	...	94¾	93½	93¾	− 1
81	70	DetE pf 7.68	z440	9.5	...	81	80	81	.....
81	68½	DetE pf 7.45	z190	9.3	...	u81	79¾	79¾	− ¾
78	67⅛	DetE pf 7.36	z360	9.4	...	u78	77½	78	+ ½
27¼	24¾	DE prF 2.75	17	10.2	...	27	26½	27	+ ¼
27⅛	24⅞	DE prB 2.75	6	10.2	...	27	26¾	27	+ ¼
100¼	94½	DetE pf9.72	...	...	...	...	...	...	...
24⅞	21¾	DetE pr 2.28	121	9.3	...	24⅞	24¼	24⅝	+ ⅛
34¾	20¼	Dexter .88	2994	4.0	13	21¾	20⅞	21¾	+ ⅝
38	19	DiagP s .24	296	.7	30	34¾	32	34¾	+ 1
35¾	22⅞	DiGior .64	256	2.1	17	30¾	30⅛	30½	− ⅛
14¾	7½	DiaSO 2.80	x3711	36.7	24	8¾	d 7½	7⅝	− ¼
28½	13¾	DShRM .44	3956	2.1	7	22¾	21¼	21⅜	− ⅛
39½	25	DShR pf 2	133	5.8	...	34⅜	32½	34⅜	+ 1⅜
8⅞	4	DianaCp	157	...	...	5½	5¼	5½	.....
47¾	34	Diebold 1.40	2026	3.8	14	37⅞	36⅜	36¾	− ⅞

Figure 11.2. NYSE prices. (*Reprinted with permission from Investor's Business Daily.*)

Bond Issues

Usually, new bond issues pay an interest rate that is competitive with existing bonds trading in the secondary market. See the issue Browning-Ferris Industries, Inc., in Fig. 11.3. This is a new bond issue of $100 million with annual interest per $1000 bond of 9.25 percent, or $92.50 per bond. The

NEW SECURITIES ISSUES

The following were among yesterday's offerings and pricings in U.S. and non-U.S. capital markets, with terms and syndicate manager, as compiled by Dow Jones Capital Markets Report:

CORPORATES

Browning-Ferris Industries Inc.—$100 million of 9.25% debentures due May 1, 2021, priced at par. The non-callable debentures were priced at a spread of 105 basis points above the Treasury's when-issued 30-year bond. Rated single-A-2 by Moody's Investors Service Inc. and single-A-plus by Standard & Poor's Corp., the issue will be sold through underwriters led by Smith Barney, Harris Upham & Co.

Harsco Corp.—$100 million of 8¾% notes, due May 15, 1996, priced at 99.92 to yield 8.77%. The noncallable notes were priced at a spread of 110 basis points above the Treasury's five-year note. Rated single-A-3 by Moody's and single-A-minus by S&P, the issue will be sold through underwriters led by Goldman Sachs & Co.

GE Capital Corp.—100 million Australian dollars (US$78 million) of 10.75% notes due April 22, 1995, priced at par. The non-callable notes were priced at 15 basis points above the 12.50% Australian governmment issue due April 1995. Rated triple-A by both Moody's and S&P, the issue will be sold through underwriters led by Merrill Lynch & Co. GE Capital is a subsidiary of **General Electric** Co.

Communications Satellite Corp.—$75 million of 8.95% notes due May 15, 2001, priced at 99.934 to yield 8.96%. The non-callable notes were priced at 95 basis points above the Treasury's when-issued 10-year note. Rated single-A-2 by Moody's and single-A by S&P, the issue will be sold through underwriters at First Boston Corp.

MUNICIPALS

Pennsylvania—$320 million of various purpose general obligation bonds, Series A and Series B, due Nov. 1 and May 1, 1992-2011, via a Goldman Sachs & Co. group. The bonds were priced for reoffering to yield from 4.50% in 1992 to 6.85% in 2010 and 2011. There are $303 million of Series A bonds due Nov. 1, 1992-2011, priced to yield from 4.50% in 1992 to 6.85% in 2010 and 2011 and $17 million of Series B bonds due May 1, 1993 and 1994, priced to yield 5.20% in 1993 and 5.40% in 1994. Bonds maturing in 1992-2004 are insured and rated triple-A by both Moody's and S&P. The remainder of the issue is rated single-A-1 by Moody's and double-A-minus by S&P.

Boise-Kuna Irrigation District, Idaho—$106.4 million of revenue refunding bonds priced by a Dean Witter Reynolds Inc. group. The 1991 Series bonds, for the Lucky Peak hydroelectric project, were priced to yield from 6% in 1998 to 6.80% in 2008. The issue is rated double-A by both Moody's and S&P. There is $36.4 million of 6% term bonds priced at 92 to yield 6.80% in 2008.

Bristol Health and Educational Facilities Board, Tenn.—$105.5 million of hospital revenue bonds due Sept. 1, 1994-2003, 2011 and 2021, tentatively priced by a Merrill Lynch group to yield from 5.60% in 1994 to 7.12% in 2021. Current interest serial bonds are priced at par to yield from 5.60% in 1994 to 6.70% in 2003. There are $26.3 million of 7% term bonds priced at 99.45 to yield 7.05% in 2011 and $60.8 million of 7% term bonds priced at 98½ to yield 7.12% in 2021. The bonds are insured and rated triple-A by Moody's and S&P.

Connecticut Housing Finance Authority—$98.5 million of mortgage finance program bonds, 1991 Series, due Nov. 15, 1996-2003, 2008 and 2009, tentatively priced by a PaineWebber Inc. group to yield from 5.95% in 1996 to 7.20% in 2008. The bonds are divided into two subseries. Subseries A-1 consists of a single tranche of $11.5 million of 7% bonds due in 2009 and priced at par. Subseries A-2 consists of bonds maturing in 1996-2003 and 2008. Current interest serial bonds are priced at par to yield from 5.95% in 1996 to 6.75% in 2003. There is $47.8 million of 7.20% term bonds priced at par due in 2008. The bonds are rated double-A by Moody's and double-A-plus by S&P. Interest on the Subseries-2 bonds will be treated as a preference item in calculating the federal alternative minimum tax that may be imposed on certain investors.

Kentucky State Property and Buildings Commission—$92.9 million of revenue bonds, Program 51, due Aug. 1, 1992-2003, 2006 and 2010, tentatively priced by a Prudential Securities Inc. group to yield from 4.75% in 1992 to 6.95% in 2010. Current interest serial bonds are priced to yield from 4.75% in 1992 to 6.65% in 2003. There are $17.7 million of 6.88% term bonds priced at par due in 2006 and $29.4 million of 6% term bonds priced at 89.99 to yield 6.95% in 2010. The bonds are rated single-A by both Moody's and S&P.

California Health Finance Authority—$71.2 million of hospital revenue bonds (Daniel Freeman Hospital issue), due May 1, 1992-2001 and 2013, were repriced by a Merrill Lynch & Co. group. The repricing lowered the yield on term bonds maturing in 2013 by five basis points. The repricing also decreased the size of the offering to $71.2 million, down from $71.5 million. The bonds are now priced to yield from 5.10% in 1992 to 7.03% in 2013, changed from 5.10% in 1992 to 7.08% in 2013. Current interest serial bonds are priced to yield from 5.10% in 1992 to 6.6% in 2001, unchanged. There are $50.3 million of 6.75% term bonds priced at 96.88 to yield 7.03% in 2013, changed from $50.56 million of 6.75% term bonds priced at 98⅜ to yield 7.08%. The bonds are insured and rated triple-A/triple-A.

Round Rock Independent School District, Texas—$70.8 million of unlimited tax school building and refunding bonds, Series 1991, due Aug. 15, 2000-2008, with capital appreciation bonds due 2009-2011, tentatively priced by a Morgan Stanley & Co. group to yield from 6.35% in 2000 to 7.05% for capital appreciation bonds due 2009-2011. Current interest serial bonds are priced to yield from 6.35% in 2000 to 6.90% in 2007 and 2008. Capital appreciation bonds are priced to yield to maturity to 7.05% in 2009-2011. The bonds are insured and rated triple-A by Moody's and S&P.

Massachusetts Educational Financing Authority—$60 million of education loan revenue bonds priced by a Goldman Sachs group. Yields on the issue D Series 1991A bonds were set at 6.10% in 1995 to 7.30% in 2009. The issue is insured and rated triple-A by both Moody's and S&P. There is $23.6 million of 7.30% term bonds priced at par due in 2009. The bonds are subject to the alternative minimum tax.

MORTGAGES

Federal National Mortgage Association—$43.1 million of real estate mortgage investment conduit securities offered by Kidder, Peabody & Co. The offering, Series 1991 G-15, is backed by **Government National Mortgage Association** 10½% securities. Further details weren't immediately available.

EUROBONDS

Germany (sovereign)—Three billion marks of 8⅜% bonds due May 21, 2001, at 100.70 to yield 8.27%, via Deutsche Bundesbank. Fees ⅞. To be placed through the traditional federal bond consortium. Auction today.

Ottawa Carleton (Canada)—100 million Canadian dollars of 10⅜% Eurobonds due June 25, 2001, at issue price 100½ via lead manager Wood Gundy Inc. Reoffered to investors at 99 to yield 10.54% (annual), spread 71 basis points above the Canadian government's 9¾% issue due in 2001. Fees 2.

Compagnie Bancaire (France)—C$75 million of 10¼% Eurobonds due June 13, 1994, issue price 101¾, via lead underwriter Hambros Bank Ltd. Yield 10.10% (annual) less full fees, spread 80 basis points over semiannual yield on benchmark three-year Canadian government bond. Fees 1⅜.

Credit Local de France (France)—150 billion Italian lire of 12.2% Eurobonds due June 12, 1996, fixed reoffer price 100.25, via Istituto Bancario San Paolo di Torino. Yield 12.13% (annual) at the fixed reoffer price. Fees 0.15.

Credit Local de France—100 million Swiss francs of 6⅝% public bonds due June 5, 1996, priced at 101¾ via Banque Paribas (Suisse). Fees 2⅛.

Western Australia Treasury Corp. (Australia)—A$100 million of 12% Eurobonds due June 24, 1998, issue price 101.80, via Hambros Bank Ltd. Yield 12.05% (annual) less full fees. Fees 2.

Yorkshire Building Society (U.K.)—£65 million of floating-rate notes due Feb. 14, 1994, issue price 99.61, via lead underwriter UBS Phillips & Drew. Notes will trade interchangeably with £100 million outstanding from payment date June 14, 1991. Coupon 10 basis points above the two-month London interbank offered rate for initial period running from June 14, 1991, to Aug. 14, 1991 (no accrued interest payable). Thereafter, coupon at 10 basis points above the three-month London interbank offered rate. Fees 0.10.

Figure 11.3. Bond new securities issues. (*Reprinted with permission from Investor's Business Daily.*)

bonds can be traded for about $100 (i.e., par of $1000 each). The current yield is $92.50 divided by $1000 (i.e., 9.25 percent). The yield to maturity is also 9.25 percent.

Tax-Exempt Bonds

Tax-exempt bonds are bonds whose interest is not taxable (for the federal income tax) to its owner. Refer to Fig 11.4, which shows the Florida Board of Education issue of 2019 selling for $95¾ each, that is, $957.50 per bond. The bond pays 7 percent, that is, $70 annual interest. The current yield ($70 ÷ $957.50) is 7.3 percent. Yield to maturity, 7.35 percent, is calculated as explained in Chaps. 12 and 13. This investment-grade bond is rated AA by Standard & Poor's (S&P).

New issues of tax-exempt bonds are described in the "official statement" (like a prospectus). The cover of a typical "official statement" is included in Fig. 11.5. The figure shows the variance in yields to maturity, depending on the year of maturity at which the issue was offered to investors. For example, the bonds maturing in 2005 are offered to provide a tax-exempt yield to maturity of 7.9 percent, and those maturing in 1998 provide a yield of 7.30 percent.

Municipal yields typically follow an ascending scale of yields (a "positive" yield curve), such that as the time to maturity increases, so does the yield to maturity. All of the bonds offered by the official statement were priced at par. As a result, the coupon interest rate for each maturity is equal to both the yield to maturity and the current yield.

Aside from determining yield rates, investors must consider a variety of fundamental and technical factors: the general level and direction of interest rates, projected inflation, callable or putable aspects of the debt, convertible features, if any, and other bond characteristics, including the creditworthiness and soundness of the issuer, the industry of the issuer, and the state of the economy. Further information concerning bond yields may be found in Chaps. 13 through 16, and 23.

Corporate Bonds

Market prices of corporate bonds are shown in Fig. 11.6. Refer to the figure, and see the entry for the issue IBM. This is a bond issue of 9.375 percent of October 2004. This means that for each $1000 bond, the annual interest is $93.75, and the bonds mature (for their face value of $1000) in 2004. "Priced at 102⅛ means that one can probably buy the bond for $1021.25 per bond. The current yield is $93.75 ÷ $1021.25 (neglecting brokerage

Moody's/S&P Ratings		Dollar Bid	Change In Bid	Yield to Maturity
	EDUCATION			
Aa/AA	FLORIDA BOARD OF ED PUBLIC EDUCATION CAPIT 7 06/01/19	95¾	- ¼	7.35
Aa/AA	FLORIDA STATE BOARD OF EDUCATION SER 89A R 7¼ 06/01/23	97⅛	- ¼	7.49
A/BBB+	NYS DORMS AUTH SER 90A CITY UNIV SYS CONSO 7⅝ 07/01/20	96⅛	- ⅛	7.97
A/A-	NYS DORMS STATE UNIV EDUCATIONAL FACILITIE 7¾ 05/15/12	97¾	- ⅛	7.92
	G.O. ET AL			
Aa/AA-	MARYLAND STADIUM AUTH SPORTS FACILITIES LE 7⅝ 12/15/19	99	- ¼	7.68
Aaa/AAA	MASSACHUSETTS G.O. CONSOLIDATED LOAN OF 7 10/01/09	94¾	- ⅛	7.51
Aaa/AAA	SOUTHEASTERN PUB SERV AUTH VA SENIOR REFUN 7 07/01/13	96⅜	- ¼	7.33
	HOSPITALS			
Aaa/AAA	CALIF HEALTH FAC FIN AUTH REVENUE SER 89A 7 07/01/20	95⅞	- ⅜	7.34
A/A-	NJ HEALTH CARE FACIL FIN AUTH REVENUE SER 7⅜ 07/01/15	96⅜	- ⅛	7.70
A/A-	NYS MED CARE FACILITIES FIN AGENCY MENTAL 7¾ 02/15/20	97⅞	- ⅛	7.94
	HOUSING			
Aaa/NR	FLORIDA HOUSING FINANCE AGENCY GNMA COLLAT 7⅞ 03/01/22	99⅜	- ⅛	7.95
NR/AAA	OHIO HOUSING FINANCE AGENCY SINGLE-FAMILY 7⅝ 03/01/29	97½	- ⅛	7.86
	POLLUTION CONTROL			
Aaa/AAA	BRAZOS RIVER AUTH TEX REFUND REV SER 89B H 7¼ 12/01/18	96½	- ¼	7.50
Aaa/AAA	MATAGORDA CO NAVIGATION DIST NO 1 TEX REFU 7¼ 12/01/18	96½	- ¼	7.50
Aaa/AAA	MATAGORDA NAVIGATION DIST .1 TEX PCR CENTR 7½ 03/01/20	98	- ¼	7.67
	POWER			
Aa3/AA-	CHICAGO ILLINOIS GAS SUPPLY SYS SER 85B&C 7½ 03/01/15	98¼	- ⅛	7.66
Aa/AA	JACKSONVILLE ELEC AUTH FLA FIRST CROSSOVER 6⅞ 10/01/13	93¾	- ¼	7.46
Aa/AA	LOS ANGELES DEPT OF WATER & POWER CALIF EL 6¾ 12/15/29	92⅜	- ¼	7.35
Aa2/AA-	NYS ENERGY RESEARCH & DEVLPMNT AUTH ELEC F 7¼ 11/01/24	93¾	- ⅝	7.77
Baa1/A-	PUERTO RICO ELEC PWR AUTH PWR REFUNDING RE 7⅛ 07/01/14	93⅞	- ⅜	7.68
Aaa/AAA	SACRAMENTO MUNICIPAL UTILITY DIST CALIF EL 7 07/01/20	95⅞	- ¼	7.34
A/A	SOUTHERN CALIF PUBLIC POWER AUTH MULTIPLE 7 07/01/09	95¼	- ⅜	7.46
A/AA-	WASH PUB PWR REFUND REV SER 89B NUCLEAR PR 7¼ 07/01/15	93⅛	- ⅛	7.88
A/AA-	WASHINGTON PUB PWR REFUND REVENUE BONNEVIL 7⅜ 07/01/12	94¾	- ¼	7.87
	TRANSPORTATION			
A3/A	ATLANTA GA REVENUE SER 89B AMT DELTA AIR L 7⅞ 12/01/18	99⅞	- ⅛	7.91
Aaa/AAA	CHICAGO O'HARE INTERNATIONAL AIRPORT SPECI 7⅝ 01/01/10	99½	- ⅛	7.67
A/A	CHICAGO O'HARE INTERNATIONAL AIRPORT SPECI 7½ 01/01/17	96	- ½	7.86
A1/AA	CONNECTICUT SPECIAL TAX OBLG TRANSPORTATIO 6¾ 12/01/09	94⅝	- ⅜	7.31
Aa/AA-	LONG BEACH CALIF HARBOR REVENUE SER 89A AM 7¼ 05/15/19	96⅝	- ⅜	7.53
A1/A	METRO WASHINGTON AIRPORTS AUTH VA AIRPORT 7⅝ 10/01/14	98⅛	- ¼	7.77
Aaa/AAA	MONROE CO AIRPORT AUTH NY GREATER ROCHESTE 7¼ 01/01/19	95½	- ⅛	7.63
A1/AA-	PORT AUTH OF NY & NJ CONSOLIDATED REVENUE 7¼ 02/15/25	95⅛	- ⅛	7.65
A1/AA-	PORT AUTH OF NY & NJ CONSOLIDATED REVENUE 6⅞ 01/01/25	92¼	- ⅛	7.50
A/A-	TEXAS TURNPIKE AUTH SER 89 NORTH DALLAS TO 7⅛ 01/01/15	95	- ¼	7.57
A/A	TRIBOROUGH BRIDGE & TUNNEL AUTH NY MORTGAG 7⅛ 01/01/19	91	- ⅛	7.92
	WATER			
Aa/AA	CALIF DEPT WATER RESOURCES SER G WTR SYS R 7⅛ 12/01/24	97⅛	- ¼	7.36
A1/A	LOS ANGELES CALIF WASTEWATER SYSTEM REVENU 6¾ 08/01/19	92⅞	- ¼	7.40
A/A-	MASSACHUSETTS WATER RESOURCES AUTH REVENUE 7½ 04/01/16	97¼	- ⅛	7.75
A/A-	MASSACHUSETTS WATER RESOURCES AUTH REVENUE 7⅝ 04/01/14	97⅞	- ¼	7.82
Aaa/AAA	TRINITY RIVER AUTH TEX REGIONAL WASTEWTR S 7⅛ 08/01/16	95½	- ¼	7.49

Figure 11.4. Tax-exempt bonds. (*Reprinted with permission from Investor's Business Daily.*)

OFFICIAL STATEMENT

NEW ISSUE

RATINGS — Moody's: A
S&P: A
(See "RATINGS" herein)

In the opinion of Bond Counsel, interest on the Bonds is excludable from the gross income of the recipients for purposes of federal income taxes under existing statutes, court decisions, regulations and published rulings, and, under existing laws, the interest on the Bonds is exempt from Kentucky income taxation, and the Bonds are exempt from ad valorem taxation (except inheritance taxes) by the Commonwealth of Kentucky and any political subdivision thereof. Included herein is a discussion of the possible federal income tax consequences of the purchase and ownership of the Bonds which could affect adversely the treatment of the interest on the Bonds for federal income tax purposes. (See "TAX EXEMPTION AND RELATED TAX MATTERS" herein).

$71,305,000
COMMONWEALTH OF KENTUCKY
State Property and Buildings Commission
Multipurpose Revenue Bonds, Project No. 48

Dated: December 1, 1988

Due: February 1 and August 1
as shown below

The Bonds, more fully described herein, are being issued by the Kentucky State Property and Buildings Commission (the "Commission") under the provisions of a Resolution and are secured by eleven separate Lease Financing Agreements which certain State Agencies have entered into as described herein. The Bonds bear interest payable on August 1, 1989 and semiannually thereafter on each February 1 and August 1 until maturity. Principal on the Bonds shall be payable at the principal corporate trust office of First Kentucky Trust Company, Louisville, Kentucky (the "Trustee"). Interest on the Bonds shall be payable by check or draft mailed to the registered owners of the Bonds as of the record date for such payment. The Bonds shall be issued only as fully registered bonds in the denominations of $5,000 or any integral multiple thereof.

$52,925,000 Serial Bonds

Maturity Date	Principal Amount	Interest Rate	Price	Maturity Date	Principal Amount	Interest Rate	Price
August 1, 1989	$1,905,000	6.20%	100%	February 1, 1998	$1,520,000	7.30%	100%
February 1, 1990	890,000	6.40	100	August 1, 1998	1,580,000	7.30	100
August 1, 1990	915,000	6.40	100	February 1, 1999	1,635,000	7.40	100
February 1, 1991	950,000	6.60	100	August 1, 1999	1,695,000	7.40	100
August 1, 1991	975,000	6.60	100	February 1, 2000	1,760,000	7.50	100
February 1, 1992	1,015,000	6.70	100	August 1, 2000	1,825,000	7.50	100
August 1, 1992	1,040,000	6.70	100	February 1, 2001	1,895,000	7.60	100
February 1, 1993	1,080,000	6.80	100	August 1, 2001	1,965,000	7.60	100
August 1, 1993	1,115,000	6.80	100	February 1, 2002	2,040,000	7.70	100
February 1, 1994	1,155,000	6.90	100	August 1, 2002	2,115,000	7.70	100
August 1, 1994	1,195,000	6.90	100	February 1, 2003	2,200,000	7.80	100
February 1, 1995	1,235,000	7.00	100	August 1, 2003	2,290,000	7.80	100
August 1, 1995	1,280,000	7.00	100	February 1, 2004	2,375,000	7.85	100
February 1, 1996	1,320,000	7.10	100	August 1, 2004	2,465,000	7.85	100
August 1, 1996	1,370,000	7.10	100	February 1, 2005	2,565,000	7.90	100
February 1, 1997	1,420,000	7.20	100	August 1, 2005	2,670,000	7.90	100
August 1, 1997	1,470,000	7.20	100				

$18,380,000 8.00% Term Bonds due August 1, 2008 — Price 100%
(Plus accrued interest)

The Bonds maturing on and after August 1, 1999 shall be subject to optional redemption as described herein. The Term Bonds shall also be subject to mandatory redemption, commencing February 1, 2006, as described herein.

The Bonds are special and limited obligations of the Commission, an independent agency of the Commonwealth of Kentucky (the "Commonwealth") and a public corporate body, issued at the request of eleven separate State Agencies for the purpose of (i) funding various State Agency projects as more fully described herein and (ii) paying the costs incident to the issuance of the Bonds.

THE BONDS DO NOT CONSTITUTE A DEBT, LIABILITY OR GENERAL OBLIGATION, WITHIN THE MEANING OF THE CONSTITUTION AND LAWS OF THE COMMONWEALTH, OF THE COMMISSION, THE COMMONWEALTH, OR ANY POLITICAL SUBDIVISION OR TAXING AUTHORITY THEREOF, OR A PLEDGE OF THE FAITH AND CREDIT OR THE TAXING POWER OF THE COMMONWEALTH OR ANY POLITICAL SUBDIVISION OR TAXING AUTHORITY THEREOF, BUT ARE PAYABLE SOLELY FROM LEASE PAYMENTS DERIVED FROM BIENNIALLY RENEWABLE LEASE FINANCING AGREEMENTS, THE PAYMENTS OF WHICH ARE SUBJECT TO APPROPRIATION BY THE GENERAL ASSEMBLY ON A BIENNIAL BASIS. THE BONDHOLDERS HAVE NO SECURITY INTEREST IN ANY PROPERTIES CONSTITUTING THE PROJECTS OR REVENUES THEREFROM.

The Bonds are offered when, as and if issued and accepted by the Underwriters, subject to prior sale, to withdrawal or modification of the offer without notice and to the approving legal opinion of Rubin and Hays, Louisville, Kentucky, Bond Counsel. Certain legal matters in connection with the Bonds will be passed upon for the Underwriters by their counsel, Greenberg, Traurig, Hoffman, Lipoff, Rosen & Quentel, P.A., Miami, Florida. It is expected that the Bonds, in definitive form, will be available for delivery in New York, New York on or about December 20, 1988.

Dean Witter Capital Markets

J. C. Bradford & Co.	Merit Financial Corporation
Merrill Lynch Capital Markets	Prescott, Ball & Turben, Inc.
Seasongood & Mayer	Stifel, Nicolaus & Company, Inc.

Dated: December 7, 1988

Figure 11.5. Typical cover page of the official statement of a new issue of tax-exempt bonds.

S&P Rating	Bond	Ex	Coupon Rate	Matures	Cur. Yld.	Yld. to Mat.	Vol.	Bond Close	Chg
AAA	IndianaBell	NY	8.000	10/14	8.5	8.6	13	93¾	+ 3¼
NR	InstrmtSys	Am	12.500	11/97	14.7	16.3	35	85	...
A –	IntlPapr	NY	5.125	11/12	8.5	9.5	3	60⅛	+ ⅛
AAA	IBM	NY	9.375	10/04	9.2	9.1	90	102⅛	– ¼
AAA	IBM	NY	10.250	10/95	9.8	8.9	186	104⅞	+ ⅜
AAA	IBM Credt	NY	9.625	03/92	9.4	7.3	5	102¼	...
B –	ICN Ph	NY	12.875	07/98	18.8	21.7	388	68⅜	+ 2⅜
B –	JonesInter	Am	13.000	05/00	15.1	16.0	70	86	+ 1¾
A	K mart	NY	8.125	01/97	8.4	8.8	8	97	– 1
A	K mart	NY	8.375	01/17	9.4	9.5	15	89	...
B –	KerrGlass	NY	13.000	12/96	14.6	16.0	25	89	+ ¼
NR	LeucdNtl	NY	14.000	05/93	13.5	12.1	10	103½	+ ¼
BBB +	Littonln	NY	11.500	07/95	11.1	10.4	10	103¾	– 1¼
A +	Lorillard	NY	6.875	12/93	7.1	8.4	72	96½	...
A –	LouⅰNash	NY	3.375	04/03	5.7	9.0	3	59	+ 1⅞
A –	LouⅰNash	NY	2.875	04/03	5.4	9.4	10	53½	+ ¾
BB +	LILCo	NY	11.500	11/14	11.1	11.1	7	103½	+ ¼
BBB –	LILCo	NY	11.875	04/15	11.0	11.0	12	107¾	+ ¾
B +	Magma	Am	14.500	06/01	14.6	14.6	112	99½	– ⅜
BBB –	MarathOil	NY	8.500	11/06	9.2	9.4	30	92⅞	+ ⅞
BBB –	MarathOil	NY	9.500	03/94	9.3	8.8	229	101⅞	+ ⅜
B	MarkIV	NY	13.375	03/99	13.2	13.2	13	101	...
B –	Mattel	NY	14.750	03/00	13.7	13.2	6	108	...
AA	McDnlds	NY	9.750	11/17	9.7	9.7	18	100½	– ½
AA	McDnlds	NY	9.750	05/19	9.5	9.4	5	103	– 1⅜
AA	McDnlds	NY	8.875	03/16	9.4	9.5	5	94	+ ⅛
AA	McDnlds	NY	ZrCpn	01/94	...	8.1	20	80⅛	– ¼
A –	MerLyn	NY	ZrCpn	10/91	...	10.0	2	95½	– ⅛
NR	MerLyn	NY	15.750	12/06	14.7	14.5	1	107½	+ ⅛
A	MerLyn	NY	ZrCpn	02/06	...	8.0	11	30⅞	...
B +	MesaCap	NY	13.500	05/99	15.0	15.7	10	90	...
B +	MesaCap	NY	12.000	08/96	13.6	15.4	6	88	+ 2
BBB +	MfrHano	NY	8.125	08/07	10.0	10.5	10	81½	...
AAA	MichBell	NY	9.600	10/08	9.4	9.3	25	102½	– ½
AAA	MichBell	NY	9.125	12/18	9.1	9.1	56	100¼	+ ¼

Figure 11.6. Corporate bond prices. (*Reprinted with permission from Investor's Business Daily.*)

costs), that is, 9.2 percent. The Standard & Poor's (S&P) ratings are furnished by that investment advisory and rating firm and attempt to rate the risk (of default) of this bond issue. Risk relates to the probability that interest will be paid on schedule and that the bond face amount will be paid at maturity. AAA is the best quality, AA is the next best, and so on. "Yld to Mat. 9.1" means that 9.1 percent is the bond's yield to maturity.

Government Issues

A variety of bonds, bills, notes, and other evidences of debt are issued by the U.S. Treasury and other governmental agencies and authorities. Prices of Treasury bonds, notes, and bills are shown in Fig. 11.7. Under "Govt. Bonds & Notes," see the bond maturing August 2019. The annual interest

Treasury Bills, Bonds & Notes

T-BILLS

Mat. Date	Bid	Asked	Bid Chg.	Yield
3-28 91	5.27	5.25	-.02	5.34
4-04 91	5.51	5.47	-.31	5.57
4-11 91	5.61	5.59	-.22	5.70
4-18 91	5.62	5.59	-.08	5.71
4-25 91	5.87	5.84	..	5.97
5-02 91	5.88	5.84	..	5.98
5-09 91	5.88	5.84	-.01	5.99
5-16 91	5.88	5.84		5.99
5-23 91	5.86	5.84	-.02	6.00
5-30 91	5.89	5.88	+.01	6.04
6-06 91	5.92	5.88	-.01	6.05
6-13 91	5.87	5.84	-.03	6.02
6-21 91	5.88	5.84	-.01	6.03
6-27 91	5.82	5.78	..	5.97
7-05 91	5.90	5.88	-.03	6.08
7-11 91	5.89	5.88	-.02	6.08
7-18 91	5.89	5.88	-.03	6.09
7-25 91	5.89	5.88	..	6.10
8-01 91	5.92	5.88	-.02	6.10
8-08 91	5.91	5.88	-.03	6.11
8-15 91	5.92	5.88	-.01	6.12
8-29 91	5.93	5.91	-.02	6.17
8-22 91	5.92	5.88	-.02	6.13
9-26 91	5.85	5.81	-.03	6.09
9-05 91	5.90	5.88	-.03	6.14
9-12 91	5.89	5.88	-.03	6.15
10-24 91	5.93	5.91	-.04	6.20
11-21 91	5.96	5.94	-.05	6.24
12-19 91	5.96	5.94	-.05	6.26
1-16 92	6.00	5.97	-.04	6.31
2-13 92	6.03	6.00	-.05	6.36
3-12 92	6.00	5.97	-.05	6.35

GOVT. BONDS & NOTES

Rate	Mat. Date	Bid	Asked	Bid Chg.	Yield
6¾s	3-91 p	99.30	100.2	..	4.09
9¾s	3-91 p	100.00	100.4	..	4.48
12⅝s	4-91 n	100.12	100.16	-.1	4.53
9¼s	4-91 p	100.10	100.14	+.1	4.99
8⅛s	5-91 p	100.7	100.11	..	5.64
14½s	5-91 n	101.6	101.10	-.1	5.36
8¾s	5-91 p	100.13	100.17	..	5.80
7⅞s	6-91 n	100.12	100.16	..	5.93
8¼s	6-91 p	100.16	100.20	..	5.84
7¾s	7-91 p	100.16	100.20	+.1	5.92
13¾s	7-91 n	102.9	102.13	+.1	5.89
7½s	8-91 p	100.15	100.19	+.1	5.95
8¾s	8-91 p	100.30	101.2	..	6.00
14⅞s	8-91 n	103.13	103.17	..	5.83
8¼s	8-91 p	100.24	100.28	..	6.18
8⅝s	9-91 p	101.1	101.5	+.1	6.10
9⅛s	9-91 p	101.13	101.17	..	6.11
7⅝s	10-91 p	100.23	100.27	..	6.17
12¼s	10-91 p	103.6	103.10	..	6.18
6½s	11-91 p	100.1	100.5	..	6.23
8½s	11-91 p	101.9	101.13	+.1	6.23
14¼s	11-91 n	104.27	105.5	..	6.00
7¾s	11-91 p	100.26	100.30	+.1	6.32
7⅝s	12-91 p	100.27	100.31	..	6.31
8¼s	12-91 p	101.10	101.14	+.1	6.30
8⅛s	1-92 p	101.10	101.14	+.1	6.37
11⅝s	1-92 p	104.00	104.4	+.1	6.34
6⅝s	2-92 p	99.31	100.3	+1	6.51
8½s	2-92 p	101.21	101.25	+.1	6.51
9⅛s	2-92 p	102.3	102.7	..	6.54
14⅝s	2-92 n	107.13	107.23	..	5.72
7⅞s	3-92 p	101.6	101.10	+.1	6.53
8½s	3-92 p	101.26	101.30	+.2	6.51
8⅞s	4-92 p	102.8	102.12	+.2	6.60
11⅝s	4-92 k	105.3	105.7	+.3	6.59
6⅝s	5-92 p	99.28	100.00	+.2	6.61
9 s	5-92 p	102.12	102.16	+.2	6.69
13¾s	5-92 n	107.17	107.21	+.2	6.70
8½s	5-92 p	101.27	101.31	+.2	6.74
8¼s	6-92 p	101.22	101.26	+.3	6.73
8⅜s	6-92 p	101.26	101.30	+.3	6.75
10⅜s	7-92 p	104.9	104.13	+.3	6.81
8 s	7-92 p	101.12	101.16	-.3	6.82
4¼s	8-87-92	95.18	96.20	+.3	6.81
7¼s	8-92	100.20	100.26	+.4	6.63
8⅛s	8-92 p	101.18	101.22	+.3	6.87
8¼s	8-92 p	101.21	101.25	+.4	6.89
7⅞s	8-92 p	101.4	101.8	+.3	6.92
8⅛s	9-92 p	101.18	101.22	+.2	6.94
8¾s	9-92 p	102.14	102.18	+.3	6.95
7¾s	10-92 p	100.31	101.3	+.3	7.01
9¾s	10-92 p	103.30	104.2	+.3	6.96
7¾s	11-92 p	100.31	101.3	+.3	7.03
8⅜s	11-92 p	101.30	102.2	+.3	7.02
10½s	11-92 n	105.5	105.9	+.2	7.04
7⅜s	11-92 p	100.14	100.18	+.3	7.01
7¼s	12-92 p	100.8	100.11	+.3	7.03
9⅛s	12-92 p	103.9	103.13	+.3	7.04
7 s	1-93 p	99.24	99.27	+.3	7.08
8¾s	1-93 p	102.23	102.27	+.4	7.05
4 s	2-88-93	94.16	95.18	+.4	6.51
6¾s	2-93	99.13	99.19	+.4	6.98
6¾s	2-93 p	99.10	99.13	+.4	7.06
7⅞s	2-93	101.10	101.16	+.4	7.01
8¼s	2-93 p	101.28	102.00	+.2	7.10
8⅜s	2-93 p	102.4	102.8	+.4	7.08
10⅞s	2-93 n	106.15	106.19	+.3	7.10
9⅝s	3-93 p	104.17	104.21	+.4	7.11
7⅜s	4-93 p	100.12	100.16	+.4	7.11
7⅝s	5-93 p	100.26	100.30	+.4	7.14
10⅛s	5-93 n	105.22	105.26	+.5	7.15
8⅝s	5-93 p	102.23	102.27	+.5	7.17
8¼s	6-93 p	101.26	101.30	+.5	7.18
7¼s	7-93 p	100.00	100.4	+.4	7.18
7½s	8-88-93	100.7	100.13	-1	6.42
8⅝s	8-93	103.00	103.6	+.7	7.15
8¾s	8-93 p	103.3	103.7	+.4	7.26
11⅞s	8-93 n	109.29	110.1	+.6	7.24
8 s	8-93 p	101.16	101.19	+.5	7.26
8¼s	9-93 p	102.3	102.7	+.4	7.27
7⅛s	10-93 p	99.15	99.19	+.4	7.30
7¾s	11-93 p	100.29	101.00	+.5	7.32
8⅝s	11-93	103.2	103.8	+.8	7.25
11¾s	11-93 n	110.9	110.13	+.6	7.35
9 s	11-93 p	103.26	103.30	+.5	7.33
7⅝s	12-93 p	100.18	100.22	+.5	7.34
7 s	1-94 p	99.1	99.5	+.6	7.33
6⅞s	2-94 p	98.23	98.26	+.6	7.33
9 s	2-94	103.31	104.5	+.4	7.38
8⅞s	2-94 p	103.22	103.26	+.5	7.39
8½s	3-94 p	102.26	102.30	+.6	7.40
7 s	4-94 p	98.26	98.30	+.6	7.39
4⅛s	5-89-94	94.11	95.13	+.7	5.74
13⅛s	5-94 p	115.12	115.18	+.2	7.48
9½s	5-94 p	105.14	105.18	+.4	7.48
8½s	6-94 p	102.26	102.30	+.8	7.47
8 s	7-94 p	101.11	101.15	+.6	7.49
8⅝s	8-94 p	103.3	103.7	+.8	7.53
8¾s	8-94	103.15	103.31	+.6	7.41
12⅝s	8-94 p	114.25	114.31	+.7	7.55
8½s	9-94 p	102.23	102.27	+.6	7.56
9½s	10-94 p	105.21	105.25	+.5	7.61
10⅛s	11-94	107.24	107.30	+.6	7.59
11⅝s	11-94 p	112.13	112.19	+.6	7.60
8¼s	11-94 p	101.29	102.1	+.7	7.60
7⅝s	12-94 p	99.30	100.1	+.6	7.61
8⅝s	1-95 p	103.00	103.4	+.7	7.66
3 s	2-95	94.13	95.15	+.6	4.27
10½s	2-95	109.7	109.13	+.7	7.66
11¼s	2-95 p	111.19	111.25	+.6	7.69
7¾s	2-95 p	100.5	100.9	+.6	7.66
8⅜s	4-95 p	102.6	102.10	+.8	7.70
8½s	5-95 p	102.20	102.24	+.8	7.71
10⅜s	5-95	108.30	109.4	+.6	7.76
11¼s	5-95 p	111.31	112.5	+.7	7.76
12⅝s	5-95	116.24	116.30	+.7	7.76
8⅞s	7-95 p	103.28	104.00	+.6	7.76
10½s	8-95 p	109.24	109.30	+.7	7.79
8½s	8-95 p	102.19	102.23	+.6	7.76
8⅝s	10-95 p	103.00	103.4	+.7	7.80
8½s	11-95 p	102.18	102.22	+.8	7.79
9½s	11-95 p	106.9	106.13	+.7	7.82
11½s	11-95	114.00	114.6	+.7	7.80
7½s	1-96 p	98.23	98.26	+.7	7.79
9¼s	1-96 p	105.14	105.18	+.9	7.84
7½s	2-96 p	98.23	98.26	+.8	7.79
7⅞s	2-96 p	100.1	100.5	+.7	7.82
8⅞s	2-96 p	104.00	104.4	+.7	7.84
9⅜s	4-96 p	105.31	106.3	+.8	7.89
7⅜s	5-96 p	97.25	97.29	+.9	7.87
7⅞s	7-96 p	99.25	99.29	+.8	7.89
8 s	10-96 p	100.5	100.9	+.9	7.93
7¼s	11-96 p	96.23	96.27	+.8	7.95
8 s	1-97 p	100.00	100.4	+.8	7.97
8½s	4-97 p	102.8	102.12	+.8	8.00
8½s	5-97 p	102.6	102.10	+.9	8.01
8½s	7-97 p	102.6	102.10	+.9	8.02
8⅝s	8-97 p	102.24	102.28	+.6	8.04
8¾s	10-97 p	103.12	103.16	+.8	8.05
8⅞s	11-97 p	104.00	104.4	+.9	8.06
7⅞s	1-98 p	99.5	99.9	+.7	8.01
8⅛s	2-98 p	100.7	100.11	+.6	8.06
9 s	5-98 p	104.23	104.27	+.11	8.09
9¼s	8-98 p	106.2	106.6	+.11	8.12
7 s	5-93-98	94.11	95.8	+.7	7.88
3½s	11-98	94.14	95.16	+.7	4.19
8⅞s	11-98 p	103.31	104.3	+.8	8.14
8⅞s	2-99 p	103.31	104.3	+.8	8.16
8½s	5-94-99	101.27	102.3	+.9	7.73
9⅛s	5-99 p	105.13	105.17	+.9	8.18
8 s	8-99 p	98.30	99.2	+.9	8.15
7⅞s	11-99 p	98.00	98.4	+.8	8.18
8½s	2-00 p	101.24	101.28	+.7	8.20
7¾s	2-01 p	31.12	31.16	+.09	8.14
7⅞s	2-95-00	98.8	98.14	+.11	8.12
8⅞s	5-00 p	104.3	104.7	+.9	8.21
8⅜s	8-95-00	100.22	101.3	+.7	8.07
8¾s	8-00 p	103.12	103.16	+.9	8.21
8½s	11-00 p	101.26	101.30	+.8	8.20
11¾s	2-01	123.20	123.26	+.11	8.19
13⅛s	5-01	133.12	133.18	+.11	8.19
8 s	8-96-01	99.00	99.10	+.10	8.10
13⅜s	8-01	135.18	135.24	+.11	8.20
15¾s	11-01	152.15	152.29	+.14	8.20
14¼s	2-02	142.10	142.24	+.14	8.23
11⅝s	11-02	124.13	124.19	+.11	8.29
10¾s	2-03	117.30	118.4	+.14	8.32
10¾s	5-03	117.29	118.3	+.11	8.35
11⅛s	8-03	120.25	120.31	+.8	8.37
11⅞s	11-03	126.25	126.31	+.11	8.37
12⅜s	5-04	131.5	131.11	+.8	8.39
13¾s	8-04	142.17	142.23	+.6	8.38
11⅝s	11-04 k	125.16	125.22	-.11	8.42
8¼s	5-00-05	99.10	99.24	+.10	8.28
12 s	5-05 k	128.31	129.5	+.11	8.43
10¾s	8-05 k	118.26	119.00	+.10	8.44
9⅜s	2-06 k	108.15	108.21	+.8	8.35
7⅝s	2-02-07	93.27	94.5	+.9	8.29
7⅞s	11-02-07	95.30	96.8	+.10	8.29
8⅜s	8-03-08	99.26	100.4	+.10	8.36
8¾s	11-03-08	102.7	102.15	+.11	8.43
9⅛s	5-04-09	105.1	105.11	+.10	8.44
10⅜s	11-04-09	114.17	114.23	+.14	8.53
11¾s	2-05-10	125.28	126.2	+.14	8.51
10 s	5-05-10	112.6	112.16	+.14	8.47
12¾s	11-05-10	134.21	134.27	+.14	8.53
13⅞s	5-06-11	144.23	144.29	+.15	8.53
14 s	11-06-11	146.16	146.22	+.15	8.53
10⅜s	11-07-12	115.30	116.2	+.13	8.55
12 s	8-08-13	130.25	130.29	+.14	8.55
13¼s	5-09-14	142.25	142.31	+.14	8.55
12½s	8-09-14k	136.8	136.14	+.14	8.54
11¾s	11-09-14k	129.19	129.25	+.13	8.53
11¼s	2-15 k	127.31	128.5	+.16	8.48
10⅝s	8-15 k	121.21	121.27	+.14	8.49
9⅞s	11-15 k	114.6	114.12	+.13	8.47
9¼s	2-16 k	107.27	108.1	+.11	8.47
7¼s	5-16 k	87.17	87.21	+.11	8.44
7½s	11-16 k	90.00	90.4	+.11	8.45
8¾s	5-17 k	103.1	103.5	+.12	8.45
8⅞s	8-17 k	104.10	104.14	+.14	8.45
9⅛s	5-18 k	107.3	107.7	+.11	8.44
9 s	11-18 k	106.00	106.4	+.12	8.42
8⅞s	2-19 k	104.21	104.25	+.13	8.43
8⅛s	8-19 k	96.26	96.30	+.9	8.41
8½s	2-20 k	101.00	101.4	+.10	8.39
8¾s	5-20 k	104.2	104.6	+.11	8.36
8¾s	8-20 k	104.00	104.4	+.10	8.37
7⅞s	2-21 k	94.27	94.31	+.10	8.33

STRIPPED SECURITIES

Mat. Date	Bid	Asked	Bid Chg.	Yield
2-91 a	99.31	100.00	..	5.75
5-91 a	99.4	99.5	+.1	5.70
8-91 a	97.19	97.20	+.2	6.03
11-91 a	96.5	96.7	+.2	6.03
2-92 a	94.11	94.14	+.2	6.44
5-92 a	92.26	92.30	+.3	6.48
8-92 a	90.28	91.1	+.3	6.81
11-92 a	89.11	89.16	+.4	6.84
2-93 a	87.13	87.20	+.4	7.06
5-93 a	85.25	86.00	+.5	7.14
8-93 a	84.2	84.9	+.6	7.24
11-93 a	82.18	82.26	+.6	7.25
2-94 a	80.21	80.28	+.7	7.45
5-94 a	78.30	79.7	+.8	7.54
8-94 a	77.9	77.18	+.6	7.61
11-94 a	75.31	76.9	+.5	7.56
2-95 a	74.1	74.11	+.4	7.74
5-95 a	72.17	72.27	+.5	7.78
8-95 a	70.31	71.10	+.4	7.83
11-95 a	69.26	70.4	+.4	7.78
2-96 a	67.29	68.7	+.2	7.95
5-96 a	66.16	66.27	+.2	7.98
8-96 a	65.1	65.12	+.2	8.02
11-96 a	63.26	64.5	+.2	8.01
2-97 a	62.5	62.16	+.3	8.12
5-97 a	60.28	61.7	+.3	8.14
8-97 a	59.18	59.29	+.4	8.16
11-97 a	58.12	58.24	+.4	8.16
2-98 a	57.1	57.13	+.5	8.20
5-98 a	55.27	56.7	+.4	8.22
8-98 a	54.20	55.00	+.6	8.24
11-98 a	53.17	53.29	+.6	8.24
2-99 a	52.5	52.17	+.6	8.31
5-99 a	51.1	51.14	+.6	8.33
8-99 a	49.28	50.9	+.5	8.35
11-99 a	48.27	49.7	+.6	8.37
2-00 a	47.24	48.5	+.5	8.38
5-00 a	46.23	47.5	+.4	8.39
8-00 a	45.23	46.4	+.6	8.40
11-00 a	44.29	45.11	+.7	8.37
2-01 a	43.25	44.6	+.7	8.42
5-01 a	42.27	43.8	+.7	8.43
8-01 a	41.30	42.11	+.7	8.43
11-01 a	41.5	41.19	+.7	8.41
2-02 a	40.3	40.17	+.7	8.46
5-02 a	39.8	39.21	+.7	8.47
8-02 a	38.12	38.25	+.6	8.48
11-02 a	37.17	37.31	+.5	8.49
2-03 a	36.20	37.1	+.7	8.52
5-03 a	35.26	36.8	+.6	8.53
8-03 a	35.1	35.14	+.6	8.54
11-03 a	34.10	34.23	+.7	8.54
2-04 a	33.16	33.29	+.8	8.56

Figure 11.7. Treasury bills, bonds, and notes. (*Reprinted with permission from Investor's Business Daily.*)

is 81.25 (8.125 percent of face value of $1000). Prices of Treasury, government, and agency issues are quoted in units of $\frac{1}{32}$ of a dollar, so a price of 96.30 means $96^{30}\!/_{32} \times 10$, that is, $969.375. The current yield is $81.25 divided by the asked price of $969.375, that is, 8.382 percent. The yield shown is the yield to maturity of 8.41 percent. Treasury bond yields are calculated using a 365-day year (as opposed to the 360-day year used in calculating yields on corporates).

Agencies

A variety of quasi-governmental agencies issue publicly traded debt. Generally, such issues are not guaranteed by the "full faith and credit" of the U.S. government. Instead the agency may have certain legislated limited rights to borrow from the Treasury or have governmental officials comprising its board of directors. Generally, agency debt sells at higher yields than U.S. Treasury debt, both because of the slightly higher risk and because of the lesser trading liquidity involved. Prices of the debt of such agencies as FNMA (Federal National Market association), World Bank, GNMA (Government National Mortgage Association), Bank for Cooperatives, Federal Land Bank, etc., are shown in Fig. 11.8.

Treasury Bills

Six-month (182-day) and three-month (91-day) Treasury bills are sold at a discount rather than at face or par value (see Fig. 11.7). Explicit interest is not paid; instead, the investor's dollar return is measured by the difference between the bill's par or maturity value and the discount price paid. Since investors purchase bills at a discount, calculation of the interest return is based on the total amount actually paid (and not on the face value that the investor will receive at maturity).

Bills are quoted differently from notes and bonds, since bills do not pay a stated rate of interest. In other words, the coupon rate on a bill is zero. An investor's return on a bill is the difference between the purchase price and the subsequent sale price or, when held to maturity, the face value paid by the Treasury. As a result, bills are quoted at a discount from face value, with the discount expressed as an annual rate based on 360 days. Quotations of all bills are therefore comparable regardless of maturity. A typical Treasury bill quotation is

Issue	Bid	Ask	Change	Yield
8/03/95	7.73	7.71	+0.02	8.29

Miscellaneous Debt Securities

FNMA ISSUES

GNMA ISSUES

FEDERAL HOME LOAN

FEDERAL LAND BANK

WORLD BANK BONDS

STUDENT LOAN MKTG.

FED FARM CREDIT

Figure 11.8. Miscellaneous debt securities. (*Reprinted with permission from Investor's Business Daily.*)

The issue represents a Treasury bill which matures August 3. Assume for purposes of this example that the current date is 55 days before the maturity date. The "bid," 7.73 percent, is the return, on a discount basis, that the buyer would receive if a seller accepts the buyer's proposed (bid) price. To obtain a 7.73 percent annual return, the buyer is offering to pay $9881.90 for a Treasury bill maturing in 55 days with a face or maturity value of $10,000. When the bill is held to maturity, the owner receives $10,000 or $118.10 more than the $9881.90 purchase price. This $118.10 represents a 7.73 percent annualized return on a discount basis.

The "ask" price of 7.71 percent is the return the seller would like to see the buyer accept on a discount basis. The seller would receive $9882.21 for the $10,000-face-value bill if the buyer agrees to accept the 7.71 percent discount return. The following examples show the calculation of price and yield based on a transaction at the 7.73 percent bid.

Price of a Treasury Bill: 6 Months or Less to Maturity

The formula for determining the price of a Treasury bill with 6 months or less until maturity is

$$P = S - \left[\frac{(S)\,(d)\,(t)}{360} \right]$$

where P = price, the purchase price for each $100 of the bill's face value (Bills are normally sold in minimum denominations of $10,000.)

t = time, the actual number of days until maturity (count the maturity date but *not* settlement date)

S = sum at maturity, the maturity value of the bills (the face value)

N = number of days in a year (use 366 if leap year and February 29 occurs between current date and maturity)

D = discount from face value (i.e., $S - P$)

d = rate of discount

For the example transaction,

$$P = S - \left[\frac{(S)\,(d)\,(t)}{360} \right]$$

$$= \$10{,}000 - \frac{(\$10{,}000)\,(0.0773)\,(55)}{360} = \$10{,}000 - \$118.097 = \$9881.90$$

Yield of a Treasury Bill:
6 Months or Less to Maturity

The difference between the purchase price and the face value is the profit, referred to as the *discount*. There are three methods of computing the yield on bills: the *discount method, simple yield,* and *the coupon equivalent method* or *equivalent coupon-issue yield method.*

Yield by Discount Method. The discount method figures the discount rate as a percentage of the face value of the bill, rather than of the purchase price. This method understates the actual yield; $118.097 divided by the $10,000 maturity value for 55 days represents a return of 7.73 percent. The discount method also uses a 360-day year. The calculation for the rate of discount is

$$d = \left(\frac{S-P}{S}\right)\left(\frac{360}{t}\right)\left(\frac{\$118.10}{\$10,000}\right)\left(\frac{360}{55}\right) = 0.0773 \quad \text{or} \quad 7.73\%$$

The *rate of discount*, calculated in the standard industry fashion as just described, *understates the rate that an investor will actually earn.* This is due to the comparison of the discount to the *face* value (rather than to the actual purchase price) and due to the use of a 360-day year (rather than the actual number of days in the year). The rate of discount is convertible into an *equivalent simple interest rate* (again understating the effective yield) by use of the following formula:

$$Y = \left(\frac{D}{P}\right)\left(\frac{360}{t}\right) = \left(\frac{\$118.1}{\$9881.9}\right)\left(\frac{360}{55}\right) = 7.823\%$$

Coupon Equivalent or Bond Equivalent Yield (6 Months or Less to Maturity). The bond equivalent yield (BEY), or coupon equivalent yield (sometimes referred to as "investment yield or rate" or "interest yield") is normally reported by the Treasury along with the yield calculated by the discount method. The BEY eliminates the two problems of the discount rate referred to earlier. This BEY formula is used for discount securities including Treasury bills with 6 months or less to maturity. It is a simple interest rate. The bond equivalent yield (BEY) formula is

$$\text{BEY} = \left(\frac{S-P}{P}\right)\left(\frac{N}{t}\right)$$

where BEY = bond equivalent yield
S = maturity value
P = current price
N = days in a year

t = actual days from the day following settlement through maturity date

Thus, in the example transaction, the bond equivalent yield is

$$\text{BEY} = \left(\frac{\$10{,}000 - \$9881.90}{\$9881.90}\right)\left(\frac{365}{55}\right) = 0.07931 \quad \text{or} \quad 7.931\%$$

The BEY can also be found as follows:

$$\text{BEY} = \left[\frac{365(d)}{360 - (d)\,(t)}\right]\left[\frac{365\,(0.0773)}{360 - (0.0773)\,(55)}\right] = 0.07931 \quad \text{or} \quad 7.931\%$$

where d is the discount rate.

Example: Finding the discount rate and the bond equivalent yield. A 6-month (182-day) bill is auctioned by the Treasury at an average price of $9,521.90 per $10,000 face value. The year, 1996, is a leap year. What is the discount rate, and what is the bond equivalent yield?

First, to find the *rate of discount*, the formula is

$$d = \left(\frac{S-P}{S}\right)\left(\frac{360}{t}\right)\left(\frac{\$10{,}000 - \$9521.90}{\$10{,}000}\right)\left(\frac{360}{182}\right) = 0.09457 \quad \text{or} \quad 9.457\%$$

Thus, the discount rate, or bank discount rate, is 9.457 percent, and simple yield is 9.932 percent.

Next, to find the *bond equivalent yield*, the formula is

$$\text{BEY} = \left(\frac{S-P}{P}\right)\left(\frac{N}{t}\right) = \left(\frac{\$10{,}000 - \$9521.90}{\$9521.90}\right)\left(\frac{366}{182}\right)$$

$$= 0.10097 \quad \text{or} \quad 10.097\%$$

The coupon equivalent or bond equivalent yield, with a 366-day year, is 10.097 percent. With a 365-day year, the BEY is 10.07 percent.

Treasury Bills with More than 6 Months to Maturity

A different formula is required to compute the yield of Treasury bills that have longer than 6 months remaining until maturity. Why? A slight digression will help explain the answer. Which would be the better investment—a $1000 bond with a maturity of 1 year with interest of $100 paid at the end of a year; or a $1000 bond with a maturity of 1 year with interest of $50 paid at the end of 6 months and $50 paid again at the end of 1 year? The $50 coupon bond would be quoted at a 10 percent yield to maturity. (In reality, the yield is 10 percent, compounded semiannually.) The $100 coupon bond would be quoted as a 10 percent yield with annual compounding. The conventional standard for quoting bond yields is to double the semiannual rate. But in this example, an investor would obviously be better off with the semiannual $50 coupon, because the investor would have the use of $50 in interest after only 6 months. If the investor chooses to reinvest the income, then he will obtain additional interest on the interest for 6 months of investing $50. And that makes the $50 coupon paid semiannually more valuable than the $100 coupon paid annually.

Back in Chap. 1 we discussed effective yields. The formula is

$$Y = \left(1 + \frac{r}{m}\right)^m - 1$$

where Y = effective annual yield
   r = conventional or nominal yield (rate)
   m = number of periods of compounding per year

The effective yield of the $50 coupon is

$$Y = \left(1 + \frac{r}{m}\right)^m - 1$$

$$= \left(1 + \frac{0.1}{2}\right)^2 - 1$$

$$= (1.05)^2 - 1$$

$$= 0.1025 \quad \text{or} \quad 10.25\%$$

Thus, a yield of 10 percent, with semiannual compounding, is equivalent to a 10¼ percent annual yield. Or, to put it another way, the conventionally quoted yield (10 percent) is understated. With a Treasury bill (or comparable security sold at a discount—a zero-coupon security) which has more than 6 months to maturity, the owner will not have an opportunity to receive interest and reinvest it at some intermediate point before maturity. Thus, a discounted yield of, say, 10 percent is not as valuable as a coupon-paying bond of the same maturity at a quoted yield of 10 percent (which means 10 percent, compounded semiannually). To make the discounted bill's yield comparable to coupon-paying instruments, the yield of the bill must be adjusted downward to reflect the fact that there will be no opportunity to receive interest prior to maturity.

Bond Equivalent Yield: More than 6 Months to Maturity.   The bond equivalent yield, based on semiannual interest payments, for a discount security with more than 6 months to maturity is given by

$$BEY = \frac{\dfrac{-2t}{365} + 2\sqrt{\left(\dfrac{t}{365}\right)^2 - \left(\dfrac{2t}{365} - 1\right)\left(1 - \dfrac{1}{P/100}\right)}}{\dfrac{2t}{365} - 1}$$

where BEY = coupon yield equivalent or bond yield equivalent
  t = time, the number of days until maturity
  P = price, the purchase price for each $100 of the bill's face value

(Bills are normally sold in minimum denominations of $10,000.)

Example: Finding coupon equivalent yield: more than 6 months to maturity. A Treasury bill is delivered on May 15, 1997. It matures April 9, 1998. The purchase price is 94.096278. What is the bond equivalent yield?

The actual number of days is 329 from delivery (settlement) to maturity. This is calculated on the actual number of days in each month. The formula given above is solved for y, as follows:

$$BEY = \frac{\dfrac{-2(329)}{365} + 2\sqrt{\left(\dfrac{329}{365}\right)^2 - \left(\dfrac{2\,(329)}{365} - 1\right)\left(1 - \dfrac{1}{0.94096278/100}\right)}}{\dfrac{2(329)}{365} - 1}$$

$$= \frac{-1.80274 + 2\sqrt{0.81247 - (0.80274)\,(-0.06274)}}{0.80274}$$

$$= \frac{-1.80274 + 1.85777}{0.80274} = 0.06856 \quad \text{or} \quad 6.856\%$$

The bond equivalent yield is 6.856 percent. This contrasts with the investment yield of 6.96 percent. The investment yield of 6.906 percent is found by the following method:

$$y = \left(\frac{\text{discount}}{\text{price}}\right)\left(\frac{365}{\text{days to maturity}}\right) = \left(\frac{5.90372}{94.096278}\right)\left(\frac{365}{329}\right)$$

$$= (0.06274)\,(1.10942) = 6.961\%$$

The bond equivalent yield is less because it is calculated as if interest were compounded 6 months from maturity. A derivation of the formula is shown in Appendix 3 as provided by The Federal Reserve Bank of New York's publication, *The Arithmetic of Interest Rates*. It is based on the use of the quadratic formula to find the root (the rate) of a second-degree equation. To obtain the publication, write: Public Information Department, Federal Reserve Bank of New York, 33 Liberty Street, New York, New York, 10045.

12

Bond Yields

After the original issuance of bonds, they are normally bought and sold at prices other than their maturity value. The maturity value, or face amount (usually $1000), is the amount which the issuer of the bond promises to pay to the owner at the bond's maturity date. The maturity date may be 1, 5, 15, or 20 years, or after some other interval from the date on which the bonds were issued (or dated). The exception is that, at original issuance, bonds are usually offered at a price equal to the maturity value. Once issued, bonds trade at varying prices as interest rates fluctuate.

The issuer of most U.S. bonds also promises to pay interest to the owner every 6 months.* The annual rate of interest (e.g., 6 percent) is expressed as a percentage of the bond face amount or maturity value. The interest may also be expressed as a dollar amount, for example, as $60, which means that the total annual interest payments are $60—equivalent to 6 percent of the $1000 maturity value. Thus, $30 would be paid each 6 months.

Bond Yield to Maturity

If today one buys for $1000 a bond with a maturity value in 20 years of $1000, and if the bond pays 6 percent per year (the interest *coupon*), then the yield to the purchaser is 6 percent. However, if the purchaser buys the bond at a *discount*, that is, he or she pays less than $1000, the *yield to maturity* (YTM) will be greater than 6 percent. Similarly, if the purchaser pays a *premium* for the bond, that is, he or she buys it for more than $1000, the YTM will be less than 6 percent.

*European bonds, on the other hand, normally pay interest annually. Thus a 10 percent yield on a European bond is worth less than a U.S. bond sold to yield 10 percent to maturity.

Short-Cut Calculation of Bond Yield to Maturity

In the previous chapter, we saw how to compute the yield of Treasury bills. Bills are discount securities (zero coupon). A major part of Treasury borrowing is by notes and bonds, which generally pay interest semiannually and have maturities of more than 1 year.

Treasury notes and bonds, as well as corporate and municipal bonds, may be sold either at a discount or at a premium. When a bond is sold at a discount, the investor pays less than the maturity value. For example, a newly issued bond or note with a purchase price of $95 means the investor receives a discount of $5 per $100 of maturity value. A security with a maturity value of $1000 would cost $950.

When a bond or note is sold at a premium, the investor pays a price greater than the maturity value. For example, if the purchase price were $110, the purchaser would pay $1100 for each $1000 of maturity value.

The actual price paid—whether at par, discount, or premium—determines the true rate of return (yield to maturity). *If the security is bought at par, the yield to maturity is the same as the coupon rate.* If it is bought at a *premium*, then the yield to maturity will be *less* than the coupon rate; and if it is purchased at a *discount*, the yield to maturity will be more than the coupon rate.

The approximate yield to maturity can be calculated using the following simple formulas, where

y = yield to maturity
D = amount of discount from maturity (face) value (or $S\text{-}P$)
n = number of years to maturity
R = regular coupon payment (semiannual payment if payments are semiannual)
S = maturity (face) value
P = purchase price
$P - S$ = amount of premium

Discount Security: Approximate Yield to Maturity

The formula for the approximate yield to maturity for a discount bond is

$$y = \frac{(2)R + (D/N)}{(S + P)/2}$$

Example: Finding approximate yield to maturity—discount bond.   A bond that has a coupon rate of 8.5 percent of face value, payable semiannually, will mature in 2 years. The purchase price is \$99.802 per \$100 of par value. What is the approximate yield to maturity?

$$y = \frac{(2)R + (D/N)}{(S + P)/2}$$

$$= \frac{(2)(\$42.50) + (1.98/2)}{(\$1000 + \$998.02)/2}$$

$$= \$0.08608 \text{ or } 8.61\%$$

This compares to the computer-calculated yield to maturity of 8.612 percent.

Premium Security: Approximate Yield to Maturity

The formula for the approximate yield to maturity for a premium bond is

$$y = \frac{(2)R - [(P - S)/N]}{(S + P)/2}$$

Example: Finding approximate yield to maturity—premium bond.   A bond has a coupon rate of 12 percent of face value, payable semiannually, matures in 10 years, and the purchase price is \$112.5 per \$100 of par value. What is the approximate yield to maturity?

$$y = \frac{(2)R - [(P - S)/N]}{(S + P)/2}$$

$$= \frac{(2)(\$60) - [(\$1125 - \$1000)/10]}{(\$1000 + \$1125)/2}$$

$$= 0.1012 \text{ or } 10.12\%$$

This compares to the computer-calculated yield of 9.968 percent for annual payments of interest.

Bond Yield to Maturity, Simplified

The following simplified formula can be used to determine approximate bond yield to maturity. This formula is for situations where: (1) whole years are the time period from settlement date until maturity or call; (2) there is

no accrued interest to consider; (3) compounding is annual. In due course
we will explore a method of handling fractional years, periodic compounding, and accrued interest.

$$P = R\left[\frac{1 - (1 + i)^{-n}}{i}\right] + S(1 + i)^{-n}$$

where i = yield to maturity, with interest compounded annually
 P = purchase price of the bond
 S = maturity value of the bond
 n = number of years from settlement date to maturity
 R = annual amount of bond interest

Both the values of the factor

$$\left[\frac{1 - (1 + i)^{-n}}{i}\right]$$

called "present worth of $1 per period or what $1 payable periodically is worth
today," and the value of expression $(1 + i)^{n}$, which is called "present worth of
$1 or what $1 due in the future is worth today," are provided in Appendix 1.

 Example: Finding the price of a bond. How much should an investor pay
for a bond to yield 10 percent to maturity (i), if the maturity value (S) is
$1000, the maturity date (n) is 20 years, and the coupon interest (R) is 8
percent or $80, neglecting transactions costs?

$$P = R\left[\frac{1 - (1 + i)^{-n}}{i}\right] + S(1 + i)^{-n}$$

$$= \$80\left[\frac{1 - (1.10)^{-20}}{0.1}\right] + \$1000\,(1.10)^{-20} = \$681 + \$149 = \$830$$

The purchase price must be about $830. Using the computer software, THE
COMPLETE BOND ANALYZER (Larry Rosen Co., 1989) (hereafter referred to as CBA), the price is $829.73. With semiannual interest payments
of $40, to yield 10 percent, the price drops to $812.54.

Using the Graphs to Find YTM

Solving the equation for the *purchase price* when the yield to maturity is
known is *not difficult.* It is more complicated, however, to solve the same
equation for the *yield to maturity, i.* In practice, the YTM is precisely the
unknown that investors often wish to determine. Figures 12.1 through
12.14, developed by the author, simplify this problem of finding the
approximate yield to maturity.

These 14 graphs provide a quick way to estimate YTM. Each graph covers a specific time period measured by years until maturity. For example, if the year of purchase of a bond by an investor is 1994 and the maturity date of the bond is 2009, there are 15 years until maturity. Figure 12.4 (tax-exempt investor) or Fig. 12.11 (28 percent tax bracket investor) is used, because each covers the situation where 15 years remain until maturity.

Figures 12.1 through 12.7 are for a tax-exempt investor, and Figs. 12.8 through 12.14 are based on an investor being in a 28 percent tax bracket for both ordinary interest and capital gains. Figures are included for maturities of 1, 5, 10, 15, 20, 25, and 30 years. The other inputs are the purchase price in the left vertical column, and the coupon interest rates paid on the bond, represented by the curves on each graph.

Using the Graphs for Tax-Exempt Investors

Figures 12.1 through 12.7 are for tax-exempt investors. Some of the appropriate users of these figures are custodians of pension funds, Keogh plans, or individual retirement accounts (IRSs), or a custodian for a child who is in a zero tax bracket.

Interestingly, for a zero tax bracket, you will note if you study the figures that, at a $1000 purchase price, the YTM is always equal to the coupon rate. For example, without looking at the figure for the moment, what do you think the IRR is for a 10 percent coupon with a $1000 purchase price and a 20-year maturity? If you said 10 percent, congratulations. If you said anything else, please reread this paragraph.

Note that Figs. 12.1 through 12.7, though for a zero tax-bracket investor, are not applicable to tax-exempt *bonds*, as compared to tax-exempt *investors*, unless the bond is purchased at its par value. Using the figures for tax-exempt bonds is discussed later.

Example: Finding YTM.   What is the approximate YTM for a bond purchased for $830, with 20 years remaining until maturity, and an 8 percent coupon?

Refer to Fig. 12.5 (20 years). The dashed lines show that the YTM is 10 percent. (Using the CBA computer software, the YTM is 9.996 percent.)

Example: Finding YTM.   What is the approximate YTM for a 3 percent bond with 1 year remaining, priced at $990?

Figure 12.1 shows the YTM to be 4 percent, as the dashed line indicates. (Using CBA, the yield is 4.04 percent.)

Example: Finding YTM.   Find the YTM for an 8 percent bond, priced at $1130, and maturing in 5 years.

Refer to Fig. 12.2, where the dashed line provides the YTM of 5 percent. (Using CBA, the YTM is 4.998 percent.)

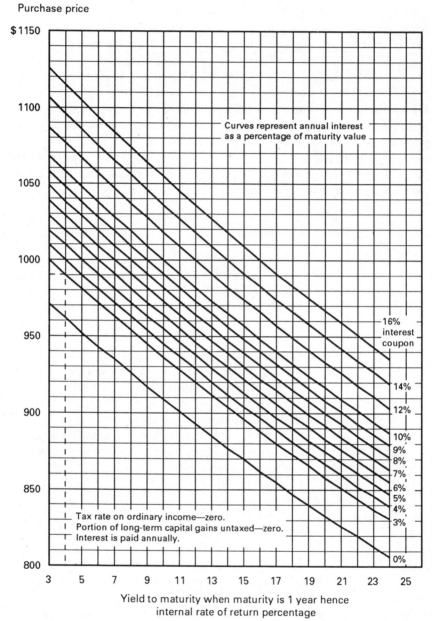

Figure 12.1. Bond yield to maturity: 1 year.

Purchase price

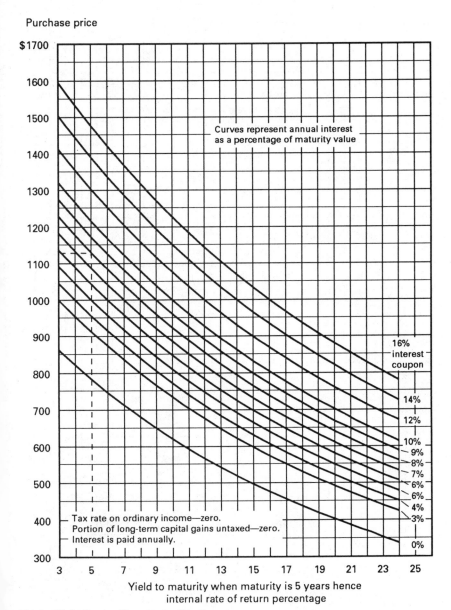

Figure 12.2. Bond yield to maturity: 5 years.

Purchase price

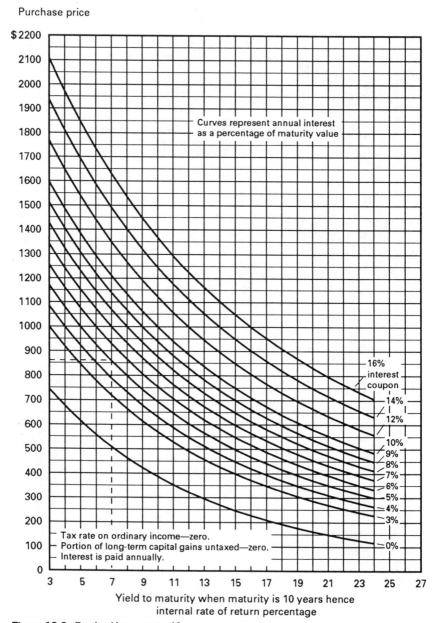

Figure 12.3. Bond yield to maturity: 10 years.

Purchase price

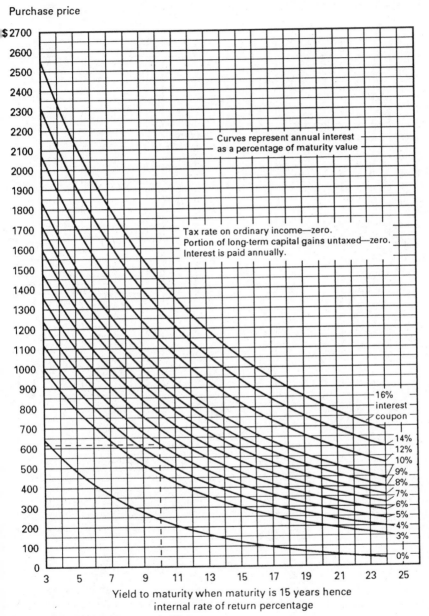

Curves represent annual interest as a percentage of maturity value

Tax rate on ordinary income—zero.
Portion of long-term capital gains untaxed—zero.
Interest is paid annually.

16% interest coupon

14%
12%
10%
9%
8%
7%
6%
5%
4%
3%
0%

Yield to maturity when maturity is 15 years hence
internal rate of return percentage

Figure 12.4. Bond yield to maturity: 15 years.

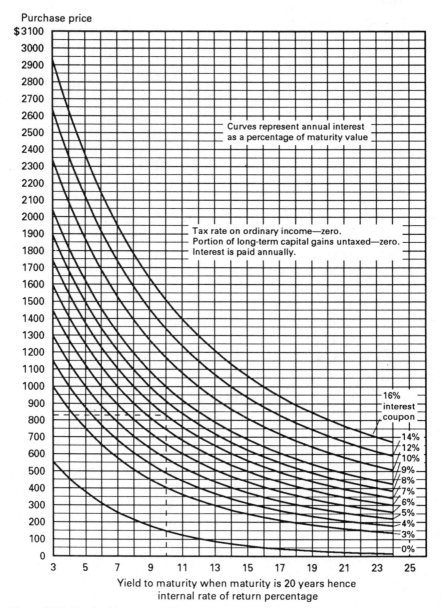

Figure 12.5. Bond yield to maturity: 20 years.

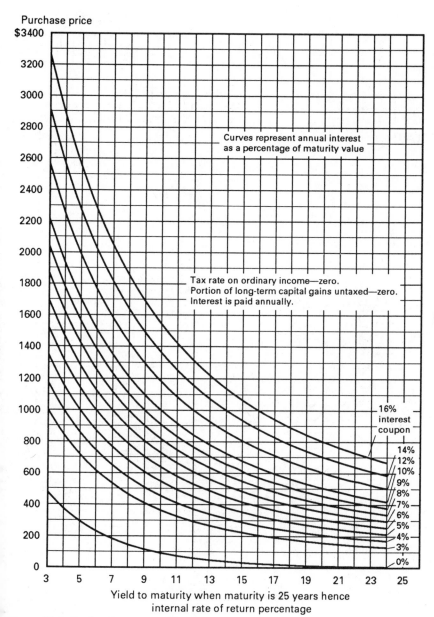

Purchase price

Curves represent annual interest
as a percentage of maturity value

Tax rate on ordinary income—zero.
Portion of long-term capital gains untaxed—zero.
Interest is paid annually.

16%
interest
coupon

14%
12%
10%
9%
8%
7%
6%
5%
4%
3%
0%

Yield to maturity when maturity is 25 years hence
internal rate of return percentage

Figure 12.6. Bond yield to maturity: 25 years.

Purchase price

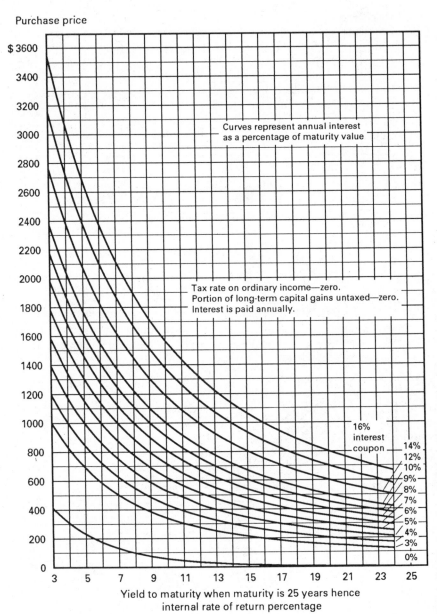

Figure 12.7. Bond yield to maturity: 30 years.

Example: Finding the price. How much may be paid to buy a bond whose maturity value 10 years hence is $1000, if the coupon interest rate is 7 percent and the investor desires a YTM of 8 percent?

Turn to the 10-year graph, Fig. 12.3. The dashed line shows that the purchase price to obtain the desired yield would be about $932. (CBA indicates $932.89 as the price.)

Using the Graphs for Taxable Investors

Figures 12.8 through 12.14 are for taxable investors. There are two cash flow elements to consider in determining the before-tax YTM for a bond investment: the annual interest yield and the proceeds of sale at the end of the holding period. If the investor is in other than a zero tax bracket, the cash flow elements are all reduced (or increased in the case of a taxable premium bond which may give birth to a capital loss at maturity) to the extent of applicable taxes. The annual cash flow from interest receipts is reduced by the appropriate level of federal and state income taxes. Finally, the proceeds of sale at the end of the holding period are reduced by the relevant capital gains tax (or increased by the tax savings resulting from a capital loss).

Figures 12.8 through 12.14 are for a 28 percent tax bracket investor and assume that the capital gains tax is 28 percent. Thus, for a 28 percent tax bracket, the tax applied to the annual cash flows is 28 percent; and 28 percent of the gain is deducted from the proceeds of sale. If the investment is sold at a loss, 28 percent of the loss is added to the sales proceeds.

Figures 12.8 through 12.14 can be used to determine the YTM for a taxable bond investment; tax-exempt bond calculations are described later in this chapter.

Two factors govern the selection of the appropriate figure: the *number of years* until the bond matures, and the applicable *tax bracket*. There are two choices for the tax bracket, 28 percent, and zero percent. (The zero percent bracket, and before-tax YTM, were discussed earlier in this chapter, and Figs. 12.1 through 7 are pertinent.) The figures may be used for any holding period from 1 to 30 years.

As an example, consider an investor in the 28 percent tax bracket, who wishes to find the YTM for a proposed taxable bond investment that matures in 30 years. Refer to Fig. 12.14, which is the graph for 30 years to maturity and a 28 percent tax bracket. The investor must determine the purchase price and the coupon rate in order to use the graph to find the YTM.

Purchase price

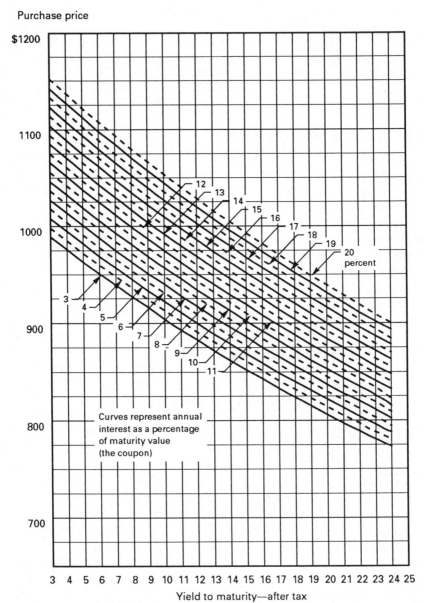

Figure 12.8. Bond yield to maturity: 1 year, 28 percent tax bracket.

Purchase price

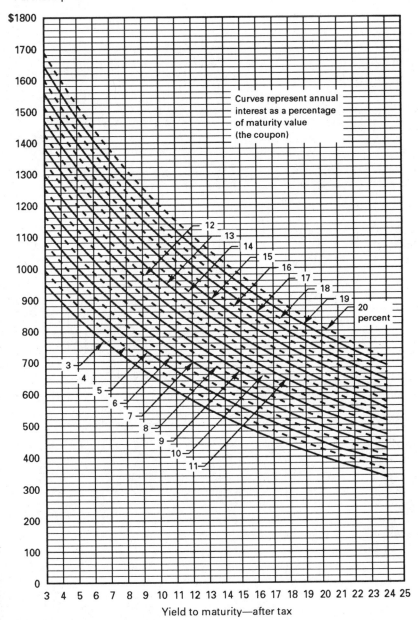

Figure 12.9. Bond yield to maturity: 5 years, 28 percent tax bracket.

Purchase price

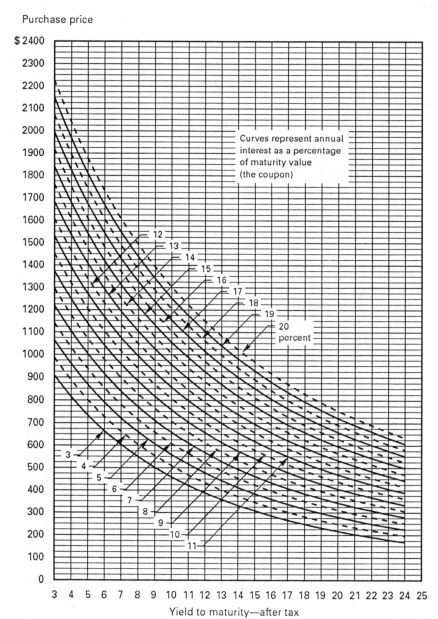

Figure 12.10. Bond yield to maturity: 10 years, 28 percent tax bracket.

Purchase price

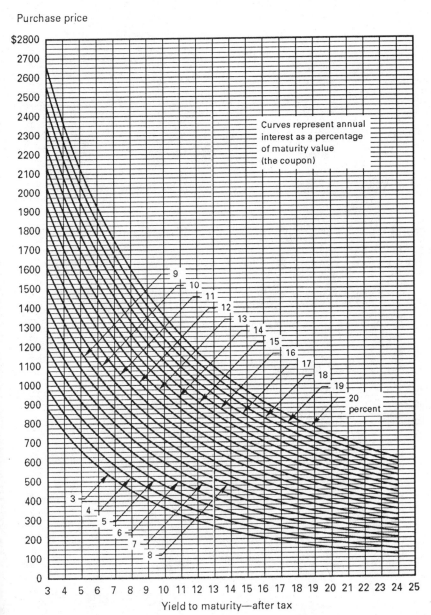

Yield to maturity—after tax

Figure 12.11. Bond yield to maturity: 15 years, 28 percent tax bracket.

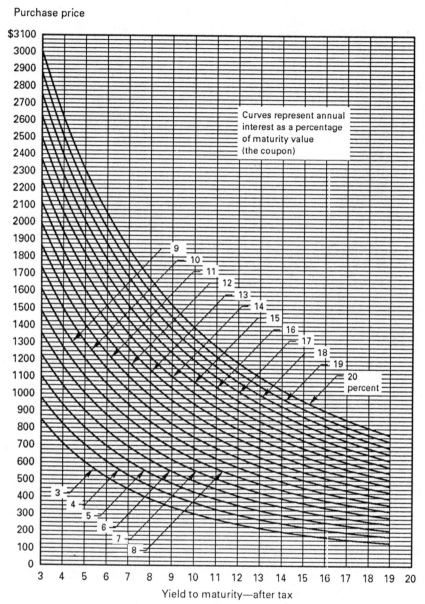

Figure 12.12. Bond yield to maturity: 20 years, 28 percent tax bracket.

Purchase price

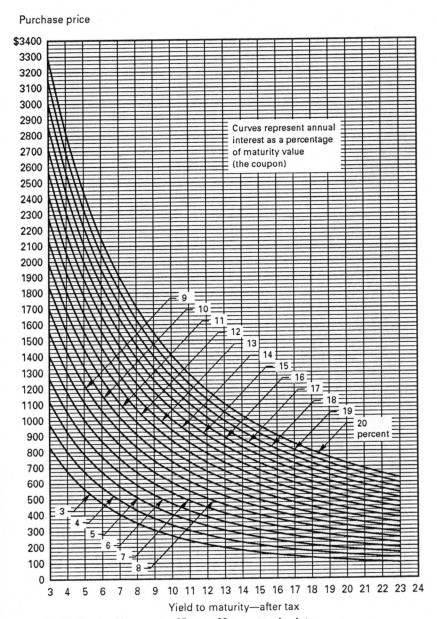

Figure 12.13. Bond yield to maturity: 25 years, 28 percent tax bracket.

Purchase price

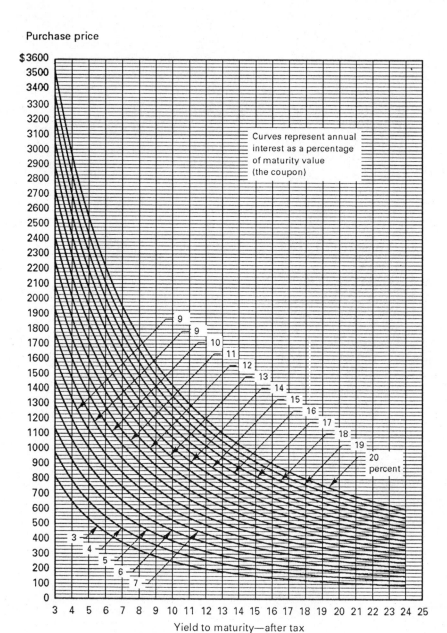

Figure 12.14. Bond yield to maturity: 30 years, 28 percent tax bracket.

The *purchase price* is simply what the name implies, the price paid for each bond, or its present market value. The left vertical axis of the graphs shows the bond purchase or market price. Our investor's bond is offered at $1050.

The *coupon rate*, or percentage annual coupon interest, are shown by the series of curves running across the graphs. The coupon rate is the annual interest divided by the bond's $1000 maturity value. Our investor's bond has a 12 percent coupon rate.

To find the YTM for this bond, enter Fig. 12.14 at the $1050 point on the vertical axis and proceed across to the 12 percent curve. From that point of intersection, drop down vertically to the bottom axis. That point of intersection with the bottom axis is the YTM, which in this case is 8.2 percent. That's all there is to it. The YTM, after 28 percent income tax and 28 percent capital gains tax, is 8.2 percent. The effect of the capital gains tax is to add $14 to the proceeds of the sale, as the redemption of the bond at maturity creates a $50 long-term capital loss ($1050 - $1000). The $14 addition to the maturity value is the tax savings—the product of the $50 loss times 28 percent (the bracket).*

Using the Graphs for Tax-Exempts (Municipals)

With slight adaptation, the figures in this chapter may be used to calculate YTM or price (after tax) from investments in municipals or tax-exempts. Although the interest receipts from a municipal bond are not normally subject to federal income tax, the capital gain upon sale or redemption at maturity is taxable.* The premium paid for a tax-exempt bond *must* be amortized to reduce the bond's tax basis. Thus, by the bond's maturity date, the adjusted basis (after such amortization) will equal the maturity value; hence there is no capital loss at maturity that may be deducted for a tax-exempt bond purchased at a premium.

The procedure for obtaining the after-tax YTM from a tax-exempt bond is as follows:

1. For discount or par tax-exempts, use the set of figures that are closer to the investor's tax bracket (zero or 28 percent).
2. For premium tax-exempts, however, one *must use* Fig. 12.1 through 12.7.

---

*See Appendix 12.1 regarding an important modification of the method of taxing "market discount" upon the disposition of tax-exempt securities. Such gains are now generally taxed as ordinary income rather than as capital gains.

3. Choose the graph which is closest to the bond's number of years until maturity (1 to 30 years).

4. Calculate an *adjusted coupon rate*, as follows:

$$\text{Adjusted coupon rate} = \frac{\text{tax--exempt bond's couponrate}}{1 - \text{investor's tax bracket}}$$

Example: Finding adjusted coupon rate. Sally Ableson, who is in a 28 percent tax bracket, is considering the purchase of a tax-exempt sewer bond for $650 with 30 years until maturity. The bond pays $72 per year in interest. The adjusted coupon rate is:

$$\text{Adjusted coupon rate} = \frac{\text{tax--exempt bond's couponrate}}{1 - \text{investor's tax bracket}}$$

$$= \frac{\$72}{1 - 0.28} = \frac{\$72}{0.72} = \$100$$

To find the YTM after capital gains tax, refer to Fig. 12.14. Enter the figure on the vertical axis at the bond's purchase price, $650. Proceed across to the *adjusted coupon rate*, 10 percent ($100), then descend to the horizontal axis. The intersection at the horizontal axis is the after-tax YTM, 11.3 percent. This value takes into consideration both the tax-free nature of the $72 annual interest as well as the ultimate capital gains tax of $98, resulting from the capital gains tax rate of 28 percent applied to $350 gain ($1000 redemption less $650 cost).* This YTM of 11.3 percent is correct even with the change described in Appendix 12.1.

Taxable investors in a tax-exempt bond *must* use an adjusted coupon rate as described. A zero percent tax bracket investor in a tax-exempt bond can use Figs. 12.1 through 12.7, without adjustment, because in a zero bracket the adjusted coupon rate will always equal the unadjusted coupon rate.

Additional Information

This chapter represents only an introduction to bond mathematics. Refer to Chap. 11 for information concerning money market instruments; Chap. 13 for mathematical methods of determining YTM; Chap. 14 for computing yield to call; and Chap. 15 for a discussion of bond price volatility and other factors. Callable bonds are discussed in Chaps. 16 through 18.

In the next chapter, we will look closer at calculating yield to maturity for bonds.

---

* The after-tax YTM is accurate provided the gain is $350 and the tax rate applicable is 28 percent. See Appendix 12.1.

Appendix 12.1: Tax-Exempt or Municipal Bonds—Disposition Gain Representing Accrued Market Discount Treated as Ordinary Income

Where securities of a municipality are originally issued at par value (or higher) and are subsequently acquired by a purchaser at a discount, such discount is not in the nature of tax-exempt interest. This discount is known as "market" discount as opposed to "issue" discount. Johan Johannson buys a tax-exempt bond (originally issued at par) for $900. The $100 is market discount. Historically such "market discount" was taxed as capital gain upon the sale or disposition at maturity. No more!

If Johannson holds the bonds until redemption, he will then realize recognized gain of the entire excess of the redemption price received ($1000) over the purchase price which he paid for the bonds ($900). If, instead, Johannson sells the bonds (say for $975), he will then realize recognized gain of the entire excess of the sales price received ($975) over the $900 purchase price (or sustain a taxable loss of the excess of such purchase price over the sales price received). Such gains or losses to the investor were formerly allowable as capital gains or losses. *However, starting in 1993, ordinary income is recognized as ordinary income instead of capital gains as described below.* The market discount rule has been extended to all tax-exempt bonds and to all market discount bonds, regardless of when such bonds were issued. Under the market discount rule, gain on the disposition of a bond that was acquired for a price less than the principal amount of the bond is treated as ordinary income to the extent of the accrued market discount. *The provisions are effective for bonds purchased after April 30, 1993.* Current owners of tax-exempt bonds and other market discount bonds issued on or before July 18, 1984, are not required to treat accrued market discount as ordinary income, provided they acquired their bonds before May 1, 1993. (Code Sec. 1276(e).) To repeat, gain realized on the disposition of a market discount bond must be recognized as *ordinary* income to the extent of the "accrued market discount" for obligations issued after July 18, 1984. Such accrued market discount is calculated by a straight-line method whereby an equal amount is computed on a daily basis unless an election is made under Code Sec. 1276(b)(2) to use the yield-to-maturity method similar to the method in Code Sec. 1272(a).

Such recognition of income is triggered by sales, exchanges, involuntary conversions, and gifts. Instead of recognizing ordinary interest income upon the sale, an election may be made under Code Sec. 1278(b) to include market discount in income currently. As most people would rather pay taxes later than sooner, the election is not likely to be popular.

13

Yield to Maturity, Accrued Interest, Bond Equivalent Yield, and Other Yields

Before we continue, it is important to note that the price and yield graphs in Chap. 12 for the most part depict a limited range of yields to maturity. Within that limited range the graphs sometimes appear to be almost straight lines. In reality, there is considerable curvature if a wide range of yields are viewed; see Fig. 13.1, which shows yields to maturity from zero to 180 percent.

Yield to Maturity

If the yield to maturity (YTM) of a bond is known, it is relatively simple to find the price by formula. On the other hand, if the price is known and the YTM is to be found, the calculation is more complex. YTM then may be determined mathematically either by a trial-and-error method, or by using a computer or a specially programmed electronic calculator. As an example, we will consider a bond purchased for $1130, which matures 5 years hence

Price P

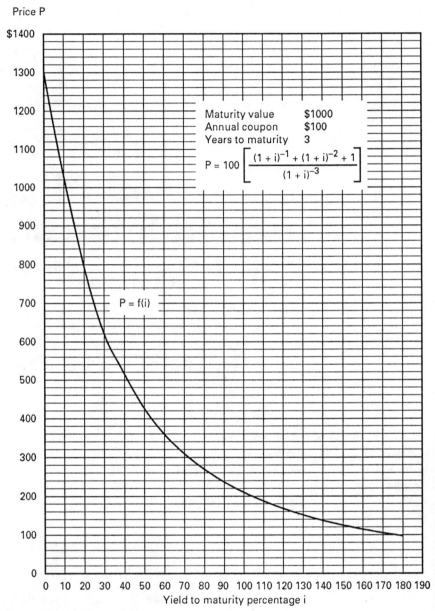

Maturity value $1000
Annual coupon $100
Years to maturity 3

$$P = 100 \left[\frac{(1 + i)^{-1} + (1 + i)^{-2} + 1}{(1 + i)^{-3}} \right]$$

P = f(i)

Yield to maturity percentage i

Figure 13.1. Yield curve—the big picture.

and has a coupon rate of 8 percent. We want to find the YTM if interest payments are made annually.

The formula for YTM with annual interest, and settlement on a coupon date, is

$$A = R \left[\frac{1 - (1 + i)^{-n}}{i} \right] + S (1 + i)^{-n}$$

where A = purchase price
R = annual interest
S = maturity of value
n = number of years to maturity
i = yield to maturity

Note that this formula is *not* valid when the bond has one coupon or less until the maturity date: In that event, the securities industry calculates YTM on a simple (not compound) interest basis.

For our example bond,

$$A = \$1130 \quad R = \$80$$

$$S = \$1000 \quad n = 5$$

Rearranging the formula and substituting for A, R and S,

$$\frac{A}{R} = \left[\frac{1 - (1 + i)^{-n}}{i} \right] + \frac{S}{R} (1 + i)^{-n}$$

$$14.125 = \left[\frac{1 - (1 + i)^{-n}}{i} \right] + 12.5 (1 + i)^{-n}$$

Trial-and-Error Solution

Various values of the two bracketed expressions can be found for values of i from Appendix 1, Table 5, column for five time periods. We seek to find the rate of i where the factors involved, when inserted in the formula, produce a total as close as possible to 14.125.

If i is	Then $\left[\dfrac{1 - (1 + i)^{-5}}{i} \right]$ is	And $12.5(1 + i)^{-5}$ is	The total is
(a) 0.03	4.579707	10.7826	15.362307
(b) 0.04	4.451822	10.274087	14.725909
(c) 0.05	4.329476	9.794075	14.123551

The total in (a) is too large, so we try a higher rate of interest.

The total in (b) is also too large, so we try a still higher rate.

The total in (c) of 14.123551 is almost exactly equal to the desired total of 14.125. Thus, the YTM is almost exactly 5 percent.

Using the computer software, COMPLETE BOND ANALYZER (Larry Rosen Co., 1986), produces 4.998 percent as the YTM. With semiannual interest, the YTM is 5.027 percent.

An approximate YTM may be found by finding the value of i in the foregoing formula using both a binomial expansion and the quadratic formula, as explained in Appendix 13.1 at the end of this chapter.

The Computer Solution: Newton's Method

The equation for yield to maturity is "high powered" in the sense that the exponent of one term will always be the product of the number of years until maturity multiplied by the number of compounding periods per year. Thus for a 30-year bond with interest compounded semiannually, one term in the equation will be to the 60th power. Think about solving an equation for i, the yield to maturity, where the equation reads something like:

$$100 \, (1 + i)^{-60} + 100 \, (1 + i)^{-59} + \ldots$$

The quadratic formula (see Appendix 13.1) can only be used to solve equations that are in a prescribed form and have an exponent of 2. Thus the quadratic formula cannot be used in most instances to solve for the yield to maturity. Nor is there any other simple method of equation solving (such as factoring) that can be used to find the root (yield to maturity) of the equation.

The computer method of solution is a trial-and-error method. Even with a trial-and-error approach, however, there are superior and inferior ways to go about solving an equation. The inferior way is just to plug "guesstimates" of i into the equation. The superior way is to use *Newton's method*, which was developed centuries ago by Sir Isaac Newton.

The first step in the computer solution is to use a formula to find an approximate starting value for the yield, and then keep trying subsequent values until the right answer is found. This type of trial-and-error method is termed an *iterative* method.

An example will serve to illustrate. If coupon payments are $100 per year paid annually, the purchase price is $1000, and the maturity is 3 years hence, what is the yield to maturity?

The formula is

$$P = \frac{C}{(1+i)^1} + \frac{C}{(1+i)^2} + \frac{C}{(1+i)^3} + \frac{S}{(1+i)^3}$$

where S = maturity value after n years
n = number of years to maturity
P = original investment (principal or present value)
i = compound annual growth rate (interest)
C = coupon payment (annual interest)

For our example,

$$\$1000 = \frac{\$100}{(1+i)^1} + \frac{\$100}{(1+i)^2} + \frac{\$100}{(1+i)^3} + \frac{\$1000}{(1+i)^3}$$

At this point, values of i are substituted in the equation one at a time until a value of i causes the right-hand side of the equation to be equal to the $1000 value of the left side. Let's try 11 percent as a first effort. At that rate, the discounted value of the right-hand side of the equation (everything to the right of the equals sign) is $244.37 for the $100 cash flows and $731.19 for the maturity value, a total of $975.56. Since this value is too low—that is, it is less than $1000, the guess of 11 percent was too high and a lower rate should be attempted.

Let's try 0.1, that is, 10 percent.

$$\$1000 = \frac{\$100}{(1+0.1)^1} + \frac{\$100}{(1+0.1)^2} + \frac{\$100}{(1+0.1)^3} + \frac{\$1000}{(1+0.1)^3}$$

$$= \frac{\$100}{(1.1000)} + \frac{\$100}{(1.2100)} + \frac{\$100}{(1.3310)} + \frac{\$1000}{(1.3310)}$$

$$= \$90.91 + \$82.64 + \$75.13 + \$751.32$$

$$= \$1000$$

Success! In other words, 10 percent is the discount rate which when applied to all the cash flows results in their sum being equal to the purchase price of the bond.

Another way of expressing the yield to maturity formula, where coupon payments are made semiannually and interest is compounded twice per year (ignoring accrued interest for the moment) is to use a summation formula:

$$P = \sum_{t=1}^{2n} \frac{C/2}{(1+i/2)^t} + \frac{S}{(1+i/2)^{2n}}$$

where P = price

     n = years to maturity

     C = annual coupon payment

     i = nominal yield to maturity

     S = maturity value of bond

Finite and infinite series are often indicated by using the Greek Letter sigma, Σ. For example, the sum $a_1 + a_2 + a_3 + \ldots + a_n$ can be written

$$\sum_{i=1}^{n} a_i$$

which is read "the sum of a_i from $i = 1$ to $i = n$.")

Expressing the formula as shown above fits into the logic pattern of computers, which have the built-in ability to do iteration. The method of programming a computer to do yield-to-maturity problems involves using the sigma equation.

First, in a trial-and-error solution, either the user supplies or the program calculates an approximate value for the yield. One method of so doing was explained earlier in Chap. 12.

Starting from that initial trial value, one may keep trying higher or lower values of i until a desired degree of accuracy is attained. This can be a time-consuming process even for a computer.

A more sophisticated approach was devised by Newton to find the roots of polynomial equations. It involves finding successive tangent lines to the yield curve equation. The yield to maturity is the value found at the tangent's intersection with the x axis. Each successive effort results in a more and more accurate value of the yield to maturity. Refer to Fig. 13.2. The curve is the equation for finding yield to maturity, where

Years to maturity = 2

Maturity value = $1000

Coupon = $100

Price = $1000

Interest payments are made annually

The equation begins with

$$\$1000 = \frac{\$100}{(1+i)^1} + \frac{\$1100}{(1+i)^2}$$

To be able to apply Newton's method, the foregoing equation is rearranged and manipulated so that it is set to zero and takes the following form:

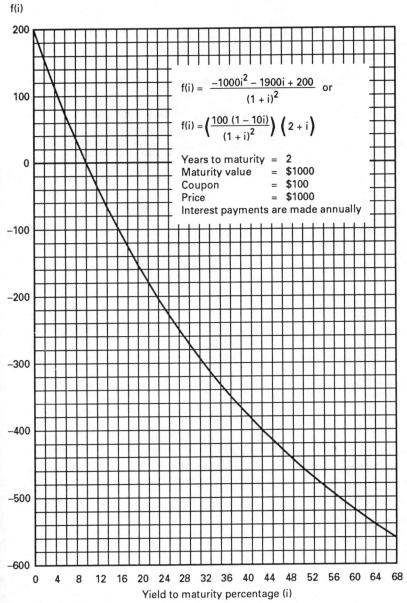

Figure 13.2. Finding yield to maturity—where curve crosses horizontal zero axis.

$$\left[\frac{100(1 - 10i)}{(1 + i)^2}\right]\left[\frac{(2 + i)}{(1 + i)^2}\right] = \left[\frac{-1000\,i^2 - 1900\,i + 200}{(1 + i)^2}\right] = 0$$

The precise *point* where the *curve* in Fig. 13.2 *crosses the horizontal axis* is the *yield to maturity*. To find that point mathematically, first start with an initial trial value, i_1. The location of that point, i_1, is selected arbitrarily or may be determined by the approximate solution for yield to maturity described in Chap. 12. Let's use 2 percent as the arbitrarily selected initial trial value. The graphic coordinates of this point are i_1, $f(i_1)$. Refer to Fig. 13.3 to see its location.

The next step in Newton's method of finding the root (which is i, the yield to maturity) of this equation is to draw a tangent (line FG) to the curve at this point, i_1. The first step in locating and drawing the tangent is to determine its slope. The slope is the first derivative $[f'(i)]$ of the equation.

$$0 = \frac{-1000\,i^2 - 1900\,i + 200}{(1 + i)^2}$$

At i_1, 0.02, then, the formula for the first derivative is

$$f'(i) = \frac{(1 + i)^2\,(-1900 - 2000i) - (200 - 1900i - 1000\,i^2)(2)(1 + i)}{(1 + i)^2}$$

$$= \frac{-2300 - 2400\,i - 100\,i^2}{(1 + i)^4}$$

(From calculus, the derivative of the product of two functions is equal to the derivative of the second function times the first function plus the derivative of the first function times the second function. And the derivative of the quotient of two functions is the denominator times the derivative of the numerator less the numerator times the derivative of the denominator, all divided by the square of the denominator.)

Substituting 0.02 for i, the *slope, m, is*

$$m = \frac{-2300 - 2400\,(0.02) - 100\,(0.02)^2}{(1 + 0.02)^4}$$

$$= \frac{-2348.04}{1.08243216} = -2169.226$$

At i_1, $i = 0.02$ and substituting that value in the equation gives the value of $f(i) = 155.32$, as follows:

f(i)

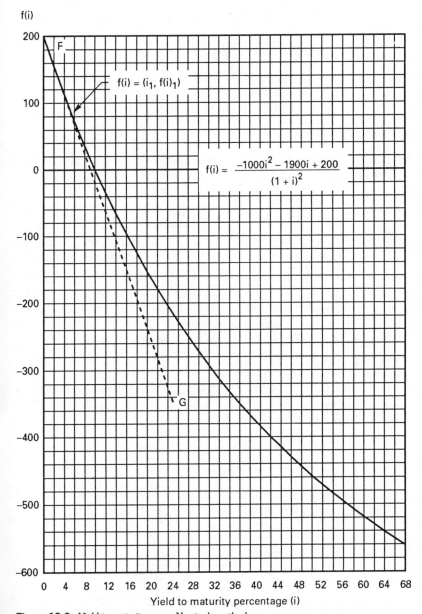

Figure 13.3. Yield-to-maturity curve: Newton's method.

$$f(i) = (-1000i^2 - 1900i + 200)/(1.02)^2$$

$$= [-1000(0.02)^2 - 1900(0.02) + 200]/1.0404$$

$$= (-0.4 - 38.0 + 200)/1.0404$$

$$= \$155.32$$

The equation for the tangent at i_1 is

$$\frac{y - 155.32}{x - 0.02} = -2169.226$$

This reduces to

$$y = 198.705 - 2169.226x$$

The above is the equation for the *tangent line* (line FG) in Fig. 13.3. By setting $y = 0$ and solving for x, we find the precise point where line FG crosses the horizontal axis. This is 0.0916. And 0.0916 is the first trial value for the yield to maturity. (As we know, the correct answer is 10 percent.) So, for a first trial, the result is remarkably accurate. To find the next trial value, refer to Fig. 13.4, which is a blown-up version of Fig. 13.3. From the point on the horizontal axis where the tangent line FG intersects (9.16 percent), draw a vertical line back to the curve. The point on the curve where it intersects is point i_2. The coordinates are 0.0916, $f(i)_2$.

Now the procedure is repeated all over again. A tangent line at i_2 is drawn and its point of intersection with the horizontal axis is the second trial value. The *slope* (m) of the new tangent line (MN) is

$$m = \frac{-2300 - 2400(0.0916) - 100(0.0916)^2}{(1.0916)^4} = -1775$$

The value of $f(i)_2$ at the point where i is 0.0916 is found by substituting the i value in the original equation, as follows: The $f(i)_2$ value at the point where $i = 0.0916$ is

$$\frac{-1000(0.0916)^2 - 1900(0.0916) + 200}{(1.0916)^2} = \frac{17.56944}{1.19159} = 14.7445$$

Thus, the coordinates of $f(i)_2$ are (0.0916, \$14.7445). And the equation for the tangent drawn to the curve at $f(i)_2$ is

$$\frac{y - 14.7445}{x - 0.0916} = -\$1775$$

$$y = -1775x + 177.335$$

F(i)

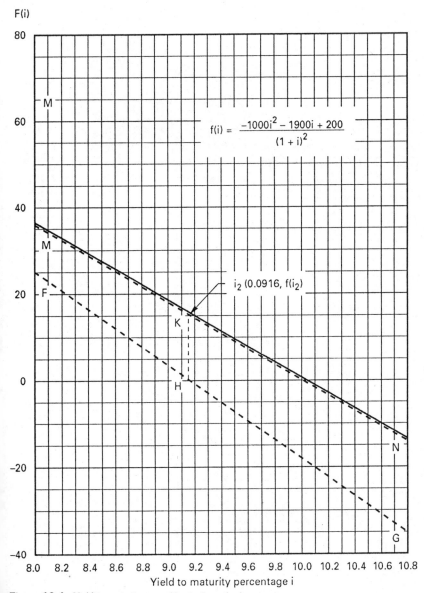

Figure 13.4. Yield-to-maturity curve: Newton's method.

By setting y equal to zero, we find the point where the tangent line intersects the horizontal axis, the *next trial value* for the yield to maturity. This is 9.991 percent, determined as follows:

$$0 = 1775x + 177.335$$

$$x = 0.09991 \text{ or } 9.991\%$$

Finally, we are in a position to perform the last step. A vertical line (RP) is drawn from 9.991 percent on the horizontal axis to the curve as shown in Fig. 13.5. It intersects the curve at i_3, where the coordinates are $(0.09991, f(i)_3)$. The problem at this point is to construct the tangent line to the curve, which is line PQ and is indistinguishable, even magnified as shown in Fig. 13.5, from the curve for the basic equation $f(i)$.

The slope (m) of the tangent line PQ is

$$M = \frac{-2300 - 2400(0.09991) - 100(0.09991)^2}{(1.09991)^4}$$

$$= \frac{-2540.78}{1.46362} = -1735.956$$

The value of $f(i)_3$ at $i = 0.09991$ is determined by substituting 0.09991 in the basic equation as follows:

$$y = \frac{-1000(0.09991)^2 - 1900(0.09991) + 200}{(1.09991)^2}$$

$$= \frac{0.18899}{1.20980} = 0.15622$$

Thus, the value of $f(i)_3$ at $i = 0.0991$ is 0.15622.

The formula for the tangent to the curve at point i_3 in Fig. 13.5 is

$$\frac{y - 0.15622}{x - 0.09991} = -1735.956$$

$$y = -1735.956x + 1735.956(0.09991) + 0.15622$$

$$= -1735.956x + 173.59558$$

To find the point where the tangent line (PQ) intersects the horizontal axis, y is set to zero, and

$$0 = -1735.956x + 173.59558$$

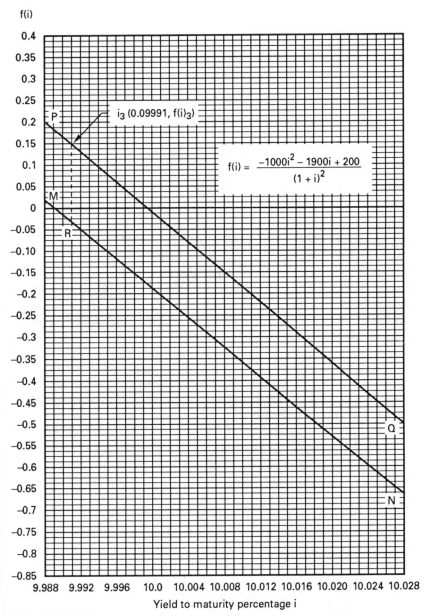

Figure 13.5. Yield-to-maturity curve: Newton's method.

$$x = 0.10000 \quad \text{or} \quad 10\%$$

This concludes the Newton iteration approach to finding the root of the equation for yield to maturity. The Newton method may be used either to find the actual YTM or to find an initial trial value when a trial-and-error approach is used. A review of the trials using the Newton method shows that:

Trial number	Trial value
1	0.02000
2	0.09160
3	0.09991
4	0.10000

This is a remarkable shortcut to finding the solution when one compares its success to the more cumbersome approach of plugging in values for i one after another until a match-up of the left and right sides of the equation occurs.* The speed of convergence of Newton's method is such that the number of decimal places of accuracy is doubled at each step. Sir Isaac did his job well.

It is Newton's basic approach that the author utilized in developing programming for the COMPLETE BOND ANALYZER computer software. In just a few seconds, the computer software calculates yield to maturity or yield to call with accrued interest and provides both the pretax and after-tax yields.

It should be noted, in closing, that Newton's method does not always converge to the root of polynomial equation. Failure to converge could occur when the first trial value is not close enough to the ultimate root to get a convergent process started. Problems are more likely to occur in finding internal rate of return in situations involving an abnormal pattern of cash flows. The author has never experiences a problem obtaining the yield to maturity of a bond using the computer software founded on Newton's method.

Today electronic calculators are capable of doing bond yield-to-maturity calculations. For example, the Hewlett Packard 17B will find the yield (10.0 percent) in the preceding problem using the steps shown in Table 13.1, and the Texas Instruments Fixed Income Securities Calculator uses the procedure shown in Table 13.2.

The financial tools mentioned above, the COMPLETE BOND ANALYZER, the HP 17B, and TI's Fixed Income Securities Calculator, all perform a variety of other functions and have other capabilities than just the calculation of yield to maturity. However, that calculation is an onerous one, especially when

---

*Another method, the bisection method, for finding the solution to a polynomial equation beyond the second degree is described in Appendix 13.4.

Table 13.1. Using the Hewlett Packard 17B to Find Yield to Maturity

Keys	Display	Remarks
clr		turns it on
fin	select a menu	picks financial functions
bond	a/a annual	chooses bond functions
type	a/a annual	
a/a	a/a annual	sets actual calendar month and year
ann	a/a annual	sets annual coupon payments
exit		moves back one menu
1.011991 SETT	sett = 01011991 TUE	sets settlement date
1.011993 MAT	mat = 01/01/1993 FRI	sets maturity or call date
10 CALL%	CPN% = 10.00	sets $100 annual coupon
more		moves to subsequent menu
100 PRICE	PRICE=100.00	sets purchase price of $1000
YLD %	YLD% = 10.000	calculates yield to maturity

Table 13.2. Using the Texas Instruments Fixed Income Securities Calculator

Key	Display	Remarks
on/off		turns it on
cor		selects corporate bonds
bnd		selects bonds
act-365		selects actual days in a 365-day year
ann	.	selects annual interest payments
dec		selects decimal values
em		selects end of month procedure
1.0191 SD	SD 01-01-1991	establishes settlement date
10 CPN	CPN 10	sets 10% coupon rate
1.0193 MAT	MAT 01-01-1993	picks maturity date
100 PRI	PRI 100	sets $1000 purchase price
Compute	YLD 10.000*	determines yield to maturity

the bond is purchased on other than a coupon date and accrued interest is a factor in the calculation, and when after-tax yields are desired.

The following printout from the COMPLETE BOND ANALYZER illustrates how easy and quick it is to use the software to find bond pretax and after-tax conventional yield to maturity or call as well as the effective annual yield, the accrued interest, and the current yield. The example given is for the purchase of a tax-exempt municipal bond with settlement on May 23 and a prerefunded call at 103 on July 1, six years later. The coupon rate is 11 percent, and the purchase price is 124.11 ($124.11).

```
                    Larry Rosen's
                Complete Bond Analyzer
                  Copyright ©1986

The user answers the following questions:

Is this a tax-exempt (1) or taxable (2) bond? [ 1 ]

Days in a year (360 or 365)? [ 360 ]

Annual coupon percent? [ 11 ]

Purchase price? [ 1241.11 ]

Time until maturity (yrs, mos, days)? [ 6,1,8 ]

Tax rate on ordinary income? [ 28 ]

Tax rate on long term or short term capital gains and losses?
[ 28 ]

Value at disposition? [ 1030 ]

The computer then replies:

Pretax yield to maturity = 3.275 % semi-annually

A nominal annual rate of 6.55 %

An effective annual rate = 6.6573 %

After tax yield to maturity = 3.275 % semi-annually

A nominal annual rate of 6.55 %

An effective annual rate of 6.657 %

Current yield = 8.86 %

Accrued interest per bond = $43.39

Note: Data in Brackets [ ] are entered by the user. Underlined
data is calculated and displayed by the software.
```

Accrued Interest

An understanding of accrued interest is important, because accrued interest is an ingredient in the calculation of yield to maturity. So far, all of our yield-to-maturity calculations have been as of a coupon date. That is, the settlement date has been assumed to be the same date that an interest payment is due. When such is the case, the buyer of the bond will receive the next interest payment in full, and he or she will be entitled to it. Accrued interest in this situation is zero. But when the settlement date is *between* interest payment dates, the buyer will still receive the next interest payment in its entirety. However, the buyer will not have owned the bond, note, or bill for the entire time period for which interest is being paid. The seller owned the instrument for part of that time period. Thus the seller is due a credit (benefit) and the buyer a debit (charge) for a portion of the next interest coupon. This is accomplished by calculating the *accrued interest*. Accrued interest is for the time period from the last coupon date (last interest payment date) until the settlement date. The seller is credited with accrued interest and receives it in addition to the sales price. The buyer is charged for accrued interest and pays it in addition to the purchase price.

There is nothing particularly difficult about calculating accrued interest. However, the method of calculation that is used depends on the type of security. For example, corporate bonds usually have interest determined on the basis of a 30-day month, 360-day year. Treasury bonds, on the other hand, have interest calculated on the basis of the actual number of days in a 365- or 366-day year.

Appendixes 13.2 and 13.3 at the end of the chapter show the rules of the National Association of Securities Dealers (NASD) and the Municipal Securities Rulemaking Board (MSRB) for calculating the number of days of accrued interest.

Table 13.3 summarizes the applicable methods of calculating accrued interest for a variety of instruments. Generally, accrued interest is calculated using a *simple* interest formula for both securities that have interest coupons as well as those sold at a discount.

These agencies follow the 30/360 pattern of "Gov't. Agencies" in Table 13.3.

Banks for Cooperatives (Co-op's) debentures

Commodity Credit Corp. (CCC)

Export-Import Bank (Ex-Im) Participation Certificates

Federal Home Loan Bank (FHLB) bonds

Federal Intermediate Credit Bank debentures (at maturity)

Federal Intermediate Credit Bank (FICB) debentures (periodic)

Federal Land Bank (FLB) bonds

Federal National Mortgage Association (FNMA) debentures

Government National Mortgage Association (GNMA) bonds

Table 13.3. Accrued Interest Methods for Various Instruments

Type of instrument	Days in month	Days in year	Compounding frequency per year	Method of price quotation	End-of-month method
Commercial paper (interest at maturity)	Actual	365	Nil	Decimal	Yes
Certificates of deposit (interest at maturity)	Actual	360	Varies	Decimal	Yes
Corporate bonds	30	360	2	Decimal	Yes
Treasury bonds and notes*	Actual	Actual	2	1/32nd	Yes
Treasury bills†	Actual	360	Nil	Decimal	
Gov't. Agencies‡	30	360	2	1/32nd	Yes
Municipals§	30	360	2	Decimal	Yes

*The actual/actual criteria for Treasury bonds are also applicable to Treasury notes, STRIP bonds (zero coupons), STRIP coupons.

†The actual/360 criteria for Treasury bills also holds for commercial paper (C/P) with interest payable at maturity, repurchase agreements (repos), U.S. Treasury Tax-Anticipation Bills (TABS), and other discount securities such as bankers' acceptances (B/As, BACs), certificates of deposit issued at discounts, and commercial paper (C/P) issued at a discount.

‡Exceptions to the 30/360 rule for government agencies are as follows: FHDA-insured notes are actual/actual; FHA debentures are actual/actual; and FNMA and TVA notes are actual/360.

§The general rule applies to muni bonds. Muni notes and warrants pay interest at maturity,

GNMA Participation Certificates

Inter-American Development Bank bonds

International Bank for Reconstruction and Development (World Bank) bonds

Merchant Marine bonds

New Communities Act debentures

Student Loan Marketing Association (SLMA) bonds

Tennessee Valley Authority (TVA) bonds

U.S. Postal Service bonds

Several agencies and other issuers use the actual number of days in the month and the actual number of days in the year:

Farmers Home Administration (FHDA) insured notes

Federal Housing Administration (FHA) debentures

The notes of two agencies and some other issuers are calculated on a discount basis for the actual number of days in a month, using a 360-day year. These are

FNMA short-term notes

TVA notes

Bankers' acceptances (B/As, BACs)

Certificates of deposit (CDs, discount, and at maturity)

Certificates of deposit (CDs, at maturity)

Commercial paper (C/P, discount)

Calculating Accrued Interest for Agencies, Municipals, and Corporates

The formula for calculating accrued interest for all debt issues that pay standard interest semiannually, annually, or at maturity is

$$a_i = (c)\left(\frac{n}{t}\right)$$

where a_i = accrued interest (accrued interest on Treasuries is covered subsequently)

c = coupon rate (expressed in dollars per year per bond)

n = number of days elapsed from the day following the last coupon date (or issuance date for a new bond) through the settlement date. The days elapsed may be regarded as the hypothetical number of days when the 30-day month/360-day year method is applicable. Where actual days are called for, the actual number of days is used. For interest payable only at maturity, use the days from issue date to maturity.

t = time in a year: 360 days, or, where actual number of days in the year is called for, 365 or 366, as appropriate. For additional information regarding counting the number of days, refer to Appendix 13.2 for the NASD Uniform Practice Code rules, and Appendix 13.3 for the Municipal Securities Rulemaking Board Rule G-33.

Example: Finding accrued interest for a municipal, agency, or corporate bond. An investor bought a $1000 face amount, New York City municipal bond with settlement on March 3. The coupon rate is 8.5 percent. It matures December 1, 22 years later. How much accrued interest will the investor be charged?

The first step is to find the number of elapsed days, on the 30/360 basis. The last interest coupon date (prior to settlement) was on December 1, in the year previous to the purchase. Thus the number of elapsed days is

December	29
January and February	60
March	3
Total days	92

$$a_i = (c)\left(\frac{n}{t}\right)$$

$$= (85)\left(\frac{92}{360}\right) = \$21.72$$

The accrued interest for the $1000 face amount is thus $21.72. Accrued interest for municipals, agencies, and corporate bonds are all computed on the 30/360 basis in the same manner.

Since the buyer pays accrued interest at settlement, his or her yield to maturity will be based on an initial cash outflow of the purchase price of the bond, plus commission and other charges, if any, *plus* the accrued interest. More about that later.

Calculating Accrued Interest for Treasury Notes and Bonds

The formula for calculating accrued interest (a_i) on a Treasury bond or note is

$$a_i = (c)\left(\frac{n}{2t}\right)$$

where c = coupon rate (expressed in dollars per year per bond)

n = actual number of days elapsed from the day following the last coupon date through the settlement date. (Do not count the date of the last coupon; start with the next day after it, and do count the date of settlement.)

t = actual number of days in the current coupon period (referred to as the *basis*). The current coupon period starts with the day after the coupon date preceding the settlement date and ends at and including the coupon date which follows the settlement date.

Example: Finding accrued interest for a Treasury bond or note. $1000 face amount of 6.875 percent U.S. Treasury notes due 5/15/99 were purchased for settlement on 4/29/94. (Interest is payable on the 15th of May and November.) What is the accrued interest?

First n must be determined, as follows: The coupon date preceding settlement was November 15, 1993. Thus the elapsed days were:

November 1993	15	(November 16–November 30 is 15 days)
December 1993	31	
January 1994	31	
February 1994	28	
March 1994	31	
April 1994	29	(April 1–April 29 is 29 days)
Total n	165 days	

Next t is calculated, as follows:

n as above	165
April 30	1
May 1–15	15
Total t	181

$$a_i = (c)\left(\frac{n}{2t}\right)$$

$$= (\$68.75)\left(\frac{\$165}{(2)(181)}\right) = \$31.336$$

Thus, the accrued interest on this Treasury note (or bond) owed by the seller at the settlement date is \$31.336 per \$1000 face amount.

Calculating Accrued Interest for Treasury Bills

As Treasury bills by definition do not pay interest and are sold at a discount from their maturity value, there is no accrued interest. Instead, when Treasury bills are sold after issuance, the price at which the sale takes place reflects a pro-ration of earned but as yet unpaid interest between seller and buyer. Treasury bills are non-interest coupon-bearing (interest is in the form of the discount from face value at which they are sold or traded), negotiable, and have an original maturity of 1 year or less. Bills are offered only in book-entry form. The return from T-bills, notes, and bonds is subject to federal income tax, but is exempt from state and local taxation. Yield calculations for Treasury bills, a discount security, *depend on whether the bill has left more than* 182 days until maturity, *or* 182 days *or less.*

Discount Security (T-Bill) with Less than 183 Days to Maturity.
The formula for determining the price of a Treasury bill (actual - 360 method) with 182 days or less until maturity is:

$$P = S - \left[\frac{(S)\,(y)\,(t)}{360} \right]$$

where P = price (in decimal form), the purchase price for each $100 of the
        bill's face value (Bills are normally sold in minimum denomina-
        tions of $10,000 with multiples of $5000 thereafter.)
      y = yield, the effective yield to maturity (can be either bid or asked)
      t = time, the number of days until maturity
      S = sum at maturity, the maturity value of the bills (the face value)
      N = number of days in a year (use 366 if Leap year and February 29
        occurs between current date and maturity)
      D = discount from face value (i.e., $S - P$)
      d = rate of discount

Example: Finding the price of a T-bill with less than 183 days to maturity.   Cautious
Charley decides to dump his stocks and invest for the moment in something
safe and secure. He calls his broker and asks about T-bills. Since the maturity
is short, there is little worry of excessive price volatility. And since the U.S.
government is the issuer, there is no credit risk. How much will it cost, asks
Charley, to buy $100,000 face amount of T-bills, maturing 180 days from
settlement, priced at a discount of 10 percent?

$$P = S - \left[\frac{(S)\,(d)\,(t)}{360} \right]$$

$$= \$100,000 - \left[\frac{(\$100,000\,)\,(0.1)\,(180)}{360} \right] = \$100,000 - \$5000 = \$95,000.00$$

As we see, the discount is $5000. Charley pays $95,000 now and in 180 days
will receive $100,000. The discount is

$$D = S - P = S \left(\frac{(y)\,(t)}{360} \right) = \$100,000 \left((0.1) \frac{(180)}{360} \right) = \$5000$$

The quoted yield is a 10 percent discount. The bond equivalent yield is
10.673 percent. Note, however, that the discount is calculated on the basis
of a 360-day year. If (contrary to practice) the discount were calculated on
the basis of a 365-day year, the discount would be less, that is $4931.51. So
Charley (and any other investors in T-bills) earns more (e.g., $5000) than is
reasonably expected to be earned (e.g., $4931.51).

Yield by Discount Method for Treasury Bills with 6 Months or Less to Maturity.
If both the face value and the current price are known, the rate of discount
on a T-bill is calculated by the following formula:

$$d = \left[\frac{S - P}{S}\right]\left[\frac{360}{t}\right]$$

Applied to the previous example, the rate of discount is

$$d = \left[\frac{\$100,000 - \$95,000}{\$100,000}\right]\left[\frac{360}{180}\right] = (0.05)(2) = 0.10 \text{ or } 10\%$$

Note that the discount *understates* yield, because it is based on the maturity value and a 360-day year rather than cost and the actual number of days in the year.

T-Bill Simple Interest Yield. If Cautious Charley merely loaned $95,000 for 180 days and received $100,000 at the end of that time, representing $5000 of interest and $95,000 of principal, the *simple interest* he earned (as conventionally calculated for the "yield" of T-bills) would be

$$I = P \times i \times T$$

where I = interest earned
P = principal
i = rate of annual interest
T = actual days divided by 360

$$\$5000 = P \times i \times T = \$95,0000 \ (i) \left(\frac{180}{360}\right)$$

$$i = \left(\frac{\$5000}{\$95,000}\right)\left(\frac{360}{180}\right) = 0.10526 \text{ or } 10.526\%$$

Thus, on a *simple interest basis* Charley earned significantly more than the stated discount rate of 10 percent. This principal is true of all Treasury bill purchases. The simple interest rate earned (10.53 percent) exceeds the stated rate of discount (10.0 percent). As noted, this method understates yield by using a 360-day year.

Bond Equivalent Yield

Discount Security (T-Bill) with 182 Days or Less to Maturity

The formula for bond equivalent yield, or *coupon equivalent yield* as it is also called, is

$$\text{BEY} = \left(\frac{S - P}{P}\right)\left(\frac{N}{t}\right)$$

where BEY = bond equivalent yield
  S = sum at maturity
  P = purchase price
  N = number of days in the year which includes the settlement date
   (365 or 366)
  t = elapsed time from settlement to maturity
For $100,000 face amount, purchased at $95,000, with 180 days to maturity,

$$BEY = \left(\frac{S-P}{P} \right) \left(\frac{N}{t} \right)$$

$$= \left(\frac{\$100,000 - \$95,000}{\$95,000} \right) \left(\frac{365}{180} \right) (0.05263)\,(2.02778) = 0.10673 \ \ \text{or} \ \ 10.67\%$$

The *bond equivalent yield* corrects the inadequacies of both the discount rate and the simple interest method. In order to make relevant and meaningful comparisons of yields or returns involving discount securities such as T-bills and coupon securities such as bonds, the discount rates (discounted yields) of the former have to be restated to the *bond equivalent yield*.

Discount Security (T-Bill) with More Than 6 Months to Maturity

The bond equivalent yield (based on theoretical semiannual interest payments) for a discount security with more than 6 months to maturity is given by the following formula:

$$BEY = \frac{[-(2)\,(t)/N] + 2\sqrt{(t/N)^2 - \{[\,(2)(t)/N\,] - 1\} - [1 - 1/(P/100)]}}{(2t/N) - 1}$$

where BEY = coupon equivalent yield or bond equivalent yield
  t = time, the number of days from settlement until maturity
  P = price, the purchase price for each $100 of the bill's face
   value (Bills are normally sold in minimum denominations
   of $10,000.)
  N = number of days in the year which includes the settlement
   date (365 or 366)

This bond equivalent yield (BEY), or coupon equivalent yield, is a rate determined in order that yields of "long" T-bills (more than 6 months to maturity) may be compared directly to yields on coupon securities. To understand the calculation of BEY, we will delve into it in more detail.

It is assumed for this determination of BEY (for T-bills of more than 6 months up to 1 year to maturity) *that the interest coupon is reinvested at the same rate as the BEY.* As will be discussed later, the general rule is that it is not necessary to reinvest to achieve the quoted bond yield to maturity. Bond equivalent yield for long T-bills is an *exception* to the general rule. It is inherent in the generally accepted formula that the one coupon payment on a comparable corporate bond is reinvested at the same rate as the bond equivalent yield. The following example demonstrates the theory of bond equivalent yield. This theory is simply that BEY is the rate that, when applied to a corporate bond, will produce the same total value at maturity as the equivalent T-bill will provide.

A 1-year T-bill is purchased at issue at a discount of 10 percent with settlement 1/1/95 and maturity 12/31/95. The corresponding dollar price is $898.8889 (quoted as 89.88889). The maturity value is, naturally, $1000. The bond equivalent yield is 10.979 percent (BEY is found by using the formula for over 182 days to maturity, but the method of calculation is not our purpose at this time), and the simple interest yield is 11.125 percent.

The essential question is: What would the yield be on a traditional corporate bond that corresponds to this T-bill quoted at a 10 percent discount or 89.88889 price? The answer is the BEY of 10.979 percent. To prove the equivalency, determine the total value at maturity of the equivalent bond at a yield-to-maturity rate of 10.979 percent, the BEY. If that total value is $1000, the value of the T-bill at maturity, the BEY is the corporate bond equivalent of the T-bill's 10.979 bond equivalent yield.

The value of the corporate bond at its 1-year maturity is the sum of:

1. The assumed first coupon 182 days before maturity
2. Interest earned for 182 days on that first coupon at an annual rate equal to the BEY
3. the second and final coupon payment
4. The maturity value of the bond

The following time line shows the cash flows:

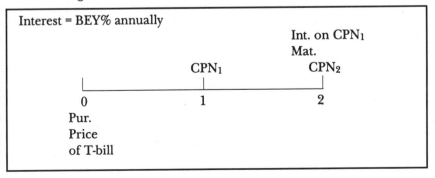

This works out as follows:

1. First coupon:

$$(0.10979)\left(\frac{182}{365}\right)(898.8889) = \$49.21$$

2. Interest earned for 182 days on first coupon at BEY:

$$\$49.21\,(0.10979)\left(\frac{182}{365}\right) = \$2.69$$

3. Final coupon payment = $49.21
4. Maturity value of a par bond: $898.89

The total of 1 through 4 above is exactly $1000.00. To recap, the theoretical bond has the same price as the T-bill, the YTM of the bond is the same as the BEY of the T-bill, the settlement and maturity dates are the same, and the 1-year bond has the penultimate coupon reinvested at the T-bill's BEY. The future value 1 year hence is $1000 for both the T-bill and the bond. Thus BEY on the T-bill is equivalent to earning 10.979 percent YTM on a corporate bond where the one coupon is reinvested at that rate.

Example: Finding bond equivalent yield for a T-bill with more than 6 months to maturity.   A T-bill is bought for settlement May 23, 1995, and it matures November 24, 1995. For a dollar price of 97.568 ($975.68), calculate the discount rate, the bond equivalent yield, and the simple interest yield.

The *discount rate* for a T-bill with more than 182 days to maturity is determined as follows. (For a bill with less than 183 days to maturity this formula also calculates the bond equivalent yield.) First the actual number of days from settlement to maturity is found:

May	8
June	30
July	31
August	31
September	30
October	31
November	24
Total	185 days from settlement to maturity

This discount is

$$d = \left(\frac{S-P}{S}\right)\left(\frac{360}{t}\right)$$

$$= \left(\frac{\$1000 - \$975.68}{\$1000.00}\right)\left(\frac{360}{185}\right) = \left(\frac{24.32}{\$1000}\right)(1.94595) = 0.04733 \text{ or } 4.733\%$$

The *simple yield* is

$$y = \left(\frac{S-P}{S}\right)\left(\frac{360}{t}\right)$$

$$= \left(\frac{\$1000 - \$975.68}{\$975.68}\right)\left(\frac{360}{185}\right) = 4.851\%$$

The *money market yield* is

$$y_{mm} = \frac{360\,(d)}{360 - (d)\,(t)} = \frac{360\,(0.04733)}{360 - (0.04733)\,(185)} = 4.851\%$$

The *bond equivalent yield* is determined by

$$\text{BEY} = \frac{[-(2)\,(t)/N] + 2\,\sqrt{(t/N)^2 - \left\{[\,(2)(t)/N\,] - 1\right\} - [1 - 1/(P/100)]}}{(2t/N) - 1}$$

$$= \frac{[-(2)(185)/365] + 2\,\sqrt{(185/365)^2 - \left\{[2\,(185)/365] - 1\right\} - [1 - 1/(97.568)/100]}}{[(2)(185)/365] - 1}$$

$$= \frac{[-370/365] + 2\,\sqrt{(0.25690) - [(370/365) - 1]\,[1 - (1/0.97568)]}}{0.01370}$$

$$= \frac{-1.01370 + 2\,\sqrt{(0.25690) - (1.01370 - 1)(1 - 1.02493)}}{0.01370}$$

$$= \frac{-1.01370 + 2\,\sqrt{(0.25690) - (0.01370)(-0.02493)}}{0.01370}$$

$$= \frac{-1.01370 + 2\,\sqrt{0.25724}}{0.01370}$$

$$= \frac{-1.01370 + 1.01437}{0.01370} = \frac{0.00067}{0.01370} = 0.04916 \text{ or } 4.916\%$$

Table 13.4. Bond Equivalent Yield Versus Discount Rate

		Equivalent bond yield				
Discount rate (%)	30-day maturity	As percent of discount rate	182-day maturity	As percent of discount rate	364-day maturity	As percent of discount rate
5	5.091	101.8	5.201	104.0	5.270	105.4
6	6.114	101.9	6.274	104.6	6.375	106.2
7	7.139	102.0	7.358	105.1	7.498	107.1
8	8.166	102.1	8.453	105.7	8.639	108.0
9	9.194	102.2	9.560	106.2	9.799	108.9
10	10.227	102.3	10.679	106.8	10.979	109.8
11	11.256	102.3	11.810	107.4	12.179	110.7
12	12.290	102.4	12.952	107.9	13.399	111.7
13	13.325	102.5	14.108	108.5	14.641	112.6
14	14.362	102.6	15.256	109.0	15.904	113.6
15	15.401	102.7	16.456	109.7	17.191	114.6

Thus, the bond equivalent yield of 4.916 percent is 18.3 basis points (a *basis point* is 1/100 of 1 percent) greater than the 4.733 discount rate. The yield on a discount basis of a T-bill with over 182 days to maturity will always be less than the bond equivalent yield. Table 13.4 shows a comparison for selected rates between the discount rate and the bond equivalent yield. It is apparent that the magnitude of the increase in yield, as measured by the bond equivalent yield, compared to the discount rate, increases as the discount rate becomes larger and as the time to maturity lengthens. For example, the bond equivalent yield of 17.191 percent for 364-day maturity with a 15 percent discount rate is 114.6% greater than the discount rate.

Alternative Solution for Bond Equivalent Yield

Another method supplied by the Federal Reserve Board may be used to determine the bond equivalent yield. The formula is

$$P\left[1 + \left(t_{sm} - \frac{N}{2}\right)\left(\frac{y}{N}\right)\left(1 + \frac{y}{2}\right)\right] = 100$$

where P = price (in decimals, e.g., 97.568)

t_{sm} = days from settlement to maturity of the T-bill (e.g., 185 days)

N = 365 unless a leap day occurs between settlement and maturity; if so, 366

Y = nominal annual interest rate of return based on semiannual interest payments

$$P\left[1+\left(t_{sm}-\frac{N}{2}\right)\left(\frac{y}{N}\right)\left(1+\frac{y}{2}\right)\right]=100$$

$$97.568\left[1+\left(185-\frac{365}{2}\right)\left(\frac{y}{365}\right)\left(1+\frac{y}{2}\right)\right]=100$$

$$\left[1+(2.5)\left(\frac{y}{365}\right)\left(1+\frac{y}{2}\right)\right]=\frac{100}{97.568}$$

$$\left(\frac{365+2.5y}{365}\right)\left(\frac{2+y}{2}\right)=1.02493$$

$$(365+2.5y)(2+y)=(1.02493)(365)(2)$$

$$2.5y^2+370y-18.19613=0$$

This is an equation in the form of $ax^2+bx+c=0$ and can be solved by using the quadratic equation, as explained in Appendix 13.1. Suffice it to say here that the root 0.04916 is a solution for y in the above equation. Thus, 4.916 percent is the bond equivalent yield by this alternative formula.

Money Market Yield

Certain money market instruments, such as certificates of deposit and such longer-term instruments as municipal bonds, are quoted in rates of interest based on a 360-day year. To compare T-bills to such 360-day investments, bill rates are sometimes converted to simple interest on a 360-day basis. The formula for money market yield, y_{mm}, for a T-bill is

$$y_{mm}=\frac{(360)(d)}{360-(d)(t)}$$

where y_{mm} = money market yield on a T-bill
        t = number of days until maturity
        d = rate of discount

Example: finding the money market yield for a T-bill.   In an earlier example, we determined that a discount rate of 10 percent applies to $100,000 face amount of 180-day bills bought for $95,000. The simple interest yield is 10.526 percent. The bond equivalent yield is 10.673 percent. What is the money market yield?

$$y_{mm} = \frac{(360)(d)}{360 - (d)(t)} = \frac{360\,(0.1)}{360 - (0.1)(180)} = 0.10526 \text{ or } 10.526\%$$

A summary of the three yield calculations for this T-bill is:

Discount rate	10.000%
Bond equivalent yield	10.673%
Money market yield (simple interest)	10.526%

Confusing? It is indeed confusing to have to deal with so many rates all applying to the same situation. The *discount rate* is what the securities and banking industries use to make quotations. It is defective because it computes yield based on the maturity value rather than the purchase price. It is also defective because it makes the calculation on the basis of a 360-day year.

For bonds with 182 days or less until maturity, the *simple interest* rate or *bond equivalent yield* corrects both of the inequities of the discount rate. Its yield calculation is based on the actual purchase price and uses a 365-day year. And, for bills with more than 182 days until maturity, the *bond equivalent yield* provides a figure which can be used in direct comparison with corporate coupon bonds, assuming that the first such coupon is reinvested at the rate of the bond equivalent yield.

The money market yield rate calculates the yield in a manner consistent with the calculation of certificate of deposit yields.

Certificates of Deposit

Yields of certificates of deposit (CDs) normally use a simple interest calculation based on the actual number of days, the actual investment, and a 360-day year with interest paid only at maturity. Thus, for the T-bill bought for $95,000 and maturing for $100,000 in 180 days, the CD rate is determined by the following yield formula (the result is the same as the simple interest or money market yield for the T-bill):

$$y_{cd} = \left(\frac{S-P}{S}\right)\left(\frac{360}{t}\right) = \left(\frac{\$100,000 - \$95,000}{\$95,000}\right)\left(\frac{360}{180}\right) = 0.10526 \text{ or } 10.526\%$$

The maturity value of a certificate of deposit is found using

$$S = P + P\left(\frac{t}{360}\right)(y_{cd})$$

where P = price of the CD (amount invested or present value)
 t = actual number of elapsed days
 y_{cd} = yield as conventionally quoted by banks
 S = maturity value, the amount one receives at maturity from the bank

The price to buy a CD is found from

$$P = \frac{S}{1 + [(t) \, (y_{cd}) \, / 360]}$$

Bond Yield to Maturity with Accrued Interest

Earlier, in discussing bond yield to maturity, it was pointed out that the formula used for simple cases ignores such complicating factors as accrued interest, fractional years, and compounding more frequently than annually. Now it is time to rectify that simplification.

Accrued interest adds to the cash outlay of the investor. However, this is *not a disadvantage*, as the investor *earns the same yield to maturity on the investment in accrued interest as he or she does on the bond itself.* In other words, accrued interest is treated as part of the investment. The base against which return is measured in calculating yield to maturity has to be adjusted to include accrued interest. The first coupon may be received after a nonstandard number of days, that is, after less than usual number of days between coupon payments. Finally, since most bond calculations are based on semiannual payments and semiannual compounding, the yield found is the semiannual rate. And the number of payment intervals is twice the number of years. A formula for the price of a coupon security that takes all this into account is

$$P = \left\{ \frac{S}{[1 + y/m]^{N - 1 + (t_{sc}/D_c)}} \right\} + \left\{ \sum_{k=1}^{N} \frac{R/m}{[1 + y/m]^{k - 1 + (t_{sc}/d_c)}} \right\} - \left[\frac{R \, (t_{cs})}{m \, (d_c)} \right]$$

where P = price, the purchase price (e.g., $1000)
 R = annual interest (annual coupon) (e.g., $100.00)
 y = annual yield, yield to maturity (as a decimal, e.g., 0.10)
 t_{sc} = time from settlement until the next coupon payment (e.g., 30)
 N = number of remaining coupon payments until maturity, call, redemption, etc. (e.g., 3)
 m = number of coupon periods per year (normally 2)
 D_c = days in the coupon period in which settlement occurs (e.g., 180)

S = maturity or redemption value (normally $1000 unless unusual call or put or redemption features are involved)

k = a summation counter (if N = 3, then the second term in braces is calculated three times, with k = 1, k = 2, and k = 3)

t_{cs} = days from beginning of coupon period to settlement date (accrued days) (e.g., 150)

The first term in braces calculates the present value of the sum (S) due at maturity; the *second term* finds the present value of all coupon payments (R); and the *third term* finds the accrued interest (due at the settlement date).

The above equation can also be used to find the yield to maturity by solving for y. To better understand the accrued interest calculation, refer to Fig. 13.6.

Example: Finding price with semiannual compounding and accrued interest. On January 15, 1997, Mr. Richardson decides to make an offer to buy the 11's of 5/1/2006 of WatchYourStep Corp. He wants a yield to maturity of 20 percent. What price should he offer if settlement is February 1, 1997?

P = price, the purchase price

R = annual interest (annual coupon) = $110

y = annual yield, yield to maturity (as a decimal) = 0.20

t_{sc} = time from settlement until the next coupon payment = 90 days

N = number of remaining coupon payments until maturity, call, redemption, etc. = 19

m = number of coupon periods per year (normally 2) = 2

D_c = days in the coupon period in which settlement occurs = 180

S = maturity or redemption value (normally $1000 unless unusual call or put or redemption features are involved) = $1000

k = a summation counter (in this example, k is 1, 2, 3, ... 19)

t_{cs} = days from beginning of coupon period to settlement date (accrued days) = 90

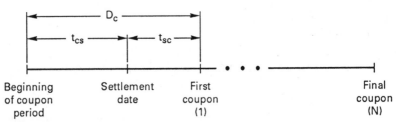

Figure 13.6. Days of accrued interest: yield to maturity.

$$P = \left\{ \frac{\$1000}{[1 + (0.2/2)]^{18 + (90/180)}} \right\} + \left\{ \sum_{k=1}^{19} \frac{110/2}{[1 + (0.2/2)]^{k - 1 + (90/180)}} \right\} - \left[\frac{\$110\,(90)}{2\,(180)} \right]$$

$$P = \left[\frac{\$1000}{1.1^{18 + (0.5)}} \right] + \left[\sum_{k=1}^{19} \frac{\$55}{(1.1)^{k - 1 + 0.5}} \right] - \left(\frac{\$990}{360} \right)$$

$$= \left(\frac{\$1000}{5.8313} \right) + \left[\sum_{k=1}^{19} \frac{\$55}{(1.1)^{k - 0.5}} \right] - (\$27.50)$$

$$= (\$171.488) + [(\$451.078 + \$55)\,(0.9534626)] - (\$27.50)$$

$$= (\$171.488) + (\$482.526) - (\$27.50) = \$626.514$$

Thus the price of the bond is $626.51, and the accrued interest is $27.50. The present value of the future maturity value is $171.488, and the present value of the future payment of 19 coupons of $55 each is $482.526.

The middle term, the present value of the coupon payments, is also the sum of the present value of an annuity of $55 of 18 payments discounted at 10 percent per semiannual period plus one first coupon of $55, all of which is discounted for 3 months at the semiannual rate of 10 percent, a discount factor of $(1.1)^{-0.5}$, that is, 0.9534623.

This calculation is admittedly not an easy one. However, computer software programs such as the *COMPLETE BOND ANALYZER* perform such calculations in seconds. In addition, the software automatically provides such other useful amounts as:

After-tax return (14.928 percent in a 28 percent bracket for income and capital gains)

Nominal annual interest (the conventionally quoted yield to maturity, which is twice the semiannual yield rate (20 percent in the example)

Annual equivalent yield (which is 21 percent)

Current yield (17.558 percent)

Finding Yield to Maturity Given Price

The formula for finding price given yield is also used to find yield to maturity given price. An iterative search process is used, trying successive values for the yield until both sides of the equation reach equality (within allowable tolerances). An alternative to the trial-and-error search process is the use of Newton's method, which was described earlier in this chapter. With Newton's method, three or four iterations normally produce a remarkably accurate solution.

It should be noted that the solution to the yield-to-maturity formula produces a value of the semiannual yield-to-maturity rate. For example, 0.05 or 5 percent semiannually is doubled, and the relevant bond is said to have a yield to maturity of 10 percent. What this means, however, is that the yield is a *nominal annual rate* of 10 percent, compounded twice per year. Alternatively, one may say that the semiannual rate is 5 percent. All yields to maturity for bonds with semiannual interest payments are quoted at double the semiannual rate. Technically, this ignores the semiannual aspect of the income stream, and for purposes of comparison with other instruments, it is advisable to find the annual or bond equivalent yield. As stated in Chap. 1, this is [(1 + semiannual rate)^2 – 1]. In this example [(1.1)^2 – 1] = 1.21 – 1 = 0.21 or 21 percent.

Effective Yield or Bond Effective Yield

In Chap. 1 we discussed the concept of *effective yield*. The following formula finds the *effective annual rate*:

$$Y = \left(1 + \frac{r}{m}\right)^m - 1$$

where Y = effective annual yield
  r = conventional or nominal yield (rate), say 20 percent
  m = number of periods of compounding per year
    for a nominal rate (r), say 2 for semiannual compounding

$$Y = \left(1 + \frac{0.20}{2}\right)^2 - 1 = 1.2100 - 1 = 0.2100 \text{ or } 21.00\%$$

Eurodollar bonds normally pay interest annually rather than semiannually. A Eurodollar bond offering a 21 percent yield to maturity as compared to a domestic U.S. bond offering only a conventionally quoted 20 percent would offer no yield advantage. The two yields are equivalent.

To find the yield to maturity of a bond, all the cash flows are discounted at a uniform rate such that the present value equals the market value or purchase price of the bond. Generally, the uniform rate at which the cash flows are discounted is the semiannual rate. Conventionally, the semiannual rate thus obtained is then multiplied by 2 in order to obtain the quoted yield to maturity. Thus, if the semiannual rate is 5 percent, that bond is said to have a yield to maturity of 10 percent. This is the way the bond industry operates. It has followed this practice for a long time, and it is doubtful that it will change.

Nevertheless, it should be emphatically noted that the quoted yield to maturity is *not* the effective annual yield, because the quoted YTM does not take into account the fact that the interest is paid twice per year rather than once. We know that it is more valuable to receive semiannual payments than annual ones, *yet the quoted YTM ignores the opportunity to invest the first coupon payment received each year.*

For a given nominal rate of interest—say, 8 percent—the more frequently the interest is compounded, the more interest will be earned and the greater will be the effective yield.

When the time period is 1 year, the effective annual rate is simply the interest earned divided by the original principal. For example, if $8160 is the interest earned and $100,000 is the original principal, the effective rate is 8.16 percent. To put it another way, if the nominal rate is 8.16 percent and compounding is annually, then the effective rate is also 8.16 percent.

Example: Bond Effective Yield. A 30-year bond pays $50 semiannually. It is bought at par. The semiannual rate is 5 percent, and doubling it gives the nominal YTM of 10 percent. What is the effective rate?

$$Y = \left(1 + \frac{r}{m}\right)^m - 1$$

$$= \left(1 + \frac{0.10}{2}\right)^2 - 1 = 1.05^2 - 1 = 1.1025 - 1 = 0.1025 \text{ or } 10.25\%$$

When the conventionally quoted YTM is 10 percent, the true effective annual yield is $10\frac{1}{4}$ percent. This will always be the case. Whenever a normal semiannual interest-paying bond YTM is quoted, the effective rate will be higher. How much higher is determined by the previously indicated formula.

Table 13.5 shows that the higher the quoted YTM, the larger is the increase in yield to reach effective annual yield. For example, with a quoted YTM of 6 percent, the increase is 9 basis points; with a quoted YTM of 20 percent, the increase is 100 basis points.

Rosen's rule of thumb allows mental calculation of the effective yield to maturity provided one knows the conventionally quoted yield. The rule of thumb (which was used to compute the last column in Table 13.5) for the multiplier is

$$\left(1 + \frac{YTM}{4}\right)(YTM) = \text{effective annual yield to maturity}$$

For example, when the quoted YTM is 10 percent, applying the rule-of-thumb multiplier, we find

$$\left(1 + \frac{0.10}{4}\right)(0.10) = 1.025\,(0.1) = 0.1025 \text{ or } 10\tfrac{1}{4}\%$$

It is the effective annual yield to maturity that should be compared to the effective annual yield of other instruments. The conventionally quoted bond yield to maturity will always understate the effective annual yield. It should be noted that bonds quoted in Europe are frequently annual interest payers, and the YTM in such cases is also equal to the effective annual yield.

Table 13.5. Bond Effective Annual Yield

Quoted bond yield to maturity (%)	Semiannual yield to maturity (%)	Effective annual yield to maturity (%)	Basis points increase for effective yield	Multiplier of YTM to obtain effective yield	Multiplier by using rule of thumb, 1 + YTM/4 (%)
4.0	2.0	4.040	4	101.00	101.00
5.0	2.5	5.063	6	101.25	101.25
6.0	3.0	6.090	9	101.50	101.50
7.0	3.5	7.123	12	101.75	101.75
8.0	4.0	8.160	16	102.00	102.00
9.0	4.5	9.202	20	102.25	102.25
10.0	5.0	10.250	25	102.50	102.50
11.0	5.5	11.302	30	102.75	102.75
12.0	6.0	12.360	36	103.00	103.00
13.0	6.5	13.422	42	103.25	103.25
14.0	7.0	14.490	49	103.50	103.50
15.0	7.5	15.562	56	103.75	103.75
16.0	8.0	16.640	64	104.00	104.00
17.0	8.5	17.723	72	104.25	104.25
18.0	9.0	18.810	81	104.50	104.50
19.0	9.5	19.903	90	104.75	104.75
20.0	10.0	21.000	100	105.00	105.00
21.0	10.5	22.103	110	105.25	105.25
22.0	11.0	23.210	121	105.50	105.50
23.0	11.5	24.323	132	105.75	105.75
24.0	12.0	25.440	144	106.00	106.00
25.0	12.5	26.563	156	106.25	106.25

So, if a European annual interest-paying bond is quoted at $10\frac{1}{4}$ percent yield to maturity, it is equivalent to a U.S. semiannual-paying bond quoted at only 10 percent. In other words, one must obtain a higher yield on the Eurodollar bond to have an equivalent result to purchase of a domestic bond.

It may desirable to find equivalent yield when odd combinations of interest payment frequency are involved. For example, suppose a bond pays interest monthly (e.g., GNMAs). What is its semiannual equivalent yield; in other words, what is the nominal yield to maturity of an equivalent bond? Appendix 5 provides a general formula that can be used to determine equivalent yields for any combination of payment frequencies of both the subject bond and the equivalent bond.

Reinvestment

It has been emphasized that, *to achieve the yield to maturity* (at purchase or otherwise), the investor *need not reinvest any of the coupon interest. On the other hand, effective annual yield* (and *bond equivalent yield*) *do assume reinvestment* of the coupons.* An example will best illustrate the reinvestment assumption included in the bond equivalent yield concept. A 5-year $50 semiannual coupon bond, bought at par of $1000, yields 10 percent at maturity (5 percent semiannual yield times 2). As we have previously determined, the effective annual yield is 10.25 percent. This means that the semiannual-paying bond is equivalent to an annual-paying bond which, bought at par, pays $102.50 per year. At the end of 5 years, a comparison of the two bonds, with reinvestment of both bonds, provides:

Bond	Rate earned reinvestment	Interest	Interest on interest	Terminal value
Semiannual $50 coupon	5% semiannually	$500.00	$128.89	$1628.89
Annual $102.50 coupon	10.25% annually	512.50	116.39	1628.89

Thus, effective annual yield makes the two bonds equivalent, provided the coupon interest from both bonds is reinvested at the respective yield rate of each bond (5 percent semiannually and $10\frac{1}{4}$ percent annually).

---

*This concept holds true for all compounding frequencies, e.g., monthly, quarterly, etc.

Yield to Maturity with Reinvestment

Some bond investors may not care about reinvestment. A 70-year-old retired teacher, who spends every dime from her bond investments before the ink on the check has a chance to dry, probably doesn't care about the YTM with reinvestment. On the other hand, investors who are still in their peak earnings years and pension plan managers, among others, should consider the yield to maturity that they will realize based on various earnings rates assumed to be earned by reinvesting the coupon interest as it is received.

The method of finding the YTM with reinvestment is the same as the determination of realized compound yield, discussed earlier. However, that approach did not consider accrued interest, which for complete accuracy ought to be considered, especially for shorter-term maturities.

Example: Yield to maturity with reinvestment. A pension manager buys a corporate bond, as follows:

Settlement date: January 1

Coupon: 10 percent ($100 per year)

Maturity date: February 1 one year later

Price: $1000

Yield to maturity (without reinvesting): 9.983 percent

Accrued interest: $41.67

Days from settlement to the next coupon: 30 days

Days in the coupon period in which settlement takes place: 180 days

Days from the last paid coupon to the settlement date: 150 days

Number of coupons to be paid after settlement through maturity: 3

Interest rate assumed to be earned on the reinvested coupons: 9.983 percent

The formula for finding the yield to maturity with reinvestment is

$$y_r = 2 \left\{ \frac{S + \sum_{k=1}^{n} (R/m) \, [1 - (x/m)]^{n-k}}{P + a_i} \right\}^{\frac{1}{k-1+(t_{sc}/d_c)}} - 1$$

where y_r = yield to maturity with reinvestment of coupon interest (as a decimal)
   x = nominal annual rate earned on reinvestment (e.g., twice the semiannual rate) (in decimal form) (e.g., 0.09983)
   P = price, the purchase price (e.g., $1000)

R = annual interest (annual coupon) (e.g., \$100)

t_{sc} = time (in days) from settlement until the next coupon payment (e.g., 30)

N = number of remaining coupon payments until maturity, call, redemption, etc. (e.g., 3)

m = number of coupon periods per year (normally 2) and compounding frequency

D_c = days in the coupon period in which settlement occurs (e.g., 180)

S = maturity or redemption value (normally \$1000 unless unusual call or put or redemption features are involved)

k = summation counter (if N = 3, then the term in braces is calculated three times, with k=1, k =2, and k = 3)

t_{cs} = days from beginning of coupon period to settlement date (accrued days) (e.g., 150)

a_i = accrued interest (e.g., 41.67) (calculated as shown under that subject)

For this example,

$$y_r = 2 \left\{ \frac{S + \sum_{k=1}^{n} (R/m) \, [1 - (x/m)]^{n-k}}{P + a_i} \right\}^{\frac{1}{k-1+(t_{sc}/d_c)}} - 1$$

$$= 2 \left(\frac{\$1157.61}{\$1041.67} \right)^{0.4615385} - 1$$

$$= 2 \, [\, (1.1113045)^{\,0.4615385} - 1]$$

$$= 2 \, [\, (1.049914 - 1)$$

$$= 2 \, (0.049914) = .009828, \text{ that is } 9.9828\% \text{ YTM with reinvestment}$$

In this example, the YTM without reinvestment is 9.9828 percent, and the same rate was chosen for the reinvestment rate. It is not unexpected that under such circumstances, the YTM with reinvestment (the *revised IRR*, or RIRR) is also 9.9828 percent. This will always be the case: If one chooses to reinvest, and the reinvestment rate selected is equal to the YTM or IRR of the investment without reinvestment, then the RIRR will not change.

The Texas Instruments Fixed Income Securities Calculator and the COMPLETE BOND ANALYZER are capable of calculating this RIRR.

Eurobonds and Other Annual Interest Payers

The standard for Eurodollar issues is annual payment of interest. Other usual characteristics of Eurodollar bonds include: (1) noncallable; (2) not secured by the pledge of any specific property; (3) 7- to 10-year maturity as measured from the offering; (4) availability of various currencies for the bond denomination and payment of interest, including marks, yen, U.S. dollars, Canadian dollars, New Zealand kiwis, ECUs (European Currency Units), etc.; and (5) probably most important and certainly not least, nondeductibility of withholding tax by any jurisdiction from the payment of interest.

For a bond which pays interest only once per year, the yield to maturity is the effective annual yield. However, a U.S. investor in such an issue who is accustomed to thinking in terms of semiannual rates may wish to convert the annual yield to the applicable semiannual rate. The following formula provides the nominal yield or yield to maturity when the effective annual yield is known:

$$r = m \, (Y + 1)^{(1/m)} - 2$$

Example: Finding yield to maturity when interest is paid annually. A Eurodollar issue pays 10.25 percent annually. The bond is purchased at par of $1000. What is the equivalent yield to maturity for a semiannual instrument?

$$r = m \, (Y + 1)^{(1/m)} - 2$$

$$= 2 \, (0.1025 + 1)^{(1/2)} - 2$$

$$= 2 \, (1.050) - 2$$

$$= 0.100 \text{ or } 10\%$$

This 10 percent yield is the semiannual coupon security's nominal annual rate or YTM—that is, 5 percent semiannually, doubled. Of course this is the result we expected to obtain, as it is a restatement of the earlier conversion from YTM to effective annual yield.

Yield/Price in Last Coupon Period

As mentioned at the beginning of this chapter, the securities industry switches to a simple interest method in calculating yield and price for transactions that take place when maturity is less than 6 months away, that is, in the last coupon period of the bond or note. This type of transaction is not a common occurrence for most, and the special calculations of yield and price have therefore been relegated to Appendix 5.

Appendix 13.1: The Binomial Expansion

The binomial expansion of the yield to maturity formula follows the formula for finding the price of a bond, which is

$$P = R \left[\frac{1 - (1 + i)^{-n}}{i} \right] + S (1 + i)^{-n}$$

where P = present value, or price (e.g., $1130)
  S = maturity of value
  n = years from the present until maturity (e.g., 5)
  i = discounted interest rate, or nominal yield to maturity
  R = annual coupon rate (e.g., $80)

For the example bond described,

$$1130 = \$80 \left[\frac{1 - (1 + i)^{-5}}{i} \right] + 1000 (1 + i)^{-5}$$

$$14.125 = \left[\frac{1 - (1 + i)^{-5}}{i} \right] + 12.5 (1 + i)^{-5}$$

$$14.125i = 1 - (1 + i)^{-5} + 12.5i (1 + i)^{-5}$$

$$14.125i (1 + i) = (1 + i)^5 - 1 + 12.5i*$$

$$14.125i (1 + 5i + 10i^2 + 10i^3 + 5i^4 + i^{5)}$$
$$= (1 + 5i + 10i^2 + 10i^3 + 5i^4 + i^{5)} - 1 + 12.5i$$

$$14.125i + 70.735i^2 + 141.25i^3 + 141.25i^4 + 70.125i^5 + 14.125i^6$$
$$= 1 + 5i + 10i^2 + 10i^3 + 5i^4 + i^5 - 1 + 12.5i^\dagger$$

---

*To determine $(1 + i)^5$, use the binomial expansion formula. For example, using the formula one obtains the following:

$(a + b)^5 = a^5 + 5a^4b + 10a^3b^2 + 10a^2b^3 + 5ab^4 + b^5$
$(a + b)^4 = a^4 + 4a^3b + 6a^2b^2 + 4ab^3 + b^4$
$(a + b)^3 = a^3 + 3a^2b + 3ab^2 + b^3$
$(a + b)^2 = a^2 + 2ab + b^2$

Where the problem is of the nature that $(a + b)$ is in the format $(1 + i)$,

$(1 + i)^5 = 1 + 5i + 10i^2 + 10i^3 + 5i^4 + i^5$
$(1 + i)^4 = 1 + 4i + 6i^2 + 4i^3 + i^4$
$(1 + i)^3 = 1 + 3i + 3i^2 + i^3$
$(1 + i)^2 = 1 + 2i + i^3$

$$0 = -3.375i + 60.625i^2 + 131.25\ i^2$$

$$0 = 131.25i^2 + 60.625i - 3.375\ \ddagger$$

$$i = \frac{-60.625 \pm \sqrt{(60.625)^2 - 4\,(131.25)\,(-3.375)}}{2\,(131.25)}$$

$$= \frac{-60.625 \pm \sqrt{(5447.265625)}}{262.5} = \frac{-60.625 \pm 73.805}{262.5}$$

$$= 0.0502$$

And 0.0502 is 5.02 percent, which is the yield to maturity.§

The binomial formula for the expansion of positive integral powers of a binomial (where r = the number of terms) is

$$(a + b)^n = a^n + na^{n-1}b + \frac{n\,(n-1)}{2!}a^{n-2}b^2 + \frac{n\,(n-1)\,(n-2)}{3!}a^{n-3}b^{n-3} + \dots$$
$$\frac{n(n-1)(n-2)\dots(n-r+2)}{(r-1)!}a^{n-r+1}b^{r-1} + \dots$$

In expanding a power of a binomial, it is usually easier to build up each successive term from the preceding one rather than substitute in the formula. Note that if the coefficient of any term is multiplied by the exponent of a in that term, and if this product is divided by the number of terms already written down, the result is the coefficient of the next term. The exponent of a decreases by one in each successive term (until the exponent becomes 0 in the last term), and the exponent of b increases by one (starting with $b^0 = 1$ in the first term). For example, to expand $(a + b)^6$, we need only remember that the first term will be a^6. Then

$$(a + b)^6 = a^6 + \frac{6 \times 1}{1} a^5b^1 + \frac{6 \times 5}{2} a^4b^2 + \frac{15 \times 4}{3} a^3b^3 + \frac{20 \times 3}{4} a^2b^4 + \frac{15 \times 2}{5} a^1b^5 + \frac{6 \times 1}{6} a^0b^6$$

$$= a^6 + 6a^5b + 15a^4b^2 + 20a^3b^3 + 15a^2b^4 + 6ab^5 + b^6$$

Usually the multiplication and division can be done mentally and the resulting coefficient written down immediately. It can be shown that the coefficients will build up to a maximum at the middle term (or two middle terms if the number of terms is even) and then decrease symmetrically as in the above example. The number of terms in the expansion is always $n + 1$.

†Values larger than i^2 or i^3 may be disregarded to simplify the solution. Such values are practically insignificant. For example, if $i = 0.04$, then $i = 0.000002$.

‡Once the equation is in the form $ax^2 + bx + c = 0$, then the quadratic formula is used to solve for x:

$$x = \frac{-b \pm \sqrt{b^2 - 4ac}}{2a}$$

§By computer the yield calculation is 4.998 percent.

Appendix 13.2: National Association of Securities Dealers Uniform Practice Code Section 46*

Interest to Be Added to the Dollar Price

(a) In the settlement of contracts in interest-paying securities other than for "cash," there shall be added to the dollar price interest at the rate specified in the security, which shall be computed up to but not including the fifth business day following the date of the transaction. In transactions for "cash," interest shall be added to the dollar price at the rate specified in the security up to but not including the date of transaction.

Basis of Interest

(b) Interest shall be computed on the basis of a 360-day year; i.e., every calendar month shall be considered to be $1/12$ of 360 days; every period from a date in one month to the same date in the following month shall be considered to be 30 days.

Note: The number of elapsed days should be computed in accordance with the examples given in the following table:

From 1st to 30th of the same month to be figured as 29 days:

From 1st to 31st of the same month to be figured as 30 days;

From 1st to 1st of the following month to be figured as 30 days;

From 1st to 28th of February to be figured as 27 days.

From the 23rd of February to the 3rd of March is to be figured as 10 days.

From the 15th of May to the 6th of June is to be figured as 21 days.

Where interest is payable on 30th or 31st of the month:

From 30th or 31st to 1st of the following month to be figured as 1 day.

From 30th or 31st to 30th of the following month to be figured as 30 days.

From 30th or 31st to 30th of the following month to be figured as 30 days.

From 30th or 31st to 1st of second following month to be figured as 1 month, 1 day.

---

*Reprinted from *NASD Manual.*

Appendix 13.3: Municipal
Securities Rulemaking Board
Rule G-33—Calculations

(a) Accrued Interest. Accrued interest shall be computed in accordance with the following formula:

$$\text{Interest} = \text{Rate} \times \frac{\text{Par Value of}}{\text{Transaction}} \times \frac{\text{Number of Days}}{\text{Number of Days in Year}}$$

For purposes of this formula, the "number of days" shall be deemed to be the number of days from the previous interest payment date (from the dated date, in the case of first coupons) up to, but not including, the settlement date. The "number of days" and the "number of days in year" shall be counted in accordance with the requirements of section (e) below.

(b) Interest-Bearing Securities.

(i) Dollar Price. For transactions in interest-bearing securities effected on the basis of yield the resulting dollar price shall be computed in accordance with the following provisions:

(A) Securities Paying Interest Solely at Redemption. Except as otherwise provided in this section (b), the dollar price for the transaction in a security paying interest solely at redemption shall be computed in accordance with the following formula:

$$P = \left[\frac{RV + \left(\dfrac{DIR}{B} \cdot R\right)}{1 + RV + \left(\dfrac{DIR - A}{B} \cdot Y\right)} \right] - \left[\frac{A}{B} \cdot R\right]$$

For purposes of this formula the symbols shall be defined as follows:

"A" is the number of accrued days from the beginning of the interest payment period to the settlement date (computed in accordance with the provisions of section (e) below);

"B" is the number of days in the year (computed in accordance with the provisions of section (e) below);

"DIR" is the number of days from the issue date to the redemption date (computed in accordance with the provisions of section (e) below);

"P" is the dollar price of the security for each $100 par value (divided by 100);

"R" is the annual interest rate (expressed as a decimal);

*Reprinted from *Municipal Securities Rulemaking Board Manual*, Oct. 1, 1989, Washington, D.C.

"RV" is the redemption value of the security per $100 par value (divided by 100); and

"Y" is the yield price of the transaction (expressed as a decimal).

(B) Securities with Periodic Interest Payments. Except as otherwise provided in this section (b), the dollar price for a transaction in a security with periodic interest payments shall be computed as follows:

(1) for securities with six months or less to redemption, the following formula shall be used:

$$
P\left[\frac{\dfrac{RV}{100}+\dfrac{R}{M}}{1+\left(\dfrac{E-A}{E}\cdot\dfrac{Y}{M}\right)}\right]-\left[\frac{A}{B}\cdot R\right]
$$

For purposes of this formula the symbols shall be defined as follows:

"A" is the number of accrued days from the beginning of the interest payment period to the settlement date (computed in accordance with the provisions of section (e) below);

"B" is the number of days in the year (computed in accordance with the provisions of section (e) below);

"E" is the number of days in the interest payment period in which the settlement date falls (computed in accordance with the provisions of section (e) below);

"M" is the number of interest payment periods per year standard for the security involved in the transaction;

"P" is the dollar price of the security for each $100 par value (divided by 100);

"R" is the annual interest rate (expressed as decimal);

"RV" is the redemption value of the security per $100 par value; and

"Y" is the yield price of the transaction (expressed as a decimal).

(2) for securities with more than six months to redemption, the following formula shall be used:

$$
P=\left[\frac{RV}{\left(1+\dfrac{Y}{2}\right)^{N-1+(E-A)/E}_{\exp}}\right]\left[\sum_{K=1}^{N}\frac{100\cdot\dfrac{R}{2}}{\left(1+\dfrac{Y}{2}\right)^{K-1+(E-A)/E}_{\exp}}\right]\left[100\cdot\frac{A}{B}\cdot R\right]
$$

For purposes of this formula the symbols shall be defined as follows:

"A" is the number of accrued days from the beginning of the interest payment period to the settlement date (computed in accordance with the provisions of section (e) below);

"B" is the number of days in the year (computed in accordance with the provisions of section (e) below);

"E" is the number of days in the interest payment period in which the settlement date falls (computed in accordance with the provisions of section (e) below);

"N" is the number of interest payments (expressed as a whole number) occurring between the settlement date and the redemption date, including the payment on the redemption date;

"P" is the dollar price of the security for each $100 par value;

"R" is the annual interest rate (expressed as a decimal);

"RV" is the redemption value of the security per $100 par value; and

"Y" is the yield price of the transaction (expressed as a decimal).

For purposes of this formula *the symbol "exp" shall signify* that the preceding value shall be raised to the power indicated by the succeeding value, for purposes of this formula the symbol "K" shall signify successively each whole number from "1" to "N" inclusive, for purposes of this formula the symbol "sigma" shall signify that the succeeding term shall be computed for each value "K" and that the results of such computations shall be summed.

(C) Transactions Where the Yield Equals the Interest Rate. A transactions in a security with a redemption value of par that is effected on the basis of a yield price equal to the interest rate of the security shall be exempt from the requirements of the subparagraph (b)(i)(B) until January 1, 1984.

(D) Interpolation. The computation of a dollar price by means of interpolation shall be deemed to be in compliance with this paragraph (b)(i) until January 1, 1984.

(ii) Yield. Yields on interest-bearing securities shale be computed in accordance with the following provisions:

(A) Securities Paying Interest Solely at Redemption. The yield of a transaction in a security paying interest with the following formula:

$$Y = \left[\frac{\left(RV + \left(\frac{DIM}{B} \cdot R\right)\right) - \left(P + \left(\frac{A}{B} \cdot R\right)\right)}{P + \left(\frac{A}{B} \cdot R\right)} \right] \cdot \left[\frac{B}{DIR - A} \right]$$

For purposes of this formula the symbols shall be defined as follows:

"A" is the number of accrued days from the beginning of the interest payment period to the settlement date (computed in accordance with the provisions of section (e) below);

"B" is the number of days in the year (computed in accordance with the provisions of section (e) below);

"DIR" is the number of days from the issue date to the redemption date (computed in accordance with the provisions of section (e) below);

"P" is the dollar price of the security for each $100 par value (divided by 100);

"R" is the annual interest rate (expressed as a decimal);

"RV" is the redemption value of the security per $100 par value (divided by 100); and

"Y" is the yield on the investment if the security is held to redemption (expressed as a decimal).

(B) Securities with Periodic Interest Payments. The yield of a transaction in a security with periodic interest payments shall be computed as follows:

(1) for securities with six months or less to redemption, the following formula shall be used;

$$Y = \left[\frac{\left(\frac{RV}{100} + \frac{R}{M}\right) - \left(P + \left(\frac{A}{E} + \frac{R}{M}\right)\right)}{P + \left(\frac{A}{E} + \frac{R}{M}\right)} \right] \times \left[\frac{M \times E}{E - A}\right]$$

For purposes of this formula the symbols shall be defined as follows:

"A" is the number of accrued days from the beginning of the interest payment period to the settlement date (computed in accordance with section (e) below);

"E" is the number of days in the interest payment period in which the settlement date falls (computed in accordance with section (e) below);

"M" is the number of interest payment periods per year standard for the security involved in the transaction;

"P" is the dollar price of the security for each $100 par value (divided by 100);

"R" is the annual interest rate (expressed as a decimal);

RV is the redemption value of the security per $100 par value; and

"Y" is the yield on the investment if the security is held to redemption (expressed as a decimal).

(2) for securities with more than six months to redemption the formula set forth in item (2) of subparagraph (b)(i)(B) shall be used.

(c) Discounted Securities.

(i) Dollar Price. For transactions in discounted securities, the dollar price shall be computed in accordance with the following provisions:

(A) The dollar price of a discounted security, other than a discounted security traded on a yield-equivalent basis, shall be computed in accordance with the following formula:

$$P = [RV] - \left[DR \cdot RV \cdot \frac{DSM}{B} \right]$$

For purposes of this formula the symbols shall be defined as follows:

"B" is the number of days in the year (computed in accordance with the provisions of section (e) below);

"DR" is the discount rate (expressed as a decimal);

"DSM" is the number of days from the settlement date of the transaction to the maturity date (computed in accordance with the provisions of section (e) below;

"P" is the dollar price of the security for each $100 par value; and

"RV" is the redemption value of the security per $100 par value.

(B) The dollar price of a discounted security traded on a yield-equivalent basis shall be computed in accordance with the formula as set forth in subparagraph (b)(i)(A).

(ii) Return on investment. The return on investment for a discounted security shall be computed in accordance with the following provisions:

(A) The return on investment for a discounted security, other than a discounted security traded on a yield-equivalent basis, shall be computed in accordance with the following formula:

$$IR = \left[\frac{RV - P}{P} \right] \times \left[\frac{B}{DSM} \right]$$

For purposes of this formula the symbols shall be defined as follows:

"B" is the number of days in the year (computed in accordance with section (e) below);

"DSM" is the number of days from the settlement date of the transaction to the maturity date (computed in accordance with section (e) below);

"IR" is the annual return on investment if the security is held to maturity (expressed as a decimal);

"P" is the dollar price of the security for each $100 par value; and

"RV" is the redemption value of the security per $100 par value

(B) The yield of a discounted security traded on a yield-equivalent basis shall be computed in accordance with the formula set forth in subparagraph (b)(ii)(A).

(d) Standards of Accuracy; Truncation.

(i) Intermediate Values. All values used in computations of accrued interest, yield, and dollar price shall be computed to not less than ten decimal places.

(ii) Results of Computations. Results of computations shall be presented in accordance with the following:

(A) Accrued interest shall be truncated to three decimal places, and rounded to two decimal places immediately prior to presentation of total accrued interest amount on the confirmation.

(B) Dollar prices shall be truncated to three decimal places immediately prior to presentation of dollar price on the confirmation and computation of extended principal; and

(C) Yields shall be truncated to four decimal places and rounded to three decimals places, provided, however, that for purposes of confirmation display as required under rule G-15(a)(viii)(N) yields accurate to the nearest .05 percentage points shall be deemed satisfactory.

Numbers shall be rounded, where required, in the following manner; if the last digit after truncation is five or above, the preceding digit shall be increased to the next highest number, and the last digit shall be discarded.

(e) Day Counting.

(i) Day Count Basis. Computations under the requirements of this rule shall be made on the basis of a thirty-day month and a three-hundred-sixty-day year, or, in the case of computations on securities paying interest solely at redemption, on the day count basis selected by the issuer of the securities.

(ii) Day Count Formula. For purposes of this rule, computations of day counts on the basis of a thirty-day month and a three-hundred-sixty-day year shall be made in accordance with the following formula:

Number of Days = (Y2 − Y1) 360 + (M2 − M1) 30 + (D2 − D1)

For purposes of this formula the symbols shall be defined as follows:

"M1" is the month of the date on which the computation period begins.

"D1" is the day of the date on which the computation period begins.

"Y1" is the year of the date on which the computation period begins.

"M2" is the month of the date on which the computation period ends;

"D2" is the day of the date on which the computation period ends.

"Y2" is the year of the date on which the computation period ends.

For purposes of this formula, if the symbol "D2" has a value of "31", and the symbol "d1" has a value of "30" of "31", the value of the symbol "D2" shall be changed to "30". If the symbol "D1" has a value of "31", the value of the symbol "D1" shall be changed to "30". For purposes of this rule time periods shall be computed to include the day specified in the rule for the beginning of the period but not to include the day specified for the end of the period.

(f) Effectiveness. The requirements of this rule shall become effective on August 1, 1982, except as provided in subparagraphs (C) and (D) of paragraph (b)(i).

Appendix 13.4: Bisection Method of Finding IRR or YTM

In addition to Newton's method and trial and error, the IRR and YTM may be found by the *bisection method*. It is both simple and reliable, but it is slow and requires many iterations or trials.

Example: Finding IRR by the bisection method. A bond may be purchased with settlement on a coupon date for $991.18. The bond has exactly 2 years remaining until maturity, and interest of $50 is paid semiannually ($100 per year). Find the YTM using the bisection method.

The equation for this situation is

$$\$991.18 = \frac{\$50}{(1+r)^1} + \frac{\$50}{(1+r)^2} + \frac{\$50}{(1+r)^3} + \frac{\$1050}{(1+r)^4}$$

Rearranging,

$$0 = \$1050 (1+r)^{-4} + \$50 (1+r)^{-3} + \$50 (1+r)^{-2} + \$50 (1+r)^{-1}$$

Refer to Fig. 13.7. Solution first requires an initial two guesses of the approximate value of the IRR, where one guess (x_1, e.g., 4 percent) is likely to produce a positive NPV (net present value, v_a) and the other (y_1, e.g., 6 percent) is likely to produce a negative present value (v_b). In other words, one trial value has to be less than the actual IRR and the other greater than the IRR. This ensures that convergence will occur. [Where there is only one change in the sign of the cash flows (plus to minus or vice-versa), if the first cash flow is negative and is smaller than the sum of the inflows, then zero is the upper bound. If the first cash flow is negative and is greater than the sum of the inflows, then zero is the lower bound.]

Next find the NPV (v_1, e.g., 8.82) of the equation at the midpoint (m_1, i.e., 5.0 percent) between the two values [i.e., ($x_1 + y_1$)/2]. Refer to Table 13.6 for details of the calculations. m_1 is an early estimate of the value of the IRR. If $v_1 = 0$, then m_1 is the IRR. Otherwise, v_1 differs in sign from (v_a) or (v_b). If v_1 (e.g., positive) is of the opposite sign as v_b (which in the example is negative), the IRR will lie in the subinterval (m_1, y_1). If the value of v_1 is of the same sign (e.g., positive) as v_b (negative in the example), the IRR will lie in the subinterval (x_1, m_1). For the appropriate subinterval (m_1, y_1), let point m_2 (i.e., 5.5 percent) be the subinterval's midpoint. Then m_2 is the next trial value of the IRR. Repeat this process until the value of m_n causes the value of v_n to be zero, or close enough to zero to meet the desired standards of precision. Refer to Fig. 13.7 and Table 13.6 to follow the method in detail. Since v_2 (i.e., -8.7057506) is of the opposite sign as v_1 (i.e., $+8.820$), the trial value of m_3 is in the subinterval (m_1, m_2). With m_3 equal to 5.25 percent, v_3 turns out to be 0.00636, which indicates that 5.25 percent is quite close to the actual solution. In this example, the net present value reaches zero to seven decimal places after 28 trials, as shown in Table 13.6.

Table 13.6. Bisection Method of Finding IRR or YTM

a	b	c	d	e	f	g	h	i	j	k	l
Trial	Trial value of r	CF	$(1+r)^{-4}$	Value of 1st term	CF	$(1+r)^{-3}$	Value of 2nd term	CF	$(1+r)^{-1}$	Value of 3rd term	CF
x_1	0.4000000	1050	0.85480	897.544	50	0.88900	44.449	50	0.92456	46.227	50
y_1	0.0600000	1050	0.79209	831.698	50	0.83962	41.980	50	0.89000	44.499	50
m_1	0.0500000	1050	0.82270	863.837	50	0.86384	43.191	50	0.90703	45.351	50
m_2	0.0550000	1050	0.80722	847.577	50	0.85161	42.580	50	0.89845	44.922	50
m_3	0.0525000	1050	0.81491	855.659	50	0.85770	42.884	50	0.90273	45.136	50
m_4	0.0537500	1050	0.81105	851.606	50	0.85465	42.732	50	0.90059	45.029	50
m_5	0.0531250	1050	0.81298	853.629	50	0.85617	42.808	50	0.90165	45.082	50
m_6	0.0528125	1050	0.81395	854.643	50	0.85693	42.846	50	0.90219	45.109	50
m_7	0.0526563	1050	0.81443	855.151	50	0.85731	42.865	50	0.90246	45.122	50
m_8	0.0525781	1050	0.81467	855.405	50	0.85751	42.875	50	0.90259	45.129	50
m_9	0.0525391	1050	0.81479	855.532	50	0.85760	42.880	50	0.90266	45.132	50
m_{10}	0.0525195	1050	0.81485	855.595	50	0.85765	42.882	50	0.90269	45.134	50
m_{11}	0.0525098	1050	0.81488	855.627	50	0.85767	42.883	50	0.90271	45.135	50
m_{12}	0.0525049	1050	0.81480	855.643	50	0.85768	42.884	50	0.90272	45.135	50
m_{13}	0.0525024	1050	0.81491	855.651	50	0.85769	42.884	50	0.90272	45.136	50
m_{14}	0.0525012	1050	0.81491	855.655	50	0.85769	42.884	50	0.90272	45.136	50
m_{15}	0.0525018	1050	0.81491	855.653	50	0.85769	42.884	50	0.90272	45.136	50
m_{16}	0.0525015	1050	0.81491	855.653	50	0.85769	42.884	50	0.90272	45.136	50
m_{17}	0.0525017	1050	0.81491	855.653	50	0.85769	42.884	50	0.90272	45.136	50
m_{18}	0.0525018	1050	0.81491	855.653	50	0.85769	42.884	50	0.90272	45.136	50
m_{19}	0.0525018	1050	0.81491	855.653	50	0.85769	42.884	50	0.90272	45.136	50
m_{20}	018.05218	1050	0.81491	855.653	50	0.85769	42.884	50	0.90272	45.136	50
m_{21}	0.0525018	1050	0.81491	855.653	50	0.85769	42.884	50	0.90272	45.136	50
m_{22}	0.0525018	1050	0.81491	855.653	50	0.85769	42.884	50	0.90272	45.136	50
m_{23}	0.0525018	1050	0.81491	855.653	50	0.85769	42.884	50	0.90272	45.136	50
m_{24}	0.0525018	1050	0.81491	855.653	50	0.85769	42.884	50	0.90272	45.136	50
m_{25}	0.0525018	1050	0.81491	855.653	50	0.85769	42.884	50	0.90272	45.136	50
m_{26}	0.0525018	1050	0.81491	855.653	50	0.85769	42.884	50	0.90272	45.136	50
m_{27}	.0525018	1050	0.81491	855.653	50	0.85769	42.884	50	0.90272	45.136	50
m_{28}	.0525018	1050	0.81491	855.653	50	0.85769	42.884	50	0.90272	45.136	50

m	n	o	p	q	r	s	t	u	v
$(1 + r)^{-1}$	Value of 4th term	Value of 5th term	Total value (NPV)		Try next value for r as below				1000 times r
.96154	46.076	-991.18	45.1189522	v_a					40.0000000
.94340	47.169	-991.18	-25.8310561	v_b					60.0000000
.95238	47619	-991.18	8.8200000	v_1	betw.	0.0600000	&	0.0500000	50.0000000
.94787	47.393	-991.18	-8.7057506	v_2	betw.	0.0500000	&	0.0550000	55.0000000
.95012	47.505	-991.18	.0063634	v_3	betw.	0.0550000	&	0.0525000	52.5000000
.94899	47.449	-991.18	-4.3622948	v_4	betw.	0.0525000	&	0.0550000	53.7500000
.94955	47.477	-991.18	-2.1811271	v_5	betw.	0.0525000	&	0.0537500	53.1250000
.94984	47.491	-991.18	-1.0881736	v_6	betw.	0.0525000	&	0.0531250	52.8125000
.94998	47.498	-991.18	-0.5411032	v_7	betw.	0.0525000	&	0.0528125	52.6562500
95005	47.502	-991.18	-0.2674195	v_8	betw.	0.0525000	&	0.0526563	52.5781250
95008	47.504	-991.18	-0.1305405	v_9	betw.	0.0525000	&	0.0525781	52.5390625
95010	47.505	-991.18	-0.0620917	v_{10}	betw.	0.0525000	&	0.0525391	52.5195312
95011	47.505	-991.18	-0.0278649	v_{11}	betw.	0.0525000	&	0.0525195	52.5097656
95011	47.505	-991.18	-0.0107510	v_{12}	betw.	0.0525000	&	0.0525098	52.5048828
95012	47.505	-991.18	-0.0021939	v_{13}	betw.	0.0525000	&	0.0525049	52.5024414
95012	47.505	-991.18	0.0020847	v_{14}	betw.	0.0525012	&	0.0525024	52.5012207
95012	47.505	-991.18	-0.0000546	v_{15}	betw.	0.0525012	&	0.0525018	52.5018311
95012	47.505	-991.18	0.0010151	v_{16}	betw.	0.0525015	&	0.0525018	52.5015259
95012	47.505	-991.18	0.0004803	v_{17}	betw.	0.0525017	&	0.0525018	52.5016785
95012	47.505	-991.18	0.0002128	v_{18}	betw.	0.0525018	&	0.0525018	52.5017548
95012	47.505	-991.18	0.0000791	v_{19}	betw.	0.0525018	&	0.0525018	52.5017929
95012	47.505	-991.18	0.0000123	v_{20}	betw.	0.0525018	&	0.0525018	52.5018120
5012	47.505	-991.18	-0.0000211	v_{21}	betw.	0.0525018	&	0.0525018	52.5018215
5012	47.505	-991.18	-0.0000044	v_{22}	betw.	0.0525018	&	0.0525018	52.5018167
5012	47.505	-991.18	0.0000039	v_{23}	betw.	0.0525018	&	0.0525018	52.5018144
5012	47.505	-991.18	-0.0000002	v_{24}	betw.	0.0525018	&	0.0525018	52.5018156
5012	47.505	-991.18	0.0000018	v_{25}	betw.	0.0525018	&	0.0525018	52.5018150
5012	47.505	-991.18	0.0000008	v_{26}	betw.	0.0525018	&	0.0525018	52.5018153
5012	47.505	-991.18	0.0000003	v_{27}	betw.	0.0525018	&	0.0525018	52.5018154
5012	47.505	-991.18	0.0000000	v_{28}	Compl.				52.5018155

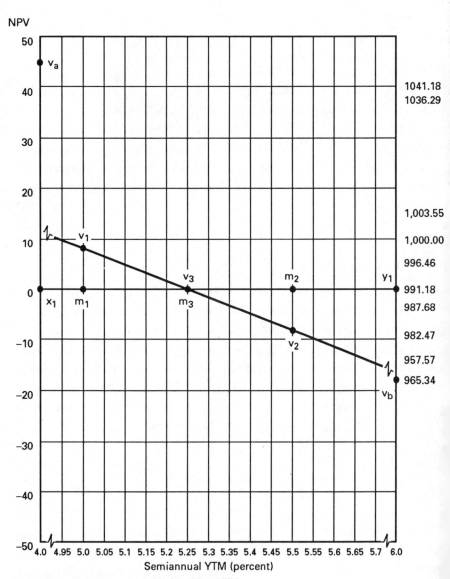

Figure 13.7. Bisection method of finding IRR or YTM.

14

Yield to Call, Average Life, and Bond Portfolio Management

Yield to Call

Most corporate and municipal bonds are callable by the issuer at a premium, declining to par, prior to the maturity date of the bonds. Both Treasury and Eurodollar bonds are an exception, however, as most are noncallable. The reason that bonds include a "callable" provision is to allow the issuer to redeem the bonds (and issue new ones) in the event that interest rates drop materially after the original issuance of the bonds. Such refinancing reduces the issuer's interest costs. Therefore, investors who purchase bonds at a premium (over $1000) must be aware of callability provisions.

Example: Finding yield to call. Charles Carew purchases a bond for $1102.70 which matures in 30 years, with a coupon rate of 10 percent (paid annually) and a yield to maturity (refer to Fig. 12.7) of 9 percent. He ignores the call provisions, which are noncallable for five years, then callable at $103.4 ($1034 per bond).

The yield to maturity (YTM) of 9 percent is dependent on the bond being held for 30 years, with annual interest payments, and being redeemed at maturity for $1000. (With semiannual interest payments the YTM is 9.004

percent.) However, if the bond is callable and the bond *is* called prior to maturity, then the yield will not be 9 percent.

Finding the yield to call (YTC) is similar to finding yield to maturity, except that the time period from the current date to the call date is shorter, and the call price is frequently in excess of the usual $1000 maturity value. Several methods are available for determining the yield to call, including formula, graphs, tables, electronic calculators, and computers.

Yield to Call by Formula

The formula for yield to call with annual interest and settlement on a coupon date is

$$A = R \left[\frac{1 - (1 + i)^{-n}}{i} \right] + S_c (1 + i)^{-n}$$

where A = purchase price or current value (e.g., $1103)
       R = annual interest (e.g., $100)
       S_c = value at the call date in n years (e.g., $1034)
       n = number of years to call date (e.g., 5)
       i = yield to call
Then

$$\$1103 = 100 \left[\frac{1 - (1 + i)^{-n}}{i} \right] + S_c (1 + i)^{-n}$$

This equation may be solved by the mathematical techniques described in Chap. 13 for yield to maturity. The yield to call (with annual payments of interest) is only 8.006 percent! (The YTC with semiannual interest payments is 8.032 percent.) Thus if the bond (with annual payments) is called, the investor's yield will be reduced by about 100 basis points, that is, from 9 percent to 8 percent. To summarize:

The 30-year YTM is 9 percent.

The 5-year yield to call is 8 percent.

Thus, if this bond is called, Mr. Carew's yield will be reduced by one-ninth, a reduction of 11.11 percent.*

---

*And he will have to reinvest the proceeds at the lower interest rates in effect at the time of call.

Yield to Call from Graphs

Graphs of bond yield to maturity (or published bond tables) may be used to determine YTC if, and only if, adjustments are made by converting the call price to a $1000 base and converting the coupon as well, as described below.

First, determine the ratio of $1000 to the call price. Continuing with the previous example,

$$\text{Ratio} = \frac{\$1000}{\$1034} = 96.7117\%$$

Then, *multiply the purchase price by this ratio*, to give the adjusted maturity value:

$$(\$1103)\,(0.967117) = \$1066.73$$

Next, *multiply the coupon rate by this ratio*, to give the adjusted coupon value:

$$(0.10)\,(0.967117) = 0.0967117$$

No adjustment is made to the number of years to call, which remains 5 years.

The above adjustments convert the terms of the bond to a $1000 base rather than $1034, and the adjustment is such that the interest per dollar invested ($0.090661) and the maturity value per dollar invested ($0.969317) remain the same. Before the adjustment, the situation was:

$$\frac{\$100 \text{ interest}}{\$1103 \text{ purchase price}} = \$0.0907 \text{ interest per dollar of purchase price}$$

$$\frac{\$1034 \text{ call value}}{\$1103 \text{ purchase price}} = \$0.93744 \text{ call value per dollar of purchase}$$

After the adjustment, the relationship is unchanged, so

$$\frac{\$96.7117 \text{ adjusted interest}}{\$1066.73 \text{ adjusted purchase price}} = \$0.0907$$

$$\frac{\$1000 \text{ adjusted call value}}{\$1066.73 \text{ adjusted purchase price}} = \$0.093744$$

Using the adjusted coupon rate and adjusted purchase price, the yield to call, 8 percent, is found in Fig. 12.2 or from conventional bond yield tables.

Dangers of Callable Bonds

One cannot ignore the risk of realizing a lower yield to call if a bond is called than what one expected in terms of yield to maturity at the time of purchase. A good rule of thumb is: *Beware whenever the purchase price of a bond exceeds the call price.* Check the yield to call. Consider that the *lower* of either (a) yield to call or (b) yield to maturity is the *minimum* yield that will be realized (if the bond is held to maturity or until called).

The purchase price of a bond can exceed the call price and the yield to maturity can still exceed the yield to call. Consider the following situation:

Settlement date	1/1/96
Maturity date	12/31/02
Coupon	8 percent
Call date	12/31/99
Call price	105

At price of	Yield to maturity (%)	Yield to call (%)	Lowest yield
$110.388	6.151	6.151	Neither
110.0	6.216	6.254	Maturity
111.0	6.049	5.990	Call

The 6.151 percent yield (at a dollar price of $1103.88) is the *crossover point*: At this level, the yield to maturity and the yield to call are equal. At prices above the crossover price, yield to call is less than yield to maturity. Conversely, at prices below the crossover price, yield to maturity is less than yield to call. (See Fig. 14.1.)

Note that at prices up to $110.388, the crossover price (which is much higher than the call price of 105), the yield to maturity is less than the yield to call. Not all purchase prices that exceed the call price lead to a lower yield to call than yield to maturity, but some do. At purchase prices above the crossover price, YTC is less than YTM; so, the wise will watch the yield to call whenever a bond is selling at a premium.

Misconceptions about Yield to Call

Academic literature generally ascribes the pricing of callable bonds to the lesser price of either call or maturity. Bond salespersons are required to provide price quotations to the lowest yield to call or yield to maturity, whichever will produce the *smaller* yield to the investor; brokers generally adhere to this practice very well.

An additional example of how bonds are conventionally priced to the lesser of call or maturity value follows. Table 14.1 shows the applicable yields to call and maturity for various prices of an 8.75 percent coupon, 30-year bond, callable in 5 years at $1070. Note that the crossover point, at which yield to call equals yield to maturity, is at a price of $1073.658. The information shown in the table is the basis for Fig. 14.1. It is readily apparent from the figure that at market prices above the crossover point, the yield to

Table 14.1. Crossover Yield to Call

Bond with 30 Years to Maturity, 5 Years to Call, at $1070 and 8.75% Coupon

Market price	YTC	YTM	YTM – YTC
$1300.00	3.4590	6.4714	3.0124
1218.78	5.0000	6.9965	1.9965
1100.00	7.4900	7.8700	.3800
1092.49	7.6636	7.9372	.2736
1073.71	8.0919	8.0926	.0007
1073.70	8.0921	8.0927	.0006
1073.67	8.0928	8.0930	.0002
1073.66	8.0930	8.0931	.0001
1073.658	8.0930	8.0930	0.0000*
1073.65	8.0933	8.0932	(.0001)
1073.45	8.0979	8.0948	(.0031)
1073.40	8.0990	8.0952	(.0038)
1073.38	8.0990	8.0950	(.0040)
1073.37	8.0997	8.0955	(.0042)
1073.35	8.1002	8.0956	(.0046)
1000.00	9.8665	8.7500	(1.1165)
900.000	12.5514	9.7878	(2.7636)
800.000	15.6373	11.0516	(4.5857)
700.000	19.2529	12.6406	(6.6123)

*Crossover point

call is less than the yield to maturity; and conversely, at prices below the crossover point, the yield to maturity is less than the yield to call.

Most investment books describe the process of finding yield to call as one of determining the yield which equates the market price of the bond to the cash flows that will result from the callable bond being called on the call date. This method was used to find the various yields to call in Table 14.1 and Fig. 14.1. *This method, however, fails to recognize* that the market price (determined by the bond's yield to maturity) may not be a good frame of reference for determining the price and yield to call. In fact, by its very nature it *causes the price to call to be equal to the price to maturity.* And *quotations to the lesser of call or maturity* also are based on prices to call and maturity that are equal to each other.

Price

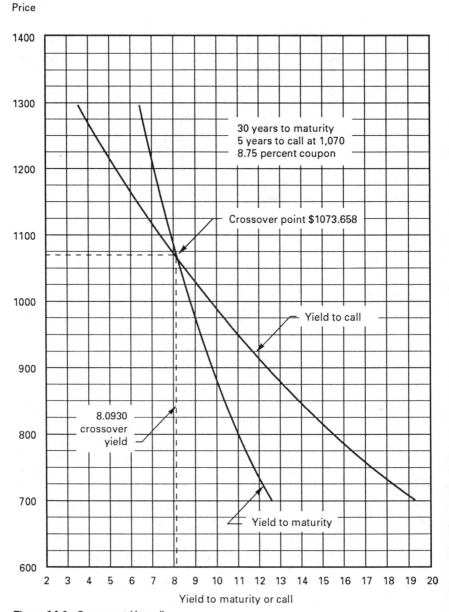

Figure 14.1. Crossover yield to call.

In the above example, we have a bond with 30 years to maturity and only 5 years to call. The price of the bond (to both call and maturity) is established by the yield to maturity. If the yield to maturity is 7.87 percent, then the price is $1100.* The normal convention of finding the yield to call requires using this $1100 as the price to call, in order to find the yield to call of 7.48 percent. This conventional approach, which is the method customarily described in investment literature, is *illogical* and would be appropriate only when the yield curve is completely flat. With a positive- or negative-sloping yield curve, however, and when the bond's price is at or above the crossover price (usually close to the maturity value plus call premium), *it makes inherently more sense to use an appropriate rate for the 5-year yield to call, and with it determine the price to call.* The price to call, so determined, becomes the operative price, and price to maturity is ignored. It is this method of finding the YTC that the author has used in the computer software, BOND PORTFOLIO MANAGER.

Example: Negatively sloped yield curve, premium bond. Let us continue with the bond priced to maturity at $1100 at a YTM of 7.87 percent. The 7.87 percent is indicative of the 30-year yield rate and, depending on the credit quality of the issuer, represents a rate adjusted upward from the rate on 30-year Treasury bonds. Let us say that the appropriate 5-year yield is 8.10 percent. (In this example the yield curve is inverted, with long rates below shorter rates.) Then the price to call is determined by discounting the cash flows to call at 8.10 percent, as follows:

Price of a conventional 5-year, 8.75% bond discounted at 8.10% (4.05% semiannually)	$1026.29
Call premium of $70 dollars discounted at the same rate.............	47.06
Price to call ($1,026.29 + $47.06)......................................	$1073.35

A prudent investor should be willing to pay less than $1073.35 to buy the bond *to yield 8.10 percent to call*, rather than the $1100.00 price commensurate with the 7.87 percent yield to maturity (which results in *only a 7.48 percent yield to call*). At this price, $1073.35, the yield to maturity is 8.096 percent as compared to 7.87 percent at the $1100 price. *The result of this difference in methodology is not trivial:* In this example, we are talking about $26.65 per bond, minimum.

We have stated that the appropriate yield to maturity for this 30-year bond is 7.87 percent. If the bond is likely to trade to maturity, then a seller normally would be unwilling to sell at the 8.10 percent yield to maturity. But if the bond is likely to be called, then the 8.10 percent, or more, yield to call is appropriate (and the rich 8.096 percent yield to maturity is a gratuitous by-product, to which the parties should attach little significance). Whether or not the seller of a bond is going to be willing to sell at the 8.10 percent, or higher, yield to call thus depends on the party's perception of the likelihood of call.

*The bond price is actually $1100.78.

Example: Positively sloped yield curve, premium bond.   Let us continue with the bond priced to maturity at $1100 at a YTM of 7.876 percent (and to call, 7.495 percent). Let us say that the appropriate 5-year yield is 7.66 percent. (In this example the yield curve is positively sloped, with long rates higher than shorter rates.) Then the price to call, at $1070, is determined by discounting the cash flows to call at 7.66 percent, as follows:

Price of a conventional 5-year, 8.75% bond discounted at 7.66% (3.83% semiannually)..	$1044.58
Call premium of $70 discounted at the same rate......................	48.07
Price to call ($1044.58 + $47.09).....................................	$1092.65

A prudent investor would be willing to pay only $1092.65, or less, to buy the bond to yield 7.66 percent to call, rather than the $1100 price commensurate with the 7.87 percent yield to maturity (which results in only a 7.49 percent yield to call). At this price, $1092.65, the yield to maturity is 7.936 percent as compared to 7.87 percent at the $1100 price. In this example, with a rising yield curve, *the difference is a substantial* $7.35, or more, per bond.

Example: Positively sloped yield curve, discount bond or par.   The bond we have been discussing was priced at a *premium*, and its conventional yield to call (7.495 percent) was less than its yield to maturity (7.876 percent). Now let us focus on a *discount or par* bond, where the yield to maturity is less than the conventional yield to call. We continue with the same bond but assume that it is currently priced to maturity at $1000 with a YTM of 8.75 percent. At the $1000 price, the conventionally calculated yield to call is 9.87 percent (due to the $1070 call). The $1000 price is well below both the crossover price of $1073 and the $1070 sum of maturity value plus call premium.

This bond is traded to its maturity of 30 years, as the bond is not expected to be called. The bond issuer is paying 8.75 percent interest. For refinancing to be profitable for the bond issuer, rates for new issues would have to fall to roughly 6.75 percent (a change of 2 percentage points to cover underwriting commissions, bond rating services, etc.).

The 5-year rate is not relevant, unless circumstances change which cause the bond to trade to call, rather than maturity. This can happen, however.

Let us say that the appropriate 5-year yield is 5.0 percent, and the perception now is that this $1000 bond is likely be called (or prerefunded) in 5 years. (In this example the yield curve is positively sloped, with long rates significantly higher than shorter rates.)

The price to call is determined by discounting the cash flows to call at 5 percent, as follows:

Price of a conventional 5-year, 8.75% bond discounted at 5% (2.50% semiannually)..	$1164.10
Call premium of $70 discounted at the same rate........................	54.68
Price to call (1164.10 + $47.09).....................................	$1218.78

Will an investor be willing to pay $1218.78 to buy the bond to yield 5 percent to call, rather than the $1000 price commensurate with the 8.75 percent yield to maturity (which results in a 9.87 percent yield to call)? At this price, $1218.78, the yield to maturity drops to 6.996 percent as compared to 8.75 percent at the $1000 price. Investors are not going to risk the chance that short rates will rise and thereby eliminate the expectation that the issuer will call the bonds. So, in this case, the bond will not sell if it is priced at the short rate of 5 percent to call. This is illustrative of the general principle that bonds priced above the crossover price will be priced to call, and bonds below the crossover price will be priced to maturity. *Only bonds which are priced to call should have the prices to call determined by the appropriate short (years to call) yield rates.*

Adverse Effects of a Call

It should be borne in mind that the effect of a call can be doubly harmful. First, the investor may receive a lower yield to call than was the initial yield to maturity, as discussed above. Second, when an investor receives, prematurely, the redemption proceeds of bonds, it is quite possible—even probable—that the interest rate environment will be one of low rates and the investor will have to invest the proceeds at lower rates than he or she was previously enjoying.

Callable bonds should sell for higher yields than otherwise comparable noncallable bonds, to compensate investors for the potential risks of the callable bond. As a result, the call price at issuance is frequently set higher than the maturity value. Several maturities of U.S. Treasury bonds (not recently issued) are callable over a 5-year period at the option of the Treasury. They show a hyphenated maturity in quotation listings. An example is the issue of Treasury bonds known as $8\frac{1}{4}$s 2000-05. They mature in 2005, but the Treasury has the right to call them at par during the 5 years starting in the year 2000.

Call Risk

Callable bonds usually have a certain period of time before the call provision becomes operative. This is called the "time of call protection." Some bonds may be *noncallable* ("NC") altogether. Others may merely be *nonrefundable* ("NR"). NR bonds may not be called to refinance the issue at lower rates, but they may be called for other purposes such as in a merger or reorganization.

Table 14.2. Typical Periods of Call Protection

Type of bond	Years of call protection	Remarks
Corporate	10	NR, callable for other reasons
Treasury	15	May be callable in years 16–20
Agencies	10	
Municipals	10	Housing issues are particularly susceptible to early redemption for purposes other than refunding

Typical periods of call protection for various categories of bonds are shown in Table 14.2.

Special Redemptions

There are also *special redemptions* with which one must be concerned. Generally, the price paid in a special redemption is just par value plus accrued interest. Among the types of special redemptions are:

Maintenance and replacement

Sinking fund

Release and substitution of property

Eminent domain

Utilities, which are major issuers of bonds, must maintain plants and replace facilities as they become obsolete. Bond indentures may require the utility to place funds in a *maintenance-and-repair fund*. If there is a deficit in the fund, the utility may be allowed to call some bonds. That reduces the exposure of the remaining bondholders. Investors should consider such factors as the size of the maintenance fund compared to the bond issue, the special redemption price, and the company's cash requirements.

Sinking funds may be either specific or funnels. *Specific funds* may be satisfied only with bonds of a specific or certain issue. *Funnel funds* may be satisfied by any bond issues of the company. Bonds chosen for redemption by either method are usually selected by a random method. Alabama Power, for one, has called in high-coupon bonds to satisfy sinking-fund requirements.

When assets are sold or liquidated, the money obtained may be required to be used to reduce debt. This debt reduction could take the form of a bond call. The bond indenture clause which would dictate this approach is called a *release and substitution of property* provision. Arizona Public Service retired $100 million of 16 percent bonds at par using this provision.

An *eminent-domain provision* allows bonds to be called with funds generated by the purchase or confiscation of assets by government exercising the right of eminent domain. Pacific Power and Light used money from the sale of a water business in Oregon to a government agency to redeem at par some $20 million of 14¾ percent bonds.

Bear in mind that *the bond issuer looks at its debt in much the same fashion as a homeowner looks at refinancing a high-rate mortgage.*

Housing Bonds

Some bonds, particularly municipal housing finance issues, contain extraordinary call provisions that allow the issuer to use unloaned funds to call bonds by random lot. In this context, unloaned funds are:

1. The portion of the bond issue that the finance authority was unable to lend to home buyers to finance home purchases; and

2. The proceeds of prepaid home mortgages.

Housing bonds may also be *prematurely repaid* (to the detriment of purchasers at a premium) in the event of foreclosure or as the result of fire, windstorm, or other casualty causing destruction of the property.

Zero-Coupon Bonds

Zero-coupon bonds present a special form of call risk. The call price is based on the accreted value. Suppose that an investor is considering buying a North Carolina Housing Finance Authority bond in the secondary market. The zero-coupon municipal was issued a few years ago at a 13 percent yield to maturity. But since the time of issuance, rates have declined to 10 percent for bonds with 15 years remaining to maturity. Thus the value of the bonds has risen. The present *accreted value* of the bond, as measured from its original issuance, is $15,989 (its maturity value in 15 more years is $100,000). But the purchase price to yield 10 percent is $23,939. If any of the variety of redemption possibilities (sinking fund, special redemption, etc.) is exercised, the investor *may be forced to sell* the bonds that just *cost $23,939 for as little as the accreted value of $15,989!* The accreted value in 5 years more will be $29,459. Suppose our investor buys the bond now and it is called 5 years hence at $29,459. The yield to call (i) is

$$\$23,939 = \$29,459 \, (1 + i)^{-5}$$

$$(1 + i) = 1.0424$$

$$i = 0.0424 \quad \text{or} \quad 4.24\%$$

Thus, with a call 5 years hence, the investor realizes only 4.24 percent instead of the 10 percent that was anticipated. The moral of the story is *Remember to investigate call and redemption provisions carefully before investing.*

Weighted-Average Life and Sinking Funds

Bonds which have active *sinking funds* require a slightly different yield calculation method than either yield to call or yield to maturity. A sinking fund requires the periodic retirement of part of the bond issue prior to maturity. The early retirement of bonds should increase the safety of the bondholder, and supports the secondary market for the issue. Historically, problems have arisen in the administration of sinking funds where the monies were used for purposes other than the intended object of retiring portions of the bond issue pursuant to a prescribed schedule (Table 14.3). To avoid the potential problems of sinking funds, issuers have largely turned to the issuance of *serial bonds*, which mature in annual segments over a period of several or many years. Normally, if rates have risen and the secondary market for bonds is below par, the issuer will buy on the open market to acquire bonds needed to meet sinking-fund obligations. On the other hand, if rates have fallen, the issue will be called by lot and redeemed for the sinking fund, usually at or near par.

For simplicity, bond yields to maturity (where there is an active sinker) are calculated on the basis of all principal payments being made as of the date of *average life*. The average life is the *weighted-average maturity* of the principal repayments of the bond. Suppose, for example, that issue SuperSinker is a $100 million, 10-year bond issue with a sinking fund starting in year 1 to retire $10 million per year. It is apparent from Table 14.4 that the average life of the issue is about $5\frac{1}{2}$ years.

The average-life calculation becomes more complex when the annual debt repayment is other than a standard fixed amount, as in the following example of a premature sinker.

Premature Sinker

(Millions of Dollars)

	Year				
	1	2	3	4	5
Principal outstanding (start)	$100	$60	$30	$20	$10
Retired during year	40	30	10	10	10
Year-end balance	60	30	20	10	0

Table 14.3. Sinking-Fund Repayment Schedule

(Millions of Dollars)

	Year									
	1	2	3	4	5	6	7	8	9	10
Principal outstanding (start)	$100	$90	$80	$70	$60	$50	$40	$30	$20	$10
Retired during year	10	10	10	10	10	10	10	10	10	10

In the above case it is apparent that the average life is less than $2\frac{1}{2}$ years.

The formula for calculating *average life* (years) or *weighted-average maturity* is

$$n_a = \sum_{t=a}^{n} \left(\frac{P_t}{S_{\text{pcf}}} \right)(t)$$

where n_a = average life or weighted-average maturity of principal repayments
a = date (year) of first principal repayment
n = year of last principal repayment
P_t = principal payment in year t
S_{pcf} = sum of all principal payments (usually $1000 per bond)
t = years (or time period)

Example: Finding yield to average life for a sinking-fund bond. A bond has 5 years remaining to final maturity. However, at the end of each year, 20 percent of the total issue is to be retired, as in the following example:

Five-Year Sinker

(Millions of Dollars)

	Year				
	1	2	3	4	5
Principal outstanding (start).....	$100	$80	$60	$40	$20
Retired during year....................	20	20	20	20	20
Year-end balance........................	80	60	40	20	0

What is the average life? The average life using the formula is 3.0 years; the calculation is described in Table 14.4.

This sinking-fund bond with 5 years to maturity would have its yield to maturity calculated on the basis of a 3-year average life. The yield to average life is tantamount to calculating yield to maturity to the average-life date.

Table 14.4. Average Life

Year (a)	P_t (b)	ab	S_{pcf}	ab/S_{pcf}
1	200	200	1000	0.2
2	200	400	1000	0.4
3	200	600	1000	0.6
4	200	800	1000	0.8
5	200	1000	1000	1.0
Total				3.0 years

Assume that this bond has an interest coupon of $100 per year (paid annually), and it is selling at $975.56. What is its yield to average life of 3 years? Yield is simply calculated to a 3-year average-life date, as if the entire $1000 principal were paid in one lump sum in 3 years. The yield to the 3-year average life is 11 percent. The yield thus calculated is not 100 percent accurate, as at an 11 percent discount rate, applied to all the cash flows, the bond price would be $976.2, a slight difference from the actual $975.56 amount. The details are given in Table 14.5. It is certainly the case, however, that this 5-year sinking-fund bond is fairly and reasonably comparable to a bullet bond yielding 11 percent to a 3-year average life. A bullet is a noncallable bond without sinking fund provisions.

Prerefunded Municipals

The phobia about buying premium bonds that exists in many minds actually creates buying opportunities. The author has made substantial purchases of municipal premium bonds that are known as either *prerefunded to call* or *escrowed to maturity in governments*. In either case, the issuer has acquired

Table 14.5. Sinking-Fund Bond

Period	Beg. Bal.	Interest	Principal	End Bal.	Cash Flow	Discount Factor	PV
1	$1000	$100	$200	$800	$300	0.9009	$270.2
2	800	80	200	600	280	0.8116	227.2
3	600	60	200	400	260	0.7311	190.1
4	400	40	200	200	240	0.6587	158.0
5	200	20	200	0	220	0.5934	130.5
Totals		$300	$1000		$1300		976.2

and placed in escrow U.S. Treasury bonds or notes, the principal and interest of which are exactly equal to the debt service requirements on an outstanding bond issue. Thus there is no credit risk. The bonds are AAA rated. However, all such prerefunded bonds have been prerefunded because they carry interest rates that were substantially higher than market rates at the time of prerefunding. Thus the bonds sell at substantial premiums above par. The yields on these excellent bonds are often 50 basis points or more higher than on other comparable credits. One should keep in mind that the yield to maturity is the rate one earns on one's investment, including accrued interest at purchase. Since the bonds are escrowed to either call or maturity, there should be no early redemption risk. This point should be verified, but if it is the case, *the extra yield these low-risk premium bonds provide should not be ignored.*

Bond Portfolio Management and Reports

When one's portfolio consists only of a couple of bonds, it is no big deal to keep track of the essentials. But even with a couple of bonds, a number of the calculations that need to be made periodically are fairly demanding.

In managing one's own bond portfolio—or the portfolios of others—there are essential items and relationships that one should track on a regular basis. A computer software program is available from the author's company, called BOND PORTFOLIO MANAGEMENT. Reports produced by this program (which are compatible with popular spreadsheets such as Lotus, Appleworks, and Excel) are used to illustrate the text in the following discussion.

Market Value of Portfolio at Lesser of Value to Maturity or Call

A callable bond with a coupon way above currently available rates will likely have a lower value to the call date than to the maturity date, even though the call price is higher than the maturity value of $1000 per bond. Table 14.6 lists, in order of ascending call date, all bonds where the value is less to the date of call than to the date of maturity. See, for example, the Brevard County issue callable on 920301 (March 1, 1992). These are the 10.625's that mature March 1, 2014 [the date shown in the reports is 1140301; the last two digits are the day (01), the next two digits (03) are the month (March), and 114 (to which 1900 must be added) is the year, 2014]. For these bonds, the market value to call is shown as $21,457 (a price of 107.285, or $1072.85 for each of 20 bonds). The value to maturity is $1397.90 per bond, or $27,958 for the 20 bonds.

Table 14.6. Reports: Lower Value to Call

Selection: 1 = ytc; 9 = ytm equals 1
Sort by call date in ascending order

Call put dte	issue	mat dte	MKT PRIC	UN-REAL GAIN	1=ytc; 9=ytm	rate	sett dte	face	rating
920301	Brevard Cty.	1140301	21457	294	1	.1063	860619	20000	1
920801	Dade Co.	1140801	11261	40	1	.1238	870817	10000	1
921001	Alamonte Springs	1081001	5458	53	1	.1030	870909	5000	1
921001	Ashland, Ky	1020801	5658	658	1	.1225	820901	5000	3
921201	Williams-burg, Ky	1081215	11069	119	1	.1030	880801	10000	1
940601	Brownsville, Tx	960601	17536	104	1	.1160	861103	15000	1
950201	Kenton Co., WS #1	1080201	5657	146	1	.0910	901217	5000	1
			78096*	1414*				70000*	

Look ahead now to Table 14.8 and inspect the same Brevard County issue. The software and the report automatically select the lesser of the value to either call or maturity. Under "MKT PRIC" the $21,457 shown for the Brevard County issue, as we have just seen, is the lesser of the values to maturity or call—in this case the value to the call date.

Certain fixed-income securities calculators calculate the *price* or value *to* the *call* date by using the *yield to maturity*. In the author's opinion this is erroneous, as the value to call should be calculated using a yield appropriate for the time period remaining to the call date and not the time until the maturity date. Only with a flat yield curve is the rate used to find the price to call the same as the yield-to-maturity rate. With a positive yield curve, the appropriate discount rate to find the price to call will be less than the yield to maturity. For bonds whose value to maturity is less than the value to call, refer to Table 14.7.

Table 14.7. Report: Lower Value to Maturity

Sort by maturity date in ascending order
Selection: 1 = ytc 9 = ytm equals 9

mat dte	issue	call put	MKT PRIC	UN-REAL GAIN	1=ytc; 9=ytm	rate	sett dte	face	ra
950501	Bowling Green Wat	950501	10662	442	9	.0790	890410	10000	
			10662*	442*				10000*	

SOURCE: BOND PORTFOLIO MANAGER, Larry Rosen Co., 1994.

Unrealized Gain or Loss for Tax Purposes of Each Bond and Overall

Any taxable entity which owns bonds, whether tax-exempt or taxable, should consider taking advantage of selling bonds which will create a taxable loss and replacing them with fairly comparable other ones. This process is generally referred to as a "tax swap." In order to make this important decision, one must know the market value and compare it to the amortized cost of the bond. For *tax-exempt* bonds purchased at a premium, the IRS requires the holder to amortize the premium over the life of the bond or other period.* (For taxable bonds, amortization is optional.) So, if one has 100 bonds that cost $120,000 and half the time period has elapsed (from date of purchase to maturity or call), then half the premium of $20,000 must be amortized. Thus the adjusted cost after amortization is $110,000. And if the present market value is $115,000, there is an unrealized gain, not a loss, for tax purposes. See Table 14.8, where the Brevard County issue is an example of a bond which at the report date had $2359 of amortization applied to its cost to determine its adjusted cost of $21,163. The bond's market value (calculated by the software) of $21,457 less the basis (adjusted cost) of $21,163 is an unrealized gain of $294 (see "UN-GAIN" column). Thus this bond is not a candidate for immediate sale to generate a tax loss, even though its market value is less than the original cost of $23,522. This report is sorted in decreasing order of unrealized gain, so the first bond on the list has the largest dollar unrealized gain, and so on.

Tax-Exempt Amortization of Premium

With respect to the method of amortizing the premium on a tax-exempt bond, the IRS, after considerable research at the author's behest, reports that: "The method of amortization generally employed by the taxpayer may be used, provided it is reasonable." IRS Regulation 1.171(2)(F) deals with the subject.† The author's rule of thumb for tax-exempts is: *the more the amortization, the more the taxable gain.* The reasoning is as follows:

Taxable gain = sales proceeds − (cost − amortization)

Taxable gain = sales proceeds + amortization− cost

It is apparent for the tax-exempts, where the amortization itself each year is not tax-deductible, that the greater the amortization, the greater is the

---

*See IRC Section 171, Amortizable Bond Premium; IRS Regulation 171, Amortizable Bond Premium Permanent Regulations; and IRS Publication 550, Investment Income and Expenses.

†IRC Section 171(b)(3) and Rev. Rul. 82-10 discuss methods of amortizing bond premiums. The "yield" method (compound type) produces less amortization in early years and more in distant years as compared to straight line. For bonds issued after September 27, 1985, the yield method is required. For bonds isused earlier, straight-line amortization could be used.

Table 14.8. Market Value and Gains

Report: gains/losses & val.
Sort by gains and losses, unrealized

issue	MKT PRIC	UNL GAIN	mat dte	call put date	cost x a-t yld	face	cost	basi
Ashland Ky.	5658	658	1020801	921001	612	5000	5000	500
Bowling Green Wat	10662	442	950501	950501	751	10000	10289	1022
Brevard Cty	21457	294	1140301	920301	1670	20000	23522	2116
Kenton Co. WS #1	5657	146	1080201	950201	378	5000	5511	551
Williamsburg Ky	11069	119	1081215	921201	757	10000	11641	1095
Brownsville Tx	17536	104	960601	940601	1243	15000	19731	1743
Alamonte Spring	5458	53	1081001	921001	382	5000	5880	540
Dade Co	11261	40	1140801	920801	814	10000	12722	1122
Totals	88758*	1856*			6607*	80000*	94296*	8690

SOURCE: BOND PORTFOLIO MANAGER, Larry Rosen Co., 1994.

gain. As to choosing the method of amortization to employ, straight-line amortization will invariably provide more amortization sooner than the constant-yield method. *Therefore it is desirable (to minimize taxable gains) to use the constant-yield method.* Figure 14.2 makes this point crystal clear. The figure shows the adjusted cost of a bond using both amortization methods. The higher the adjusted cost, the lower is the taxable gain upon sale. As the figure shows, the use of the constant-yield method provides a lower tax throughout the 10-year bond's life. For *taxable* bonds, however, the amortization is deductible or offsets taxable interest income and a straight-line method would be preferable.*

*A *taxable* bond that is *subject to a call* before it matures can be redeemed by the issuer before the scheduled maturity date. The *bond premium is determined by reference to the amount the issuer will pay at the earlier call* date if the call results in a smaller amortizable bond premium for the period ending on the call date. For *callable tax-exempts,* the premium should be amortized to the first call date, and the premium amortized is the excess of cost over the call price. See IRS Reg. 1.171-2 for details. In the case of a callable tax-exempt bond, the earlier call date will be considered as the maturiy date. The amount due on the earlier call date will be considered as the amount payable on maturity unless it is determined under a different method of amortization regularly employed by the taxpayer that another amount shall be the amount payable on maturity. Hence, in the case where a bond premium is to be amortized to the earlier call date, the bond premium on such bond is required to be spread over the period from the date as of which the basis for loss of the bond is established down to the earlier call date, rather than to the maturity date. The earlier call date may be the earliest call date specified in the bond as a day certain, the earliest interest payment date if the bond is callable at such date, the earliest date at which the bond is callable at par, or such other call date, prior to maturity, specified in the bond as may be selected by the taxpayer. Where a deduction for amortizable bond premium may be determined with respect to alternative call dates, the amount of amortizable bond premium calculated with reference to a particular call date must be calculated thereafter with reference to the same call date. However, if, upon such

rate	sett dte	credit rate	1=ytc 9=ytm	orig %	gain %	% chg per yr	int peri	curr yld
.1225	820901	3	1	.0613	.1320	.0160	306	.1080
.0790	890410	2	9	.0365	.0430	.0260	395	.0740
.1063	860619	1	1	.0355	.0140	.0030	1062	.0990
.0910	901217	1	1	.0343	.0260		228	.0800
.1030	880801	1	1	.0325	.0110	.0050	515	.0930
.1160	861103	1	1	.0315	.0060	.0010	870	.0990
.1030	870909	1	1	.0325	.0100	.0030	258	.0940
.1238	870817	1	1	.0325	.0040	.0010	619	.1100
							4252*	

Aggregate Annual or Monthly Interest Income

Bondowners may wish to structure their portfolios so that a fairly consistent income is received each month. Alternatively, they may wish to have larger amounts of income in certain months. Table 14.9 provides the needed information: a month-by-month summary of expected coupon interest.

Investors who own many bonds, or who manage several portfolios, must be concerned that all the coupon interest to which they are entitled is in fact received. Not only is it important to receive the interest, but it is important that it be received in a timely manner. Table 14.9 provides the necessary management tool. With this report it is a simple matter to check on the interest payments as they arrive each month, and to clip the coupons of those bonds identified as "CPN."

Date of Maturity, Call, or Put

Serious financial loss can result from overlooking vital dates. For example, "put" bonds give the holder the option of selling the bond to a third party

---

call date originally selected, the bond has not in fact been called, the bond premium then unamortized must be amortized to a succeeding call date or to maturity. Thus, assume a $100 bond is acquired at time of issue for $125. The bond is callable in five years at $115 and in 10 years at $110. The taxpayer may amortize $10 of premium during the first five years and, if the bond is not then called, an additional $5 of premium during the next five years. If the bond is not called at the end of ten years, the remaining $10 of premium must be amortized to maturity.

Bond price

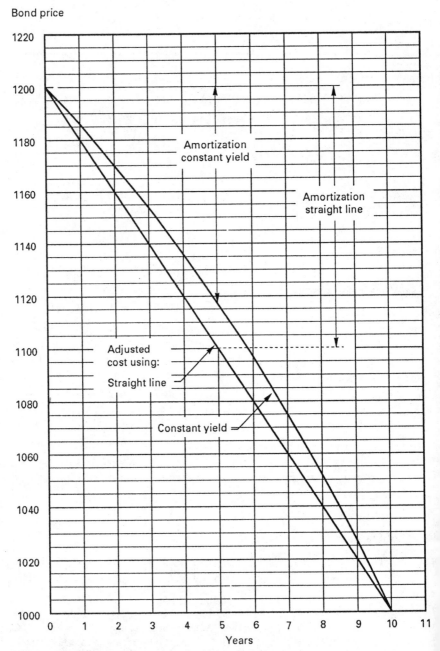

Figure 14.2. Straight-line versus constant-yield amortization.

able 14.9. Interest Payments Report

eport: interest pmts
ort by location (A-Z); then, month of interest (0-9) (in col. A)

o mo day		issue	int per period	location	rate %	mat dte	face	remarks
nt int int								
8 15		Kenton Co. WS #1	227.50		.0910	1080201	5000	
8		Dade Co	618.75	file CPN	.1238	1140801	10000	pre-ref @103
b-total			864.25					
9		Brevard Cty	1062.50	Gabriele	.1063	1140301	20000	pre-ref @102
b-total			1062.50					
10		Alamonte Springs	257.50	file 1277 Stoever reg	.1030	1081001	5000	pre-ref @102
10		Ashland, Ky	306.25	file CPN	.1225	1020801	5000	
b-total			563.75					
11		Bowling Green Wat S	395.00	file R-CIB 1921 Stoever	.0790	950501	10000	moody's AAA
-total			395.00					
12 15		Williamsburg, Ky	515.00	file 586, 587 CPN Stoever	.1030	1081215	10000	pre-ref @103
-total			515.00					
12		Brownsville Tx	870.00	Gabriele	.1160	960601	15000	pre-ref @100
-total			870.00					
nd total			4252.50*				80000*	

ource: BOND PORTFOLIO MANAGER, Larry Rosen Co., 1994.

or to the issuer at a specified time and price. The price at which the bonds may be "put" can be much higher than the market value of the bonds without the put feature. If one fails to exercise the option to put (sell) the bonds, substantial losses may be incurred. In planning cash flows that will be received, and how such monies are to be reinvested or disposed of, a report such as that shown in Table 14.10 is essential. The first column of this report is in ascending order of either the call date or the maturity date.

Table 14.10. Expiration Dates Report

Report: Value by Expiration Date

maturity or call date	yrs hence	issue	rate	maturity date	face	call date	1=ytc and 9=ytm	market value	VALUE YR OF EXPIRY	VALUE % of total	unreali gai
920301	1	Brevard C	10.63%	1140301	20,000	920301	1	21,457	21,457	24.2%	29
920801	2	Dade Co	12.38%	1140801	10,000	920801	1	11,261			4
921001	2	Alamonte	10.30%	1081001	5,000	921001	1	5,458			5
921001	2	Ashland	12.25%	1020801	5,000	921001	1	5,658			65
921201	2	Williamsb	10.30%	1081215	10,000	921201	1	11,069	33,446	37.7%	1
940601	3	Brownsvil	11.60%	960601	15,000	940601	1	17,536	17,536	19.8%	1
950201	4	Kenton Co	9.10%	1080201	5,000	950201	1	5,657			1
950501	4	Bowling G	7.90%	950501	10,000	950501	9	10,662	16,319	18.4%	4
Totals					80,000				88,758	100.0%	18

SOURCE: BOND PORTFOLIO MANAGER, Larry Rosen Co., 1994.

The software automatically uses the date which produces the lower yield or price. The column "value year of expiry" shows the total value of bonds which will mature or are expected to be called in each year. The percentage that each year's value represents of the total portfolio is shown in the column "value % of total."

Alphabetical List by Issuer

An alphabetical listing of bonds in the portfolio is frequently used as the quickest source of an extensive amount of information about that bond. Table 14.11 is an example that shows characteristics of each bond, such as whether it is registered or bearer, where it is located, identification numbers of the certificates, and call price. The column "Location" shows where each bond is located, certificate numbers, and the brokerage firm from which the bond was acquired. It also indicates if the bond is a bearer instrument with coupons (CPN).

Quality Report

A bond owner/manager should have guidelines as to how he wishes to structure his portfolio. Portfolios can be broken down in several categories, including (1) year of maturity or call—structuring the portfolio so that price volatility is controlled by controlling the duration or time; (2) creditworthiness—arranging the portfolio with the desired concentration of AAA, AA, A, BBB, or other credit ratings; (3) geographic diversification—spreading the risk among issuers in various parts of the country or the world; (4) type

`able 14.11.` Alphabetical Listing of Bonds by Issuer

eport: alpha
ort alphabetically by issue

issue	rate	mat dte	put call date	face	MKT price	rat	mo	mo	remarks	location	inter period
lamonte Springs	.103	1081001	921001	5000	5458	1	4	10	pre-ref @102	file 1277 Stoever reg	258
shland Ky	.123	102080	921001	5000	5658	3	4	10		file CPN	306
owling Green Wat wr	.079	950501	950501	10000	10662	2	5	11	moody's AAA	file R-CIB 1921 Stoever	395
evard Cty	.106	1140301	920301	20000	21457	1	3	9	pre-ref @103	Gabriele	1062
owns- ille Tx	.116	960601	940601	15000	17536	1	6	12	pre-ref @102	Gabriele	870
de Co	.124	1140801	920801	10000	11261	1	2	8	pre-ref @103	file CPN	619
nton Co. S #1	.091	1080201	950201	5000	5657	1	2	8			228
lliamsburg y	.103	1081215	921201	10000	11069	1	6	12	pre-ref @102	file CPN 586,587 Stoever	515
als				80000*	88758*						4252*

SOURCE: BOND PORTFOLIO MANAGER, Larry Rosen Co., 1991.

of issuer diversification—varying the portfolio among general obligations, corporates, municipals, utilities, industrial revenue issues, etc. In Table 14.12, AAA bonds are identified as "1," AAs as "2," etc. The report shows the value of the bonds in the portfolio in each credit category.

Duration Report

Duration, and how it is calculated, are discussed in detail in the next chapter. Suffice it to say at this point that *duration is an excellent measure of the price risk or volatility of a bond*; and a *weighted duration measure for an entire portfolio gives a meaningful indication for it of the price fluctuation that will occur with changes in market rates of interest*. In the sample report, Table 14.13, the entire portfolio's weighted duration is 2.738 years. This means that if interest rates shift by 100 basis points (i.e., 1 percent), the value of the portfolio will increase or decrease by about 2.738 percent. The column "mod dur" shows the actual modified duration for each bond. If the portfolio manager wishes to raise or lower the portfolio duration, the "mod dur" amount will indicate which bonds should be considered for sale.

Table 14.12. Quality Report

Report: quality
Sort by rating with sub-totals (AAA=1, AA=2, A=3, BBB=4, (BBB=5)

rating	issue	rate	mat dte	call put date	face	1=ytc	MKT PR	UN- GAIN	int per	mod dur
1	Alamonte Springs	.103	1081001	921001	5000	1	5458	53	258	1.6
1	Brevard Cty	.106	1140301	920301	20000	1	21457	294	1062	1.1
1	Browns- ville Tx	.116	960601	940601	15000	1	17536	104	870	2.8
1	Dade Co	.124	1140801	920801	10000	1	11261	40	619	1.4
1	Kenton Co. WS #1	.091	1080201	950201	5000	1	5657	146	228	3.3
1	Williams- burg Ky	.103	1081215	921201	10000	1	11069	119	515	1.7
sub-total		.643			65000	6	72438	756	3551	12.1
2	Bowling Green Wa	.079	950501	950501	10000	9	10662	442	395	3.6
sub-total		.079			10000	9	10662	442	395	3.6
3	Ashland Ky	.123	1020801	921001	5000	1	5658	658	306	1.5
sub-total		.123			5000	1	5658	658	306	1.5
grand total					80000*		88758*	1856*	4252*	

SOURCE: BOND PORTFOLIO MANAGER, Larry Rosen Co., 1994.

Convexity Report

Convexity and how it is calculated are described in Chap. 16. Knowing the convexity of a bond or a portfolio assists investors and managers in maximizing the "reward–risk ratio." Let us call the reward–risk ratio (RRR) the result of the following calculation:

$$RRR = \frac{\text{Increase in bond price from a downward shift in yields}}{\text{Decrease in bond price from an equal upward shift in yields}}$$

Thus, if a par bond would increase to $1100 (for a downshift) and decrease to $950 for an upshift the RRR is 115.8 percent with the given yield shift. The RRR is

Table 14.13. Duration Report

wgt dur	mod dur	isuue	rate %	mat dte	face	dte call	value
.124	2.16	Alamonte Springs	.103	1081001	5000	921001	5559
.127	2.13	Ashland Ky	.1225	1020801	5000	921001	5796
.235	1.97	Dade Co.	.12375	1140801	10000	920801	11584
.262	2.26	Williamsburg Ky	.103	1081215	10000	921215	11273
.380	1.68	Brevard Cty	.10625	1140301	20000	920301	21936
.440	4.01	Bowling Green Wat S	.079	950501	10000	950501	10660
.575	4.48	Alaska ST HSG 0%	0	941201	20000	941201	12468
.595	3.24	Brownsville Tx	.116	960601	15000	940601	17818
2.738*					95000*		97094*

SOURCE: BOND PORTFOLIO MANAGER, Larry Rosen Co., 1994.

$$RRR = \frac{(\$1100/\$100)}{(\$950/\$1000)} = \frac{110}{95} = 115.8\%$$

The convexity of a bond or portfolio gives an indication of the RRR. Convexity is basically a proxy for knowing the RRR. The convexity for each bond in a small sample portfolio, as well as the portfolio convexity, is shown in Table 14.14.

Portfolio Summary Report

The summary report for an entire portfolio (tax-exempt bonds) is shown in Table 14.15. The portfolio has a favorable reward–risk ratio as shown in lines *a*, *b*, and *c*. The RRR is 107.277 percent. The actual percentage price increase is 3.75 percent for a yield shift of 1 percent (line *ac*), as opposed to a decrease of only 3.5 percent from the same shift in the reverse direction (line *v*).

The face amount of the portfolio is $940,000 (line *f*). However, the cost price is $1,053,787. Thus the portfolio is weighted toward bonds that were selling at premiums at the time of acquisition. The current market value (computed to the lesser of the values at call or maturity) is $1,018,048 (line *g*). The adjusted basis (after amortization) is $992,918 (line *i*). The adjusted basis represents original cost adjusted for premiums using the *constant yield* (also referred to as *scientific yield*) method of amortization. Adjustment to basis is made in accordance with the procedure that an investor would follow in terms of IRS reporting. Thus premiums are amortized. Acquisition premium for OID (original issuance discount, as, for example, zero-coupon bonds) issues is amortized. Bonds bought at a discount (without OID) are

Table 14.14. Convexity Report

Weighted portfolio adjusted convexity	Bond	rate %	date for mkt val calc	LESS OF MKT PRICE TO MAT OR CALL	convexity per period squared	Adj. cvx 1/2 CVX times 1.000% squared	Price with YLD chg of +1%	Actual % price change with +1.0% shift	Price with YLD chg of -1%	Actual % price change with -1.0% shift	Value of 01 (avg) to mat or call
.00001	Almonte Springs	10.300%	921001	5,458	3.56	.018%	5,370	-1.6%	5,549	1.7%	.0164%
.00001	Ashland Ky	12.250%	921001	5,658	3.51	.018%	5,567	-1.6%	5,750	1.6%	.0162%
.00002	Dade Co	12.375%	920801	11,261	2.99	.015%	11,096	-1.5%	11,430	1.5%	.0148%
.00002	Brevard Cty	10.625%	920301	21,457	1.85	.009%	21,216	-1.1%	21,702	1.1%	.0113%
.00003	Williamsburg Ky	10.300%	921201	11,069	4.13	.021%	10,875	-1.8%	11,268	1.8%	.0178%
.00005	Kenton Co. WS #1	9.100%	950201	5,657	14.72	.074%	5,465	-3.4%	5,857	3.5%	.0347%
.00010	Bowling Green Wat	7.900%	950501	10,662	16.60	.083%	10,277	-3.6%	11,064	3.8%	.0369%
.00010	Brownsville Tx	11.600%	940601	17,536	10.56	.053%	17,037	-2.8%	18,054	3.0%	.0290%
.00034	Totals			88,758			86,903		90,674		

SOURCE: BOND PORTFOLIO MANAGER, Larry Rosen Co., 1994.

Table 14.15. Summary Report

Reward Risk Ratio	
a. Actual portfolio % price chg fm yld chg +1.00% :	−3.4997%
b. Actual portfolio % price chg fm yld chg −1.00% :	3.7526%
c. Portfolio % price increase div by % price decrease	<u>107.227%</u>

Unrealized Gain or Loss	
d. Original yield × cost divided by total cost	7.152%
e. Annual interest	90,522
f. Face amount	940,000
g. Market price (to lesser of call or maturity values)	1,018,048
h. Cost (original, unadjusted)	1,053,787
i. Adjusted basis (after amortization)	992,918
j. Unrealized gain or (loss)—market less adjusted basis	<u>25,130</u>

Portfolio Duration and Convexity	
k. Weighted portfolio modified duration	3.566%
l. Weighted portfolio convexity	.125%
m. Combined portfolio mod. dur & cvx—for rate increase	−3.441%
n. Combined portfolio mod. dur & cvx—for rate decrease	3.691%
o. Combined ratio, "n" divided by "m"	<u>107.265%</u>

Yield Shift Up—Losses from	
p. Portfolio price sensitivity frm rate chg +100.00% :	
q. −Weighted modified duration × mkt value × yield chg	(36,304)
r. Weighted adj convexity × market value	$1,272.6
s. Projected change in portfolio value in money	(35,031)
t. Projected change / total market value in percent	−3.441%
u. Actual change in money	(35,629)
v. Actual change in percent	−3.500%

Yield Shift Down—Benefits of	
w. Portfolio price sensitivity frm YLD shft −1.00 :	
x. −Weighted modified duration × mkt value × yield chg	$36,303.6
y. −Weighted adjusted convexity × market value	$1,272.6
z. Projected change in portfolio value in money	$37,576.2
aa. Projected change / total market value in percent	3.691%
ab. Actual change in money	$38,203.6
ac. Actual change in percent	3.753%

not amortized.* The difference between market value and adjusted basis is the *unrealized gain or loss* (line *j*) of $25,130.

The duration for the whole portfolio is 3.566 percent (line *k*). This means that a yield increase of 1 percent would result in a price decrease of the portfolio of about 3.6 percent. When convexity is combined with duration, the result is a more refined measure of predicted price change (than from duration alone). The combined convexity plus duration figures are given in lines *m* and *n*.

The convexity percentage for the entire portfolio is 0.125. Investors and managers of portfolios should seek to increase convexity if such an increase can be obtained without disproportionate cost (in the form of reduced yield, increased maturity, etc.).

The "Yield shift up—losses from" section of the summary report shows that the portfolio will decrease about $36,000 in value from a 1 percent upward shift. The combined duration plus convexity *predicted* price decrease is $35,031 (line *s*), which is quite close to the actual price decrease of $35,629 (line *u*). In percentages, the *predicted* decrease is 3.4 percent (line *t*) versus the *actual* decrease of 3.5 percent (line *v*).

The "Yield shift down—benefits from" section of the summary report shows that the portfolio will increase about $37,600 in value from a 1 percent downward yield shift (line *z*). The combined duration plus convexity *predicted* price increase is $37,576, which is quite close to the *actual* increase of 3.75 percent (line *ac*).

The author's computer software, BOND PORTFOLIO MANAGER, produced the various reports shown in this section. The user needs to enter only seven yield figures (current yield to maturities for AAA bonds of various maturities) and four gradation yields (yield differentials between credit categories such as AAA and AA issues) and the date of the valuation or report. With only that minimal input from the user, the software then makes all the calculations of values to maturity, values to call, yields, durations, convexities, and so forth. We developed this software to manage our own bond accounts and have found it invaluable. The software turned potential chaos into precise order.

---

*Amortization of discount on taxable bonds would result in the creation of taxable income in each year of amortization. Not amortizing postpones the taxation until sale or disposition.

15

Bond Selection, Tax Considerations, Price Volatility, and YTM Misconceptions

Discount bonds, premium bonds, or par bonds—which should one buy?

A bond may be purchased at a *discount* from its maturity value—e.g., a $1000 bond may be purchased for $600; or at a *premium* from its maturity value—e.g., a $1000 bond may be acquired for $1200; or at *par*—e.g., a $1000 bond may be bought for that amount, $1000.

Taxable Premium Bonds

One may choose to amortize the premium one pays to buy *taxable* bonds. If an investor makes this choice, he or she reduces the cost basis (original cost) of the bonds by a part of the premium each year, spread out or *amortized* over the life of the bonds. An investor in taxable premium bonds may deduct from taxable income the amount by which the basis is reduced for each year as an offset to interest income (for bonds acquired after 1987). The choice applies for the year the election is made and for all later years. It applies to all similar bonds one owns in the year the election is made, and to similar bonds one acquires in later years. The method of amortization employed for taxables is the constant-yield method, described in Chap. 14.*

The portion of the premium that should be allocated to a particular year, called the *amortizable bond premium* of such year, is determined by spreading the premium, cost less maturity—or, if amortized to call, call value (less, if applicable, the amount paid for a convertible feature)—over the period from the date of purchase to the maturity (or earlier call date, if applicable).† If the taxable bond is called prior to or at maturity, the then-unamortized portion of the premium is deductible in that year (which reduces the basis and increases the taxable gain). The adjustment to taxable basis of the bond is made by reducing the basis each year, beginning with the date of acquisition or with a later year in which the election is made, by the amortizable bond premium for such year.

When the bond is sold, the difference between the sale price and the adjusted basis (cost price less amortization) represents a capital gain or loss—long-term or short-term, depending on the holding period.

For example, a new taxable bond is bought at issuance for $1200. The bond has a 20-year maturity. The premium is $200 ($1200 less $1000 maturity value). The annual amortization (deductible from both taxable income and basis) is $14 for the first year, and it increases each year. It is $27 for the last year.

Tax-Exempt Premium Bonds

One must amortize the premium and reduce the basis of tax-exempt bonds. This prevents the investor from claiming an unrealistic capital loss when the bonds mature or are sold. However, one may *not* deduct the amortized premium from taxable income.

Tax-Exempt Discount Bonds

And, if the investor buys tax-exempt bonds at a discount, the gain when the bond is sold for more than cost is taxable. That is, the amount of the *market*

---

*Full details, for tax purposes, are found in IRC Sec. 171.

†Amortization to call may be elected only if the annual deduction is *less* than would be the deduction if amortized to maturity.

discount is *not* tax-exempt interest.* For example, a municipal (tax-free) bond is bought for \$600 and later sold for \$900. The \$300 difference is taxable.†

**Market discount.* Market discount is the excess of the stated redemption price of a bond at maturity over your basis in the bond immediately after you acquire it. You can disregard market discount and treat it as zero if the market discount is less than one-fourth of 1 percent (.0025) of the stated redemption price of the bond multiplied by the number of full years to maturity (after you acquire the bond). If a market discount bond also has OID, the market discount is the sum of the bond's issue price, plus the total OID includible in the gross income of all holders before you acquired the bond, reduced by your basis in the bond immediately after you acquired it.

A *market discount* bond is any bond having market discount except: (1) short-term obligations (those with fixed maturity dates of up to one year from the date of issue), (2) tax-exempt obligations that you bought before May 1, 1993, (3) U.S. savings bonds, and (4) certain installment obligations. Market discount arises when the value of a debt obligation decreases after its issue date, generally because of an increase in interest rates. If you buy a bond on the secondary market, it may have market discount.

If you dispose of a market discount bond, you generally must recognize the gain as taxable interest income up to the amount of the bond's *accrued market discount,* if: (1) the bond was issued after July 18, 1984, or (2) you purchased the bond after April 30, 1993. The rest of the gain is a capital gain if the bond was a capital asset.

A different rule applies if you dispose of a market discount bond that was: (1) issued before July 19, 1984, *and* (2) purchased by you before May 1, 1993.

The accrued market discount is figured in one of two ways.

Ratable accrual method. Treat the market discount as accruing in equal daily installments during the period you hold the bond. The daily installments are determined by dividing the market discount by the number of days after the date you acquired the bond, up to and including its maturity date. Multiply the daily installments by the number of days you held the bond to determine your accrued market discount.

Constant interest method. Instead of using the ratable accrual method, you can choose to determine the accrued discount using the constant interest method. Make this choice by attaching to your timely filed return a statement identifying the bond and stating that you are making a constant interest rate election. The choice takes effect on the date you acquired the bond. If you choose to use this method for any bond, you cannot change your choice for that bond.

If you are using this computation method for a market discount bond, treat the bond as being issued on the date you acquire it. Treat the amount of your basis (immediately after you acquire the bond) as the issue price.

†Any gain from *market discount* on tax-exempt bonds is taxable when you dispose of or redeem the bonds. If you bought the tax-exempt bonds after April 30, 1993, the gain from market discount is *ordinary* income. If you bought the tax-exempt bonds before May 1, 1993, the gain from market discount is *capital* gain.

You figure market discount by subtracting the price you paid for the bond from the total of the original issue price of the bond and the amount of OID that represented interest to any earlier holders.

Premium on Convertible Bonds

If one paid a premium to buy a convertible bond, the portion of the premium that relates to the conversion feature of the bond may not be amortized or deducted. Amortization is not allowed for any part of a premium that is paid for the conversion feature of a convertible bond. To find the value of the conversion feature, first determine the market value of a bond that has no conversion feature and that is of the same character and grade as the convertible issue. Second, determine the yield to maturity of this similar bond. Third, find the theoretical cost of the convertible issue that would produce the same yield to maturity as that of the similar nonconvertible issue. The difference between the latter and the cost of the convertible is the value of the conversion feature.

Taxable Discount Bonds

The coupon income on taxable discount bonds is reported each year as interest income. The discount produces no effect until the bond is sold, unless one chooses to amortize the discount. (Exceptions apply to zero-coupon bonds, or other debt *originally* issued at more than a minimal discount.) At the time of sale, the investor realizes a gain or loss based on the difference between the sale price and the original cost.*

The gain on sale for bonds *issued* after July 18, 1984, and *purchased* after April 30, 1993, generally must be recognized as ordinary interest income to the extent of *accrued market discount.* Market discount accrues in equal daily installments during the period one holds the bond; see IRS Publication 550 for details.

Thus, it is apparent that a discount bond, if held to maturity, will automatically create a capital gain, ordinary income, or both, for the investor. The ultimate payment of tax on that gain ought to be considered in comparing the relative merits of bonds that might be purchased at premiums, par, or discounts. *Many brokers fail miserably in this regard, in that they fail to quote to prospective investors the after-tax yield of discount bonds.*

For example, a taxable discount bond, originally issued before July 19, 1984, is purchased for $833 by an investor who pays 40 percent tax (federal, state, and local). The bond pays $80 per year interest and is held until it matures in 20 years. Each year the $80 interest is included in taxable interest income of the owner, leaving $48 after tax, and upon receiving $1000 at maturity, the investor will owe tax on the capital gain. The gain is $167

---

*See earlier footnotes regarding taxability of gain resulting from market discount.

($1000 maturity value less the $833 original cost). Assuming that the capital gains tax is $66.80, the maturity value may be regarded as $933.20, that is, $1000 less the estimated tax of $66.80. The yield to maturity, ignoring the capital gains tax, is 9.938 percent. The *after-tax* yield to maturity is reduced to about 6.079 percent. At a 28 percent tax rate on both income and gains, the after-tax yield is about 7.247 percent.

Income Tax Considerations

After-tax return on investment should be the primary concern of the investor. Assume that one pays 50 percent tax (federal, state, local) on ordinary income, and a more favorable 20 percent on long-term gains. The investor is considering the purchase of one of the three bonds described in Table 15.1. Yields are calculated on the basis of annual payments of coupon interest. The pretax YTM of the three bonds is an identical 10 percent. Based only on *after-tax* YTM, which bond should be purchased?

Taxable Premium Bond

The after-tax results of buying the taxable premium bond may be determined by treating the annual $120 in interest as being reduced by an offset of the annual amortization of the premium. If one elects to amortize, this treatment is mandatory for bonds acquired after 1987 and optional for bonds acquired after October 22, 1986. For bonds acquired before that, the investor is able to take a miscellaneous deduction of the annual amortization. All investors are eligible to claim the miscellaneous deduction. The minimum threshold of 2 percent of adjusted gross income does not apply. The annual amortization is calculated by apportioning the $171.59 premium over the 20 years remaining to maturity, by the *scientific* or *yield-to-maturity method*. The first year's amortization is $2.92.

Table 15.1. What Type of Bond to Buy?

	Purchase cost	Coupon (%)	Years to maturity	Conventional pretax yield to maturity (%)
Premium bond	$1171.59	12%	20	10
Par bond	1000.00	10%	20	10
Discount bond	828.40	8%	20	10

The scientific or yield-to-maturity method involves finding the price for the nineteenth year, the eighteenth year, etc., at which the yield to maturity (YTM) remains constant—in this case, at 10 percent. The difference between the previous year's price and the current year's price is the amortization for that year.* The first year's after-tax annual interest is then:

Interest coupon..	$120.00
Less: amortization...	2.92
Subtotal..	$117.08
Less: 50% federal, state, and local tax...	58.54
After-tax interest..	$ 61.46

The after-tax YTM using scientific or YTM amortization is 5.0 percent. With respect to the premium bond, no capital loss will be recognizable at maturity, since the annual amortization of premium reduces the cost basis, which at maturity will have been reduced to $1000. *With straight-line amortization,* the quoted or conventional yield drops from 10 percent *pretax* to only *5.055* percent *after tax.* However, if the premium is *not amortized* over the ownership period, the after-tax YTM is only *4.764* percent.

After-tax YTM of 4.764 percent when the premium is not amortized is calculated on the following basis: Annual cash flow after 50 percent tax is $60; cash flow at maturity is $1034, which is the sum of the $1000 maturity plus the tax benefit of $34 ($171.59 loss at an assumed tax rate of 20 percent on long-term gains). At a tax rate of 40 percent for both ordinary income and capital gains, the after-tax YTM (when the premium is not amortized) is 5.910 percent. And at a 28 percent tax on ordinary income and 19.6 percent tax on capital gains, the after-tax yield is 7.099 percent. Thus, *one should definitely elect to amortize the premium,* as electing to do so results in a significant increase in the after-tax yield to maturity.

Taxable Discount Bond

The after-tax results of the 8 percent, 20-year discount bond may be determined by treating the tax, payable at sale or maturity, as a reduction in the maturity value:

Maturity value...	$1000
Less: purchase cost..	830
Capital gain...	170
Less: tax at 20%..	34
Adjusted maturity value...	$ 966

*The same amount of amortization results from the following methodology: (a) multiply bond's adjusted basis by semiannual YTM at purchase; (b) subtract the amount in (a) from the semiannual interest payment. Repeat this process every six months. The adjusted basis is continually reduced by the previous period's amortization.

The after-tax yield to maturity is 5.304 percent, at 50 percent tax on ordinary income and 20 percent on long-term gains. Recognizing both the taxability of annual interest, which reduces the annual interest to $40, and the capital gains tax at maturity, which reduces the maturity value to $966 after tax, the investor's after-tax yield is reduced from the conventional pretax 10 percent to only 5.304 percent. (It is assumed that this bond was issued prior to July 19, 1984, and none of the gain was converted to ordinary income under the market discount rules.)

Par Bond

The after-tax yield of the par bond may be found by reducing the *annual* interest income of $100 by the tax of $50. No adjustment is required to the maturity value. Thus, for a $1000 bond, purchased for the same amount, with an after-tax yield of $50 per year, and a 20-year maturity, the after-tax YTM is 5 percent. The pretax YTM of 10 percent is cut in half.

A summary of the pretax and after-tax yields of the premium, discount, and par bonds discussed in this section is given in Table 15.2. The table shows that the *discount* bond would be a *superior* purchase to the alternatives. (For discount bonds issued after July 18, 1984, part or all of the capital gain upon sale or maturity is converted to ordinary income under the market *discount* rules.) This holds true at both the 50 percent/20 percent tax rate as well as at the 28 percent rate. Discount bonds have a built-in after-tax advantage over par bonds which are priced at the same pretax YTM, even when capital gains are taxed at the same rate as coupon income.

Table 15.2. Comparison After Tax: 20 Years to Maturity (Semiannual Coupons)

	Purchase cost	Coupon (%)	Pretax yield to maturity (%)	After-tax yield to maturity 50/20* (%)	After-tax yield to maturity 28/28 † (%)
Premium bond (amortized)	$1171.59	12	10.000	5.000	7.200
Premium bond (no amort.)	1171.59	12	10.000	4.764	7.129
Discount bond	828.40	8	10.000	5.304	7.294
Par bond	1000.00	10	10.000	5.000	7.200

* At 50% tax on ordinary income and 20% on capital gains.
† At 28% tax on both ordinary income and capital gains.

Municipals

In the municipals market, it would be unlikely that 20-year premium, par, and discount bonds would all be priced to yield 10 percent, pretax.

Discount bonds usually offer the highest YTM, followed by premiums, then by par bonds. The saying, "DIscover PRetty PAstures" can be an aid to remembering the normal pattern of yields—from high to low—for the three categories of bonds (having equal times until maturity and credit ratings).

One reason why discount bonds tend to have the highest yields is that banks and other corporations or institutions are important purchasers, and these investors often are subject to a higher corporate capital gains tax (say, 34 percent) than are private individuals (say, 15 to 28 percent). The price on discount municipals must be set low enough so that the after-capital-gains tax yield to such corporations will be attractive. Corporations pay no capital gains tax on a muni bought at par or a premium.

Premium municipal bonds almost always *yield more* than comparable par bonds. This may be due to one or more factors, including the following: first, the psychological factor invoked by the word "premium." (A premium is something we like to receive, but don't like to pay.) Second, an investor who buys at a premium may have a greater risk of realizing future results that are less than anticipated due to an early call redemption for sinking-fund requirements, or other special redemption.

Bond Price Volatility

It is well known that as economic conditions change, the yields to maturity and thus the prices of bonds fluctuate. Volatility measures the percentage price fluctuations of bonds, and relative volatility is a comparison of such fluctuations among various bonds. Volatility varies according to:

Coupon rate—*low* coupon issues are *more* volatile than those with high coupons

Table 15.3. Price Volatility

Bond feature	Characteristics of low volatility	Characteristics of high volatility
Coupon rate	Higher coupons	Lower coupons
Maturity	Near or short	Distant
Duration	Low	High
Initial YTM	Lower	Higher

Maturity—the *more distant* the maturity, the higher the volatility

Duration—the *higher* the duration, the higher the volatility

Initial YTM—issues with *higher* YTMs at time of purchase are more volatile than issues with lower YTMs at time of purchase.

The factors that influence volatility are summarized in Table 15.3.

Short versus Long Maturity

A given change in bond YTM has a progressively greater effect on the bond price as the time until maturity lengthens. For example, consider a 6 percent coupon, $1000 bond, bought at par to yield 6 percent until maturity. For various maturities, the change in bond price (with annual coupons) that results from an increase in YTM from 6 to 9 percent is shown in Table 15.4.

While the price volatility generally increases with longer maturities, the incremental increase (rate of increase) lessens as maturity lengthens. Nevertheless, a 50 percent increase in YTM results in an 11.7 percent drop in bond price for a 5-year maturity versus a 30.8 percent drop for a 30-year maturity, as shown in Table 15.4.

High versus Low Coupons

The lower the coupon rate of a bond, the greater is the change in the bond price that takes place from a given change in yield to maturity. For example, consider a 6 percent coupon, $1000 bond, bought at par to yield 6 percent until maturity. For various coupon rates, the change in bond price that results from an increase in YTM from 6 to 9 percent, for a bond with a 20-year maturity, is shown in Table 15.5.

Table 15.4. Effect on Volatility of Time to Maturity*

	Yield to maturity			Bond price		
Years to maturity	Original (%)	Revised (%)	Percent change	Original	Revised†	Percent change
5	6	9	50	$1000	$883	−11.7
10	6	9	50	1000	807	−19.3
15	6	9	50	1000	758	−24.2
20	6	9	50	1000	726	−27.4
25	6	9	50	1000	705	−29.5
30	6	9	50	1000	692	−30.8

*Results are based on annual coupon payments.
†Revised price after YTM increases from 6% to 9%.

Table 15.5. Effect on Volatility of Coupon*

Coupon (%)	Yield to maturity			Bond price		
	Original (%)	Revised (%)	Percent change	Original	Revised†	Percent change
12	6	9	50	$1688	$1274	−24.5
10	6	9	50	1459	1091	−25.2
8	6	9	50	1229	909	−26.0
6	6	9	50	1000	726	−27.4
4	6	9	50	771	544	−29.4
2	6	9	50	541	361	−33.3
0	6	9	50	312	178	−42.9

*Results are based on annual coupon payments.
†Revised price after YTM increases from 6% to 9%.

Thus, with a $120 coupon (12 percent), a 50 percent increase in YTM results in a price drop of 24.5 percent, but with a $20 coupon (2 percent), the price decreases by 33.3 percent from the same yield change; a zero-coupon bond has the greatest volatility of all—a 42.8 percent decline.

Magnitude of Yield to Maturity at Purchase

Is volatility greater if the yield to maturity at the time of purchase is high (e.g., 8 percent), as compared to low (e.g., 2 percent)? The answer is emphatically *yes*. The *higher* the YTM at time of purchase, the *greater* is the bond price volatility. This principle is evidenced by Table 15.6, which shows

Table 15.6. Volatility and Yield at Purchase*

Yield to maturity			Bond price		
Original (%)	Revised (%)	Percent change	Original	Revised†	Percent change
2	3	50	$1654	$1446	−12.6
4	6	50	1272	1000	−21.4
6	9	50	1000	726	−27.4
8	12	50	804	552	−31.3
10	15	50	659	437	−33.7

*Revised price is based on $60 coupon, 20 years to maturity, with interest paid annually.
†Price for revised yield to maturity.

that a 50 percent increase in YTM results in only a 12.6 percent drop in bond price at an at-purchase level of 2 percent YTM, but results in a much larger 31.3 percent drop at an at-purchase YTM level of 8 percent. The point, however, is more of academic than of practical interest as there is little that one can do with this knowledge.

Summary

The volatility, that is, the percentage price change of a bond, is a function of four factors: maturity, coupon rate, duration, and the starting level of yields. The longer the maturity or duration, the lower the coupon rate, and the higher the initial yield to maturity, the greater is the price volatility. Conversely, the shorter the maturity or duration, the higher the coupon rate, and the lower the initial yield to maturity, the lower is the price volatility. The subject of volatility is discussed further in Chap. 16.

Is Yield to Maturity the True Yield?

Is a buyer of a bond with a yield to maturity of 10 percent assured that 10 percent will actually be earned if the bond is held until maturity? Assuming that the interest and principal are paid by the debtor on schedule, the answer is *yes*—provided the investor simply spends the interest and principal as it is received. In this case the bond investment (or any investment) earning a 10 percent YTM is equivalent to having a bank account earning 10 percent, where the interest is paid in cash periodically and the depositor spends the interest. In other words, when the income is spent, the YTM is equivalent to a *simple* interest rate on the same account earned on a bank deposit.

If, instead of spending the cash flow from the bond (or deposit), the money is reinvested, then the actual YTM realized by the investor will vary according to the rate earned on such reinvestment. If it is assumed that future reinvestments of interest receipts are made, the after-reinvestment YTM depends on the rate earned on such reinvestment. In this case, the YTM is equivalent to the rate earned on a bank deposit, where the interest is compounded (reinvested) instead of being paid out in cash.

Bond yield-to-maturity calculations include an implicit assumption that the periodic receipts of interest by the bondholder will not, contrary to popular opinion, be reinvested. An exception is the bond equivalent yield calculation on a Treasury bill of more than 182 days' maturity, where reinvestment is assumed at the bond equivalent yield rate. This exception applies only to bond equivalent yield calculations.

Table 15.7. Effect of Interest Reinvestment Rate on Yield to Maturity

Stated yield to maturity at purchase: 10%
Purchase price:$1000
Annual interest: $100 (10%), paid annually
Years until maturity: 10

Interest reinvestment rate (%)	Interest without reinvestment	Interest including reinvestment at reinvestment rate	Total value including principal	Interest reinvestment divided by total interest (%)	YTM or IRR (pretax)(%)
0*	$1000	$1000	$2000	0.00	10.00
10	1000	1594	2594	37.00	10.00
12	1000	1755	2755	43.00	10.67
15	1000	2030	3030	51.00	11.72

*Zero reinvestment rate is taken to mean no reinvestment at all. If reinvestment occurs at a zero rate, in contrast, the YTM plunges to 7.2 percent.

Effect on YTM of Reinvestment

The owner of a 10-year, $1000 bond, purchased at par with 10 percent annual interest coupons, would actually experience a varying YTM depending on the "reinvestment rate," the rate at which the periodic $100 receipts are reinvested. The fully compounded YTM, at various reinvestment rates, is shown in Table 15.7. It is evident that the YTM, though stated at 10 percent, will actually be equal to or greater than or less than 10 percent, depending on the rate at which earnings are reinvested. A similar effect of the reinvestment rate on YTM will be experienced if the bonds are originally purchased at a discount or premium rather than at par.

Interest Reinvestment and Maturity

The dollar value of the interest reinvested compared to total interest receipts varies in Table 15.7 from zero to 51 percent. As the rate earned on interest reinvestment increases, so does the importance or effect of the interest reinvestment component of the total return. Total return, in the case where interest is reinvested, includes coupon receipts, interest on interest, and the final maturity or sales proceeds.

As the time period until maturity of a bond lengthens (e.g., a 20-year maturity as opposed to a 5-year maturity), the percentage of total return represented by interest reinvestment also increases, as shown in Table 15.8.

Table 15.8. Interest Reinvestment and Maturity

Interest rate: 10% coupon, paid annually

Purchase price: $1000

Rate earned on reinvestment: 10%

Maturity	Interest paid until maturity without reinvestment	Interest earned including reinvestment of interest at 10%	Interest from reinvestment only	Interest reinvestment divided by total interest (%)
1	$ 100	$ 100	0	0
10	1000	1594	594	37
20	2000	5728	3728	65

As shown in this table, the longer the period to maturity, other factors being equal, the greater is the importance of interest reinvestment earnings.

Practical Significance

Suppose that a bond buyer expects interest rates in future years to average less than the rates at the time of purchase. Should the investor buy discount, par, or premium bonds? If the investor is not planning to reinvest interest receipts and expects lower rates in the future, then the characteristics of high volatility—to maximize capital appreciation—are appropriate, including low coupon, distant maturity, and high duration. But if interest is to be reinvested, then the investor should buy discount or zero-coupon bonds because the YTM, considering reinvestment, is higher. With lower rates expected, the discount bond provides the least portion of total return from the coupon payments. As Table 15.9 shows, with 5 percent interest on reinvested amounts, the YTM for the premium bond is 7.5 percent versus 7.68 percent for the discount bond.

Conversely, suppose that an investor expects interest rates to rise in future years. He will find that par or premium bonds, as compared to discount bonds, will provide a higher yield to maturity. More of the total return from those bonds (when interest is reinvested) comes from interest on interest, and will benefit from the expected higher future reinvestment rate.

When the future reinvestment rate (5 percent) is less than the initial (10 percent) yield to maturity at purchase, the discount bond provides the best yield to maturity (7.68 percent), as shown in Table 15.9. And if the future reinvestment rate (15 percent) is greater than the yield to maturity at purchase (10 percent), the premium bond provides the best yield to maturity (12.92 percent).

Table 15.9. Effect on Par, Discount, and Premium Bonds of Future Reinvestment Rate*

Yield to maturity at purchase: 10%
Maturity: 20 years
Interest paid annually

Price at purchase	Coupon (%)	At maturity, sum of cash flow including interest reinvestment, and principal at reinvestment rate of			Yield to maturity with reinvestment rate of		
		0%	5%	15%	0%	5%	15%
$1,170	12	$3,400	$4,968	$13,293	10.00%	7.50%	12.92%
1,000	10	3,000	4,307	11,244	10.00	7.57	12.86
830	8	2,600	3,645	9,195	10.00	7.68	12.78

*With no reinvestment, YTM is the yield at purchase, 10%. With reinvestment at a zero rate, YTM with reinvestment is 5.479% for the premium bond, 5.64% for the par bond, and 5.88% for the discount bond.

Finally, any bond purchased without reinvesting interest—whether premium, par, or discount—provides a 10 percent yield to maturity.

The values at maturity in Table 15.9 are not directly comparable without adjustment, as the initial purchases ("Price at purchase") were unequal. One bond was purchased in each case. However, the YTMs are directly comparable.

Misconceptions and the Reality of YTM or IRR Assumptions

Yield to maturity is synonymous with internal rate of return (IRR). IRR is the term that prevails in business analysis (capital budgeting) and in real estate analysis; yield to maturity predominates in the bond markets. Again, however, YTM and IRR mean the same thing.

A generalized formula for YTM is

$$P = \left[\sum_{n=1}^{N} \frac{R_n}{(1 + y/m)^n} \right] + \frac{S_N}{[1 + (y/m)]^N}$$

where YTM = $y \times m$ (as defined below)
P = price, the capital or initial cash investment
R_n = cash flow during the nth time period

n = a summation counter, representing the number of a particular time period

y = *periodic* yield to maturity (as a decimal)

m = number of *compounding periods* per year

N = total number of time periods (e.g., the *last* period)

S_N = maturity, redemption value, or net equity reversion at the end of the Nth time period

Although the generalized formula seems imposing, it simply means that *the periodic yield to maturity (e.g., the semiannual rate) is the discount rate, y, which causes the present value (price) to equal the discounted values of the future cash flows.* Since y is the *periodic rate*, the convention (although not quite accurate) is to multiply it by the number of compoundings per year (e.g., 2) to obtain the *nominal annual yield* to maturity or internal rate of return. The IRR is thus an interest rate that summarizes the investment results of a project. It does not depend on the prevailing level of interest rates in the market; it is *internal* to the project's cash flows. Hence, it is called the *internal* rate of return, or yield to maturity.

Any combination of cash investment(s) and future cash flows may be analyzed by the IRR method. The IRR may be calculated for a stock investment, a bond investment, or a real estate holding. The after-tax IRR is an exceedingly accurate measure of true investment performance. Depending on the objectives of the investor, IRR may be "with reinvestment" or "without reinvestment."

Yield to Maturity without Reinvestment

IRR is like a bank deposit interest rate: no reinvestment is required. IRR is technically the rate earned on the adjusted investment balance (referred to as "unrecovered investment"). In like manner, a bank interest rate is the rate earned on the bank balance. In any event, you only earn at IRR or a bank rate on the balance in the account; and you don't earn on what you have withdrawn or recovered. The beginning adjusted balance is the initial investment (the purchase price of a bond). The ending adjusted balance is the disposition proceeds (the bond's maturity value or other sales proceeds). For a bond bought at par, the beginning and ending adjusted balances are the same, $1000. But for premium, discount, and zero-coupon bonds (which are just an extreme form of discount bonds), the beginning and ending adjusted balances are different.

An annual modification (or amortization) of the adjusted balance gradually changes it, such that over the life of the holding, the initial difference between the beginning and ending balances is fully eliminated. The annual modification is determined as *IRR* times prior years' adjusted balance, less cash flow distribution for the year. For a $30 coupon bond bought for $800 at an IRR of 8 percent, the first annual modification would be (0.08 × $800) − $30, that is, $34. Thus the adjusted balance for the next year becomes $800 plus $34, that is, $834.

Thus, the use of IRR allows an investor to earn at the IRR rate on the adjusted balance of an investment and at the same time amortizes the difference, if any, between the initial beginning balance and the ultimate sales or disposition proceeds: The IRR is the magic number that makes the projected results happen.

To illustrate the comparability of YTM to a bank deposit interest rate, let's now consider a par, discount, and premium bond, as described in Table 15.10.

The result of investing in a bond, at par, is exactly comparable to making a bank deposit of the same amount, where the earnings on the bank account are at the same rate as the YTM of the bond, as shown in Table 15.10. In neither case, bond nor bank, is one penny of the interest income reinvested. Hence, in order to achieve the YTM at purchase of a bond, where all the

Table 15.10. Par Bond Compared to Bank Deposit Account

Years to maturity: 5
Purchase price (initial deposit): $1000
Coupon (annual interest): $100
Maturity value (withdrawal of ending balance): $1000
YTM (bank interest rate): 10%
Tax bracket: 0%

	Year					
	1	2	3	4	5	Total
Purchase price of bond (initial bank deposit)	$1000	$1000	$1000	$1000	$1000	
Plus: YTM times balance (credits to account)	100	100	100	100	100	$500
Less: coupon interest (interest from bank spent)	(100)	(100)	(100)	(100)	(100)	−500
Less: maturity value					(1000)	−1000
Cash balance (end of year)	1000	1000	1000	1000	0	

Summary:

Initial bank deposit (purchase price of bond)	$1000
Plus: sum of annual credits to account (YTM times balance)	500
Less: interest from bank spent (coupon interest)	−500
Less: maturity value	−1000
Ending bank balance	0

coupon interest is spent as it is received, *no reinvestment is assumed, either implicity or explicitly. Thus, the YTM is equivalent to the simple (without reinvestment) rate earned on the bank account.*

In the case of a discount bond, exactly the same conclusions are in order, no reinvestment is required to achieve the YTM, and the YTM is comparable to the simple interest rate earned on a bank deposit, as shown in Table 15.11.

By this time, it should be no surprise that the results of ownership of a premium bond produce exactly analogous conclusions: The YTM from owning the bond is comparable to the simple interest rate earned on a bank account, and no reinvestment is required to achieve the YTM, as shown in Table 15.12.

Table 15.11. Discount Bond Compared to Bank Deposit Account

Years to maturity: 5
Purchase price (initial deposit): $800.36
Coupon (annual interest): $30
Maturity value (withdrawal of ending balance): $1000
YTM (bank interest rate): 8%
Tax bracket: 0%

	Year					
	1	2	3	4	5	Total
Purchase price of bond (initial bank deposit)	$800.36	$834.39	$871.14	$910.83	$ 953.70	
Plus: YTM times balance (credits to account)	64.03	66.75	69.69	72.87	76.31	$ 349.64
Less: coupon interest (bank interest spent)	−30.00	−30.00	−30.00	−30.00	−30.00	−150.00
Less: maturity value					−1000.00	−1000.00
Cash balance (end of year)	834.39	871.14	910.83	953.70	−0.01	

Summary:

Initial bank deposit (purchase price of bond)	$800.36
Plus: sum of annual credits to account (YTM times balance)	349.64
Less: interest bank interest spent (coupon interest)	−150.00
Less: maturity value	−$1000.00
Ending bank balance	0

Table 15.12. Premium Bond Compared to Bank Deposit Account

Years to maturity: 5
Purchase price (initial deposit): $1199.87
Coupon (annual interest): $100
Maturity value (withdrawal of ending balance): $1000
YTM (bank interest rate): 5.34%
Tax bracket: 0%

	Year					
	1	2	3	4	5	Total
Purchase price of bond (initial bank deposit)	$1199.87	$1163.94	$1126.10	$1086.23	$1044.24	
Plus: YTM times balance (credits to account)	64.07	62.15	60.13	58.00	55.76	$300.13
Less: coupon interest (bank interest spent)	−100.00	−100.00	−100.00	−100.00	−100.00	−500.00
Less: maturity value					−1000.00	−1000.00
Cash balance (end of year)	1163.94	1126.10	1086.23	1044.24	0.00	

Summary:

Initial bank deposit (purchase price of bond)	$1199.87
Plus: sum of annual credits to account (YTM times balance)	300.13
Less: interest from bank spent (coupon interest)	−500.00
Less: maturity value	−1000.00
Ending bank balance	0

Par, discount, and premium bonds (Tables 15.10 through 15.12) have been examined, and in each case, without reinvesting so much as one penny of the interest receipts, the investment results have been shown to be comparable to depositing money in a bank savings account, where the rate of simple interest earned is the bond's yield to maturity.

By definition, the YTM is the discount rate which, when applied to a bond's cash flows, equates the present values of those cash flows to the purchase or current price. (As we shall see in Chap. 20, it is also the rate which results in a zero net present value.)

Let us now examine the cash flows (which contain absolutely nothing from reinvesting) of the three bonds (Tables 15.10 through 15.12). We will discount, at the applicable YTM, the relevant cash flows, which contain nothing from interest on interest or reinvestment. If the discounted present value of such cash flows is the current or market price of the bond, then it will be evident that *no reinvestment is required to achieve the yield to maturity*.

Discounted Present Values of Cash Flows (No Reinvestment)

	Par bond		Discount bond		Premium bond	
Years to maturity	5		5		5	
Purchase price	$1000.00		$ 800.36		$1199.87	
Coupon	100.00		30.00		100.00	
Maturity value	1000.00		1000.00		1000.00	
Yield to maturity	10.00%		8.00%		5.34%	
Year	Cash flows	Cash flows' present value discounted at 10.00%	Cash flows	Cash flows' present value discounted at 8.00%	Cash flows	Cash flows' present value discounted at 5.34%
1	$ 100.00	$ 90.91	$ 30.00	$ 27.78	$100.00	$94.93
2	100.00	82.64	30.00	25.72	100.00	90.12
3	100.00	75.13	30.00	23.81	100.00	85.55
4	100.00	68.30	30.00	22.05	100.00	81.21
5	1100.00	683.01	1030.00	701.00	1100.00	848.06
Discounted present value		1000.00		800.36		1199.87

Thus, the sum of the discounted (at YTM) present values of each bond's cash flows equals each bond's purchase price. And the cash flows, so discounted, consist of the regular coupon interest and maturity value. The cash flows include no interest on interest or compounding or proceeds of reinvestment. *With such incontestible proof, how can any reasonable person argue that it is necessary to reinvest in order to achieve the (at purchase) yield to maturity?*

Yield to Maturity with Optional Reinvestment

Many, if not most, investors are not concerned with the subject of reinvestment of cash flow received from a bond, bank deposit, or other investment. They invest to produce money to spend. Some investors, however, are concerned about reinvestment: they include pensions plans where most participants are some years from retirement, insurance companies whose premium income exceeds benefits being paid to policyholders, and the like.

If one does choose to reinvest the cash flows from investments, then the overall results will of course depend on the rate of interest earned from reinvesting the cash flows. If reinvestment is taken into consideration (at whatever rate), then only two cash flows exist, the cash outflow at the start and the cash inflow when the investment including reinvested interest is liquidated. *Revised IRR* or *revised YTM* (RYTM) is the return when reinvestment takes place. It will be shown that if the reinvestment rate is equal to the at-purchase YTM or IRR, then the RYTM equals the at-purchase yield to maturity.

If one assumes as a prerequisite that all coupon interest is reinvested, then the original yield to maturity is no longer applicable. A revised yield to maturity [also termed *compound realized yield* (CRY), *realized compound yield* (RCY), *horizon return*, or *modified internal rate of return* (MIRR)] must be calculated.

Only two cash flows are recognized with full reinvestment or compounding of all coupon interest. These are the first cash outflow (the investment at the beginning); and a single cash inflow at maturity or sale of the investment which includes the maturity value, the interest coupons, and interest on interest on the coupons.

Thus, for example, if reinvestment is assumed at a zero percentage rate, the revised yield to maturity will be much less than the original yield to maturity because, in computing RYTM, all the semiannual coupon payments are assumed to come at maturity rather than periodically. Rather, the coupon payments are isolated as received and reinvested at, in this case a zero rate, and are unavailable to the owner until maturity.

When reinvestment is opted for, it is analogous to saying that interest is to be compounded. Compounded interest entails reinvesting; with simple interest the cash flows are spent as received. With reinvestment, the comparison continues to hold between the RYTM earned on a bond and the compound interest rate earned from a bank deposit.

To illustrate, we continue with the example of the par bond described in Table 15.10, except that now we will find the results assuming that reinvestment occurs at the 10 percent rate of the original YTM.

Table 15.13. Revised Yield to Maturity, Par Bond, with Reinvestment

BONDS	Enter %'s as decimals! Input data at arrows ←	
Enter "1" if taxable, "2" if tax-exempt	2 ←	
Tax bracket	0.00% ←	
No. of Years to Maturity	5.00 ←	(1 to 40 years)
Maturity Value	1,000.00 ←	
% Rate Earned on Reinvestment—Pretax	10.00% ←	
Purchase Price of Bond	1000.00 ←	
Coupon Rate in Dollars	$100.00 ←	(annual interest)
Portion of LTCG untaxed	0.00% ←	

YEAR	Cash Flow Tax Exempt	Cash Flow Pre-reinvestment	Cumulative Balance Pre-reinvestment	INTEREST REINVESTMENT Original Balance	Annual Interest	Ending Balance	TOTAL CASH FLOW
0	−1000	−1000	0	0	0	0	−1000
1	100	100	100	0	0	100	100
2	100	100	200	100	10	210	110
3	100	100	300	210	21	331	121
4	100	100	400	331	33	464	133
5	1100	1100	1500	464	46	1611	1146
		500			111		611

WITH REINVESTMENT THE IRR IS 10 PERCENT
WITHOUT REINVESTMENT THE IRR IS 10 PERCENT

SOURCE: INVESTMENT IRR ANALYSIS (AFTER TAX) FOR STOCKS, BONDS & REAL ESTATE, Larry Rosen Co., 1994.

The results are shown in Table 15.13. The total value, $1611, is composed of:

Maturity value	$1000
Coupon receipts	500
Interest on interest	111
Total	$1611

The same total value is obtained more simply when the reinvestment rate equals the original YTM, by adding the maturity value (M) to the future value of an annuity (S) resulting from the compounding at the reinvestment rate (i) of the annual coupon interest (R):

$$\text{Total value} = S + M = R \left[\frac{(1 + i/m)^{(n)(m)} - 1}{i/m} \right] + M$$

where S = future value of a series of equal payments (annuity)
 i = periodic interest rate (0.10)
 m = number of times interest is compounded per year (1)
 R = amount of each regular future periodic payment (100)
 n = number of years (5)
 M = maturity value

or

$$\text{Total value} = \$100 \left[\frac{(1.1)^{(5)} - 1}{0.1} \right] + \$1000$$

$$= \$100\ (6.11) + \$1000 = \$611 + \$1000 = \$1611$$

This $1611 is the same total value as is calculated in Table 15.13 and is directly comparable to the reporting of a bank account balance.

The Reinvestment Misconception

A misstatement concerning interest reinvestment and yield to maturity frequently appears as: "To achieve the yield to maturity, all coupon receipts must be reinvested at a reinvestment rate equal to the yield to maturity at purchase." As we have seen, this simply is not true.

The following quotations are indicative of the widespread misconception concerning reinvestment and yield to maturity:

> As explained in Chapter 4, the quoted yield-to-maturity is a promised yield. It reflects the yield if the security is held to maturity and if coupon interest payments are reinvested at the yield-to-maturity. Marcia Stigum and Frank J. Fabozzi, ("U.S. Treasury Notes and Bonds," in Frank J. Fabozzi and Irving M. Pollack, eds., *The Handbook of Fixed Income Securities*, 2d ed., Dow Jones-Irwin, Homewood, Il, 1987, p. 217).

> When using the yield-to-maturity as a measure of investment return, it is assumed that the coupon interest can be reinvested at a rate equal to the yield-to-maturity. That is, if the yield-to-maturity is 12 percent, it is assumed that the coupon interest payments can be reinvested to yield 12 percent (Frank J. Fabozzi, "Bond Yield Measures and Price Volatility Properties," in Frank J. Fabozzi and Irving M. Pollack, eds., *The Handbook of Fixed Income Securities*, 2d ed., Dow Jones-Irwin, Homewood, Il, 1987, pp. 71–72).

> The yield to maturity that any note or bond offers is a function of three key variables:
> 1. The known (or assumed) cash flows the security will generate

2. The frequency of compounding
3. The reinvestment rate
(Marcia Stigum, *Money Market Calculations–Yields, Break-evens, and Arbitrage*, Dow Jones-Irwin, Homewood, IL, p. 113)

Unlike the current yield, the yield-to-maturity does take into account any capital gain or loss. The yield-to-maturity does consider the reinvestment of the contracted periodic payments; *however, it implicitly assumes that these payments are reinvested at the yield-to-maturity.* (Frank J. Fabozzi, "Bond Yield Measure and Price Volatility Properties," in Frank J. Fabozzi and Irving M. Pollack, eds., *The Handbook of Fixed Income Securities*, 2d ed., Dow Jones-Irwin, Homewood, IL, 1987, p. 67).

On the other hand, the yield-to-maturity tells the investor what the bond would yield if held to maturity and is the yield to be used for comparing alternative bond investments. The approximation assumes that the bond is held to maturity and all interest payments received can be reinvested at the yield-to-maturity rate, an unlikely event in a volatile interest rate environment (John Markese, "A Simple Format for Comparing bonds," *AAII Journal*, vol. viii, no. 1, Jan. 1986, p. 31)

The yield to maturity for regular notes and bonds, however, is based on a standardized formula and is seldom realized by the small investor. For example, the 11⅞ percent Treasury bonds, due in 2003 were recently offered at a price of 101 per $1000, with a yield to maturity of 11.77 percent. That yield to maturity, however, assumes that each of the forty interest payments received during the next twenty years will be reinvested at 11.77 percent (Michael Quint, "Zero Coupons Can Add Up to Big Numbers," *The Courier-Journal*, Louisville, Ky, Feb. 26, 1984, copyright New York Times News).

The yield to maturity quoted on ordinary bonds assumes that you reinvest the bonds' coupons at the same rate as when you bought the bonds (Lisa R. Sheeran, "Investing for College," in the column "Your Money," *Inc.*, July 1984, p. 140).

The yield-to-maturity does consider the reinvestment of the contracted interest payments; *however, it implicitly assumes that these payments are reinvested at the yield-to-maturity* (Frank J. Fabozzi, "Bond Yield Measures and Price Volatility Properties," in Frank J. Fabozzi and Irving M. Pollack, eds., *The Handbook of Fixed Income Securities*, 2d ed., Dow Jones-Irwin, Homewood, IL, 1987, p. 64).

The stated yield to maturity on a bond assumes that each coupon is clipped every six months and reinvested at that yield (Randall W. Forsyth, *Barron's*, "Dig Those CATS, Why the Pros Like Zero Coupon Bonds for IRAs." Apr. 2, 1984, p. 41).

The yield-to-maturity on other bonds assumes that you'll always invest the interest income at the same rate paid by the underlying bond, which is not always possible (Jane Bryant Quinn, *The Courier Jornal*, Louisville, KY, Feb. 14, 1985, p. B-17; © The Washington Post).

That eliminates reinvestment risk, an important matter because a bond's yield-to-maturity calculation assumes that each interest coupon is reinvested at the same yield (Randall W. Forsyth, "Current Yield," *Barron's*, Sept. 24, 1984).

One other bond yield that is reported in the financial press is the yield to maturity. This concept of yield assumes that the bond is held to maturity and all interest payments are reinvested and compounded at the yield to maturity (John Markese, "Defining Yield," *AAII Journal*, vol. ix, no. 8, Sept. 1987, p. 34).

As an internal rate of return, YTM assumes that all cash flows are reinvested at the YTM rate and that the bond is held to maturity (Livingston G. Douglas, *Yield Curve Analysis*, NYIF Corp., New York, 1988, p. 60).

Recall that the YTM assumes the reinvestment of coupons at the internal rate of return of the bond. (Thomas S. Y. Ho, *Strategic Fixed Income Investment*, Dow Jones-Irwin, Homewood, IL, 1990, p. 18).

These quotations are all overtly incorrect. The reader may wonder how this misconception originated and why it has been perpetuated. The source of the misconception is probably a misinterpretation of the following and other similar passages from the classic *Inside the Yield Book* by Martin Leibowitz and Sidney Homer (Prentice-Hall and The New York Institute of Finance, 1972): "The Investor will achieve a fully compounded yield equal to the bond's stated yield-to-maturity at the time of purchase only if he can reinvest all coupons at his purchase yield." This statement, though true, can be—and it is suggested has been—easily misinterpreted. The accuracy of the statement depends entirely on Homer and Leibowitz's newly coined definition of "a fully compounded yield." The crux of the matter is that Homer and Leibowitz's definition of realized compound yield requires by its terms, the reinvestment of income. On p. 64 they state: "the term 'realized compound yield' was used to describe the total effective compound yield obtained from a bond purchased at a given price when the coupon income is reinvested and thus compounded at a specified 'reinvestment rate' over the entire life of the bond. Only when the reinvestment rate equals the yield-to-maturity at purchase, does the realized compound yield coincide with the yield book's yield to maturity!" And, realized compound yield is not the internal rate of return, nor is it the yield to maturity—neither of which require reinvestment either implicitly or explicitly.

Some adherents to the incorrect notion that one must reinvest at the rate of the original IRR in order actually to realize the IRR over the life of the investment base their erroneous conclusion on the following reasoning: The present value of a "reference bond" may be viewed as comprised of a bundle of zero-coupon bonds each of which represents a future cash flow of either interest or principal of the reference bond. Since the current or present value of each such zero-coupon bond is determined by the application of compound-interest discounting to the future cash flows, it is axiomatic that the current value of the zero is compounded to the date of the pertinent future cash flow. The erroneous reasoning is that, since the foregoing is true—which it is—it is necessary to reinvest to achieve the IRR. The mistake in logic is that the foregoing example *requires* the bond owner to reinvest. A zero-coupon bond owner is explicitly required to reinvest at the YTM. But the owner of the "reference bond" can choose to reinvest or not to reinvest. The correct interpretation is simply that if one chooses to reinvest, then if one reinvests at the YTM, one realizes a compound return equal to the YTM. But if one does not reinvest, one will realize a simple-interest return equal to the IRR, as has been previously demonstrated in this chapter.

One minor aberration exists, concerning reinvestment, in the case of T-bills with more than 182 days and up to 1 year to maturity. The industry method of calculating *bond equivalent yield* assumes in this case the reinvestment of theoretical coupon interest at the bond equivalent yield rate.

Readers may wish to refer to the Bibliography at the end of the book for additional references on the question of reinvestment. In particular, the following are recommended: C. L. Dudley's article in *The Journal of Finance*; and Jack Lohmann's articles in *The Engineering Economist*. Quotations from two other sources who agree that reinvestment is not required to achieve the IRR follow:

> The internal rate of return of an investment can be computed without any assumption about the utilization of the funds generated by the investment (Bierman, 1986).*
>
> It is frequently claimed that the present value method assumes reinvestment at the rate of discount, and that the internal rate of return method assumes reinvestment at the internal rate of return.... At best this assumption is inexact. In the first place the internal rate of return of an investment can be computed without any assumption about the utilization of the funds generated by the investment.... This IRR is not dependent on any assumption about reinvestment opportunities.... The term *internal rate of return* emphasizes that the value of this measure depends only on the cash flows from the investment and not on any assumptions about reinvestment rates.... We conclude that one does not need to know the reinvestment rates to compute the internal rate of return (Bierman, Jr. 1984).†

*Harold Bierman, Jr. and Seymour Smidt, *Financial Management for Decision Making*, Macmillan, New York, 1986, p. 214.

†Harold Bierman, Jr. and Seymour Smidt, *The Capital Budgeting Decision, Economic Analysis of Investment Projects*, 6th ed., Macmillan, New York, 1984, pp. 57–59.

These results do not require any reinvestment rate other than zero. They show that the percentage return on an investment does not depend on the available reinvestment rate. The actual gain to the investor (or lender) may, of course, be higher than this minimum amount if the available reinvestment rate is greater than zero, but that is a condition *external* to the investment. The IRR is concerned with the internal characteristics only, and therefore provides a measure of the minimum return on the investment. In summary, the conceptual difficulty with the reinvestment rate assumption arises from focusing on the superficial aspects of the mathematics of the IRR while neglecting the economic interpretation of the initial investment and the subsequent cash flows.... The IRR might be called more properly *return on invested capital* to make clear its economic assumptions (Herbst, 1982).*

Surprisingly, many sources of the reinvestment misconception, when apprised of the author's views on the subject, remain adamant in their convictions and continue to perpetuate their incorrect views. Notable exceptions, who have changed their publications to reflect this author's views, include Erich A. Helfert author of *Techniques of Financial Analysis* (Richard D. Irwin, Homewood, IL 1987); and the Federal Reserve Board of New York, author and publisher of *The Arithmetic of Interest Rates* (1988).

Zero-Coupon Yield

Zero-coupon bonds are discussed in detail in Chap. 19. Here we shall discuss only their yields and prices. A formula is derived later in this section that relates the purchase price of a zero-coupon bond and the sum received at maturity. The formula for zero-coupon bond pricing is

$$S = P (1 + i)^n$$

where S = maturity value
      P = purchase price
      i = annual interest rate
      n = number of years until maturity

Consider the following example:

Purchase price	$ 1,000
Maturity value	$17,449.40
Number of years until maturity	30

---

*Anthony F. Herbst, *Capital Budgeting, Theory, Quantitative Methods, and Applications,* Harper & Row, New York, 1982, p. 92.

Find the internal rate of return, or yield to maturity.

$$S = P(1 + i)^n$$

$$\$17,449.40 = \$1000 (1 + i)^{30}$$

$$17.449 = (1 + i)^{30}$$

$$(17.449)^{1/30} = (1 + i)$$

$$1.1 = (1 + i)$$

$$i = 0.1 \text{ or } 10\%$$

Reinvestment of interest from a zero-coupon bond is compulsory: The owner does not have the option of receiving interest in cash. An investment of $1000 will grow into $17,449.40 in 30 years at a compound interest rate of 10 percent. A compound interest rate requires that all earnings be reinvested. In the absence of reinvestment of earnings, there is nothing to compound. During the 30 years while the investment augments from $1000 to $17,449, the value of the investment is continuously increasing. The value at the end of the first year is 10 percent more than at the beginning; the value at the end of the second year is 10 percent more than at the end of the first year; and so on.

Although there is no cash flow to the investor from a zero-coupon bond, the nature of compounding is such that there is an "imputed cash flow" which is reinvested each year. That "imputed cash flow" is the increase in value each year. In the first year it is $100, in the second year it is $110, in the third year it is $121, and so forth.

To judge the return from such an investment, consider the initial investment to be the first (negative) cash flow, and the imputed cash flow each year to be the cash flow, which is reinvested at a rate equal to the YTM (10 percent). In other words, this is the same as buying a bond for $1000 that pays $100 per year interest, which is reinvested at a reinvestment rate of 10 percent. Such a conventional bond will grow into $17,449 after 30 years. Thus, the 10 percent revised YTM or *compound realized yield* is the same as investing at a 10 percent YTM and reinvesting the cash flows at a 10 percent reinvestment rate. The YTM and RYTM for a zero-coupon bond, by definition, have to be the same, since reinvestment or compounding of the theoretical interest (annual accretion) is compulsory.

It can be shown that the pricing formula for a zero is exactly comparable to the pricing formula for a conventional bond. The derivation of the pricing formula for a zero-coupon bond is as follows.

The formula for determining the present value of a conventional bond is

$$A = R\left[\frac{1-(1+i)^{-n}}{i}\right] + S(1+i)^{-n}$$

where A = purchase price
       R = annual interest
       S = maturity value
       n = number of years to maturity
       i = yield to maturity

The foregoing assumes YTM with annual interest and settlement on a coupon date. For a zero-coupon bond, $R = 0$, hence

$$A = \frac{S}{(1+i)^n}$$

$$S = A(1+i)^n$$

Thus, we have arrived at the pricing formula for a zero coupon bond, which is the same as the formula for finding the value of a future sum at compound interest.

It is thus apparent that the return from a zero bond (purchased at a compounded yield of *x* percent) is identical to that from a conventional bond (purchased at a YTM of *x* percent) when all cash flows are reinvested at the *rate of the initial YTM.* The amount invested in the zero-coupon bond is used to purchase the same dollar amount of the conventional bond at par.

What is the practical significance of all of this? Simply this: When a broker tells you that the rate of return or yield to maturity of a zero-coupon bond is 10 percent, he or she is referring to the compound growth rate that equates the purchase price to the maturity value. This requires that all cash flow (imputed, in this case) be reinvested for the entire term at a rate of earnings on reinvestment (which is fixed and inflexible) equal to the YTM (10 percent in this case).

Although "Invest $57,000 and receive $1,000,000 in U.S.-backed Treasuries" sounds exciting, consider what it means. The investor will not be receiving any cash flow for 30 years. This is the same as obtaining a conventional 10 percent YTM and reinvesting all "imputed cash flows" at a reinvestment rate of 10 percent. This may be good, or it may not: Success depends on market conditions. Nevertheless, *the price volatility as interest rates change is about three times greater for the zero than the conventional bond.*

Price Patterns of Bonds Based on Ratings

Assume that the quality ratings and years until maturity are the same for a group of bonds. All such bonds would normally trade at a price that will produce approximately equal yields to maturity. Some differences will occur, of course, among other things due to varying tax treatment to various categories of investors and volatility variation between high and low coupons. Utility bond issues that are all rated equally (AAA, A, or BBB–) by Standard and Poor's, which all mature in the same year, 20 years hence, are shown in Table 15.14. Their coupons and market closing prices (on the same day), as well as current yields and yields to maturity are also shown. The bonds in each rating category are listed in order of price magnitude from high to low.

Yields to maturity within each rating category do not vary significantly, either from high to low or from the average for the group. The yield variations are summarized in Table 15.15. However, although the difference in yield to maturity in the AAA category from lowest to highest (10.7 to 11.24 percent) does not seem great, $100,000 in bonds purchased today at the higher YTM, with reinvestment at the purchase yield, would produce $49,800 more interest over the 20-year life of the bonds.

The higher-priced, higher-coupon bonds do not seem to trade at YTMs that vary greatly from those of the lower-priced, lower-coupon bonds, as indicated in Table 15.16. In general, however, discount bonds are normally priced at slightly higher yields to maturity.

The higher the quality rating of a bond, the lower one may expect its YTM to be; and the lower the bond rating, the higher one may expect its YTM to be. It is of course assumed that the bonds have equal times remaining until maturity. This relationship is shown in Table 15.17.

Analysis of the foregoing information indicates that bond conventional yields to maturity increase as the bond rating declines, but that there is not absolute uniformity in the rate of increase. Nor are yields uniform within a quality category. Uniformity would not be expected, of course, as the bonds differ in terms of call protection, risk of sinking-fund call, coupon rates, and liquidity. Thus, investors should investigate alternatives before purchasing and should consider such factors as (1) earlier refund terms—determine the earliest call price and date; (2) sinking-fund call price, amounts to be called, years of call, and sliding scale of call prices and year when sinking fund starts; (3) yield to maturity; (4) current yield; (5) rating; (6) where traded and liquidity; (7) spread in pricing between bid and asked prices; (8) volatility; (9) after-tax results; (10) effect of reinvestment rates, if any; (11) income, gain, inheritance and estate, and AMT (alternative minimum) taxes.

Table 15.14. Bond Yields and Ratings

Description	Price ($)	Current yield (%)	Yield to maturity (%)
AAA rated bonds:			
Dallas Power and Light 9⅜%	863	10.87	11.10
Texas Power and Light 8⅞	813	10.92	11.24
Texas Electric Service 8⅞	813	10.92	11.24
American Tel and Tel 6%	615	9.76	10.70
Mountain States Tel & Tel 5%	521	9.59	10.99
New Jersey Bell Tel 4⅞	506	9.63	11.01
Southern Bell 4¾	494	9.62	11.09
Pacific Northwest Bell Tel 4½	471	9.55	11.10
New York Telephone Co. 4¼	464	9.16	<u>10.98</u>
Average			11.05
A rated bonds:			
Dayton Power & Light 9½	819	11.60	11.89
Empire Dist. Elect. 9½	806	11.78	12.09
Central Louisiana Elect 9⅛	791	11.53	11.90
Kansas City Power & Lt. 9⅛	790	11.55	11.90
Consolidated Edison, N.Y. 9⅜	788	11.90	12.23
Carolina Power & L. 8¾	764	11.46	11.89
Consolidated Edison, N.Y. 8.90	763	11.67	12.09
Pennsylvania Power Co. 9¼	755	12.25	12.65
Virginia Electric & Pwr 9s	755	11.92	12.34
Delmarva Pwr & Light 8¾	751	11.65	12.10
Virginia Electric & Pwr 8⅞	744	11.93	12.35
Public Service Colorado 1st 8¾	743	11.78	12.21
General Tel Fla. 8⅝	741	11.64	12.10
Mississippi Power Co. 8⅛	701	11.59	12.10
Gulf States Utilities 7⅞	683	11.54	12.10
Iowa Electric Lt. & Powr. 7⅞	670	11.75	12.33
Pacific Tel & Tel 4⅝	460	10.05	<u>11.68</u>
Average			12.11
BBB– rated bonds:			
Portland General Electric 9⅞	784	12.60	12.90
Arkansas Power & Lt. 1st 9⅝	781	12.32	12.65
Boston Edison 1st 9⅜	764	12.27	12.64
Jersey Central Pwr. & Lt. 10s	750	13.33	13.68
Louisiana Power & Lt. 9⅜	735	12.76	13.14
Alabama Power 1st 9s	718	12.54	12.97
Jersey Central Pwr. & Lt. 8¾	685	12.77	<u>13.25</u>
Average			13.03

Table 15.15. Comparison of Yield Variations by Bond Rating

Group	Yield to maturity (%)		
	Average	Highest	Lowest
AAA	11.05	11.24	10.70
A	12.11	12.65	11.68
BBB–	13.03	13.68	12.64

Table 15.16. Yield to Maturity by Price

Years to maturity: 20

Group	Yield to maturity		
	Highest-priced bond (%)	Average yield	Lowest-priced bond (%)
AAA	11.10	11.05	10.98
A	11.89	12.11	11.68
BBB–	12.90	13.03	13.25

Table 15.17. Ratings and Yields to Maturity (for bonds with the same maturity)

Standard and Poor's quality	Issue	Yield to rating (%)
Aaa	Dallas Power & Lt 9⅜	11.10
Aa+	General Tel Illinois 8½	11.39
Aa	Public Service E & G 9⅛	11.39
Aa–	Utah Power & Lt. 9¼	11.70
A+	Atlantic City Elect. 8⅞	11.89
A	Central Louisiana Elect 9⅛	11.90
A–	Rochester Gas & Elect. 9⅛	12.34
Bbb+	Mississippi Pwr & Lgt. 9¼	12.35
Bbb	Public Service New Hampshire 9's	12.90
Bbb-	Jersey Central Pwr & Lt. 8¾	13.25
Bb+	Public Service New Hampshire 14½	14.27

Municipal Bond Quality

Municipal bonds have, in general, demonstrated a good record of paying interest and principal when due. However, there have been defaults, and one should not rely blindly on a credit rating by Moodys, Standard & Poor's, or other rating service.

Municipals may be categorized in terms of safety into four general categories:

1. *Highest safety.* U.S. government-backed tax-exempt bonds. Public Housing Authority (PHA) bonds, which are unconditionally guaranteed by the U.S. Department of Housing and Urban Development (HUD). Also, bonds which have been "prerefunded in governments" or "escrowed until maturity in governments.

2. *Next highest safety.* General obligations backed by the full faith and credit of a creditworthy issuer, and essential service revenue bonds such as water, sewer, and electric bonds.

3. *Third level.* Housing Finance Agency bonds, and revenue bonds for roads, tunnels, bridges, and airports.

4. *Least safe.* Industrial revenue bonds, and bonds for hospitals, nursing homes, and extended-care facilities.

The quality or safety of a bond may also be judged by the existing condition of the issuer. The rankings in this regard from higher to lower degrees of quality are:

1. Issues of an existing, fully operational facility—for example, a highway authority

2. Issues of successful revenue producers that are expanding—for example, a hospital adding some additional beds

3. Issues for totally new projects, which rely upon engineering and accountants' estimates of projected financial results

Dangers of Price Fluctuation

Yields and prices of long-term U.S. government bonds from 1973 to 1990 are shown in Fig. 15.1. The two curves on the figure represent the high and low of yields to maturity for each year. For example, yields peaked in 1981 at over 15 percent. The lowest yield was in 1973, about 5.75 percent. The left axis of the graph depicts the YTM, and the right vertical axis shows the approximate bond price (for a 30-year issue with an 8 percent coupon). The following observations arise from studying the figure:

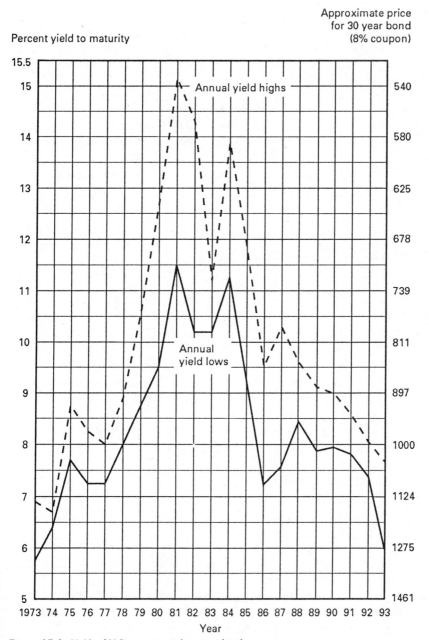

Figure 15.1. Yields of U.S. government long-term bonds.

1. During the 1970s, most of the time, yields were rising and prices were falling; in the 1980s the reverse held true.
2. Prices are volatile. A purchase in 1973 at the yield low would have been above $1275 per bond. Similar bonds purchased in 1981 could have been acquired for about $540 at their low.

However, for some nonactive investors, who are not seeking to maximize their investment returns, some think the volatility of bonds may not be of too much importance. For example, a bond buyer who purchases a bond with the intention of holding it until maturity would have little cause to worry about the ups and downs of prices in the intervening years.

Bond Yields Compared to Stock Dividend Yields

Bond yields in recent years have been higher than stock dividend yields. This was not the case from the 1940s through the 1960s, however, as shown in Fig. 15.2. The rationale for bond yields exceeding stock dividend yields is that bonds are perceived to lack the opportunity for appreciation that stocks might provide. This logic is dubious, however. Bond yields are based largely on inflationary expectations plus a real rate of interest above inflation of 3 to 4 percent. Explanation of various theories regarding the levels of interest rates (term structure) is given in Chap. 8. Historically, the common view was that stocks were riskier and therefore stock investors deserved higher yields than bond investors.

Long-Term Bond Yields versus Short-Term Rates

Long-term and short-term rates tend to follow the same trend, up or down, but short-term rates are considerably more volatile, as shown in Fig. 15.3. Yields for AAA corporate bonds are the annual averages for selected bonds of all types of corporations rated AAA by Standard & Poor's. Yields are for 30-year bonds, as compiled by the National Bureau of Economic Research, Inc., and Scudder, Stevens and Clark. The commercial paper rates are the annual average of monthly figures. Most of the time since the 1940s, bond yields have been rising.

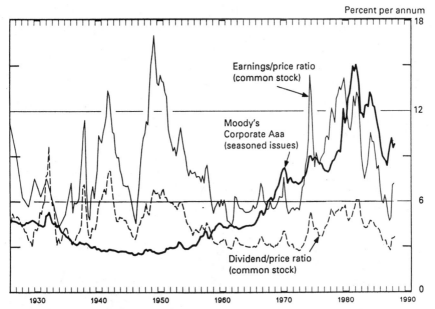

Figure 15.2. Stock market stock and bond yields. Earnings/price ratio: annually, 1926–1935; end of quarter, 1936; quarterly, 1937–.

Trading Bonds

Long-term bond yields have been rising most of the time since the 1970s. If yields are rising, prices are falling. If you think many people, including institutions, have lost a lot of money in the bond market, you would be absolutely correct: They have. But that does not mean there is no money to be made in bonds.

The most successful investment strategy in the past 25 years or so would have been to buy bonds when yields are high, then sell after a relatively small decrease in yields, say, 14 to 20 percent. Then wait for a much larger percentage increase in yields, say, 40 percent or more, before buying again. Please don't interpret this as a formula to follow. Use the charts and a crystal ball to develop your own method. In the past, it seems that the best results in bond investing would have been achieved by holding for a small drop in yields, and waiting for a large rise in yields before buying again. However, in the early 1990s the reverse has been true, as yields have dropped by major proportions. One major change in the economic environment, post-1990, is that the United States has shifted from being a creditor nation to being the world's largest debtor nation. This, together with ceaseless Federal budget deficits, may result in some upward pressure on yields, in order to continue to induce foreign investors to invest in the United States.

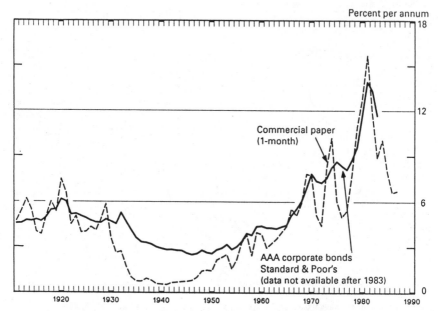

Figure 15.3. Long- and short-term interest rates (annually).

Why such a difference in the percentages that would have triggered successful trading activity in the past? The mathematics of percentages account for most of this wide variance; the rest is accounted for by the fact that the bond market has been a falling price market most of the time since the 1940s. The mid- to late 1980s and 1990s until 1994 were the exception to the rule: During this period rates fell and prices rose. Consider the example shown in Table 15.18 of a bond that first increases by 100 basis points in yield and then drops by the same 100 basis points. In rising from 100 to 200, the increase was 100 percent; but to return to the start level required a drop of only 50 percent to decrease by the same 100 points.

Incidentally, if the rise occurred in year 1 and the fall in year 2, some people would (erroneously) say that the average annual increase was 25 percent, using the following reasoning:

$$+ 100 - 50 = 50$$

$$\frac{50}{2} = 25\% \text{ average per year}$$

Yet the level of rates, 100, was the same at the end of year 2 as it was at the beginning of year 1. The moral is to watch out for "average annual increase" figures. Also, remember the adage: "Figures don't lie, but liars can figure!"

Table 15.18. Figures Don't Lie, but Liars Can Figure

	Start level	End level	Percent change	Points change
Rise	100	200	100	+100
Fall	200	100	50	−100

Another possibly misleading result occurs when the *quantity* of assets is ignored. Suppose that a fund of $100 million increases 50 percent in year 1, and in year 2, when it is $150 million, it decreases 40 percent. The average annual increase could be claimed by one measure to be 5 percent, as follows:

$$+ 50 - 40 = 10\% \text{ in 2 years}$$

$$\frac{10}{2} = 5\% \text{ average per year}$$

Buy let's see where the money is:

From $100 million to $150 million (50 percent increase)

Then from $150 million to $90 million (40 percent decrease)

Overall, from $100 million to $90 million

Not a bad result: a 5 percent average annual increase claimed as the result of losing $10 million!

Of course, computing the yield for this investment with a present value of 100 and a future value of 90, for 2 years, provides the real return: −5.13 percent compounded.

16

Duration, Modified Duration, and Convexity

Duration: An Aid to Predicting Price Fluctuation

The magnitude of the fluctuation of bond prices resulting from interest rate changes, in general, and changes in yields to maturity, in particular, is known as *volatility*. A method of measuring such volatility is through a concept known as *duration*, which was introduced by Professor F. R. Macaulay (*Some Theoretical Problems Suggested by Movements on Interest Rates, Bond Yields, and Stock Prices in the United States since 1856*, National Bureau of Economic Research, New York, 1938). Other measures of volatility include the "dollar value of a basis-point change" and the "yield value of a price change of $\frac{1}{32}$." Duration gives a useful indication of the volatility (interest-rate risk exposure) of a bond. It is essentially a time-weighted present value measure, that is, the weighted-average time until the payment of the bond's cash flows. Duration thus measures the average life of a bond. Duration provides a bond portfolio manager with a tool to *measure the interest-rate risk of an entire portfolio.*

Calculating Duration

Duration is a measure of the average time that it takes to realize the present value of the projected cash flows from an investment. A formula for its calculation is

$$D = \frac{\left[\dfrac{c}{(1+r/m)}\right] + \left[\dfrac{2c}{(1+r/m)^2}\right] + \left[\dfrac{3c}{(1+r/m)^3}\right] + \cdots + \left[\dfrac{nc}{(1+r/m)^n}\right] + \left[\dfrac{nS}{(1+r/m)^n}\right]}{P}$$

where n = number of time periods to maturity or redemption
P = price of the bond or its market value
S = maturity or redemption value
m = number of coupon payments per year
c = periodic coupon payment
r = periodic yield to maturity
D = duration in periods

Duration is calculated in Table 16.1 for a 10-year, $1000 bond, with a $60 coupon, selling at par for a yield to maturity or IRR of 6 percent. The cash flows are shown in the third column. The fourth column is the present value factor which is applied to the amounts in the third column, discounting at the 6 percent YTM rate. The duration in this case, based on annual payments of interest, is 7.8. With semiannual interest payments, the duration is 7.67.

Modified Duration: Estimating Price Fluctuation

A slight modification to the duration formula allows a rule-of-thumb estimation of the specific bond price fluctuation that will occur. *Modified duration* is a measure of the price sensitivity of a bond to changes in its yield to maturity. The modification to duration is simply to divide it by $(1 + r/m)$, where r is the yield to maturity and m is the annual number of coupon payments.

For the bond in Table 16.1, the modified duration is

$$D_m = \frac{7.80}{1+.06} = \frac{7.80}{1.06} = 7.36$$

For a zero-coupon bond the duration is equal to the number of years to maturity. So, if the bond just described had been a zero-coupon issue, the

Table 16.1. Duration and Modified Duration

Shift in rates: 3.000%
Face amount: $1000
Coupon rate: 6.00%
Term in years: 10
Initial yield to maturity: 6.00%
Price: $1000
Coupon payments per year: 1

Period (t)	Cash flow	$\dfrac{1}{1 + \text{YTM}/m}$	PV of cash flow	(PV)(t)
1	1	60	0.943396	56.604	56.604
2	2	60	0.889996	53.400	106.800
3	3	60	0.839619	50.377	151.131
4	4	60	0.792094	47.526	190.102
5	5	60	0.747258	44.835	224.177
6	6	60	0.704961	42.298	253.786
7	7	60	0.665057	39.903	279.324
8	8	60	0.627412	37.645	301.158
9	9	60	0.591898	35.514	319.625
10	10	1060	0.558395	591.898	5918.985

Totals   1000.000   7801.7

First derivative   7802

Duration per period $\dfrac{7802}{1000.000} = 7.8017$

Macaulay duration in years $\dfrac{7.8017}{1} = 7.80$

Modified duration   7.360

Percentage price change from shift in rates due to duration:
– Modified duration (–7.36) × shift in rates (3%) = –22.080%

Dollar price change resulting from shift due to duration:
% price change (–22.08%) × initial price ($1000) = $220.80

SOURCE: BOND PORTFOLIO MANAGER, Larry Rosen Co., 1989–1994.

duration would have been 10. A coupon bond's duration will never exceed the number of years until its maturity. A perpetual with a $60 annual coupon rate (6 percent) has a duration of 17.7 years, determined from

$$D = \frac{1 + (r/m)}{r/m} = \frac{1 + (0.06/1)}{0.06/1} = \frac{1.06}{0.06} = 17.7 \text{ years}$$

where r = yield to maturity
$\quad\quad\ D$ = number of periods of time
$\quad\quad\ m$ = number of compounding periods per year

To predict or estimate a price change in a bond using the modified duration, the method is simply:

Price change = (– modified duration)

× (change in YTM, in decimal form)(100)

Example: Finding percentage price change using modified duration. For the 10-year bond shown in Table 16.1, if the yield to maturity increases from 6 percent to 9 percent, the change in yield to maturity is 0.03. And the product of the negative modified duration (–7.36 and the 3 percent absolute change) is an *estimated* price change of –22.1 percent. The *actual* price change is –19.3 percent.

Factors Affecting Duration

Duration is affected by the same three factors which affect volatility: years until maturity, yield to maturity, and coupon rate. Short durations correspond to reduced volatility

Coupon Effect

A higher bond coupon (as compared to an otherwise comparable bond with a lower coupon) means a shorter duration and less volatility. Other characteristics of lower volatility and shorter duration are lower levels of yield to maturity and shorter time periods until maturity. Figure 16.1 shows how the duration of various bonds varies with changes in maturity. Included are perpetuals, premiums, par, discounts, and zero-coupon bonds. The bond coupon rate is kept constant at 10 percent, and YTM is allowed to change.

Duration, years

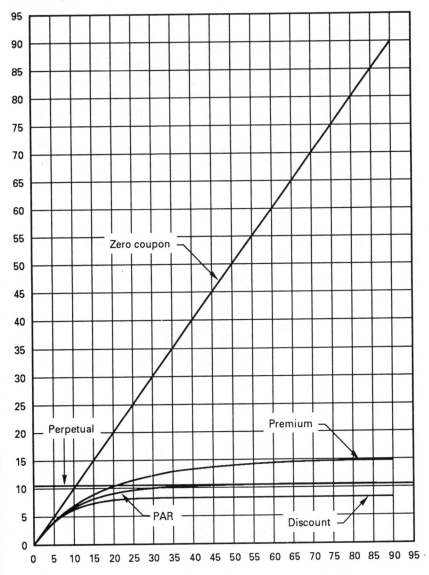

Years to maturity

Figure 16.1. How maturity affects duration. All bonds are 10 percent coupon, except for the zero. Yields to maturity are: premium, 7 percent; discount, 13 percent; par, 10 percent; and perpetual, 10 percent. Interest is paid semiannually.

When YTM is kept constant and coupons are changed, as maturity lengthens, the effect on duration varies according to the type of bond, such as zero coupon, discount, par, premium, or perpetual. The duration of *perpetuals* remains unchanged as maturity changes. The duration of *zero-coupon* bonds increases at a constant (linear) rate. The behavior of the duration of *premium* and *par* bonds resembles a zero in the early maturity years (say, less than 10 years) and resembles a perpetual at long maturities (say, more than 20 years).

Discount bonds exhibit more complex behavior. For short- and medium-length maturities (say, 18 years or so), they resemble zero coupons. Eventually, as maturity continues to lengthen, the duration of discounts begins to emulate a perpetual. Very low coupon discount bonds may actually decline in duration as maturity lengthens in fairly distant maturities. For example, for a 1 percent coupon, 20-year zero selling to yield 10 percent, the duration is 15.2; for a 90-year maturity, the duration declines to 10.6 years.

Provided other conditions (e.g., liquidity and credit quality) are equal, bonds with similar durations should sell at comparable yields. The degree of correlation of yields is much higher with respect to duration than that of mere years until maturity.

As the level of yields increase, prices decrease and so does duration. This can be seen most easily in the case of a perpetual bond. As annual yields increase from 5 percent to 10 percent, duration drops from 21 to 11 years. See Fig. 16.2.

Duration (years)

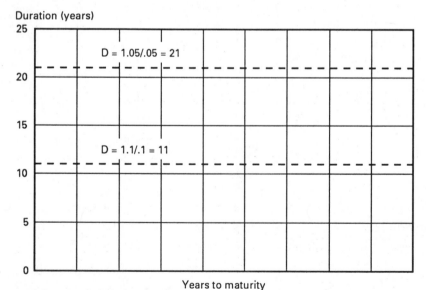

Years to maturity

Figure 16.2. Effect of yield level on duration. Interest is compounded annually.

$$D = \frac{1+(r/m)}{r/m} = \frac{1+(0.05/1)}{(0.05/1)} = \frac{1.05}{0.05} = 21 \text{ years}$$

$$D = \frac{1+(r/m)}{r/m} = \frac{1+(0.10/1)}{(0.10/1)} = \frac{1.10}{0.10} = 11 \text{ years}$$

A higher bond coupon (as compared to an otherwise comparable bond with a lower coupon) means a shorter duration and less volatility. See Fig. 16.3.

Modified Duration of a Bond Portfolio

Consider the bond portfolio shown in Table 16.2. It contains five bonds, ranging in coupon from zeros to 16 percent and ranging in maturity from 5 to 30 years. The face amounts range from $10,000 (1 bond) to $80,000 (8 bonds). An owner or manager of a bond portfolio is concerned with the degree of price risk of the portfolio when yields to maturity or the level of interest rates change. We have seen earlier in this chapter the factors that influence such price sensitivity or volatility and the effect of changes in coupon, yield levels, and maturity on price and duration. We shall now look at a convenient method of getting a handle on the price sensitivity to interest-rate changes of a whole portfolio.

In Table 16.2, actual market values (column e) are shown at a 10 percent YTM and again when rates increase by 100 basis points (1 percent) to 11 percent (column j). Column k shows the actual price decline that occurs for each individual bond, which ranges from 24.8 percent to as little as 3.5 percent. A handy tool for maintaining an acceptable degree of risk resulting from changes in interest rates is given for the entire portfolio by a *portfolio modified duration*. This is shown (in column i) as "weighted modified duration" for both the whole portfolio as well as each individual bond. For the whole portfolio it is 5.147 years. Applying the previously discussed formula,

Percent price change = − modified duration × change in yield × 100

$$x = (-D)(r)(100)$$

$$= (-5.147)(0.0100)(100) = -5.15\%$$

This 5.1474 percent is the *predicted* decrease in market value of the portfolio with a 1 percent increase in yields. A comparison of the totals of market value (column e) of $195,122.70 and the adjusted market value after the

Duration, years

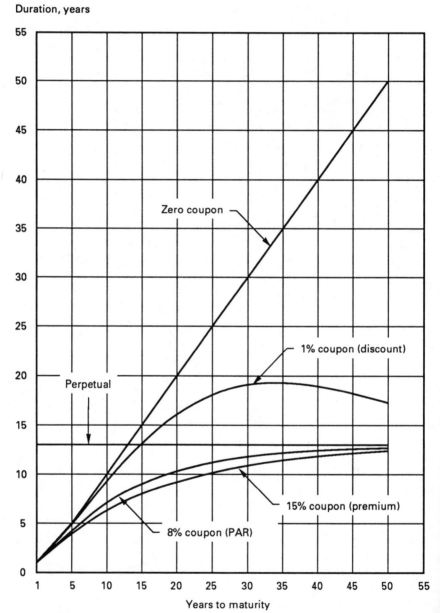

Figure 16.3. Effect of coupon changes on duration. All yields to maturity are 8 percent. Interest is compounded semiannually.

Table 16.2. Modified Duration of a Bond Portfolio

(a)	(b)	(c)	(d)	(e)	(f)	(g)	(h)	(i)	(j)	(k)
Face amount	Issue	Coupon rate	Maturity (years hence)	Market value (including accrued)	Duration	Modified duration	Market value as percent of total	Weighted modified duration $(g \times h)$	Market value adjusted for +1% change in YTM	Percent change in market value
$10,000	Bond A	0	30	$ 535.3	30.000	28.571	0.274	0.078	$ 402.5	−24.81
20,000	Bond B	0	30	1070.6	30.000	28.571	0.549	0.157	805.0	−24.81
50,000	Bond C	10	15	50,000.0	8.071	6.686	25.625	1.713	46,366.5	−7.27
40,000	Bond D	12	10	44,984.8	6.311	6.010	23.055	1.386	42,390.0	−5.77
80,000	Bond E	16	5	98,532.0	3.771	3.591	50.497	1.813	95,075.2	−3.51
Totals				$195,122.7			100.000	5.147	$185,039.2	

Market value change resulting from 1% increase in YTM from 10% to 11% [(h − j)/h]:

Change in market by weighted-average duration method:

− market value weighted modified duration	−5.147%
Percent increase in yield to maturity (decimal)	0.010
Predicted decline in market value	−5.1474%
Actual decline in market value	−5.1678%
Difference between predicted and actual	0.0204%

$\downarrow$ −5.168%

Notes: All bonds are initially priced at a 10% YTM. Repricing in column j is at an 11% YTM.

change in rates (column j), \$185,039.20, shows an *actual* decline of 5.17 percent. Thus, the portfolio modified duration proves to be a good indicator of the price sensitivity to rate changes for the whole portfolio.

The portfolio weighted modified duration is the sum of the weighted modified durations of each individual bond. For each individual bond, the weighted modified duration (WMD) is

$$WMD = \frac{\text{present market value of the bond}}{\text{total market value of the portfolio} \times \text{that bond's modified duration}}$$

For bond A the WMD is

$$WMD = \frac{\$535.30}{\$195,122.7} \times 28.571 = 0.078 \text{ years}$$

Using WMD as a tool, bond owners or managers can *determine a goal* for the entire portfolio WMD that is commensurate with the desired degree of price risk they are willing to assume.

Using Duration to Control Risk

Controlling price risk which results from interest-rate fluctuations should be an objective of every bond owner. If one knows a bond portfolio's modified duration, the task of managing price risk is greatly simplified. The rule of thumb to use is *desired maximum modified duration* (MMD):

$$MMD = \frac{L \text{ (tolerable loss \%)}}{dy \text{ (shift in interest rates \%)}}$$

where L = tolerable loss (e.g., 15%)
dy = percent shift in interest rates (e.g., 2%)

Example: Finding maximum desired portfolio modified duration. Charlie Cautious manages a large bond portfolio. The current level of long-term interest rates on AAA bonds is 10 percent. Charlie figures that rates may move up or down by 20 percent, that is, up to 12 percent or down to 8 percent. If rates should increase to the 12 percent level, Charlie does not want the value of his portfolio to decline by more than 15 percent. He should structure his portfolio so that the portfolio modified duration does not exceed what amount?

$$MMD = \frac{L}{dy} = \frac{15}{2} = 7.5$$

which is the maximum desired portfolio modified duration. In other words, to find the *desirable maximum portfolio modified duration*, just divide the maximum tolerable decline in portfolio value by the indicated shift in interest rates.

Price Value of a Basis Point

When *yields* change by 1/100th of 1 percent, that is, 1 basis point, the accompanying *price* change is known as the price value of 0.01. The effect of a change in YTM by 1 basis point, when yield is at 6 percent and when yield is at 10 percent, is shown in Fig. 16.4. Table 16.3 details the change in price that occurs. It is evident that a bond has greater price sensitivity to a stated change in yield when yield levels are low. As the table shows, at the 3 percent yield level, the percentage price change resulting from a move of 1 basis point is 17/100 percent, while at the 10 percent yield level the corresponding change is much less, about 10/100 percent. Thus the price value of a basis point is another way of looking at bond price sensitivity to changes in yields. Another similar measure is the *yield value of* $^1\!/_{32}$. *Since modified duration values relate to a move of 100 basis points, to compare them to "price change from 0.01, an adjustment factor of 100 is required.*

The figures in Chap. 12 show the effect of varying coupons for a given maturity. The curves of higher-coupon bonds have steeper slopes than those

ble 16.3. Price Value of Yield Change of 1 Basis Point

-Year Bond with 6% Coupon)

TM %)	Price	Price change from 0.01 (chg YTM)	Percent change divided by original price	Duration	Modified duration	Price increase + by decrease	Modified duration predicted price change*	Modified duration predicted price change†
010	$1587.97	$(2.73)	−0.172					
000	1590.70			17.409	17.151	1.000	−272.821	−2.728
990	1593.43	2.73	0.172					
010	998.61	(1.39)	−0.139					
000	1000.00			14.253	13.838	0.993	−138.380	−1.384
990	1001.38	1.38	0.138					
010	620.78	(0.63)	−0.101					
000	621.41			10.629	10.123	1.000	−62.905	−.629
990	622.04	0.63	0.101					

For a 100-basis-point change in yields.
For a 1-basis-point move; previous column amount divided by 100.

of lower-coupon bonds with the same maturity. This might imply, intuitively, that the higher-coupon bond thus has a higher level of price sensitivity because of the steeper yield curve. The appearance is deceiving, because the change in price at the higher yield is relative to a much higher base or starting price than that of the low-coupon bond. *Higher-coupon bonds have lower volatility* and *lower durations* than lower-coupon bonds of the same maturity and at the same level of YTM.

Yield Value of $\frac{1}{32}$

Since the price of Treasury bonds is quoted in increments of $\frac{1}{32}$ ($0.03125), it is convenient to think of yield sensitivity to price changes of $\frac{1}{32}$ of a dollar. The process of finding the change in yield when price changes by $\frac{1}{32}$ is comparable, in theory, to that just discussed for a yield change of 1 basis point.

Convexity

The degree of curvature of the yield curve is referred to as its *convexity*. As shown in Fig. 16.4 and Table 16.3, for minuscule changes in yield, the estimated changes in price are nearly equal when determined by *modified duration* (which is a function of the yield curve tangent line *BC*) as compared to the actual change in price (determined by the curve *DAE*). For larger changes in yield, the convexity effect is that actual changes in price increase more than is indicated by the modified duration. The magnitude of the difference is shown by the distance between point P_x and point P_y on Fig. 16.4. [Mathematically, negative modified duration (times current price) is the slope of the tangent line at a given point on the yield curve. Modified duration divided by price is the first derivative of the yield-curve equation (price with respect to yield). The second derivative of the equation shows the actual rate of change at a given point on the curve itself. Convexity (divided by price) is the second derivative of the price–yield equation.]

An interesting aspect of positive convexity (the upward curvature of the yield curve for noncallable bonds, or bonds with no embedded options) is that for a given change in interest rates, both up and down from a given yield level, *the price increase in the bond* (from, say, a 1 percent yield decrease) *is greater than the price decrease* (from the same 1 percent yield increase). For example, for a 40-year-maturity zero-coupon bond, when yields change by 1 basis point from a starting level of 12 percent, the price increase of $0.0357 exceeds the price decrease of only $0.0356. The upward

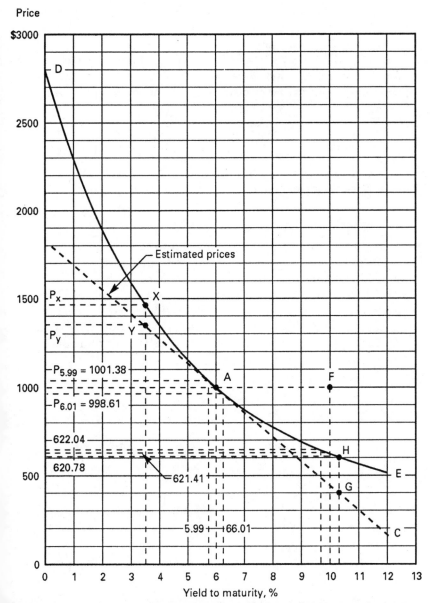

Figure 16.4. Duration and price yield curve. Bond is a 30-year, 6 percent coupon (paid semiannually). The slope of the line *BC* equals: (– modifed duration) (current market price of bond). The downward slope (from left to right) of *BC* connotes positive modified duration and vice versa.

price movement exceeds the downward by $0.00014. This results from a shift in yield of only 1 basis point. For larger yield changes, the results are magnified. For example, a 1 percent shift in rates to 13 or 11 percent results in prices of $6.48 or $13.79, respectively. Thus the price increase is 45.9 percent versus a decrease of 31.4 percent for a 100-basis-point shift.

One method of calculating *convexity*, C, is by the following formula:

$$C = \frac{(10)^8 (P_1 + P_3 - 2P_2)}{P_2}$$

where C = convexity of a bond with no embedded call options
P_1 = price after yield increase of 1 basis point
P_2 = price of original bond before yield change
P_3 = price after yield decrease of 1 basis point

Example: Finding the convexity. A 40-year zero-coupon bond's market value is $9.4521538 (per $1000), and its yield to maturity is 12 percent, compounded semiannually. What is the convexity?

First, one must find the market value of the bond at yields of 11.99 and 12.01 percent, that is, the current yield to maturity ± 0.0001 (1 basis point). These prices are for 11.99 percent, $9.4878905 and for 12.01 percent, $9.4165533. (The duration is 40.0, and the modified duration is 37.736.) Then the above formula is used to find the convexity, C.

$$C = \frac{(10)^8 (P_1 + P_3 - 2P_2)}{(P_2)}$$

$$= \frac{(10)^8 [9.4878905 + 9.4165533 - 2(9.4531538)]}{(9.4531538)}$$

$$= \frac{(10)^8 (0.0001363)}{(9.4531538)} = 1441.83$$

The convexity is 1441.83 for a shift of 1 basis point.

Predicting New Price Using Duration and Convexity

When yields *decline* from a point on the price–yield curve, as from point A in Fig. 16.4, the change in price is a function of the price *increase* from duration plus the price *increase* from convexity. In Fig. 16.4, when yield to maturity decreases from 6 percent to 3.5 percent, the new price, P_x, is the sum of the *increase* from modified *duration* (shown in the figure as the distance from 1000 to point y) *plus* the *increase from convexity* (the distance from y to x). On the other hand, when the yield to maturity *increases* from a shift upward (e.g., from 6 percent to 10 percent), the new price is a function of the *decrease* from modified duration (shown by line *FG*) and the *increase* from convexity (shown by line *GH*).

Price changes resulting from a yield change can be estimated if one knows the present price, the yield change, and the convexity and modified duration. The smaller the change in yield, the more accurately can the estimation be made.

$$P_n = P_2 + (-D_m)(y_2 - y_1)(P_2) + [(C_x)(y_2 - y_1)^2(P_2)(\tfrac{1}{2})]$$

where

P_n = new dollar price of the bond

P_2 = original dollar price of the bond at yield to maturity of y_1

$-D_m$ = modified duration at yield to maturity of y_1

y_2 = new yield to maturity

$(y_2 - y_1)$ = increase or decrease in YTM

C_x = convexity at original price with change of 1 basis point in YTM

$(-D_m) (y_2 - y_1) (P_2)$ = change in price from duration effect

$[(C_x) (y_2 - y_1)^2(P_2)(\tfrac{1}{2})]$ = change in price from convexity effect

Example: Finding estimated price change using duration and convexity. For the previous case of a 40-year zero-coupon bond, selling at \$9.4521538, to yield 12 percent to maturity, what is the price estimate from a yield increase of 100 basis points (a change of 0.01, or 1 percent, to 13 percent YTM)? The modified duration is -37.736, and the convexity is 1441.83.

$$P_n = P_2 + (-D_m)(y_2 - y_1)(P_2) + [(C_x)(y_2 - y_1)^2(P_2)(\tfrac{1}{2})]$$

$$= 9.4521538 + (-37.736)(0.01)(9.4521538)$$

$$+ [(1441.83)(0.01)^2(9.4521538)(\tfrac{1}{2})]$$

$$= 9.4521538 - 3.5668648 + 0.6814199$$

$$= \$6.566709 \quad \text{the } \textit{estimated} \text{ price}$$

The price *estimate* (using modified duration and convexity) is close to the *actual* new price at 13 percent YTM of \$6.48. (The residual difference is due to the effect of derivatives beyond two, as in a Taylor series.) The price estimate, where yield to maturity is increased, equals price decreased by the effect of modified duration and increased by the effect of convexity. The remaining $0.08 difference between the predicted price, $6.56, and the actual price, $6.48, is a residual effect. Modified duration and convexity explain most of the change in price, but not all.

Portfolio Management Considerations

We have seen that modified duration can be a useful tool in structuring a portfolio so that price risk due to changes in yield levels is kept at tolerable limits. Other things being equal, it would be better to achieve this objective with bonds which have a higher degree of convexity so that the bond portfolio convexity is also higher. The *convexity* (degree of upward curvature of the price–yield curve) for individual bonds *increases*, as follows:

With increasing maturity (except for perpetuals and within a limited range of long maturities for certain low-coupon issues)

With decreasing yield (where maturity and coupon are constant)

With increased duration

With decreasing coupon (where maturity and yield are constant)

For a bond portfolio, convexity can be *increased* by:

Adding bonds which have a greater convexity than the portfolio as a whole.

Replacing bonds with shorter maturities by bonds with longer maturities—even where both bonds have equal duration, as, for example, replacing a zero-coupon bond with 13 years to maturity with a 30-year, 7 percent Treasury. Both have a 12.56 modified duration and a 7 percent YTM. Yet the convexity of the long-maturity bond is almost four times greater than that of the shorter-term issue.

Replacing a straight bond (sometimes referred to as a "bullet") with other bonds which have longer and shorter modified durations, creating a "barbell" effect with cash flows concentrated at each end of a time spectrum.

A portfolio with increased positive convexity is highly desirable because for a given change in interest rates the *rewards outweigh the risks*. However, if one must give up yield to obtain the extra convexity, it could be money ill-spent if interest rates do not fluctuate much or the shape of the yield curve changes unfavorably (for example, if increased convexity is gained by eliminating a short-term bond and purchasing a long-term bond, and long-term yields move adversely while short-term yields move favorably).

On the other hand, if one must give up modified duration as the cost of achieving increased convexity, the trade-off is unlikely to be beneficial. This is due to the fact that most of the change in bond prices due to a change in yields is due to the effect of modified duration and relatively little is due to the impact of convexity.

Convexity, combined with duration, is useful in understanding predicted price behavior of bonds. Convexity is also interesting as a means of comparing the reward/risk ratio of one bond to another. Other things being equal, it is certainly advantageous to own a bond with higher convexity than another, as for a change in yield, the increase in price will exceed the decrease. However, the use of convexity in comparing two bonds or portfolios requires that the subjects of the comparison have equal or approximately equal durations. Since the effect of convexity is more important when yield shifts are relatively large, convexity is more significant when high interest-rate volatility is expected.

The discussion of convexity and duration in this chapter has been applicable to bonds which do not contain embedded options (such as callable bonds, or put bonds). The next chapter discusses bonds with embedded options.

17
Callable Bonds: Duration and Convexity

Callable Bonds

In earlier discussions of duration and convexity, it was emphasized that the analysis was for noncallable bonds, that is, bonds with no embedded options. Owning a callable bond is tantamount to owning two securities, a straight bond and a short position in a call option (writing a call). In this case the issuer of the bond owns the call option, and the owner of the bond is the writer of (or short) the theoretical option.

To find the value of a callable bond, the value of the call option must be *subtracted* from the value of an otherwise comparable, noncallable bond. A put bond also contains an embedded option. The owner of a put bond can sell the bond back to the issuer prior to maturity, under stated conditions. To find the value of a put bond, the value of the put option (owned by the bond owner and written by the bond issuer), must be *added* to the value of an otherwise comparable straight bond. Since the volume of transactions in callable bonds dwarfs those of put bonds, we will confine the rest of this discussion to callable bonds.

With a noncallable bond, the timing of the cash flows (in the absence of a default) is known. With a callable bond, however, the timing of the cash flows becomes uncertain. The uncertainty is due to the unpredictable nature of future interest-rate movements. One simply does not know whether the bond will be allowed to mature or whether the issuer will redeem it earlier by exercising the issuer's right to call. For a 30-year bond callable in 5 years, this means that the maturity value could be paid anytime after 5 years, perhaps in 10 years, perhaps in 30. Since the timing of the cash flows is uncertain, duration and convexity cannot be calculated with certainty using the previously described methods. New methods are required.

Bond owners may be paid off prior to maturity as the result of several different occurrences. Most frequently, early payoff is due to a currently prevailing level of interest rates which is less than that of the bond (the refinancing is generally called a *refunding*). There are motivations other than interest-rate levels, as well, for example, the issuer's desire to eliminate a bond issue, the indenture for which contains onerous clauses. Usually, refunding calls are restricted for a period of years (the call deferment period) after original issuance. And, depending on the terms of a particular issue, when refunding is operative, the redemption price may be at premium, at a gradually reducing premium, or at par. Some bonds may be restricted for refunding calls, but may allow calls for cash (where the source of funds is from earnings or asset sales) or for sinking funds.

Since redemptions or calls are invariably at a price at least equal to the bond's par value (usually $1000), it is only in the case of bonds purchased at a premium that an investor can suffer potentially severe loss from an early redemption, whether by refunding, cash call, sinking fund, or other cause. *It behooves any investor in a premium bond to ascertain all facts about early redemption possibilities, not just those of a refunding call.* Most corporate and municipal bonds are callable for refunding purposes. Most Treasury and agency bonds are noncallable.

We have noted that noncallable bonds have positive convexity. That is, the price–yield curve is like a cup sitting on top of the line depicting duration. See Fig. 17.1, where the curve *DBC* shows the price–yield relationship for a 30-year, 6 percent coupon (paid semiannually), *noncallable bond*. The slope of the straight line, *EF*, indicates the modified duration of the bond at a 6 percent yield to maturity. Let's compare this to the same bond, made *callable* now at par of $1000. At yields to maturity of less than 6 percent, the issuer may find it desirable to call the bond, that is, pay off the bonds which have a 6 percent coupon with the proceeds of a new issue at a lower rate. Since the issuer can redeem at the call price of $1000, the callable bonds' price will not exceed that value. Thus the price curve for the callable bond at low yields is capped by the price where the yield is figured to the call date—in this case, $1000 (line *AB* in Fig. 17.1). Since there is some chance that rates will increase so that the call will not be exercised, the callable bond price will be less than that of a noncallable bond priced to the call date. At yields higher than 6 percent, the bond price is capped by curve *BC*, a portion of the curve of the noncallable issue. Curve *BC* represents the price of the bond held to maturity. Line *AB* represents the price if the bond is called. The price of the callable bond, whether priced

Price

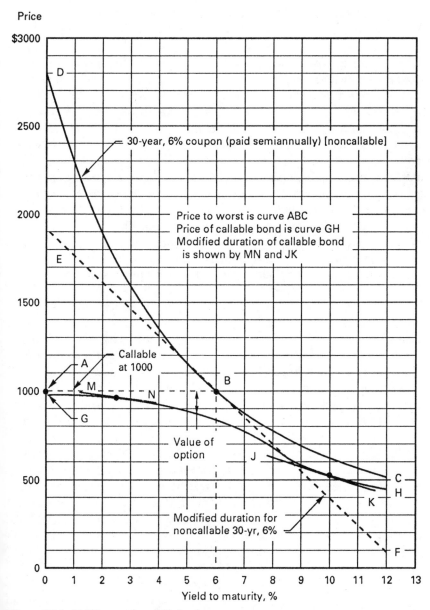

Figure 17.1. Yield to worst for callable bond.

to call or to maturity, will normally be less than the price of the noncallable bond because the possibility normally exists that interest rates will fall to the point where the issuer will call the bond.

Line *ABC* is the theoretical *maximum* price for the bond, and the bond should not trade at this high a price. The reason is that *ABC* represents the price for a *noncallable* bond redeemed either at maturity (*BC*) or earlier (*AB*), if called. But a *callable* bond will have to be priced below the price–yield curves of the noncallable priced to either maturity or call date, because the value of the call option retained by the issuer must be deducted. If an investor can buy a noncallable bond for $1000, she would not pay as much for a comparable callable bond. There is virtually no limit to the price increase that can occur for the noncallable bond, but *the price of the callable issue is capped at its redemption price*. Hence the title of the figure is "yield to worst," that is, the worst possible price or yield. Thus, a callable bond would have a price–yield curve somewhat along the lines of curve *GH*. Exactly where that price curve will lie depends on the option pricing method used to determine the value of the call option at various yields. Only after the value of the call option (and the callable bond's price–yield curve) is determined can one find the duration, modified duration, and convexity for the callable bond.

The duration for the callable bond's price–yield curve, *GH*, varies as shown by duration line *MN* (where the curve is now concave, and duration and convexity are negative) and duration line *JK*, where the curve is convex, and duration and convexity are positive. Naturally, where the curve is convex, the opposite effect of positive convexity applies, and for a given change in yield, the percentage increase in price is less than the percentage decrease.

The terms of the call option, whether call is deferred for a period of years from the present, or whether the call price is at par or a higher price, also affect the callable bond's price–yield curve, duration, modified duration, and convexity. Figure 17.2 shows revised curves for the same bond as before, callable at par in 5 and 10 years, and for a 10-year call at a premium, $1090. Increasing the period of call deferment or increasing the call price results in higher potential prices for the bond, at given levels of yield to maturity, and an upward shift in the price–yield curve. At low yields, a callable bond (selling at a premium) is generally regarded as *priced to call* (since the yield to call is less than the yield to maturity). At high yields, a callable bond (selling at a discount) is generally regarded as *priced to maturity* (since the yield to maturity is less than the yield to call). In other words, it is priced to the worst yield alternative, the call date or maturity date. At yields near the coupon rate (where the bond is priced near par), the bond's yields to call and to maturity are nearly equal, and the pricing is approximately the same to either. The *effective or option-adjusted duration* of a callable bond lies

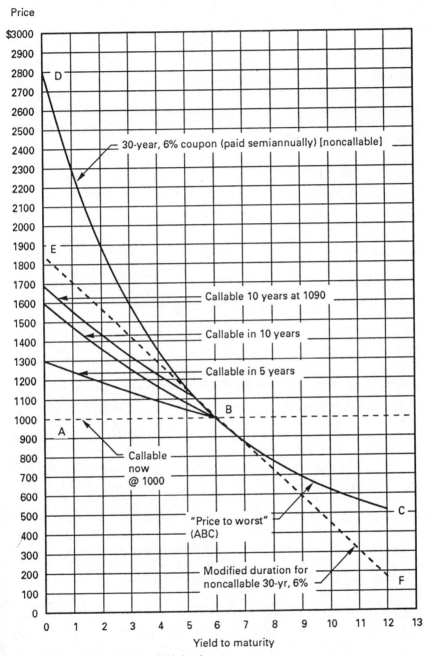

Figure 17.2. Price to worst for callable bond.

somewhere between the duration to first call and the duration to maturity. The option pricing model (Chap. 18) allows a more exact determination of the true effective duration, which is not provided by conventional yield and duration calculations. It should be noted that the standards established by the Securities Industry Association (SIA) for calculating duration are based on either call or maturity. Bond calculators that adhere to the SIA standards for duration calculations will give a result that is either to call or to maturity, which, as discussed, is not as accurate as the effective duration calculated with an option pricing model.

Finding Option Values for Callable Bonds

The value of a call option, referred to as its *premium*, is affected by several factors, including:

1. *The strike price* (which is the call or redemption price). The strike price determines how much "in the money," "at the money," or "out of the money" the option is at the time of valuation. The higher the strike price for a call option, the lower is the option's value, and the higher is the value of the underlying callable bond.

2. *Estimated volatility* (which may be thought of as the fluctuations in yield to maturity levels). The higher the volatility level of interest rates, the more likely it is that the bond will be called, and the higher is the value of the option. Refer to Fig. 17.3 to see the effect on the price–yield curve of changing interest-rate volatility. Estimating volatility of interest-rate movements is an inexact science. Professionals may use past performance to gauge volatility and determine the past percentage increases and decreases from a mean rate. This guide may be determined for 67 percent probability (one standard deviation from the mean) or 95 percent probability (two standard deviations). But despite the scientific nature of the approach, it still represents past history. And there is no guarantee or even probability that the future will emulate the past. Suffice it to say the interest rates may be quite volatile. (*Kappa* or *vega* of an option, discussed later, is the ratio of the change in option price to a 1 percent change in expected volatility of interest rates.)

3. *Time until the option expires* (which is until the call option ceases). Generally, the longer the time until the expiration of the option, the greater is its *time value*. (Consider that a 30-year bond with call protection for 5 years has an operative call option for up to 25 years.) However, the greater time value may be offset by changes (reductions) in the bond's *intrinsic value* resulting from the increased time until expiry. (*Theta* of

Price of bond

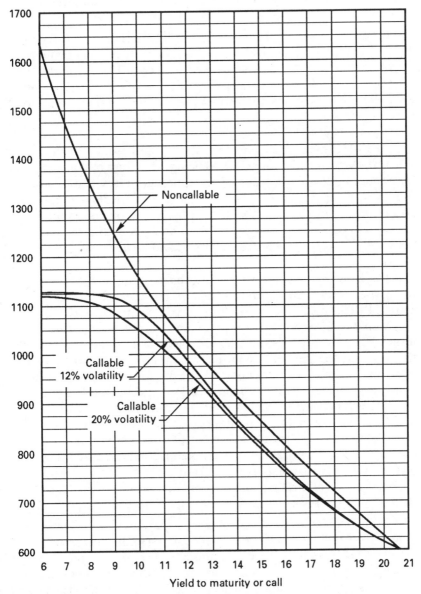

Yield to maturity or call

Figure 17.3. Effect of interest volatility assumption for a 12 percent bond, noncallable for 2 years, callable thereafter for 15 years at $1020, at par for noncallable. Callable bond values determined from option pricing model—short-term rate 6 percent; volatilities of 12 percent and 20 percent.

an option, discussed later, is the ratio of change in option price to the decrease in time until option expiration.)

4. *Cash flows of the bond.* The embedded call option represents the right to purchase the future cash flows of the bond. The value of that option is related directly to the present values of those cash flows. If other factors are equal, *adding* to or increasing the cash flow of the underlying bond will cause the option value to *diminish* and the value of the callable bond to be higher.

Adding cash flows is analogous to reducing the duration of the bond. Think of the value of the call option as being a function of duration; that is, if duration increases, the value of the option increases, and if duration decreases, so does the value of the option. Adding cash flows reduces the bond's duration, and reduces the value of option on that bond (provided other factors are equal). Low- or zero-coupon bonds (as compared to higher-coupon bonds) have higher durations and higher option values.

5. *Short-term interest-rate levels.* The higher the short-term interest rate, the higher is the value of the call option (assuming other factors are constant). This results from the alternative to owning a bond, of buying a call on the bond for a small premium and putting the rest of the investment in a certificate of deposit. Assume that both investments (bond versus CD plus call) require equal outlays of cash. If short-term rates rise and call premiums do not, investors will sell bonds (due to the higher cost of financing the bond position) and instead buy the combined CDs (and earn the higher rates) and calls. To keep such arbitrage from occurring, as short-term rates rise, so must the value of calls. The relationship of the short rate to option values is more pronounced and clear for options on stocks than for options on bonds because, for options on bonds, changes in the short rate will also affect bond prices. The effect on bond prices of a change in the short rate pushes option prices (on the bond) in the reverse direction from that described above.

6. *The current price of the bond.* Options that are deeply "out of the money," and with relatively little volatility of the underlying security, will have little or no value because of the obviously remote possibility of making a profit from their ownership. On the other hand, options which are "in the money" should sell for at least their intrinsic value. The middle ground, where the option is neither deeply in nor out of the money, is where the time value of the option is greatest. Refer to Fig. 17.4. At bond price levels corresponding to yields of 9 to 12 percent, the value of the call option is very little (deeply out of the money). On the other hand, at yield levels of 4 to 5 percent, the value of the call (in the money) approaches its intrinsic value. At par (6 percent YTM), the time value

Bond price

Value of call option

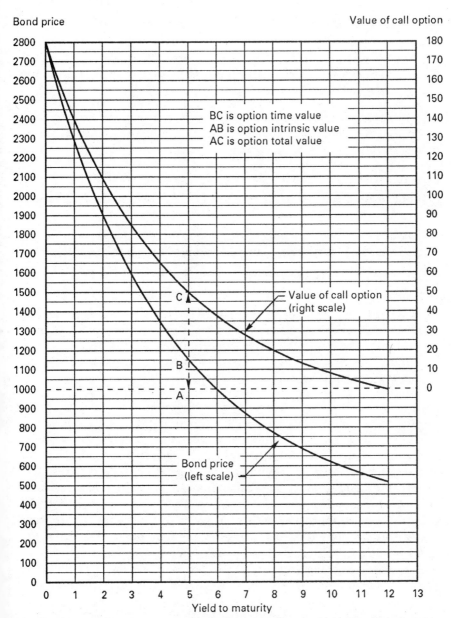

Figure 17.4. Value of a call option. Thirty-year 6 percent coupon bond; call option to buy one bond at $1000.

comprises all of the options value. (The *delta* of an option, described later, is a measure of the relationship between option value and the price change of the underlying bond. Another measure, *lamda*, is the ratio of percentage change in the option price to the percentage change in the underlying (noncallable) bond's price.)

To summarize the factors that will *increase* the value of the call *option*, and *reduce* the value of a callable *bond*, as compared to an otherwise comparable bullet or noncallable issue:

1. Lower strike price (which is the call or redemption price).

2. Higher estimated volatility (which may be thought of as the fluctuations in yield to maturity levels).

3. Longer amount of time until the option expires (which is until the call option ceases)—as it pertains to time value, but not intrinsic value.

4. Lower cash flows of the bond from coupon interest.

5. Higher short-term interest rate levels.

6. The closer the current price of the bond is to par, the higher is the time value of the option; the deeper the option is in the money, due to a higher bond price, the higher is the total value of the option. In other words, as the price of the underlying callable bond increases, the value of the call option tends to increase.

There is no simple closed-form formula for determining the value of a long-term call option. Formulas used to value short-term options on stocks, such as that developed by Black-Scholes, are not pertinent because, among other reasons, they assume constant interest rates and do not reflect the changing yield-curve values over a protracted period of time. As a result, to estimate the value of a long-term call option, an *option pricing model* must be used. Option pricing models are explored in Chap. 18. Such a model needs to have certain characteristics, including the following: No arbitrage possibilities are allowed among comparable straight bonds. Put–call parity must be preserved; that is, ownership of the security plus a put option must be equivalent to owning a term bond which matures on the option exercise date (with redemption price equal to the option striking price and with a coupon equal to the coupon of the underlying bond) plus a call option (with the same striking price and expiration date).

Put–Call Parity

Just as nature abhors a vacuum, so does the financial world abhor riskless profits. In order to prevent such riskless profits, in an efficient market, arbitrage activity, where one instrument is bought and another sold, drives prices to levels which eliminate such riskless profits. (Nevertheless, those arbitrageurs doing the driving are making riskless profits in the process.)

A sacred tenet in the world of options is *put–call parity*. The basic strategy (ignoring for the moment the time value of money) is "Buy a bond: Buy a European put option on the bond and simultaneously sell a European call option on the bond." European options can be exercised only on their expiry date, not before. The put and call options are both exercisable at the same price at which the bond was purchased, and expire at the same time. The investor is guaranteed (ignoring the time value of money for the moment) a riskless profit equal to the excess of the call premium received less the put premium paid. Let's say the cost to buy the bond is $1000. The call premium received is $40 and the put premium paid is $30. At various future prices of the bond, here's what happens when the options expire:

Original cost of the bond: $1000
Premium from sale of call: $40
Cost of purchase of put: $30

(a) Future price of the bond	(b) Prelimi- nary profit (loss) (a − $1000)	(c) Intrinsic value of put option	(d) Intrinsic value of short call option	(e) Gain or loss from price change (b + c + d)	(f) Income from sale of call	(g) Cost of purchase of put option	(h) Net profit or loss (e + f + g)
$1100	$100	0	$−100	0	$40	$30	$10
1075	75	0	−75	0	40	30	10
1050	50	0	−50	0	40	30	10
1025	25	0	−25	0	40	30	10
1000	0	0	0	0	40	30	10
975	−25	$ 25	0	0	40	30	10
950	−50	50	0	0	40	30	10
925	−75	75	0	0	40	30	10
900	−100	100	0	0	40	30	10

Thus, the $10 difference between the sale of the call and the cost of the put would be a locked-in profit, if the put and call were priced at the hypothetical amounts of $40 and $30. However, in an efficient market this situation would exist only momentarily, as the actions of buyers and sellers who act to capture this riskless profit would either bid up the price of the put or drive down the price of the call. Still ignoring the time value of money (the cost of financing the riskless transaction), the prices of the put and call option must be equal. Thus, at any time, for a European option and ignoring the time value of money:

$$P_{ub} - E - \text{CPN} + P_{poub} - C_{coub} = 0 \qquad (17.1)$$

where P_{ub} = price of the underlying bond (equal to the exercise price E of the options)

E = exercise price of the options (e.g, $1000)

P_{poub} = price of a put option on the underlying bond at striking price E (e.g., $30)

C_{coub} = price of a call option on the underlying bond at striking price E (e.g., $40)

CPN = periodic coupon payments payable on the underlying bond from settlement date through the option exercise date

Alternatively, Eq. (17.1) may be written:

$$P_{ub} + P_{poub} = C_{coub} + E + \text{CPN} \qquad (17.2)$$

Or, expressed in terms of the value of the put:

$$P_{poub} = C_{coub} + E - P_{ub} + \text{CPN} \qquad (17.3)$$

For European options, when the time value of money is taken into consideration, the adjusted equation expressing put–call parity is

$$P_{poub} = C_{coub} + \frac{E}{(1+i)^t} - P_{ub} + \text{CPN}_{pv} \qquad (17.4)$$

where i = riskless cost of money

t = years until expiration of the option

P_{ub} = price of the underlying bond (equal to the exercise price E of the options)

E = exercise price of the options

P_{poub} = price of a put option on the underlying bond at striking price E (e.g., $30)

C_{coub} = price of a call option on the underlying bond at striking price E (e.g., $40)

CPN_{pv} = present value of coupons $\left[\sum_{k=1}^{t} \dfrac{\text{CPN}}{(1+i)^k} \right]$

Example: Put-call parity.   Buy a bond for $1000, which carries a 10 percent coupon, simultaneously sell a call option exercisable at $1000 after 1 year, and buy a put option for $40 exercisable at $1000 at the end of 1 year. The riskless rate is 10 percent. Find the price of the call option.

$$P_{poub} = C_{coub} + \frac{E}{(1 + i)^t} + CPN_{pv} - P_{ub}$$

$$C_{coub} = P_{poub} - \frac{E}{(1 + i)^t} - CPN_{pv} + P_{ub}$$

$$= \$40 - \frac{\$1000}{(1.1)^1} - \frac{\$100}{(1.1)^1} + \$1000 = \$40$$

The theoretical value of the European call option is $40, which equals the put value of $40. Thus put–call parity exists.

Duration of a Callable Bond

The duration of a callable bond, as well as a call option, is found in the same manner as the duration of a bullet. The duration of a callable bond, referred to as the *effective* or *option-adjusted* duration, is the percentage change in price that results from a change in interest rates (of, for example, 1 percent). The method of determining the duration of the call option (D_c) is first to use the option pricing model (described in Chap. 18) to determine the call value at a given yield (C_0), and then to change the yield by the percentage that results from the change in interest rate (say, 1 percent), and again determine the value of the call (C_1). The change in yield must be applicable to the entire structure of rates in the interest-rate tree.

$$D_c = \frac{(C_0 - C_1)/C_0}{\text{change in yield (say, 1 percent)}}$$

Once the durations for both the call option (D_c) and the underlying bond (D_{ub}) are known, the duration for the callable bond (D_{cb}) can be determined from the formula

$$D_{cb} = (x)(D_{ncb}) + (1 - x)(D_c)$$

where x = value of the bullet divided by the total value of the callable bond
   D_{cb} = duration of the callable bond
   D_{ncb} = duration of the bond underlying the call
   D_c = duration of the call option

Example: Duration of a callable bond.   The price of a bullet is $956.80. The price of an otherwise comparable callable bond is $920. The value of the embedded call option is $36.80. The duration of the call option is 100 (years). The duration of the bullet is 10 (years). What is the duration of the callable bond?

$$x = \frac{\text{value of the bullet}}{\text{value of the callable bond}} = \frac{\$956.80}{\$920} = 1.04$$

$$D_{cb} = (x)(D_{ncb}) + (1 - x)(D_c) = 10.4 + (-0.04)(100) = 6.4 \text{ (years)}$$

The duration of the callable bond is 6.4 years, compared to 10 years for the bullet and 100 years for the option alone.

Effective or Option-Adjusted Spread

The lower the credit quality, and the less the liquidity of a fixed-income security, the higher should be its yield to maturity, as compared to a Treasury issue of the same maturity and coupon rate. Another measure of the difference in pricing (besides yield to maturity) is the *option-adjusted* or *effective spread.* The spread is the interest-rate adjustment to the Treasury short-term rate tree (described in Chap. 18) that causes the present value of any fixed-income bond to be calculated correctly. For example, let us say that the price of a BBB-rated bond is calculated correctly with an adjustment of 150 basis points to each short-term rate on the tree. The BBB bond is said to sell at an *effective* spread of 150 basis points over Treasuries. There is no certain correlation between that spread and the differential in yields to maturity ("the yield spread") of the two issues, because the methods of calculation are different. The difference results from the fact that the spread is added to the future short-term rates in the tree rather than to the yield to maturity itself. The effective spread of a bullet corporate bond will be similar to its yield spread over a benchmark Treasury. And the effective spread (or *option-adjusted spread* for a callable issue) for a callable bond will be less than its yield-to-maturity spread. The effective spread is that which causes the price of the callable bond calculated by the option pricing model to be exactly equal to its observed market price.

Option-Adjusted or Effective Convexity

As shown in Fig. 17.1, the convexity of a callable bond may be either positive or negative. The significance of convexity for callable bonds is analogous to that of a noncallable bond. However, the calculation of convexity for a callable bond depends on its call-adjusted or effective duration. A formula for calculating *option-adjusted* or *effective convexity* is

$$C_{cb} = \frac{P_{ncb}}{P_{cb}} \, [C_{ncb}(1 - \text{delta}) - (P_{ncb})(\text{gamma})(D_{ncb})^2]$$

where C_{cb} = convexity of the callable bond (call-adjusted convexity)
　　P_{cb} = price of callable bond
　　C_{ncb} = convexity of noncallable (reference) bond
　　D_{ncb} = modified duration of noncallable (reference) bond
　　P_{ncb} = price of noncallable (reference) bond

　　delta = $\dfrac{dP_o}{dP_{ncb}}$

　　P_o = price of the option

　　gamma = $\dfrac{\text{change in option's Delta}}{\text{change in noncallable price}}$

For noncallable bonds, convexity is always positive and is added to duration. But for callables, when the yield level is such that convexity is negative, then negative convexity is added to duration.

Example: Determining call-adjusted duration and convexity. A callable 12 percent coupon corporate bond priced at $1069.333 has 17 years until maturity and is callable after 2 years at $1020. Its yield to maturity is 10.474 percent, and yield to call is 6.461 percent at the noncallable's market value of $1120. An option pricing model (using a 6 percent short-term rate, and interest volatility of 12 percent) provides the value of the embedded call option as $50.667. (See Fig. 17.5.) The modified duration of the noncallable bond is 7.67, and its convexity is 91.82. Delta at $1110 P_{ncb} is 0.4616, and at $1120 it is 0.4711. What is the option-adjusted duration and convexity? The implied value of a noncallable bond with the same maturity is

$$P_{ncb} = P_{cb} + P_o = \$1069.333 + \$50.667 = \$1120.00$$

At the $1110 market price of the noncallable bond, the option value is $45.956 (from the option pricing model). As shown earlier, the option-adjusted duration of the callable bond is

$$D_{cb} = (D_{nc}) \left(\frac{P_{nc}}{P_{cb}}\right) \left(1 - \frac{dP_{co}}{dP_{nc}}\right)$$

$$= (7.67) \left(\frac{1120}{\$1069.333}\right) \left(1 - \frac{\$50.667 - \$45.956}{10}\right) = 4.249$$

The option-adjusted convexity of the callable bond is

Call option price

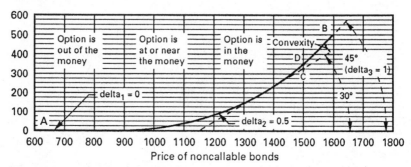

Figure 17.5. Callable bond: option value. The bond has a coupon of 12 percent, is noncallable for 2 years, and is callable thereafter for 15 years at $1020. The option pricing model uses a 12 percent volatility and a 6 percent short-term rate.

$$C_{cb} = \frac{P_{ncb}}{P_{cb}} \left[(C_{ncb}) \left(1 - \frac{dP_o}{dP_{ncb}} \right) - (P_{ncb}) \, (\text{gamma}) \, (d_{ncb})^2 \right]$$

$$= \frac{\$1120}{\$1069.33} \left[(\$91.82) \left(1 - \frac{\$50.667 - \$45.956}{\$1120 - \$1110} \right) - (\$1120)(0.00095)(6.67^2) \right]$$

$$= -14.6951$$

$$\text{Gamma} = \frac{d\text{Delta}}{dP_{ncb}} = \frac{0.4711 - 0.4616}{10} = 0.00095$$

The option-adjusted modified duration of 4.25 indicates that a 1 percent change in yields will result in about a 4.25 percent change in the price of the callable bond.

Just as with noncallable bonds, option-adjusted duration and convexity can be used to predict price changes of a callable bond when yields change.

The embedded call option reduces a bond's price volatility with respect to interest-rate movements. *When the option has little value* (e.g., many years of call protection, low current price of the bond relative to the call price, etc.), then the callable bond's duration will more closely approximate the duration of a straight bond or bullet priced to maturity. On the other hand, *when the option has great value* (few years of call protection, high current price relative to the call price, etc.), then the callable bond's duration will more closely approximate the duration of a bullet priced to the date of call. The duration of a callable bond (option-adjusted or effective duration) is bounded by the duration of a straight bond's duration to maturity and its duration to call date. Call-adjusted (or effective) duration measures the price volatility of the callable bond with respect to changes in yield.

Call-Adjusted Yields

The *call-adjusted yield* provides a useful means of determining the relative richness or cheapness of the price at which a particular callable bond is trading. Earlier it was noted that the price of a callable bond should equal the price of a noncallable bond *minus* the value of the embedded call option. In order to determine the call-adjusted yield, if one knows both the price of the callable issue (as quoted in the market) and the value of the call option (from an option pricing model, as described in the next chapter), then the value of the underlying noncallable or "reference" bond is their sum. That reference bond's price (of the noncallable) can be compared to other noncallable issues of comparable duration and credit quality to ascertain its relative value.

The formula for call-adjusted yield begins with

$$P_{nc} = P_c + P_o$$

where P_{nc} = price of the noncallable underlying bond
P_c = price of the callable bond
P_o = price of the embedded option
n = time periods until maturity of the noncallable bond

Then a normal yield-to-maturity calculation is performed to find the call-adjusted yield to maturity of the reference bond, where the price of the noncallable bond is treated as the current market price of the callable plus the option value, n is the time periods until maturity, and the coupon is the same as that of the noncallable bond.

Example: Finding call-adjusted yield to maturity.   A 30-year bond is selling at par, has an 11 percent coupon, is noncallable for 5 years, and thereafter is callable at $1040. The value of the call option (determined from an option pricing model is $50. Then the call-adjusted yield (YTM_{ca}) is the YTM for a reference bond currently priced at $1050 ($1000 callable price plus $50 option value), with 30 years until maturity and a coupon of $110. The YTM_{ca} is 10.452 percent. The call terms (5 years at $1040) do not enter the calculation of call adjusted yield directly, but are reflected in the $50 value of the embedded option.

Other factors (such as credit quality, duration, and convexity) being equal, the 10.452 percent YTM$_{ca}$ may be used to compare the relative value of the reference bond to the YTM of other noncallable bonds. The callable bond is overpriced if its option-adjusted yield is less than that of comparables, and vice versa.

Of paramount significance is the accuracy of the option price as determined by the option pricing model. Computing call-adjusted yield using an inappropriate price for the option is an exercise in futility.

The chances are good that with a good model and accurate computation, one will find that many callable bonds are overpriced. Latainer and Jacob (1987, p. 269) report finding callable bonds that are so mispriced that their call-adjusted yields are actually less than U.S. Treasuries.*

Implied Volatility

Frequently the marketplace assesses the fairness of the price of an option (and thus the price of a callable bond) by analyzing the *implied volatility* of the data contained in the pricing model.

If an investor forms his own independent judgment as to appropriate yield volatility (the standard), he can then compare his standard to the implied volatilities of available options. To do so, the investor accepts the price at which the option is quoted, and determines, using a pricing model, the volatility that is implied by the model (the implied volatility). A comparison is then made with the standard.

If the volatility of the standard is greater than the implied volatility, the option is undervalued (and a callable bond would be overvalued). *Investors should beware of buying callable bonds priced by a broker/dealer which uses a pricing model with an implied volatility that is too low.*

If the volatility of the standard is less than the implied volatility of the model, the option is overvalued (and callable bonds priced in reliance thereon would be undervalued).

As discussed previously, another means of determining the relative richness or cheapness of option prices or callable bonds, is by comparing their call-adjusted yields. Latainer and Jacob used a 25-basis-point difference as significant, and found that buying the identified "cheap" bonds resulted in incremental returns of a very impressive 1.27 percent relative to the rich bonds.

---

*Latainer, Gary and David Jacob, "Modern Techniques for Analyzing Value and Peformance of Callable Bonds," *Advances in Bond Analysis & Portfolio Strategies* (Chicago: Probus, 1987).

Realized Compound Yield for Callables

As with a noncallable bond, total return including reinvestment of cash flows can be measured to some future (or horizon) date. The price of the callable bond at the horizon date, assumption of a reinvestment rate, the coupon rate, and the time period from the current date to the horizon date are all factors in the calculation. The price of the callable bond at the horizon date is itself dependent on the value of a noncallable bond less the embedded option's value. The embedded option's value can be determined using the option pricing model described in the next chapter. At the horizon date, the values of both the noncallable and the option are dependent on the level of interest rates at that time.

Summary

Because of options, understanding the price/yield behavior of callable or putable bonds becomes much more complex than the relatively simple application of discounted cash flow procedures to a known series of cash flows. Options (including embedded options in callable bonds, put bonds, certificates of deposit, GNMAs, convertible bonds, single-premium deferred annuities, and mortgage-backed securities) introduce uncertain cash flows. And these now uncertain cash flows are a function of both changes in current interest-rate levels and the volatility of interest rates in the term structure. To determine yields, or prices, a measure of probability must be applied to changes in interest-rate levels. An option pricing model, which takes into consideration the volatility of the term structure of interest rates and establishes a tree of short-term interest rates, is the appropriate means of valuing embedded options. With the model, the financial instrument which contains an embedded option can be priced, and its option-adjusted yield, effective duration, and call-adjusted convexity can be calculated. An understanding of these principles can lead to better risk control and the ability to extract greater profitability from one's investments.

18

Option Pricing Model (Arbitrage Free)

The securities industry practice of pricing callable bonds to the lesser of yield to call or to maturity does not provide investors with the whole or even a reasonable picture of likely experience. This pricing practice results from the mathematical complexity of using a more accurate measure. An option pricing model, as described in this chapter, can be used to determine more accurately the option-adjusted yield, duration, and convexity of financial instruments with embedded options.

Professionals and academicians disagree over the best way to find the value of a long-term call option. Nor is there a simple equation for finding the solution. The method presented in this chapter is intended to be consistent with that presented by Black, Derman, and Toy. Thanks are due to Cal Johnson, of the Salomon Brothers bond pricing analysis group, for his advice concerning this chapter.*

Our objective is to find the effective yield, the effective modified duration, and the effective convexity of a callable bond. Although the discussion centers on callable bonds, the principles described in this chapter are applicable to such other financial instruments as guaranteed investment

*Fisher Black, Emanuel Derman, and William Toy, "A One-Factor Model of Interest Rates and Its Application to Treasury Bond Options. *Financial Analysts Journal*, Jan.–Feb., 1990, pp. 33–39.

contracts (GICs), single-premium deferred annuities (SPDAs), mortgage pass-throughs, collateralized mortgage obligations (CMOs), and certificates of deposit (CDs). All these financial instruments often have early redemption or prepayment privileges, which are equivalent to a fixed-income security with an embedded put option.

Before one can find the price or duration of a callable bond, determining the value of the embedded option is a prerequisite. To find the value of the embedded call option, certain sophisticated investors utilize an "option pricing model." The *option pricing model* (OPM) establishes probable future levels of interest rates (which directly affects the probability that it will be profitable to exercise a call or put option).

The backbone of an OPM is a *short-rate yield tree*. From this tree of short rates (the rates can be annual, semiannual, or for shorter periods), any financial instrument can be priced, including the value of an option or the value of the callable or putable instrument. The greater the number of time periods (e.g., one if annual, two if semiannual, 12 if monthly), the greater is the effectiveness and accuracy of the output from the OPM. Construction of an OPM is not a simple procedure, but understanding the option pricing model is essential for understanding the pricing and interest-rate sensitivity or volatility of callable or putable bonds.

The timing and amount of cash flows of a bond must be known or predicted in order to find effective yield, effective duration, and convexity. With a callable bond, the timing and amount of cash flows depends on future interest rates. It is obvious that an issuer's decision to call a bond will depend on the future level of rates. If current interest rates are low relative to a bond's coupon rate, the bond will likely be called; conversely, if rates are high, the bond will continue to maturity. The option pricing model allows one to estimate the likely or probable timing and amount of cash flows. Thus the model is a "stochastic" process, which implies a *probability estimate* of the distribution of interest rates.

Term Structure of Interest Rates and Volatility

The first step in developing an option pricing model is to determine the term structure of long-term rates. Table 18.1 shows a sample term structure for U.S. Treasury issues for a 10-year period. The first part of the table shows the mean (average) yield for each type of bond for the year in question. For example, the mean yield for a 30-year bond for 1990 was 8.61 percent. (The actual high rate during the year for this bond was 9.18 percent, and the low was 8 percent.) The short rates developed for the OPM must be consistent with the term structure rates. However, the term structure rates are average rates: for example, for this year, 8.61 percent is the rate which, uniformly applied as a discount rate to all the cash flows of the 30-year bond, results in its price. A different set of short rates, valid for one time period (e.g., 1 year), can be derived from the term structure. For example, the 1-year rate in year 30 might be 9.5 percent, and the 1-year rate in year 2 might be 6.0 percent. These short rates, when applied to discount the future cash flows of the 30-year bond, will also result in its present price.

The second part of Table 18.1 shows the volatility of the rates for each instrument for each year. For example, for the 30-year bond, in 1990, the annualized volatility was 11.14 percent. The volatility of the interest rate is a measure of its variability from the average or mean rate. Volatility is determined using ordinary statistical methodology and is the standard deviation from the mean.

The calculation of the annualized volatility (11.14 percent) for the 30-year treasury issue for 1990 is shown in Table 18.2, mean and annualized

Table 18.1. Term Structure and Annualized Volatility of U.S. Treasury Bonds and Bills

Year	3-month bill	5-year	10-year	30-year
	Bond Equivalent Yield or Yield to Maturity (%)			
1982	11.07	13.09	13.09	12.77
1983	8.93	10.80	11.09	11.82
1984	9.89	12.27	12.45	12.41
1985	7.72	10.14	10.62	10.79
1986	6.14	7.30	7.66	7.78
1987	5.93	7.94	8.38	8.58
1988	6.88	8.48	8.84	8.95
1989	8.40	8.48	8.49	8.44
1990	7.74	8.36	8.54	8.61
Average	8.08	9.65	9.91	10.02
	Annualized Volatility (%)			
1982	43.03	20.81	19.30	15.72
1983	15.28	12.66	11.61	11.56
1984	16.46	12.08	12.16	11.55
1985	16.03	14.36	13.90	12.04
1986	14.54	19.74	18.68	16.27
1987	34.41	18.73	17.40	16.46
1988	15.76	12.02	11.59	11.66
1989	15.39	13.40	10.90	9.86
1990	11.11	11.57	11.46	11.14
Average	20.22	15.04	14.11	12.92

SOURCE: Adapted from data provided by First Boston Corp.

Table 18.2. Mean and Annualized Volatility Calculation

	Date	Yield	Yield % chg	Yield % change less mean	Deviation squared
0	12/29/89	7.980			
1	1/02/90	8.000	0.251	0.235	0.055
2		8.030	0.375	0.360	0.129
3		8.030	0.000	-0.015	0.000
.					
.					
.					
.					
254		8.280	0.730	0.715	0.511
255		8.350	0.845	0.830	0.689
256		n/a			
257		8.350	0.000	-0.015	0.000
258		8.255	-1.138	-1.153	1.329
259		8.300	0.545	0.530	0.281
260	12/31/90	8.240	-0.723	-0.738	0.545
Sum =		2168.52	3.823	0	123.561
Observations (n) =		252			
Trading days =		252			
Mean ($\overline{u}$) =			0.0152		

Variance (sd^2) = 123.56/(252 – 1) = 0.4923

Standard deviations (s) = $0.4922763^{0.5}$ = 0.7016

Annualized volatility = $(252)^{0.5}$ = (0.7016) (15.88) = 11.14%

Note: Instead of basing the above calculations on "yield percentage changes," similar results arise from using "price relatives (which are the natural logarithms of (1 + yield % change).

volatility calculation. Further information concerning the term structure of interest is in Appendix 18.1.

Constructing an Arbitrage-Free Option Pricing Model

The quickest way to grasp the mechanics of constructing and using an OPM is to build one. To construct the option pricing model, begin with a Treasury zero-coupon bond's yield to maturity for each year as well as the volatility of each year's yield. (Further insight into the causes of the slope or shape of the yield curve is offered in Appendix 18.1 at the end of this chapter.) Refer to Table 18.3, a hypothetical term structure for long-term rates. The yields to maturity are shown for a representative Treasury zero-coupon bond

Table 18.3 Term Structure of Long-Term Rates

(a)	(b)	(c)	(d)	(e)	(f)
Years to maturity (n)	Yield to maturity (y) (%)	Standard deviation (sd)	Volatility (c/b) (%)	$\dfrac{y+sd}{y-sd}\,0.5 \times \ln\left(\dfrac{y+sd}{y-sd}\right)$ (volatility) (%)	
1	10.00	0.02000	20.00	1.500	20.3
2	11.00	0.02090	19.00	1.469	19.2
3	12.00	0.02064	17.20	1.415	17.4
4	12.50	0.01912	15.30	1.361	15.4
5	13.00	0.01755	13.50	1.312	13.6

Note: The yield to maturity in column (b) is the YTM of a zero-coupon Treasury bond of n years until maturity. These zero-coupon rates are derived from coupon Treasury bonds (using bonds priced near par, when possible). Derived zero-coupon rates are preferable to using actual price quotes of zeros for various technical reasons, including the differences in liquidity between treasuries and zeros and odd tax consequences attendant to zeros. A "zero-coupon spot rate" yield calculation method is described in Chap. 19. In the table, the YTM for a 4-year zero-coupon Treasury is 12.5%.

for each maturity. The volatility calculation for the first year is shown in Table 18.4. This table is based on observed rates for 1-year maturity at various times being 10.5, 10.25, 9.75, and 9.361 percent. The four observations (plus an initial yield of 11.055 percent) allow calculation of the mean rate (9.965 percent) and the variance from the mean, the square of the standard deviation (sd^2), which is 0.0001587. From this, one standard deviation of the daily percentage change in yields is found to be 0.0126, and the annualized volatility is 0.2, or 20 percent. It is important to note that the daily percentage changes in yield (or relative yields) serve as the base of the calculation, not the actual yields themselves. The distribution of the percentage change in daily rates is a more normal distribution than the actual yield rates (which are considered to be log-normally distributed).

About two-thirds of the time, the probability, for a normal distribution is that yields will lie between the mean plus and minus one standard deviation. And the probability is about 95 percent that it will lie between the mean plus and minus 1.96 standard deviations. The probability is 99 percent that the mean plus and minus 2.58 standard deviations will encompass the yield.

Method 1:

$$a = \frac{1}{(n-1)} = 0.3333333 \quad b = \text{sum } x_i^2 = 0.0073925$$

Table 18.4. Yield Volatility Calculation (for 1 Year to Maturity)

Obser-vation number (n)	Daily yield obser-vation (Y)	Relative yield (Y_n/Y_{n-1})	Daily return: natural log of relative yields (X_i)	Square of natural logs of relative yields (X_i^2)	Deviation from mean of Xi's (X_{i-u})	Deviation squared square of (X_{i-u})
0	11.055					
1	10.500	0.949796	−0.051508	0.0026531	−0.0099252	0.0000985
2	10.250	0.976190	−0.024098	0.0005807	0.0174848	0.0003057
3	9.750	0.951220	−0.050010	0.0025010	−0.0084272	0.0000710
4	9.361	0.960103	−0.040715	0.0016577	0.0008678	0.0000008
Sum	39.861		−0.166331	0.0073925	0.0000000	0.0004760

Mean of X_i's = sum X_i's / 4 = $\bar{u}$ =   −0.0415828

Mean of Y's = sum Y's / 4 =   9.965

$$c = \frac{1}{n(n-1)} = 0.0833333 \quad d = \text{sum } x_i^2 = 0.0276660$$

Variance $= (a * b) - (c * d) = 0.0001587$

Standard deviation = squareroot of value of the variance = 0.0126

Annualized volatility for daily yields =

square root of number of trading days times standard deviation

Square root of trading days (252 days) = 15.8745

Standard deviation = 0.0126

Annualized volatility = 0.2000 or 20%

Method 2:

$$a = \frac{1}{(n-1)} = 0.3333333 \quad b = \text{sum } (X_{i-\bar{u}})^2 = 0.000476$$

Variance $= a \times b = 0.0001587$

Standard deviation = square root of variance = 0.0125963

Annualized volatility $= 252^{0.5} \times \text{sd} = 0.2000$

If weekly rates were used instead of daily, to find annualized volatility multiple by the square root of 52; and if monthly rates are used, multiply by the square root of 12 (instead of the square root of 252).

It is the percentage change in yield which is the basis for the calculation of volatility (rather than the actually observed yields). The reason for using daily percentage changes (or the natural logarithm of the relative yields) is that the distribution of the percentage changes (or the natural logarithm of the relative yields) will be more *normally* distributed than the original rates (or prices) from which the changes are derived.

Since volatility is used in reference to annual yields, daily variance must be annualized. In statistical jargon, where a sample (of daily changes in rates) is *identically and independently distributed (iid)* as compared to the entire population (all the changes in yields for the year), then:

$$(\sigma)^2 = (sd^2)(n)$$

and

$$(\sigma) = (sd)(n)^{0.5}$$

where $(\sigma)^2$ = the population's variance or standard deviation squared
sd^2 = the sample's variance or standard deviation squared
n = the number of trading days in the year (approximately equal to 52 weeks times 5 business days per week, from which the number of holidays falling during the business week is subtracted; statistically, it is assumed that the sample includes the daily change of rates for all trading days in the year)
σ = the population's annualized volatility of changes in rates
sd = the sample's standard deviation

For further information regarding the calculation of volatility (standard deviation of the daily percentage changes in yields, refer to Table 18.2. It contains, for an entire year, for a 30-year treasury bond, the daily yield to maturity and the author's calculation of standard deviation and volatility.

The OPM requires one to determine the *short interest rate* (defined as the 1-year forward rate of a zero-coupon bond) at each point in time throughout the time period of the analysis. In this example, we must find the short rates for the next 5 years. We know from Table 18.3 that the YTM for a 1-year zero-coupon bond is 10 percent. This 10 percent is also the current short rate. All other short rates will have to be calculated. For the 5-year analysis, we will designate each point in time and possible interest rate or price as shown in Fig. 18.1, an interest rate tree. Such a tree is sometimes referred to as a *lattice*.

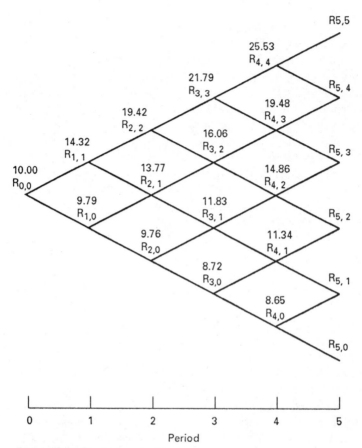

Figure 18.1. Short rates, complete.

For example, the interest rate at the current date (the beginning of the study) is shown as $R_{0,0}$. From the beginning of the first period (1 year is equal to 1 period), we will assume that rates will either go up to $R_{1,1}$ or down to $R_{1,0}$, and that the probability is 50/50 as to which will occur. Each subscript identifies the location or node on the lattice. The first subscript represents the time period, and the second subscript shows the various rate possibilities for each year, counting up from the bottom ray.

To determine the short rates for the first year, we start with the known short rate at $R_{0,0}$, which is 10 percent (from Table 18.3). We seek to find two unknowns, the rate at period 1 if rates rise ($R_{1,1}$), and the rate at period 1 if rates fall ($R_{1,0}$). We know two relationships involving those rates, as follows.

First, the present price ($P_{0,0}$) is found by discounting the $100 maturity values of a zero-coupon bond at period 2 (lattice nodes $P_{2,2}$, $P_{2,1}$, and $P_{2,0}$) to the values at $P_{1,1}$ and $P_{1,0}$ at rates $R_{1,1}$ and $R_{1,0}$, and again discounting those prices (at $P_{1,1}$ and $P_{1,0}$) to the present at the initial short-term rate of 10 percent. See Fig. 18.2.

$$P_{0,0} = \frac{\$100(1 + R_{1,1})^{-1}(1.1)^{-1}}{2} + \frac{\$100(1 + R_{1,0})^{-1}(1.1)^{-1}}{2} \quad (18.1)$$

Let

$$x = (R_{1,1}) \quad y = (R_{1,0}) \qquad P = P_{0,0} \quad (18.2)$$

Then

$$\frac{(1.1)(2P)}{\$100} = \frac{1}{1 + x} + \frac{1}{1 + y} \quad (18.3)$$

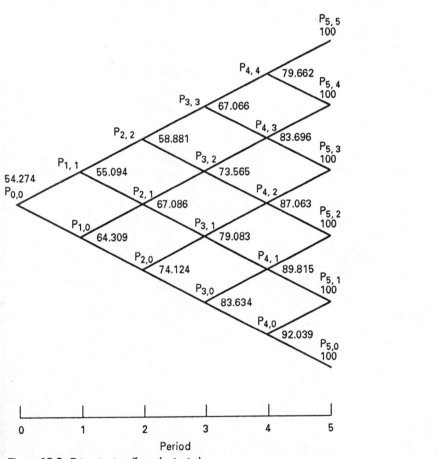

Figure 18.2. Price structure (from short rates).

which reduces to (see Appendix 18.2 for the derivation):

$$(1.78556)(xy) + (0.78556)(x) + (0.78556)(y) - 0.21444 = 0 \quad (18.4)$$

We shall substitute equivalent values for x in the above form of the equation by obtaining x from a second relationship, which expresses the known volatility of 19 percent (from Table 18.3) at 2 years to maturity. This is

$$\frac{\ln(x/y)}{2} = 0.19 \quad (18.5)$$

$$\frac{x}{y} = 1.4623 \quad (18.6)$$

$$x = 1.4623\,y \quad (18.7)$$

Substituting $1.4623y$ for the value of x in (18.4) gives

$$(1.78556)(1.4623\,y)(y) + (0.78556)(1.4623y) + 0.78556y - 0.21444 = 0$$

$$(18.8)$$

and

$$2.61156y^2 + 1.93452y - 0.21444 = 0 \quad (18.9)$$

This is solvable by the quadratic equation for the value of y, as follows:

$$y = \frac{-b \pm (b^2 - 4ac)^{0.5}}{2a} = \frac{0.511301}{5.22312} = 0.0978 \text{ or } 9.79\% \quad (18.10)$$

Also,

$$x = 1.4623y = 1.4623(0.097892) = 0.1431767 \text{ or } 14.32\% \quad (18.11)$$

Since $x = (R_{1,1})$,

$$R_{1,1} = 14.32\% \quad (18.12)$$

and since $y = (R_{1,0})$,

$$R_{1,0} = 9.79\% \quad (18.13)$$

These rates are now posted to the short-rates tree of Fig. 18.1.

The price tree so far determined is shown in Fig. 18.2. Each price is determined as follows:

$$P_{1,1} = \frac{P_{2,2}\,(1+0.1432)^{-1}}{2} + \frac{P_{2,1}(1+0.1432)^{-1}}{2} = 87.474 \qquad (18.14)$$

$$P_{1,0} = \frac{P_{2,1}\,(1+0.0979)^{-1}}{2} + \frac{P_{2,0}(1+0.0979)^{-1}}{2} = 91.083 \qquad (18.15)$$

$$P_{0,0} = \frac{P_{1,1}\,(1+0.010)^{-1}}{2} + \frac{P_{1,0}(1+0.10)^{-1}}{2} = 81.162 \qquad (18.16)$$

The rate and price tree calculated so far must satisfy *two tests* for validity: the *YTM test* and the *volatility test*. The YTM test for a 2-year zero maturity is that the price just computed of 81.162 should be the value obtained when the 2-year YTM term rate (of 11 percent) from Table 18.3 is applied to the 2-year face amount of the bond. Since $100(1.11)^{-2}$ is 81.162, the first test is passed.

The volatility of short rates at year 1 is determined by taking one-half of the natural logarithm of each pair of rates at that year. See Appendix 18.3 at the end of the chapter for a derivation of the volatility test.

$$\text{Volatility} = (0.5)\ln\left(\frac{R_{1,1}}{R_{1,0}}\right) = (0.05)\ln\left(\frac{0.1432}{0.0979}\right)$$

$$= (0.5)(0.38) = 0.19 \ \text{ or } \ 19\% \qquad (18.17)$$

Checking Table 18.3 for the term structure volatility for a 2-year maturity, we find that 19 percent is correct.

Because the YTM and volatility tests validate the calculations, we know that no matter what interest rate path is selected from the initial price to the last year, the resulting price at period 2 will be the same. Thus one can proceed forward or backward in the price tree (of Fig. 18.2) using the short rates (of Fig. 18.1), and no matter which path is selected from the root (e.g., up, up; or up, down; or down, up; or down, down), the resulting price will be 100; and vice versa if the starting point is at year 2. The price at $P_{0,0}$ represents that price determined from assigning equal probabilities of occurrence to each price in the price tree in year 2.

The next task is to find the 2-year short rates ($R_{2,0}$, $R_{2,1}$, and $R_{2,2}$). Since, by definition, the volatilities of the short rates must match the given volatility of the 3-year term structure (17.4%), it can be shown that

$$(R_{2,1})^2 = (R_{2,2})(R_{2,0}) \qquad (18.18)$$

The proof is as follows:

$$\ln\left(\frac{R_{2,2}}{R_{2,1}}\right) = \ln\left(\frac{R_{2,1}}{R_{2,0}}\right) \tag{18.19}$$

$$\ln(R_{2,2}) - \ln(R_{2,1}) = \ln(R_{2,1}) - \ln(R_{2,0}) \tag{18.20}$$

$$2\ln(R_{2,1}) = \ln(R_{2,2}) + \ln(R_{2,0}) \tag{18.21}$$

Since the middle rate can be found from the upper and lower rates, we must find only the upper and lower rates (which must match the term structure for YTM and volatility). Generally, matching two unknowns (the two rates) with two quantities (the term rate YTM and volatility) will produce a unique solution. Using a mathematical process like the one used to find the 1-year short rates, the 2-year short rates are found to be $(R_{2,2})$ = 19.42, $(R_{2,1})$ = 13.77, and $(R_{2,0})$ = 9.76. These values are now added to the short rates tree (Fig. 18.1). It is to be noted that if one cannot find the short rates by algebraic solution, the values may be found by trial and error, substituting values for each unknown rate until values are found that also meet the validation criteria for volatility and term YTM. By this process, the short rates that comprise the entire structure have been added to Fig. 18.1.

With the short rate structure intact (Fig. 18.1), the corresponding pricing structure can be determine from the short rates. This price tree is shown in Fig. 18.2 The price at any node on the tree is determined by discounting backward one year at a time (using the rates from the short rate tree) from the maturity value in the fifth year. For example, the price at $P_{4,0}$ is found as

$$\frac{\$100\,(1 + 0.0865\,)^{-1}}{2} + \frac{\$100\,(1 + 0.0865\,)^{-1}}{2} = (2)(\$46.019\,) = \$92.039 \tag{18.22}$$

Validation of the price structure of Fig. 18.2 (which was constructed by using the short rates) is found by comparing the price at $P_{0,0}$, \$54.274, to the price that would be obtained by using the term structure rate (Table 18.3) of 13 percent to find the price:

$$P_{0,0} = \frac{\$100}{(1 + 0.13)^5} = \$54.27$$

Thus the price at the root is the same, \$54.27, regardless of whether it is found by walking the price back from maturity through the short rate table or by using the YTM from the term rate structure.

The additional test of the validity of the short rate structure is that the volatilities of rates for each year must match each other and also match the volatility of the term rate (Table 18.3). These relationships are shown in Table 18.5.

Table 18.5. Validation of Short-Term Rates by Volatility

Short rate structure

Year	0	1	2	3	4	5
Ray 4						25.53%
Ray 3					21.79%	19.48%
Ray 2				19.42%	16.06%	14.86%
Ray 1			14.32%	13.77%	11.83%	11.34%
Ray 0		10.00%	9.79%	9.76%	8.72%	8.65%
Volatility of short rates: ratio of rates within each year						
e.g., 25.53/19.48 = 1.31						1.31
					1.36	1.31
				1.41	1.36	1.31
			1.46	1.41	1.36	1.31
Volatility of short rates: by natural log method (see Appendix 18.3)						
e.g., (0.5)[ln(0.2553/.1948)]						13.5%
					15.4%	13.5%
				17.2%	15.4%	13.5%
			19.0%	17.2%	15.4%	13.5%

The *probability* of each node's occurrence is shown in Fig. 18.3. For example, after 5 periods, the probability that an upward movement will occur at *each* node is 3.125 percent.

The value $2n$ (where n is the number of periods) is the *number of nodes* that are created at each time period, counting the double nodes which are shared. Not counting each shared node as two, the number is $n + 1$.

Finding the Value of an Embedded Bond Call Option

The value (theoretical price) of an embedded call option is determined using the structure of 1-year short rates, the *strike price* of the option (the exercise price of a bond's call option), and a breakdown of the bond's cash flows into a series of comparable zero-coupon bonds. As an example, consider a 3-year Treasury bond, callable at 95 until its maturity, with a 10 percent coupon rate.

The first step is to break down the cash flows into a series of comparable zero-coupon bonds, as shown in Table 18.6 under "Cash flows." The cash flows of these three zero-coupon bonds are identical to the cash flows of the parent bond. The present value of the three zeros is determined by

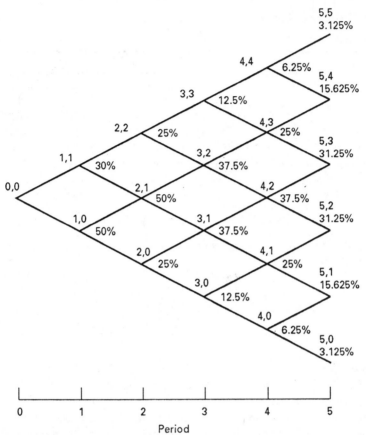

Figure 18.3. Probability of each node's occurrence.

Notes:

1. The total number of nodes at time $n = 0.5 (n + 1) (n + 2)$. For example, with 5 periods, the total number of nodes is $0.5 (5 + 1)(5 + 2) = 21$. The number of nodes in the fifth period is $n + 1$, or 6.

2. The probability of the occurrence of the paths from any particular node, n, j, where n = the time period and j = the number of rows up, starting from zero, is a fraction, the numerator of which is the coefficient of a binomial expansion and the denominator of which is the total number of paths.

3. The denominator or number of possible paths is 2^n.

4. The coefficient or numerator is $n!/[j !(n - j)!]$, where n is the time period and j is the number of rows for the particular node.

5. Example at $n = 5$, $j = 1$: *The probability is*

$$\text{Numerator} = \frac{5!}{1!(5 - 1)!} = 5 \quad \text{Denominator} = 2^n = 2^5 = 32$$

$$\text{Probability} = \frac{5}{32} = 0.15625 \text{ or } 15.625\%$$

Table 18.6. Value of Embedded Call Option

Value of a 3-year Treasury determined by short rates
$100 maturity value
10.00% coupon rate
Cash flows, if divided into corresponding zero-coupon bonds

Year	Cash flow
1	10
2	10
3	110

Year 0	Year 1	Year 2	Year 3

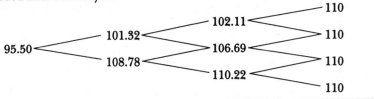

Short Rates:

```
                         19.42%
              14.32%
  10.00%                 13.77%
               9.79%
                          9.76%
```

Part A. *Price of 1-year zero:*

```
              10
  $9.09
              10
```

Part B. *Price of 2-year zero:*

```
                          10
               8.75
  8.12                    10
               9.11
                          10
```

Part C. *Price of 3-year zero:*

```
                                    110
                         92.11
               82.57                110
  78.29                  96.69
               89.67                110
                        100.22
                                    110
```

Part D. *Combined portfolio* of 1-, 2-, and 3-year zeros: $10.00 of *accrued* interest is included after current year

```
                                    110
                        102.11
              101.32                110
  95.50                 106.69
              108.78                110
                        110.22
                                    110
```

Table 18.6. Value of Embedded Call Option (*Continued*)

Year 0	Year 1	Year 2	Year 3

Part E. Combined portfolio of 1-, 2-, and 3-year zeros: (*without* accrued interest)

```
                                                        ┌─ 100
                                    ┌─ 92.11 ─┤
                        ┌─ 91.32 ─┤           └─ 100
              95.50 ─┤            ├─ 96.69 ─┤
                        └─ 98.78 ─┤           └─ 100
                                    └─ 100.22 ─┤
                                                        └─ 100
```

Part F. *Value of a call option* at each node (bond price less strike price, minmum 0)

                              95 = strike price (call price)
                              3 = years to call

```
                                                        ┌─ 5.00
                                    ┌─ 0.00 ─┤
                        ┌─ 0.00 ─┤           └─ 5.00
              0.50 ─┤            ├─ 1.69 ─┤
                        └─ 3.78 ─┤           └─ 5.00
                                    └─ 5.22 ─┤
                                                        └─ 5.00
```

Part G. *Call value tree* (discounted values; applicable to European options)

```
                                                        ┌─ 5.00
                                    ┌─ 4.19 ─┤
                        ┌─ 3.75 ─┤           └─ 5.00
              3.56 ─┤            ├─ 4.39 ─┤
                        └─ 4.08 ─┤           └─ 5.00
                                    └─ 4.56 ─┤
                                                        └─ 5.00
```

Part H. *Bond price less strike price* (option exercise price)

```
                                                        ┌─ 5.00
                                    ┌─ -2.89 ─┤
                        ┌─ -3.68 ─┤           └─ 5.00
              0.50 ─┤            ├─ 1.69 ─┤
                        └─ 3.78 ─┤           └─ 5.00
                                    └─ 5.22 ─┤
                                                        └─ 5.00
```

Part I. *American option* valued at the greater of value if held or value if option is exercised (at each node)

```
                                                        ┌─ 5.00
                                    ┌─ 4.19 ─┤
                        ┌─ 3.75 ─┤           └─ 5.00
              3.70 ─┤            ├─ 4.39 ─┤
                        └─ 4.38 ─┤           └─ 5.00
                                    └─ 5.22 ─┤
                                                        └─ 5.00
```

applying the short rates (Table 18.5) to the cash flows of each of the three zeros. Each zero's present value is shown in Table 18.6, parts A, B, and C. The combined value of the three zeros, $95.50, is shown in part D. The prices of each bond at each node are the average of the prices (upper node and lower node) 1 year forward, discounted back at the applicable short rate.

The discount price results from the fact that the bond's conventional yield to maturity is about 11.87 percent (on an annual-payment basis), which is below the term structure (12 percent) used to compute the short rates. Stated another way, the 10 percent coupon is less than current prevailing rates, therefore the bond is priced at a discount.

Part E of Table 18.6 shows the combined portfolio with the prices reduced (from Part D) by the $10 value of accrued interest included in the prices of Part D. The prices in Part E are used to find the value of the embedded call option.

The bond price less the $95 strike price, minimum zero, at each node is shown in Part F. Part G shows the call value of a *European option*, which is exercisable only at the option's expiration at the end of 3 years. Since the bond price at maturity is $100, and the strike price is 95, the third-year value in each case is $5.00. Discounting back at the rates of the short rate structure (Fig. 18.1) produces the value at each node. The present value of the described call option, if European, is $3.56.

An *American option* can be exercised at any time, not just at the expiration date of the option. The call option value at each node is the greater of either the discounted values of the two forward values *or* the value of the current price less strike price. The greater of the two values is used at that node. It then is issued to discount back to the previous node. Thus, as shown in Part I, the current value of the embedded option, if American, is 3.70 per $100 par, or $37.00 per $1000. A European option's call value is determined only by the discounted values of the two forward values.

In the example, the call option is in effect throughout the entire period of the study. If the call option exists for a shorter term than that of the study, then, in the noncall years, the value at each node is the discounted value (as in the European option) without reference to the difference between price and strike call price. For example, the noncall years would be the first 10 years in the case of a 30-year bond which is noncallable for 10 years. The callable years would be the last 20 years. The call value at each node is determined American-style for the last 20 years, and is found European-style for the first 10 years.

The accuracy of an option pricing model depends on computer memory limitations. Ideally, a tree is needed that is graded in 1-day steps rather than 1-year steps, and that can handle up to a full 40 years of maturity for long-term bonds. Coupon and option exercise dates would always fall on a node in such a model. Computer memory limitations may be alleviated by using two trees, one for rough estimation and the other for fine tuning. The rough model would value the option from maturity to the present; and the fine tree would cover the period from option expiration to today. Dates that fall between nodes (e.g., coupon, expiration, and maturity) would be interpolated to the nearest node. In the final analysis, calculations of yields, prices, duration, and convexity of financial instruments with embedded options are no better than the accuracy of the option pricing model.

Fine-tuning the Model

The "proof of the pudding" as far as pricing models are concerned is whether they work. That is, does application of the model accurately produce the value that the model purports to calculate?

Values of call options can be tested against benchmarks of liquid, relevant securities in the marketplace. For example, certain callable U.S. Treasuries are highly liquid, with narrow spreads between bid and asked prices. Nearby maturities exist which are noncallable. Thus the marketplace value of the embedded call option is easily ascertainable. Comparison of the pricing option model calculation against the market value of the option shows the accuracy or lack thereof of the market, assuming that the issues chosen for the test are not under- or overvalued.

One of the more subjective inputs to the model is the term structure of interest rates and the volatility of such rates (Table 18.1 and 18.2). It may be necessary or beneficial to fine tune those inputs by adjusting the chosen sample data (which will cause the volatilities of the chosen rates to change). Naturally, such changes will cause the entire term structure of short-term rates to change.

Model Constraints

The one-factor binomial option pricing model developed from the term structure of interest rates has great utility: It can be used to price bonds, call options, put options, callable bonds, put bonds, etc. However, there is no universal agreement on the manner and method of constructing a pricing model.

However, if the model is structured incorrectly, the results obtained from its use will be incorrect as well. The axiom for a badly constructed model is "garbage out" regardless of how accurate is the data provided as input.

As a minimum, the pricing model should include freedom from arbitrage possibilities and maintenance of the put–call parity relationship.

Freedom from Arbitrage Possibilities

Freedom from arbitrage possibilities means that using the interest rate structure developed in the model, it will not be possible to better one's results by, for example, owning a long bond as compared with rolling over a series of short-term holdings, and vice versa. The investment results should be the same either way. For example, let's illustrate using the short rate structure developed in Fig. 18.1. If a 3-year zero-coupon bond is purchased at the long-term rate (from Table 18.3) of 12 percent, its cost is $711.78 [price = $1000 $(1.12)^{-3}$]. And for that current investment of $711.78, one receives in 3 years the maturity value of $1000. If instead, the $711.78 is invested at the 10 percent 1-year short rate (from Fig. 18.1) and, in each subsequent year, a new bond is purchased at the average of the 1-year short rates for that year, the result of that investment, and reinvestment at the average of the pertinent rates at each time period, should also be $1000 in 3 years. Let's say that the path chosen is represented by the following nodes and rates:

Year	Average short rates (%)	Price	
0		$711.78	
1	10.00	782.95	
2	12.05	877.29	where 12.05 = (0.5) (9.79 + 14.32)
3	14.00	1000.00	where 14.0 = (0.333) (19.42 + 13.77 + 9.76)

Thus, the investment results (of $711.02) will be the same in 3 years in either the case where a 3-year term bond is purchased, or a series of 1-year bonds is acquired. In using the average short rates for each time period, it is implied that there is equal probability that any particular interest rate path will be followed.

Put–Call Parity

Put–call parity holds that a put option with a striking price of E and an expiration of N on an underlying bond plus a position in the bond itself should be equivalent to ownership of a call option with a striking price of E and an expiration of N on the underlying bond plus a term bond maturing at N and with a redemption value equal to E and the same coupon as the underlying bond. In testing for put–call parity, only European (option is exercisable only at expiration date) type option values may be used. See Chap. 17 for further discussion of put–call parity.

Black-Scholes Option Pricing Formula

The Black-Scholes option pricing model (BSOPM) was a major advancement in finance and remains the industry standard, in appropriate circumstances. (See Black and Scholes, 1973.) Without adaptation however, the BSOPM is principally effective only for European options on non-dividend-paying stocks.* The BSOPM is not effective for valuing options on bonds for the following reasons.

First, the BSOPM assumes that the logarithm of a stock return follows a normal distribution. Such an assumption results in a skewed distribution where higher prices are more likely to occur than lower prices, and there is some probability that a price can reach virtually any positive price. However, it is inapplicable to bonds, since bond prices are limited to a minimum value of zero and a maximum value equal to the sum of remaining cash flows.

The binomial model described in this chapter is based on a *log-normal* distribution of *yields*, which means that yields are skewed to the right of the mean, and do not fall below zero. The resulting distribution of bond *prices* for short-term bonds is skewed to the left of the mean; and for longer-term bonds, the skewness is to the right of the mean.

* The Black-Scholes option pricing formula is

$$c = SN(d_1) - Xe^{-r(T-t)}N(d_2)$$

where

$$d_1 = \frac{\ln(S/X) + (r + \sigma^2/2)(T-t)}{\sigma\sqrt{T-t}}$$

$$d_2 = \frac{\ln(S/X) + (r + \sigma^2/2)(T-t)}{\sigma\sqrt{T-t}} = d_1 - \sigma\sqrt{T-t}$$

where c = value of European call option to buy one share
S = stock price per share
X = exercise price per share of the option
t = current date
T = expiration date of option
σ = volatility of stock
r = risk-free interest rate

Second, the BSOPM assumes that the volatility of a stock's return is constant over time. It is inapplicable to valuing options on bonds, both because the volatility of bond yields and prices change over time and because (for all bonds except perpetuals) the price volatility approaches zero as a bond approaches maturity.

Third, the BSOPM assumes that the underlying stock pays no dividend. Most bonds, however, are coupon paying, and the original BSOPM requires adjustment even for stocks that pay dividends.

Fourth, the BSOPM was developed for European options. American-options, however, are generally worth more. Since the issuer of a callable bond, or the holder of a putable bond, can usually exercise the option in a manner more like an American option than a European, the BSOPM does not handle this eventuality.

Hence, though the BSOPM represented a great step forward in pricing short-term options on non-dividend-paying stocks, it is inappropriate for valuing instruments other than those it was designed to value.

Summary

Because of options, understanding the price/yield behavior of bonds becomes much more complex than the relatively simple application of discounted cash flow procedures to a known series of cash flows. Options (including embedded options in callable bonds, put bonds, certificates of deposit, GNMAs, single-premium deferred annuities, and mortgage-backed securities) introduce uncertain cash flows. And these now uncertain cash flows are a function of changes in interest rate levels. To determine yields, or prices, a measure of probability must be applied to changes in interest rate levels. An option pricing model, which takes into consideration the volatility of interest rates and establishes a short-term tree of interest rates, is the appropriate means of valuing embedded options. With the model the financial instrument which contains an embedded option can be priced, and its effective yield, duration, and convexity can be calculated. An understanding of these principles can lead to better risk control and the ability to extract greater profitability from one's investments.

The short-term rates tree or lattice, once constructed, can be used to determine the spread between the rates of liquid and riskless (as to payment of principal and interest) Treasuries which were used to construct the tree, and appropriate rates for any other fixed-income security.

Other desired characteristics of the binomial model include (1) preserving put–call parity and being arbitrage free (by making the model consistent with the yields and varying volatility of the term structure of interest rates); (2) avoiding the production of negative interest rates (by using a log-normal distribution of yields); and (3) modeling more reasonably the behavior of the yield curve (again by making the model consistent with the term structure).

The methodology of binomial models was first suggested by Sharpe (1978), and soon after was expanded by Cox, Ross, and Rubinstein (1979). Suggested further reading on the inherent problems in developing option pricing models and their method of construction includes: Vasicek (1977); Brennan and Schwartz (1982); Courtadon (1982); Bookstaber (1991); and Cox, Ingersoll, and Ross (1985). More recent works include: Lord, Jacob, and Tilley (1987): Boyce, Koenigsberg, and Tatevossian (1987): Ho (1990); and Black, Derman, and Toy (1990).

Appendix 18.1: Term Structure of Interest Rates

The term structure of long-term rates or yields generally depicts the yields to maturity of Treasury bonds at maturities from 1 to 30 years, with annual or semiannual gradations. A three-dimensional representation of the term structure is shown in Fig. 18.4.

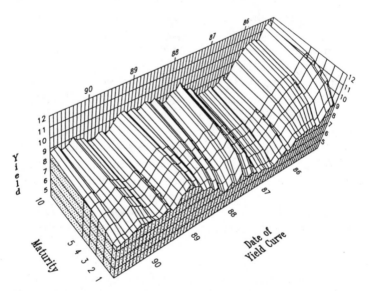

Figure 18.4. Term structure of interest rates (January 1986 to October 1990). (*Courtesy of Solomon Bros.*)

In selecting specific bonds to include in the term structure, care must be exercised to eliminate bonds having yields that are affected by special circumstances. Such special circumstances might include tax benefits or detriments that accrue to the owner of a particular issue, such as for *flower bonds* [certain low-coupon bonds which may be used at *par* value (even though the bonds would otherwise sell at enormous discounts) by the estate of a decedent to pay federal estate tax]. (In the zero-coupon arena, the Japanese tax treatment of zeros has had a varying effect. For example, if zero corpus instruments are not taxed and other stripped coupons are taxed, yields can be distorted.) In some instances, there may be more than one Treasury bond having the same maturity, but with different coupons, and different yields to maturity. The yield difference is at least partially due to the different durations of the two bond, as well as to potentially different after-tax yields to taxable investors. Other pitfalls in selecting specific issues for inclusion in the term structure include the facts that some maturities will have no issues outstanding, and some maturities will have only callable issues.

At least three theories attempt to explain the relative changes of short-term interest rates as compared to long-term rates: the expectations theory, the liquidity-preference theory, and the institutional or hedging-pressure theory.

The Expectations Theory

The expectations theory holds that the yield curve shape is explained by investors' expectations of future rates.

When investors think that current yields to maturity are high and that lower rates are probable in the future, they will buy long-term bonds and sell short-term ones. This will cause the yield curve to level or become inverted.

When the reverse is the case, and investors think that currently yields to maturity are low and that higher rates are probable in the future, they will sell long-term bonds and invest in short-term bonds. This will cause the yield curve to be positive, or upward sloping.

The expectations theory leads to a conclusion that the long-term yield to maturity is a *geometric average* of current and expected shorter-term rates. (Technically, if n rates are being averaged, the procedure is to take the nth root of the product of $(1 +$ each rate$)$. The rationale is that investors will attempt to maximize their return by buying and selling bonds so that their holdings will produce maximum returns over the period of time that their investment funds are available (their investment horizon). Such buying and selling alters the yield structure until an *equilibrium* level is reached, where the differential in returns for a specified time horizon is eliminated. This leads to higher volatility of short-term rates as compared to long-term rates.

To better understand the foregoing, think of a pretty girl standing at a pier waving goodbye to her boyfriend, who is aboard ship and sailing away. Her arm represents long- and short-term rates. The upper arm, anchored to her shoulder, represents long-term rates, and her hand represents short-term rates.

The expectations theory explains all the varieties of yield curves. If future short-term rates are expected to be less than the long rate (which equals an average of the short rates), then the long rate will lie below the short rate. And conversely, if rates are expected to be higher in the future, short rates will lie below the long rate.

Inflation is taken into account in this theory in that inflationary expectations influence the expected future interest rates. Irving Fisher first set forth the argument that the nominal market rate of interest is composed of two parts, the *real rate* paid as a reward for forgoing present consumption, and *an inflation component* to compensate investors for the expected loss of purchasing power.*

Forward rates (the rate on a security of a stated maturity for a certain period in the future) are implied and determinable by simple algebra if the term structure is known. For example, if the 1-year rate is 6 percent yield to maturity and 7 percent is the yield to maturity for 2-year securities, the consensus forecast for yields 1 year hence for 1-year securities is 8 percent. The calculation is

$$R_F = \frac{(1 + R_2)^2}{(1 + R_1)} - 1$$

where R_F = forward rate for a 1-year maturity 1 year hence
R_2 = actual 1-year yield to maturity for a 2-year Treasury
R_1 = actual 1-year yield to maturity for a 1-year Treasury

For example,

$$R_F = \frac{(1 + 0.07)^2}{(1 + 0.06)} - 1 = 1.0801 - 1 = 0.0801, \text{ or } 8.01\%$$

Tests of the theory have been performed by numerous economists and academicians, including W. Braddock Hickman, Frederick R. Macaulay, David Meiselman, Malkiel, Edwar J. Kane, Frank De Leeuw, Franco

---

*I. Fisher, *Theory of Interest* (New York: Macmillan, 1930).

Modigliani, and Richard Sutch. Meiselman, in particular, is credited with devising a test that did not simply look for accurate forecasting, but rather allowed for the market's ability to correct forecasting errors as time elapses. The Modigliani and Sutch tests offer great support for the expectations theory.

The Liquidity-Preference or Biased Expectations Theory

The liquidity-preference or biased expectations theory holds that longer-term rates should enjoy a premium over short-term rates as compensation to the investor for the risk of greater price fluctuation in the event of an *unexpected* change in the level of rates. This contrasts with the expectations theory, which holds that long and short rates should be equal if no change is expected in future rates.

Liquidity in the sense used here implies both the ability to convert the bond into cash and being able to do so without appreciable loss or gain of principal. Thus, these theorists suggest that a premium is appropriate for long-term yields due to loss of liquidity.

The Institution or Market Segmentation Theory

Life insurance companies (issuers of annuities, endowment contracts, and guaranteed investment contracts), banks (issuers of long-term certificates of deposit), pensions funds, and other institutions attempt to match the duration of their liabilities (the payments to their customers) with their assets (their investments in Treasury bonds, and other investments) in order to immunize their risk from interest-rate fluctuations. As a result, their demand for investments is affected by considerations of matching assets and liabilities, and the maturities selected result from such pressures. This results, so the institution or market segmentation theory holds, in effective segmentation of maturities. At an extreme, theorists hold that certain investors would never purchase maturities outside their particular preferred range in order to take advantage of yield differentials. These theorists hold that yields are determined by supply and demand in two or more (long, and short or additional maturities) markets.

Summary

The three theories are not mutually exclusive. There is considerable support for holding that combinations of the theories are in fact the most accurate way of analyzing the term structure.

Innumerable books have been written on the subject of term structure, and countless research has been performed. For further reading on this subject, the following are suggested (see the Bibliography for full details): Van Horne (1978), Meiselman (1962); Malkiel (1970); and Chambers, Carleton, and Waldman (1984). Despite all the research, no generally accepted overall theory has yet been accepted. Nevertheless, the study of term structure is important to portfolio managers, corporate and public issuers of debt, as well as to the government officials who manage monetary and fiscal affairs.

Appendix 18.2: Derivation of Equation (18.4)

$$P_{1,1} = \frac{\$100(1+x)^{-1}}{2} + \frac{\$100(1+x)^{-1}}{2} = (\$50)(2)(1+x)^{-1} = \$100(1+x)^{-1} \quad (1)$$

$$P_{1,0} = \frac{\$100(1+y)^{-1}}{2} + \frac{\$100(1+y)^{-1}}{2} = (\$50)(2)(1+y)^{-1} = \$100(1+y)^{-1} \quad (2)$$

$$P_{0,0} = \frac{P_{1,1}(1+0.1)^{-1}}{2} + \frac{P_{1,0}(1+0.1)^{-1}}{2} \quad (3)$$

Substituting $P_{1,0}$ (2) and $P_{1,1}$ (1) in (3):

$$P_{0,0} = \frac{\$100(1+x)^{-1}(1.1)^{-1}}{2} + \frac{\$100(1+y)^{-1}(1.1)^{-1}}{2} \quad (4)$$

$$\frac{(2)(P_{0,0})}{\$100} = \frac{1}{(1+x)(1.1)} + \frac{1}{(1+y)(1.1)} \quad (5)$$

$$\frac{2(1.1)(P_{0,0})}{\$100} = \frac{1}{(1+x)} + \frac{1}{(1+y)} \quad (6)$$

From Table 18.3 we know the 2-year YTM is 11 percent. Therefore,

$$P_{0,0} = \$100(1+0.11)^{-2} \quad (7)$$

$$P_{0,0} = \$81.162 \quad (8)$$

Substituting (8) in (6), we find:

$$0.022(\$81.162) = \frac{1}{(1+x)} + \frac{1}{(1+y)} \quad (9)$$

$$1.78557(1+x)(1+y) = 1 + y + 1 + x \quad (10)$$

$$1.78557 (1 + x + y + xy) - 2 - x - y = 0 \quad (11)$$

$$1.78557 + 1.78557x + 1.78557y + 1.78557xy - 2 - x - y = 0 \quad (12)$$

$$1.78557xy + 0.78557x + 0.78557y - 0.21444 = 0 \quad (13)$$

Appendix 18.3: Volatility Test

The option pricing model is constructed such that, within the lattice or tree, each up and down movement of rates satisfies the term structure volatility for the particular year. The volatility test is

$$0.5 \ln \left(\frac{r_u}{r_d} \right)$$

where r_u = upper rate
r_d = downward or lower rate
ln = natural logarithm

It is intuitively next to impossible to understand why the above test is used. The derivation of the formula as a measure of volatility follows.

First, practitioners tend to use interest rates in the term structure which are continuously compounded, rather than compounded semiannually or at some other interval. The formula for *continuously compounded* interest is

$$S = Pe^{rt}$$

where S = accumulated sum at the expiration of time t
P = initial principal
e = approximately 2.71828 (the base of the natural logarithm system)
r = continuously compounded rate of interest
t = time in years

For example, an interest rate of 10 percent compounded annually is equivalent to a continuously compounded rate of only 9.531 percent.

If the initial node interest rate is r_0, then the rate increase or decrease are functions of the mean (m) and standard deviation from the mean (sd), as shown below:

$$r_0 \begin{cases} r_u = (r_0)\,(e^{m + \text{sd}}) \\ \\ r_d = (r_0)\,(e^{m - \text{sd}}) \end{cases}$$

$$r_u = r_0 e^{m + \text{sd}} \tag{1}$$

$$r_d = r_0 e^{m - \text{sd}} \tag{2}$$

Dividing (1) by (2) and canceling the r_0's produces

$$\frac{r_u}{r_d} = \frac{e^{m + sd}}{e^{m - sd}}$$

Taking the natural logarithm of both sides gives

$$\ln\left(\frac{r_u}{r_d}\right) = \ln\left(\frac{e^{m + sd}}{e^{m - sd}}\right) = \ln e^{m + \text{sd}} - \ln e^{m - \text{sd}} \tag{4}$$

And

$$\ln\left(\frac{r_u}{r_d}\right) = m + \text{sd} - (m - \text{sd}) = 2(\text{sd}) \tag{5}$$

$$\left(\frac{1}{2}\right)\ln\left(\frac{r_u}{r_d}\right) = \text{sd} \quad \text{i.e., volatility} \tag{6}$$

19

Zero-Coupon Bonds

Not since the go-go years of the late 1960s has the investment world been mesmerized by any development as it has by zero-coupon bonds. Since their introduction in 1982, some hundreds of billions in zero-coupon bonds have been originated and sold. "Zeros" have not only become the hottest new investment medium for tax-exempt investors, but they have also created new markets for U.S. Treasury securities, which are the foundation and backing for most zero-coupon bonds.

The advertisements for zeros present an enticing picture for investors:

- Quadruple your money in 11 years!
- Safety!
- Security!
- Tax-free income!
- Backed by U.S. Treasuries!
- Eliminate Reinvestment risk!
- Invest $33,000 now. Start earning $10,000 a year tax-free in 11½ years!

Are zeros the answer to everyone's investment dilemma? Definitely *not*. To invest successfully in zeros, timing is crucial.

Surprisingly, some of the most attractive and enticing aspects of zero-coupon bonds are not the features that are advertised. Three noteworthy examples of such features are:

1. The noncallable nature of most zero-coupon bonds. This feature alone can be worth its weight in gold to an investor who has bought fortuitously

in a period of near-peak interest rates. Just consider the value of being able to hold a bond yielding 15 percent for 30 years rather than being forced to surrender it for redemption after 5 years, and then being forced to reinvest the proceeds at a rate of 7 percent.

2. The possible use of zeros to increase a company's market value and earnings per share by reducing pension plan costs through "dedicating" zero-coupon bonds to match certain specified pension plan liabilities for benefits.

3. The possible benefit from the Federal Reserve policy of allowing up to 100 percent borrowing against the full market value of zeros; and the opportunity to make profits as high as 100 percent in a year, after taxes.

Zero-coupon bonds are an intriguing subject. They afford investors remarkable profit-making (or -losing) opportunities and special uses. On the other hand, there are major pitfalls and risks. There are indeed many complex issues with which investors owe it to themselves to be familiar. The result of unfamiliarity with such issues can be financially devastating.

What Zero-Coupon "Yield" Really Means

A zero-coupon bond is one which pays no periodic annual or semiannual income. Instead its holder receives only the maturity value, usually $1000, at the maturity date. Zero-coupon certificates of deposit are similar, except that they are issued by a bank or savings and loan and may be insured by the Federal Deposit Insurance Corporation (FDIC). Zero-coupon instruments may be taxable, such as those tied to Treasury bonds; or they may be partially tax-exempt, as are those issued by municipalities. And zeros may be short term or long term.

Consider a zero-coupon bond that is bought for $30.31, and that matures 30 years later for $1000. It is purchased to yield 12 percent (with semiannual compounding). Between the time of purchase and the time of maturity the investor receives not one penny, one yen, or one franc of interest. The theoretical or accreted value of the bond increases each 6 months by 6 percent over the ending balance of the previous period. The investor can sell the bond on the market prior to maturity but will receive only the accreted or theoretical value if interest rates in general and those for zeros in particular are at the same levels as they were at the time of original purchase. If interest rates have risen, the bond will sell for less than its accreted value; and if rates have fallen, it will bring more money than the accreted value. The accumulated sum of money at maturity for the zero is identical to that which would result from buying a par bond for $30.31 that pays $1.82 semiannually (6 percent of par semiannually), and that matures for the purchase price of $30.31. It is mandatory that the $1.82 semiannual interest be reinvested at 6 percent semiannually (nominally, 12 percent per year). If one purchases the $30.31 par bond and reinvests as stated, the financial effect is the same as buying the $30.31 zero which matures for $1000. In both cases the investor will have accumulated $1000 at maturity.

Thus the zero-coupon holder is "locked in" to a fixed interest reinvestment rate. Being locked in may be beneficial or harmful, depending on what happens to the level of interest rates in the future.

A formula has been established that relates the purchase price of a zero-coupon bond to the sum received at maturity. It is the often-stated equation for compound interest:

$$S = P (1 + i)^n$$

where S = maturity value
P = purchase price
i = annual interest rate
n = number of years until maturity

Example: Finding the YTM of a zero-coupon bond.   Zero Zalman acquires a zero-coupon bond for $1000, which matures for $17,449.40 in 30 years. What is the yield to maturity?

$$S = P (1 + i)^n$$

$$\$17,449.40 = \$1000(1 + i)^{30}$$

$$17.449 = (1 + i)^{30}$$

$$(17.449)^{1/30} = 1 + i$$

$$1.1 = 1 + i$$

$$i = 0.1 \text{ or } 10\%$$

This means that Mr. Zalman's $1000 will grow into $17,449.40 in 30 years at a compound interest rate of 10 percent. A compound interest rate requires that all earnings be reinvested. In the absence of reinvestment of earnings, there is nothing to compound. During the 30 years while the investment augments from $1000 to $17,449, the value of the investment is continuously increasing. The value at the end of the first year is 10 percent more than at the beginning; the value at the end of the second year is 10 percent more than at the end of the first year, etc. Although there is no cash flow to the investor from a zero-coupon bond, the nature of compounding is such that there is an "imputed cash flow" which is reinvested each year.

That "imputed cash flow" or "accretion" is the value increase each year. In the first year it is $100, in the second year it is $110, in the third year $121, and so forth.

Thus, the 10 percent YTM of Zalman's zero is comparable to *compound realized yield* and is the same as investing at a 10 percent YTM and reinvesting the cash flows at a 10 percent reinvestment rate; in other words, both the YTM and the revised YTM are the same—10 percent.

Although "Invest $57,000 and receive 1,000,000 in U.S.-backed Treasuries" may sound exciting, consider what it means. The investor must forget about the investment and not receive any cash flow for 30 years. The investor obtains a conventional 10 percent YTM and reinvests all "imputed cash flows" at a reinvestment rate of 10 percent. This may be well and good, or it may not, depending on market conditions.

If a person could buy a 30-year Treasury at a 12 percent YTM and on the same day is offered the above zero-coupon bond at 10 percent, he would certainly be wise to consider passing the zero, buying the Treasury, and taking his chances on whether he would be able to reinvest the cash flow from the conventional Treasury bond at rates averaging 10 percent.

Graphs for Quick Zero-Coupon Price–Yield Solutions

Figures 19.1 through 19.4 can be used to determine in seconds the YTM resulting from most zero-coupon bond investments. The figures assume a zero tax bracket, or a tax-exempt investor, and do not take into effect possible call provisions that could cause the bond to be retired prior to the stated maturity date.

Example: Finding yield to maturity for a zero-coupon bond. Roger Shafer, a stockbroker, calls a prospective investor, David Melin, an affluent elderly investor, with the following proposition:

Roger: "David, I've got a hot investment for you! It couldn't be safer; it's based on U.S. Treasury bonds, and what could be safer than the government? You simply invest $33,378 now and in 30 years you get back $1 million. That's almost 30 times or 3000 percent on your original investment. Shall I go ahead and buy?"

David: "Just a minute, please, Roger." Mr. Melin turns to Fig. 19.3. Let's see, he reasons, $1,000,000 at maturity divided by the purchase price of $33,378 is 29.96—let's say 30. So the proposed investment would multiply by about 30 times in 30 years. That would produce the same YTM as an increase from $1000 to $30,000 in 30 years. Mr. Melin draws a line horizontally across the graph starting from the $30,000 point on the left vertical axis, and draws a vertical line up until the $30,000 line is reached.

Value

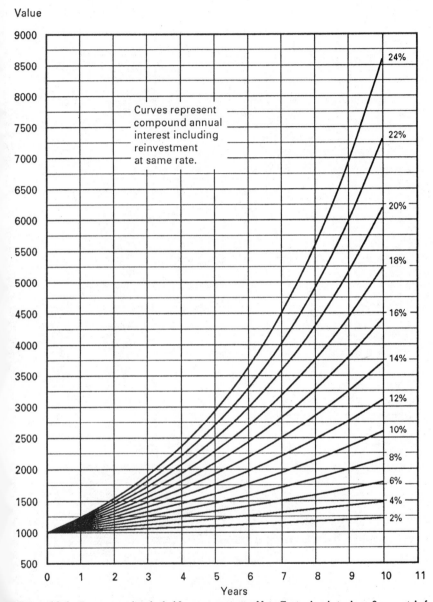

Curves represent compound annual interest including reinvestment at same rate.

Years

Figure 19.1. Zero-coupon bonds: 1–10 years to maturity. *Note:* For tax brackets above 0 percent, before using the graph, multiply the compound interest rate by (1 – tax bracket) and use the amount so determined in the graph. For example, tax bracket 50 percent, compound interest 20 percent, 0.20 (1 – 0.5) = 0.20(0.5) = 10%. Use the 10 percent curve.

Value

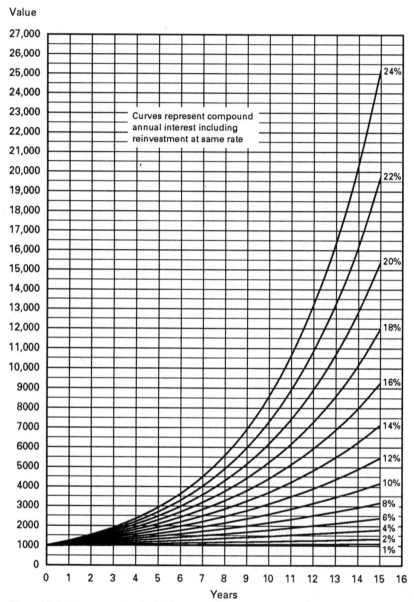

Figure 19.2. Zero-coupon bonds: 1–15 years to maturity. *Note:* For tax brackets above 0 percent, before using the graph, multiply the compound interest rate by (1 − tax bracket) and use the amount so determined as the curve in the graph. For example, tax bracket 30 percent, compound interest 10 percent, 0.10 × (1 − 0.3) = 0.10(0.7) = 7%. Use the 7 percent curve.

Value

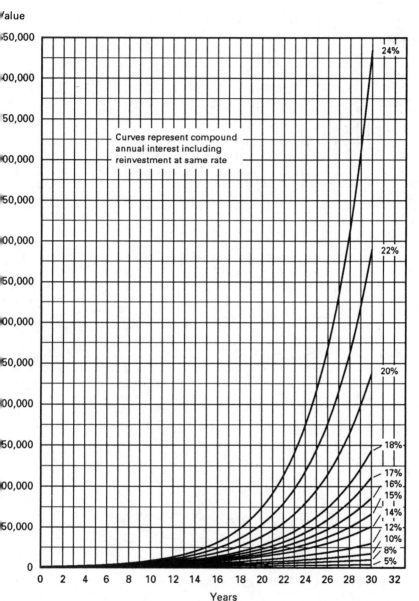

Figure 19.3. Zero-coupon bonds: 1–30 years to maturity. *Note:* For tax brackets above 0 percent, before using the graph, multiply the compound interest rate by (1 – tax bracket) and use the amount so determined as the curve in the graph. For example, tax bracket 50 percent, compound interest 20 percent, 0.20 × (1 – 0.5) = 0.20(0.5) = 10%. Use the 10 percent curve.

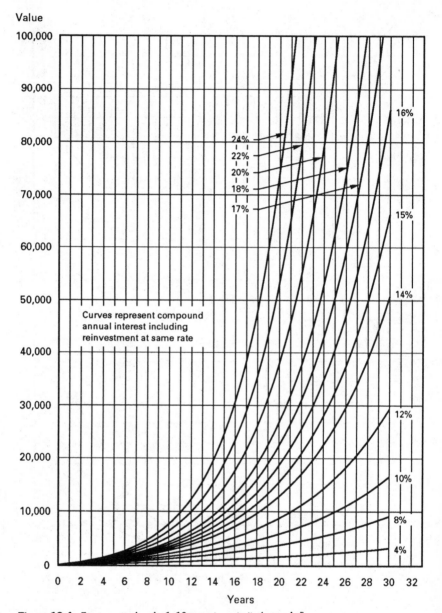

Figure 19.4. Zero-coupon bonds: 1–10 years to maturity (expanded).

The curve that passes through (or closest to) the junction or point of intersection of the two lines indicates the YTM. In this case, the YTM is about 12 percent. "Why should I invest at a 12 percent YTM," Mr. Melin says, "when much higher yields are currently available to me. No thanks, not today," he tells Roger.

The Theoretical Spot Rate Curve

Yields to maturity, at purchase, of a zero-coupon bond in some instances should be *higher* than the YTM of a conventional Treasury bond of the same maturity. For example, if a 20-year Treasury is selling at par to yield 12 percent, it is possible that a 20-year zero-coupon bond should sell at a price to yield 13 or 14 percent to maturity. Conversely, it is also possible that zero-coupon yields ought to be less than YTMs for comparable maturities of Treasury bonds. Confused? There is a relationship between the yield level at which zero-coupon bonds ought to sell and the YTM for comparable maturities of coupon-paying treasuries. The relationship, which depends principally on the shape of the T-bond yield curve, can be determined mathematically.

The YTM is an *average rate* in the sense that the same rate of YTM is applied to all cash flows from a particular bond, whether the first such cash flow due in 6 months or the last cash flow, which may be at maturity 30 years hence. Because the YTM applies the same discount rate to all future cash flows, it is inappropriate to use the YTM for valuing a zero-coupon instrument, where a single, unique maturity is involved. Just because the YTM of a 3-year conventional Treasury bond is 10 percent, this is no reason that a 3-year zero coupon bond should be sold to yield 10 percent. For the conventional bond, 10 percent may represent an average (geometric mean) or compilation of an 8 percent yield for the first coupon payment, 9 percent for the second coupon, and 11 percent for the third, or an almost infinite variety of other combinations. The relevant rate for a 3-year zero would be the 11 percent applicable to 3-year maturies (and not the 10 percent average YTM at which conventional 3-year bonds are priced). Thus a completely different yield curve (as compared to the traditional Treasury bond curve) is required for zero-coupon issues. The necessary curve is the *spot rate yield curve*.

It is possible to construct an entire spot rate yield curve from the conventional Treasury bond price–yield curve. The Treasury bond price/yield quotations at a random date have been plotted and the curve thus formed makes up the Treasury bond yield curve, as shown in Fig. 19.5. Such a yield curve has historically been *the benchmark of value in the fixed-income markets*, against which all other yields are measured and

Percent yield to maturity

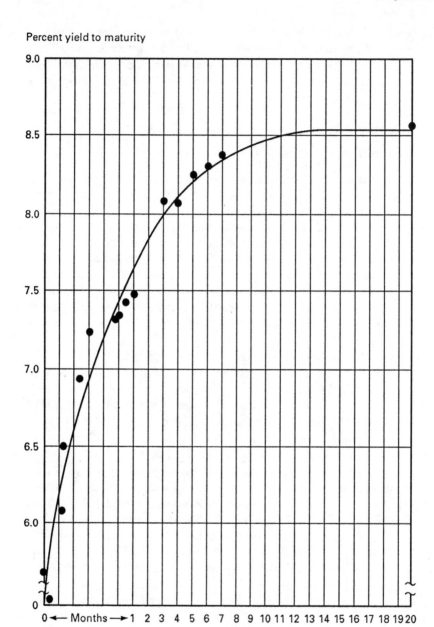

Figure 19.5. Yield curve for U.S. Treasury securities—bills, notes, and bonds. Dots represent observed yields; yield curve is fitted to them.

compared. The broad, liquid, and well-understood conventional Treasury bond market, in effect, serves as the basis for the determination of appropriate yields for zero-coupon instruments.

Derivation of the Spot Rate

The spot rate for any year is the YTM of a zero-coupon security with a maturity in that year. Spot rates may be derived from an initial T-bill (pure discount security) of 1 year or less until maturity, and appropriately chosen conventional Treasury bonds for the other maturities in the term structure. Care must be taken to avoid such issues as flower bonds (redeemable at par in the estate of a decedent) as well as callable issues. The following formula gives the *spot rate* for any time period (where previous periods spot rates are known):

$$y_n = \left(\frac{(R/m) + \$1000}{P_n - \left\{ (R/m) \sum_{k=1}^{n=1} \left[1/(1 + y_k)^k \right] \right\}} \right)^{1/k} - 1$$

where k = counter for each coupon payment or time interval; if semiannual, $k = 1$ for the first 6 months, $k = 2$ for the second 6 months, $k = 3$ for the third 6 months, etc. If the bond has 10 time periods until maturity, and one is finding the spot rate for the fifth period, then k equals 5.

$\quad y_n$ = spot rate for a bond maturing in n time periods.

$\quad m$ = number of coupon payments per year (frequency of compounding per year)

$\quad n$ = number of periods until each maturity; e.g., for 10-year maturity $n = 20$ with semiannual interest

$\dfrac{n}{m}$ = years until maturity

$\quad y_n$ = spot rate per period at time interval n

$(y_n)\,(m)$ = annualized spot rate at time interval n

$\quad R$ = annual interest (annual coupon) (e.g., \$100)

$\dfrac{R}{m}$ = coupon payment per period (e.g., \$50 if semiannual)

$\quad P_n$ = current price of a Treasury bond with n periods until maturity to yield YTM_n at period n (the value of P_n is calculated using the normal equation for finding the price of a bond where its YTM is known; however, the prices of T-bonds are readily available); this is the link between the spot rate and the T-bond yield curve; the T-bond price for each maturity is taken from the T-bond yield curve.

Example: A 3-year T-bond has an annual coupon of $82.50 and is priced at $993.61 to yield 8.50 percent to maturity. Find the spot rate at the end of 3 years, where the 1-year bill rate and the 2-year spot rate are as follows:

Annual Coupon	Period	T-bill YTM %	T-bond YTM %	Bill/bond price	Spot rate %	$(1+y_k)^k$	$\dfrac{1}{(1+y_k)^k}$
0	1	8.00			8.00	1.08000	0.92593
8.25	2		8.25	$1000.00	8.26	1.17200	0.85324
8.25	3		8.50	993.61	?		
						Total	1.77917

$$y_3 = \left(\frac{(\$82.5/1) + \$1000}{\$993.61 - \left\{ (\$82.5/1) \displaystyle\sum_{k=1}^{3-1} \left[1/(1+y_k)^k \right] \right\}} \right)^{1/3} - 1$$

$$= 1.085285 - 1 = 8.5285\%$$

Thus, the 3-year spot rate is 8.5285 percent. In similar fashion, working one year at a time, the spot rates for the entire term structure can be found. A comparable calculation is required to determine each spot rate for each period. Thus, to construct the theoretical spot rate curve, with semiannual interest, going out to 30 years, 60 such calculations will be necessary. The software, COMPLETE BOND ANALYZER (published by the author) calculates in seconds the entire spot rate (generally referred to as *the term structure of interest rates*). Comparison of the spot rates thus determined to the actual rates at which zero-coupon bonds are being offered allows one immediately *to spot under- and overvalued offerings.*

The Link among YTM, Zero Spot Rates, and Forward Rates

The yield curve comprised of yields to maturity of bonds of various maturities serves as the basis from which the theoretical spot rate curve is determined, as has been demonstrated earlier in this chapter. The zero-coupon rates thus determined are the theoretical rates applicable to a zero-coupon bond with a given maturity—for example, the zero theoretical spot rate for a 20-year maturity.

From the theoretical zero-coupon rates thus determined, a new set of rates, *forward rates*, can be calculated. A 1-year forward rate might be, for example, the 1-year rate applicable 10 years from now and would apply to a transaction commencing in 10 years and ending 1 year thereafter.

Table 19.1 shows for a coupon bond the linkage between YTM, theoretical zero spot rates, and 1-year forward rates. The 3-year bond is priced at $993.610 to yield 8.5 percent to maturity (with annual interest payments of $82.50). The price of $993.610 was determined by the usual method of finding YTM. However, once spot rates and forward rates have been determined, either may be used to also calculate the value of this bond. The present value using the theoretical zero spot rates is shown in column(d). And the value of the bond is also calculated using the 1-year forward rates as shown in column(n). Regardless of the basis of the calculation, whether YTM, theoretical zero spot rates, or 1-year forward rates, the result is the same $993.610 value for the bond.

The "theoretical" spot rate curve depicts the yields that should be effective for varying maturities of zero coupon issues. *The theoretical curve is based on the premise that the value of a bond should be the same regardless of whether one owns it in the conventional manner (i.e., with all interest coupons attached) or whether one owns all the parts of a "stripped" bond.* The premise is that the whole (conventional bond) is worth no more and no less than the sum of its parts (after conversion to a series of zero-coupon issues). If actual STRIPS or other zero-coupon Treasuries, as quoted in the marketplace, differ from the corresponding theoretical spot rate, arbitrage possibilities are created. Variations between actual zero prices and theoretical spot rates are due to such factors as the fact that zero-coupon liquidity is less than that of Treasuries, and tax advantages or disadvantages may affect investor preferences for zeros.

Yield Curve Slope

Let us now consider an *upward-sloping* yield curve and then a *downward-sloping* curve. For the hypothetical upward-sloping curve, we start with a 1-year Treasury bill yield of 8 percent, with yields increasing at the rate of 0.25 percent for each subsequent year, until in the twentieth year the yield is 12.75 percent. Applying the spot rates to the cash flows of the 20-year par bond results in a correct determination of its par price. The theoretical spot rates range from a low of 8 percent to a high of 22.8 percent for this conventional bond, priced at a 12.75 percent yield to maturity. This illustrates that with an upward-sloping yield curve it is appropriate that spot rate yields (and YTMs) for zero-coupon bonds are *higher* than for those of conventional bonds with the same maturity.

Table 19.1. Link among YTM, Theoretical Spot Rates, and 1-Year Spot Rates

Three-year bond, priced at $993.610 to yield 8.500% percent (paid annually)
Coupon $82.50 per year

(a) Year, n	(b) Cash flow	(c) Zero spot rate, %	(d) Present value at spot rate	(e) Conventional bond YTM	(f) Conventional modified duration	(g) Value	(h) Change in value	(i) Marginal return	(j) Geometric mean calculation	(k)	(l) One year forward, %	(m) Future value factor at spot rates	(n) Present value discounted at forward rates
1	$ 82.5	8.0000	$ 76.389	8.00	0.926	$ 995.7355	$2.12545	0.0851697	1.02762			$1.08000	$ 76.3889
2	82.5	8.2600	70.391	8.25	1.777	997.8654	2.13000	0.0849925	1.02756	1.05595	8.5206	1.17202	70.3911
3	1082.5	8.5285	846.831	8.50	2.554	1,000.0000	2.13455	0.0848156	1.02751	1.08499	9.0675	1.27830	846.8305
Total			$993.61054				$6.39000			8.499%			$993.6105

Notes:

1. Spot rates source: COMPLETE BOND ANALYZER, Larry Rosen Co., 1986–1994.
2. Column (d): for year 2, (82.5) $(1 + 0.0826)^{-2}$.
3. Column (e): conventioal bond YTM is from the T-bond yield curve.
4. Column (f): Source: COMPLETE BOND ANALYZER.
5. Column (g): for year 2, value is ($995.7355 + $2.13).
6. Column (h): for year 2, change in value is $[9($1000/$995.610)^{1/3} - 1]$ ($995.7355).
7. Column (i): for year 2, marginal reutrn is ($2.13 + $82.5)/$995.7355.
8. Column (j):for year 2, $(1 + 0.0849925)^{1/3}$.
9. Column (k): for year 2, (1.02762)(1.02756).
10. Column (l): for year 2, $[(1 + 0.0826)^2/(1 + 0.0800)^1] - 1$.
11. Column (m): for year 2, (1 + 0.085206)(1.08000).
12. Column (n): for year 2, (82.5)/(1.17202).

It is frequently stated that a zero should sell at a YTM commensurate with a Treasury of the same *duration* (as opposed to maturity). This does *not* appear to be well founded. For example, the 7-year zero (with a duration of 7) should be priced at bout 9.72 percent, the spot rate. A Treasury with similarly duration has a 15-year maturity (modified duration, 6.997), which is priced at 11.50 percent YTM. With an *upward-sloping* yield curve, the more distant the maturity of the zero-coupon bond, the *higher* (as compared to Treasury bonds of the same maturity) the zero coupon bond's yield should be.

With a *downward-sloping* yield curve, the more distant the maturity of the zero coupon bond, the *less* its yield should be as compared to Treasury bonds of the same maturity.

Buying or Selling Zeros

When trading a zero-coupon bond, first consider the number of years until maturity and compare the quoted zero YTM to that of a Treasury bond of the same duration. Such comparison may show the yield of the zero security to be either above or below that of the Treasury. Either may be fair, as discussed previously. Second, make a rough sketch of the Treasury bond yield curve. If it is upward sloping, then you know that the YTM of the zero should be *higher* than that of a Treasury bond of the same maturity. If the yield curve is downward sloping, then the YTM of the zero should be *less* than that of the Treasury bond of the same maturity.

Above all, don't judge the reasonableness of price and yield by what you see on the New York Stock Exchange (NYSE). An extraordinary aspect of the zero-coupon pricing situation involves certain zero-coupon bonds in the form of CATS (Certificates of Accrual on Treasury Securities) that are listed and traded on the NYSE. The trading activity on the exchange has taken place at incredibly high prices and amazingly low yields.

The simple guidelines just expressed will help, but they are not a panacea because the rules of thumb do not indicate how much higher or how much lower the YTM of the zero should be compared to the Treasury bond of the same maturity. An accurate determination of the YTM at which the zero security should be purchased (the spot rate) may be accomplished by the method described previously, or by a computer program, such as the COMPLETE BOND ANALYZER.

Another safeguard before trading a zero is to check at least three active dealers, including a bank, to obtain competitive quotes. This is no guarantee that all three are not mischarging, but it is certainly better than not checking the market thoroughly.

Munis Are Not Tax-Exempt!

Contrary to conventional wisdom, tax-exempt municipals (munis) are *not* wholly tax exempt. Such bonds are exempt from the federal income tax on interest; but their owners may be subject to state tax on interest (from out-of-state issuers) and are subject to the federal capital gains or income tax upon sale, as well as gift and estate taxes. In addition, ownership of tax exempts may trigger the taxability of otherwise untaxable benefits from Social Security. Other municipals whose interest may be subject to federal income tax include certain federally guaranteed munis, mortgage revenue bonds, arbitrage bonds, and private activity bonds. And certain munis may cause the holder to be subject to the alternative minimum tax (AMT). For definitive tax information, readers are advised to obtain the free publications of the IRS, *Investment Income and Expenses*, Publication 550, as well as *List of Original Issue Discount Instruments*, Publication 1212.

Original issue discount (OID) is the difference between the redemption price of a bond (say, $1000) and the *issue price* (say, $100, for a zero-coupon bond). The OID in this case is $900, that is, $1000 less $100.*

Generally, municipal bond interest receipts are not taxed, nor is the accrual of interest, as in the case of a zero-coupon municipal to the extent of the OID. The interest accrued (by either the straight-line or the YTM method depending on dates of issuance or acquisition involved) is added to the purchase price to obtain the "tax-adjusted basis" of the bond. Thus the accrual, by increasing the tax basis, reduces the taxable capital gain upon sale or redemption.

Market Discount on Taxable OIDs

Market discount (MD) is the excess of the redemption price of a bond at maturity over the investor's original *cost* basis. If a market discount bond also has OID, the market discount is the sum of the bond's issue price plus the total OID includable in the gross income of all prior holders (before the current purchase by an investor) less the current investor's cost basis.

A gain from bonds issued after July 18, 1984, attributable to market discount is includable in gross income to the extent of bond's *accrued market discount*. The balance of the gain (in excess of accrued market discount) is taxable if the bond is a capital asset.† Accrued market discount

---

*See IRS publications 550 and 1212 regarding taxability of zeros and OID. See also the following discussion "Market Discount on Taxable OIDs."

†The gain may be taxed as ordinary income or capital gain depending on when the bond was issued and when it was purchased.

may be found by either a straight-line method or by a constant interest method. Historically, if one bought a taxable "discount" bond (bought for, let's say, $700, originally issued at par of $1000) in the secondary market (other than at the original issuance), the interest received during the year was taxable as ordinary income and a gain at redemption or earlier sale was a *capital gain*, long or short term depending on the holding period. After-tax yields were based on application of ordinary rates to the periodic interest and usually long-term capital gain rates to the gain upon disposition. No more! The Deficit Reduction Act of 1984 quietly changed the rules of the game, and *amazingly few people seem to be aware of the changes.*

For market discount bonds issued after July 18, 1984, or purchased after April 30, 1993, taxpayers (except certain non-U.S. citizen residents) are required on disposition to report as *ordinary income* any accrued part of the gain, up to the amount of any *market discount* on the obligation (that accrued while the taxpayer held the obligation). The market discount rules do not apply to obligations maturing within a year, municipal bonds, purchased before May 1, 1993, installment-sale obligations, and U.S. Savings Bonds. And the market discount is considered to be zero and is disregarded if the market discount is less than $\frac{1}{4}$ of 1 percent of the redemption price times the number of years to maturity.

Taxpayers are permitted to calculate the accrued market discount on a compound interest basis ("scientific yield," yield to maturity, or internal rate of return) instead of straight-line basis. Normally, the taxpayer will *benefit by electing the compound interest method* (YTM or IRR), because the calculated accrued market discount will be less than with straight line.

Check out the tax consequences of proposed investments carefully before investing, and consult your tax advisor. Remember, its the after-tax (not the pretax) yield to maturity that matters.

Immunization, Dedication, and Pension Plans

Pension plans, life insurance annuity policies (that pay a benefit for one or more persons lives), and other insurers have in common the problem of having to pay a fixed, determinable or estimatable benefit in the future. In the case of a pension plan, it is the payment of monthly income for life or as provided in the pension plan. Managers of pension plans, insurance assets, etc., have the problem of meeting those future liabilities by investing their assets in a manner which will produce enough cash flow (at as low a cost to the sponsor or corporation as possible while maintaining a sensible level of risk).

The cash flows of a bond investment portfolio consist of interest, redemptions of bonds at maturity, and the interest on interest earned from reinvestment. With normal coupon bond investments, the interest-on-interest proceeds in the future are unpredictable, because the rate at which future reinvestment will occur is unknown.

Zero-coupon bond investment provides a valuable tool for portfolio management by "locking in" a reinvestment rate and eliminating that unpredictable element in managing pension plan assets.

Immunization

Immunization is the term that applies to the attempt to insulate or "immunize" a bond portfolio from the risks of interest-rate fluctuation. As just mentioned the primary risk is that of the rate to be earned on reinvestment. Zero-coupon bonds do a magnificent job of immunizing.

Another technique which preceded the availability of zero-coupon bonds involves the concept of duration, discussed earlier. The three elements of total return from a bond, if one reinvests the income, are coupon interest, interest on interest from reinvesting, and maturity value. Let's say that as a pension plan manager you plan to meet a $1 million liability in x years with $600,000 in bonds, with a coupon annually of $70,000 and interest on interest from reinvesting at a 9 percent rate. The first step is to match the average durations of the assets and liabilities. If the bonds are selected so that the portfolio also has an average duration of x years, and the portfolio is continuously adjusted to maintain that duration, then it should be possible to wind up with the targeted $1 million, no matter what happens to interest rates in the interim. If the durations are equal, should interest rates decline, then capital gains from the bond portfolio will offset the reduced interest on interest from reinvesting. And should rates rise, then the capital losses from the bond portfolio will be offset by the higher rate earned on reinvestment.

The mathematics involved is such that it may be impossible to immunize a portfolio for as long a time period as desired. As noted earlier, the duration (except for zero-coupon bonds) is shorter than the bond's term to maturity. Zero-coupon bonds offer a simple solution because their duration is equal to their maturity; hence a 30-year zero-coupon bond has a duration of 30 as well.

Dedication of Pension Assets

A variant of immunizing a portfolio is the concept of *dedication*. The objective of dedication is to raise the actuarial funding rate assumption used. A higher rate allows reduction or elimination of contributions to the plan by the plan sponsor. Alternatively, unfunded pension liabilities may be funded, or benefit levels increased. To accomplish this objective, certain fund liabilities such as those of already retired persons are determined actuarially. Then an immunized bond portfolio is structured to provide the cash flows that will be needed to fully meet such future liabilities. As compared to the actuarial assumed rate (e.g., 7 percent) used for a certain pension plan, it may be that the yield is much higher (say, 13 percent) on this particular portfolio dedicated to meeting the specified liabilities. Discounting the future liabilities at 13 percent (with the actuaries' consent) instead of 7 percent will produce a materially smaller present liability. In other words, certain of the pension plans assets are "dedicated" to meeting a specified portion of the plan's liabilities.

Again, zero-coupon bonds lend themselves beautifully to this concept, because of the ability to lock in the rate at which reinvestment will occur. With any other bond, an actuary is not likely to agree to a reinvestment rate assumption of 13 or 14 percent. But if the high rate is locked in with a zero-coupon bond, what choice does the actuary have? The actuary's agreement to the high rate locked in by the zero means that the pension plan needs less money and management can make a lower contribution, and have higher income, higher earnings per share, and a higher market price.

Volatility

The lower the coupon rate of a bond, the greater is the change in the bond price that takes place from a given change in YTM. And coupon rates do not get any lower than with a zero-coupon bond. Thus, other things being equal, zero-coupon bonds are the *most volatile* of all bonds (except for perpetuals). Prices will fluctuate more with zeros, when interest rates change, than with any other type of bond. This can be a blessing; or it can be disastrous. Investors who think they have spotted a yield peak in the market may intentionally buy zeros to maximize capital gain potential, when and if yields decline as expected. On the other hands, investors who wish to avoid substantial changes in the value of their assets may wish to shun zeros altogether.

20

Internal Rate of Return, Capital Budgeting, Net Present Value, and Pretax IRR for Stocks

Internal Rate of Return

If you are going to make intelligent, savvy, and logical investment decisions, it is essential to look at the big picture. If you were going to buy a video recorder, you wouldn't buy it just because the case was your favorite color, would you? And if you needed a new car, you would want to consider more than just the passenger capacity. Obviously, there are a number of criteria in either case that you would want to check out and analyze before making a decision.

Investments are no different. Some of the factors that need to be considered in the case of an investment in a common stock include:

Expected growth rate

Price at the time of purchase

Expected sale price

Cash return from dividends while the investment is held

In the final analysis, the only thing that matters is what you get back in return, and what you get back usually consists of three benefits:

1. *Periodic income.* Cash receipts, either monthly, annually, or quarterly, in the form of dividends, interest, or rents.

2. *Sales proceeds.* The amount of money you expect to receive when the investment is eventually sold.

3. *Tax benefits or cost.* Both the periodic income and the sales proceeds need to be adjusted for the cost of taxes. In some cases of tax-favored investments, there may be tax savings in some years to take into consideration. For example, in a given year, the investment may produce tax deductions that exceed the revenues—in other words, a net tax loss. If such is the case, then the reduced income taxes that you pay in that year are equivalent to cash received, just as if you had received it in the form of tax-free interest from a municipal bond.

For example, Tommy Taxed is in 50 percent tax bracket (including federal, state, and local income taxes), and his investment in widgets produces a net loss of $10,000 for the year. If the loss can be included on Tommy's personal income tax return, this deductible loss of $10,000 will result in his paying $5000 less in income taxes for the year. The deductible loss of $10,000 times the tax rate of 50 percent equals the tax savings. Tommy's $5000 tax savings is equivalent to his receiving $5000 in tax-free income: Tommy has $5000 more after taxes to spend in that year as the result of the investment. But beware of the possibility that the deductions that make a tax loss possible will come back to haunt the investor in a future year. More about that later.

The elements of investment decision making are not very complicated. There are only four basic considerations: the cash investment, the periodic cash flow, the proceeds from sale, and the adjustment for taxes. However, complications arise in making the assumptions and judgments necessary to obtain the cash flow projections.

Example: Choosing between investment alternatives. Beulah Berich has $10,000 to invest, and she is offered two alternatives.

Alternative 1: A high-quality corporate bond which she can buy for $9000 that matures in 20 years for $10,000. It pays annual interest of $1400.

Alternative 2: Nine hundred shares of a high-quality electric utility common stock that Beulah can buy at $10 per share for a total investment of $9000. The utility presently pays a dividend of $1000 ($1.11 per share) per year. Buelah checks with various sources and concludes that it is likely that the dividend will increase at 5 percent per year. When she sells the stock in 20 years, the value will have increased at the same 5 percent per year that the dividend is expected to increase.

How should Beulah compare these two alternatives to decide which is the better choice? Let's make a comparison chart of what we know about the two alternatives:

Criteria	The bond	The stock
Amount invested	$9,000	$9,000
Periodic, annual income (initially)	$1,400	$1,000
Current yield (annual income ÷ amount invested)	15.56%	11.11%
Income 5 years hence	$1,400	$1,276
Current yield in 5 years	15.56%	14.18%
Number of years investment is expected to be held	20	20
Proceeds of sale at end of 20 years	$10,000	$23,880

Which is the better investment? The bond provides more current income, but the stock, based on appreciation at 5 percent per year, should produce higher sales proceeds 20 years from now. The annual income from the bond, though higher than that of the stock, does not change. The annual income from the stock should increase periodically.

Which is the better investment is not an easy question to answer unless Beulah Berich has the right tools at hand to help her. This book is her tool. When she has completed the book, she will be able to determine the answer in seconds—and without using much math. Certainly, she will not need to use any math that is any more complicated than that used by a high school student.

The determination of the answer is based on the principle that *the value of any investment is the sum of the present values of the future cash flows from that investment.* However, we know that a sum of money—say, $10,000— that is due to be received at some time in the future is not worth as much as $10,000 received today. Why? Because the $10,000 received today can be invested to produce more money over the years. The $10,000 to be received in the future cannot be invested until it is received. Therefore, the future cash flows must be reduced in value by a *discount factor*, like a negative interest rate, to compare them to money that is in hand today.

A Magic Number

If only there were some *magic number*, an interest rate that could be used to make the initial investment, $9000 in the above example, equal to the future cash flows from that investment (the periodic annual income and the sales proceeds). That magic number would be applied to each of the periodic cash flows and future sales proceeds, and after doing so, the sum would equal the initial investment. Then whichever investment alternative had the higher magic number would be the better investment. Or a series of possible investments could all be ranked by magic number. The magic number would tell us what the true rate of return actually would be from each alternative investment.

Happily there is a magic number. Sometimes it is called *yield to maturity* (YTM) in the case of a bond, or in the case of real estate investments it may be called *internal rate of return* (IRR). We use both terms: IRR and YTM have the same meaning. This book, in many cases, allows investors to determine YTM or IRR in seconds, by using graphs produced by the author's computer software, INVESTMENT IRR ANALYSIS (AFTER TAX) FOR STOCKS, BONDS, AND REAL ESTATE (Larry Rosen Co., copyright 1990).

To return to Beulah Berich's two alternative investments, the stock is the better investment, as can be seen in Fig 20.1. Enter the graph on the vertical axis at 11.11 percent (the initial yield); proceed horizontally to the 5 percent curve (representing the 5 percent annual increase in both the dividend and market value); then descend to the bottom axis, where the graph shows the magic number or IRR to be 16+ percent.

For the bond, refer to Fig. 20.2, which provides the magic number. Enter the graph on the vertical axis at the purchase price of one bond, $900. (Note: 10 bonds were purchased at $900 each, for a total investment of $9000.) Proceed horizontally to the 14 percent curve (which represents the $140 annual interest revenue divided by the $1000 maturity value of the bond); then move vertically to the bottom axis, where the YTM is shown to be about 15.65 percent.

That's all there is to it!

A Little Interest Makes a Big Difference

The difference between 15.65 percent in the case of Beulah's bond and 16 percent in the case of the stock may not sound like much. Consider, however, that if one invests $9000 today and earns 15.65 percent compound annual interest, at the end of 20 years the account will be worth $164,875. The same investment at 16 percent would be worth $175,147. The difference, $10,272, is more than the entire initial $9000 investment—from just 35/100 of 1 percent per year.

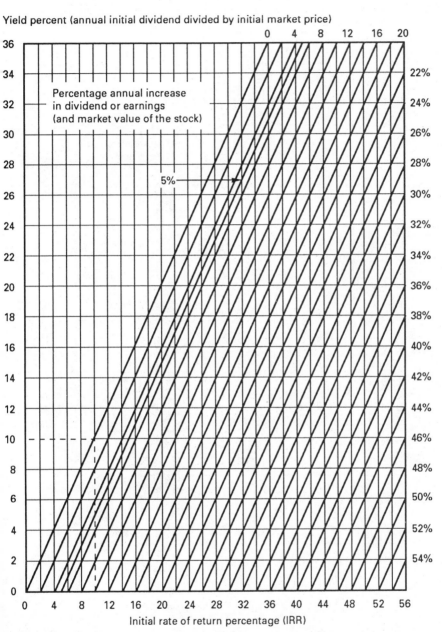

Figure 20.1. Stocks: before-tax internal rate of return (holding period 0–100 years). (*Source: INVESTMENT IRR ANALYSIS (AFTER TAX) FOR STOCKS, BONDS, AND REAL ESTATE, Larry Rosen Co., 1990*).

Purchase price

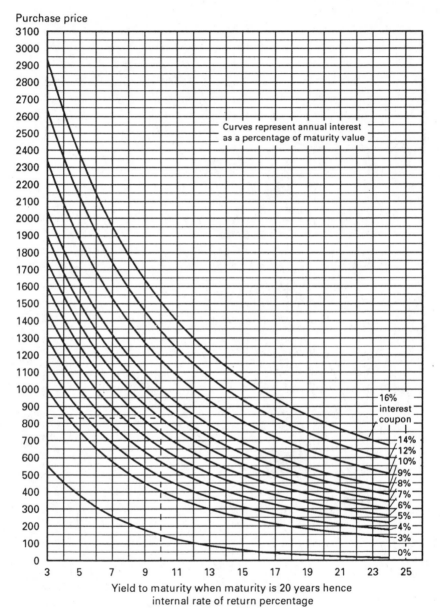

Yield to maturity when maturity is 20 years hence
internal rate of return percentage

Figure 20.2. Bond yield to maturity: 20 years. (*Source: INVESTMENT IRR ANALYSIS (AFTER TAX) FOR STOCKS, BONDS, AND REAL ESTATE, Larry Rosen Co., 1990.*)

The moral of this story is that when it comes to interest rates, and internal rates of return in particular, a molehill can become a mountain. Every little bit counts.

As we continue, we shall see how all forms of investment—stocks, bonds, real estate, company investments in new machinery, and the like—may be evaluated using IRR as the yardstick for comparison. First, let's look at business decision making, referred to as "capital budgeting."

Capital Budgeting

A businessman has proposed to him by his staff two alternative courses of action.

Proposal 1. Proposal 1 requires a capital investment of $100,000. The estimated economic life of the project is 5 years, and the estimated revenues for the 5-year economic life are as follows:

Year	Estimated revenues
1	0
2	$ 10,000
3	10,000
4	50,000
5	60,000
Total	$130,000

The revenues forecasted are net, after expenses, taxes, and so on—and the businessman has investigated the underlying assumptions, which he believes to be accurate. The capital assets acquired with the $100,000 original investment are assumed to be worthless at the end of the 5-year economic life. If there were a salvage or residual value, it would be included in the fifth (last) year's estimated revenues.

Proposal 2. The capital investment required for proposal 2 is also $100,000, and revenues are forecasted to be

Year	Estimated revenues
1	$ 40,000
2	20,000
3	20,000
4	20,000
5	20,000
Total	$120,000

Net Present Value and Discounted Cash Flow

The businessman's financial limitations are such that he must choose between the two proposals. He decides that he will select the one that offers the best return on investment during the estimated 5-year life. Which proposal should he choose?

In both cases, it is necessary to determine what the future revenues are worth today based on discounting such revenues back from the date they occur to the present at an appropriate interest rate. This is called the *present value*. The interest rate selected should be at least what the company could obtain by investing its funds elsewhere. This discount or interest rate is referred to by such designations as minimum attractive rate of return, *cutoff rate, hurdle rate, marginal growth rate,* rate of return, or *cost of capital.*

Let's assume that 10 percent per year is the rate selected. Many users of net present value prefer to discount at a rate equal to the company's cost of capital.

Net Present Value

Our businessman calculates the net present value of the two alternatives from the formula,

$$\text{NPV} = a(1 + i)^{-n} + b(1 + i)^{-n_1} + \cdots - I$$

where NPV = net present value
$\quad I$ = initial investment
$\quad a$ = first cash flow, due n years from now
$\quad b$ = next cash flow, due n_1 years from now
$\quad i$ = annual cost of capital
$\quad n$ = time in years until cash flow a
$\quad n_1$ = time in years until cash flow b, etc.

Proposal 1: $\text{NPV} = a(1 + i)^{-n} + b(1 + i)^{-n_1} + \cdots - I$

$\qquad\qquad = \$10,000(1.1)^{-2} + \$10,000(1.1)^{-3} + \$50,000\,(1.1)^{-4}$
$\qquad\qquad\quad + \$60,000(1.1)^{-5} - \$100,000$

$\qquad\qquad = \$8,264 + \$7,513 + \$34,151 + \$37,653 - \$100,000$
$\qquad\qquad = -\$12,817$

Proposal 2: $\qquad = \$40,000(1.1)^{-1} + \$20,000(1.1)^{-2} + \$20,000(1.1)^{-3}$
$\qquad\qquad\quad + \$20,000(1.1)^{-4} + \$20,000(1.1)^{-5} - \$100,000$

$\qquad\qquad = \$36,364 + \$16,259 + \$15,026 + \$13,660 + \$12,418$
$\qquad\qquad\quad - \$100,000 = -\$6003$

The calculations indicate that at a 10 percent discount rate, the NPVs of both proposals are *negative*. Since the NPV is the present value of the cash flows less the initial investment, neither proposal should be selected, because the present value of the future revenue in both cases is less than the $100,000 initial investment. In other words, the investment return is less than the 10 percent discount factor used to determine NPV.

Proposal 2 affords the businessman the prospect of about $6800 more in present value of future income, even though proposal 1 would produce more total cash over the entire 5-year period.

This type of analysis is commonly known as the *net present value* or *discounted cash flow* method of investment analysis. It illustrates a key element in decision making with respect to investments: that it is important to consider both the *amount* of money one expects to earn as well as when one will receive it.

The present value of proposal 1 is $87,183 when the discount rate is 10 percent, and the NPV is ($12,816.44). But using NPV can be very confusing. Why use 10 percent as the discount rate? What if a different discount rate is chosen? The NPV analysis does show that proposal 2 is better than proposal 1. How much better is it? The difference between $87,183 and $93,997, if money is worth 10 percent.

The curves in Fig. 20.3 show the NPVs of proposal 1 and proposal 2. A number of important points can be seen by looking at this figure. First, at a 10 percent cost of capital, it is apparent that proposal 2's NPV (NPV$_2$ in Fig. 20.3) is better than proposal 1's (NPV$_1$ in the figure). Second, at about a 5 percent cost of capital the curves of proposal 1 and proposal 2 cross each other. The cost of capital rate at which this occurs is called, aptly, the *crossover rate*. By inspection, it is evident that, at rates below the crossover rate, the situation reverses and the NPV of proposal 1 is higher than that of proposal 2.

NPV and IRR

However, wouldn't it be much better if we could simply analyze the two proposals in terms of some common denominator? The magic number concept, or IRR, provides a unique answer, and is equally applicable in this type of situation. In this case, the IRR is the compound interest rate which will equate the initial cash outflow of $100,000 to the future cash inflows in years 1 through 5. In other words, it is the true rate of return on the money invested.

Again, refer to Fig. 20.3. The IRR for each proposal is the rate which equates the present values of the cash flows to the initial $100,000 investment. In other terms, it is the *rate where the net present value is zero*. For

Net present and present value (000's of $)

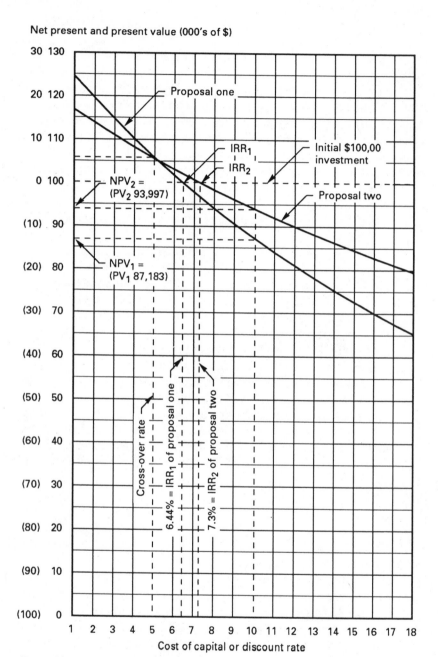

Figure 20.3. NPV at various costs at capital.

each proposal, it is the rate where the NPV curve crosses the $100,000 initial investment line. The IRRs for each proposal are shown in the figure as IRR$_1$ and IRR$_2$.

The IRR for proposal 1 is 6.44 percent, and for proposal 2 it is 7.3 percent. Besides telling us that proposal 2 is superior to proposal 1, the IRR also reveals the true earnings percentage for each proposal. (In this example, one should really be asking, if the rate of return on both proposals is so low, should I be making this investment at all?)

The magic number, IRR, allows one to compare alternate proposals or to compare the prospective results from such diverse investment possibilities as stocks, bonds, and real estate. Tables 20.1 and 20.2 compare NPV to IRR for the example proposals.

To repeat, IRR, is the interest rate that equates the expected cash inflows from an investment to the initial (and subsequent, if any) cash outlays. Without a computer, special electronic calculator, or without this book, IRR is found by *trial and error*. The present value of the expected cash inflows from the investment is calculated using an estimated interest rate. The present value obtained from the first trial is compared to the initial cash outlay. If it is larger than the cash outlay, the next trial interest rate should be a higher number. On the other hand, if the present value of the cash inflows is smaller than the initial cash outlay, the next trial should be performed with a lower interest rate. This process of repeated trials is continued until the present value of the cash inflows is equal to the initial cash outlay. At this point, when the present value of the cash inflows equals the initial cash investment, the NPV is zero. *The interest rate that equates the present value of the cash inflows to the initial investment is the IRR.*

IRR Is Rate Earned on Unrecovered Investment

The IRR is the rate earned on the *unrecovered capital investment*. The initial unrecovered capital investment for proposals 1 and 2 is $100,000. Neither proposal has a return of capital in the final year of the analysis. Instead the capital is used up or dissipated over its life. The IRR method allows for the recovery of the capital investment during the period of analysis through the cash flows, including the ending or residual value, if any.

Refer to Table 20.3, which shows that the IRR is the rate earned on unrecovered investment. Applying the IRR rate to each year's beginning investment balance, one obtains the earnings. To obtain each year's ending investment balance, the cash flow distributed or withdrawn for each proposal is subtracted, and the earnings are added to each year's beginning

Table 20.1. NPV at Various Rates of Cost of Capital

	Cash Flows	
Year	Proposal 1	Proposal 2
0	($100,000)	($100,000)
1	0	40,000
2	10,000	20,000
3	10,000	20,000
4	50,000	20,000
5	60,000	20,000

Present Values and Net Present Values
at Various Discount Rates

	Proposal 1		Proposal 2	
Rate (%)	PV	NPV	PV	NPV
1	$124,646	$24,646	$116,871	$16,871
2	119,571	19,571	113,877	13,877
3	114,758	14,758	111,012	11,012
4	110,191	10,191	108,267	8,267
5	105,855	5,855	105,637	5,637
6	101,736	1,736	103,115	3,115
7	97,821	(2,179)	100,696	696
8	94,098	(5,902)	98,373	(1,627)
9	90,556	(9,444)	96,142	(3,858)
10	87,184	(12,816)	93,998	(6,002)
11	83,972	(16,028)	91,936	(8,064)
12	80,911	(19,089)	89,953	(10,047)
13	77,994	(22,006)	88,044	(11,956)
14	75,211	(24,789)	86,205	(13,795)
15	72,555	(27,445)	84,434	(15,566)
16	70,020	(29,980)	82,727	(17,273)
17	67,598	(32,402)	81,081	(18,919)
18	65,284	(34,716)	79,493	(20,507)

Table 20.2. IRR Compared to Discounted Present Value and Net Present Value

Year	Revenues: proposal 1	Revenues: proposal 2
0	($100,000)	($100,000)
1	0	40,000
2	10,000	20,000
3	10,000	20,000
4	50,000	20,000
5	60,000	20,000
Total revenues	$130,000	$120,000
Present value at 10% discount rate	$87,183	$93,997
NPV	(12,817)	(6,003)
IRR	6.440%	7.300%

Table 20.3. IRR: The Rate Earned on Unrecovered Investment

Year	Beginning investment balance	Earnings: balance × IRR	Cash flow: amount withdrawn	Ending investment balance
		Proposal 1: IRR = 6.437%		
1	$100,000	$ 6,437	0	$106,437
2	106,437	6,852	$10,000	103,289
3	103,289	6,649	10,000	99,938
4	99,938	6,433	50,000	56,371
5	56,371	3,629	60,000	0
Total		$30,000	$130,000	
		Proposal 2: IRR = 7.295%		
1	$100,000	$7,295	0	
2	0	0	$40,000	($40,000)
3	(40,000)	(2,918)	20,000	(62,918)
4	(62,918)	(4,590)	20,000	(87,508)
5	(87,508)	(6,384)	20,000	(113,892)
Total		($6,597)	$100,000	0

balance. The IRR method treats each investment as if it were a bank account. In the case of proposal 1, the bank pays 6.437 percent interest (the IRR). The account holder puts the earnings in the account and withdraws from the account each year the amount of the cash flow. At the end of the fifth year the balance in the account is zero. This means that the IRR earnings rate was just enough, no more and no less, to allow the depositor to receive the desired or projected cash flows.

A similar result occurs for proposal 2: and comparable results will occur for any investment proposal.

Notice that no reinvestment is involved in either of the proposals. IRR does not require reinvestment of the cash flows. If reinvestment does occur, a modified or revised IRR results, as described in Chapter 15.

Another View: Mao's Method

Another view of the relationship between NPV and IRR is given by J. C. T. Mao in *The Quantitative Analysis of Financial Decisions*, (Macmillan, New York, 1969, p. 196). Mao shows that

$$\text{NPV} = \sum_{t=0}^{N} R_t \left[(1+r)^{-t} - (1+k)^{-t}\right]$$

Table 20.4. Mao's Method: The Relation between NPV and IRR

IRR = 20.6981%
k = 12.0000%
Investment = $10,000

(a)	(b)	(c)	(d)	(e)	(f)	(g)	(h)
n		$(1+r)^{-t}$	$(1+k)^{-t}$	(c) - (d)	(b)(e)	(b)(d)	(b)(c)
1	$ 8,000	0.8285	0.8929	-0.0643	($515)	$ 7,143	$ 6,628
2	2,000	0.6864	0.7972	-0.1108	(222)	1,594	1,373
3	2,000	0.5687	0.7118	-0.1431	(286)	1,424	1,137
4	1,000	0.4712	0.6355	-0.1643	(164)	636	471
5	1,000	0.3904	0.5674	-0.1770	(177)	567	390
Totals	$14,000				($1,364)	$11,364	$10,000
						(10,000)	(10,000)
NPV						1,364	0

The table demonstrates the interrelationship of NPV and IRR. Column (e) for each time period is the product of columns (c) and (d), as called for in Mao's method. Column (f) shows the product of column (e) multiplied by the cash flow in column (b). The sum of column (f), by Mao's method, is the NPV of $1364. This is the same result for the NPV when conventionally determined, as shown in column (g), that is, $1364. [Column (h) shows that the NPV is zero when the cash flows are discounted at the IRR rate of 20.6981%.]

where NPV = net present value
r = internal rate of return per period
k = cost of capital or NPV discount rate per period
N = number of time periods
t = number of time periods

Example: Mao's Method. Consider an initial investment of $10,000, with cash flows in periods 1 through 5 of $8000, $2000, $2000, $1000, and $1000, respectively. The IRR is 20.698 percent. If the cost of capital is 12 percent, Table 20.4 shows the accuracy of Mao's method.

Payback and Average Return on Investment

Two commonly used but inferior methods of evaluating investment decisions are *years to payback* and *average return on investment (ROI)*. Both methods fails to account properly for the time value of money. As a result, their use should be avoided.

Years to payback is simply the amount of investment divided by the average annual cash flow produced by the investment. In other words, it measures how long it takes to recover the original investment. One might say that the investment "pays back" in 4.2 years, or that the payback is 4.2 years. The formula for determining years to payback is

$$y = \frac{I}{R}$$

where y = years to payback
     I = total investment
     R = cash flow each year

Another problem with years to payback is that it ignores all cash flows that occur after the payback period. The above example, for instance, ignores all cash flows that take place after 4.2 years.

The *average return on investment* is found by dividing the average income by the average investment. Average income is found after deducting the depreciation necessary to recover the original investment. Average investment for a $100,000 original investment that is worth zero in 6 years is (100 + 80 + 60 + 40 + 20 + 0) ÷ 6; that is, the average investment is $50,000.

For proposals 1 and 2 considered earlier, evaluation by these *ill-advised* methods shows:

	Proposal 1	Proposal 2
Annual average cash flow	$26,000	$24,000
Depreciation (of original investment)	(20,000)	(20,000)
Average annual cash flow after depreciation	6,000	4,000
Investment	100,000	100,000
Life of investment (years)	5	5
Years to payback	3.8	4.17
	(100/26)	(100/24)
ROI (average income/average investment)	12% (6/50)	8% (4/50)
IRR	6.44%	7.3%

In summary, neither method (payback or ROI) is reliable, and neither should be used. Instead, use IRR or NPV, which are founded in logical and sound time-value-of-money concepts.

Negative Cash Flows

Soon, we will determine the IRR of stocks and real estate investments. Both before-tax and after-tax calculations will be performed. By using simple graphs, you will be able to make these calculations yourself for varying investment possibilities. But first, let's briefly consider the implications of negative cash flows.

A tax shelter deal is proposed to you as follows. Invest $100,000 in widgets now and receive tax deductions in the first year of $300,000; second-year deductions of $250,000; third-year deductions of $200,000; and fourth-year deductions of $100,000. In the fifth year, the widgets will be sold for $750,000 to end the investment. For an investment of only $100,000, you will receive $850,000 in deductions. You can't lose, right?

If the deductions are valid, and the stringent passive loss rules introduced by the 1986 Tax Act are not violated, and there is economic substance to the deal so that it is not disallowed with penalties by the IRS as a "tax sham," how good a deal is it? Can we apply IRR analysis? Of course. Set it up as follows for a 50 percent tax bracket (for federal, state, and local taxes):

	Year	Cash flow	Net tax deductions
Initial cash investment	0	($100,000)	0
From tax savings	1	150,000	$300,000
From tax savings	2	125,000	250,000
From tax savings	3	100,000	200,000
From tax savings	4	50,000	100,000
Tax payable on sale	5	(375,000)	(750,000)
Cash from sale	5	750,000	0
Repay loan	5	(750,000)	0
Total		($50,000)	$100,000

The widgets were bought for $850,000 in year 0 for $100,000 cash, and with the proceeds of a $750,000 loan, payable interest only for 5 years, with a balloon payment in the fifth year. When the widgets are sold in year 5 for $750,000, the entire sales proceeds repay the outstanding loan balance. At this point, the widgets have been fully depreciated, so the tax "cost basis" is zero, and the entire gain of $750,000 is recapturable as ordinary income. The resulting tax of $375,000 must be paid out of pocket by the investor, because there are no investment proceeds left (after repaying the loan) with which to pay the taxes.

So we have negative cash flows of $100,000 at point 0, and $375,000 at the end of year 5. Here's the IRR formula:

$$\$100,000 = \frac{\$150,000}{(1+i)^1} + \frac{\$125,000}{(1+i)^2} + \frac{\$100,000}{(1+i)^3} + \frac{\$50,000}{(1+i)^4} - \frac{\$375,000}{(1+i)^5}$$

The rate of interest, i, which satisfies the equation is the IRR. The equation may be solved by trial and error, substituting trial values for i, and continuing to try new values for i until the right-hand side of the equation is equal to $100,000 (the value of the left side). By any method, i is about 1.16853, or 117 percent. This is the IRR for this investment. If this mythical investment were real, the return would be terrific.

However, it is also the case that 6.67815, or about 6.7 percent, also solves this equation. Both 117 percent and 6.7 percent are mathematically correct. This multiple IRR situation results from more than one negative cash flow, and is discussed further in Chap. 22. A legitimate criticism of IRR evaluations is that multiple solutions (e.g., 117 percent and 6.7 percent) are possible. These multiple possibilities do *not* occur in a conventional cash flow situation, where "conventional" means one or more negative cash flows followed by one or more positives. Multiple real solutions occur only with *nonconventional* cash flows. When nonconventional cash flows occur, use modified IRR as described in Chap. 22. With modified IRR only one positive, real solution will exist. Be cautious when nonconventional cash flows are involved: *Would you like to be in the position of a lawyer, accountant, or advisor who recommended the above investment to a client because of the 117 percent return, without realizing or mentioning that the return is also 6.7 percent?*

The critical factor in tax shelter situations is to be sure to provide for the unpleasant tax effects in the year of sale, disposition, or foreclosure. This is the year when all or part of those wonderful deductions in prior years suddenly come back to haunt you as ordinary income, capital gains, or both.

Bear in mind that the above analysis is an economic one. Equally important in any proposed deal whose merits reside in the availability of large tax deductions is the legal or accounting analysis. Read the legal "tax opinion" carefully. Does it state that the proposed accounting and tax treatment is valid, or does it raise the various tax issues and hedge the conclusion with wording like "It is more likely than not that the tax deductions are valid"? In any event, have your own tax expert advise you on the tax and accounting aspects (not the investment merits) before you invest one penny. (The ability to offset passive losses from investments against income from one's profession or portfolio was severely curtailed by the 1986 Tax Act.) Subsequently the limitations were eased slightly.

Capital Budgeting and Weighted-Average Cost of Capital

Capital budgeting is the process of allocating a company's capital to alternative investments. It is the process that we have just experienced in choosing between proposal 1 and proposal 2. The economic number crunching is best performed by internal rate of return (IRR) or net present value (NPV) analysis. Both IRR and NPV properly take the time value of money of the cash flows into consideration.

Various names given to the discount rate used to determine NPV include minimum attractive rate of return, cutoff rate, *hurdle rate,* marginal growth rate, rate of return, or *cost of capital.* Whatever the name, it is the rate of return that a capital investment must generate in order for the project to be a desirable economic undertaking. Perhaps the most appealing discount rate to use in determining NPV is the *weighted-average cost of capital*

(WACC). The WACC recognizes that a company may employ both equity and debt capital, that each has different cost characteristics, and that an appropriate discount rate will take both into consideration. In the example shown in Fig. 20.3, a 10 percent discount rate was used in finding NPV. However, let's assume that the investor is a company which borrows money at 12 percent and is in a 46 percent tax bracket. The after-tax cost of borrowing is then $12 \times (1 - \text{tax rate})$; that is, $12(0.54) = 6.48$. Say 6.5 percent is the after-tax cost of borrowing for that company.

The company's plans may call for it to maintain one part debt to two parts equity (common stock). Thus one-third of the capital structure is debt and two-thirds is equity. For the debt portion, in determining the WACC,

$$\text{Portion of capital} \times \text{after-tax cost} = \text{weighted cost}$$

$$\tfrac{1}{3} \times 0.065 = 0.0217$$

This figure, 0.0217, is the debt contribution to WACC.

For the equity portion, the cost of equity is earnings per share divided by price per share. Called the earnings-price ratio, it is the reciprocal of the price-earnings (P-E) ratio. If the P-E ratio for this company is 12, then the cost of equity is $\tfrac{1}{12}$ or 0.085. This amount, 0.085, multiplied by $\tfrac{2}{3}$, is the equity contribution to the WACC.

The WACC for the entire company is then:

	Portion of capital	After-tax cost	Weighted cost
Debt	$\tfrac{1}{3}$	0.065	0.0217
Equity	$\tfrac{2}{3}$	0.085	0.0567
Total WACC			0.0784 or 7.84%

Thus, for this company, an appropriate discount rate to use would be the WACC of 7.84 percent. In other words, an investment that provides 7.84 percent will be adequate to cover the after-tax cost of interest on the company's normal debt, and provide the existing return on the company's common stock.

The *weighted-average cost of capital* (WACC) is found from the following formula:

$$\text{WACC} = \frac{S}{B + S}(R_s) + \frac{B}{B + S}(1 - t)(R_b)$$

where S = total equity (common stock) value
$\quad B$ = total value of debt
$\quad R_s$ = cost of equity (earnings ÷ price)
$\quad R_b$ = cost of debt capital (pre-tax)

$t =$ tax bracket

The process of determining the WACC can be further refined by considering various portions of equity and debt as well as allowing for the risk of the project itself by varying the P-E (more accurately the E-P) ratio used in the equity portion. For example, with a 6.5 percent after-tax cost of debt, and various P-Es and various debt-to-equity relationships, the WACC ranges from 6.9 percent to 20 percent, as follows:

P-E ratio	Portion of debt in capital structure		
	80%	33%	Zero
12:1	6.9	7.7	8.3
8:1	7.7	10.5	12.5
5:1	9.2	15.5	20.0

NPV will vary considerably depending on the discount rate selected. In determining the WACC (discount rate), the debt-to-equity mixture may be adjusted to reflect the normal financial structure for the type of business in which the investment is to be made. Low-risk businesses will typically have higher debt ratios and lower WACCs, and conversely, high-risk businesses, at the extreme, may be financed entirely by equity and have correspondingly higher WACCs.

The P-E ratio, or its reciprocal (the E-P ratio), should reflect independent third-party companies engaged in the type of industry for which the capital investment is targeted. High-growth, higher-risk businesses with high P-E multiples will have lower WACCs than more mature, stable businesses with lower P-E multiples.

It is to be emphasized that the selection of the rate of earnings per share for determining WACC is *based on the purpose* of the investment (e.g., to acquire real estate or manufacture a new widget) and is not based on the nature of the proposer of the investment (e.g., a drug company).

Naturally, the rate selected for WACC and for discounting to find NPV is a "moving target"; that is, it is not a static, unchanging rate. It can be expected to change as time passes to reflect changes in inflationary expectations as well as changes in the cost of borrowing, and taxation.

Capital budgeting is a process that goes beyond the economic evaluation of alternatives by NPV or IRR analysis. The IRR or NPV analysis is the conclusion of the capital budgeting process. Components of the process itself, to which many entire books are devoted, include:

Economic assumptions underlying the cash flow projections

Detailed economic studies

Detailed cash flows

Details of project worth

Market research studies

Details of alternatives

Engineering studies

Environmental factors

Risk studies

For further reading on the capital budgeting process, including forms, procedures, authorizations levels, company manuals, and the like, see Mike Kaufman (ed)., *The Capital Budgeting Handbook*, (Dow Jones-Irwin, Homewood, IL, 1986). (Be advised, however, that Thomas J. Hindelang's chapter, "Portfolio Management: How to Manage the Corporate Investment Portfolio," falls into the mistaken reinvestment assumption trap regarding IRR.)

Mutually Exclusive Investment Proposals

If unlimited capital is available, or if enough capital is available to select all proposals which meet one's IRR or NPV criteria, all such proposals that meet one's criteria can be selected. But unlimited capital is generally not available. And sometimes there are two or more projects where the acceptance of one precludes the acceptance of any other. Such cases are called *mutually exclusive*.

Let's consider a case where only $100,000 is available to invest in either proposal A ($20,000) or proposal B ($100,000). Obviously the investments are mutually exclusive, as there is not enough cash to invest in both. The facts are as follows:

	Cash flows				NPV @ 10%	NPV @ 12.944%
	Year 0	Year 1	Year 2	IRR, %		
Proposal A	($20,000)	$12,000	$ 14,400	20.0	$2,810	$1,913
Proposal B	(100,000)	12,000	116,450	14.1	7,150	1,913
Difference (B - A)	(80,000)	0	102,050	12.944	4,339	0

At a 10 percent discount rate, proposal A has a *higher* IRR but *lower* NPV and lower investment. Which investment, A or B, should be chosen, bearing in mind that only one may be selected?

First, the differences between the cash flows of proposal A and B are determined, as shown above under "Difference (B - A)." These differences or incremental cash flows, if added to the cash flows of proposal A, result in the flows of proposal B. The IRR of these differences (or incremental cash flows) is 12.944 percent. When this 12.944 percent is used as the discount factor to redetermine the NPVs of proposals A and B, it is seen that their NPVs of $1913 are equal.

As shown in the NPV profile in Fig. 20.4, proposal A has a lower NPV at all discount rates below the 12.944 crossover percentage. At rates higher than 12.944 percent, the reverse holds true and proposal B's NPV is lower. Thus, if the company's weighted-average cost of capital (WACC) is below 12.944 percent, proposal B should be selected; if the WACC is above 12.944 percent, then proposal A is appropriate.

Terminal Value (with Reinvestment)

In this unusual case, proposal A has the higher IRR, a lower investment, and lower NPV at discount rates below the 12.944% crossover. Another means of deciding between the proposals is to determine the *terminal value* at some investment horizon. In this case, let's say that the investment horizon is 2 years hence, and that the available cash flows are reinvested at selected rates. The $80,000 difference between investments A and B will be added to the results of proposal A with interest at the selected rate as well. The terminal values are as follows.

At 12.944 percent, the crossover rate, the proposals are equivalent.

Proposal A: $12,000(1.12944)^1 + 14,400 + 80,000(1.2944)^2 = \$130,004$

Proposal B: $12,000(1.2944)^1 + 116,450 = \$130,004$

At 15 percent, proposal A should be selected.

Proposal A: $12,000(1.15)^1 + 14,400 + 80,000(1.15)^2 = \$134,000$

Proposal B: $12,000(1.15)^1 + 116,450 = \$130,250$

At 10 percent, selection of proposal B is indicated.

Proposal A: $12,000(1.10)^1 + 14,400 + 80,000(1.10)^2 = \$124,000$

Proposal B: $12,000(1.10)^1 + 116,450 = \$128,450$

Net present value (NPV)

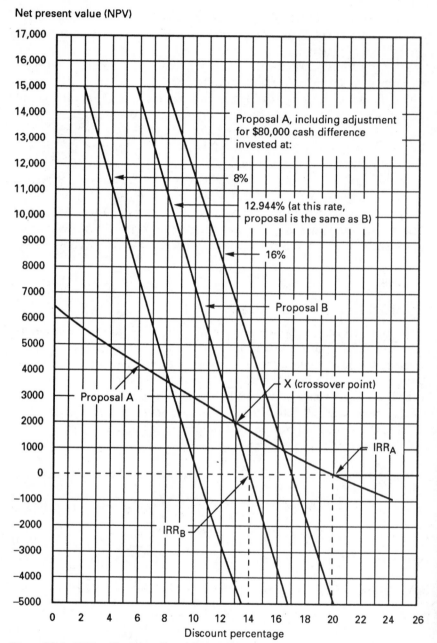

Figure 20.4. NPV profile of mutually exclusive investments.

Thus, as expected, proposal B should be selected based on the terminal value of the cash flows when the reinvestment rates are less than 12.944 percent (the crossover rate), and vice versa.

Although no reinvestment is necessary for the IRR to be achieved, in cases where IRR and NPV give uncertain or contradictory indications, consciously deciding to find terminal value at assumed reinvestment rates can make the picture clear—as it did in the case of proposals A and B.

The key concept in the above determination is to find the IRR for the incremental cash flows. This determines the crossover point x in Fig. 20.4, where the NPVs of the two alternative capital investments are equal. At discount rates higher than the crossover rate, one proposal will be better than the other, and conversely, at lower rates the other proposal will have the higher NPV.

Another way to look at mutually exclusive proposals with apparent contradictions between IRR and NPV is to find the adjusted NPV of the investment which has the smaller original cash investment, by adjusting that proposal (e.g., proposal A) for the "excess cash" (the $80,000 cash difference between proposals A and B). To adjust, the excess cash is assumed to earn interest (or to be itself invested), and the cash flows thus generated, together with the excess cash itself, are added to the preadjustment cash flows (of proposal A). The adjusted figures, at rates of 8 percent, 12.944 percent, and 16 percent, are as follows:

	Percent rate earned on excess cash	Year 0	Year 1	Year 2	IRR, %	NPV at 12.944%
Proposal A (unadjusted)		($20,000)	$12,000	$14,400	20.00	$1,913
Cash flows from investing excess cash	8.000	(80,000)	6,400	86,400		
Proposal A, adjusted		(100,000)	$18,400	$100,800	10.02	($4,689)
		($20,000)	$12,000	$14,400		
Cash flows from investing excess cash	12.944	(80,000)	10,355	90,355		
Proposal A, adjusted		($100,000)	$22,355	$104,755	14.10	$1,913
		($20,000)	$12,000	$14,400		
Cash flows from investing excess cash	16.000	(80,000)	$12,800	92,800		
Proposal A, adjusted		($100,000)	$24,800	$107,200	16.68	$5,994

Refer to Fig. 20.4 to see the effect of the adjustments. At all discount rates there is no longer an ambiguity or contradiction. With 8 percent earned on the $80,000 excess cash, proposal B is superior; at 12.944 percent (the crossover rate), proposals A and B are equivalent; and at 16 percent, proposal A is superior. These results correspond to those obtained earlier by comparing the terminal values.

Before-Tax IRR Analysis for Stocks

Why would anyone be interested in the before-tax rate of return from an investment in a stock? There could be several reasons. The investor might be tax-exempt, such as a pension fund, Keogh plan, or individual retirement account (IRA). Or the investor might be the custodian for a child who is in a zero tax bracket, due to the effect of the child's personal income tax exemption.

In order to determine the IRR from a stock investment, all you have to do is use Fig. 20-5, and the IRR can be found in mere seconds. Only two values must be determined in order to use the graph and make the determination.

1. *Percent current yield.* Percent yield is the annual dividend from the security divided by the initial market price of the stock. For example, if the purchase price of the stock is $100 and the initial dividend per year is $6 per share, then the percent current yield is 6 percent ($6 ÷ $100). Refer to Fig. 20.5. The left axis of the graph is "percent yield," and whatever amount you determine as the yield will be your starting point on the left axis.

2. *Percentage annual increase in dividend (and market value of the stock).* The curves running across Fig. 20.5 represent percentage annual increases in earnings and dividends ranging from 0 to 54 percent per year. You must decide, for the particular stock you are contemplating purchasing or evaluating, your best estimate for the percentage annual increase in earnings and dividends. Stock market analyst reports may help in making this estimate, as may brokerage firms, discussions with officers of the company, or your own analysis. For example, let's assume you decide that the best estimate of such future growth is 6 percent. To find the IRR for this stock, enter the graph at the 6 percent point on the left axis, go across until you reach the 6 percent curve; then proceed down until you reach the bottom axis. The point of intersection with the bottom axis is the IRR, which in this case is 12 percent. That's all there is to it. If the stock does not pay any dividend, simply enter the graph at the zero

Yield percent (annual initial dividend divided by initial market price)

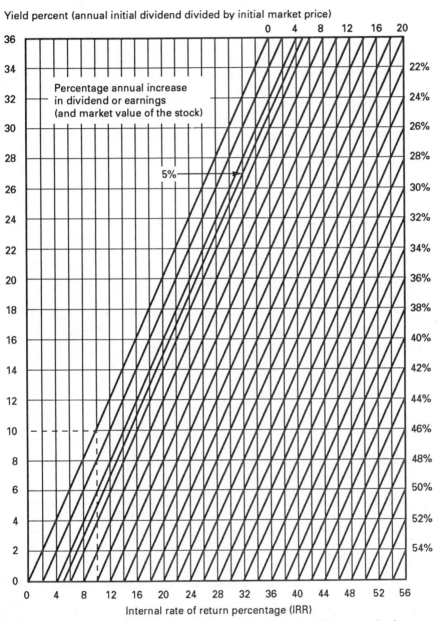

Figure 20.5. Stocks: before-tax internal rate of return (holding period 0–100 years, tax bracket zero, static P-E multiple. (*Source: INVESTMENT IRR ANALYSIS (AFTER TAX) FOR STOCKS, BONDS, AND REAL ESTATE, Larry Rosen Co., 1990.*)

point on the left axis and proceed to the curve that represents your estimate of the annual increase in earnings per share.

There are two implicit assumptions in Fig. 20.5; first, that the market value of the stock will increase over the long term at the same rate as the annual increase in earnings per share. This is a reasonable assumption, but it may not always be the case. This is because the figure assumes that the price-earnings ratio will remain constant or static. In actual practice, a rapid-growth company is likely to see its price-earnings multiple decrease as time passes, and a depressed company that is "turned around" may enjoy an expanded or increased price-earnings ratio. Where the P-E multiple shrinks with the passage of time, the realized IRR will be less than that obtained from Fig. 20.5. In such cases, Fig. 20.5 overstates the IRR. The second assumption is that the annual increase in dividends is at the same rate as the annual increase in earnings per share.

Any holding period may be used with Fig. 20.5; it does not matter whether the time period is 5 years or 50 years. This single graph does it all for a zero tax bracket, provided the price-earnings ratio is the same at purchase and sale.

Interestingly, for a zero tax bracket, *the IRR is always the sum of the initial yield percentage and the annual increase in dividend or earnings per share.* For example, without looking at the figure for the moment, what do you think the IRR is for a stock with 10 percent initial yield and 6 percent annual increases in earnings per share? If you said 16 percent, congratulations! If you said anything else, please reread this paragraph.*

*The analysis of IRR and revised IRR throughout this text presumes, for stocks, that the price at which the stock is sold is based on earnings per share (EPS) at the *end* of the holding period. The earnings per share utilized for this purpose would be effective on the first day *following* the date of sale. For example, if the holding period is 10 years, then the EPS used in determining sales proceeds in the tenth year is that EPS that would have become effective at the beginning of the eleventh year. By using this method, the before-tax IRR for all stocks, regardless of the holding period, can be displayed on one graph. If the EPS at the *beginning* of the year of sale had been used instead in determining sales proceeds, one graph would be required for each holding-period year. (Let's refer to the latter procedure as the "other method.") The IRR for stocks, as determined by the method employed, will normally be very close to the IRR that would result from the other method. For example, with a 20-year projection, the method used shows an IRR of 12 percent, while the other method produces 11.83 percent. The closeness of the result for the two methods holds for time periods of 6 years or more (less than 1 percent difference). For periods shorter than 6 years, the other method will result in progressively lower IRRs as the time period shortens, and the difference becomes more significant. For example, with a 3-year holding period, the method used shows an IRR of 12 percent and the other method produces 10.08 percent; and for 1 year, the results would be 12 percent versus 6 percent. Aside from the simplicity resulting from the method used, it is logical to assume that the earnings per share reflected in the market price are those about to occur, as opposed to those that have already occurred.

Shrinking P-E Multiples

That the rate of change in both dividends and earnings per share will be the same is a reasonable assumption in most instances. In other words, if a company's earnings per share are increasing at 8 percent per year, then its dividend is also likely to increase at about that rate.

And it is reasonable that the P-E multiple for an average stock will remain stable provided that the stock is selling at a P-E multiple near that of the stock market averages. In other words, if the market averages are selling at a P-E multiple of 12, and Hagaan Ice Cream Company is selling at a P-E multiple of 11, then 3, 5, or 10 years later, it is reasonable to expect that Hagaan Ice Cream's multiple will still be around that of the stock market averages.

However, for a company which is presently anticipated to increase dividends and earnings per share at a growth rate substantially greater than the market averages, it is likely that, over a period of years, its P-E multiple will decrease.

For example, the Jerome Hotel Company was started 10 years ago and has enjoyed 50 percent growth in earnings per share. Its annual revenues are now $2 million, and its P-E multiple is a lofty 40. As the company matures and gets bigger, it is likely that its rapid growth rate will subside, and that its P-E multiple will shrink to a figure nearer the market averages. To see the effects of a shrinking multiple, refer to Fig. 20.6. The assumptions underlying this graph are that the P-E multiple shrinks from 30:1 at purchase, to 10:1 at sale; the stock is held for 10 years before sale; and the owner's tax bracket is zero.

For a stock with a dividend rate of zero, and thus an initial yield of 0 percent, an expected growth rate of 40 percent per year in earnings per share, refer to Fig. 20.6. The figure shows that the IRR is 25.4 percent. This is true despite a drop in the P-E multiple from 30:1 at purchase to 10:1 at sale. Had the multiple remained unchanged, the IRR would have been 40 percent, as shown in Fig. 20.5. Thus it is evident that a large drop in the P-E multiple will cause a significant decrease in investor results, as measured by the IRR.

What is the effect if the P-E multiple drops by half, from let's say a multiple at purchase of 20:1 to a multiple at sale of 10:1? Figure 20.7 provides the answer: The stock described in the preceding paragraph would show an IRR of 30.6 percent with a 50 percent drop in the multiple over the 10-year holding.

The following table summarizes the illustrations of the effect of a shrinking P-E multiple on a stock paying zero dividend:

Annual percent increase in earnings per share

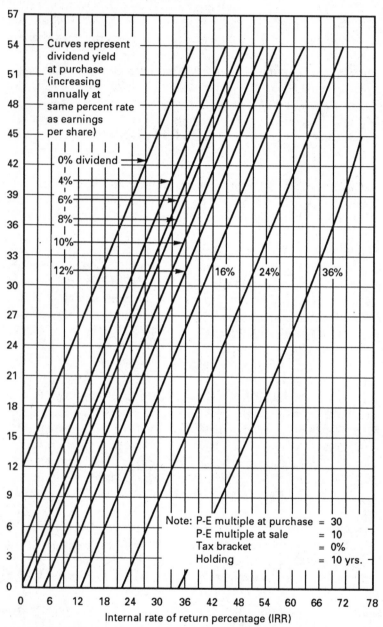

Figure 20.6. IRR of stocks: 67 percent drop in P-E multiple (10 years); tax bracket: zero. (*Source: INVESTMENT IRR ANALYSIS (AFTER TAX) FOR STOCKS, BONDS, AND REAL ESTATE, Larry Rosen Co., 1990.*)

Annual percent increase in earnings per share

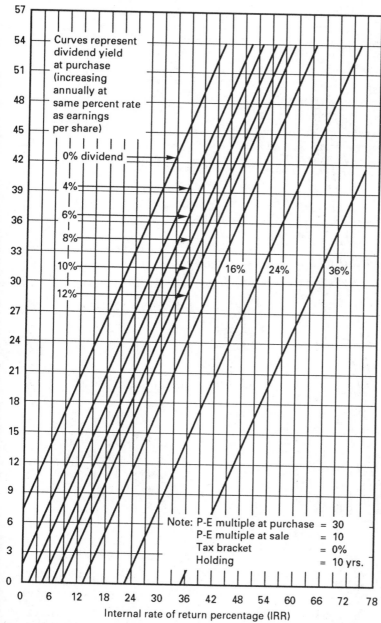

Figure 20.7. IRR of stocks: 50 percent drop in P-E multiple (10 years); tax bracket: zero. (*Source: INVESTMENT IRR ANALYSIS (AFTER TAX) FOR STOCKS, BONDS, AND REAL ESTATE, Larry Rosen Co., 1990.*)

Annual percent increase in earnings per share

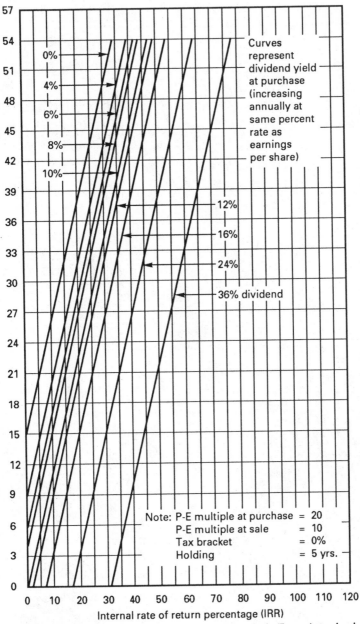

Figure 20.8. IRR of stocks: 50 percent drop in P-E multiple (5 years); tax bracket: zero. (*Source: INVESTMENT IRR ANALYSIS (AFTER TAX) FOR STOCKS, BONDS, AND REAL ESTATE, Larry Rosen Co., 1990.*)

P-E multiple decrease, %	Earnings growth rate, %	IRR, %
0.00	40.00	40.00
50.00	40.00	30.63
66.67	40.00	25.40

What happens to the IRR if the holding period, the length of time between purchase and sale, is shortened from 10 years? The effect of a shrinking P-E multiple becomes more significant; that is, the drop in IRR is more dramatic. Figure 20.8 shows the results of a 5-year holding period with a 50 percent drop in the P-E multiple from a 20:1 ratio at purchase to a 10:1 ratio at sale, and Fig. 20.9 shows the results of a 5-year holding period with a 66.67 percent drop in the P-E multiple from a 30:1 ratio at purchase to a 10:1 ratio at sale.

To visualize the concepts involved, it may help you to think of the P-E ratio as "how many dollars do I have to invest to acquire $1 of company earnings?"

Let's continue with the example of a stock paying zero dividend, held for 5 years, with an expected earnings-per-share growth rate of 40 percent per year. Refer to Fig. 20.8. Enter the left axis at 40 percent (EPS growth rate) and proceed horizontally across to the 0 percent dividends and earnings curve. At that intersection, drop vertically to the intersection with the bottom axis. That point of intersection shows the IRR to be about 22 percent. For a 66.67 percent drop in the P-E multiple, Fig. 20.9 shows the IRR to be about 12.5 percent. To summarize, the results for a 5-year holding are

P-E multiple decrease, %	Earnings growth rate, %	IRR, %
0.00	40.00	40.00
50.00	40.00	22.00
66.67	40.00	12.50

Mounting P-E Multiples

If the P-E multiple at purchase is less than the multiple at sale, we have a *mounting multiple*. For example, the stock of Ableson R-T Envelopes Company is selling at a P-E multiple of 10, and pays no dividend. In the past, the company has increased its earnings per share annually at a rate of only 3 percent per year. However, you have met the management and studied analytical information about the company. The president, Sally Ableson, tells you that the company is going to enter a new field, stationery for home computers—including personalized form-fed checks, envelopes, and stationery. Your best estimate is that earnings per share will increase at a compound

Annual percent increase in earnings per share

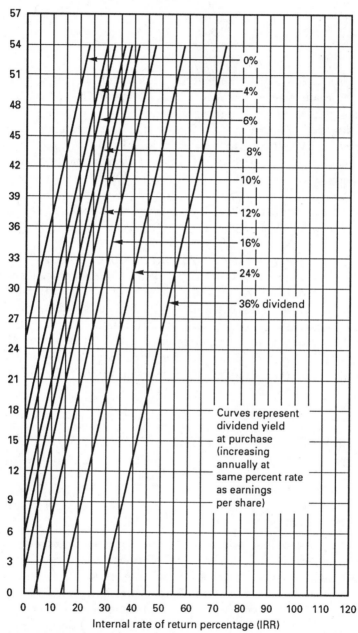

Figure 20.9. IRR of stocks: 67 percent drop in P-E multiple (5 years); tax bracket: zero. (*Source: INVESTMENT IRR ANALYSIS (AFTER TAX) FOR STOCKS, BONDS, AND REAL ESTATE, Larry Rosen Co., 1990.*)

Annual percent increase in earnings per share

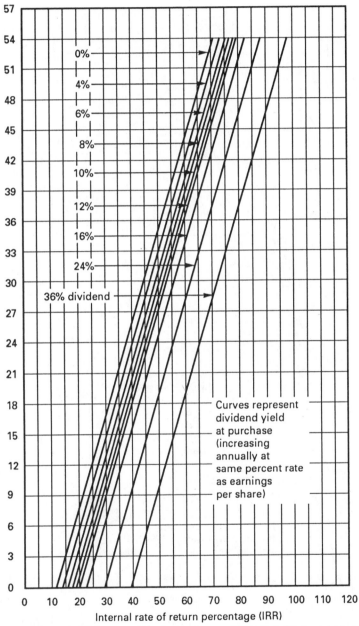

Figure 20.10. IRR of stocks: 200 percent increase in P-E multiple (10 years); tax bracket: zero. (*Source: INVESTMENT IRR ANALYSIS (AFTER TAX) FOR STOCKS, BONDS, AND REAL ESTATE, Larry Rosen Co., 1990.*)

Annual percent increase in earnings per share

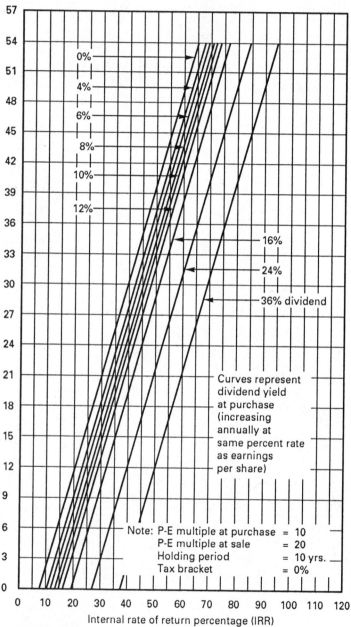

Internal rate of return percentage (IRR)

Figure 20.11. IRR of stocks: 100 percent increase in P-E multiple (10 years); tax bracket: zero. (*Source: INVESTMENT IRR ANALYSIS (AFTER TAX) FOR STOCKS, BONDS, AND REAL ESTATE, Larry Rosen Co., 1990.*)

Annual percent increase in earnings per share

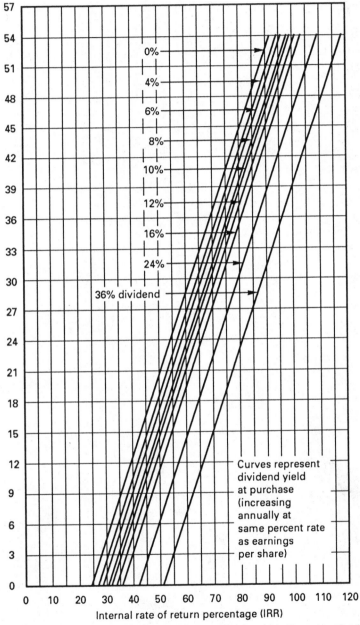

Figure 20.12. IRR of stocks: 200 percent increase in P-E multiple (5 years); tax bracket: zero. (*Source: INVESTMENT IRR ANALYSIS (AFTER TAX) FOR STOCKS, BONDS, AND REAL ESTATE, Larry Rosen Co., 1990.*)

Annual percent increase in earnings per share

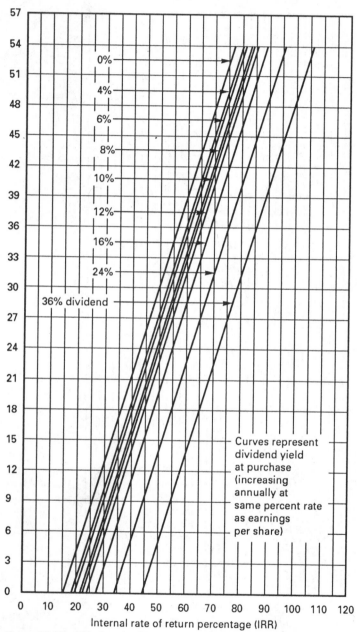

Internal rate of return percentage (IRR)

Figure 20.13. IRR of stocks: 100 percent drop in P-E multiple (5 years); tax bracket: zero. (*Source: INVESTMENT IRR ANALYSIS (AFTER TAX) FOR STOCKS, BONDS, AND REAL ESTATE, Larry Rosen Co., 1990.*)

rate of 30 percent annually for the next 10 years and that, as a result of this growth, the P-E multiple will mount to 30:1 by the end of 10 years. Under such circumstances, what will be the IRR from buying this stock?

Enter Fig. 20.10 on the left axis at 30 percent; proceed horizontally to the 0 percent dividend curve; at its intersection, descend to the bottom axis. The point of intersection at the bottom axis is the IRR, 45 percent. Had the P-E multiple remained constant, the IRR would have been only 30 percent (Fig. 20.1).

But suppose you were too optimistic in your projection and the P-E multiple for Abelson R-T Envelopes increases, but only by double instead of triple. What would the IRR be then? Refer to Fig. 20.11. The IRR in this case would be 39.5 percent.

Perhaps you aren't comfortable projecting earnings and P-E multiples for as long a period as 10 years. You might feel that Abelson R-T Envelopes will boom, but only for the next 5 years. If its earnings per share increase at 30 percent annually for 5 years and the P-E multiple mounts, what will the IRR be? If the P-E multiple triples, then the IRR will be a rousing 62.5 percent. Figure 20.12 provides the analysis in seconds. And if the P-E multiple merely doubles, then you will still derive a highly respectable IRR of 49.5 percent from your intelligent investing (Fig. 20.13).

A summary of the results of investing in Abelson R-T Envelopes shows:

P-E multiple increase, %	Years held	Earnings growth rate, %	IRR, %
300	10	30.00	45.0
200	10	30.00	39.5
0	10	30.00	30.0
300	5	30.00	62.5
200	5	30.00	49.5
0	5	30.00	30.0

A mounting multiple has a more significant effect on the IRR realized when the holding period is shorter. This is true because the proceeds of sale, which are magnified by the mounting multiple, are realized sooner.

In the next chapter we will explore the IRR on stocks—after taxes.

21

Stocks: After-Tax IRR Analysis

The four cash flow elements to consider in determining the IRR for a stock investment are (1) the initial yield, (2) the yield in subsequent years, (3) the proceeds of sale at the end of the holding period, and (4) the initial investment. When the investor is in other than a zero tax bracket (as in the preceding chapter), the analysis becomes just a bit more complicated.

For taxable investors, the cash flow elements are reduced to the extent of applicable income and capital gains taxes. Dividends are reduced by applicable federal, state (if any), and local (if any) levies. Finally, the proceeds of sale at the end of the holding period are reduced by the relevant capital gains tax.

Tax Treatment of Capital Gains

The Tax Act of 1986 generally causes the federal tax on long- and short-term capital gains to be levied at the same 28 percent rate as ordinary income. Before that act, 60 percent of the capital gain was waived, leading to, in most instances, a capital gains tax of 40 percent of the ordinary rate, with the top brackets being 50 percent on ordinary income and a legislated maximum tax on long term-gains of 20 percent. Subsequent to the 1986 Act, rates on ordinary income have increased at incremental levels of income to 31 percent, 36 percent, and 39.6 percent, while the rate on long-term capital gains has remained unchanged at 28 percent. As a result, capital gains are in some instances taxed more favorably than ordinary income. It is likely that preferential treatment for capital gains will again be enacted someday.

Taxing long-term capital gains at the same rate of taxation as ordinary earned income is *unfair* and *inequitable*. It is tantamount to giving the government a license to steal. Many developed, industrialized countries have no capital gains tax at all—and for good reason. That reason is inflation, and because of it capital gains should be taxed favorably or not at all. Consider a person who spent $3000, as part of a college education savings program, to buy a stock 18 years ago. That was enough, then, to pay for a year of tuition at many universities. Those same universities today are charging about $10,000 instead of $3000. The Consumer Price Index (CPI) today is about 3.15 times what it was 18 years ago. By the same measurement (the CPI yardstick), $3000 then is equivalent to $9450 now. If the stock investment appreciated no more and no less than inflation, then the $3000 original investment would be worth $9450 today. It would be fair and equitable for that stock to be sold or exchanged for at least 1 year of education today. If it merely buys 1 year of college today, the purchasing power has not increased at all. If capital gains were not taxed, it would be possible to sell the stock and pay for 1 year's tuition. But with a capital gains tax, the stock cannot be sold and produce enough money after tax to pay for 1 year of tuition.

It is unreasonable to expect U.S. citizens (or residents) to pay tax on illusory gains. And is a true gain realized by the sale of an investment for no more purchasing power than that with which one started? The measure of gain should be purchasing power—what one can do with the money. If an investment, whether in a house, a stock, a bond, or widgets, produces no increase in purchasing power from the time it was bought until it is sold, then it is confiscatory to tax that investment when it is sold. The gains are illusory, not real.

The extent to which capital gains are taxed is frequently manipulated, either for political or fiscal reasons. The figures in this chapter, which show after-tax IRRs for stock investments, include a variety of tax combinations for ordinary income and capital gains, as follows: 28 percent on both ordinary income and long-term capital gains; 50 percent on ordinary income and 20 percent on long-term gains; and 30 percent on ordinary income and 12 percent on capital gains. For tax-exempt investors, the figures in Chap. 20 are pertinent.

There are four choices of tax bracket, three taxable rates (for figures in this chapter), and the zero tax bracket (for figures in Chap. 20). Select the bracket closest to that of the investor. Let's say the investors, Joyce and Dan, are in the 28 percent tax bracket and they wish to find the IRR for a proposed stock investment to be held for 5 years. Figure 21.1 is used for a

Yield percentage
(annual initial dividend
divided by initial market price)

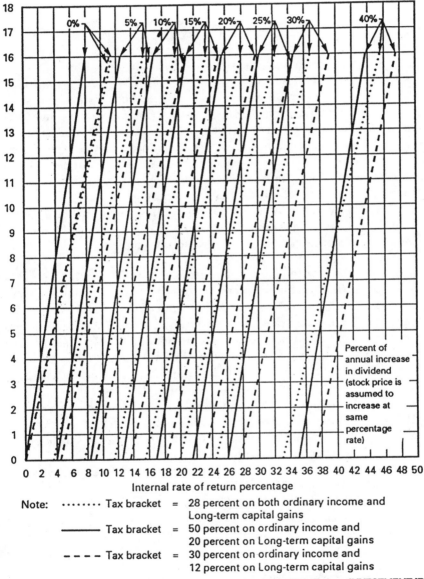

Figure 21.1. Five-year holding of stocks: static P-E multiple; after-tax IRR. (*Source: INVESTMENT IRR ANALYSIS (AFTER TAX) FOR STOCKS, BONDS, AND REAL ESTATE, Larry Rosen Co., 1990–1994.*)

taxable 5-year holding with a static P-E multiple. Joyce and Dan need only two values in order to use the figure to calculate the IRR:

1. *Percent yield.* Percent yield is the annual dividend divided by the initial market price of the stock. For example, if the purchase price of the stock is $100 and the initial dividend per year is $6 per share, then the percent yield is 6 percent ($6 ÷ $100). The left axis of Fig. 21.1 is percent yield, and 6 percent, in this case, is the starting point on the left axis.

2. *Percent annual increase in earnings or dividends per share.* The lines running across the graph represent percent annual increases in dividends or earnings per share ranging from 0 to 40 percent per year. Estimate the percent annual increase in earnings or dividends per share for the particular stock you are evaluating. Stock market analyst reports may help in making this estimate, as may brokerage firms, discussions with officers of the company, or your own analysis. For example, let's assume that Joyce and Dan decide that the best estimate of such future growth is 5 percent per year. (The choices provided in the figure in this chapter include 0, 5, 10, 15, 20, 25, 30, and 40 percent. Values other than these would lie proportionately between the curves for the next smaller and larger values.)

To find the IRR for the proposed investment, enter Fig. 21.1 at 6 percent on the left vertical axis and go across to the 5 percent curve (for 5 percent growth) for the 28 percent tax bracket (the dotted curve; dashed curves are for the 30 percent tax bracket, and solid lines are for 50 percent). From that point of intersection, proceed down to the bottom axis. The intersection with the bottom axis is the IRR, which in this case is about 8 percent.

There is an implicit assumption in the figure that dividends and earnings per share will increase at the same rate over the long term. This is a reasonable assumption, but exceptions will inevitably occur.

If the stock pays no dividend, simply enter the graph at the zero point on the left axis and proceed to the curve that represents the estimate of the annual increase in earnings per share.

The graphs were prepared using the author's computer software, IN-VESTMENT IRR ANALYSIS (AFTER TAX) FOR STOCKS, BONDS, AND REAL ESTATE (Larry Rosen Co., 1990). Because of space limitations, the figures in this chapter cover only 5-year holding periods.

Shrinking P-E Multiples

A reasonable assumption in most cases is that the rate of change of both dividends and earnings per share will be about the same. In other words, if a company's earnings per share are increasing at 8 percent per year, then its dividend is also likely to increase (over the long term) at about that rate. This assumption underlies all the figures in this chapter.

The "static multiple" graphs assume that the P-E multiples at purchase and eventual sale are the same. For an average stock, the P-E multiple is likely to remain stable, provided the stock is selling at a P-E multiple near that of the stock market averages and no major changes occur in the company's prospects. In other words, if a stock is selling at the market's P-E multiple of 9, then it is reasonable to expect that its multiple will still be near that of the market averages some years later. And if the multiple for the market as a whole remains static, so will the multiple of the individual stock.

But for a stock that is anticipated to increase earnings per share at a growth rate substantially less than the market averages, it is likely that, over a period of years, the P-E multiple will decrease. For example, Pidgeons Pottery opened its doors 10 years ago and has increased its earnings per share 40 percent each year since. Its annual sales are now $75 million, and its P-E multiple is 36. As the company matures, it is likely that its rapid growth rate will subside, and in anticipation of that occurrence, its P-E multiple will *shrink* from the elevated 36 level to about 12, where the market averages generally reside. The drop in multiple is 67 percent. Assume that the company plows its earnings back into the business and pays no dividend. What will be the IRR for an investment in Pidgeons Pottery?

Enter Fig. 21.2 on the left axis at the 40 percent earnings per share growth rate; proceed horizontally to the 0 percent dividend curve for the 50/20 percent tax bracket. Then drop vertically to the bottom axis. The intersection at the bottom axis is the IRR, about 10.3 percent.

Compare this result to the following:

Tax bracket, %	Change in P-E multiple	IRR, %
0	No change	40
50	No change	35
50	Drop from 30 to 10	11
50	Drop from 20 to 10	19
30	No change	37
30	Drop from 30 to 10	12
30	Drop from 20 to 10	12
28	No change	33
28	Drop from 30 to 10	10
28	Drop from 20 to 10	17.5

What conclusions can you draw from the foregoing? First, think carefully about your proposed investment, and the assumptions that underlie your

Annual percent increase in earnings per share

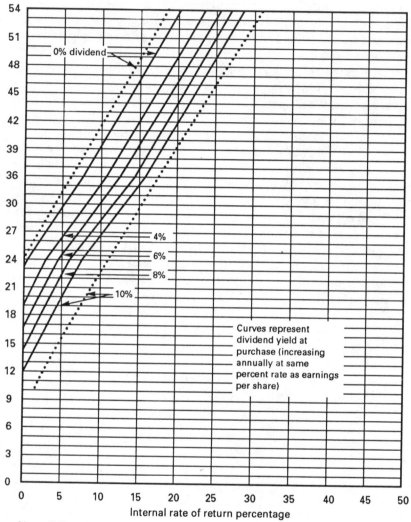

Figure 21.2. Five-year holding of stocks: 67 percent drop in P-E multiple; after-tax IRR. (*Source:*
INVESTMENT IRR ANALYSIS (AFTER TAX) FOR STOCKS, BONDS, AND REAL ESTATE, Larry
Rosen Co., 1990–1994.)

analysis. Apply the same criteria to your alternative investment possibilities, stocks, bonds, tax-exempts, and real estate. Second, if you must buy high-growth stocks at lofty P-E multiples, by all means get rid of them before they enter the shrinking-multiple stage.

Mounting P-E Multiples

A *turnaround* or *special-situation* stock may exhibit characteristics quite the opposite of the shrinking-multiple company. Suppose you are considering an investment in McGrewders Muffler Company (MMC). As a muffler company, it has exhibited unspectacular growth, increasing earnings per share at only an average of 8 percent per year over the past 10 years. However, a year ago it formed a research-and-development arm that has been engaged in research on an electrically powered automobile motor. You have reason to think that a commercially viable product will result that will allow the consumer to drive at a cost of only 2 cents per mile, and with the motor in mass production, the cost of cars will decline by 20 percent. MMC is selling at only seven times its $1 per-share earnings. You buy it on the expectation that its earnings will increase 40 percent per year over the next 5 years, and that its P-E multiple will triple from 7:1 to 21:1. MMC pays no dividend, and you are in a 50 percent tax bracket for ordinary dividends and 20 percent for capital gains. What will be your IRR if this investment works out as you anticipate?

Enter Fig. 21.3 on the left axis at 40 percent growth of earnings per share; proceed horizontally to the intersection with the 0 percent dividend curve; then drop to the bottom axis, where it is seen that the IRR for this investment is 66.5 percent. Compare this to several other possibilities at 40 percent earnings per share growth, as follows:

Tax bracket, %	Change in P-E multiple	IRR, %
0	No change	40
50	200% increase	66
50	100% increase	55
30	100% increase	57
30	200% increase	70

It is so much better to own a stock with a mounting, rather than a shrinking multiple!

Annual percent increase in earnings per share

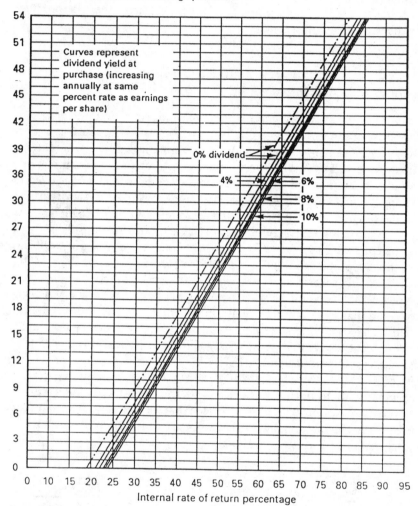

Note: P-E multiple at purchase = 10
   P-E multiple at sale = 30
   ———— tax bracket = 50 percent on ordinary income;
          20 percent for Long term gains
   ·· —·— tax bracket = 28 percent on both ordinary income
          and Long term gains
   holding period = 5 years

Figure 21.3. Five-year holding of stocks:200 percent increase in P-E multiple; after-tax IRR. (*Source: INVESTMENT IRR ANALYSIS (AFTER TAX) FOR STOCKS, BONDS, AND REAL ESTATE, Larry Rosen Co., 1990–1994.*)

22

Modified IRR and Negative Cash Flows

Newton's highly innovative method for finding yield to maturity was discussed in Chap. 13, and it was evident that Sir Issac's method was superior to a trial-and-error approach to finding the yield. We also saw that the usual methods for finding the roots (solutions) to linear (straight-line) and quadratic polynomial equations (second degree or power) will not work for yield to maturity. This chapter continues the discussion of Newton's method.

Convergence and Divergence

Newton's method is the cornerstone of many computer programs (including spreadsheets) and electronic calculators which compute internal rate of return, but it is not perfect. Refer to Fig. 22.1, where curve AZ is a typical yield-to-maturity curve for a noncallable bond. Newton's first tangent to the curve is line AB, and the second tangent is line CD; the third tangent EF intersects the horizontal axis at a point that is indistinguishable in the graph from the yield to maturity, which is located at point E, where the curve crosses the horizontal axis. The successive tangents are said to *converge* on the root of the equation. However, Newton's method may not always result in convergence. Instead the successive tangents may *diverge* from the root. And if a divergence occurs, the correct yield or IRR will not be found.

Two major factors affect the process of convergence. The first is the selection of the initial trial value of IRR or YTM. If the initial trial value is

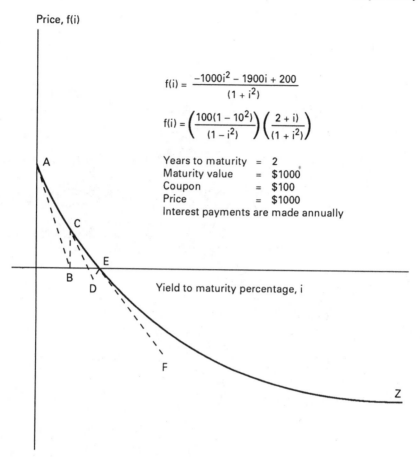

Figure 22.1. Yield to maturity: Newton's method.

too far from the root, depending on the shape of the curve, convergence may not occur. Figure 22.2 shows a situation where divergence will occur. If point A on the curve is the initial trial value, then the tangent will not intersect the horizontal axis at a point which converges on either of the solutions R_1 or R_2. On the other hand, if point B is chosen as the first trial value, then the successive tangents rapidly converge on solution R_1.

The general formula for IRR is found from

$$P = \left| \sum_{n=1}^{N} \frac{R_n}{(1+y/m)^n} \right| + \frac{S_N}{(1+y/m)^{-N}}$$

where P = price, the capital or initial cash investment
R_n = cash flow during the nth time period

ce

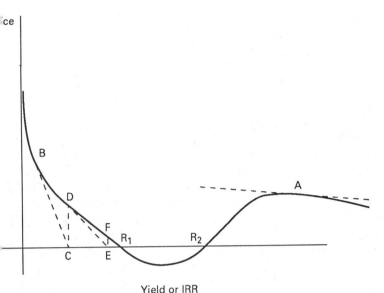

Yield or IRR

Figure 22.2. Divergence with Newton's method.

$n =$ a summation counter, representing the number of a particular time period

$y =$ *periodic* yield to maturity (as a decimal) or *periodic* interval rate of return

$m =$ number of compounding periods per year

$N =$ total number of time periods (e.g., the *last* period)

$S_N =$ maturity, redemption value, or net equity reversion at the end of the Nth time period

The initial term of the formula is the summation of all cash flows discounted to the inception date at the periodic yield or IRR. The nominal annual rate (where compounding and cash flows are more frequent than once per year) is $y \times m$. Thus, if the periodic semiannual rate is 0.05, the nominal annual IRR is 0.10.

Multiple Roots and Negative Cash Flows

The typical IRR equation or bond yield-to-maturity formula is a polynomial equation of Nth degree. For example, the equation for a 30-year bond, with semiannual interest, would be of the 60th degree or power. As a result, the equation has N different roots or solutions (e.g., 60). However, in a *normal* situation only one root is a *positive real* number. The other roots, which can be ignored, are either imaginary or negative numbers. As used here, a *normal* situation is one that has one or more cash outflows or costs (negative cash flows) followed by a series of cash inflows or receipts (positive cash flows). Descarte's rule of signs states: "The number of real positive roots ... does not exceed the number of variations (changes) of sign (of the coefficients of a polynomial equation)." And, if the number of positive, real roots is less than the number of sign changes, the number is less by any even number.

An *abnormal* situation occurs when there are additional negative cash flows which follow previous positive cash flows. In such an abnormal case there is the possibility of *multiple positive* real roots to the equation. (For a discussion limited to bonds, see Gary Bronson, "Determining Bond Yield," *The Fixed Income Quarterly Report*, vol. 1, issue 4, 1989.) This means that more than one solution may be correct. For a given situation, the IRR may be both 15 percent and 300 percent, and both are mathematically correct. Figure 22.2 represents such a situation. Both R_1 and R_2 are solutions and represent positive real IRRs for the equation represented by the curve. Each time cash flows switch from positive to negative, the possibility of one more IRR solution which may be a positive real number is created.

Doubt may arise as to which root of multiple solutions is the most appropriate IRR to use. In such cases neither is a correct measure of return, and use of modified IRR (MIRR) or financial management rate of return (FMRR) is appropriate. These will be discussed in a moment. Another approach to resolving the multiple-solutions dilemma is to compound the cash flows at the rate of IRR, both positive and negative (except the initial cost), to the future terminal date. The interest rate (IRR) that equates this terminal sum to the initial investment cost may be deemed to be the revised IRR. An example will make this clear.

The cash flows for an investment are:

Number	Amount	Remarks
1	–160	The initial investment
2	1000	
3	–1000	Note the negative cash flow

As a result of the sign changes of cash flow 3, it would be expected that two positive, real roots exist. Such is the case, as is shown in Tables 22.1 and 22.2. The IRR for these cash flows is *both* 25 percent and 400 percent.

It is also true that *both* solutions satisfy the criteria for determining terminal value or realized compound yield. Realized compound yield requires reinvestment of the cash flows. If the cash flows are reinvested at

Table 22.1. Modified IRR

25.00% IRR

| Cash flow number | Cash flow | Discount factor | Present Value | Terminal values | |
				Accum. factor	Future value
0	-$160	1.0	-$160.0		
1	1000	1.2	800.0	2.0	$ 1953
2	-1000	1.6	-640.0	1.6	-1562
		Present value sum	0.0	Future value sum	$ 391
$160 accumulated at IRR to terminal date					$ 391
Difference between future value sum and initial investment accumulated at IRR rate					0.000

the rate of either IRR (25 percent or 400 percent), then in both cases the initial investment compounded at the IRR equals the *terminal value*. However, at this point, it becomes apparent that 25 percent is the more realistic realized compound yield, since it is in all probability much more likely that cash flows could be reinvested at 25 percent than at the lofty rate of 400 percent per year.

Modified IRR

It is apparent that the negative cash flows are discounted at the IRR just as are the positive cash flows. But such negative cash flows probably will have to be funded by additional funds from either bank borrowing or equity investment. As it is not likely that the *external* rate of interest charged by a

Table 22.2. Modified IRR

400.00% IRR

| Cash flow number | Cash flow | Discount factor | Present Value | Terminal values | |
				Accum. factor	Future value
0	-$160	1.0	-$160.0		
1	1000	5.0	200.0	125.0	$125,000
2	-1000	25.0	-40.0	25.0	-25,000
		Present value sum	0.0	Future value sum	$100,000
$160 accumulated at IRR to terminal date					$100,000
Difference between future value sum and initial investment accumulated at IRR rate					0.000

lender will be the same as the *internal* rate of return, a *modified IRR* (MIRR) is suggested for use in situations where there are negative cash flows that occur after the first positive cash flow. There are at least three methods of determining the MIRR.

First MIRR Method (Also Referred to as a *Sinking-Fund* Method or *Initial Investment* Method). The negative cash flows can be eliminated from being discounted at the IRR by discounting such negative cash flows to the date of initial investment at the investor's "safe" rate (the rate that can be earned on a riskless investment for the time period involved from inception to the date of the negative cash flows). The MIRR is then calculated on the basis of the revised initial investment, which is the sum of the actual initial investment and the discounted (at the safe rate) present value of the future negative cash flows. In effect, this procedure is tantamount to placing on deposit in a supplementary fund enough money that when it is invested at the safe rate it will grow to an amount equal to the future cash outflow. In the author's opinion, *this is the preferred method of computing IRR when multiple negative cash flows occur.* It does not require consideration of reinvestment. The cash flows can be spent by the investor just as they can from a bond or certificate of deposit, and the MIRR will still be accurate.

An example will illustrate the difference between IRR and MIRR when negative cash flows are involved. Tables 22.3 and 22.4 show the results of a single series of cash flows (−816, +900, +300, 0, 0, −400) where the two IRR solutions are 5.1 percent and 11.81 percent. To find the MIRR for the cash flows shown in these two tables, the first step is to find the discounted present value of the $−400 cash flow in year 5 at an appropriate rate (sometimes referred to as a "safe rate")—say, 11 percent. (Some practitioners use as the safe rate either the T-bill rate or the T-bond rate.) The fifth-year negative cash flow, when discounted to the present at 11 percent, is ($237.38). This ($237.38) is then added to the initial investment ($816), making the adjusted initial negative cash flow ($1053). *The MIRR* of 11.08 percent is *found for the modified cash flows* as shown in Table 22.5. The following timeline illustrates the example:

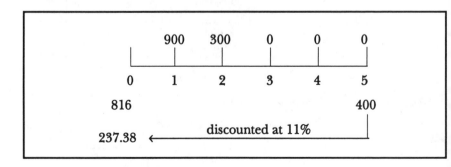

Table 22.3. Modified IRR

5.10% IRR

Cash flow number	Cash flow	Discount factor	Present Value	Terminal values	
				Accum. factor	Future value
0	−$816	1.0	−$816.0		
1	900	1.1	857.1	1.2	$1094
2	300	1.1	272.1	1.2	347
3	0	1.2	0.0	1.1	0
4	0	1.2	0.0	1.1	0
5	−400	1.3	−313.4	1.0	(400)
		Present value sum	0.2	Future value sum	$1041

$816 accumulated at IRR to terminal date $1041

Difference between future value sum and initial investment accumulated at IRR rate 0

Table 22.4. Modified IRR

11.81% IRR

Cash flow number	Cash flow	Discount factor	Present Value	Terminal values	
				Accum. factor	Future value
0	−$816	1.0	−$816.0		
1	900	1.1	805.2	1.6	$1405
2	300	1.2	240.1	1.4	419
3	0	1.4	0.0	1.2	0
4	0	1.6	0.0	1.1	0
5	−400	1.7	−229.2	1.0	(400)
		Present value sum	0.0	Future value sum	$1424

$816 accumulated at IRR to terminal date $1424

Difference between future value sum and initial investment accumulated at IRR rate 0

Table 22.5. Modified IRR: Initial Investment or Sinking-Fund Method

11.0785% MIRR

Cash flow number	Original cash flow	Adjust-ment at 11.00%	Adjusted cash flow	Discount factor	Present value	Terminal value	
						Accum. factor	Futur value
0	-$816	($237.38)	($1053.38)	1.000	-$1053.38		
1	900		900.00	1.111	810.24	1.522	$1370.
2	300		300.00	1.234	243.14	1.371	411.
3	0		0.00	1.371	0.0	1.234	0.
4	0		0.00	1.522	0.0	1.111	0.
5	-400	400.00	0.00	1.691	0.00	1.000	0.
				Present value sum	-0.00	Future value sum	$1781.2

$1053.38 accumulated at IRR to terminal date $1781.

Difference between future value sum and initial investment accumulated at
IRR rate −0.

Second MIRR Method. Another approach to handling negative cash flows is to assume that the negative cash flow is funded by the *nearest preceding years' positive* cash flows, which are reinvested until the year of the negative cash flow at the safe (external) rate. The cash flows involved in funding the negative cash flow as well as the negative cash flow itself are then removed from the analysis and the MIRR is found of the remaining cash flows. This approach is sometimes referred to as the *traditional sinking-fund method.* By this method the MIRR is 11.124 percent, as shown in Table 22.6.

Third MIRR Method. A variation of the traditional sinking-fund method is called the *financial management rate of return* (FMRR).* The FMRR is the rate which equates the present value of the cash outflows (negative cash flows), discounted at an appropriate safe rate, to the future value of the cash inflows (positive cash flows), compounded at an appropriate inflation or reinvestment rate. With the FMRR, negative cash flows are first offset against positives occuring at the same time. Any remaining negative balance is discounted to the beginning at the safe rate and is thus

---

*FMRR results in consideration of only two cash flows—*inception,* which includes the present value of all future negative cash flows, and *terminal,* which includes all positive cash flows compounded to the terminal date.

Table 22.6. Modified IRR: Traditional Sinking-Fund Method

11.1240% MIRR

Cash flow number	Original cash flow	Adjust-ment at 11.00%	Adjusted cash flow	Discoun t factor	Present value	Terminal values Accum. factor	Terminal values Future value
0	−$816		($816.00)	1.000	(−$816.00)		
1	900		900.00	1.111	809.91	1.525	$1372.38
2	300	(−$292.48)	7.52	1.235	6.09	1.372	10.32
3	0		0.00	1.372	0.00	1.235	0.00
4	0		0.00	1.525	0.00	1.111	0.00
5	−400	400.00	0.00	1.694	0.00	1.000	0.00
					Present value sum −0.00		Future value sum $1382.70

$816.00 accumulated at IRR to terminal date $1382.70

Difference between future value sum and initial investment accumulated at IRR rate   −0.00

considered a part of the initial investment. Any remaining positive cash flows are compounded to the terminal date at the reinvestment rate and are added to the sale or maturity proceeds. In the author's opinion this method is less desirable, as it requires the assumption that cash flows are reinvested.* This introduces more uncertainty into the calculation.

In this MIRR method, reinvestment is also compulsory. The steps are:

1. Calculate the present value of the negative cash flows at the safe rate and add it to the initial investment.
2. Calculate the terminal value of the positive cash flows with interest reinvestment at a rate which reflects the return on other investments of comparable risk, the "reinvestment rate." (In the author's opinion, this introduces a major uncertainty into the calculation. Who knows at what level interest rates will be in 3 months, let alone 5 or 10 years in the future?)

*FMRR also depends on the accuracy of the selected "safe rate" as well as the "inflation rate." IRR requires neither "external" rate assumption.

3. Determine the compound rate which equates the present values to the terminal value. The result is FMRR or financial modified IRR. The formula is

$$\text{MIRR} = \left(\frac{S_p}{P_p}\right)^{1/n} - 1$$

where MIRR = modified periodic internal rate of return (in decimal form)
n = total number of compounding periods
S_P = net future value of positive cash flows
P_P = net present value of negative cash flows

Table 22.7 presents at set of cash flows, the IRR of which is 14.92 percent. In Table 22.8 the MIRR using method 3 is determined as 14.3 percent.

FMRR probably came into being because the math calculations are relatively simple. Nothing more is involved than discounting to find present value, finding the compound future value of either an annuity or individual cash flows, and finding the rate of interest which equates the present and future values. However, simplicity does not mean quality. And for the reasons noted above, this author does not recommend method 3, even though it is the MIRR method described by Hewlett-Packard's *Business Calculator (HP-17B) Owner's Manual* as well as the *HP-12C Owner's Handbook and Problem-Solving Guide*. The Texas Instruments *Financial*

Table 22.7. Terminal Value and IRR

14.9225 IRR

Cash flow number	Original cash flow	Adjust-ment at 9.00%	Adjusted cash flow	Discount factor	Present value	Terminal values	
						Accum. factor	Future value
0	−$75.00		($75.00)	1.000	−$75.00		
1	−9.50		(9.50)	1.149	8.27	1.744	($16.57)
2	27.00	0.00	27.00	1.321	20.44	1.518	40.98
3	−11.00		(11.00)	1.518	−7.25	1.321	(14.53)
4	50.00		50.00	1.744	28.66	1.149	57.46
5	83.00	0.00	83.00	2.005	41.40	1.000	83.00
				Present value sum	−0.00	Future value sum	$150.34

$75.00 accumulated at IRR to terminal date $150.34

Difference between future value sum and initial investment accumulated at IRR rate −0.00

Table 22.8. Modified IRR: Method 3, FMRR

9.00% "safe" rate at which negative cash flows are discounted
14.3140% MIRR, or FMRR
14.0000% reinvestment rate at which positive cash flows are invested

Cash flow number	Original cash flow	Adjust-ment at 9.00%	Adjusted cash flow	Discount factor	Present value	Terminal values Accum. factor	Future value
0	-$75.00	($17.210)	($92.21)	1.000	-$92.21		
1	-9.50	9.50	0.00	1.143	0.00	1.708	0.00
2	27.00	-27.00	0.00	1.307	0.00	1.494	0.00
3	-11.00	11.00	0.00	1.494	0.00	1.307	0.00
4	50.00	(50.00)	0.00	1.708	0.00	1.143	0.00
5	83.00	97.00	180.00	1.952	92.21	1.000	$180.00
	64.50						

	Present value sum	Future value sum
	0.00	$180.00

$92.21 accumulated at IRR to terminal date	$180.00
Difference between future value sum and initial investment accumulated at IRR rate	0.00

Adjusted initial value of negative cash flows $ 92.210

Adjusted ending value of positive cash flows 180.002

Number of periods 5.000

Rate which equates initial value to end value 14.314%

Notes:
1. $97 = $27(1.14)^3 + $50 (1.14)^1$
2. $17.21 = $9.5 (1.09)^{-1} + $11(1.09)^{-3}$

Application Guide and Fixed Income Securities Calculator are silent on the subject of MIRR.

Summary

Internal rate of return analysis allows an investor to compare alternative investment possibilities in a logical, scientific, and intelligent fashion. The use of IRR allows the investor to compare without distortion the returns from investments that may be for different capital sums and for varying periods of time. On the other hand, *net present value* is the discounted present value of the cash inflows and outflows of an investment. It requires the investor to select the interest rate, such as weighted-average cost of capital at which the discounting takes place. The higher the net present value, the better is the investment return. The IRR, on the other hand, is the rate at which the net present value is zero. The *normal* pattern of an investment is one or more negative cash flows (the investment) followed by a series of positive cash flows including the proceeds of eventual sale of the investment. Such normal situations will have only one positive, real IRR (that is greater than zero). However, in *abnormal* situations, when one or more negative cash flows occur after the first positive cash flow, more than one positive real IRR may occur. To eliminate confusion, in such abnormal situations, MIRR (i.e., the sinking-fund method) can be used. MIRR may be computed in at least three different ways, and the pros and cons of each have been described and the author's preferred method has been indicated.

Sometimes one fails to see the forest for the trees. If $1000 grows into $10,000 in 10 years, what is the return? The wrong answer is $9000 profit divided by $1000 investment for a 900 percent return in 10 years, and then dividing by 10 to get 90 percent per year. The right answer is 25.89 percent per year. This is the IRR. No MIRR calculation is needed, because there were no negative cash flows after the first positive cash flow. Where the MIRR approach is utilized, the MIRR may be more or less than the normally computed IRR. Whether it is more or less depends on whether the assumed rate earned on reinvestment is more or less than the normal IRR, as well as how the safe rate compares to the normal IRR. If the safe rate and the reinvestment rate are both the same as the IRR, then the MIRR will be equal to the IRR.

MIRR is generally unnecessary for stock and bond investments, because there generally are no subsequent-year negative cash flows with such investments. However, MIRR is of considerable interest to companies that make capital investments and to real estate investors. With both capital and real estate investments, sometimes sales don't always materialize, tenants sometimes go bankrupt, or vacancies exceed projections—all of which may lead to negative cash flows in a year or years after the first positive cash flow. Real estate investment is the subject of the following chapters.

23

Real Estate
Investing
and IRR Analysis

Well-selected real estate investments can be extremely rewarding, notwith-standing credit crunches, savings and loan scandals, overbuilding, and other well-publicized abuses of the late 1980s and early 1990s. Nevertheless, real estate as an investment shares one major characteristic with all invest-ments: *risk*. However, even supposedly risk-free investments such as certifi-cates of deposit have a purchasing-power risk: Will the depositor be able to buy as much at maturity, considering inflation, as could have been pur-chased at the inception of the deposit? Real estate is no panacea for the potential ills and difficulties of investing.

Generally, well-selected and properly purchased "income property" should initially provide owners with cash flow considerably higher than the yields on high-grade, long-term corporate bonds. Such yields fluctuate according to economic and political trends, and the volatility of such long-term yields is much less than for short-term yields.

Income property includes industrial buildings, shopping centers, apart-ment complexes, office buildings, and commercial buildings.

Cash flow is the excess of rental income over property operating ex-penses, excluding noncash charges such as depreciation and amortization, but including the cost of servicing principal and interest on mortgage loans. Let's look at cash flow another way. If you open a new bank account for your income property at the beginning of each year, deposit all receipts to it, and make all disbursements from it, then the balance in the account at the end of the years is the *annual cash flow*. The cash flow, as a percent of cash invested, from higher-quality real estate investments, at the time of purchase, will tend to be closer to the annual yield from U.S. government issues than to the higher-yielding, lower-quality corporate issues.

Little information is available about yields and returns obtained by real estate investors. There is no Dow Jones Average of Real Estate Yields. In our business at the Larry Rosen Co., we devote substantial time to analyzing, selecting, negotiating, purchasing, and managing income property. In order to provide an idea of the actual financial results from income property investment, we have selected from our records all eight properties purchased prior to 1979 in which we were participants. The average annual cash flow (for each property for each year) divided by the initial cash investment was: for one property 7.6 percent; for three properties, between 10 and 20 percent, and for four properties, greater than 20 percent. This ratio is commonly referred to as the annual *cash-on-cash return on investment*.

Cash expenditures have been deducted in arriving at the cash flow figures above and include mortgage loan principal payments. Such payments are direct reductions in the property owner's outstanding mortgage loan balance. As they reduce the debt owed by the property owner, such payments are often said to increase the owner's "equity." *Equity*, in the real estate sense, is the excess of property market value over indebtedness. For example, consider the following:

At origin:	
Purchase price	$1,000,000
Initial loan	750,000
Cash investment	250,000
Five years later:	
Market value	1,250,000
Loan outstanding	650,000
Equity	600,000

For example, Joy Keller buys a mansion for $1,000,000. She borrows $750,000 from a savings and loan and invests $250,000 of her own money. Her initial *equity* is $250,000, which equals her initial cash investment. After some years, due to various factors including inflation, property maintenance, location, community economic factors, etc., the value of Joy's property has increased to $1,250,000. At this moment, her loan balance has been reduced from $750,000 to $650,000, as the result of her monthly payments of mortgage principal (and interest). At this point, Joy's equity is the difference between the market value of the house, $1,250,000, and her outstanding loan balance, $650,000; that is, she has $600,000 in equity. So Joy's home equity, or worth, has increased from $250,000 initially to $600,000, an increase of $350,000 which, relative to her initial investment, is quite substantial.

Let's return to discussing mortgage loan principal payments. Such payments reduced cash flow and thus reduce the *cash-on-cash* return percentage. However, some recognition needs to be given to such principal payments. *Payments of principal represent an increase in equity, provided the market value of the property has not diminished.* If the market value of Joy's home had not increased at all and still remained at $1,000,000 after 5 years, her equity would have increased by $100,000, the amount of the reduction in her debt. But if the market value *decreased*, such a decrease would have reduced the equity increase from loan principal reduction.

To continue in the real world, let's look at the eight properties from the point of view of increase in equity, or equity buildup resulting from loan principal payments. The mortgage loan principal payments for each year divided by the owners' cash investment in the property, for five properties averaged between 3.9 and 10.0 percent per year, and for three properties exceeded 10.0 percent per year. Assuming that each property's market value has not decreased, this ratio represents the *equity buildup* as a percentage of the original cash investment.

If we add the percentage returns from cash-on-cash to the equity buildup, does that give us the complete picture? Absolutely not, for two reasons. First, there are still tax effects, pro or con, to be considered. Second, the percentage returns on a year-by-year basis have not been weighted for the time factor of money. Remember, money due to be paid in the future is not worth as much as money in hand today. So we must take both taxes and time into consideration.

For the purpose of calculating taxable income (for U.S. federal income taxation), buildings are assumed to depreciate in value every year. Therefore, after completing construction, the *theoretical depreciation* of a building may result in annual *losses* for income tax purposes. These losses may continue to shelter all or part of income (cash flow) for many years. Depreciation *deductions* from taxable income are allowable even though the property is, in fact, *appreciating* in value as a consequence of market conditions, good management, proper maintenance, and so forth. And though the property may show a tax loss, it can have a *positive* cash flow, which the owners may spend, hold in reserve, or whatever.

To determine tax cost or tax savings and taxable income or loss from a real estate investment, several adjustments have to be made to cash flow as follows:

Cash flow:

(a) Cash receipts	$100,000	
(b) Less: cash expenditures	80,000	(includes loan principal payments)
(c) Cash flow	$ 20,000	(a) - (b)
(d) Taxable Income:		

(e) Cash flow (as above)	20,000	
(f) Less: depreciation	60,000	(depreciation was not included in cash expenditures)
(g) Add: mortgage loan principal payments	8,000	(loan repayments are not a tax deductible expense)
(h) Taxable income (loss)	($32,000)	(e) - (f) + (g)
Income Tax:		
(i) Taxable loss	($32,000)	
(j) Tax bracket rate	40.0%	(for a 40 % bracket)
(k) Income tax savings	$12,800	(i) × (j)

Suppose that Dr. Sam Wang, an investor in a 40 percent tax bracket, owned the above property. The taxable loss shown in (i) winds up on his income tax return as a deduction from income. A deduction only lessens his income, it does not directly reduce the tax owed. After Dr. Wang's tax bracket *rate* is applied to the taxable loss, the resulting amount is the actual reduction in current-year income tax that he would pay as a result of the transaction. This is the amount shown in line (k), $12,800.

Under the Tax Reform Act of 1986, income tax savings may be realized by offsetting losses against income from other investment real estate. Severe "passive loss" restrictions apply to prevent offsetting losses against professional and portfolio income. Further information concerning this is available free from the IRS in Publication 925, *Passive Activity and At-Risk Rules.*

This simple example is not far, in terms of proportion, from actual situations. The important things to note are *positive cash flow* and *negative taxable income.* As a result of the investment, Dr. Wang could spend, lend, or do whatever he wishes with the $20,000 cash flow. The negative taxable income of $32,000 in a 40 percent tax bracket, produced $12,800 in *tax savings.* In other words, Dr. Wang, as a result of this investment, paid $12,800 less in income taxes and has $12,800 more to spend, invest, or lend. So the actual spendable cash from the investment is $32,800: $20,000 in cash flow and $12,800 in tax savings (or deferral). Thus cash flow after tax is $32,800; that is, line (c) plus line (k).

Real estate investment has several potential pitfalls. First, there are the problems of evaluation, selection, negotiation, and management. Second, the deduction generated by depreciation accumulates over the years and serves to reduce the tax *basis* of the property. If Dr. Wang's original cost for the entire property was a $200,000 cash investment and $800,000 loan, then his original basis was $1,000,000. But when he sells the property, the revised or adjusted basis that must be used to calculate his capital gain or loss is the original cost of $1,000,000 less all depreciation that he has deducted over the years. Let's say that those accumulated depreciation deductions amount to $400,000. Then his adjusted taxable basis is

$1,000,000 less $400,000, or $600,000. If he sells the property for $1,000,000, his long-term capital gain, $400,000, is equal to the sales price, $1,000,000, less his taxable basis of $600,000.*

The Tax Reform Act of 1986 affected the preferential tax rate that was previously applied to long-term capital gains and taxes such gains, generally, at 28 percent. The Deficit Reduction Act of 1990 restores, in some cases, limited favorable long-term capital gains taxation by increasing ordinary income rates above the 28 percent rate on such capital gains. Taxation in the year of sale may also depend upon the IRS code provisions that were in effect when the asset was acquired and the depreciation method(s) that have been utilized. For example, depreciation deductions using accelerated methods (faster than the straight-line method) may give rise to taxation of all or part of the gain as ordinary income rather than capital gain. This is termed "recapture" (of accelerated depreciation as ordinary income rather than capital gain).

From the point of view of taxation, over a period of years, Dr. Wang deducted $400,000 in depreciation from his taxable income. This saved him $160,000 in income taxes. He could have spent or invested the $160,000 as the savings occurred. When he sold the property, the $400,000 in deductions reduced his taxable basis and created a capital gain of the same amount. *And capital gains are frequently taxed more favorably than ordinary income.*

Even if capital gains were taxed at the same 40 percent tax rate (federal, state, and local) as ordinary income, the doctor benefits by postponing the payment of $160,000 in taxes until the year of sale.

Now let's see what the tax effects were of the eight properties. For each property, for each year, the tax cost or tax savings divided by the original cash investment averaged a loss of 20.5 percent.

Finally, let's put the results from all three components of return together, cash-on-cash return, equity buildup, and tax savings or cost. The actual investment experiences for the eight properties was: for five properties, a gain of between 18 and 25 percent per year; and for three properties, a gain exceeding 40 percent per year.

Among the investment *objectives* that one should have when dealing with income real estate are:

Preserve and protect the original investment capital. This may be achieved by buying structurally sound, environmentally clean properties that have a proven earnings record or that are substantially preleased to experienced and responsible tenants.

---

*The gain on the sale of income property, under IRS section 1231, is a capital gain, if the holding period requirements are met, unless the gain is subject to the recapture rules. Loss is an ordinary loss.

Provide capital gains through appreciation of the property's value. Through the years, well-selected property investments have yielded high profits to investors who bought and sold intelligently.

Shelter distributions of cash. Through the operation of the combined effects of mortgage financing and depreciation, tax shelter of all or part of the income from the property as well as other investment income may be generated.

Build up equity through reduction of mortgage loans on properties (out of cash flow) and appreciation of market value.

Purchase property at well below reproduction cost. Properties that can be purchased at prices below reproduction cost include offerings from distressed sellers who desire a quick sale and properties that are producing less than market rates of income or that are older.

Select properties where the rentals are at below-market rates. The main reason for this objective is that in the event that the tenant defaults or moves out and a replacement tenant must be found, the new rental under such circumstances should at least equal the old and hopefully exceed it.

Sell the property at the appropriate time based on changing market factors, available reinvestment opportunities, and tax considerations.

In summary, many key concepts have been explored in this chapter, including: cash-on-cash return, equity buildup, tax savings or cost, combining all three return factors with estimated after-tax proceeds of sale to determine an internal rate of return, investment management, and real estate investment objectives.

In the next chapter, we develop *models* of real estate investment that allow one to estimate IRR for either existing holdings or properties being considered for acquisition.

24

Real Estate: IRR Models

The IRR for a wide variety of income-producing real estate investments may be found in seconds using the unique graphs provided in this chapter. Performing the calculations that were required to prepare these graphs, as well as determining the IRR, is a somewhat complex and laborious task. *The beauty of these graphs is that they provided an accurate, yet simple, solution to the problem of determining the IRR of a real estate investment.* Some *250,000 calculations* were required to prepare *each* graph, and about *1 million calculations* were involved in preparing all the graphs in this chapter.

Perhaps the easiest way to become familiar with the process of finding IRR for a real estate investment is simply to do it. Let's say that Judy Whitecloud is considering acquiring an office building, and her projections are as follows:

Rate of inflation	6%
Initial percent return: net operating income ÷ total investment	10%
Tax bracket	35%
Loan as a percentage of total investment	75%
Loan interest rate	10%
Years of loan amortization	25
Building cost ÷ total investment cost	90%
Years of straight-line depreciation	31.5
Years hence when the property will eventually be sold	10
Capitalization rate for determining eventual sales price based on net operating income in the year of sale	10%

Based on the above estimates, to find the IRR for this proposed investment, Miss Whitecloud needs to find the graph that comes closest to corresponding to her assumptions. In this case, it is Fig. 24.1 at the end of the chapter. Table 24.A, the *Match-up Worksheet*, allows Miss Whitecloud to quickly find the graph that matches the estimates of her proposed real estate investment. The assumptions underlying Fig. 24.1 are identical, in this case, to her estimates.

To find the IRR, Miss Whitecloud enters the figure on the vertical axis at the 10 percent level, which represents the initial net operating income (NOI) as a percentage of the total investment. She proceeds horizontally to the 6 percent curve, which represents the assumed annual inflation rate. At the intersection with the 6 percent curve, she proceeds toward the bottom of the graph until the bottom horizontal axis is reached. That point of intersection is the IRR for this investment, 19.8 percent.

The same graph may be used to find the IRR for other rates of initial NOI to total investment and other rates of inflation. For example, refer to Fig. 24.1. How would the IRR change if inflation were 10 percent instead of 6 percent? Entering the left axis at 10 percent for initial yield, proceed horizontally to the 10 percent curve, then descend to the bottom axis. The point of intersection is 26.2 percent, which is the new IRR. So if inflation, in this example, increases from 6 to 10 percent, the IRR increases from 19.8 to 26.2 percent.

The same figure may be used to determine the IRR for varying levels of initial yield. If the initial yield is 7 percent (instead of 10 percent), what happens to the IRR? Enter the figure at the 7 percent point on the left axis, then go across to the 6 percent inflation curve, then descend to the bottom axis, where the IRR is about 7.9 percent. Thus the effect of a drop in the initial yield level from 10 to 7 percent is a decrease in IRR from 19.8 to 7.9 percent. The *sensitivity* of the IRR *to changes in the initial yield level* is thus apparent.

Following the figures at the end of this chapter is Table 24.1, a printout of the entire 10-year projection for *one point* on one curve for Fig. 24.1.

In order to understand the figures and tables, several comments regarding the methodology may be helpful.

Inflation. The inflation rate is applied on an annual compound basis to increase the initial year's NOI. This is equivalent to increasing all items of rent and other income, as well as all operating expenses (except depreciation and interest) by the inflation rate.

Loan principal and interest. This is the annual debt service amount including both principal and interest. It is calculated from the stated assumptions in terms of loan amount, years of amortization, and loan interest rate.

Table 24.A. Match-up Worksheet: Real Estate IRR

	Figure number			
Assumptions	1	2	3	4
Rates of inflation: 0–10%	Yes	Yes	Yes	
Other				5%
Initial percentage return				
NOI/total investment: 0–16%	Yes	Yes	Yes	
NOI/total investment: 10%				Yes
Tax bracket: 0%				
28%				Yes
30%				
35%	Yes	Yes	Yes	
40%				
Loan as a percent of total investment: 75%	Yes		Yes	Yes
50%				
0%		Yes		
Loan interest rate percentage: 6–16%				Yes
10%	Yes			
12%			Yes	
No loan		Yes		
Years of loan amortization: 25 years	Yes			Yes
Interest only			Yes	
No loan		Yes		
Building/total investment: 90%	Yes	Yes	Yes	Yes
Years of straight-line depreciation: 31.5 years	Yes	Yes	Yes	
27.5 years				Yes
15 years				
Year of sale: 10 years hence	Yes	Yes	Yes	Yes
15 years hence				
Capitalization rate at sale: 10%	Yes			Yes
12%		Yes	Yes	
16%				
Percentage of capital gains not taxed: 0%	Yes	Yes	Yes	Yes

Initial depreciable assets. Land is not depreciable, but buildings and equipment are. Therefore a breakdown of the total investment amount is necessary between land on the one hand and buildings on the other. Initial depreciable assets are determined by multiplying the fraction shown in "Building divided by total investment" times the total investment.

Depreciation. Depreciation is found by dividing the "initial depreciable assets" by the amount shown as "years, straight-line depreciation." Pursuant to the provisions of the Tax Reform Act of 1986, depreciable lives are generally 27.5 years for residential and 31.5 years (39 years for property acquired after May 12, 1993) for other, including commercial and industrial, property. This Modified Accelerated Cost Recovery System (MACRS) applies to real property placed in service after 1986. Other investments made prior to that date continue to be depreciated using *much more realistic and liberal methods* based on earlier IRS provisions.

Sales proceeds and year of sale.   The acquired property is assumed to be sold in the last year of the analysis. The gross sales price is determined by dividing the net operating income in the year of sale (e.g., the tenth year) by the capitalization rate stated in the assumptions. Generally, the capitalization rate would be at a higher level than yields to maturity on long-term Treasury bonds (at the time of sale).

Capital gains tax on sale.   The sales proceeds less the original cost less accumulated depreciation are the taxable long-term gain. Prior to the Tax Reform Act of 1986, 60 percent of this gain was disregarded, or waived. The remaining 40 percent of the gain was multiplied by the tax bracket rate stated in the assumptions. The Tax Reform Act eliminated the preferential treatment of long-term capital gains. The Deficit Reduction Act of 1990 restores a minute element of favorable long-term capital gains treatment by limiting to 28 percent the tax on such gains.

The figures include no waiver of gain.

Cash from sale after tax and loan repayment.   Both the outstanding loan balance remaining in the year of sale as well as capital gains tax are deducted from the sale proceeds to determine "cash from sale after tax and loan repayment."

Cash flow after tax.   It is the after-tax cash flow in each year that forms the principal basis for the calculation of the investment's IRR. In the year of sale, the "cash flow after tax" also includes the "cash from sale after tax and loan repayment."

Internal rate of return.   *This is the "magic number" that summarizes the results of the entire projection. It is an after-tax percentage including deduction of both ordinary income and capital gains taxes. This rate relates the after-tax cash flows to the initial cash investment.*

To find the figure needed to perform the desired IRR calculation, refer to the Match-up Worksheet, Table 24.A. Select the figure that has the same characteristics as the proposed investment. If the worksheet does not contain exactly the characteristics desired, select the figure that comes closest to having the correct assumptions. That's all there is to it!

Sample IRR Calculations for Real Estate

Table 24.B contains one IRR calculation for each of 13 real estate situations, using the assumptions stated. Several things worth noting in Table 24.B include:

ıble 24.B. Sample IRR Calculations

Assumptions	\multicolumn{13}{c}{Situation}
	24-1	24-2	24-3	24-4	24-5	24-6	24-7	24-8	24-9	24-10	24-11	24-12	24-13
ıtes of Inflation %)	6	6	6	6	6	6	6	6	6	6	6	6	6
ıtial percent ¡eturn (NOI/total ¡nvestment) (%)	10	10	10	10	10	10	10	10	10	10	10	10	10
.x rate on capital ¡ains (%)	35	35	35	12	12	35	16	0	28	28	12	12	0
›an as a percent of ›tal investment (%)	75	75	0	75	75	75	75	75	50	75	50	75	0
›an interest rate %)	10	12	–	12	12	12	12	12	12*	12*	10*	10*	–
¡ars of loan ˛mortization	25	25	–	25	99	999	25	25	25	25	25	25	–
˛ilding/total ¡nvestment (%)	90	90	90	90	90	90	90	90	90	90	90	90	90
˛ars, straight-line ˛epreciation	31.5	31.5	31.5	15	15.5	31.5	15	10	27.5	27.5	15	15	31.5
˛ar of sale x years ˛ence	10	10	10	15	15	10	15	10	10	10	15	15	10
˛pitalization rate ˛t sale (%)	10	10	12	10	12	12	16	12	10	10	10	10	12
y Results													
›an principal + ˛nterest per year	83	96	–	96	90	90	96	96	64	96	55	82	–
›ortgage constant ˛principal + ˛nterest as percent ›f original loan) (%)	11.0	12.8	–	12.8	12.0	12.0	12.8	12.8	12.8	12.8	11.3	10.9	–
˛es proceeds after ˛apital gains tax ˛nd payment of ˛utstanding loan ˛alance ($000)	0.72	0.70	1.16	1.14	0.9	0.41	0.7	0.76	0.87	0.65	1.1	1.5	1.4
˛ternal rate of ¡eturn (%)	19.8	17.5	10.2	21.2	21.2	15.7	18.8	18.7	13.5	16.6	17.7	23.3	14.4

*Interest rate varies; IRR is determined based on various loan rates.

1. *Effect of reducing loan amount.* Compare the results of situations 24.2 and 24.3. they are nearly identical except that situation 24.2 is based on a 75 percent loan (75 percent of the purchase price is borrowed and 25 percent is invested in cash). Situation 24.3 is an *all-cash* transaction. The IRR *drops* from 17.5 percent for the leveraged investment to only 10.2 percent for the all-cash transaction. However, there are other situations where the reverse effect would be true—everything depends on the cost of the borrowed money and the repayment terms.

Also, see Table 24-B, situations 24.9 and 24.10 for a similar comparison. With a 75 percent loan (24.10) the IRR is 16.6 percent, and when the loan is *reduced* to 50 percent (24.9), the IRR drops to 13.5 percent.

2. *Effect of differing tax brackets.* When the tax bracket is 35 percent (situation 24.6), the IRR is 15.7 percent. At the lowest bracket rate of 0 percent (24.8), the IRR increases to 18.7 percent. Here again there are multiple forces at work, and the results could be reversed depending on the circumstances. Tax losses in the early years of ownership may benefit the high-bracket investor. But when the investment is showing taxable income, tax cost benefits the lower-tax-bracket investor. The Tax Reform Act of 1986 limits one's ability to offset such losses against professional and portfolio income, but allows such losses to be offset against other passive income.*

3. *Effect of altering the capitalization (CAP) rate at sale.* When the capitalization rate is *increased* from 10 percent (situation 24.4) to 12 percent (24.5), the IRR *remains unchanged* at 21.2 percent. However, if the years of loan amortization were the same for both situations, the IRR would *drop* to 20.17 percent at the higher 12 percent capitalization rate. The lack of material effect on IRR of changes in the CAP rate at sale is due to the relative unimportance of sums due at far-distant future dates, as a result of the discounting process. Compare also the results of situations 24.1 and 24.6.

4. *Effect of increasing the number of years of loan amortization.* When the amortization time period is *increased* from 25 years (situation 24.4) to 99 years (equivalent to an interest-only loan with no amortization of principal (24.5), the IRR remains 21.2 percent. However, in situation 24.5, the CAP rate at sale increases from 10 percent to 12 percent. Had the CAP rate remained 10 percent, the IRR (for 24.5) would have increased to 22.2 percent.

Generally, where the effect of leverage is favorable, stretching out the loan amortization period, or taking an interest-only loan, will increase the IRR. This is in sharp contrast to the conventional wisdom of paying off loans as

---

*IRS publication 925 discusses "Passive Activity and At-Risk Rules." Beginning in 1994, real estate activities in which you materially participate will no longer be passive activities if you meet certain eligibility requirements. Losses from these activities will not be limited by the passive activity rules.

rapidly as possible. Study the figures and discover for yourself the benefits of *not* paying off the loan principal. The loan principal payments reduce nearby cash flows (at the expense of distant cash flows), which reduces the IRR. Further, loan principal payments are not tax deductible. *In general, then, it is likely to be advantageous to avoid paying off the loan.*

5. *Effect of changing loan interest rates.* When the loan interest rate *increases* from 10 percent (situations 24.12) to 12 percent (24.4), the IRR *decreases* from 23.3 percent to 21.2 percent. There is nothing surprising about this, as the higher the interest rate, the more is the reduction of cash flow; and the less the cash flow, the lower is the IRR.

Importance of the Level of Initial Yield

The assumptions underlying Fig. 24.1 are fairly typical of the real world at the time of this writing. A change in the magnitude of the "initial yield percentage" has a *dramatic effect* on the IRR. The initial yield percentage is net operating income (before debt service) divided by total investment.

	Before	After	Relative change
Initial yield percentage	8%	10%	25%
IRR	12.5%	19.8%	58%

Thus just a 2 percent increase (from 8 to 10 percent, an increase of 25 percent) in the initial yield results in over a 7 percent increase (from 12.5 to 19.8 percent, an increase of 58 percent) in the internal rate of return.

Figures 24.1 through 24.4 show various real estate models (graphs) for the determination of IRR.

It must be emphasized that the above comparisons are not rules of thumb. The interplay of many, many variables is involved in determining the annual cash flows—and the IRR. The above effects are valid only for the figure presented and the assumptions contained therein.

Initial yield percent

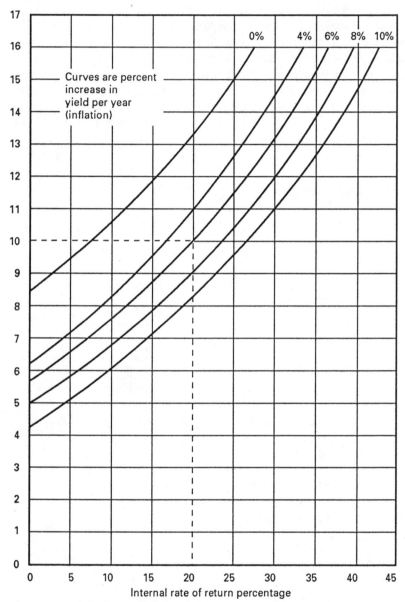

Figure 24.1. After-tax real estate IRR: 35 percent tax bracket, 75 percent loan, 25-year amortization; 10 percent interest; 0–10 percent inflation; various initial yields; 90 percent building/total investment; 31.5 years straight-line depreciation; 10 percent cap rate at sale in 10 years; 0 percent of capital gains not taxed. *(Source: INVESTMENT IRR ANALYSIS (AFTER-TAX) FOR STOCKS, BONDS, AND REAL ESTATE, Larry Rosen Co., copyright © 1990–1994.)*

Initial yield percent

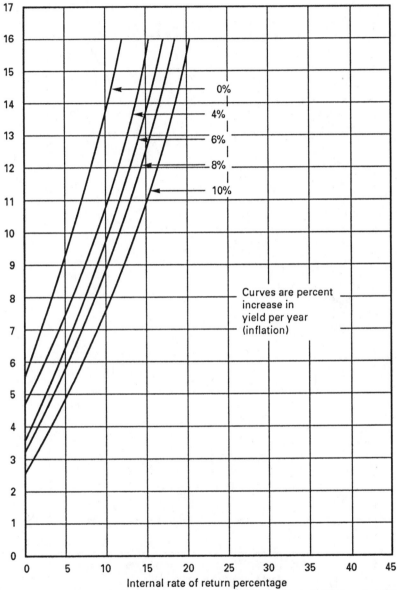

Figure 24.2. After-tax real estate IRR: 35 percent tax bracket, zero loan; 0–10 percent rate of inflation; 0–16 percent, initial percent return; 90 percent, building + total investment; 31.5 years, straight-line depreciation; 12 percent cap rate at sale, 10 years hence; 0 percent of capital gains tax waived. *(Source: INVESTMENT IRR ANALYSIS (AFTER-TAX) FOR STOCKS, BONDS, AND REAL ESTATE, Larry Rosen Co., copyright © 1990–1994.)*

Initial yield percent

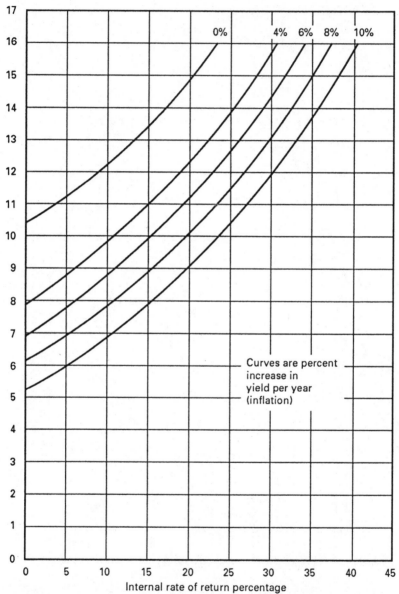

Internal rate of return percentage

Figure 24.3. After-tax real estate IRR: 35 percent tax bracket, interest-only 12 percent loan; 0–10 percent, rate of inflation; 0-16 percent, initial percent return; 75 percent loan; 90 percent, building + total investment; sale 10 years hence at 12 percent cap rate; 0 percent of capital gains tax waived. *(Source: INVESTMENT IRR ANALYSIS (AFTER-TAX) FOR STOCKS, BONDS, AND REAL ESTATE, Larry Rosen Co., copyright © 1990–1994.)*

Loan interest rate percentage

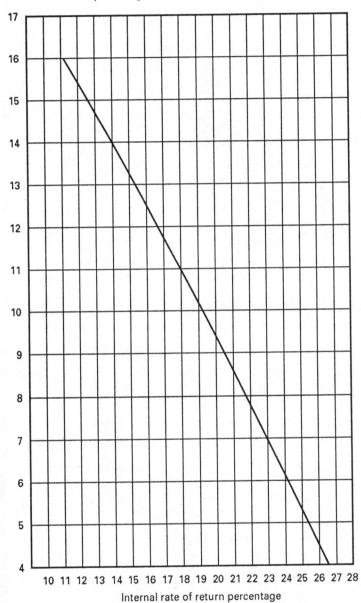

Internal rate of return percentage

Figure 24.4. After-tax real estate IRR: 28 percent tax bracket; effect of loan rate on IRR; 5 percent inflation; 10 percent initial percentage return; 75 percent loan, 25-year amortization; 4–16 percent loan interest; 90 percent, building + total investment; 27.5 years, straight-line depreciation; sale 10 years hence at 10 percent cap rate; 0 percent of capital gains tax waived; 5 percent increase in rents (and expenses) per year. (*Source: INVESTMENT IRR ANALYSIS (AFTER-TAX) FOR STOCKS, BONDS, AND REAL ESTATE, Larry Rosen Co., copyright © 1990–1994.*)

Table 24.1. Real Estate IRR after Tax

Inflation 6%
Initial yield 10%

Annual Increase in Rents (enter decimal)	6.00%
Annual Increase in Expenses (decimal)	6.00%
Year 1 Rents are: 10.0% total inv	100
First Year Operating Expenses	0
Interest Rate on Reinvesting (decimal)	30.52%
Tax Bracket (decimal)	35.00%
CASH INVESTMENT	250
LOAN	750
Total Investment	1,000
Years of Loan Amortization	25
Loan Interest % (enter as decimal)	10.00%
Loan principal & interest	83
Building divided by Total Investment	90.00%
Depreciable assets	900
Years of Straight Line Depreciation	31.5
No. of Years of Analysis and Year of Sale	10
Capitalization Rate at Sale	10.00%
Portion of Long Term C. Gain Not Taxed	0.000%
Mortgage constant	11.017%

```
<*><*><*><*><*><*><*><*><*><*><*><*><*><*>
<*>
<*>   Enter percents as decimals, e.g. 5% as 0.05      <*>
<*>   Do not enter data in cells containing formulas   <*>
<*>   Years of Analysis--from 1 to 15                   <*>
<*>   Enter your assumptions in Column E, E2 to E20     <*>
<*>              GOTO A1 to                             <*>
<*>              Continue                               <*>
<*>
<*><*><*><*><*><*><*><*><*><*><*><*><*><*>
```

	YEAR 0	YEAR 1	YEAR 2	YEAR 3	YEAR 4	YEAR 5	YEAR 6	YEAR 7	YEAR 8	YEAR 9	YEAR 10	TOTALS
NO USER ENTRIES BELOW THIS!	0											
(Is year of sale reached?)		0	0	0	0	0	0	0	0	0	0	
Annual Depreciation		29										
(Has loan maturity been reached?)		0	0	0	0	0	0	0	0	0	0	
Loan Beginning		750	742	734	725	715	703	691	678	663	646	0
Interest, Annual		75	74	73	72	71	70	69	68	66	65	705
Principal relocation		8	8	9	10	11	12	14	15	16	18	122
Loan (Ending)		742	734	725	715	703	691	678	663	646	628	
Net Operating Income (NOI)		100	106	112	119	126	134	142	150	159	169	1,318

	1	2	3	4	5	6	7	8	9	10	T
Cash flow (pre tax)	17	23	30	36	44	51	59	68	77	86	492
Cash flow/cash investment	6.95%	9.35%	11.89%	14.59%	17.45%	20.48%	23.69%	27.09%	30.70%	34.56%	
(Is maximum yrs. of deprec. reached?)											
Depreciation (cumulative)	0	29	57	86	114	143	171	200	229	257	286
Less: depreciation	29	29	29	29	29	29	29	29	29	29	
Plus: loan principal	8	8	9	10	11	12	14	15	16	18	122
(Is this the year of sale?)	0	0	0	0	0	0	0	0	0	1	
TAXABLE INCOME	(4)	3	10	18	26	35	44	54	65	76	328
Income tax if savings "-" savings	(1)	1	4	6	9	12	15	19	23	27	115
CASH FLOW after tax and pre-sale	19	22	26	30	34	39	44	49	54	60	377
Sales proceeds in year (10)	0	0	0	0	0	0	0	0	0	1689	1689
Capital gains tax on sale	0	0	0	0	0	0	0	0	0	341	341
Cash from sale after tax & loan payment	0	0	0	0	0	0	0	0	0	720	720
CASH FLOW AFTER TAX	19	22	26	30	34	39	44	49	54	780	1097

REINVESTMENT OF CASH FLOW ANALYSIS:

Reinvestment rate 30.52%

	YEAR 1	YEAR 2	YEAR 3	YEAR 4	YEAR 5	YEAR 6	YEAR 7	YEAR 8	YEAR 9	YEAR 10	
Beginning balance with reinvestment	0	19	45	80	125	185	260	356	475	624	
Interest reinvestment earned for year	0	4	9	16	25	37	52	71	94	124	430
Cash flow after tax incl interest reinv.	19	26	35	46	59	76	95	119	148	903	1527
ENDING BALANCE	19	45	80	125	185	260	356	475	624	1527	
	E	F	G	H	I	J	K	L	M	N	T

A B C D

THE REVISED IRR PERCENTAGE is 19.857% with reinvestment.
THE IRR PERCENTAGE is 19.840 without reinvestment.

SOURCE: INVESTMENT IRR ANALYSIS (AFTER TAX) FOR STOCKS, BONDS, AND REAL ESTATE, Larry Rosen Co., 1984-1994.

25

IRR and Beyond: Partitioning IRR, Marginal IRR and Revised IRR, Geometric Mean, and Average Discounted Return

Partitioning IRR

Even though the concept of IRR is both useful and informative, it does not completely eliminate the need for thoughtful consideration on the part of investors. IRR is subject to even further refinement to fine-tune the decision-making process. Three additional refinements are possible: *partitioning* the IRR, determining the *marginal* IRR, and using the *revised* IRR (with reinvestment).

Consider the two alternative real estate investments presented in Table 25.1. Both have the same IRR, 39.08 percent. In the case of Dr. Markman's property, there are no before-tax cash flow benefits; the entire return is derived from tax benefits, interest expense on loan and depreciation (21.95

Table 25.1. Partitioning IRR

Seller	Year						Total	Percent of total	Present value at IRR rate	Present value as percent of total
	0	1	2	3	4	5				
Dr. Markman:										
Cash investment	$100,00									
Cash flow before tax		0	0	0	0	0	0	0.00	0	0.00
Tax benefits (cost)		$20,000	$19,000	$18,000	$17,000	$16,000	$90,000	21.95	$ 38,511	38.51
Subtotal		20,000	19,000	18,000	17,000	16,000			38,511	38.51
Sales proceeds (after tax and loan)						320,000	320,000	78.05	61,489	61.49
Cash flow (after tax)	–100,00	20,000	19,000	18,000	17,000	336,000	410,000	100.00	100,000	100,000
Internal rate of return						39.08%				
Mr. McClintock:										
Cash investment	100,000									
Cash flow before tax		29,000	29,000	29,000	29,000	$29,000	145,000	44.02	59,943	59.94
Tax benefits (cost)		5,000	4,000	3,000	2,000	1,000	15,000	4.55	7,504	7.50
Subtotal		34,000	33,000	32,000	31,000	30,000			67,447	67.45
Sales proceeds (after tax and loan)						169,425	169,425	51.43	32,553	32.55
Cash flow (after tax)	–100,00	34,000	33,000	32,000	31,000	199,425	329,425	100.00	100,000	100.00
Internal rate of return						39.08%				

percent of benefits), and the projected sales proceeds in the fifth year (78.05 percent of benefits).

Mr. McClintock's property, on the other hand, projects a strong annual before-tax cash flow, 44.02 percent of benefits, has normal tax advantages (4.55 percent of benefits), and is expected to produce reasonable after-tax proceeds at sale (51.43 percent of benefits).

Even though Dr. Markman's property and Mr. McClintock's property have the same projected IRR (39.08 percent), which would be likely to be a superior investment?

Certainly, the IRR that is ultimately realized, as opposed to projected, for Mr. McClintock's property is much more likely to equal or exceed stated projections than is Dr. Markman's. Consider the following breakdown of the IRR composition, after first obtaining the net present value of each cash flow stream discounted at the overall IRR rate of 39.08 percent:

	Dr. Markman	Mr. McClintock
As a percentage of total benefit:		
Before-tax cash flow	0.00	59.95
Tax benefits	38.51	7.50
Subtotal	38.51	67.45
Sales proceeds, after tax	61.49	32.55
Total	100.00	100.00

Since projected cash flows from operations (e.g., annual net rentals) are much more likely to be accurately predicted than are those from future years' tax benefits and sales proceeds 5 years down the road, the intelligent choice would be Mr. McClintock's property, where 59.9 percent of the IRR (compared to 0 percent for Dr. Markman) results from the more predictable stream of cash flows (see Fig. 25.1).

The problem in real estate investing, like investing in anything, is to identify the risk as well as the potential rewards. And what better way is there to choose intelligently among alternative investments than by partitioning the IRR? Partitioning IRR means determining the present value proportion of each important component of overall return.

Ranked in order of security or safety, the components to partition are:

1. Initial or guaranteed before-tax cash flow (such as base rent on a retail lease that also has a percentage or overage rent. Include future rent increases that are contractually binding in existing leases). For a stock, the cash flow from a presently secure dividend would also fall in this category.

2. Tax benefits (subject to the risk of change in tax laws and a change in the investor's marginal tax rate).

Percent

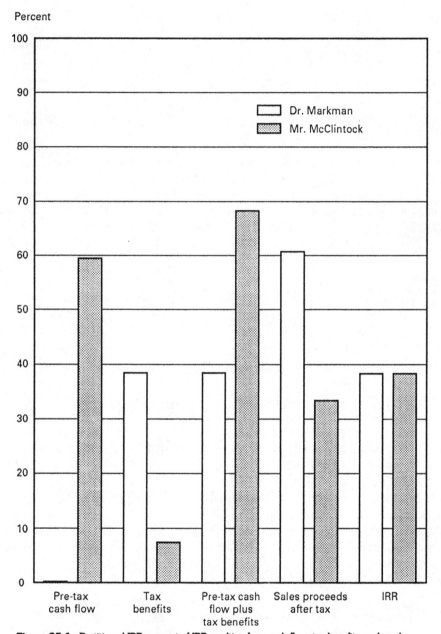

Figure 25.1. Partitioned IRR: percent of IRR resulting from cash flow, tax benefits, and resale.

3. Growth in cash flow above initial or base level (such as income from percentage rents or future increases in rent that are not contractually binding). For a stock, future increases in the level of dividends are comparable.

4. Sales proceeds, after repayment of any debt financing, which thus also recognizes equity buildup through loan principal amortization. Sales proceeds includes expected future appreciation in the value of the property, and reflects estimated changes in cash flows and capitalization rates. For stocks, sales proceeds reflect future levels of earnings per share and price-earnings multiples.

Marginal IRR

When to Sell the Investment

When the rate of return to be gained by holding the investment is less than the rate of return that is obtainable by investing the after-tax sales proceeds in a different investment, then *it is time to sell.* Because of the eventual extinction or demise of tax benefits that result from finite depreciation, replacement investments eventually become an alluring possible alternative to continuing to hold a property. For stocks, diminishing rates of earnings-per-share growth, which frequently accompany an aging company, have a similar effect.

A 15-year analysis for a hypothetical investment with $250 cash invested and a $750 loan, for an investor in a 40 percent tax bracket, is presented in Table 25.2. The 15-year IRR is 23.17 percent. However, Part B of the table determines cash flows for holding periods of 1 to 14 years as well. Notice that the element that changes each year is the after-tax proceeds of sale, which increases with the length of the holding period.

Gross sales proceeds are found by capitalizing at a stated CAP rate, 10 percent in the example, the projected net operating income (NOI) in the year of sale. For example, in year 10 the NOI is $169, and the sales proceeds are 169 ÷ 0.10, or $1690.

Part B, "Cumulative IRR: Holdings of 1 to 15 years," shows the IRR for varying holding periods. In this example the IRR increases each year until it peaks in the sixth year, after which it diminishes slightly each year. However, from year 2 through year 15, it is never less than 21.66 percent.

Bear in mind that this IRR is an *average* in that it always includes the results from the first year through the last year of the desired holding period. If the first 4 years' results were particularly beneficial, they will continue to favorably affect the results for a 10- or 12-year analysis.

Table 25.2. Marginal IRR

Tax bracket	40%		Building/total investment	90%
Cash investment	$250		Initial depreciable assets	$900
Loan	$750		Years straight-line depreciation	15
Total investment	$1000		Year of sale	15
Years loan amortization	25		Capitalization rate at sale	10%
Loan interest	10%		Inflation	6%
Loan principal and interest	$83		Mortgage constant	11.017%

Year

Part A

	1	2	3	4	5	6	7	8	9	10	11	12	13	14	15	Totals
Loan (beginning of year)	750	742	734	725	715	703	691	678	663	646	628	609	587	563	537	
Annual interest	75	74	73	72	71	70	69	68	66	65	63	61	59	56	54	997
Principal reduction during year	8	8	9	10	11	12	14	15	16	18	20	22	24	26	29	242
Loan (end of year)	742	734	725	715	703	691	678	663	646	628	609	587	563	537	508	
Net operating income (NOI)/cash investment 10.00%																
Net operating income	100	106	112	119	126	$34	142	150	159	169	179	190	201	213	226	2328
NOI/total investment, %	10.00	10.60	11.24	11.91	12.62	13.38	14.19	15.04	15.94	16.89	17.91	18.98	20.12	21.33	22.61	
Less: Loan principal and interest	83	83	83	83	83	83	83	83	83	83	83	83	83	83	83	1239
Cash flow before tax	17	23	30	36	44	51	59	68	77	86	96	107	119	131	143	1088
Cash flow/cash investment, %	6.95	9.35	11.89	14.59	17.45	20.48	23.69	27.09	30.70	34.53	38.58	42.88	47.44	52.27	57.39	
Less: Depreciation	60	60	60	60	60	60	60	60	60	60	60	60	60	60	60	900
Plus: Loan principal repayment during year	8	8	9	10	11	·12	14	15	16	18	20	22	24	26	29	242

(savings in tax)	-14	-11	-8	-5	-2	-2	1	5	9	13	18	22	28	33	39	45
Cash flow after tax, before sale	31	35	38	42	46	50	54	59	64	69	74	80	86	92	98	916
Sales proceeds in year of sale															2261	2261
Capital gains tax on sale															346	346
Cash from sale after tax and loan repayment															1407	1407
Cash flow after tax	31	35	38	42	46	50	54	59	64	69	74	80	86	92	1506	2323
Internal rate of return																23.17%

Part B: Marginal IRR based on sale at each year-end:

	-14	-11	-8	-5	-2	-2	1	5	9	13	18	22	28	33
Sale proceeds	1000	1060	1124	1191	1262	1338	1419	1504	1594	1689	$791	1898	2012	2133
Capital gains tax on sale	10	29	49	69	90	112	134	157	181	206	232	259	287	316
Cash from sale after tax and loan repayment	248	297	350	407	469	535	607	683	766	855	950	1052	1162	1281
Cash flow sale in year 1	279													
Cash flow sale in year 2	31	332												
Cash flow sale in year 3	31	35	388											
Cash flow sale in year 4	31	35	38	449										
Cash flow sale in year 5	31	35	38	42	515									
Cash flow sale in year 6	31	35	38	42	46	585								
Cash flow sale in year 7	31	35	38	42	46	50	661							
Cash flow sale in year 8	31	35	38	42	46	50	54	742						
Cash flow sale in year 9	31	35	38	42	46	50	54	59	830					
Cash flow sale in year 10	31	35	38	42	46	50	54	59	64	923				
Cash flow sale in year 11	31	35	38	42	46	50	54	59	64	69	1024			
Cash flow sale in year 12	31	35	38	42	46	50	54	59	64	69	74	1132		

Table 25.2. Marginal IRR (Continued)

	Year															Totals
	1	2	3	4	5	6	7	8	9	10	11	12	13	14	15	
Cash flow sale in year 13	31	35	38	42	46	50	54	59	64	69	74	80	1248			
Cash flow sale in year 14	31	35	38	42	46	50	54	59	64	69	74	80	86	1372		
Cash flow sale in year 15	31	35	38	42	46	50	54	59	64	69	74	80	86	92	1506	
Cumulative IRR: Holdings of 1 to 15 years, %	11.76	21.66	24.29	25.12	25.32	25.25	25.05	24.81	24.55	24.29	24.04	23.80	23.58	23.37	23.17	
Marginal IRR: Percent return from holding 1 more year, %	11.76	33.81	30.69	28.27	26.33	24.76	23.44	22.33	21.37	20.54	19.81	19.16	18.58	18.07	17.60	
Part C: Proof that no reinvestment is needed to achieve the stated (23.17%) IRR 15-year analysis																
Outstanding (unrecovered) cash investment	$250	$277	$306	$339	$375	$417	$463	$517	$578	$648	$729	$824	$936	$1067	$1222	
Cash flow (after tax) for year	31	35	38	42	46	50	54	59	64	69	74	80	86	92	1506	2323
IRR × outstanding cash investment	58	64	71	78	87	97	107	120	134	150	169	191	217	247	283	2073
Reduction in outstanding investment (recovery)	-27	-29	-33	-37	-41	-47	-53	-61	-70	-82	-95	-111	-131	-155	1223	250
Outstanding cash investment at end of year	277	306	339	375	417	463	517	578	648	729	824	936	1067	1222	0	250

This "average" syndrome can be avoided by using the *marginal return concept*. Introductory economics says that the *marginal* return is that obtained from adding one more unit to what you already have. It is the return on that *one more* unit, not the average for all the units. The margin concept is often thought of in terms of taxes. The important consideration in looking at tax cost or tax savings is the marginal rate of tax—how much tax am I going to pay by adding or subtracting $1 of income to what I already have?

In this example, we want to know when to sell the investment. We have set forth the proposition that *the time to sell is when the return for holding is less than the return obtainable by investing the after-tax sales proceeds in an alternate investment*. The marginal IRR is an accurate measure of the rate obtained by continuing to hold the investment. *The marginal IRR for year n is a measure of how much more cash the investor will have by selling in year n compared to what he or she would have from selling the previous year, year (n − 1). The increase in cash by selling in year n is divided by the cash that would have resulted from a sale in year (n − 1).*

A. The increase in cash by selling year *n* is the cash from the sale after tax and loan, plus the cash flow after tax, before sale in that year, less the cash from sales proceeds after tax and loan repayment at the end of year (*n* − 1).

B. The cash that would have resulted from a sale in year (*n* −1) is the cash from sales proceeds after tax and loan repayment at the end of year (*n* − 1).

The marginal IRR is simple A + B. For a sale in year 6, this would be 24.8 percent [($50 + $535 − $469) + $469]. *Thus, the marginal return is the percent return from holding the investment one more year.* The marginal return so obtained is directly comparable to IRRs obtained from alternative investments.

In our example, the marginal return is greater than the average IRR for holdings of 1 to 5 years and is less than the average IRR for holdings of 6 years or more, as shown in Table 25.2, Part B.

If, in year 8, an investment with an IRR of 25 percent is available, then the existing investment should be considered for sale to obtain the alternative, because the marginal return resulting from continuing to hold the existing investment for year 8 is only 22.3 percent.

Another possibility, with such attractive investments, would be to obtain *both*—by refinancing the existing investment and using the proceeds of the loan to acquire the alternative.

Although Table 25.2 illustrates a *real estate* situation, *exactly the same principles apply to stock and bond investments.*

The Real McCoy

You may be thinking, "All these illustrations are so farfetched. Where can you buy a property for $1000 with $250 cash? What I want to see is an analysis of a real situation." OK, but if you dislike detail you are not going to be happy with the response. A real pro forma analysis which was prepared for an actual property that we purchased is presented in Table 25.3. It is a freestanding retail store of 3000 square feet in Louisville. The lot is 75 feet by 200 feet. The property is leased to a national firm, that together with franchisees, sold at the time of acquisition about $500 million per year. In addition to a base rent of $6000 per year, the tenant pays a percentage rent equal to 1 percent of sales in excess of $375,000 per year. The year before acquisition, the store sold $614,000, so percentage rents were already being paid. Sales are assumed to increase at the rate of inflation, which in the pro forma analysis is projected at 6 percent per year. Loan financing is at the prime rate plus ½ percent, interest only.

Any of the assumptions can be changed and the results instantly recomputed, using a typical spreadsheet and the author's real estate analysis computer software, INVESTMENT IRR ANALYSIS AFTER TAX FOR STOCKS, BONDS, AND REAL ESTATE (Larry Rosen Co., 1990–1994). For example, analyzing the effects of varying assumptions in the following areas are useful:

Tax bracket

Inflation rate

Size of loan

Interest rate

Capitalization rate upon resale

Analysis of Table 25.3 shows that 25 to 30 percent interest would be required for a fully taxed investment to produce returns equal to those from this property (see equivalent return on a fully taxed investment). The *after-tax* IRR is projected to be almost 15 percent. The *marginal* IRR peaks in the third year at 17.48 percent but remains above 15 percent for holdings of anywhere from 2 to 15 years.

The results of *partitioning the IRR* of the investment (shown in Table 25.3) are given in Table 25.4. Here, a 5-year holding period has been used

Table 25.3. Pro Forma Analysis with Marginal IRR

Sales starting	$614,000 (present annualized amount)	Initial depreciable assets	$54,240
Tax bracket	50.00%	Years straight-line depreciation	15.00 (whole years)
Cash investment	$46,800	Year of future sale of property	15.00 (from year of purchase)
Loan	$31,200	Capitalization rate at sale	10.00%
Total investment	$78,000	Inflation rate	6.00% (applies to most expenses)
Total investment includes leases of	$16,260	Mortgage constant	10.0008% (principal and interest)
Years amortization, leases	3.50	Annual sales increase	6.00%
Total investment includes personal property	$0	Sales breakpoint for percent rent	$375,000
Years amortization, personal property	0.00 (whole years)	Additional rent percent of sales greater than breakpoint	1.000%
Purchase price of land	$7,500 (per contract)	Maximum real estate tax paid by owner	$0
Years loan amortization	99.00 (interest only, no amortization)	Maximum insurance paid by owners	$0
Loan interest	10.00%	Building square feet	3,000
Fixed or minimum rental per year	$6,000		

	Year															
	1	2	3	4	5	6	7	8	9	10	11	12	13	14	15	Totals
Income:																
Sales, $	614,000	650,840	689,890	731,284	775,161	821,671	870,971	923,229	978,623	1,037,340	1,099,580	1,165,555	1,235,489	1,309,618	1,388,195	14,291,445
Fixed or minimum rent	6,000	6,000	6,000	6,000	6,000	6,000	6,000	6,000	6,000	6,000	6,000	6,000	6,000	6,000	6,000	90,000
Percentage rent additional	2,390	2,758	3,149	3,563	4,002	4,467	4,960	5,482	6,036	6,623	7,246	7,906	8,605	9,346	10,182	86,664
Total rent	8,390	8,758	9,149	9,563	10,002	10,467	10,960	11,482	12,036	12,623	13,246	13,906	14,605	15,346	16,182	176,664
Vacancy allowance (0.00%)	0	0	0	0	0	0	0	0	0	0	0	0	0	0	0	
Effective gross income (EGI)	8,390	8,758	9,149	9,563	10,002	10,467	10,960	11,482	12,036	12,623	13,246	13,906	14,605	15,346	16,182	176,664
Expenses:																
Management fee (6.00%)	503	526	549	574	600	628	658	689	722	757	795	834	876	921	968	10,600

Table 25.3. Pro Forma Analysis with Marginal IRR (Continued)

							Year									
	1	2	3	4	5	6	7	8	9	10	11	12	13	14	15	Totals
Utilities	0	0	0	0	0	0	0	0	0	0	0	0	0	0	0	0
Real estate tax	617	654	694	735	779	826	876	928	984	1,043	1,106	1,172	1,242	1,317	1,396	14,371
Proceeds from limit on owner tax	−617	−654	−694	−735	−779	−826	−876	−928	−984	−1,043	−1,106	−1,172	−1,242	−1,317	−1,396	−14,371
Insurance	0	0	0	0	0	0	0	0	0	0	0	0	0	0	0	0
Proceeds from limit on insurance	0	0	0	0	0	0	0	0	0	0	0	0	0	0	0	0
Repairs and maintenance	0	0	0	0	0	0	0	0	0	0	0	0	0	0	0	0
Professional fees, $	125	133	140	149	158	167	177	188	199	211	224	237	252	267	283	2,909
Advertising	0	0	0	0	0	0	0	0	0	0	0	0	0	0	0	0
Roof reserve or allowance	0	0	0	0	0	0	0	0	0	0	0	0	0	0	0	0
Asphalt reserve or allowance	0	0	0	0	0	0	0	0	0	0	0	0	0	0	0	0
Other expenses	0	0	0	0	0	0	0	0	0	0	0	0	0	0	0	0
Total expenses, $	628	658	689	723	758	795	835	877	921	969	1,019	1,072	1,128	1,187	1,251	13,509
Loan (beginning balance)	31,200	31,200	31,199	31,199	31,199	31,198	31,198	31,198	31,197	31,197	31,196	31,195	31,195	31,194	31,193	
Interest per year	3,120	3,120	3,120	3,120	3,120	3,120	3,120	3,120	3,120	3,120	3,120	3,120	3,119	3,119	3,119	46,796
Principal of loan reduction	0	0	0	0	0	0	0	0	1	1	1	1	1	1	1	7
Loan (ending balance)	31,200	31,199	31,199	31,199	31,198	31,198	31,198	31,197	31,197	31,196	31,195	31,195	31,194	31,193	31,192	
Net operating income (NOI)	7,762	8,100	8,460	8,840	9,244	9,671	10,125	10,605	11,115	11,655	12,227	12,834	13,477	14,159	14,881	163,155
NOI total investment, %	9.95	10.39	10.85	11.33	11.85	12.40	12.98	13.60	14.25	14.94	15.68	16.45	17.28	18.15	19.08	

																Total
income tax	4,641	4,980	5,339	5,720	6,123	6,551	7,005	7,485	7,995	8,535	9,107	9,714	10,357	11,059	11,761	116,551
Cash flow/cash investment, %	9.92	10.64	11.41	12.22	13.08	14.00	14.97	15.99	17.08	18.24	19.46	20.76	22.13	23.59	25.18	
Less depreciation, $	3,616	3,616	3,616	3,616	3,616	3,616	3,616	3,616	3,616	3,616	3,616	3,616	3,616	3,616	3,616	54,240
Plus loan principal reduction	0	0	0	0	0	0	0	1	1	1	1	1	1	1	1	8
Less amortization of leases	4,646	4,646	4,646	2,323	0	0	0	0	0	0	0	0	0	0	0	16,260
Less amortization of personal property	0	0	0	0	0	0	0	0	0	0	0	0	0	0	0	0
Taxable income:	−3,620	−3,281	−2,922	−219	2,508	2,936	3,389	3,870	4,379	4,919	5,492	6,098	6,742	7,423	8,146	45,859
Income tax (− = tax savings)	−1,810	−1,641	−1,461	−109	1,254	1,468	1,695	1,935	2,190	2,460	2,746	3,049	3,371	3,712	4,073	22,930
Cash flow after tax (presale)	6,451	6,621	6,800	5,829	4,870	5,083	5,310	5,550	5,805	6,075	6,361	6,664	6,986	7,327	7,688	93,422
Sales proceeds in year 15															148,814	148,814
Capital gains tax on sale in year 15															28,263	28,263
Cash from sale after tax and loan repayment															89,359	89,359
Cash flow after tax	6,451	6,621	6,800	5,829	4,870	5,083	5,310	5,550	5,805	6,075	6,361	6,664	6,986	7,327	97,047	182,781
Assessed value for real estate tax, $	61,740	65,444	69,371	73,533	77,945	82,622	87,579	92,834	98,404	104,308	110,567	117,201	124,233	131,687	139,588	
Real estate tax rate, %	1.000	1.000	1.000	1.000	1.000	1.000	1.000	1.000	1.000	1.000	1.000	1.000	1.000	1.000	1.000	
Annual rent per square foot, $	2.80	2.92	3.05	3.19	3.33	3.49	3.65	3.83	4.01	4.21	4.42	4.64	4.87	5.12	5.38	
Annual sales per square foot	204.67	216.95	229.96	243.76	258.39	273.89	290.32	307.74	326.21	345.78	366.53	388.52	411.83	436.54	462.73	
Return on cash investment of $46,800:																
Before-tax cash flow/cash investment, %	9.92	10.64	11.41	12.22	13.08	14.00	14.97	15.99	17.08	18.24	19.46	20.76	22.13	23.59	25.18	

Table 25.3. Pro Forma Analysis with Marginal IRR (Continued)

	1	2	3	4	5	6	7	8	9	10	11	12	13	14	15	Totals
								Year								
Tax savings or cost (−)/(cash investment	3.87	3.51	3.12	0.23	−2.68	−3.14	−3.62	−4.13	−4.68	−5.26	−5.87	−6.52	−7.20	−7.93	−8.70	
Equity—loan principal/cash investment	0.00	0.00	0.00	0.00	0.00	0.00	0.00	0.00	0.00	0.00	0.00	0.00	0.00	0.00	0.00	
Total return on cash investment, %	13.79	14.15	14.53	12.46	10.41	10.86	11.35	11.86	12.41	12.98	13.59	14.24	14.93	15.66	16.43	
Equivalent return on fully taxed investment, %	27.57	28.30	29.06	24.91	20.81	21.73	22.69	23.72	24.81	25.96	27.19	28.48	29.86	31.31	32.86	
Internal rate of return for this property, %																14.97
Marginal internal rate of return:																
Sales proceeds at end of each year, $	77,616	81,004	84,595	88,402	92,437	96,714	101,248	106,054	111,148	116,548	122,272	128,339	134,771	141,588	148,814	
Capital gains tax on sale	1,576	3,905	6,276	8,225	9,755	11,334	12,964	14,648	16,390	18,194	20,062	21,998	24,008	26,094	28,263	
Cash from sale after tax and loan, $	44,841	45,899	47,120	48,978	51,483	54,182	57,086	60,208	63,561	67,158	71,015	75,146	79,569	84,301	89,359	
Cash flow, sale in year 1	51,292															
Cash flow, sale in year 2		52,520														
Cash flow, sale in year 3	6,451	6,621	53,920													
Cash flow, sale	6,451															

Cash flow, sale	Year 1	Year 2	Year 3	Year 4	Year 5	Year 6	Year 7	Year 8	Year 9	Year 10	Year 11	Year 12	Year 13	Year 14	Year 15
Cash flow, sale in year 5	6,451	6,621	6,800	5,829	56,353										
Cash flow, sale in year 6	6,451	6,621	6,800	5,829	4,870	59,266									
Cash flow, sale in year 7	6,451	6,621	6,800	5,829	4,870	5,083	62,397								
Cash flow, sale in year 8	6,451	6,621	6,800	5,829	4,870	5,083	5,310	65,759							
Cash flow, sale in year 9	6,451	6,621	6,800	5,829	4,870	5,083	5,310	5,550	69,366						
Cash flow, sale in year 10	6,451	6,621	6,800	5,829	4,870	5,083	5,310	5,550	5,805	73,233					
Cash flow, sale in year 11	6,451	6,621	6,800	5,829	4,870	5,083	5,310	5,550	5,805	6,075	77,876				
Cash flow, sale in year 12	6,451	6,621	6,800	5,829	4,870	5,083	5,310	5,550	5,805	6,075	6,361	81,811			
Cash flow, sale in year 13	6,451	6,621	6,800	5,829	4,870	5,083	5,310	5,550	5,805	6,075	6,361	6,664	86,555		
Cash flow, sale in year 14	6,451	6,621	6,800	5,829	4,870	5,083	5,310	5,550	5,805	6,075	6,361	6,664	6,986	91,627	
Cash flow, sale in year 15	6,451	6,621	6,800	5,829	4,870	5,083	5,310	5,550	5,805	6,075	6,361	6,664	6,986	7,327	97,047
IRR—Sale at end of each year, %	9.60	13.05	14.32	14.72	14.77	14.82	14.85	14.88	14.90	14.92	14.94	14.95	14.96	14.97	14.97
Marginal IRR—Percent return from holding 1 more year, %	9.60	17.13	17.48	16.31	15.06	15.12	15.16	15.19	15.21	15.22	15.21	15.20	15.18	15.15	15.12

and the average after-tax IRR was 14.77 percent. The results of the partitioning show that:

Source	IRR percentage
Cash flow before tax	37.88
Tax benefits (cost)	6.89
Subtotal	44.76
Sales proceeds after tax	55.24
Total	100.00

What Reinvestment Rate Is Needed to Achieve IRR?

Maria Bertolucci is thinking of making a real estate investment, and she has studied the projected financial results including the IRR, which is estimated to be 20 percent. She realizes that the IRR is an after-tax result, but, she wonders, is it necessary to reinvest the cash flow each year at a rate equal to the IRR in order to wind up with true results equal to the IRR at purchase?

This is a very significant question. If the answer is "yes," Maria must reinvest at a rate equal to the IRR, which means that a reinvestment rate that is lower than the initial IRR rate will result in a true IRR that is less than that calculated initially. There is a lot of confusion over this point in the literature and even among academics.

The answer is that *no reinvestment of cash flow is required to achieve the IRR!* (See Chap. 15.) Maria can spend every penny she receives from the real estate without reinvesting at all, and her IRR will be as originally calculated (if the projections hold true). Proof of this can be seen in Part C of Table 25.2.

Geometric Mean and Average Discounted Return

Two measures of cost or return that, like IRR, take into account both the timing and the size of periodic cash flows are the *geometric mean* (GM) and the average discounted return (AD).

A serious detriment of both GM and AD is that neither method has the IRR characteristic of being the rate earned on unrecovered investment, which makes the IRR comparable to an interest rate earned on a bank account. The IRR is more useful than either GM or AD in that it can be compared directly to bank interest or yields to maturity on bonds, whereas GM and AD cannot. Both GM and AD are sensitive to marginal returns (changes in market value without immediate accompanying cash flows), while IRR recognizes changes in asset values only at the end of the valuation period when the cash is actually received from the change in asset value.

Table 25.4. Partitioning IRR

	Year						Total	Percent of total	Present value at IRR rate	Present value as percent of total
	0	1	2	3	4	5				
Cash investment	$46,800									
Cash flow before tax		$4,641	$4,980	$5,339	$5,720	$ 6,123	$26,803	32.67%	$17,727	37.88%
Tax benefits (cost)		1,810	1,641	1,461	109	−1,254	3,767	4.59	3,222	6.89
Subtotal		$6,451	$6,621	$6,800	$5,829	$ 4,869	$30,570	37.26%	$20,949	44.76%
Sales proceeds (after tax and loan)						51,483	51,483	62.74%	25,851	55.24%
Cash flow (after tax)	−46,800	$6,451	$6,621	$6,800	$5,829	$56,352	$82,053	100.00%	$46,800	100.00%
Internal rate of return			14.77%							

Geometric Mean

The computation of GM can best be understood by computing it in a two-stage process, as follows:

$$m_j = \frac{e_j - e_{j-1} + c_j}{e_j}$$

where m_j = a form of marginal return
$\quad\quad e_j$ = equity in investment at the end of period j
$\quad\quad j$ = time period (1, 2, 3, . . . , etc.)
$\quad\quad c_j$ = cash flow (net) in period j

$$r_g = \left[\prod_{j=1}^{n} (1 + m_j) \right]^{(1/n)} - 1$$

where r_g = geometric mean return.

Twelve examples with varying patterns of cash flows and changes in asset value are given in Table 25.5, with details of the computation given in Table 25.6, Parts A through L.

For Part A of Table 25.6, the details of the calculation are as follows:

$$m_1 = \frac{\$1000 - \$1000 + 0}{\$1000} = 0$$

$$m_2 = \frac{\$1000 - \$1000 + \$50}{\$1000} = 0.05$$

$$m_3 = \frac{\$1000 - \$1000 + \$100}{\$1000} = 0.10$$

$$m_4 = \frac{\$1000 - \$1000 + \$150}{\$1000} = 0.15$$

$$m_5 = \frac{\$1000 - \$1000 + \$200}{\$1000} = 0.20$$

and

$$r_g = (1 + 0)^{\frac{1}{5}} (1 + 0.05)^{\frac{1}{5}} (1 + 0.1)^{\frac{1}{5}} (1 + 0.15)^{\frac{1}{5}} (1 + 0.2)^{\frac{1}{5}} - 1$$

$$= (1.0)(1.0098)(1.0192)(1.0283)(1.0371) - 1 = 9.772\%$$

Table 25.5. Illustrations of IRR, Geometric Mean, and Average Discounted Return

| | | | Period | | | | | | Geometric | Ave. |
	0	1	2	3	4	5	Sum	IRR R_c, %	mean R_g, %	discount R_a, %
Cash flow only; no change in value										
Example A Cash flows	−$1000	0	$50	$100	$150	$1200	$500	9.1292	9.7720	9.1290
Change in value	0	0	0	0	0	0	0			
Example B Cash flows	−1000	$100	100	100	100	1100	500	10.000	10.0000	10.0000
Change in value	0	0	0	0	0	0	0			
Example C Cash flows	−1000	200	150	100	50	1000	500	11.0425	9.7720	11.0425
Change in value	0	0	0	0	0	0	0			
No cash flows; value change only										
Example D Cash flows	−1000	0	0	0	0	1000	0	8.4472	8.4470	7.9910
Change in value	0	50	100	150	200	0	500			
Example E Cash flows	−1000	0	0	0	0	1000	0	8.4472	8.4470	8.5690
Change in value	0	100	100	100	100	100	500			
Example F Cash flows	−1000	0	0	0	0	1000	0	8.4472	8.4470	9.5720
Change in value	0	200	150	100	50	0	500			
Level cash flows; value changes										
Example G Cash flows	−1000	200	200	200	200	1200	1000	18.6192	18.3410	18.5990
Change in value	0	0	−10	−20	−30	−40	−100			
Example H Cash flows	−1000	200	200	200	200	1200	1000	18.6192	18.7650	18.6350
Change in value	0	−20	−20	−20	−20	−20	−100			
Example I Cash flows	−1000	200	200	200	200	1200	1000	18.6192	19.2120	18.7020
Change in value	0	−40	−30	−20	−10	0	−100			
Variable cash flows and value change										
Example J Cash flows	−1000	200	200	200	200	1000	800	27.0279	26.1200	27.7390
Change in value	0	100	100	200	200	200	800			
Example K Cash flows	−1000	100	200	200	200	1100	800	25.4611	22.5100	35.2090
Change in value	0	700	100	0	0	0	800			
Example L Cash flows	−1000	400	100	100	100	1100	800	28.4233	25.8700	31.0000
Change in value	0	100	100	300	300	0	800			

Table 25.6. Computation of Geometric Mean and Average Discounted Return

Principal sum received at maturity: $1000
Number of periods, n: 5
Initial investment: $1000

							Average discounted rate of return R_a	
Period j	CF C_j	R_c IRR 9.1292%	Value change	Invest. equity E_j	Marginal return M_j	Geometric rate of return R_g	Numerator 9.129%	Denominator
0	−$1000	−$1000.000		$1000				
1	0	0.000	0	1000	0.00	1.0000	0.0000	0.9163
2	50	41.984	0	1000	0.05	1.0098	0.0420	0.8397
3	100	76.944	0	1000	0.10	1.0192	0.0769	0.7694
4	150	105.761	0	1000	0.15	1.0283	0.1058	0.7051
5	1200	775.310	0	1000	0.20	1.0371	0.1292	0.6461
Totals	$ 500	0.000	0			9.772%	0.3539	3.8766

Part A

Summary: $R_a = \dfrac{0.3539}{3.8766}$

$= 9.129\%$

R_c = internal rate of return = 9.129%
R_g = geometric mean return = 9.772%
R_a = average discounted rate = 9.129%

Part B

							Average discounted rate of return R_a	
Period j	CF C_j	R_c IRR 10.0000%	Value change	Invest. equity E_j	Marginal return M_j	Geometric rate of return R_g	Numerator 10.000%	Denominator
0	−$1000	−$1000.000		$1000				
1	100	90.909	0	1000	0.1	1.0192	0.0909	0.9091
2	100	82.645	0	1000	0.1	1.0192	0.0826	0.8264
3	100	75.131	0	1000	0.1	1.0192	0.0751	0.7513
4	100	68.301	0	1000	0.1	1.0192	0.0683	0.6830
5	1100	683.013	0	1000	0.1	1.0192	0.0621	0.6209
Totals	$ 500	0.000	0			10.000%	0.3791	3.7908

Summary: $R_a = \dfrac{0.3791}{3.7908}$

$=10.0\%$

R_c = internal rate of return =10.000%
R_g = geometric mean return = 9.772%
R_a = average discounted rate = 9.129%

Table 25.6. Computation of Geometric Mean and Average Discounted Return *(Continued)*

Part C

Period *j*	CF C_j	R_c IRR 11.0425%	Value change	Invest. equity E_j	Marginal return M_j	Geometric rate of return R_g	Average discounted rate of return R_a Numerator 11.0420%	Denominator
0	-$1000	-$1000.000		$1000				
1	200	180.111	0	1000	0.20	1.0371	0.1801	0.9006
2	150	121.650	0	1000	0.15	1.0283	0.1217	0.8110
3	100	73.035	0	1000	0.10	1.0192	0.0730	0.7304
4	50	32.886	0	1000	0.05	1.0098	0.0329	0.6577
5	1000	592.317	0	1000	0.00	1.0000	0.0000	0.5923
Totals	$ 500	$ -0.001	0			9.772%	0.4077	3.6920

Summary:
$$R_a = \frac{0.4077}{3.6920}$$
$$= 11.042\%$$

R_c = internal rate of return = 11.042%
R_g = geometric mean return = 9.772%
R_a = average discounted rate = 11.042%

Part D

Period *j*	CF C_j	R_c IRR 0.4472%	Value change	Invest. equity E_j	Marginal return M_j	Geometric rate of return R_g	Average discounted rate of return R_a Numerator 7.9910%	Denominator
0	-$1000	-$1000.000		$1000				
1	0	0.000	0	1000	0	1.0000	0.0000	0.9260
2	0	0.000	$ 50	1050	0.05	1.0098	0.0429	0.8575
3	0	0.000	100	1150	0.09523	1.0184	0.0756	0.7940
4	0	0.000	150	1300	0.13043	1.0248	0.0959	0.7353
5	1500	1000.000	200	1500	0.15384	1.0290	0.1047	0.6809
Totals	$ 500	-0.000	$500			8.447%	0.3192	3.9937

Summary:
$$R_a = \frac{0.3192}{3.9937}$$
$$= 7.991\%$$

R_c = internal rate of return = 8.447%
R_g = geometric mean return = 8.447%
R_a = average discounted rate = 7.991%

Table 25.6. Computation of Geometric Mean and Average Discounted Return *(Continued)*

Part E

Period j	CF C_j	R_c IRR 8.4472%	Value change	Invest. equity E_j	Marginal return M_j	Geometric rate of return R_g	Average discounted rate of return R_a	
							Numerator 8.5690%	Denominator
0	−$1000	−$1000.000		$1000				
1	0	0.000	$100	1100	0.10000	1.0192	0.0921	0.9211
2	0	0.000	100	1200	0.09090	1.0176	0.0771	0.8484
3	0	0.000	100	1300	0.08333	1.0161	0.0651	0.7814
4	0	0.000	100	1400	0.07692	1.0149	0.0554	0.7197
5	1500	1000.000	100	1500	0.07142	1.0139	0.0474	0.6629
Totals	$ 500	−0.000	$500			8.447%	0.3371	3.9335

Summary:

$$R_a = \frac{0.3371}{3.9335}$$

$$= 8.569\%$$

R_c = internal rate of return = 8.447%
R_g = geometric mean return = 8.447%
R_a = average discounted rate = 8.569%

Part F

Period j	CF C_j	R_c IRR 8.4472%	Value change	Invest. equity E_j	Marginal return M_j	Geometric rate of return R_g	Average discounted rate of return R_a	
							Numerator 9.5720%	Denominator
0	−$1000	−$1000.000		$1000				
1	0	0.000	$200	1200	0.20000	1.0371	0.1825	0.9126
2	0	0.000	150	1350	0.01250	1.0238	0.1041	0.8329
3	0	0.000	100	1450	0.07407	1.0144	0.0563	0.7602
4	0	0.000	50	1500	0.03448	1.0068	0.0239	0.6937
5	1500	1000.000	0	1500	0.00000	1.0000	0.0000	0.6331
Totals	$ 500	−0.000	$500			8.447%	0.3669	3.8326

Summary:

$$R_a = \frac{0.3669}{3.8326}$$

$$= 9.572\%$$

R_c = internal rate of return = 8.447%
R_g = geometric mean return = 8.447%
R_a = average discounted rate = 9.572%

ble 25.6. Computation of Geometric Mean and Average Discounted Return *(Continued)*

Part G

Period j	CF C_j	R_c IRR 18.6192%	Value change	Invest. equity E_j	Marginal return M_j	Geometric rate of return R_g	Average discounted rate of return R_a	
							Numerator 18.5990%	Denominator
0	−$1000	−$1000.000		$1000				
1	200	168.607	0	1000	0.20000	1.0371	0.1686	0.8432
2	200	142.141	−$ 10	990	0.19000	1.0354	0.1351	0.7109
3	200	119.830	− 20	970	0.18181	1.0340	0.1090	0.5995
4	200	101.021	− 30	940	0.17525	1.0328	0.0886	0.5054
5	1100	468.401	− 40	900	0.17021	1.0319	0.0725	0.4262
Totals	$ 900	−0.000	−$100			18.341%	0.5738	3.0852

Summary:

$$R_a = \frac{0.5738}{3.0852}$$

$$= 18.599\%$$

R_c = internal rate of return = 18.619%
R_g = geometric mean return = 18.341%
R_a = average discounted rate = 18.599%

Part H

Period j	CF C_j	R_c IRR 18.6192%	Value change	Invest. equity E_j	Marginal return M_j	Geometric rate of return R_g	Average discounted rate of return R_a	
							Numerator 18.6350%	Denominator
0	−$1000	−$1000.000		$1000				
1	200	168.607	$− 20	980	0.18000	1.0337	0.1517	0.8429
2	200	142.141	− 20	960	0.18367	1.0343	0.1305	0.7105
3	200	119.830	− 20	940	0.18750	1.0350	0.1123	0.5989
4	200	101.021	− 20	920	0.19148	1.0357	0.0967	0.5048
5	1100	468.401	− 20	900	0.19565	1.0364	0.0833	0.4255
Totals	$ 900	−0.000	−$100			18.765%	0.5745	3.0827

Summary:

$$R_a = \frac{0.5745}{3.0827}$$

$$= 18.635\%$$

R_c = internal rate of return = 18.619%
R_g = geometric mean return = 18.765%
R_a = average discounted rate = 18.635%

Table 25.6. Computation of Geometric Mean and Average Discounted Return *(Continued)*

Part I

Period j	CF C_j	R_c IRR 18.6192%	Value change	Invest. equity E_j	Marginal return M_j	Geometric rate of return R_g	Average discounted rate of return R_a Numerator 18.7020%	Denom inato
0	−$1000	−$1000.000		$1000				
1	200	168.607	−$ 40	960	0.16000	1.0301	0.1348	0.842
2	200	142.141	− 30	930	0.17708	1.0331	0.1257	0.709
3	200	119.830	− 20	910	0.19354	1.0360	0.1157	0.597
4	200	101.021	− 10	900	0.20879	1.0387	0.1052	0.503
5	1100	468.401	0	900	0.22222	1.0410	0.0943	0.424
Totals	$ 900	− 0.000	−$100			19.212%	0.5757	3.078

Summary: $R_a = \dfrac{0.5757}{3.0781}$

$= 18.702\%$

R_c = internal rate of return = 18.619%
R_g = geometric mean return = 19.212%
R_a = average discounted rate = 18.702%

Part J

Period j	CF C_j	R_c IRR 27.0279%	Value change	Invest. equity E_j	Marginal return M_j	Geometric rate of return R_g	Average discounted rate of return R_a Numerator 27.7390%	Denom inato
0	$1000	−$1000.000		$1000				
1	200	157.446	$100	1100	0.30000	1.0539	0.2349	0.782
2	200	123.946	100	1200	0.27272	1.0494	0.1671	0.612
3	200	97.574	200	1400	0.33333	1.0592	0.1599	0.479
4	200	76.813	200	1600	0.28571	1.0515	0.1073	0.375
5	1800	544.223	200	1800	0.12500	1.0238	0.0368	0.294
Totals	$1600	0.001	$800			26.120%	0.7060	2.545

Summary: $R_a = \dfrac{0.7060}{2.5451}$

$= 27.739\%$

R_c = internal rate of return = 27.028%
R_g = geometric mean return = 26.120%
R_a = average discounted rate = 27.739%

Table 25.6. Computation of Geometric Mean and Average Discounted Return *(Continued)*

							Average discounted rate of return R_a	
				Invest. equity E_j	Marginal return M_j	Geometric rate of return R_g	Numerator	Denominator
Period j	CF C_j	R_c IRR 25.4611%	Value change				35.2090%	
0	−$1000	−$1000.000		$1000				
1	100	79.706	$700	1700	0.80000	1.1247	0.5917	0.7396
2	200	127.061	100	1800	0.17647	1.0330	0.0965	0.5470
3	200	101.275	0	1800	0.11111	1.0213	0.0450	0.4046
4	200	80.722	0	1800	0.11111	1.0213	0.0332	0.2992
5	1900	611.236	0	1800	0.05555	1.0109	0.0123	0.2213
Totals	$1600	0.000	$800			22.510%	0.7787	2.2117

Summary:

$$R_a = \frac{0.7787}{2117}$$

$$= 35.209\%$$

R_c = internal rate of return = 25.461%
R_g = geometric mean return = 22.510%
R_a = average discounted rate = 35.209%

Part L

							Average discounted rate of return R_a	
				Invest. equity E_j	Marginal return M_j	Geometric rate of return R_g	Numerator	Denominator
Period j	CF C_j	R_c IRR 28.4233%	Value change				31.0025%	
0	−$1000	−$1000.000		$1000				
1	400	311.470	$100	1100	0.50000	1.0845	0.3817	0.7633
2	100	60.633	100	1200	0.18181	1.0340	0.1059	0.5827
3	100	47.214	300	1500	0.33333	1.0592	0.1483	0.4448
4	100	36.764	300	1800	0.26666	1.0484	0.0905	0.3395
5	1900	543.919	0	1800	0.05555	1.0109	0.0144	0.2592
Totals	$1600	0.001	$800			25.877%	0.7408	2.3895

Summary:

$$R_a = \frac{0.7408}{2.3895}$$

$$= 31.0026\%$$

R_c = internal rate of return = 28.423%
R_g = geometric mean return = 25.877%
R_a = average discounted rate = 31.003%

Oddly, GM favors uniform distribution of cash flows. Compare the results in Table 25.5, Examples A, B, and C. All have net dollar cash flows for the life of the investment of $500. But in case C, where the cash flows arrive sooner, the GM is lower than in case B, where the cash flows take longer to achieve.

When the only investment return is from changes in value, GM assigns the same rate of return regardless of the time period in which the changes in value occurs. See Examples D, E, and F.

Peculiarly, and contrary to intuition, GM assigns a higher return to situations involving an early rather than a late decrease in asset value. Compare the GM in Examples G, H, and I. Example I shows the highest return even though its asset values are lower in every period except the last.

Finally, the GM method bias for uniform cash flows is illustrated by comparing the GMs in Examples J, K, and L. Example J (with uniform or level cash flows) has the highest return even though the cash flows and increased asset values occur sooner in Examples K and L.

For all the above reasons, in the author's opinion the geometric mean method *should not be utilized* in preference to IRR.

Average Discounted Rate of Return

The average discounted rate of return (AD) is the only method of the three under discussion which recognizes, in the form of a higher return, an early augmentation in asset value (see Part F of Table 25.5). The heart of this method is that it discounts the average of the marginal rates to itself. The formula for AD is

$$r_a = \frac{\displaystyle\sum_{j=1}^{n} m_j (1 + r_a)^{-j}}{\displaystyle\sum_{j=1}^{n} (1 + r_a)^{-j}}$$

where r_a = average discounted rate of return
m_j = a form of marginal return
j = time period (1, 2, 3, ..., etc.)
n = number of time periods, total

For the example cited in Part A of Table 25.6, the details of the calculation of AD are as follows:

j	$m_j[(1 + r_a)^{-j}]$	Where $[(1 + r_a)^{-j}]$ = 0.09129	Where $[(1 + r_a)^{-j}]$ = 0.09129
1	$0[(1 + r_a)^{-1}]$	0	0.9163467
2	$0.05[(1 + r_a)^{-2}]$	0.0419846	0.8396913
3	$0.1[(1 + r_a)^{-3}]$	0.0769448	0.7694484
4	$0.15[(1 + r_a)^{-4}]$	0.1057622	0.7050815
5	$0.2[(1 + r_a)^{-5}]$	0.1292198	0.6460991
Total		0.3539114	3.8766669

$$r_a = \frac{0 + 0.0419846 + 0.0769448 + 0.1057622 + 0.1292198}{0.9163467 + 0.8396913 + 0.7694484 + 0.7050815 + 0.6460991}$$

$$= \frac{0.3539114}{3.8766669} = 9.129\%$$

The AD recursively discounts the marginal returns in each year at the AD rate itself. The AD method shows higher returns (compared to IRR and GM), other things being equal, for those investments which have early appreciation in value. Both IRR and GM recognize changes in value only at the time when cash flow is received from such changes, normally at the end of the investment horizon. In fact, IRR and GM will produce the same result when the only cash flows result from changes in value, as shown in Parts D, E, and F. Those same parts show how AD recognizes, in the form of a higher return, the increase in value of the investment, with a greater return being commensurate with early appreciation (see Part F). One ambiguity of AD is illustrated in Parts G, H, and I. Comparing the AD results for these parts shows the highest return for Part I, where the earliest depreciation of the value of the investment is recorded. This peculiar result is due to the lower base created for marginal returns, and dividing by this lower base results in relatively higher marginal returns in each year.

The problem with using AD can be easily seen with the following example. An investment is made of $1000. One year later, it doubles, that is, its value increases by $1000, but there is no cash flow accompanying the change in value. At the end of the second year, the value falls by $1000. Thus the marginal change at the end of the first year is an increase of 100 percent, and the marginal change at the end of the second year is a decrease of 50 percent. Over the life of the investment the investor had no economic gain, as $1000 was invested at the beginning and $1000 was received back at the end of two years. As shown in Table 25.7, the IRR and the GM are both zero. Yet the average discounted return is 36.602 percent, which obviously makes no sense.

Table 25.7. Breakdown of Average Discounted Return

Principal sum received at maturity: $1000
Number of periods, n: 2
Initial investment: $1000

Period j	CF C_j	R_c IRR 0.0000%	Value change	Invest. equity E_j	Marginal return M_j	Geometric rate of return R_g	Average discounted rate of return R_a Numerator 36.6020%	Denominator
0	−$1000	−$1000.000		$1000				
1	0	0.000	$1000	2000	100.0%	1.4142	0.7321	0.7321
2	1000	1000.000	−1000	1000	−50.0%	0.7071	−0.2680	0.5359
Totals	0	0.000	0			0.000%	0.4641	1.2680

Summary:

$$R_a = \frac{0.4641}{1.2680}$$

$$= 36.602\%$$

R_c = internal rate of return = 0.000%
R_g = geometric mean return = 0.000%
R_a = average discounted rate = 36.602%

Where there are variable cash flows and changes in asset values, the three methods may disagree on the ranking of the relative merits of the investment proposals, as shown in Parts J, K, and L. First ranking is given (for the same set of cash flows) by IRR for Part L, by GM for Part J, and by AD for Part K.

When only one time period is involved, the three methods will all give the same result. And when the cash flows are uniformly distributed from year to year (and no changes in value occur), the three methods also yield the same result (see Part B). Otherwise, differences occur in the results yielded by the three methods. However, only IRR produces a result which is the rate of return on the unrecovered investment (e.g., bank balance), and which is directly comparable to the yield to maturity on bonds.

For the reasons stated, this author prefers the use of IRR to the alternatives. However, it is useful to augment the use of IRR by the techniques described in this chapter, including the use of marginal IRR, and by partitioning the IRR.

26

Revised IRR for Bonds, Stocks, and Real Estate

What counts in investing are the results after consideration of all relevant factors. Among these pertinent factors are the effects of taxes and, in some cases, the interest on interest earned from reinvestment. In this chapter we shall see how to determine the *revised IRR* (RIRR) for bonds, stocks, and real estate.

First, graphs are presented that allow the determination of RIRR for taxable bond investments. These bond RIRR graphs have the following characteristics:

1. Any or all purchase prices are applicable
2. Ten or 25 years until maturity
3. A choice of three pretax reinvestment rates at which all interest income is presumed to be reinvested: 6, 8, and 12 percent
4. Ordinary income taxation at a rate of 28 or 0 percent
5. Capital gains taxation at 28 or 0 percent on the gain or loss resulting from the disposition of the bond at maturity
6. Bond coupon rates of 0, 2, 5, 8, 11, or 14

In the case of taxable bonds purchased at a premium, the tax benefit from the capital loss is included in the results and is recognized when the bond matures at less than the purchase price.

Revised IRR (RIRR) for a bond is the same as modified IRR (MIRR) or the financial management rate of return (FMRR).

Example: Finding RIRR for a bond. Connie Watanabe, an astute investor who is in a 28 percent tax bracket for ordinary income and capital gains, is considering the possible purchase of two taxable bonds, both of which are priced with an after-tax yield to maturity (YTM) of 8.59 percent. Bond A is a *premium* bond that Connie can purchase for $1156.90. It pays interest annually of $140 and has 25 years until maturity. The stated YTM of 8.59 percent is after taxes, but ignores reinvestment. The pretax, prereinvestment YTM is 12.00 percent. Bond B is offered at a *discount* to Connie at $474.37, pays interest annually of $50, also matures in 25 years, and at the offering price provides a YTM of 8.59 percent after taxes and ignoring reinvestment. Bond B's YTM is 11.445 percent, pretax and prereinvestment. The alternatives are summarized as follows:

	Bond A	Bond B
After-tax YTM	8.59%	8.59%
Offering price	$1156.90	$474.37
Annual coupon	$140.00	$50.00
Pretax YTM	12.000%	11.445%
Maturity (years hence)	25	25

After consulting with her accountant, Connie decides that it is unwise to ignore either taxes or reinvestment, because her intention is to reinvest all the earnings to build up funds for the purchase of a vacation condo in Aspen. She anticipates that she will earn at least 8 percent (before taxes) on the interest receipts that are reinvested as she receives them. The problem, then, is to see which bond—premium or discount—is the better investment at a pretax reinvestment rate of 8 percent.

Connie turns to Fig. 26.5, which covers reinvestment of interest at a pretax rate of 8 percent, in a tax bracket of 28 percent, and where the bond has 25 years until maturity. The 8 percent interest reinvestment rate is a before-tax amount. However, the RIRR determined from the figure is after taxes.

Reinvestment rate after tax less than YTM. For the *premium* bond, Connie enters Fig. 26.5 along the vertical axis at the $1156.90 purchase price, proceeds horizontally to the $140 coupon curve, then down to the bottom axis where it intersects at the 7.08 percent point. For bond A, the premium bond, 7.08 percent is the RIRR, after taxes and after reinvesting all interest receipts at 8 percent pretax, 5.76 percent after tax.

Next, for the discount bond, Connie enters the same figure along the left axis at the $474.37 purchase price, proceeds horizontally to the $50 coupon curve, then down to the bottom axis, where the point of intersection is 7.3 percent.

The end result is that the premium bond produces a RIRR of only 7.08 percent versus 7.3 percent for the discount bond, even though both bonds were priced to yield 8.59 percent after taxes, but before considering reinvestment returns. Clearly, then, for Connie Watanabe's purposes, the discount bond is the more attractive purchase.

In this example the YTM after tax, 8.59 percent, is greater than the after-tax interest reinvestment rate of 5.76 percent. So the RIRR is less than the YTM.

Reinvestment rate after tax equals YTM. But what if the interest reinvestment rate after tax is equal to the YTM after tax? In this case no graph is needed: The RIRR for the premium bond after reinvestment of earnings at 8.59 percent, after taxes, is also 8.59 percent, and for the discount bond it is 8.59 percent, as well. *If the after-tax reinvestment rate equals the after-tax YTM, the RIRR remains unchanged.*

Reinvestment rate after tax exceeds YTM. If the interest reinvestment rate after tax is 10 percent, and the bond is priced at an after-tax YTM of 8.59 percent, which is then the better investment after considering reinvestment of cash flows? Here, the premium bond is still priced at $1156.90 with a coupon of $140 to provide an after-tax YTM of 8.59 percent, and the discount bond provides the same 8.59 percent after-tax YTM with a $474.37 purchase price and a coupon of $50.* Under these circumstances, the RIRRs, after reinvestment at an after-tax 10 percent rate, are *9.41 percent for the premium* bond versus *9.31 percent for the discount* bond. Thus, if the after-tax reinvestment rate exceeds the YTM, the premium bond is the better choice.

If one is planning to reinvest, and the projected after-tax reinvestment rate is *higher* than the original YTM, then the faster one obtains cash flows, the better will be the overall results because the quicker the cash flows arrive, the more will be earned from reinvesting. A *premium* bond will provide more cash flows, earlier, than either a par or a discount bond. But if the reverse is the case, and the projected after-tax reinvestment rate is *lower* than the original YTM, then a *discount* bond will provide superior results to either a par or a premium alternative.

In the three situations presented, where the YTM after-tax was greater than, equal to, or less than the after-tax rate on reinvestment, the premium bond performs best at the high reinvestment rate, and the discount bond provides better results at a low reinvestment rate. The decision of which bond to acquire depends on the investor's assessment of the level of the future reinvestment rate. For a summary of the results see the table on the next page.

For a complete year-by-year view of the effects of reinvesting interest, see Table 26.1. The $60 entries in the first column represent each year's interest receipts of $75 less 20 percent income tax, leaving $60 after taxes. The column entitled "Before-reinvestment balance" is the cumulative sum

---

*A tax rate of 28% is applied on both ordinary income and capital gains and losses.

	Premium	Discount
After-tax YTM	8.59%	8.59%
Offering price	$1156.90	$474.37
Annual coupon	$140.00	$50.00
Pretax YTM	12.000%	11.445%
Maturity (years hence)	25	25

Case 1: low reinvestment rate (5.76% after taxes):
| After-tax RIRR | 7.08% | 7.30% |

Case 2: same as IRR reinvestment rate (8.59% after taxes equals YTM):
| After-tax RIRR | 8.59% | 8.59% |

Case 3: high reinvestment rate (10% after taxes):
| After-tax RIRR | 9.41% | 9.31% |

of all cash flow receipts, excluding interest earned from reinvesting. The three columns under the heading "Interest reinvestment" are comparable to a bank account, to which is credited the coupon interest and interest earned on such coupon interest, after taxes at 20 percent. The ending "New balance" of $1252 reflects the after-tax cash flows, receipt of bond maturity value, annual interest coupons, and interest earned on interest—all after applicable income or long-term capital gains taxes. The earnings from reinvestment after taxes are $12.24 in the example: the YTM after taxes without reinvestment is 13.78 percent, decreasing to 12.336 percent with reinvestment.

Another term which describes RIRR, after taxes with reinvestment of earnings, is *realized compound yield*. The two terms are synonymous.

The RIRR is the interest rate that relates the original cost of the investment to its terminal value. The detailed process is displayed in Tables 26.1 and 26.2 for a bond with 5 years until maturity, purchased for $700, and paying $75 per year in interest that is reinvested at 2.5 percent pretax per year. The tax bracket is 20 percent. The cash flows displayed are after taxes, as such cash flows have already been reduced 20 percent. Cash flow in the fifth year includes the maturity value less capital gains tax, plus the interest coupon for the fifth year, after ordinary income tax. The tax on gain at maturity and cash flow in the fifth year is shown in Table 26.2.

Revised IRR for Bonds at Various Reinvestment Rates

The revised IRR (RIRR) or realized compound yield is the interest rate that relates the cost of the investment to the terminal value. The terminal value is the sum of:

Table 26.1. Bonds: After-Tax with Reinvestment

Pretax YTM: 16.84%
Number of years until maturity: 5
Maturity value: $1000
Tax bracket for ordinary income: 20.0%
Percentage interest on reinvestment, pretax: 2.5%
Purchase price: $700
Coupon: $75
Capital gains tax rate: 20.0%

After-tax and before-rein- vestment cash flows*	Year	Before-rein- vestment balance	Old balance	Interest on interest	New balance
				Interest reinvestment	
($700.00)	0	0.00	0.00	0.00	0.00
60.00	1	$ 60.00	0.00	0.00	$ 60.00
60.00	2	120.00	60.00	1.20	121.20
60.00	3	180.00	121.20	2.42	183.62
60.00	4	240.00	183.62	3.67	247.30
1000.00	5	1240.00	247.30	4.95	1252.24
$1240.00				$12.24	

After-tax IRR	13.78%	without reinvestment
After tax RIRR	12.33%	with reinvestment

*The 5th year entry of $1000 is composed of $60 after-tax coupon, $1000 sales proceeds, and tax on market discount of $60 on the $300 gain.

Table 26.2. Tax on Gain at Maturity

(a)	Maturity value	$1,000	
(b)	Less: cost	700	
(c)	Long-term capital gain	$ 300	
(d)	Capital gains tax [(c) × 0.2]	60*	
(e)	Proceeds after tax [(a − d)]		$940
(f)	Interest coupon before reinvestment	75	
(g)	Tax on interest [0.2 × (f)]	15	
(h)	Interest after tax		60
(i)	Cash flow in fifth year before income from reinvestment		$1,000

*Since the example uses the same tax rate, 20% on both ordinary income and capital gain, the tax of $60 is correct, irrespective of whether the gain is capital gain or ordinary income under the market discount rules.

1. Sales proceeds less capital gains tax

2. After-tax coupons

3. After-tax interest on interest from reinvestment

The calculation is a simple one, as it requires little more than calculating the future value of an annuity (in the case of bonds) or the future value of specific individual cash flows (where the cash flows are irregular in amount, unlike the uniform coupon payments of a bond).

It is likely that the simplicity of RIRR fostered its popularity. It is much easier to calculate RIRR for a bond than it is to calculate IRR or YTM. The calculation of IRR or YTM has been discussed extensively in this book; it is hardly a simple matter. Calculating RIRR, on the other hand, is simple.

The RIRR, by definition, requires reinvestment of coupons at some given interest rate to be earned on such reinvestment. If the reinvestment rate is the same as the IRR, then and only then will the RIRR equal the IRR.

When an investor has definite feelings about the future direction of interest rates, and where that investor intends to reinvest coupon income, then RIRR can play a useful role. RIRR can be usefully employed to see which alternative investment possibilities offer the best returns under stated future reinvestment rate projections.

For investors who intend to spend their investment income rather than reinvest, IRR (which contains no reinvestment assumptions) has more significance than RIRR.

RIRR or realized compound yield, y, is calculated from

$$y = \frac{(T)^{1/n}}{P} - 1$$

where T = terminal value (sales proceeds after tax, cash flows after tax, and interest on interest after tax from reinvesting cash flows),

$$T = (1 - t_o)\,(R) \left\{ \frac{[1 + (1 - t_o)\,(r)^n - 1]}{(1 - t_o)\,(r)} \right\} + S - (t_{cg})\,(S - p)$$

where t_o = tax rate on ordinary income

t_{cg} = tax rate on capital gains

p = initial investment or cost

r = reinvestment rate earned pretax

n = years from initial investment until disposition of the investment

R = coupon receipts

S = maturity value

For a 5-year bond with $120 coupon purchased for $700, with 4 percent coupon pretax reinvestment, 20 percent capital gains tax, and 50 percent tax on interest, and IRR of 13.78 percent after taxes, the calculation of RIRR is as follows: First, find the terminal value, using the formula. The formula seems rather imposing. It's easier to remember that the formula simply represents the maturity value or sales proceeds, less tax on the gain if any, plus the coupons or cash flow (after taxes) throughout the investment, plus the interest on interest (after taxes) earned from reinvesting those cash flows.

$$T = (1 - 0.5)(\$120) \left\{ \frac{[1 + (1 - 0.5)(0.04)]^5 - 1}{(1 - 0.5)(0.04)} \right\} + \$1000 - (0.2)(\$1000 - \$700)$$

$$= (\$60) \left(\frac{1.10408 - 1}{0.02} \right) + \$1000 - \$60$$

$$= (\$60)(5.2040) + \$940$$

$$= \$312.24 + \$940 = \$1252.24$$

Thus, $1252.24 is the terminal value. The next step is to find the RIRR, as follows:

$$y = \frac{(T)^{1/n}}{P} - 1$$

$$= \left(\frac{\$1252.24^{1/5}}{\$700} \right) - 1 = 1.78891^{0.2} - 1$$

$$= 1.12336 - 1 = 0.12336 \quad \text{or} \quad 12.336\%$$

The after-tax RIRR, then, is 12.336 percent.

It should have been expected that at a pretax reinvestment rate of 4 percent, the RIRR will be less than the IRR of 13.78 percent. It is interesting to note the following rates, all of which are applicable to this bond:

IRR before tax and without reinvestment	22.61%
IRR after tax and without reinvestment	13.78%
RIRR after tax and with reinvestment at 4% (pretax)	12.34%

Stock and bond brokers, in this author's experience, frequently offer tax-exempt bonds that sell at a discount and quote a yield to maturity for the bond. Inquiry usually establishes that the quoted YTM is a before-tax yield and ignores the very important fact that the buyer is acquiring a built-in tax liability of the gain upon sale, at call, or at maturity.* *Only after-tax results should be considered.*

---

* This tax liability may be at either ordinary rates or capital gains rates depending on when the bond was issued and when it was acquired.

Municipals or Tax-Exempt RIRRs

RIRR, the revised YTM after tax with interest reinvestment from investments in municipals or *tax-exempts* purchased at *par* or a *premium*, may be found by using Figs. 26.1 through 26.3. Figures 26.4 and 26.5 with slight adaptation, may be used to find RIRRs of municipals purchased at a *discount*. Although the interest receipts from a municipal are not normally subject to federal income tax, the *capital gain or loss upon sale or redemption at maturity is taxable*. When tax-exempt bonds are purchased at a premium, that is, for more than $1000 the premium *must* be amortized over the life of the bonds or until call, whichever is the shorter period. Such amortization each year reduces the "taxable basis." At the call or maturity date, the "taxable basis" will have been reduced to an amount equal to the maturity value. Thus, there is *no taxable loss* at the maturity of a tax-exempt bond purchased at a premium. The procedure to follow for obtaining the after-tax YTM from an investment in a tax-exempt bond by an investor in a tax bracket of r is as follows:

1. Choose the figure closest to the bond's number of years until maturity (10–30 years). For *par* or *premium* bonds, use Figs. 26.1 through 26.3 in the normal manner. For *discount* bonds, use Figs. 26.4 and 26.5 and *adjust* the coupon rate.

2. Calculate an adjusted coupon rate for *discount* bonds, as follows:

$$\text{Adjusted coupon rate} = \frac{\text{tax exempt bond's coupon rate}}{(1 - r)}$$

Example: Finding adjusted coupon rate.   John White, who is in a 28 percent tax bracket, is considering the purchase of a tax-exempt sewer bond for $600, with 25 years until maturity. The bond's pretax YTM is 17.03 percent. It pays $100.80 per year in interest per bond. The adjusted coupon rate (for the figures) for the bond is:

$$\text{Adjusted coupon rate} = \frac{\$100.80 \ (\text{tax exempt's coupon rate})}{0.72 \ (1 - \text{tax bracket})}$$

$$= \frac{\$100.80}{0.72} = \$140.00$$

White estimates that he can reinvest the interest receipts at 12 percent (before tax) in taxable CDs. To find the YTM after capital gains tax and with

Purchase price of bond

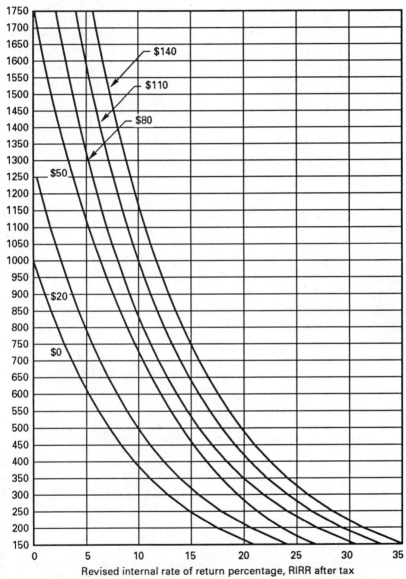

Figure 26.1. Bond interest reinvestment (RIRR) rate of 8 percent for 10 years for 0 percent tax bracket.

Purchase price of bond

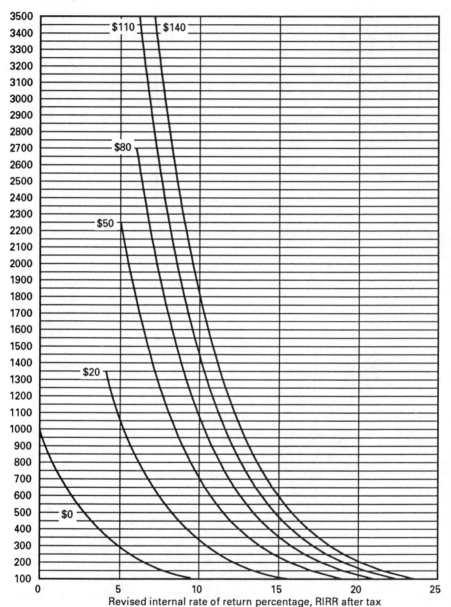

Figure 26.2. Bond interest reinvestment (RIRR) rate of 12 percent for 25 years for 0 percent tax bracket.

Purchase price of bond

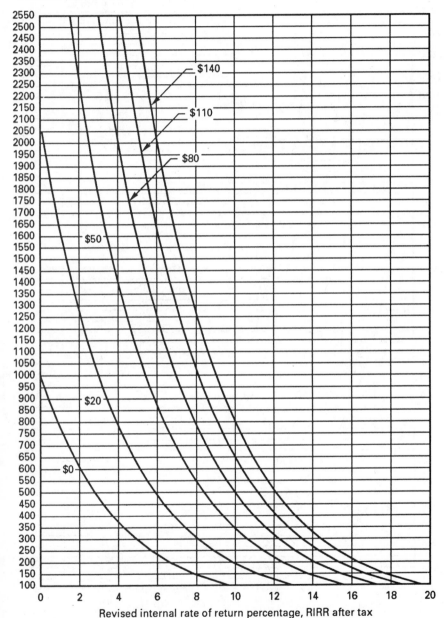

Figure 26.3. Bond interest reinvestment (RIRR) rate of 6 percent for 25 years for 0 percent tax bracket.

Purchase price of bond

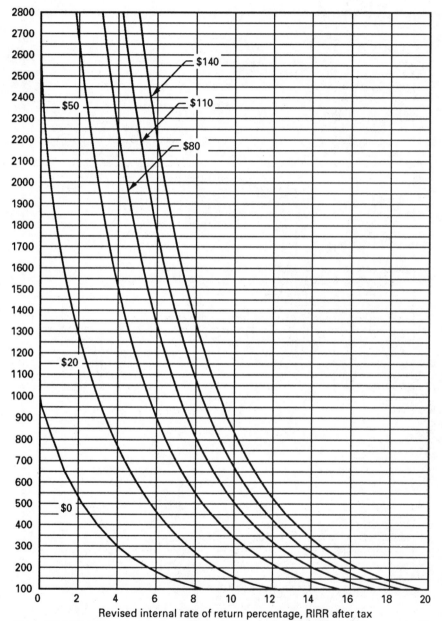

Figure 26.4. Bond interest reinvestment (RIRR) rate of 12 percent for 25 years for 28 percent tax bracket.

Purchase price of bond

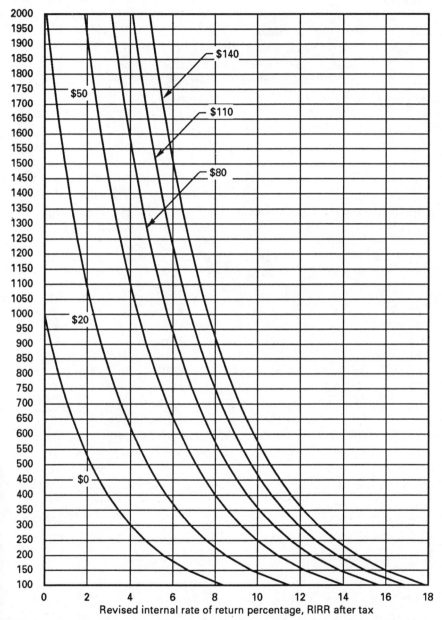

Figure 26.5. Bond interest reinvestment (RIRR) rate of 8 percent for 25 years for 28 percent tax bracket.

reinvestment at 12 percent, refer to Fig. 26.4. Enter the figure on the vertical axis at the bond's purchase price, $600. Proceed horizontally to the adjusted coupon rate, 14 percent ($140); then descend to the horizontal axis. The intersection with the horizontal axis is the after-tax YTM with reinvestment of interest, 11.43 percent. This RIRR, 11.43 percent, for White's purchase, takes into consideration reinvestment of interest, the tax-free nature of the $110.80 annual interest, as well as the ultimate capital gains tax of $112—28 percent of the $400 gain (i.e., $1000 redemption less $600 cost). The RIRR at an 8 percent reinvestment rate (before tax) is 9.82 percent (use Fig. 26.5); at a 6 percent reinvestment rate it is 9.82 percent. The YTM without reinvestment, pretax, is 17.03 percent, and it is 16.965 percent after 28 percent capital gains tax.

A taxable investor in a *tax-exempt discount* bond *must* use an adjusted coupon rate, as determined above, and use Figs. 26.4 and 26.5. Only the figures for taxable investors calculate the tax on the gain at maturity.

Example: Finding the RIRR for a tax-exempt par bond. Pilar Delgado, a successful proprietor of a book distribution company, is in a 28 percent tax bracket. Miss Delgado is considering the purchase of a tax-exempt San Jose Sewer and Water bond at its par value of $1000. The tax-exempt bond matures in 25 years and has a $110 coupon. Miss Delgado has no immediate need for the income from the investment and estimates that she can conservatively reinvest the coupon income at 6 percent, after taxes, in taxable CDs or the like (i.e., a rate of earnings on reinvestment of 8.33 percent before tax in a 28 percent tax bracket). But Miss Delgado wants to know what her RIRR will be after reinvesting all the income.

To find the RIRR for a tax-exempt par bond, use Figs. 26.1 through 26.3. These figures are for a zero-tax-bracket investor. Since a tax-exempt investor in either a par or a premium tax-exempt bond is not subject to tax on the coupon income and cannot deduct a capital loss at maturity, these figures may be used in the normal fashion without any adjustments. The reinvestment percentage rate, that is, 6 percent, should be the rate the investor anticipates earning *after* paying applicable taxes on the reinvested earnings. Miss Delgado enters Fig. 26.3 (the figure for 25 years to maturity, 6 percent after-tax reinvestment rate) along the vertical axis at the $1000 purchase price, crosses to the $110 coupon curve, then descends to the bottom axis where the RIRR is found, 8.12 percent.

Miss Delgado wonders what the results will be if she is able to reinvest the income at higher rates. If she can reinvest at a 12 percent, after-tax, reinvestment rate, the RIRR soars to 11.63 percent (Fig. 26.2).

Thus, at after-tax reinvestment rates higher than the initial YTM of 11 percent, the with-reinvestment RIRR exceeds 11 percent: at reinvestment rates below 11 percent, the RIRR drops below 11 percent.

Example: Finding the RIRR for a tax-exempt premium bond. Stefan Michalski is also in a 28 percent bracket, and is considering the purchase of a tax-exempt premium bond at a purchase price of $1450. The bond's annual coupon is $140, and it matures in 25 years. The YTM without reinvesting is 9.305 percent. Stefan can determine the RIRR in the same manner as Pilar Delgado did by choosing the appropriate figures from Figs. 26.1 through 26.3. At a reinvestment rate of 6 percent after tax, the RIRR is 7.42 percent (Fig. 26.3); at 12 percent after tax, Stefan reaps the rewards of a 10.99 percent RIRR (Fig. 26.2).

Tax-Exempt Investors

Tax-exempt investors, such as pension funds, individual retirement accounts (IRAs), Keogh (HR-10) retirement plans for the self-employed, and simplified employee pension (SEP) plans, enjoy a status even more favorable than investors in tax-exempt securities. That may sound a bit peculiar at first reading. The tax-exempt investor is normally free from any taxation. On the other hand, a tax-exempt security such as a municipal bond is normally free of federal income tax and state tax of the issuer, but it is subject to federal tax on gains and usually the interest is taxable in states other than the state in which the bond was issued.

Now let's look at the tax-exempt *investor*. Figures 26.1 through 26.3 show RIRR, after reinvesting cash receipts at various percentage rates, for the tax-exempt investor. Nothing has been deducted for taxes—either from the regular coupon, the interest-on-interest receipts from reinvestment, or as the result of the capital gain or loss at maturity. These figures cover periods of 10 and 25 years until maturity and three rates of interest reinvestment: 6, 8, or 12 percent.

For example, to find the RIRR of a 10-year bond, with reinvestment at 8 percent, use Fig. 26.1. The figures follow the typical pattern found throughout this text. Enter along the left axis at the bond purchase price, proceed horizontally to the curve representing the appropriate interest coupon rate, then descend to the bottom axis to find the RIRR.

Zero-Coupon Bonds

Zero-coupon bonds have been actively promoted by brokers in recent years. They have been discussed in detail in Chap. 19. Typically the investor is offered a bond at an extraordinarily low purchase price. The bond matures in *x* years for $1000. No interest is received during the intervening years. Such a bond is precisely equivalent to a conventional bond at the *same* purchase price, with coupon interest equal to the purchase price times the YTM of the zero, reinvesting all income at that same rate, and maturity at a value equal to the purchase price. The rate earned on reinvestment is fixed and irrevocable at the rate of YTM at purchase.

Normally, ordinary tax-paying citizens should *not* buy these bonds because taxpayers must pay tax on income *each year* even though they have not received any cash flow and will not receive any until the bond's disposition or maturity. For the *tax-exempt investor*, however, such bonds may have appeal, depending on quality, pricing, and timing.

Revised IRR for Stocks at Various Reinvestment Rates

In Chap. 21 we found that a number of variables affect the IRR, including such factors as:

Whether the P-E multiple is static, mounting, or shrinking

Earnings growth rate

Dividend yield initially

Growth in dividends

Tax rate on ordinary income

Tax rate on capital gains

Time the investment is held

The reinvestment of cash flows from a stock investment follows the same general principles as for a bond investment. One must look at the after-tax interest rate earned on reinvestment. For example, in a 28 percent tax bracket, if the pretax rate earned on reinvestment is 10 percent, then the after-tax rate is 7.2 percent.

If the after-tax rate earned on reinvestment is equal to the IRR without reinvestment, then the RIRR will equal the IRR.

If the after-tax rate earned on reinvestment is greater than the IRR without reinvestment, then the RIRR will be greater than the IRR.

If the after-tax rate earned on reinvestment is less than the IRR without reinvestment, then the RIRR will be less than the IRR.

If the earnings and dividends in a stock investment grow (although this certainly does not always happen), the IRR will be higher at higher growth levels. And at a given level of earnings and dividend growth, the higher the initial yield of the stock, the higher is the IRR and the RIRR. Refer to Fig. 26.6. Notice the curves for the IRR (without reinvestment) and the RIRRs (with reinvestment). As the initial yield increases, so does the IRR and so do the RIRRs.

The curves in Fig. 26.6 represent different *pretax* rates of interest earned on reinvestment. For example, the 10 percent curve is for interest reinvestment at a pretax rate of 10 percent. In a 28 percent tax bracket, however, the after-tax rate applied to reinvestment is 7.2 percent. At very low initial yield rates, the IRR exceeds the after-tax 7.2 percent rate, and the RIRR is greater than the IRR. At higher initial yield rates (6 percent and higher), the reverse is true: The IRR is higher than the after-tax 7.2 percent rate and the RIRR is less than the IRR. Table 26.3 shows the details at the point where the initial yield is 6 percent. Notice that the IRR at this point is 8.26 percent and the RIRR is 7.89 percent. The IRR is less because the after-tax rate earned on reinvestment of 4.32 percent is less than the 8.26 percent IRR without reinvestment. Thus the effect of reinvesting is to reduce the return to the RIRR of 7.89 percent.

Finding the RIRR for a Stock

The RIRR for a stock can be found mathematically in a fashion similar to that of a bond. The interest rate that relates the terminal value to the initial investment is the RIRR. The terminal value includes the sales proceeds after tax, the dividends after tax, and the reinvestment interest earned on the dividends, after tax.

In dealing with RIRRs, remember that there are only two cash flows: the initial investment and the terminal value. Why, you may be wondering. What about the cash flows each year from dividends? What about the cash flows each year from interest earned on those dividends? These cash flows each year take place, but the funds are unavailable to the investor because the decision was made to reinvest. Once the decision to reinvest is made, the investment is like a zero-coupon bond. The periodic cash flows are unavailable to the investor, the investor does not receive them, and they do not count in determining the RIRR (except as part of the terminal value).

Example: Finding the RIRR for a stock. An investor in the 28 percent tax bracket for both ordinary income and capital gains is considering the purchase of a stock with P-E multiple of 10. He expects the multiple to be static when he disposes of the investment in 6 years. He expects 6 percent growth in dividends and earnings. The current or initial yield is also 6 percent. If he reinvests the dividends at 6 percent (pretax), what are the IRR and the RIRR of the investment? Table 26.3 shows the details of calculating

Percent yield (annual initial dividend divided by initial market price)

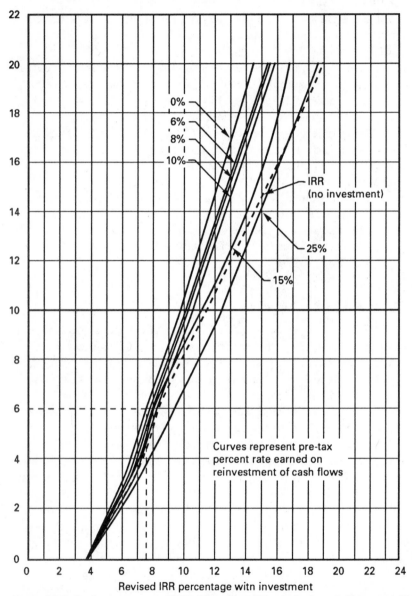

Figure 26.6. Stock reinvestment and RIRR. (Notes: Static P-E multiple; 6-year holding period; 10:1 P-E ratio at purchase and sale; 28% ordinary income and capital gain tax bracket; 6% earnings and dividend growth rate.)

Table 26.3 Stocks: IRR

Dividend growth rate: 6.00%
Initial investment: $100.00
Initial dividend rate: 6.00%
Price-earnings ratio at purchase: 10.00
Price-earnings Ratio at sale: 10.00
Earnings growth rate: 6.00%
Earnings per share at purchase: $1.00
No. of years investment is held: 6.00
Rate at which cash flow is reinvested: 6.00%, pretax; 4.32%, after tax.
Tax bracket: 28.00%

CF w/o reinvestment, including sale, after tax	Starting balance	Interest after tax	Ending balance	Year
−$100.00	0.00	0.00	0.00	0
4.32	0.00	0.00	$ 4.32	1
4.58	$ 4.32	$0.19	9.09	2
4.85	9.09	0.39	14.33	3
5.15	14.33	0.62	20.10	4
5.45	20.10	0.87	26.42	5
130.13	26.42	1.14	157.69	6

RIRR: 7.89%
IRR: 8.26%

Source: INVESTMENT IRR ANALYSIS (AFTER TAX) FOR STOCKS, BONDS, AND REAL ESTATE (Larry Rosen Co., 1990–1994).

the RIRR. The RIRR is the rate that relates the terminal value of $157.69 (ending balance in the sixth year in the table) with the initial investment of $100 over 6 years.

The formula for RIRR is

$$y = \left[\frac{(T)^{1/n}}{P} - 1 \right]$$

where y = RIRR or compound realized yield) (MIRR or FMRR)
  T = terminal value (sales proceeds after tax and cash flows and interest on interest from reinvesting cash flows)
  P = initial investment or cost

n = years from initial investment until disposition of the investment

For this example,

$$y = \left[\frac{(\$157.69)^{1/6}}{\$100} - 1 \right] = 1.07887 - 1 = 0.07887 \text{ or } 7.89\%$$

The RIRR can also be found from **Fig. 26.6.** Enter the graph on the left vertical axis at the 6 percent initial yield, proceed horizontally to the intersection with the after tax rate of interest on reinvestment of 6 percent, then drop vertically to the horizontal bottom axis, where the point of intersection is about 7.9 percent, the RIRR.

Analysis shows that a 1 percent increase in the RIRR usually results in between 18 and 22 percent more money after tax at the conclusion of the investment. This holds for a 20-year holding period.

Rosen's rule of thumb is that *for a 1 percent increase in RIRR* (say, from 9 to 10 percent), *the percentage increase in the terminal value equals roughly the number of years in the accumulation period.*

Thus, for example, if one wonders how much the increase in terminal value would be at an RIRR of 10 percent instead of 9 percent for a 10-year holding, the terminal value would increase by about 10 percent. The same increase in terminal value would apply to an RIRR increase from 4 percent to 5 percent or from 13 to 14 percent.

How can this handy rule of thumb be applied? Let's talk retirement. To have a $30,000 annual income in the form of an annuity, something on the order of a $300,000 nest egg is needed at retirement. Now, what if one's RIRR can be increased by only *1 percent* during the savings period? What will this 1 percent increase in the RIRR do to the nest egg over a 20-year savings period? The rule of thumb says that it will increase the nest egg from $300,000 to $360,000—that is, by $60,000. Rosen's rule of thumb says for every 1 percent increase in RIRR, the increase in the nest egg will be a percentage equal to the number of years in the accumulation period. A 20 percent increase in the nest egg is 0.2 × $300,000 or $60,000.

Further details of terminal values that will be accumulated at various rates of RIRR are shown in Table 26.4.

The percentage increase in terminal value that results from a 1 percent increase in RIRR is shown in Table 26.5. For example, if RIRR increases from 10 to 11 percent, by what percent will terminal value increase over 20 years? As Table 26.5 indicates, the terminal value increases by 20 percent.

Table 26.4. Terminal Values and RIRRs

Present value or initial investment: $100

											Terminal value									
RIRR %	Year 1	Year 2	Year 3	Year 4	Year 5	Year 6	Year 7	Year 8	Year 9	Year 10	Year 11	Year 12	Year 13	Year 14	Year 15	Year 16	Year 17	Year 18	Year 19	Year 20
1	$101	$102	$103	$104	$105	$106	$107	$108	$109	$110	$112	$113	$114	$115	$116	$117	$118	$120	$121	$122
2	102	104	106	108	110	113	115	117	120	122	124	127	129	132	135	137	140	143	146	149
3	103	106	109	113	116	119	123	127	130	134	138	143	147	151	156	160	165	170	175	181
4	104	108	112	117	122	127	132	137	142	148	154	160	167	173	180	187	195	203	211	219
5	105	110	116	122	128	134	141	148	155	163	171	180	189	198	208	218	229	241	253	265
6	106	112	119	126	134	142	150	159	169	179	190	201	213	226	240	254	269	285	303	321
7	107	114	123	131	140	150	161	172	184	197	210	225	241	258	276	295	316	338	362	387
8	108	117	126	136	147	159	171	185	200	216	233	252	272	294	317	343	370	400	432	466
9	109	119	130	141	154	168	183	199	217	237	258	281	307	334	364	397	433	472	514	560
10	110	121	133	146	161	177	195	214	236	259	285	314	345	380	418	459	505	556	612	673
11	111	123	137	152	169	187	208	230	256	284	315	350	388	431	478	531	590	654	726	806
12	112	125	140	157	176	197	221	248	277	311	348	390	436	489	547	613	687	769	861	965
13	113	128	144	163	184	208	235	266	300	339	384	433	490	553	625	707	799	902	1020	1152
14	114	130	148	169	193	219	250	285	325	371	423	482	549	626	714	814	928	1058	1206	1374
15	115	132	152	175	201	231	266	306	352	405	465	535	615	708	814	936	1076	1238	1423	1637
16	116	135	156	181	210	244	283	328	380	441	512	594	689	799	927	1075	1247	1446	1678	1946
17	117	137	160	187	219	257	300	351	411	481	562	658	770	901	1054	1233	1443	1688	1975	2311
18	118	139	164	194	229	270	319	376	444	523	618	729	860	1015	1197	1413	1667	1967	2321	2739
19	119	142	169	201	239	284	338	402	479	569	678	806	960	1142	1359	1617	1924	2290	2725	3243
20	120	144	173	207	249	299	358	430	516	619	743	892	1070	1284	1541	1849	2219	2662	3195	3834
21	121	146	177	214	259	314	380	459	556	673	814	985	1192	1442	1745	2111	2555	3091	3740	4526
22	122	149	182	222	270	330	402	491	599	730	891	1087	1326	1618	1974	2409	2938	3585	4374	5336
23	123	151	186	229	282	346	426	524	644	793	975	1199	1475	1814	2231	2745	3376	4152	5107	6282
24	124	154	191	236	293	364	451	559	693	859	1066	1321	1639	2032	2520	3124	3874	4804	5957	7386

Table 26.5. Percent Increase in Terminal Value per 1% Increase in RIRR

RIRR, %	Year																			
	1	2	3	4	5	6	7	8	9	10	11	12	13	14	15	16	17	18	19	20
2	1.0	2.0	3.0	4.0	5.0	6.1	7.1	8.2	9.3	10.4	11.4	12.6	13.7	14.8	15.9	17.1	18.2	19.4	20.6	21.8
3	1.0	2.0	3.0	4.0	5.0	6.0	7.1	8.1	9.2	10.2	11.3	12.4	13.5	14.6	15.8	16.9	18.0	19.2	20.4	21.5
4	1.0	2.0	2.9	3.9	4.9	6.0	7.0	8.0	9.1	10.1	11.2	12.3	13.4	14.5	15.6	16.7	17.9	19.0	20.2	21.3
5	1.0	1.9	2.9	3.9	4.9	5.9	6.9	8.0	9.0	10.0	11.1	12.2	13.2	14.3	15.4	16.5	17.7	18.8	19.9	21.1
6	1.0	1.9	2.9	3.9	4.9	5.9	6.9	7.9	8.9	9.9	11.0	12.0	13.1	14.2	15.3	16.4	17.5	18.6	19.7	20.9
7	0.9	1.9	2.9	3.8	4.8	5.8	6.8	7.8	8.8	9.8	10.9	11.9	13.0	14.0	15.1	16.2	17.3	18.4	19.5	20.7
8	0.9	1.9	2.8	3.8	4.8	5.7	6.7	7.7	8.7	9.7	10.8	11.8	12.9	13.9	15.0	16.0	17.1	18.2	19.3	20.4
9	0.9	1.9	2.8	3.8	4.7	5.7	6.7	7.7	8.6	9.7	10.7	11.7	12.7	13.8	14.8	15.9	17.0	18.0	19.1	20.2
10	0.9	1.8	2.8	3.7	4.7	5.6	6.6	7.6	8.6	9.6	10.6	11.6	12.6	13.6	14.7	15.7	16.8	17.9	18.9	20.0
11	0.9	1.8	2.8	3.7	4.6	5.6	6.5	7.5	8.5	9.5	10.5	11.5	12.5	13.5	14.5	15.6	16.6	17.7	18.8	19.8
12	0.9	1.8	2.7	3.7	4.6	5.5	6.5	7.4	8.4	9.4	10.4	11.4	12.4	13.4	14.4	15.4	16.5	17.5	18.6	19.6
13	0.9	1.8	2.7	3.6	4.5	5.5	6.4	7.4	8.3	9.3	10.3	11.3	12.2	13.3	14.3	15.3	16.3	17.4	18.4	19.5
14	0.9	1.8	2.7	3.6	4.5	5.4	6.4	7.3	8.3	9.2	10.2	11.2	12.1	13.1	14.1	15.1	16.2	17.2	18.2	19.3
15	0.9	1.8	2.7	3.6	4.5	5.4	6.3	7.2	8.2	9.1	10.1	11.0	12.0	13.0	14.0	15.0	16.0	17.0	18.1	19.1
16	0.9	1.7	2.6	3.5	4.4	5.3	6.2	7.2	8.1	9.0	10.0	11.0	11.9	12.9	13.9	14.9	15.9	16.9	17.9	18.9
17	0.9	1.7	2.6	3.5	4.4	5.3	6.2	7.1	8.0	9.0	9.9	10.9	11.8	12.8	13.7	14.7	15.7	16.7	17.7	18.7
18	0.9	1.7	2.6	3.5	4.3	5.2	6.1	7.0	8.0	8.9	9.8	10.8	11.7	12.7	13.6	14.6	15.6	16.6	17.6	18.6
19	0.8	1.7	2.6	3.4	4.3	5.2	6.1	7.0	7.9	8.8	9.7	10.7	11.6	12.5	13.5	14.5	15.4	16.4	17.4	18.4
20	0.8	1.7	2.5	3.4	4.3	5.1	6.0	6.9	7.8	8.7	9.6	10.6	11.5	12.4	13.4	14.3	15.3	16.3	17.2	18.2
21	0.8	1.7	2.5	3.4	4.2	5.1	6.0	6.9	7.8	8.7	9.6	10.5	11.4	12.3	13.3	14.2	15.2	16.1	17.1	18.1
22	0.8	1.7	2.5	3.3	4.2	5.1	5.9	6.8	7.7	8.6	9.5	10.4	11.3	12.2	13.1	14.1	15.0	16.0	16.9	17.9
23	0.8	1.6	2.5	3.3	4.2	5.0	5.9	6.7	7.6	8.5	9.4	10.3	11.2	12.1	13.0	14.0	14.9	15.8	16.8	17.7
24	0.8	1.6	2.5	3.3	4.1	5.0	5.8	6.7	7.6	8.4	9.3	10.2	11.1	12.0	12.9	13.8	14.8	15.7	16.6	17.6

Percentage increase in terminal value per 1% increase in RIRR

Revised IRR for Real Estate at Various Reinvestment Rates

The RIRR for real estate investments is like that for stocks in that cash flows are hopefully increasing from year to year. Also, like stocks, the investor anticipates a sales proceeds after taxes that is in excess of the original cash investment. Unlike stocks, it sometimes happens that negative cash flows occur in subsequent years after the initial investment. *Revised IRR* (RIRR), *modified IRR* (MIRR), compound realized return, and *financial management rate of return* (FMRR) are essentially synonymous: They all are the IRR calculation after giving effect to the reinvestment of available cash flows.

A typical method involves taking all positive cash flows to the terminal date with interest compounded at the after-tax rate earned on reinvestment, where they are added to the after-tax sales proceeds. Negative cash flows are discounted at a "safe" T-bill rate to the time of original investment and added to the original investment. The MIRR or FMRR is the rate that equates the terminal value and adjusted initial investment. On the other hand, the RIRR as calculated throughout this book (unless otherwise indicated) treats negative cash flows in the same manner as positive cash flows.

An RIRR calculation was performed in Chap. 24 in Table 24.1. It involved a reinvestment rate after-tax which equaled the IRR.

The IRR of a real estate investment is a function of many variables, including:

Annual increase in rents and other income

Annual increase in operating expenses

Debt service costs of principal and interest on one or more mortgage loans

Tax rate for both income and capital gains

Number of years the investment is held

Amount of future sale of the property

These figures can be reduced to an annual after-tax cash flow and, just as in the case of stocks or bonds, the IRR and RIRR can be determined by methods described previously.

Just as in the case of both bonds and stocks, if the after-tax rate earned on reinvestment is equal to the IRR without reinvestment, then the RIRR will equal the IRR. (This is not true of MIRR or FMRR.)

If the after-tax rate earned on reinvestment is greater than the IRR without reinvestment, then the RIRR will be greater than the IRR. (Neither this statement nor the next is true for MIRR or FMRR calculations.)

If the after-tax rate earned on reinvestment is less than the IRR without reinvestment, then the RIRR will be less than the IRR.

The foregoing principles are apparent in Fig. 26.7, which depicts both the IRR (left vertical axis) and RIRR (bottom horizontal axis) for a typical real estate investment. The various assumptions underlying the analysis are stated in the figure. The typical pattern of initial yield as percent of net operating income is in the range of 6 to 10 percent. Within that range, it is clear that all the reinvestment curves are to the left of the pure IRR line (the IRR without any reinvesting). This means that the IRR is higher than the after tax rate earned on reinvestment. The after-tax rate earned on reinvestment in a 28 percent bracket would be, in this case, only 72 percent of the pretax rate. Whenever the after-tax rate earned on reinvestment is less than the IRR, the RIRR will be less than the IRR. The greater the difference, the less RIRR will be relative to IRR. This is evident in Fig. 26.7, as, for example, at an initial yield of 10 percent at the highest after-tax reinvestment rate shown of 12 percent:

$$IRR = 23.7 \%$$

$$RIRR = 20.5 \%$$

This situation occurs because of the relatively high IRRs of well-selected real estate investments. It is just not likely that it will be possible to reinvest the after-tax cash flows at an after-tax reinvestment rate of the magnitude of the IRR. Thus the RIRR is dragged down (as compared to the original IRR). If one intends to spend the income from the real estate, the IRR is what matters—not the RIRR. But if income is to be reinvested, the real estate RIRR should be compared to the RIRRs of alternative investments.

Appendix 6 shows the calculations necessary to find just one point on one curve of Fig. 26.7. It happens to be the point where the after-tax interest rate earned on reinvestment (the RIRR) is equal to the IRR. Thus, as shown, the IRR and RIRR are equal at 23.7 percent. This corresponds to the indicated point on the figure. This real estate analysis, along with similar stock and bond programs, are contained on the computer disk called INVESTMENT IRR ANALYSIS (AFTER TAX) FOR STOCKS, BONDS AND REAL ESTATE (Larry Rosen Co., 1990-1994).

Summary

If one is going to reinvest the available after-tax cash flows from any investment—stock, bond, real estate, or whatever—then one must make assumptions regarding the after-tax interest rate that can be earned on such reinvestment.

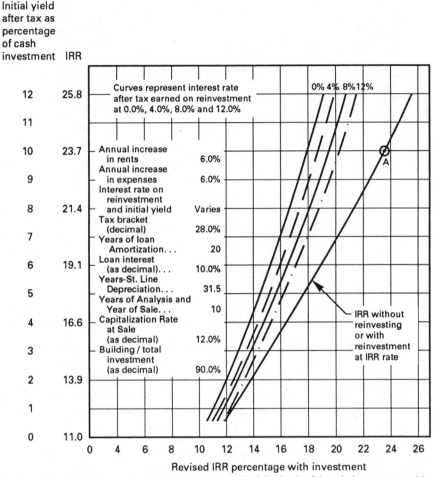

Figure 26.7. Real estate investment: RIRR. (See Appendix 6 for details of the calculation at point A.)

If future rates are expected to be high, then high current income is desirable from the investment so that more money will be available to invest sooner at the high rates. This could take the form of high rents, high coupons, or high dividends.

Conversely, if reinvestment rates are expected to be low, then it is more desirable to give up high current income for gain in the form of sales proceeds, which would favor zero-coupon or deep-discount bonds, real estate with low rents but high appreciation potential, or stocks with great earnings growth potential and little or no dividends.

In any case, the guide to the most intelligent investment decision, when cash flows are to be reinvested, is the RIRR, MIRR, or FMRR. The investment offering the highest RIRR is the best choice—other factors such as risk, volatility, liquidity being equal.

27

The Cost of Procrastination

Everyone should be aware of the cost of procrastination. It is obvious that the longer you wait to begin a savings program for a particular goal, the more you will have to save or invest. It doesn't matter what that goal is—a retirement nest egg, a college fund for a son or daughter, or even a yacht. The critical factors are time and the rate of earnings on investment. What is not so obvious is how the cost of procrastination escalates the amount that has to be saved.

Example: Finding the cost of procrastination in starting a retirement fund. Jacob Youngman is 46 and figures he will need to accumulate $500,000 in a retirement fund to continue to live in retirement in the style to which he has become accustomed. He knows that at 12 percent after-tax earnings he must save $7881.50 per year starting *now. How much more will he have to save if he delays starting the plan for 5 more years?*

Enter Fig. 27.1 on the vertical axis at 46 years (19 years until funds are needed) and proceed horizontally across the graph until the curve for a 5-year delay is reached. From that point, drop vertically to the bottom, horizontal axis. The point of intersection with the horizontal axis is about 101 percent. A little more precision is possible by referring to Table 27.1, where the increase in cost is indicated to be 100.6 percent.

Thus, no matter how you figure it, Jacob Youngman's cost will be 101 percent more if he waits 5 years to start his savings plan. In money terms that means an increase of 101 percent of $7881.50, or a total cost of $15,841.82 per year each and every year starting at age 51. When you hear phrases like "the power of compound interest," it is this kind of situation that is being referred to. Doubling the annual cost of providing a retirement plan just by procrastinating for 5 years is nothing to sneeze at.

Age   Years until funds needed

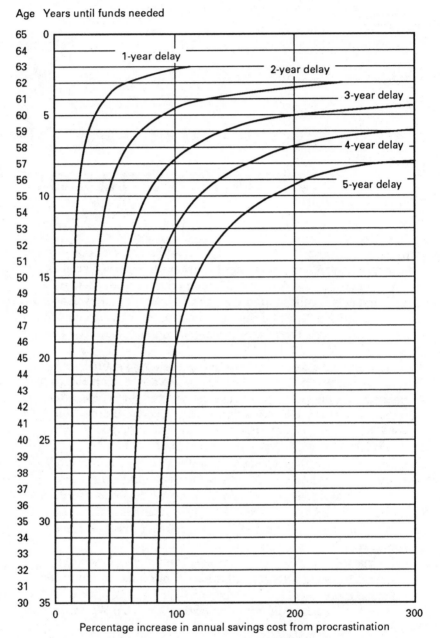

Percentage increase in annual savings cost from procrastination

Figure 27.1. How delay in starting a saving program affects the cost when money earns 12 percent.

Table 27.1. Impact of Procastination on the Cost of Funding a Savings Program

Annual rate of interest earned on savings fund: 12.00%
Total sum to be accumulated, including interest: $100,000
Age at which total sum is needed: 65
Number of compounding periods per year: 12

Years until funds are needed	Age	Compound growth factor	Percent increase in cost of periodic investment needed to fund the same total benefit if commencement of the fund is delayed n years				
			$n = 1$	$n = 2$	$n = 3$	$n = 4$	$n = 5$
35	30	6431	12.9	27.5	44.0	62.8	84.0
34	31	5696	12.9	27.6	44.2	63.0	84.3
33	32	5044	13.0	27.7	44.3	63.2	84.7
32	33	4465	13.0	27.7	44.5	63.5	85.1
31	34	3951	13.0	27.8	44.7	63.8	85.5
30	35	3495	13.1	28.0	44.9	64.1	86.0
29	36	3090	13.1	28.1	45.1	64.5	86.6
28	37	2731	13.2	28.2	45.4	64.9	87.3
27	38	2413	13.3	28.4	45.7	65.4	88.0
26	39	2130	14.4	28.6	46.0	66.0	88.9
25	40	1879	13.4	28.8	46.4	66.7	89.9
24	41	1656	13.6	29.1	46.9	67.4	91.1
23	42	1458	13.7	29.4	47.4	68.3	92,4
22	43	1283	13.8	29.7	48.0	69.3	94.0
21	44	1127	14.0	30.1	48.8	70.5	95.9
20	45	989	14.1	30.5	49.6	71.9	98.0
19	46	867	14.4	31.1	50.6	73.5	100.6
18	47	758	14.6	31.7	51.7	75.4	103.6
17	48	661	14.9	32.4	53.0	77.7	107.3
16	49	576	15.2	33.2	54.7	80.4	111.7
15	50	500	15.6	34.2	56.6	83.7	117.2
14	51	432	16.1	35.4	58.9	87.8	124.0
13	52	372	16.7	36.9	61.8	93.0	132.7
12	53	319	17.3	38.7	65.4	99.5	144.2
11	54	272	18.2	41.0	70.0	108.1	159.7
10	55	230	19.3	43.8	76.0	119.7	181.7
9	56	193	20.6	47.6	84.2	136.2	215.1
8	57	160	22.4	52.7	95.8	161.2	271.3
7	58	131	24.8	60.0	113.4	203.3	384.4
6	59	105	28.2	71.0	143.1	288.2	725.6
5	60	82	33.4	89.6	202.8	544.0	n/a
4	61	61	42.1	127.0	382.7	n/a	n/a
3	62	43	59.7	239.7	n/a	n/a	n/a
2	63	27	112.7	n/a	n/a	n/a	n/a
1	64	13	n/a	n/a	n/a	n/a	n/a
0	65	0	n/a	n/a	n/a	n/a	n/a

That is a startling statement, but here's the proof. The monthly investment starting at age 46 to accumulate a capital fund of, say, $100,000, is

$$\frac{\$100,000}{\$866.7} = \$115.39 \text{ per month}$$

and the monthly investment to accumulate the same 100,000 fund starting from age 51 is

$$\frac{\$100,000}{\$432.1} = \$231.43 \text{ per month}$$

The cost increase of 100.6% percent from Table 27.1 is determined as follows:

$$\frac{\text{cost at age 51} - \text{cost at age 46}}{\text{cost at age 46}} = \frac{\$231.43 - \$115.39}{\$115.39} = 100.6\,\%$$

Next, let's consider whether the percentage increase in cost due to delay increases or decreases with the interest rate.

At higher interest rates, the percentage increase in cost due to delay increases; at lower interest rates, the percentage increase in cost decreases. Though this result might not be what one would expect, it is true. Think of it in these terms. The effect of delay is to lose one or more years of accumulation—both payments and the interest on those payments. The higher the interest rate, the greater is the value of what is lost due to delay. Everything that is lost will have to be recouped in a shorter time period when the savings actually do start; and the higher the value of what is lost, the more that will have to be made up by higher savings amounts.

What is the percentage increase in cost resulting from a 5-year delay from age 46 to age 51, if money earns 8 percent?

Enter Fig. 27.2 enter on the vertical axis at 46 years (19 years until funds are needed) and proceed horizontally across the graph until the curve for a 5-year delay is reached. From that point, drop vertically to the bottom, horizontal axis. The point of intersection with the horizontal axis is about 73 percent. A little more precision is possible by referring to Table 27.2, where the increase in cost is indicated to be 72.8 percent.

Example: Effect of delay in starting a college fund.   Paul Prudhomme has an infant daughter. He wants to start a college fund for her and will need the money in 17 years. It is reasonable to expect 8 percent earnings on the fund. If he procrastinates for 5 years in starting the fund, how much more will he have to save each month?

Enter Fig. 27.2 on the vertical axis at age 48 year (17 years until funds are needed) and proceed horizontally across the graph to the curve for a 5-year delay. From that point, drop vertically to the bottom, horizontal axis. The point of intersection with the horizontal axis is about 80 percent. A little

Age   Years until funds needed

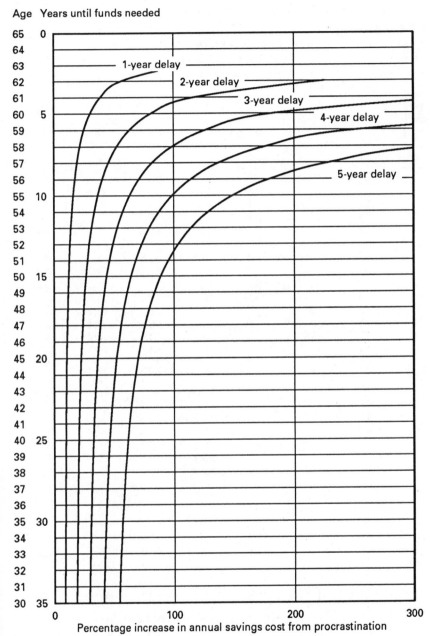

Figure 27.2. How delay in starting a saving program affects the cost when money earns 8 percent.

Table 27.2. Impact of Procrastination on the Cost of Funding a Savings Program

Annual rate of interest earned on savings fund: 8.00%
Total sum to be accumulated, including interest: $100,000
Age at which total sum is needed: 65
Number of compounding periods per year: 12

Years until funds are needed	Age	Compound growth factor	Percent increase of cost of periodic investment needed to fund the same total benefit if commencement of the fund is delayed n years				
			$n = 1$	$n = 2$	$n = 3$	$n = 4$	$n = 5$
35	30	$2294	8.9	18.6	29.3	41.0	53.9
34	31	2107	8.9	18.8	29.5	41.3	54.4
33	32	1934	9.0	18.9	29.7	41.7	54.9
32	33	1774	9.1	19.0	30.0	42.1	55.4
31	34	1627	9.1	19.2	30.3	42.5	56.0
30	35	1490	9.2	19.4	30.6	43.0	56.7
29	36	1365	9.3	19.6	30.9	43.5	57.5
28	37	1249	9.4	19.8	31.3	44.1	58.3
27	38	1141	9.5	20.0	31.7	44.7	59.2
26	39	1042	9.6	20.3	32.2	45.4	60.3
25	40	951	9.7	20.6	32.7	46.2	61.5
24	41	867	9.9	20.9	33.3	47.1	62.8
23	42	789	10.0	21.3	33.9	48.2	64.3
22	43	717	10.2	21.7	34.6	49.3	66.0
21	44	650	10.4	22.2	35.5	50.6	68.0
20	45	589	10.6	22.7	36.4	52.1	70.2
19	46	532	10.9	23.3	37.5	53.9	72.8
18	47	480	11.2	24.0	38.7	55.9	75.9
17	48	432	11.5	24.8	40.2	58.2	79.5
16	49	387	11.9	25.7	41.9	61.0	83.9
15	50	346	12.3	26.8	43.9	64.3	89.1
14	51	308	12.9	28.1	46.3	68.4	95.7
13	52	273	13.5	29.6	49.2	73.4	103.9
12	53	241	14.2	31.5	52.8	79.7	114.5
11	54	211	15.1	33.8	57.3	87.8	128.8
10	55	183	16.2	36.7	63.2	98.8	149.0
9	56	157	17.6	40.4	71.1	114.3	179.4
8	57	134	19.4	45.5	82.2	137.6	230.2
7	58	112	21.8	52.6	99.0	176.6	332.3
6	59	92	25.2	63.3	127.0	254.9	639.2
5	60	73	30.4	81.3	183.3	490.2	n/a
4	61	56	39.0	117.3	352.6	n/a	n/a
3	62	41	56.3	225.6	n/a	n/a	n/a
2	63	26	108.3	n/a	n/a	n/a	n/a
1	64	12	n/a	n/a	n/a	n/a	n/a
0	65	0	n/a	n/a	n/a	n/a	n/a

more precision is possible by referring to Table 27.2, where the increase in cost is indicated to be 79.5 percent.

This means that a 5-year delay will cost Paul about 80 percent more in the size of monthly payments. It is not unreasonable to assume that 17 years from now, a college fund of the order of $325,000 will be needed to pay for four years of tuition, books, and room and board at a private institution. The cost to accumulate such a sum starting now, with 17 years to go, with 8 percent earnings compounded monthly, is about $753 per month. But if Paul procrastinates for 5 years in starting the monthly savings program, the cost will increase by 80 percent of $753, that is, $602 more per month, making the increased cost $1355 per month.

The moral of this chapter is: "Don't delay, start today."

28

The Summing Up

In the twilight of his life, the marvelous novelist and quasi-philosopher, W. Somerset Maugham, wrote a book bearing the title, *The Summing Up*. It is no accident that this chapter bears the same title. Maugham's book summarized the results of his years of study and observations—and succinctly stated his beliefs, many of which he had previously voiced through the mouths of the characters in his novels. This chapter is intended to sum up my observations, in the hope that it will help readers to invest their assets more efficiently and intelligently—whether these assets are presently large or small. Even small assets may become large over time if the methods presented throughout the text are adopted.

The Concept of IRR

Throughout this volume, much as been said about IRR, RIRR, realized compound yield, partitioning IRR, marginal IRR, and so forth. It is easy to become so enmeshed in details that one loses track of basic tenets. Think of IRR as being equivalent to the interest rate quoted conventionally on a bank account. Of course there are nuances and fine points, such as whether rates are compounded daily or at some other frequency, whether interest is figured on a 360- or a 365-day year, and the oddity in the case of bonds that the quoted yield to maturity (IRR) is double the semiannual rate. Nevertheless, the fact remains, that IRR is directly comparable to the interest rate paid on a bank savings account. If one takes the income from an investment or a bank account and spends it as it is received, the interest rate or IRR is clearly a *simple* (as opposed to compound) rate. IRR is an average simple rate of interest, even though it is calculated by using compound-interest discounting methods.

On the other hand, if one allows all of one's earnings to accumulate and be reinvested at some reinvestment rate, which may be equal to or differ from the IRR, then one is *compounding* one's investment. When an investment is compounded, there are only two relevant cash flows, the initial investment and the proceeds at the termination of the investment. RIRR or realized compound yield is an accurate measure of such compounded returns.

Investment results, whether projected into the future or historical, require measurement. If the ruler one uses is inaccurate, the results are sure to be wrong no matter how painstaking the analysis. The first point I wish to emphasize is: *Use IRR as the ruler; don't be hoodwinked into analyzing investments by other, inferior measures.*

The second point to remember is: *Check out the tax implications of proposed investments before you invest.*

IRR isn't the only consideration. The third key point is that it is important to consider the degree of reliability of the assumptions. The less reliable the assumptions are, the less reliable the projected IRR will be. Also, at least three other factors must be considered: *liquidity* (how easy or difficult it is to sell the investment, if necessary); *volatility* (how much the price of the investment is likely to fluctuate); and *risk* (how likely it is that the dividend will be maintained, the principal and interest paid, that you will become involved in litigation, or that the building will stay rented and not have unprojected expenses). These factors must be taken into account along with the after-tax IRR.

The Market Situation

Ralla Richie wants to know where to invest her surplus cash. She doesn't want any highly risky investments, she doesn't expect to need the money for many years, and she wants to know the alternatives.

The only sure thing about markets, as Bernard Baruch once said when asked to predict the stock market, is that they will fluctuate.

Ralla has three basic choices: bonds, stocks, or real estate. Suppose that Ralla applies the techniques in this volume and finds that, with current market conditions, she can expect to receive the following after-tax yields (with taxes at 28 percent on both ordinary income and capital gains):

Corporate or government bond	About 9.0%
Municipal or tax-free bond	About 7.7%
Income-producing real estate	About 19.3%
Utility common stock	About 9.3%

How can there be such a difference, Ralla wonders. Why doesn't everyone buy real estate?

That's what makes up a market, Ralla. Forces of supply and demand interact, prices change, yields change, and the good investment of today may be the poor choice of tomorrow. In addition, remember that the results above were tailored to Ralla Richie's tax bracket. If the investor were tax-free, then the IRR of the government or corporate bonds would increase, and the IRR from the real estate would stay about the same, in spite of the lack of value of any tax-shelter benefits to the tax-free investor.

The only generalization I will make is not about which investment should be purchased, but rather about how the decision should be made. And that is, to use precise measures, *IRR, revised IRR, or marginal IRR, as the magic number that puts all investments on a directly comparable basis.*

There are a considerable number of financial decisions that we are called upon to make. Among them are:

- Should I make biweekly mortgage payments on my home loan?
- Should I refinance my home mortgage loan?
- How much more will it cost to finance my retirement if I start saving in 5 years instead of now?
- With the savings I have, how much can I withdraw each month for retirement income for my expected lifespan?
- Should I take a reverse mortgage?
- Am I better off with a tax-exempt bond than a corporate bond?
- Which bonds are better to buy—discount, premium, or par bonds?
- Is a zero-coupon bond better than a conventional bond?
- How much more yield should I receive if I buy a callable bond rather than a noncallable one?
- Which is better for me: stocks, bonds, or real estate?
- Do I have to reinvest my income in order to achieve the return on investment indicated at purchase?
- What is the true cost of my loan, considering the up-front points that I have to pay?
- How much do I need to save to retire in comfort and dignity, pay for college education for my children, or build up enough funds for a down payment on a house? How about if I want to buy a yacht, or take a trip around the world?

The list can be continued almost indefinitely. The world of investments is like a desert, with constantly shifting sands. Today, bonds may offer the best possibilities; tomorrow it may be real estate or stocks. *But no matter how long the list of financial decisions that face us, and no matter how many different possible investments one may be offered, the one unchanging factor is that the principles described in this book, at all times, will aid in making the most intelligent financial decisions.*

Good luck with your investments, and good fortune.

Appendixes

Appendix 1 gives *factors for future and present values* for both single payments and for a series of payments. The first pages of Appendix 1 give an overview of the factors and their use.

Appendix 2 explains how to use *logarithms*. Log tables are readily available and have not been included due to space limitations. Logarithms can be very helpful in dealing with high-powered equations. Somehow situations do arise when one needs an answer now, but the battery in the calculator is dead and it's after closing time at the store. Logarithms might just save the day.

A derivation of the formula for calculating the *yield of a 1-year Treasury bill* is shown in Appendix 3.

A method of figuring both price and yield for interest-paying *securities traded within 6 months of maturity* or redemption is shown in Appendix 4.

A generalized approach to *finding equivalent yields* (e.g., the semiannual equivalent of monthly payments) is provided in Appendix 5.

Appendix 6 shows the calculations necessary to find the revised IRR for a real estate investment.

Tables of Factors for Future and Present Values of Single Payments and a Series of Payments*

The tables of Appendix 1 cover the factors that are underlined in the following formulas:

$$S = P\underline{(1 + i)^n}$$ How P (principal) left at compound interest will grow

$$P = S\underline{(1 + i)^{-n}}$$ What S (value of account) due in the future is worth today

$$V = R\underline{\left[\frac{(1 + i)^n - 1}{i}\right]}$$ How R (regular future payments) deposited periodically will grow

*Tables 1 through 20 of Appendix 1 are reprinted with the permission of: Financial Publishing Company, 82 Brookline Avenue, Boston, Mass. 02215. Readers who require more extensive information on the computation of interest will find the purchase of Financial Publishing Company's Publication #376 a most valuable investment.

$$R = S \left[\frac{i}{(1 + i)^n - 1} \right]$$ Periodic deposit that will grow into S at future date

$$A = R \left[\frac{1 - (1 + i)^{-n}}{i} \right]$$ What R payable periodically is worth today

$$R = A \left[\frac{i}{1 - (1 + i)^{-n}} \right]$$ Periodic payment necessary to pay off an original loan of A

The tables contain values for each of the factors identified for the following interest rates and number of periods (e.g., years, months, quarterly period):

Interest rate %	Number of periods	Table number
$\frac{1}{2}$	180*	1
1	180*	2
$1\frac{1}{2}$	45	3
2	10	4
3	20	5
4	10	6
5	20	7
6	30	8
7	20	9
8	30	10
9	25	11
10	30	12
11	25	13
12	10	14
13	10	15
14	10	16
15	15	17
16	15	18
17	15	19
18	30	20

* Entire range of periods is not included.

Table 1. Rate of ½%

Periods	Amount of $1 (how $1 left at compound interest will grow)	Amount of $1 per period (how $1 deposited periodically will grow)	Sinking fund (periodic deposit that will grow to $1 at future date)	Present worth of $1 (what $1 due in the future is worth today)	Present worth of $1 per period (what $1 payable periodically is worth today)	Partial payment (annuity worth $1 today; periodic payment necessary to pay off a loan of $1)
1	1.005 000	1.000 000	1.000 000	.995 024	.995 024	1.005 000
2	1.010 025	2.005 000	.498 753	.990 074	1.985 099	.503 753
3	1.015 075	3.015 025	.331 672	.985 148	2.970 248	.336 672
4	1.020 150	4.030 100	.248 132	.980 247	3.950 495	.253 132
5	1.025 251	5.050 250	.198 009	.975 370	4.925 866	.203 009
6	1.030 377	6.075 501	.164 595	.970 518	5.896 384	.169 595
7	1.035 529	7.105 879	.140 728	.965 689	6.862 074	.145 728
8	1.040 707	8.141 408	.122 828	.960 885	7.822 959	.127 828
9	1.045 910	9.182 115	.108 907	.956 104	8.779 063	.113 907
10	1.051 140	10.228 026	.097 770	.951 347	9.730 411	.102 770
11	1.056 395	11.279 166	.088 659	.946 614	10.677 026	.093 659
12	1.061 677	12.335 562	.081 066	.941 905	11.618 932	.086 066
13	1.066 986	13.397 240	.074 642	.937 219	12.556 151	.079 642
14	1.072 321	14.464 226	.069 136	.932 556	13.488 707	.074 136
15	1.077 682	15.536 547	.064 364	.927 916	14.416 624	.069 364
16	1.083 071	16.614 230	.060 189	.923 300	15.339 925	.065 189
17	1.088 486	17.697 301	.056 505	.918 706	16.258 631	.061 505
18	1.093 928	18.785 787	.053 231	.914 136	17.172 768	.058 231
19	1.099 398	19.879 716	.050 302	.909 588	18.082 356	.055 302
20	1.104 895	20.979 115	.047 666	.905 062	18.987 419	.052 666
21	1.110 420	22.084 011	.045 281	.900 560	19.887 979	.050 281
22	1.115 972	23.194 431	.043 113	.896 079	20.784 058	.048 113
23	1.121 552	24.310 403	.041 134	.891 621	21.675 680	.046 134
24	1.127 159	25.431 955	.039 320	.887 185	22.562 866	.044 320
25	1.132 795	26.559 115	.037 651	.882 771	23.445 638	.042 651
26	1.138 459	27.691 910	.036 111	.878 379	24.324 017	.041 111

Table 1. Rate of ½% (Continued)

Periods	Amount of $1 (how $1 left at compound interest will grow)	Amount of $1 per period (how $1 deposited periodically will grow)	Sinking fund (periodic deposit that will grow to $1 at future date)	Present worth of $1 due (what $1 due in the future is worth today)	Present worth of $1 per period (what $1 payable periodically is worth today)	Partial payment (annuity worth $1 today; periodic payment necessary to pay off a loan of $1)
27	1.144 151	28.830 370	.034 685	.874 009	25.198 027	.039 685
28	1.149 872	29.974 521	.033 361	.869 661	26.067 689	.038 361
29	1.155 621	31.124 394	.032 129	.865 334	26.933 024	.037 129
30	1.161 400	32.280 016	.030 978	.861 029	27.794 053	.035 978
...						
106	1.696 690	139.338 035	.007 176	.589 382	82.123 441	.012 176
107	1.705 173	141.034 726	.007 090	.586 450	82.709 891	.012 090
108	1.713 699	142.739 899	.007 005	.583 532	83.293 424	.012 005
109	1.722 267	144.453 599	.006 922	.580 629	83.874 054	.011 922
110	1.730 879	146.175 867	.006 841	.577 741	84.451 795	.011 841
111	1.739 533	147.906 746	.006 761	.574 866	85.026 661	.011 761
112	1.748 231	149.646 280	.006 682	.572 006	85.598 668	.011 682
113	1.756 972	151.394 511	.006 605	.569 160	86.167 829	.011 605
114	1.765 757	153.151 484	.006 529	.566 329	86.734 158	.011 529
115	1.774 586	154.917 841				

N	$(1+i)^N$	$\dfrac{(1+i)^N-1}{i}$	$\dfrac{i}{(1+i)^N-1}$	$(1+i)^{-N}$	$\dfrac{1-(1+i)^{-N}}{i}$	$\dfrac{i}{1-(1+i)^{-N}}$
116	1.783 459	156.691 827	.006 361	.560 708	87.658 578	.011 361
117	1.792 376	158.475 287	.006 310	.557 918	88.416 296	.011 310
118	1.801 338	160.267 663	.006 239	.555 142	88.971 439	.011 239
119	1.810 345	162.069 001	.006 170	.552 380	89.523 820	.011 170
120	1.819 396	163.879 346	.006 102	.549 632	90.073 453	.011 102
...						
171	2.346 370	269.274 068	.003 713	.426 190	114.761 963	.008 713
172	2.358 102	271.620 438	.003 681	.424 069	115.186 033	.008 681
173	2.369 892	273.978 540	.003 649	.421 960	115.607 993	.008 649
174	2.381 742	276.348 433	.003 618	.419 860	116.027 854	.008 618
175	2.393 650	278.730 175	.003 587	.417 771	116.445 626	.008 587
176	2.405 619	281.123 826	.003 557	.415 693	116.861 319	.008 557
177	2.417 647	283.529 445	.003 526	.413 625	117.274 944	.008 526
178	2.429 735	285.947 092	.003 497	.411 567	117.686 512	.008 497
179	2.441 884	288.376 828	.003 467	.409 519	118.096 032	.008 467
180	2.454 093	290.818 712	.003 438	.407 482	118.503 514	.008 438

SOURCE: *Financial Compound Interest and Annuity Tables*, 5th ed. (Financial Publishing Co., Boston, 1970).

Table 2. Rate of 1%

Periods	Amount of $1 (how $1 left at compound interest will grow)	Amount of $1 per period (how $1 deposited periodically will grow)	Sinking fund (periodic deposit that will grow to $1 at future date)	Present worth of $1 (what $1 due in the future is worth today)	Present worth of $1 per period (what $1 payable periodically is worth today)	Partial payment (annuity worth $1 today; periodic payment necessary to pay off a loan of $1)
1	1.010 000	1.000 000	1.000 000	.990 099	.990 099	1.010 000
2	1.020 100	2.010 000	.497 512	.980 296	1.970 395	.507 512
3	1.030 301	3.030 100	.330 022	.970 590	2.940 985	.340 022
4	1.040 604	4.060 401	.246 281	.960 980	3.901 965	.256 281
5	1.051 010	5.101 005	.196 039	.951 465	4.853 431	.206 039
6	1.061 520	6.152 015	.162 548	.942 045	5.795 476	.172 548
7	1.072 135	7.213 535	.138 628	.932 718	6.728 194	.148 628
8	1.082 856	8.285 670	.120 690	.923 483	7.651 677	.130 690
9	1.093 685	9.368 527	.106 740	.914 339	8.566 017	.116 740
10	1.104 622	10.462 212	.095 582	.905 286	9.471 304	.105 582
11	1.115 668	11.566 834	.086 454	.896 323	10.367 628	.096 454
12	1.126 825	12.682 503	.078 848	.887 449	11.255 077	.088 848
13	1.138 093	13.809 328	.072 414	.878 662	12.133 740	.082 414
14	1.149 474	14.947 421	.066 901	.869 962	13.003 703	.076 901
15	1.160 968	16.096 895	.062 123	.861 349	13.865 052	.072 123
16	1.172 578	17.257 864	.057 944	.852 821	14.717 873	.067 944
17	1.184 304	18.430 443	.054 258	.844 377	15.562 251	.064 258
18	1.196 147	19.614 747	.050 982	.836 017	16.398 268	.060 982
19	1.208 108	20.810 895	.048 051	.827 739	17.226 008	.058 051
20	1.220 190	22.019 003	.045 415	.819 544	18.045 552	.055 415
21	1.232 391	23.239 194	.043 030	.811 430	18.856 983	.053 030
22	1.244 715	24.471 585	.040 863	.803 396	19.660 379	.050 863
23	1.257 163	25.716 301	.038 885	.795 441	20.455 821	.048 885
24	1.269 734	26.973 464	.037 073	.787 566	21.243 387	.047 073
25	1.282 431	28.243 199	.035 406	.779 768	22.023 155	.045 406
26	1.295 256	29.525 631	.033 868	.772 047	22.795 203	.043 868
27	1.308 208	30.820 887	.032 445	.764 403	23.559 607	.042 445
28	1.321 290	32.129 096	.031 124	.756 835	24.316 443	.041 124
	1.334 503	33.450 387	.029 895	.749 349	25.065 785	.039 895

N	$(1+i)^N$	$\dfrac{(1+i)^N - 1}{i}$	$\dfrac{i}{(1+i)^N - 1}$	$(1+i)^{-N}$	$\dfrac{1-(1+i)^{-N}}{i}$	$\dfrac{i}{1-(1+i)^{-N}}$
30	1.347 848	34.784 891	.028 748	.741 922	25.807 708	.038 748
31	1.361 327	36.132 740	.027 675	.734 577	26.542 285	.037 675
32	1.374 940	37.494 067	.026 670	.727 304	27.269 589	.036 670
33	1.388 690	38.869 008	.025 727	.720 103	27.989 692	.035 727
34	1.402 576	40.257 698	.024 839	.712 973	28.702 665	.034 839
35	1.416 602	41.660 275	.024 003	.705 914	29.408 580	.034 003
36	1.430 768	43.076 878	.023 214	.698 924	30.107 505	.033 214
37	1.445 076	44.507 647	.022 468	.692 004	30.799 509	.032 468
38	1.459 527	45.952 723	.021 761	.685 153	31.484 663	.031 761
39	1.474 122	47.412 250	.021 091	.678 369	32.163 032	.031 091
40	1.488 863	48.886 373	.020 455	.671 653	32.834 868	.030 455
41	1.503 752	50.375 237	.019 851	.665 003	33.499 689	.029 851
42	1.518 789	51.878 989	.019 275	.658 418	34.158 108	.029 275
43	1.533 977	53.397 779	.018 727	.651 899	34.810 008	.028 727
44	1.549 317	54.931 757	.018 204	.645 445	35.455 453	.028 204
45	1.564 810	56.481 074	.017 705	.639 054	36.094 508	.027 705
46	1.580 458	58.045 885	.017 227	.632 727	36.727 236	.027 227
47	1.596 263	59.626 344	.016 771	.626 463	37.353 699	.026 771
48	1.612 226	61.222 607	.016 333	.620 260	37.973 959	.026 333
49	1.628 348	62.834 833	.015 914	.614 119	38.588 078	.025 914
50	1.644 631	64.463 182	.015 512	.608 038	39.196 117	.025 512
...						
171	5.482 200	448.220 052	.002 231	.182 408	81.759 149	.012 231
172	5.537 022	453.702 252	.002 204	.180 602	81.939 752	.012 204
173	5.592 392	459.239 275	.002 177	.178 814	82.118 566	.012 177
174	5.648 316	464.831 668	.002 151	.177 043	82.295 610	.012 151
175	5.704 799	470.479 984	.002 125	.175 290	82.470 901	.012 125
176	5.761 847	476.184 784	.002 100	.173 555	82.644 465	.012 100
177	5.819 466	481.946 632	.002 074	.171 837	82.816 293	.012 074
178	5.877 660	487.766 098	.002 050	.170 135	82.986 429	.012 050
179	5.936 437	493.643 759	.002 025	.168 451	83.154 880	.012 025
180	5.995 801	499.580 197	.002 001	.166 783	83.321 663	.012 001

SOURCE: *Financial Compound Interest and Annuity Tables*, 5th ed. (Financial Publishing Co., Boston, 1970).

Table 3. Rate of 1½%

Periods	Amount of $1 (how $1 left at compound interest will grow)	Amount of $1 per period (how $1 deposited periodically will grow)	Sinking fund (periodic deposit that will grow to $1 at future date)	Present worth of $1 (what $1 due in the future is worth today)	Present worth of $1 per period (what $1 payable periodically is worth today)	Partial payment (annuity worth $1 today; periodic payment necessary to pay off a loan of $1)
1	1.015 000	1.000 000	1.000 000	.985 221	.985 221	1.015 000
2	1.030 225	2.015 000	.496 277	.970 661	1.955 883	.511 277
3	1.045 678	3.045 225	.328 382	.956 316	2.912 200	.343 382
4	1.061 363	4.090 903	.244 444	.942 184	3.854 384	.259 444
5	1.077 284	5.152 266	.194 089	.928 260	4.782 644	.209 089
6	1.093 443	6.229 550	.160 525	.914 542	5.697 187	.175 525
7	1.109 844	7.322 994	.136 556	.901 026	6.598 213	.151 556
8	1.126 492	8.432 839	.118 584	.887 711	7.485 925	.133 584
9	1.143 389	9.559 331	.104 609	.874 592	8.360 517	.119 609
10	1.160 540	10.702 721	.093 434	.861 667	9.222 184	.108 434
11	1.177 948	11.863 262	.084 293	.848 933	10.071 117	.099 293
12	1.195 618	13.041 211	.076 679	.836 387	10.907 505	.091 679
13	1.213 552	14.236 829	.070 240	.824 027	11.731 532	.085 240
14	1.231 755	15.460 382	.064 723	.811 849	12.543 381	.079 723
15	1.250 232	16.682 137	.059 944	.799 851	13.343 233	.074 944
16	1.268 985	17.932 369	.055 765	.788 031	14.131 264	.070 765
17	1.288 020	19.201 355	.052 079	.776 385	14.907 649	.067 079
18	1.307 340	20.438 375	.048 805	.764 911	15.672 560	.063 805
19	1.326 950	21.796 716	.045 878	.753 607	16.426 168	.060 878
20	1.346 855	23.123 667	.043 245	.742 470	17.168 638	.058 245
21	1.367 067	24.470 522	.040 865	.731 497	17.900 136	.055 865
22	1.387 568	25.837 579	.038 703	.720 687	18.620 824	.053 703

N	$(1+i)^N$	$\dfrac{(1+i)^N-1}{i}$	$\dfrac{i}{(1+i)^N-1}$	$(1+i)^{-N}$	$\dfrac{1-(1+i)^{-N}}{i}$	$\dfrac{i}{1-(1+i)^{-N}}$
23	1.408 377	27.225 143	.036 730	.710 037	19.330 861	.051 730
24	1.429 502	28.633 520	.034 924	.699 543	20.030 405	.049 924
25	1.450 945	30.063 023	.033 263	.689 205	20.719 611	.048 263
26	1.472 709	31.513 968	.031 731	.679 020	21.398 631	.046 731
27	1.494 800	32.986 678	.030 315	.668 985	22.067 617	.045 315
28	1.517 222	34.481 478	.029 001	.659 099	22.726 716	.044 001
29	1.539 980	35.998 700	.027 778	.649 358	23.376 075	.042 778
30	1.563 080	37.538 681	.026 639	.639 762	24.015 838	.041 639
31	1.586 526	39.101 761	.025 574	.630 307	24.646 145	.040 574
32	1.610 324	40.688 288	.024 577	.620 992	25.267 138	.039 577
33	1.634 479	42.298 612	.023 641	.611 815	25.878 954	.038 641
34	1.658 996	43.933 091	.022 761	.602 774	26.481 728	.037 761
35	1.683 881	45.592 087	.021 933	.593 866	27.075 594	.036 933
36	1.709 139	47.275 969	.021 152	.585 089	27.660 684	.036 152
37	1.734 776	48.965 108	.020 414	.576 443	28.237 127	.035 414
38	1.760 798	50.719 885	.019 716	.567 924	28.805 051	.034 716
39	1.787 210	52.480 683	.019 054	.559 531	29.364 582	.034 054
40	1.814 018	54.267 893	.018 427	.551 262	29.915 845	.033 427
41	1.841 228	56.081 912	.017 831	.543 115	30.458 960	.032 831
42	1.868 847	57.923 141	.017 264	.535 089	30.994 050	.032 264
43	1.896 879	59.791 988	.016 724	.527 181	31.521 231	.031 724
44	1.925 333	61.688 867	.016 210	.519 390	32.040 622	.031 210
45	1.954 213	63.614 200	.015 719	.511 714	32.552 337	.030 719

SOURCE: *Financial Compound Interest and Annuity Tables*, 5th ed. (Financial Publishing Co., Boston, 1970).

Table 4. Rate of 2%

Periods	Amount of $1 (how $1 left at compound interest will grow)	Amount of $1 per period (how $1 deposited periodically will grow)	Sinking fund (periodic deposit that will grow to $1 at future date)	Present worth of $1 (what $1 due in the future is worth today)	Present worth of $1 per period (what $1 payable periodically is worth today)	Partial payment (annuity worth $1 today; periodic payment necessary to pay off a loan of $1)
1	1.020 000	1.000 000	1.000 000	.980 392	.980 392	1.020 000
2	1.040 400	2.020 000	.495 049	.961 168	1.941 560	.515 049
3	1.061 208	3.060 400	.326 754	.942 322	2.883 883	.346 754
4	1.082 432	4.121 608	.242 623	.923 845	3.807 728	.262 623
5	1.104 080	5.204 040	.192 158	.905 730	4.713 459	.212 158
6	1.126 162	6.308 120	.158 525	.887 971	5.601 430	.178 525
7	1.148 685	7.434 283	.134 511	.870 560	6.471 991	.154 511
8	1.171 659	8.582 969	.116 509	.853 490	7.325 481	.136 509
9	1.195 092	9.754 628	.102 515	.836 755	8.162 236	.122 515
10	1.218 994	10.949 720	.091 826	.830 348	8.982 585	.111 326
	$(1+i)^N$	$\dfrac{(1+i)^N - 1}{i}$	$\dfrac{i}{(1+i)^N - 1}$	$(1+i)^{-N}$	$\dfrac{1-(1+i)^{-N}}{i}$	$\dfrac{i}{1-(1+i)^{-N}}$

SOURCE: Financial Compound Interest and Annuity Tables, 5th ed. (Financial Publishing Co., Boston, 1970).

Table 5. Rate of 3%

Periods	Amount of $1 (how $1 left at compound interest will grow) $(1+i)^N$	Amount of $1 per period (how $1 deposited periodically will grow) $\dfrac{(1+i)^N - 1}{i}$	Sinking fund (periodic deposit that will grow to $1 at future date) $\dfrac{i}{(1+i)^N - 1}$	Present worth of $1 (what $1 due in the future is worth today) $(1+i)^{-N}$	Present worth of $1 per period (what $1 payable periodically is worth today) $\dfrac{1-(1+i)^{-N}}{i}$	Partial payment (annuity worth $1 today; periodic payment necessary to pay off a loan of $1) $\dfrac{i}{1-(1+i)^{-N}}$
1	1.030 000	1.000 000	1.000 000	.970 873	.970 873	1.030 000
2	1.060 900	2.030 000	.492 610	.942 595	1.913 469	.522 610
3	1.092 727	3.090 900	.323 530	.915 141	2.828 611	.353 530
4	1.125 508	4.183 627	.239 027	.888 487	3.717 098	.269 027
5	1.159 274	5.309 135	.188 354	.862 608	4.579 707	.218 354
6	1.194 052	6.468 409	.154 597	.837 484	5.417 191	.184 597
7	1.229 873	7.662 462	.130 506	.813 091	6.230 282	.160 506
8	1.266 770	8.892 336	.112 456	.789 409	7.019 692	.142 456
9	1.304 773	10.159 106	.098 435	.766 416	7.786 108	.128 433
10	1.343 916	11.463 879	.087 230	.744 093	8.530 202	.117 230
11	1.384 233	12.807 795	.078 077	.722 421	9.252 624	.108 077
12	1.425 760	14.192 029	.070 462	.701 379	9.954 003	.100 462
13	1.468 533	15.617 790	.064 029	.680 951	10.634 955	.094 029
14	1.512 589	17.066 324	.058 526	.661 117	11.296 073	.088 526
15	1.557 967	18.598 919	.053 766	.641 861	11.937 935	.083 766
16	1.604 706	20.156 881	.049 610	.623 166	12.561 102	.079 610
17	1.652 847	21.761 587	.045 952	.605 016	13.166 118	.075 952
18	1.702 433	23.414 435	.042 708	.587 394	13.753 513	.072 708
19	1.753 506	25.116 868	.039 813	.570 286	14.323 799	.069 813
20	1.806 111	26.870 374	.037 215	.553 675	14.877 474	.067 215

SOURCE: *Financial Compound Interest and Annuity Tables*, 5th ed. (Financial Publishing Co., Boston, 1970).

Table 6. Rate of 4%

Periods	Amount of $1 (how $1 left at compound interest will grow)	Amount of $1 per period (how $1 deposited periodically will grow)	Sinking fund (periodic deposit that will grow to $1 at future date)	Present worth of $1 (what $1 due in the future is worth today)	Present worth of $1 per period (what $1 payable periodically is worth today)	Partial payment (annuity worth $1 today; periodic payment necessary to pay off a loan of $1)
1	1.040 000	1.000 000	1.000 000	.961 538	.961 538	1.040 000
2	1.081 600	2.040 000	.490 196	.924 556	1.886 094	.530 196
3	1.124 864	3.121 600	.320 348	.888 996	2.775 091	.360 348
4	1.169 858	4.246 464	.235 490	.854 804	3.629 895	.275 490
5	1.216 652	5.416 322	.184 627	.821 927	4.451 822	.224 627
6	1.265 319	6.632 975	.150 761	.790 314	5.242 136	.190 761
7	1.315 931	7.898 294	.126 609	.759 917	6.002 054	.166 609
8	1.368 569	9.214 226	.108 527	.730 690	6.732 744	.148 527
9	1.423 311	10.582 795	.094 492	.702 586	7.435 331	.134 492
10	1.480 244	12.006 107	.083 290	.675 564	8.110 895	.123 290
	$(1+i)^N$	$\dfrac{(1+i)^N - 1}{i}$	$\dfrac{i}{(1+i)^N - 1}$	$(1+i)^{-N}$	$\dfrac{1-(1+i)^{-N}}{i}$	$\dfrac{i}{1-(1+i)^{-N}}$

SOURCE: *Financial Compound Interest and Annuity Tables*, 5th ed. (Financial Publishing Co., Boston, 1970).

Table 7. Rate of 5%

Periods	Amount of $1 (how $1 left at compound interest will grow) $(1+i)^N$	Amount of $1 per period (how $1 deposited periodically will grow.) $\dfrac{(1+i)^N-1}{i}$	Sinking fund (periodic deposit that will grow to $1 at future date) $\dfrac{i}{(1+i)^N-1}$	Present worth of $1 (what $1 due in the future is worth today) $(1+i)^{-N}$	Present worth of $1 per period (what $1 payable periodically is worth today) $\dfrac{1-(1+i)^{-N}}{i}$	Partial payment (annuity worth $1 today; periodic payment necessary to pay off a loan of $1) $\dfrac{i}{1-(1+i)^{-N}}$
1	1.050 000	1.000 000	1.000 000	.952 380	.952 380	1.050 000
2	1.102 500	2.050 000	.487 804	.907 029	1.859 410	.537 804
3	1.157 625	3.152 500	.317 208	.863 837	2.723 248	.367 208
4	1.215 506	4.310 125	.232 011	.822 702	3.545 950	.282 011
5	1.276 281	5.525 631	.180 974	.783 526	4.329 476	.230 974
6	1.340 095	6.801 912	.147 017	.746 215	5.075 692	.197 017
7	1.407 100	8.142 008	.122 819	.710 681	5.786 373	.172 819
8	1.477 455	9.549 108	.104 721	.676 839	6.463 212	.154 721
9	1.551 328	11.026 564	.090 690	.644 608	7.107 821	.140 690
10	1.628 894	12.577 892	.079 504	.613 913	7.721 734	.129 504
11	1.710 339	14.206 787	.070 388	.584 679	8.306 414	.120 388
12	1.795 856	15.917 126	.062 825	.556 837	8.863 251	.112 825
13	1.885 649	17.712 982	.056 455	.530 321	9.393 572	.106 455
14	1.979 931	19.598 631	.051 023	.505 067	9.898 640	.101 023
15	2.078 928	21.578 563	.046 342	.481 017	10.379 658	.096 342
16	2.182 874	23.657 491	.042 269	.458 111	10.837 769	.092 269
17	2.292 018	25.840 366	.038 699	.436 296	11.274 066	.088 699
18	2.406 619	28.132 384	.035 546	.415 520	11.689 586	.085 546
19	2.526 950	30.539 003	.032 745	.395 733	12.085 320	.082 745
20	2.653 297	33.065 954	.030 242	.376 889	12.462 210	.080 242

SOURCE: *Financial Compound Interest and Annuity Tables*, 5th ed. (Financial Publishing Co., Boston, 1970).

Table 8. Rate of 6%

Periods	Amount of $1 (how $1 left at compound interest will grow) $(1+i)^N$	Amount of $1 per period (how $1 deposited periodically will grow) $\frac{(1+i)^N-1}{i}$	Sinking fund (periodic deposit that will grow to $1 at future date) $\frac{i}{(1+i)^N-1}$	Present worth of $1 (what $1 due in the future is worth today) $(1+i)^{-N}$	Present worth of $1 per period (what $1 payable periodically is worth today) $\frac{1-(1+i)^{-N}}{i}$	Partial payment (annuity worth $1 today; periodic payment necessary to pay off a loan of $1) $\frac{i}{1-(1+i)^{-N}}$
1	1.060 000	1.000 000	1.000 000	.943 396	.943 396	1.060 000
2	1.123 600	2.060 000	.485 436	.889 996	1.833 392	.545 436
3	1.191 016	3.183 600	.314 109	.839 619	2.673 011	.374 109
4	1.262 475	4.374 616	.228 591	.792 093	3.465 105	.288 591
5	1.338 225	5.637 092	.177 396	.747 258	4.212 363	.237 396
6	1.418 519	6.975 318	.143 362	.704 960	4.917 324	.203 362
7	1.503 630	8.393 837	.119 135	.665 057	5.582 381	.179 135
8	1.593 848	9.897 467	.101 035	.627 412	6.209 793	.161 035
9	1.689 478	11.491 315	.087 022	.591 898	6.801 692	.147 022
10	1.790 847	13.180 794	.075 867	.558 394	7.360 087	.135 867
11	1.898 298	14.971 642	.066 792	.526 787	7.886 874	.126 792
12	2.012 196	16.869 941	.059 277	.496 969	8.383 843	.119 277
13	2.132 928	18.882 137	.052 960	.468 839	8.852 682	.112 960
14	2.260 903	21.015 065	.047 584	.442 300	9.294 983	.107 584
15	2.396 558	23.275 969	.042 962	.417 265	9.712 248	.102 962
16	2.540 351	25.672 528	.038 952	.393 646	10.105 895	.098 952
17	2.692 772	28.212 879	.035 444	.371 364	10.477 259	.095 444
18	2.854 339	30.905 652	.032 356	.350 343	10.827 603	.092 356
19	3.025 599	33.759 991	.029 620	.330 513	11.158 116	.089 620
20	3.207 135	36.785 591	.027 184	.311 804	11.469 921	.087 184
21	3.399 563	39.992 726	.025 004	.294 155	11.764 076	.085 004
22	3.603 537	43.392 290	.023 045	.277 505	12.041 581	.083 045
23	3.819 749	46.995 827	.021 278	.261 797	12.303 378	.081 278
24	4.048 934	50.815 577	.019 679	.246 978	12.550 357	.079 679
25	4.291 870	54.864 511	.018 226	.232 998	12.783 356	.078 226
26	4.549 382	59.156 382	.016 904	.219 810	13.003 166	.076 904
27	4.822 345	63.705 765	.015 697	.207 367	13.210 534	.075 697
28	5.111 686	68.528 111	.014 592	.195 630	13.406 164	.074 592
29	5.418 387	73.639 798	.013 579	.184 556	13.590 721	.073 579
30	5.743 491	79.058 186	.012 648	.174 110	13.764 831	.072 648

SOURCE: *Financial Compound Interest and Annuity Tables*, 5th ed. (Financial Publishing Co., Boston, 1970).

Table 9. Rate of 7%

Periods	Amount of $1 (how $1 left at compound interest will grow)	Amount of $1 per period (how $1 deposited periodically will grow)	Sinking fund (periodic deposit that will grow to $1 at future date)	Present worth of $1 (what $1 due in the future is worth today)	Present worth of $1 per period (what $1 payable periodically is worth today)	Partial payment (annuity worth $1 today; periodic payment necessary to pay off a loan of $1)
1	1.070 000	1.000 000	1.000 000	.934 579	.934 579	1.070 000
2	1.144 900	2.070 000	.483 091	.873 438	1.808 018	.553 091
3	1.225 043	3.214 900	.311 051	.816 297	2.624 316	.381 051
4	1.310 796	4.439 943	.225 228	.762 895	3.387 211	.295 228
5	1.402 551	5.750 739	.173 890	.712 986	4.100 197	.243 890
6	1.500 730	7.153 290	.139 795	.666 342	4.766 539	.209 795
7	1.605 781	8.654 021	.115 553	.622 749	5.389 289	.185 553
8	1.718 186	10.259 802	.097 467	.582 009	5.971 298	.167 467
9	1.838 459	11.977 988	.083 486	.543 933	6.515 232	.153 486
10	1.967 151	13.816 447	.072 377	.508 349	7.023 581	.142 377
11	2.104 851	15.783 599	.063 356	.475 092	7.498 674	.133 356
12	2.252 191	17.888 451	.055 901	.444 011	7.942 686	.125 901
13	2.409 845	20.140 642	.049 650	.414 964	8.357 650	.119 650
14	2.578 534	22.550 487	.044 344	.387 817	8.745 467	.114 344
15	2.759 031	25.129 022	.039 794	.362 446	9.107 914	.109 794
16	2.952 163	27.888 053	.035 857	.338 734	9.446 648	.105 857
17	3.158 815	30.840 217	.032 425	.316 574	9.763 222	.102 425
18	3.379 932	33.999 032	.029 412	.295 863	10.059 086	.099 412
19	3.616 527	37.378 964	.026 753	.276 508	10.335 595	.096 753
20	3.869 684	40.995 492	.024 392	.258 419	10.594 014	.094 392
	$(1+i)^N$	$\dfrac{(1+i)^N-1}{i}$	$\dfrac{i}{(1+i)^N-1}$	$(1+i)^{-N}$	$\dfrac{1-(1+i)^{-N}}{i}$	$\dfrac{i}{1-(1+i)^{-N}}$

SOURCE: *Financial Compound Interest and Annuity Tables*, 5th ed. (Financial Publishing Co., Boston, 1970).

Table 10. Rate of 8%

Periods	Amount of $1 (how $1 left at compound interest will grow) $(1+i)^N$	Amount of $1 per period (how $1 deposited periodically will grow) $\dfrac{(1+i)^N-1}{i}$	Sinking fund (periodic deposit that will grow to $1 at future date) $\dfrac{i}{(1+i)^N-1}$	Present worth of $1 (what $1 due in the future is worth today) $(1+i)^{-N}$	Present worth of $1 per period (what $1 payable periodically is worth today) $\dfrac{1-(1+i)^{-N}}{i}$	Partial payment (annuity worth $1 today; periodic payment necessary to pay off a loan of $1) $\dfrac{i}{1-(1+i)^{-N}}$
1	1.080 000	1.000 000	1.000 000	.925 925	.925 925	1.080 000
2	1.166 400	2.080 000	.480 769	.857 338	1.783 264	.560 769
3	1.259 712	3.246 400	.308 033	.793 832	2.577 096	.388 033
4	1.360 488	4.506 112	.221 920	.735 029	3.312 126	.301 920
5	1.469 328	5.866 600	.170 456	.680 583	3.992 710	.250 456
6	1.586 874	7.335 929	.136 315	.630 169	4.622 879	.216 315
7	1.713 824	8.922 803	.112 072	.583 490	5.206 370	.192 072
8	1.850 930	10.636 627	.094 014	.540 268	5.746 638	.174 014
9	1.999 004	12.487 557	.080 079	.500 248	6.246 887	.160 079
10	2.158 924	14.486 562	.069 029	.463 193	6.710 081	.149 029
11	2.331 638	16.645 487	.060 076	.428 882	7.138 964	.140 076
12	2.518 170	18.977 126	.052 695	.397 113	7.536 078	.132 695
13	2.719 623	21.495 296	.046 521	.367 697	7.903 775	.126 521
14	2.937 193	24.214 920	.041 296	.340 461	8.244 236	.121 296
15	3.172 169	27.152 113	.036 829	.315 241	8.559 478	.116 829
16	3.425 942	30.324 283	.032 976	.291 890	8.851 369	.112 976
17	3.700 018	33.750 225	.029 629	.270 268	9.121 638	.109 629
18	3.996 019	37.450 243	.026 702	.250 249	9.371 887	.106 702
19	4.315 701	41.446 263	.024 127	.231 712	9.603 599	.104 127
20	4.660 957	45.761 964	.021 852	.214 548	9.818 147	.101 852
21	5.033 833	50.422 921	.019 832	.198 655	10.016 803	.099 832
22	5.436 540	55.456 755	.018 032	.183 940	10.200 743	.098 032
23	5.871 463	60.893 295	.016 422	.170 315	10.371 058	.096 422
24	6.341 180	66.764 759	.014 977	.157 699	10.528 758	.094 977
25	6.848 475	73.105 939	.013 678	.146 017	10.674 776	.093 678
26	7.396 353	79.954 415	.012 507	.135 201	10.809 977	.092 507
27	7.988 061	87.350 768	.011 448	.125 186	10.935 164	.091 448
28	8.627 106	95.338 829	.010 488	.115 913	11.051 078	.090 488
29	9.317 274	103.965 936	.009 618	.107 327	11.158 406	.089 618
30	10.062 656	113.283 211	.008 827	.099 377	11.257 783	.088 827

Source: Financial Compound Interest and Annuity Tables, Ed. et al. (Financial Publishing Co., Boston, 1970).

Table 11. Rate of 9%

Periods	Amount of $1 (how $1 left at compound interest will grow)	Amount of $1 per period (how $1 deposited periodically will grow)	Sinking fund (periodic deposit that will grow to $1 at future date)	Present worth of $1 (what $1 due in the future is worth today)	Present worth of $1 per period (what $1 payable periodically is worth today)	Partial payment (annuity worth $1 today; periodic payment necessary to pay off a loan of $1)
1	1.090 000	1.000 000	1.000 000	.917 431	.917 431	1.090 000
2	1.188 100	2.090 000	.478 468	.841 679	1.759 111	.568 468
3	1.295 029	3.278 100	.305 054	.772 183	2.531 294	.395 054
4	1.411 581	4.573 129	.218 668	.708 425	3.239 719	.308 668
5	1.538 623	5.984 710	.167 092	.649 931	3.889 651	.257 092
6	1.677 100	7.523 334	.132 919	.596 267	4.485 918	.222 919
7	1.828 039	9.200 434	.108 690	.547 034	5.032 952	.198 690
8	1.992 562	11.028 473	.090 674	.501 866	5.534 819	.180 674
9	2.171 893	13.021 036	.076 798	.460 427	5.995 246	.166 798
10	2.367 363	15.192 929	.065 820	.422 410	6.417 657	.155 820
11	2.580 426	17.560 293	.056 946	.387 532	6.805 190	.146 946
12	2.812 664	20.140 719	.049 650	.355 534	7.160 725	.139 650
13	3.065 804	22.953 384	.043 566	.326 178	7.486 903	.133 566
14	3.341 727	26.019 189	.038 433	.299 246	7.786 150	.128 433
15	3.642 482	29.360 916	.034 058	.274 538	8.060 638	.124 058
16	3.970 305	33.003 398	.030 299	.251 869	8.312 558	.120 299
17	4.327 633	36.973 704	.027 046	.231 073	8.543 631	.117 046
18	4.717 120	41.301 337	.024 212	.211 993	8.755 625	.114 212
19	5.141 661	46.018 458	.021 730	.194 489	8.950 114	.111 730
20	5.604 410	51.160 119	.019 546	.178 430	9.128 545	.109 546
21	6.108 807	56.764 530	.017 616	.163 698	9.292 243	.107 616
22	6.658 600	62.873 338	.015 904	.150 181	9.442 425	.105 904
23	7.257 874	69.531 938	.014 381	.137 781	9.580 206	.104 381
24	7.911 083	76.789 813	.013 022	.126 404	9.706 611	.103 022
25	8.623 080	84.700 896	.011 806	.115 967	9.822 579	.101 806
	$(1+i)^N$	$\dfrac{(1+i)^N - 1}{i}$	$\dfrac{i}{(1+i)^N - 1}$	$(1+i)^{-N}$	$\dfrac{1-(1+i)^{-N}}{i}$	$\dfrac{i}{1-(1+i)^{-N}}$

SOURCE: *Financial Compound Interest and Annuity Tables*, 5th ed. (Financial Publishing Co., Boston, 1970).

Table 12. Rate of 10%

Periods	Amount of $1 (how $1 left at compound interest will grow)	Amount of $1 per period (how $1 deposited periodically will grow)	Sinking fund (periodic deposit that will grow to $1 at future date)	Present worth of $1 due in the future (what $1 at future is worth today)	Present worth of $1 per period (what $1 payable periodically is worth today)	Partial payment (annuity worth $1 today; periodic payment necessary to pay off a loan of $1)
1	1.100 000	1.000 000	1.000 000	.909 090	.909 090	1.100 000
2	1.210 000	2.100 000	.476 190	.826 446	1.735 537	.576 190
3	1.331 000	3.310 000	.302 114	.751 314	2.486 851	.402 114
4	1.464 100	4.641 000	.215 470	.683 013	3.169 865	.315 470
5	1.610 510	6.105 100	.163 797	.620 921	3.790 786	.263 797
6	1.771 561	7.715 610	.129 607	.564 473	4.355 260	.229 607
7	1.948 717	9.487 171	.105 405	.513 158	4.868 418	.205 405
8	2.143 588	11.435 888	.087 444	.466 507	5.334 926	.187 444
9	2.357 947	13.579 476	.073 640	.424 097	5.759 023	.173 640
10	2.593 742	15.937 424	.062 745	.385 543	6.144 567	.162 745
11	2.853 116	18.531 167	.053 963	.350 493	6.495 061	.153 963
12	3.138 428	21.384 283	.046 763	.318 630	6.813 691	.146 763
13	3.452 271	24.522 712	.040 778	.289 664	7.103 356	.140 778
14	3.797 498	27.974 983	.035 746	.263 331	7.366 687	.135 746
15	4.177 248	31.772 481	.031 473	.239 392	7.606 079	.131 473
16	4.594 972	35.949 729	.027 816	.217 629	7.823 708	.127 816
17	5.054 470	40.544 702	.024 664	.197 844	8.021 553	.124 664
18	5.559 917	45.599 173	.021 930	.179 858	8.201 412	.121 930
19	6.115 909	51.159 090	.019 546	.163 507	8.364 920	.119 546
20	6.727 499	57.274 999	.017 459	.148 643	8.513 563	.117 459
21	7.400 249	64.002 499	.015 624	.135 130	8.648 694	.115 624
22	8.140 274	71.402 749	.014 005	.122 845	8.771 540	.114 005
23	8.954 302	79.543 024	.012 571	.111 678	8.883 218	.112 571
24	9.849 732	88.497 326	.011 299	.101 525	8.984 744	.111 299
25	10.834 705	98.347 059	.010 168	.092 295	9.077 040	.110 168
26	11.918 176	109.181 765	.009 159	.083 905	9.160 945	.109 159
27	13.109 994	121.099 941	.008 257	.076 277	9.237 223	.108 257
28	14.420 993	134.209 936	.007 451	.069 343	9.306 567	.107 451
29	15.863 092	148.630 929	.006 728	.063 039	9.369 605	.106 728
30	17.449 402	164.494 022	.006 079	.057 308	9.426 914	.106 079
	$(1+i)^N$	$\dfrac{(1+i)^N - 1}{i}$	$\dfrac{i}{(1+i)^N - 1}$	$(1+i)^{-N}$	$\dfrac{1-(1+i)^{-N}}{i}$	$\dfrac{i}{1-(1+i)^{-N}}$

SOURCE: *Financial Compound Interest and Annuity Tables*, 5th ed. (Financial Publishing Co., Boston, 1970).

Table 13. Rate of 11%

Periods	Amount of $1 (how $1 left at compound interest will grow) $(1+i)^N$	Amount of $1 per period (how $1 deposited periodically will grow) $\dfrac{(1+i)^N - 1}{i}$	Sinking fund (periodic deposit that will grow to $1 at future date) $\dfrac{i}{(1+i)^N - 1}$	Present worth of $1 (what $1 due in the future is worth today) $(1+i)^{-N}$	Present worth of $1 per period (what $1 payable periodically is worth today) $\dfrac{1 - (1+i)^{-N}}{i}$	Partial payment (annuity worth $1 today; periodic payment necessary to pay off a loan of $1) $\dfrac{i}{1 - (1+i)^{-N}}$
1	1.110 000	1.000 000	1.000 000	.900 900	.900 900	1.110 000
2	1.232 100	2.110 000	.473 933	.811 622	1.712 523	.583 933
3	1.367 631	3.342 100	.299 213	.731 191	2.443 714	.409 213
4	1.518 070	4.709 731	.212 326	.658 730	3.102 445	.322 326
5	1.685 058	6.227 801	.160 570	.593 451	3.695 897	.270 570
6	1.870 414	7.912 859	.126 376	.534 640	4.230 537	.236 376
7	2.076 160	9.783 274	.102 215	.481 658	4.712 196	.212 215
8	2.304 537	11.859 434	.084 321	.433 926	5.146 122	.194 321
9	2.558 036	14.163 972	.070 601	.390 924	5.537 047	.180 601
10	2.839 420	16.722 008	.059 801	.352 184	5.889 232	.169 801
11	3.151 757	19.561 429	.051 121	.317 283	6.206 515	.161 121
12	3.498 450	22.713 187	.044 027	.285 840	6.492 356	.154 027
13	3.883 280	26.211 637	.038 150	.257 514	6.749 870	.148 150
14	4.310 440	30.094 918	.033 228	.231 994	6.981 865	.143 228
15	4.784 589	34.405 358	.029 065	.209 004	7.190 869	.139 065
16	5.310 894	39.189 948	.025 516	.188 292	7.379 161	.135 516
17	5.895 092	44.500 842	.022 471	.169 632	7.548 794	.132 471
18	6.543 552	50.395 935	.019 842	.152 822	7.701 616	.129 842
19	7.263 343	56.939 488	.017 562	.137 677	7.839 294	.127 562
20	8.062 311	64.202 832	.015 575	.124 033	7.963 328	.125 575
21	8.949 165	72.265 143	.013 837	.111 742	8.075 070	.123 837
22	9.933 574	81.214 309	.012 313	.100 668	8.175 739	.122 313
23	11.026 267	91.147 883	.010 971	.090 692	8.266 431	.120 971
24	12.239 156	102.174 150	.009 787	.081 704	8.348 136	.119 787
25	13.585 463	114.413 307	.008 740	.073 608	8.421 744	.118 740

SOURCE: *Financial Compound Interest and Annuity Tables*, 5th ed. (Financial Publishing Co., Boston, 1970).

Table 14. Rate of 12%

Periods	Amount of $1 (how $1 left at compound interest will grow) $$(1+i)^N$$	Amount of $1 per period (how $1 deposited periodically will grow) $$\frac{(1+i)^N - 1}{i}$$	Sinking fund (periodic deposit that will grow to $1 at future date) $$\frac{i}{(1+i)^N - 1}$$	Present worth of $1 (what $1 due in the future is worth today) $$(1+i)^{-N}$$	Present worth of $1 per period (what $1 payable periodically is worth today) $$\frac{1-(1+i)^{-N}}{i}$$	Partial payment (annuity worth $1 today; periodic payment necessary to pay off a loan of $1) $$\frac{i}{1-(1+i)^{-N}}$$
1	1.120 000	1.000 000	1.000 000	.892 857	.892 857	1.120 000
2	1.254 400	2.120 000	.471 698	.797 193	1.690 051	.591 698
3	1.404 928	3.374 400	.296 348	.711 780	2.401 831	.416 348
4	1.573 519	4.779 328	.209 234	.635 518	3.037 349	.329 234
5	1.762 341	6.352 847	.157 409	.567 426	3.604 776	.277 409
6	1.973 822	8.115 189	.123 225	.506 631	4.111 407	.243 225
7	2.210 681	10.089 011	.099 117	.452 349	4.563 756	.219 117
8	2.475 963	12.299 693	.081 302	.403 883	4.967 639	.201 302
9	2.773 078	14.775 656	.067 678	.360 610	5.328 249	.181 678
10	3.105 848	17.548 735	.056 984	.321 973	5.650 223	.176 984

SOURCE: *Financial Compound Interest and Annuity Tables*, 5th ed. (Financial Publishing Co., Boston, 1970).

Table 15. Rate of 13%

Periods	Amount of $1 (how $1 left at compound interest will grow)	Amount of $1 per period (how $1 deposited periodically will grow)	Sinking fund (periodic deposit that will grow to $1 at future date)	Present worth of $1 (what $1 due in the future is worth today)	Present worth of $1 per period (what $1 payable periodically is worth today)	Partial payment (annuity worth $1 today; periodic payment necessary to pay off a loan of $1)
1	1.130 000	1.000 000	1.000 000	.884 955	.884 955	1.130 000
2	1.276 900	2.130 000	.469 483	.783 146	1.668 102	.599 483
3	1.442 897	3.406 900	.293 521	.693 050	2.361 152	.423 521
4	1.630 473	4.849 797	.206 194	.613 318	2.974 471	.336 194
5	1.842 435	6.480 270	.154 314	.542 759	3.517 231	.284 314
6	2.081 951	8.322 705	.120 153	.480 318	3.997 549	.250 153
7	2.352 605	10.404 657	.096 110	.425 060	4.422 610	.226 110
8	2.658 444	12.757 263	.078 386	.376 159	4.798 770	.208 386
9	3.004 041	15.415 707	.064 868	.332 884	5.131 655	.194 868
10	3.394 567	18.419 749	.054 289	.294 588	5.426 243	.184 289
	$(1+i)^N$	$\dfrac{(1+i)^N - 1}{i}$	$\dfrac{i}{(1+i)^N - 1}$	$(1+i)^{-N}$	$\dfrac{1-(1+i)^{-N}}{i}$	$\dfrac{i}{1-(1+i)^{-N}}$

SOURCE: *Financial Compound Interest and Annuity Tables*, 5th ed. (Financial Publishing Co., Boston, 1970).

Table 16. Rate of 14%

Periods	Amount of $1 (how $1 left at compound interest will grow)	Amount of $1 per period (how $1 deposited periodically will grow)	Sinking fund (periodic deposit that will grow to $1 at future date)	Present worth of $1 (what $1 due in the future is worth today)	Present worth of $1 per period (what $1 payable periodically is worth today)	Partial payment (annuity worth $1 today; periodic payment necessary to pay off a loan of $1)
1	1.140 000	1.000 000	1.000 000	.877 192	.877 192	1.140 000
2	1.299 600	2.140 000	.467 289	.769 467	1.646 660	.607 289
3	1.481 544	3.439 600	.290 731	.674 971	2.321 632	.430 731
4	1.688 960	4.921 144	.203 204	.592 080	2.913 712	.343 204
5	1.925 414	6.610 104	.151 283	.519 368	3.433 080	.291 283
6	2.194 972	8.535 518	.117 157	.455 586	3.888 667	.257 157
7	2.502 268	10.730 491	.093 192	.399 637	4.288 304	.233 192
8	2.852 586	13.232 760	.075 570	.350 559	4.638 863	.215 570
9	3.251 948	16.085 346	.062 168	.307 507	4.946 371	.202 168
10	3.707 221	19.337 295	.051 713	.269 743	5.216 115	.191 713
	$(1+i)^N$	$\dfrac{(1+i)^N-1}{i}$	$\dfrac{i}{(1+i)^N-1}$	$(1+i)^{-N}$	$\dfrac{1-(1+i)^{-N}}{i}$	$\dfrac{i}{1-(1+i)^{-N}}$

SOURCE: *Financial Compound Interest and Annuity Tables*, 5th ed. (Financial Publishing Co., Boston, 1970).

Table 17. Rate of 15%

Periods	Amount of $1 (how $1 left at compound interest will grow) $(1+i)^N$	Amount of $1 per period (how $1 deposited periodically will grow) $\dfrac{(1+i)^N - 1}{i}$	Sinking fund (periodic deposit that will grow to $1 at future date) $\dfrac{i}{(1+i)^N - 1}$	Present worth of $1 (what $1 due in the future is worth today) $(1+i)^{-N}$	Present worth of $1 per period (what $1 payable periodically is worth today) $\dfrac{1-(1+i)^{-N}}{i}$	Partial payment (annuity worth $1 today; periodic payment necessary to pay off a loan of $1) $\dfrac{i}{1-(1+i)^{-N}}$
1	1.150 000	1.000 000	1.000 000	.869 565	.869 565	1.150 000
2	1.322 500	2.150 000	.465 116	.756 143	1.625 708	.615 116
3	1.520 875	3.472 500	.287 976	.657 516	2.283 225	.437 976
4	1.749 006	4.993 375	.200 265	.571 753	2.854 978	.350 265
5	2.011 357	6.742 381	.148 315	.497 176	3.352 155	.298 315
6	2.313 060	8.753 738	.114 236	.432 327	3.784 482	.264 236
7	2.660 019	11.066 799	.090 360	.375 937	4.160 419	.240 360
8	3.059 022	13.726 819	.072 850	.326 901	4.487 321	.222 850
9	3.517 876	16.785 841	.059 574	.284 262	4.771 583	.209 574
10	4.045 557	20.303 718	.049 252	.247 184	5.018 768	.199 252
11	4.652 391	24.349 275	.041 068	.214 943	5.233 711	.191 068
12	5.350 250	29.001 667	.034 480	.186 907	5.420 618	.184 480
13	6.152 787	34.351 917	.029 110	.162 527	5.583 146	.179 110
14	7.075 705	40.504 705	.024 688	.141 328	5.724 475	.174 688
15	8.137 061	47.580 410	.021 017	.122 894	5.847 370	.171 017

SOURCE: *Financial Compound Interest and Annuity Tables*, 5th ed. (Financial Publishing Co., Boston, 1970).

Table 18. Rate of 16%

Periods	Amount of $1 (how $1 left at compound interest will grow) $(1+i)^N$	Amount of $1 per period (how $1 deposited periodically will grow) $\dfrac{(1+i)^N-1}{i}$	Sinking fund (periodic deposit that will grow to $1 at future date) $\dfrac{i}{(1+i)^N-1}$	Present worth of $1 due in the future (what $1 due in the future is worth today) $(1+i)^{-N}$	Present worth of $1 per period payable periodically (what $1 payable periodically is worth today) $\dfrac{1-(1+i)^{-N}}{i}$	Partial payment (annuity worth $1 today; periodic payment necessary to pay off a loan of $1) $\dfrac{i}{1-(1+i)^{-N}}$
1	1.160 000	1.000 000	1.000 000	.862 068	.862 068	1.160 000
2	1.345 600	2.160 000	.462 962	.743 162	1.605 231	.622 962
3	1.560 896	3.505 600	.285 257	.640 657	2.245 889	.445 257
4	1.810 639	5.066 496	.197 375	.552 291	2.798 180	.357 375
5	2.100 341	6.877 135	.145 409	.476 113	3.274 293	.305 409
6	2.436 396	8.977 477	.111 389	.410 442	3.684 735	.271 389
7	2.826 219	11.413 873	.087 612	.353 829	4.038 565	.247 612
8	3.278 414	14.240 093	.070 224	.305 025	4.343 590	.230 224
9	3.802 961	17.518 507	.057 082	.262 952	4.606 543	.217 082
10	4.411 435	21.321 469	.046 901	.226 683	4.833 227	.206 901
11	5.117 264	25.732 904	.038 860	.195 416	5.028 644	.198 860
12	5.936 027	30.850 169	.032 414	.168 462	5.197 107	.192 414
13	6.885 791	36.786 196	.027 184	.145 226	5.342 333	.187 184
14	7.987 517	43.671 987	.022 897	.125 195	5.467 529	.182 897
15	9.265 520	51.659 505	.019 357	.107 927	5.575 456	.179 357

SOURCE: *Financial Compound Interest and Annuity Tables*, 5th ed. (Financial Publishing Co., Boston, 1970).

Table 19. Rate of 17%

Periods	Amount of $1 (how $1 left at compound interest will grow)	Amount of $1 per period (how $1 deposited periodically will grow)	Sinking fund (periodic deposit that will grow to $1 at future date)	Present worth of $1 (what $1 due in the future is worth today)	Present worth of $1 per period (what $1 payable periodically is worth today)	Partial payment (annuity worth $1 today; periodic payment necessary to pay off a loan of $1)
1	1.170 000	1.000 000	1.000 000	.854 700	.854 700	1.170 000
2	1.368 900	2.170 000	.460 829	.730 513	1.585 214	.630 829
3	1.601 613	3.538 900	.282 573	.624 370	2.209 584	.452 573
4	1.873 887	5.140 513	.194 533	.533 650	2.743 235	.364 533
5	2.192 448	7.014 400	.142 563	.456 111	3.199 346	.312 563
6	2.565 164	9.206 848	.108 614	.389 838	3.589 184	.278 614
7	3.001 242	11.772 012	.084 947	.333 195	3.922 380	.254 947
8	3.511 453	14.773 254	.067 689	.284 782	4.207 162	.237 689
9	4.108 400	18.284 707	.054 690	.243 403	4.450 566	.224 690
10	4.806 828	22.393 108	.044 656	.208 037	4.658 603	.214 656
11	5.623 989	27.199 936	.036 764	.177 809	4.836 413	.206 764
12	6.580 067	32.823 925	.030 465	.151 974	4.988 387	.200 465
13	7.698 678	39.403 993	.025 378	.129 892	5.118 279	.195 378
14	9.007 454	47.102 671	.021 230	.111 019	5.229 299	.191 230
15	10.538 721	56.110 126	.017 822	.094 888	5.324 187	.187 822
	$(1+i)^N$	$\dfrac{(1+i)^N-1}{i}$	$\dfrac{i}{(1+i)^N-1}$	$(1+i)^{-N}$	$\dfrac{1-(1+i)^{-N}}{i}$	$\dfrac{i}{1-(1+i)^{-N}}$

SOURCE: *Financial Compound Interest and Annuity Tables*, 5th ed. (Financial Publishing Co., Boston, 1970).

Table 20. Rate of 18%

Periods	Amount of $1 (how $1 left at compound interest will grow) $(1+i)^N$	Amount of $1 per period (how $1 deposited periodically will grow) $\frac{(1+i)^N - 1}{i}$	Sinking fund (periodic deposit that will grow to $1 at future date) $\frac{i}{(1+i)^N - 1}$	Present worth of $1 (what $1 due in the future is worth today) $(1+i)^{-N}$	Present worth of $1 per period (what $1 payable periodically is worth today) $\frac{1-(1+i)^{-N}}{i}$	Partial payment (annuity worth $1 today; periodic payment necessary to pay off a loan of $1) $\frac{i}{1-(1+i)^{-N}}$
1	1.180 000	1.000 000	1.000 000	.847 457	.847 457	1.180 000
2	1.392 400	2.180 000	.458 715	.718 184	1.565 642	.638 715
3	1.643 032	3.572 400	.279 923	.608 630	2.174 272	.459 923
4	1.938 777	5.215 432	.191 738	.515 788	2.690 061	.371 738
5	2.287 757	7.154 209	.139 777	.437 109	3.127 171	.319 777
6	2.699 554	9.441 967	.105 910	.370 431	3.497 602	.285 910
7	3.185 473	12.141 521	.082 361	.313 925	3.811 527	.262 361
8	3.758 859	15.326 995	.065 244	.266 038	4.077 565	.245 244
9	4.435 453	19.085 854	.052 394	.225 456	4.303 021	.232 394
10	5.233 835	23.521 308	.042 514	.191 064	4.494 086	.222 514
11	6.175 925	28.755 144	.034 776	.161 919	4.656 005	.214 776
12	7.287 592	34.931 070	.028 627	.137 219	4.793 224	.208 627
13	8.599 359	42.218 662	.023 686	.116 287	4.909 512	.203 686
14	10.147 243	50.818 022	.019 678	.098 548	5.008 061	.199 678
15	11.973 747	60.965 266	.016 402	.083 516	5.091 577	.196 402
16	14.129 022	72.939 013	.013 710	.070 776	5.162 353	.193 710
17	16.672 246	87.068 036	.011 485	.059 979	5.222 333	.191 485
18	19.673 250	103.740 282	.009 639	.050 830	5.273 164	.189 639
19	23.214 436	123.413 533	.008 102	.043 076	5.316 240	.188 102
20	27.393 034	146.627 970	.006 819	.036 505	5.352 746	.186 819
21	32.323 780	174.021 004	.005 746	.030 936	5.383 683	.185 746
22	38.142 061	206.344 785	.004 846	.026 217	5.409 901	.184 846
23	45.007 632	244.486 846	.004 090	.022 218	5.432 119	.184 090
24	53.109 006	289.494 479	.003 454	.018 829	5.450 948	.183 454
25	62.668 627	342.603 485	.002 918	.015 956	5.466 905	.182 918
26	73.948 980	405.272 112	.002 467	.013 522	5.480 428	.182 467
27	87.259 796	479.221 093	.002 086	.011 460	5.491 888	.182 086
28	102.966 560	566.480 890	.001 765	.009 711	5.501 600	.181 765
29	121.500 541	669.447 450	.001 493	.008 230	5.509 831	.181 493
30	143.370 638	790.947 991	.001 264	.006 974	5.516 805	.181 264

SOURCE: *Financial Compound Interest and Annuity Tables*, 5th ed. (Financial Publishing Co., Boston, 1970).

Logarithms

The use of Logarithms ("logs") provides a mathematical shortcut for multiplying, dividing, taking square roots, and finding powers of numbers. Most log tables are to the base 10, which means that the log of a number is

$$10^y = x$$

where x is the number and y is its log.

Negative Powers of a Number

To find the logarithm of a number with a negative exponent (power), it is first necessary to recast the number in a positive form. Thus, to find the value of $(1.12)^{-9}$ using logs, it is first necessary to eliminate the negative power by changing the number to the form

$$\frac{1}{(1.12)^9}$$

Then normal methods are used to find the quotient.

Natural Logarithms

Heretofore, the discussion of logarithms has been about *common* logs, that is, logs to the base 10. In Chaps. 1 and 2, in the sections dealing with continuous compounding, the concept of e was introduced. The Swiss mathematician Leonard Euler proved that the value of e is about 2.71828. As a result, it became known as Euler's constant, or simply e. Early in the seventeenth century a Scot, John Napier, developed a table of logs to the base e, and appropriately the tables became known as Napierian logs, or *natural* logs.

The rules, methods, or laws concerning the use of logs are the same whatever the base happens to be—10, e, or some other base. And if a table of logs to a particular base, e.g., 10, has been developed, it is possible to convert from that table to another base. To effect such a change, one must find a *conversion constant* and then multiply the logs of the first table by that constant to obtain the logs of the second table. The formula for conversion from base 10 to base e is

$$\log_e x = (\log_e 10)(\log_{10} x) = \frac{\log_{10} x}{\log_{10} e}$$

where x = the number whose log is being converted from one base to another.

Example: Find the natural log of 9. The log of 9 is 0.95424. With $x = 9$, then

$$\log_e 9 = (\log_e 10)(\log_{10} 9) = \frac{\log_{10} 9}{\log_{10} e} = \frac{0.95424}{0.43429448} = 2.1972188$$

By convention, when logs to the base 10 of a number x are used, the terminology is: "log x"; and when the natural log of a number x is referred to, it is expressed as "ln x."

By the same token, natural logs may be converted to base 10 logs by dividing the natural log by $(1/0.43429448)$, that is, dividing by 2.302585103. Most hand-held calculators and computers have built-in natural log functions.

The log of a positive number z, with a positive base b, is defined as the exponent x to which b must be raised to obtain z. Thus,

$$\log_b z = x \quad \text{and} \quad b^x = z$$

The above foundation for logarithmic systems applies equally to base 10, natural logs, and logs using any other base.

Derivation of Yield Formula for 1-Year Treasury Bills*

Computing the yield for a Treasury bill with more than 6 months to maturity is more involved than for 3- and 6-month bills. The complexity arises because it is customary to state the yield on a basis that is directly comparable to the quoted yields on coupon securities. The coupon equivalent yield (also called the bond equivalent yield) reflects the opportunity for the reinvestment of the semiannual coupon paid holders of interest-paying securities (i.e., notes and bonds). The coupon equivalent yield is calculated as if interest were compounded 6 months from maturity. It is less than the investment yield.

The derivation of the equation is straightforward (symbols are defined below).

$$\frac{P\,[D - (Y/2)]R}{Y} \quad \text{interest that would be earned at 6 months from maturity}$$

$$P\left[1 + \left(D - \frac{Y}{2}\right)\left(\frac{R}{Y}\right)\right] \quad \text{principal plus interest earned at 6 months from maturity}$$

* Source: Federal Reserve Bank of New York, *The Arithmetic of Interest Rates*.

$\left(\dfrac{R}{2}\right)$ interest rate for the remaining 6 months

$$P\left[1 + \frac{(D - Y/2)}{Y}(R)\right]\left(1 + \frac{R}{2}\right) = 100$$

$$1 + \frac{(D - Y/2)}{Y}(R) + \left(\frac{R}{2}\right) + \frac{R^2}{2Y}\left(D - \frac{Y}{2}\right) = \frac{100}{P}$$

$$\left(\frac{1}{2Y}\right)\left(D - \frac{Y}{2}\right)(R^2) + \left[\left(D - \frac{Y}{2}\right)\left(\frac{1}{Y}\right) + \frac{1}{2}\right](R) + 1 - \frac{100}{P} = 0$$

$$\left(\frac{1}{2Y}\right)\left(\frac{D - Y}{2}\right)(R^2) + \left(\frac{D}{Y} - \frac{1}{2} + \frac{1}{2}\right)R + \left(\frac{P - 100}{P}\right) = 0$$

$$\left(\frac{D}{2Y} - 0.25\right)R^2 + \left(\frac{D}{Y}\right)R + \left(\frac{P - 100}{P}\right) = 0$$

which is a quadratic equation of the general form $AX^2 + BX + C = 0$, where

$$A = \frac{D}{2Y} - 0.25$$

$$B = \frac{D}{Y}$$

$$C = \frac{P - 100}{P}$$

$$X = R$$

The solution to such an equation is given by

$$R = \frac{\sqrt{B^2 - 4 \times A \times C} - B}{2 \times A}$$

In the above formula, the terms are defined as follows:

A is the ratio of the total number of days (D) between the bill's issue and maturity dates and 2 times the number of days in the year (Y) following the issue date, minus 0.25. In other words,

$$A = \frac{D}{2 \times Y} - 0.25$$

B is the ratio of the total number of days (D) between the bill's issue and maturity dates and the number of days in the year (Y) following the issue date. In other words,

$$B = \frac{D}{Y}$$

C is the ratio of the bill's purchase price ($\$P$) per $100 minus $100 and the purchase price. In other words,

$$C = \frac{\$P - \$100}{\$P}$$

Interest-Paying Securities Traded within 6 Months of Redemption or Maturity

Price

The formula for determining the price of an interest-paying instrument within 6 months of redemption or maturity is

$$P = \left\{ \frac{S + [100(r)/m]}{1 + [(e-a)/e](y/m)} \right\} - \left\{ \left(\frac{a}{e} \right) \left[\frac{100(r)}{m} \right] \right\}$$

where P = price, the purchase price for each $100 of the bond's face value

r = annual interest rate (expressed as a decimal) (coupon rate)

m = number of coupon periods per year

e = time, the number of days in the coupon period

S = sum at maturity, the maturity or redemption value of the bond (the face value) per $100 par value

a = number of days from the start of the coupon period until the settlement date (the number of days of interest accrual)

y = yield, annually; yield price of the transaction, expressed as a decimal

$e - a$ = days from settlement to redemption or maturity

The first term in the formula represents the present value of the maturity value, including interest, discounted at the yield rate for the invested period of time. The second term finds the accrued interest.

Example 1. A corporate bond is bought with settlement date of November 1, 1997, with coupon rate of 12.5 percent, and maturing March 1, 1998. Interest is paid semiannually, and the 30/360 day-count method is applicable. If the yield to maturity is 12.500, what is the purchase price?

In this example, to make life easier, the following date-related items are given: a = 60; $e - a$ = 120; e = 180.

$$P = \left\{ \frac{\$100 + [\$100(0.125)/2]}{1 + [(120/180)(0.125/2)]} \right\} - \left\{ \left(\frac{60}{180} \right) \left[\frac{\$100(0.125)}{2} \right] \right\}$$

$$= \left(\frac{\$100 + \$6.25}{1.04166670} \right) - (\$2.083333)$$

$$= \$101.9999967 - \$2.083333 = \$99.916$$

That is, $999.16 is the price.

Example 2. A municipal bond is purchased with settlement on February 7, 1994. It matures August 1, 1998. The interest coupon is $4\frac{1}{2}$ percent. At a yield to maturity of 5.35 percent, what is the purchase price?

For simplicity, the day counts are: a = 6; $a - e$ = 174; e = 180. The day-count method is 30/360.

$$P = \left\{ \frac{\$100 + [\$100(0.045)/2]}{1 + (174/180)(0.0535/2)} \right\} - \left\{ \left(\frac{6}{180} \right) \left[\frac{\$100(0.045)}{2} \right] \right\}$$

$$= \frac{\$102.25}{1.02586} - \$0.07500 = \$99.597$$

That is, the price is $995.97.

Yield to Maturity

The formula for yield to maturity for interest-paying securities traded within 6 months of redemption or maturity is

$$y = \left\{ \frac{(s/100) + (r/m) - [(P/100) + (a/e)(r/m)]}{(P/100) + (a/e)(r/m)} \right\} \left[\frac{(m)(e)}{e - a} \right]$$

where y = annual yield on the investment if the security is held to redemption (expressed as a decimal)

P = dollar price per $100 par value

S = maturity or redemption value of the security per $100 par value

r = annual interest rate (expressed as a decimal)

a = number of accrued days from the start of the interest payment period to the settlement date

e = number of days in the interest payment period in which the settlement date falls

m = number of interest payment periods per year

$e - a$ = number of days from settlement date to maturity or redemption

The first term in braces determines the yield on invested dollars; the second term annualizes the yield.

Example 3. A U.S. Treasury bond is purchased with settlement on February 7, 1996, with a maturity of May 15, 1996. The coupon rate is 4.75 percent. The purchase price is 99 $^{28}\!/_{32}$ (i.e., 99.875 in decimal form). Given that a = 84 days, $a - e$ = 98 days, and e = 182 days. Interest is paid semiannually. What is the annual yield?

$$y = \left\{ \frac{(\$100/\$100) + (0.0475/2) - [(\$99.875/100) + (84/182)(0.0475/2)]}{(\$100/\$100) + (84/182)(0.0475/2)} \right\}$$

$$\times \left[\frac{(2)(182)}{182 - 84} \right]$$

$$= \left[\frac{(1 + 0.02375) - (0.099875 + 0.0109615)}{0.99875 + 0.1101374} \right] \left(\frac{364}{98} \right)$$

$$= (0.0139034)(3.7142857) = 0.05164$$

that is, 5.164 percent.

The above formulas for price and yield are for the special circumstance when a coupon instrument is traded with less than 6 months remaining to maturity. When more than 6 months are left, the normal yield-to-maturity formula is used.

Equivalent Yields

It may be desirable to find yield equivalency when odd combinations of interest payment frequency are involved. For example, a bond (e.g., a GNMA) pays interest monthly. What is its semiannual equivalent yield, or in other words, what is the nominal yield to maturity of an equivalent bond? The following general formula can be used to determine equivalent yields for any combination of payment frequencies of both the subject bond and the equivalent bond.

Equivalent Yields for Various Payment Frequencies

$$\text{YTM}_2 = m_2 \left[\left(1 + \frac{\text{YTM}_1}{m_1} \right)^{m_1/m_2} - 1 \right]$$

where YTM$_1$ = nominal yield to maturity of subject bond
m_1 = number of times interest is paid annually for subject bond
YTM$_2$ = equivalent yield to maturity for target bond
m_2 = number of times interest is paid per year for target bond

Example: Finding equivalent yield. Subject bond pays interest annually, and its quoted nominal yield to maturity is 10 percent. For a bond which pays semiannual interest (the target bond), what is the equivalent yield to maturity?

$$\text{YTM}_2 = 2 \left[\left(1 + \frac{0.10}{12} \right)^{12/2} - 1 \right]$$

$$= 2 [(1.00833)^6 - 1] = 0.1021066 \ \text{ or } \ 10.211\%$$

Thus the 10 percent nominal yield to maturity of the subject bond, which pays monthly, is equivalent to a semiannual-paying target bond with a quoted nominal yield to maturity of 10.211 percent.

By a similar approach, the annual equivalent yield is found to be 10.471 percent.

Revised IRR, Real Estate

Table 1. Revised IRR, Real Estate, Calculation of One Point on One Curve of Fig. 26.7

Annual increase in rents	6.0%	
Annual increase in expenses	6.0%	
First Year Rents....	116.80	
First year operating expenses	0	IRR
Interest rate on reinvestment (decimal)	32.9%	without
Tax Bracket (decimal)	28.0%	Reinveestment
CASH INVESTMENT	250	
LOAN	750	23.68%
Total Investment	1000	
Years of Loan Amortization....	20	
Loan Interest (as decimal)	10.0%	
Loan principal and interest (NO ENTRY)	88	Revised
Building/total investment (as decimal)	90.0%	IRR
Initial Depreciable Assets (NO ENTRY)	900	with
Years-St. Line Depreciation....	31.5	Reinvestment
Years of Analysis and Year of Sale....	10	
Capitalization Rate at Sale (as decimal)	12.0%	23.68%
Portion of Long Term Gain not Taxed	0.0%	
Mortgage Constant DO NOT CHANGE	11.75	

	Year			
NO USE ENTRIES BELOW THIS!	0	1	2	3
ANNUAL DEPRECIATION		28.57		
LOAN (BEGINNING)		750.00	736.91	722.50
INTEREST, ANNUAL		75.00	73.69	72.25
PRINCIPAL REDUCTION		13.09	14.40	15.84
LOAN (ENDING)		736.91	722.50	706.66
NET OPERATING INCOME (NOI)		116.80	123.81	131.23
NOI/TOTAL INVESTMENT		11.7%	12.4%	13.1%
LESS: LOAN PRINCIPAL & INTEREST		88.09	88.09	88.09
CASH FLOW PRE-TAX		28.70	35.71	43.14
CASH FLOW/CASH INVESTMENT		11.5%	14.3%	17.3%
DEPRECIATION (CUMULATIVE)		0.00	28.57	57.14
LESS DEPRECIATION		28.57	28.57	28.57
PLUS: LOAN PRINCIPAL		13.09	14.40	15.84
TAXABLE INCOME		13.23	21.54	30.41
INCOME TAX, IF "-" TAX SAVINGS		3.70	6.03	8.52
CASH FLOW AFTER TAX, PRE-SALE		25.00	29.68	34.62
SALES PROCEEDS IN YEAR....	10	0.00	0.00	0.00
CAPITAL GAINS TAX ON SALE		0.00	0.00	0.00
CASH FROM SALE AFTER TAX & LOAN REPAYMENT		0.00	0.00	0.00
CASH FLOW AFTER TAX	−250.00	25.00	29.68	34.62
REINVESTMENT OF CASH FLOWS ANALYSIS:				
REINVESTMENT RATE	32.9%	1	2	3
BEGINNING BALANCE WITH REINVESTMENT		0.00	25.00	60.60
INTEREST REINVESTMENT EARNED FOR YEAR		0.00	5.92	14.35
CASH FLOW WITH REINVESTMENT	−250	25.00	35.60	48.97
ENDING BALANCE...		25.00	60.60	109.57

SOURCE: REAL ESTATE ANALYSIS BY IRR (Copyright © 1989 Larry Rosen Co.).

4	5	6	7	8	9	10	TOTALS
706.66	689.23	670.06	648.97	625.77	600.25	572.18	672.25
70.67	68.92	67.01	64.90	62.58	60.03	57.22	208.70
17.43	19.17	21.09	23.20	25.52	28.07	30.88	
689.23	670.06	648.97	625.77	600.25	572.18	541.30	
139.11	147.46	156.30	165.68	175.62	186.16	197.33	1539.40
13.9%	14.7%	15.6%	16.6%	17.6%	18.6%	19.7%	
88.09	88.09	88.09	88.09	88.09	88.09	88.09	880.95
51.01	59.36	68.21	77.59	87.53	98.06	109.23	658.55
20.4%	23.7%	27.3%	31.0%	35.0%	39.2%	43.7%	
85.71	114.29	142.86	171.43	200.00	228.57	257.14	
28.57	28.57	28.57	28.57	28.57	28.57	28.57	285.71
17.43	19.17	21.09	23.20	25.52	28.07	30.88	208.70
39.87	49.96	60.73	72.21	84.47	97.56	111.54	581.53
11.16	13.99	17.00	20.22	23.65	27.32	31.23	162.83
39.85	45.37	51.20	57.37	63.87	70.75	78.00	495.72
0.00	0.00	0.00	0.00	0.00	0.00	1644.40	1644.40
			0.00	0.00			
0.00	0.00	0.00			0.00	260.43	260.43
0.00	0.00	0.00	0.00	0.00	0.00	842.66	842.66
39.85	45.37	51.20	57.37	63.87	70.75	920.67	1338.38
4	5	6	7	8	9	10	
109.57	175.36	262.26	375.54	521.81	709.23	947.88	
25.94	41.52	62.09	88.91	123.54	167.91	224.41	754.58
65.79	86.89	113.20	146.28	187.41	238.66	1145.08	2092.96
175.36	262.25	375.54	521.81	709.23	947.88	2092.96	

Bibliography

Anderson, Keith. "Measuring, Interpreting and Applying Volatility within the Fixed Income Market." In F. J. Fabozzi (ed.), *Handbook of Fixed-Income Options*. Chicago: Probus, 1989, pp. 173–188.

Bierman, Harold, Jr., Charles P. Bonini, and Warren Hausman. *Quantitative Analysis for Business Decisions*. Homewood, Ill.: Richard D. Irwin, 1981.

Bierwag, G. O., George Kaufman, and Cynthia Latta. "Duration: Response to Critics." *Journal of Portfolio Management*, Winter 1987, pp. 49–52.

Bierwag, G.O., George Kaufman, and Cynthia Latta. "Duration Models: A Taxonomy. *Journal of Portfolio Management*, Fall 1988, pp. 50–54.

Black, Fisher, Emanuel Derman, and William Toy. "A One-Factor Model of Interest Rates and Its Application to Treasury Bond Options." *Financial Analysts Journal*, Jan.–Feb. 1990, pp. 33–39.

Black, Fischer, and Piotr Karasinski. 'Bond and Option Pricing When Short Rates Are Lognormal." *Financial Analysts Journal*, July–Aug. 1991, pp. 52–59.

Black, Fischer, and Myron Scholes. "The Pricing of Options and Corporate Liabilities." *Journal of Political Economy*, May–June 1973, pp. 637–654.

Bookstaber, Richard. *The Complete Investment Book–Trading Stocks, Bonds, and Options with Computer Applications*. Glenview, Ill.: Scott, Foresman, 1985.

Bookstaber, Richard M. *Option Pricing & Investment Strategy*. Chicago: Probus, 1987.

Bookstaber, R. W., Haney, and P. Noris. "Are Options on Debt Issues Undervalued?" Morgan Stanley, December 1984.

Bookstaber, R., and J. McDonald. "A Generalized Option Valuation Model for the Pricing of Bond Options." *Review of Research in Future Markets*, vol. 4, 1985, pp. 60–73.

Boyce, William, M. Koenigsberg, and Armand Tatevossian. "Effective Duration of Callable Bonds–The Salomon Brothers Term Structure-Based Option Pricing Model." New York: Salomon Brothers, 1987.

Brealey, Richard A., and Stewart C. Myers. *Principles of Corporate Finance*, 4th ed. New York: McGraw-Hill, 1988.

Brennan, M. J., and E. S. Schwartz. "An Equilibrium Model of Bond Pricing and a Test of Market Efficiency." *Journal of Finance and Quantitative Analysis*, Sept. 1982.

Brenner, Menachem (ed.). *Option Pricing, Theory and Applications*. Lexington, Mass.: Lexington Books, 1983.

Brooks, Robert, and Miles Livingston. "A Closed-Form Equation for Bond Convexity." *Financial Analysts Journal*, Nov.–Dec. 1989, pp. 78–79.

Brown, Steven J., Mark P. Kritzman (eds.). *Quantitative Methods for Financial Analysis*. Homewood, Ill.: Dow Jones-Irwin, 1987.

Chambers, Donald, Willard Carleton, and Donald Waldman. "A New Approach to Estimation of the Term Structure of Interest Rates." *Journal of Financial and Quantitative Analysis*, Sept. 1984.

Chua, Jess. "A Generalized Formula for Calculating Bond Duration." *Financial Analysts Journal*, Sept.–Oct. 1988, pp. 65–67.

Courtadon, G. "The Pricing of Options on Default Free Bonds." *Journal of Finance and Quantitative Analysis*. Sept. 1982.

Courtadon, Georges R., and John J. Merrick, Jr. "The Option Pricing Model and the Valuation of Corporate Securities." *The Revolution in Corporate Finance*. Basil Blackwell, Cambridge, Mass.: pp. 197–212.

Cox, J. C., J. E. Ingersoll, and Stephen A. Ross. "An Intertemporal General Equilibrium Model of Asset Prices." *Econometrica*, vol. 53, no. 2, Mar. 1985, pp. 363–384.

Cox, J. C., J. E. Ingersoll, and Stephen A. Ross. "A Theory of the Term Structure of Interest Rates." *Econometrica*, Mar. 1985, pp. 385–407.

Cox, J. C., and Mark Rubinstein. *Option Markets*. Englewood Cliffs, N.J.: Prentice-Hall, 1985.

Cox, J. C., Stephen A. Ross, and Mark Rubinstein. "Option Pricing: A Simplified Approach." *Journal of Financial Economics*, Sept. 1979, pp. 229–263.

Dattatreya, Ravi E., and F. Fabozzi. "A Simplified Model for Valuing Debt Options." *Journal of Portfolio Management*, Spring 1989, pp. 64–72.

Douglas, Livingston G. *Yield Curve Analysis*. New York: New York Institute of Finance, 1988.

Douglas, Livingston G. *Bond Risk Analysis*. New York: New York Institution of Finance, 1990

Dudley, C. L., Jr. "A note on Reinvestment Assumptions in Choosing Between Net Present Value and Internal Rate of Return." *The Journal of Finance*, vol. 27, no. 4, pp. 907–915.

Dunetz, Mark, and James Mahoney. "Using Duration and Convexity in the Analysis of Callable Bonds." *Financial Analysts Journal*, May–June 1988, pp. 53–72.

Dyer, Lawrence J., and David P. Jacob. "Guide to Fixed Income Option Pricing Models." In F. J. Fabozzi (ed.), *Handbook of Fixed-Income Options*. Chicago: Probus, 1989.

Fabozzi, Frank J. (ed.). *The Handbook of Fixed-Income Options*. Chicago: Probus, 1989.

Fabozzi, Frank, and T. Garlicki (eds.). *Advances in Bond Analysis & Portfolio Strategies*. Chicago: Probus, 1987.

Farragher, Edward J. "Clarifying the Confusion about IRR Reinvestment Assumptions." *The Real Estate Review*, vol. 13, Summer 1983, pp. 56–60.

Figlewski, Stephen. "What Does an Option Pricing Model Tell Us about Option Prices?" *Financial Analysts Journal,* Sept.–Oct. 1989, pp. 12–15.

Financial Publishing Company Staff. *Financial Compound Interest and Annuity Tables.* Boston: Financial Publishing, 1970.

Finnerty, John D., and Michael Rose. "Arbitrage-Free Spread: A Consistent Measure of Relative Value." *Journal of Portfolio Management,* Spring 1991, pp. 65–79.

Fong, H. Gifford, and Frank J. Fabozzi. *Fixed Income Portfolio Management.* Homewood, Ill.: Dow Jones-Irwin, 1985.

Herbst, Anthony F. *The Handbook of Capital Investing.* New York: Harper Business, 1990.

Ho, S. Y. *Strategic Fixed Income Investment.* Homewood, Ill.: Dow Jones-Irwin, 1990.

Homer, Sidney, and Martin L. Leibowitz. *Inside the Yield Book.* Englewood Cliffs, N.J.: Prentice-Hall, 1972.

Hull, John. *Options, Futures and Other Derivative Securities.* Englewood Cliffs, N.J. Prentice-Hall, 1989.

Jarrow, Robert, A., and Andrew Rudd. *Option Pricing.* Homewood, Ill.: Dow Jones-Irwin, 1983.

Kahn, Ronald, and Roland Lochoff. "Convexity and Exceptional Return." *Journal of Portfolio Management,* Winter 1990, pp. 43–47.

Kaufman, George, G. Bierwag, and Alden Toevs (eds.). *Innovations in Bond Portfolio Management.* Greenwich, Conn.: JAI Press, Inc., 1983.

Kritzman, Mark. "What Practitioners Need to Know about Estimating Volatility." *Financial Analysts Journal,* July–Aug. 1991, pp. 22–37.

Lapin, Lawrence L. *Quantitative Methods for Business Decisions: With Cases,* 3d ed. San Diego, Calif.: Harcourt Brace Javanovich, 1985.

Latainer, Gary, and David Jacob. "Modern Techniques for Analyzing Value and Performance of Callable Bonds." *Advances in Bond Analysis & Portfolio Strategies.* Chicago: Probus, 1987, pp. 263–302.

Leibowitz, Martin. "Total Portfolio Duration: A New Perspective on Asset Allocation." *Financial Analysts Journal,* Sept.–Oct. 1986, pp. 18–29.

Leibowitz, Martin, William Krasker, and Ardavan Nozari. "Spread Duration: A New Tool for Bond Portfolio Management." *Journal of Portfolio Management,* Spring 1990, pp. 46–53.

Litterman, Robert, and Jose Schienkman. "Common Factors Affecting Bond Returns." *The Journal of Fixed Income,* June 1991, pp. 54–61.

Litterman, Robert, Jose Scheinkman, and Laurence Weiss. "Volatility and the Yield Curve." *The Journal of Fixed Income,* June 1991, p.. 49–53.

Lohmann, Jack R. "The IRR, NPV and the Fallacy of the Reinvestment Rate Assumptions." *The Engineering Economist,* vol. 33, no. 4, pp. 303–329.

Lord, Graham, David Jacob, and James Tilley. "The Valuation of Fixed Income Securities with Contingent Cash Flows." *Advances in Bond Analysis & Portfolio Strategies.* Chicago: Probus, 1987, pp. 237–259.

Malkiel, Burton. *The Term Structure of Interest Rates: Theory, Empirical Evidence, and Applications.* New York: McCaleb-Seiler, 1970.

Maloney, Kevin, and Mark J. Byrne. "An Equilibrium Debt Option Pricing Model in Discrete Time." *Journal of Banking and Finance,* July 1989, pp. 421–442.

Marsh, Terry A., and Eric R. Rosenfeld. "Stochastic Processes for Interest Rates and Equilibrium Bond Prices." *Journal of Finance,* May 1983, pp. 635–647.

McMillan, Lawrence G. *Options as a Strategic Investment,* 2d ed. New York: New York Institute of Finance, 1986.

Meiselman, David. *The Term Structure of Interest Rates.* Englewood Cliffs, N.J.: Prentice-Hall, 1962.

Nawalkha, Sanjay. "Closed-Form Solutions of Convexity and M-Square." *Financial Analysts Journal,* Jan.–Feb. 1990, pp. 75–77.

Nelson, Daniel B., and Krishna Ramaswamy. "Simple Binomial Processes as Diffusion Approximations in Financial Models." *Review of Financial Studies,* vol. 3, no. 3, 1990.

Oakford, R. V., S. A. Bhimjee, and J. V. Jucker. "The Internal Rate of Return, the Pseudo Internal Rate of Return, and Their Use in Financial Decision Making." *The Engineering Economist,* vol. 22, no. 3, pp. 187–201.

Richards, Scott F., and Richard Roll. "Prepayments on Fixed-Rate Mortgage-backed Securities." *Journal of Financial Management,* Spring 1989, pp. 73–82.

Rosen, Lawrence R. *The Dow Jones-Irwin Guide to Calculating Yields–Quick Solutions for Investment Selection Using Computer Generated Internal Rate of Return Analysis.* Homewood, Ill.: Dow Jones-Irwin, 1985.

Rosen, Lawrence R. *Investing in Zero Coupon Bonds–All about CATs, STRIPS, TIGRs, LIONs, and TBRs.* New York: John Wiley & Sons, 1986.

Rosen, Lawrence R. *The Dow Jones-Irwin Guide to Interest: What You Should Know about the Time Value of Money,* rev. ed. Homewood, Ill., Dow Jones-Irwin, 1981.

Rosen, Lawrence R. *Go Where the Money Is–A Guide to Understanding and Entering the Securities Business.* Homewood, Ill., Dow Jones-Irwin, 1968.

Rosenberg, Jerome R. *Managing Your Own Money.* New York: Newsweek Books, 1979.

Ross, Stephen A., Randolph W. Westerfield, and Jeffrey F. Jaffe. *Corporate Finance,* 2d ed. Homewood, Ill.: Richard D. Irwin, 1990.

Rubinstein, Mark. "Displaced Diffusion Option Pricing." *Journal of Finance,* Mar. 1983, pp. 213–217.

Rudd, Andrew, and Henrik K. Clasing, Jr. *Modern Portfolio Theory.* Homewood, Ill.: Dow Jones-Irwin, 1982.

Schnabel, Jacques A. "Is Benter Better? A Cautionary Note on Maximizing Convexity." *Financial Analysts Journal.* Jan.–Feb. 1990, pp. 78–79.

Sharpe, William F., and Gordon J. Alexander. *Investments*, 4th ed., Englewood Cliffs, N.J.: Prentice-Hall, 1990.

Stigum, Marcia L. *The Dow Jones-Irwin Guide to Bond and Money Market Investments.* Homewood, Ill.: Dow Jones-Irwin, 1987.

Stigum, Marcia L. *The Money Market*, rev. ed. Homewood, Ill.: Dow Jones-Irwin, 1983.

Stigum, Marcia L. *Money Market Calculations: Yields, Break-Evens, and Arbitrage.* Homewood, Ill.: Dow Jones-Irwin, 1981.

Taylor, Richard. "Bond Duration with Geometric Mean Returns." *Financial Analysts Journal*, Nov.–Dec. 1988, pp. 82–84.

Trippi, Robert R. "A Discount Rate Adjustment for Calculation of Expected Net Present Values; Internal Rates of Return of Investments Whose Lives Are Uncertain." *Journal of Economics and Business*, vol. 41, May 1989, pp. 143–151.

Van Horne, James C. *Financial Market Rates and Flows.* Englewood Cliffs, N.J.: Prentice-Hall, 1978.

Vasicek, O. A. "An Equilibrium Characterization of the Term Structure." *Journal of Financial Economics*, Nov. 1977, pp. 177–188.

Vasicek, Oldrich A., and H. Gifford Fong. "Term Structure Modeling Using Exponential Splines." *Journal of Finance*, May 1982, pp. 339–348.

Weston, J. F., and E. F. Brigham. *Managerial Finance*, 6th ed. Hinsdale, Ill.: Dryden, 1981.

Wilson, Richard S. "A Comprehensive Review of the Call Features Found in Corporate Bond Indentures." In F. J. Fabozzi (ed.), *Handbook of Fixed-Income Options.* Chicago: Probus, 1989, pp. 441–485.

Winklemann, Kurt. "Uses and Abuses of Duration and Convexity (Callable and Noncallable Bonds)." *Financial Analysts Journal*, Sept.–Oct. 1989, pp. 72–75.

Yawitz, Jess, Kevin Maloney, and William Marshall. "The Term Structure and Callable Bond Yield Spreads." *Journal of Portfolio Management*, Winter 1983, pp. 57–63.

Zarb, Frank G. and Frank J. Fabozzi (eds.). *Handbook of Financial Markets.* Homewood, Ill.: Dow Jones-Irwin, 1986.

Index

About the Author

Lawrence R. Rosen is widely recognized internationally as a leading financial and real estate expert. He is managing director of Larry Rosen Co., a Louisville, Kentucky-based investment management firm that manages an eight-figure portfolio of U.S. real estate and global bonds. Mr. Rosen often provides litigation support or expert testimony in financial controversies. He is the author of seven investment books, including the best-selling *Dow Jones-Irwin Guide to Interest,* the *Dow Jones-Irwin Guide to Calculating Yields,* and *Go Where the Money Is.* Prior to forming his present company in 1975, he spent 13 years in Japan and Switzerland in investment and banking during which time he founded mutual funds in Australia and Sweden. In 1959, he graduated Phi Beta Kappa from Miami University (Ohio).

Author's Software Available

1 Complete Bond Analyzer

Nearly every bond-related calculation can be performed in seconds with the *Complete Bond Analyzer*. This program finds:

- Purchase price given yield to maturity.
- Yield to maturity (pre-tax and after tax) given purchase price, with or without reinvestment of coupons.
- Yield to call.
- Precise results for exact time periods.
- Accrued interest at purchase or sale.
- Modifed duration which predicts the price fluctuation of bonds based on changes in market interest rates.
- Spot rates. Knowledge of spot rates is essential for trading zero coupon bonds at fair prices, either in taxable or tax-free zero's.

3 Mortgage Loans: Is It Time to Refinance?

When asked for his views on the market, Bernard Baruch, financier and advisor to five presidents, said, "It will fluctuate my good man, it will fluctuate." For borrowers these fluctuations may mean great opportunity.

Determining whether or not to refinance one's loan involves the following considerations:

- The interplay between the old and new interest rates.
- The costs to obtain the new loan appraisal.
- Up-front fees known as 'points' to the lender.
- Origination fees.
- Number of years remaining on the old loan compared to the number of years over which the new loan is repayable.
- The length of time which the borrower is likely to keep the new loan (before selling the asset).
- The amount of the new loan.
- Pay-off penalties on both old and new loans.

This is an indispensable program for properly analyzing the question of whether or not to refinance.

This program is used with a spreadsheet.

2 Investment Analysis: For Stocks, Bonds, and Real Estate

These programs compute:

- A detailed, year-by-year pre-tax and after-tax cash flow analysis, printable on a single page.
- An Internal Rate of Return for an existing or proposed investment, both pre-tax and after-tax.
- A revised Internal Rate of Return (compound realized yield) showing the results with reinvestment of after-tax cash flows at an earnings rate for reinvestment determined by the investor.

This program is used with a spreadsheet (Lotus 1-2-3, Microsoft Excel, Microsoft Works, Appleworks, or Claris Works).

4 Bond Portfolio Manager

The Bond Portfolio Manager keeps track of:

- The market value of each bond and the entire portfolio, priced to the lesser value of call or maturity.
- Duration, convexity, and reward-risk indicators for changes in yield for individual bonds as well as the entire portfolio.
- The month and day each interest payment is due.
- Unrealized gain or loss for each bond, ranked in order of magnitude from the largest loss to the largest gain. Calculations are made using taxable basis adjusted for "constant yield" amortization.
- Portfolio evaluations and reports by:
  - (a) Credit worth of the bond issuer. For example, 25% of the portfolio is rated AAA.
  - (b) Date of maturity, call or put. For example, 18% of the portfolio matures or is expected to be called in 1998.
- House-keeping information such as bond location, serial number, status (registered or coupon), the transaction broker, and key dates including call, put, and maturity in chronological order.

This program is used with a spreadsheet.

5 Financial and Interest Calculator

The *Financial and Interest Calculator* performs the following analyses:

- Prepares loan amortization schedules for fixed rate mortgages and variable rate loans.
- Finds the future value of a single investment or a series of investments (constant or increasing annuity).
- Determines the present value of a single future payment or the value of a constant or increasing annuity. For example, the Financial and Interest Calculator can determine the amount one must invest each year to accumulate one million dollars over a stated period of time, provided each year's contribution is X% greater than the preceding year, and the account earns Y%.
- Calculates the true cost of a loan involving the payment of Mortgage Points.
- Finds the Internal Rate of Return (IRR). Unlike the vast majority of IRR calculators, this program accommodates multiple cash flows within the same calendar year and at irregular time intervals.

6 Options: Finding Their Value

The importance of determining a proper value for an option goes far beyond merely determining the value of a call option on a stock. Many securities contain implicit or embedded options. These include callable bonds, putable bonds, mortgage backed securities and the like.

In order to obtain valid option values the methodology must be "arbitrage free" among other criteria.

These programs compute option values for stocks, European bond embedded options and American bond embedded options.

Additionally, programs are included which calculate:

- Time spread or elapsed time
- Average weighted life
- Macaulay Duration
- Modifed Duration
- Spot Rates and Forward Rates
- Volatility of price or yield changes
- Probability
- Conversion to continuous interest

- -

Order Form
The following computer software is available. Please list the quantity of the programs you would like in the boxes below:

- ❑ *1 Complete Bond Analyzer*
- ❑ *2 Investment Analysis: For Stocks, Bonds, and Real Estate*
- ❑ *3 Mortgage Loans: Is It Time to Refinance?*
- ❑ *4 Bond Portfolio Manager*
- ❑ *5 Financial and Interest Calculator*
- ❑ *6 Options: Finding Their Value*

The disks include full documentation explaining how to use the programs. The software is available for the following computers: Apple II Series, Macintosh, IBM PC's and compatibles.

Each program costs $89.00.
For orders of three or more, deduct 15%.
For orders of all six disks, deduct 20%.

Name _____

Address _____

Home Phone _____

Office Phone _____

Computer _____

RAM _____ K _____

Operating System _____

Spreadsheet _____ Version _____

Choose: ❑ DOS   ❑ Windows

Type of Disk Drive to be used: ❑ 5¼″ ❑ 3½″

Please send this form with check or money order made payable to Larry Rosen Company to:

Larry Rosen Company
7008 Springdale Road
Louisville, KY 40241